Android Cookbook

Date: 11/1/12

005.276 DAR
Darwin, Ian F.
Android cookbook /

Ian F. Darwin

PALM BEACH COUNTY
LIBRARY SYSTEM
3650 SUMMIT BLVD.
WEST PALM BEACH, FL 33406

O'REILLY®

Beijing · Cambridge · Farnham · Köln · Sebastopol · Tokyo

Android Cookbook

by Ian F. Darwin

Copyright © 2012 O'Reilly Media, Inc.. All rights reserved.
Printed in the United States of America.

Published by O'Reilly Media, Inc, 1005 Gravenstein Highway North, Sebastopol, CA 95472.

O'Reilly books may be purchased for educational, business, or sales promotional use. Online editions are also available for most titles (*http://my.safaribooksonline.com*). For more information, contact our corporate/institutional sales department: (800) 998-9938 or *corporate@oreilly.com*.

Editors: Mike Loukides and Courtney Nash
Production Editor: Teresa Elsey
Copyeditor: Audrey Doyle
Proofreader: Stacie Arellano

Indexer: Lucie Haskins
Cover Designer: Karen Montgomery
Interior Designer: David Futato
Illustrators: Robert Romano and Rebecca Demarest

April 2012: First Edition.

Revision History for the First Edition:
2012-04-05   First release

See *http://oreilly.com/catalog/errata.csp?isbn=9781449388416* for release details.

Nutshell Handbook, the Nutshell Handbook logo, and the O'Reilly logo are registered trademarks of O'Reilly Media, Inc. *Android Cookbook*, the image of a marine iguana, and related trade dress are trademarks of O'Reilly Media, Inc.

Many of the designations used by manufacturers and sellers to distinguish their products are claimed as trademarks. Where those designations appear in this book, and O'Reilly Media, Inc., was aware of a trademark claim, the designations have been printed in caps or initial caps.

While every precaution has been taken in the preparation of this book, the publisher and authors assume no responsibility for errors or omissions, or for damages resulting from the use of the information contained herein.

ISBN: 978-1-449-38841-6

[LSI]

1333643019

To Dennis M. Ritchie (1941–2011), language pioneer and co-inventor of Unix, who showed us all where the braces go, and so much more…

Table of Contents

Preface

Preface

Ian Darwin

Android is "the open source revolution" applied to cellular telephony and mobile computing. At least, part of the revolution. There have been many other attempts to provide open source cell phones, ranging from the mostly defunct Openmoko FreeRunner (*http://wiki.openmoko.org*) to QT Embedded, Moblin, LiMo, Debian Mobile, and Maemo to the recently open sourced (*http://news.bbc.co.uk/2/hi/technology/8496263.stm*) Symbian OS (*http://symbian.org*) and the recently defunct HP WebOS. And let's not forget the established closed source stalwarts: BlackBerry OS, Apple's iPhone, and Microsoft Windows Mobile (these all have developer toolkits, but their OS is not available as open source and often has other "click-wrap" restrictions).

"Nobody's armchair is a good predictor of the future," though, as Mike O'Dell once said. Does Android have a place in the sun alongside these other players? We thought it did when we set out to crowdsource this book, and time has proven us right: Android is definitely here to stay! This book is here to help the Android developer community share the knowledge that will make it happen. Those who contribute knowledge here are helping to make Android development easier for those who come after.

About Android

Android (*http://www.android.com/*) is a mobile technology platform that provides cell phones, tablets, and other handheld and mobile devices (even netbooks) with the power and portability of the Linux operating system and the reliability and portability of a standard high-level language and API. Android apps are written in the Java language, using tools such as Eclipse, compiled against the Android API, and translated into bytecode for the Dalvik VM.

Android is thus related by OS family to Openmoko, QT Embedded, MeeGo (the 2010 merger of Nokia's Maemo and Intel's MobLin: *http://www.engadget.com/2010/02/15/ meego-nokia-and-intel-merge-maemo-and-moblin*), OPhone, LiMo, and other Linux-based cell phone projects. Android is also related by programming language to

BlackBerry and Java ME phones, and to Java and the wider realm of Java Enterprise applications.

Android sales have continued to climb; a report from NPD states that first-quarter 2010 sales of all Android devices exceeded sales of the iPhone (*http://www.npd.com/press/ releases/press_100510.html*), moving Android into second place (although still well behind the BlackBerry platform). Surely its growth was due in part to major carrier Verizon's two-for-one sale, but that doesn't account for all of it...

Who This Book Is From

This book was written by several dozen Android developers from the Android community at large. Development occurred in the open, on the website *http://androidcook book.com/*, which I built to allow people to contribute, view, review, and comment on the recipes that would make up this book. A complete list can be found in "Acknowledgments" on page xviii. I am deeply grateful to all the contributors, who have helped moved this book from a dream to the reality that you have in your hands (or on-screen if you are reading the ebook format). Thank you all!

Who This Book Is For

We assume you know the basics of the Java language. If not, see Recipe 1.2. We also assume you know the basics of the Java Standard Edition API (since this forms the basis of Android's runtime libraries) as well as the basics of Android. The terms *activity*, *intent*, *service*, and *content provider*, while not necessarily being what you dream about at night, should at least be familiar to you. If not, see Recipe 1.6.

What's in This Book?

Chapter 1, *Getting Started*, takes you through the steps of setting up the Android development environment and building several simple applications of the well-known "Hello, World" type pioneered by Brian Kernighan.

Chapter 2, *Designing a Successful Application*, covers some of the differences in mobile computing that will hit developers coming from desktop and enterprise software environments, and talks about how mobile design (in particular, Android design) differs from those other environments.

Testing is often an afterthought for some developers, so we discuss this early on, in Chapter 3, *Testing*. Not so that you'll skip it, but so that you'll read and heed. We talk about unit testing individual components as well as testing out your entire application in a well-controlled way.

Android provides a variety of mechanisms for communicating within an application and across applications. In Chapter 4, *Inter-/Intra-Process Communication* we discuss intents and broadcast receivers, services, `AsyncTask`s, and handlers.

Another communication mechanism is about allowing controlled access to data that is usually in an SQL database. In Chapter 5, *Content Providers*, we show you how to make an application that can be used by other applications through something as simple but ubiquitous (in Android) as the URL.

Chapter 6, *Graphics*, covers a range of topics related to graphics, including use of the graphical drawing and compositing facilities in Android as well as using desktop tools to develop graphical images, textures, icons, and so on that will be incorporated into your finished application.

Every mobile app needs a GUI, so Chapter 7, *Graphical User Interface*, covers the main ins and outs of GUI development for Android. Examples are given both in XML and, in a few cases, in Java-coded GUI development.

Chapter 8, *GUI Alerts: Menus, Dialogs, Toasts, and Notifications*, covers all the pop-up mechanisms—menus, dialogs, and toasts—and one that doesn't pop up but is also for interaction outside your application's window, Android's notification mechanism.

Chapter 9, *GUI: ListView*, focuses on one of the most important GUI components in Android, the `ListView`.

Android is rich in multimedia capabilities. Chapter 10, *Multimedia*, shows how to use the most important of these.

Chapter 11, *Data Persistence*, shows how to save data into files, databases, and so on. And how to retrieve it later, of course.

Android started out as an operating system for mobile telephones. Chapter 12, *Telephone Applications*, shows how to control and react to the telephone device that is in most mobile devices nowadays.

Mobile devices are, for the most part, always-on and always-connected. This has a major impact on how people use them and think about them. Chapter 13, *Networked Applications*, shows the coding for traditional networked applications. This is followed by Chapter 14, *Gaming and Animation*, and Chapter 15, *Social Networking*.

The now-ubiquitous Global Positioning System has also had a major impact on how mobile applications work. Chapter 16, *Location and Map Applications*, discusses how to find your location, how to get map data from Google and OpenStreetMap, and how applications can be location-aware in ways that are just now being explored.

Chapter 17, *Accelerometer*, talks about the sensors built into most Android devices and how to use them.

Chapter 18, *Bluetooth*, talks about the low-energy very-local area networking that Bluetooth enables, going beyond connecting your Bluetooth headset to your phone.

Android devices are perhaps unique in how much control they give the developer. Some of these angles are explored in Chapter 19, *System and Device Control*. Since Android is Linux-based, a few of the recipes in this chapter deal with traditional Unix/Linux commands and facilities.

In Chapter 20, *Other Programming Languages and Frameworks*, we explore the use of other programming languages to write all or part of your Android application. Examples include C, Perl, Python, Lisp, and other languages.

While this edition of this book is in English, and English remains the number-one technical language worldwide, it is far from the only one. Most end users would rather have an application that has its text in their language and its icons in a form that is culturally correct for them. Chapter 21, *Strings and Internationalization*, goes over the issues of language and culture and how they relate to Android.

Most Android developers hope other people will use their applications. But this won't happen if users can't find the applications. Chapter 22, *Packaging, Deploying, and Distributing/Selling Your App*, shows how to prepare your application for distribution via the Android Market, and to use that as well as other markets to get your application out to the people who will use it.

Conventions Used in This Book

The following typographical conventions are used in this book:

Italic
> Indicates new terms, URLs, email addresses, filenames, and file extensions.

`Constant width`
> Used for program listings, as well as within paragraphs to refer to program elements such as variable or function names, databases, data types, environment variables, statements, and keywords.

`Constant width bold`
> Shows commands or other text that should be typed literally by the user.

`Constant width italic`
> Shows text that should be replaced with user-supplied values or by values determined by context.

This icon signifies a tip, suggestion, or general note.

This icon indicates a warning or caution.

Getting and Using the Code Examples

Contributors of each recipe have the option to provide a download URL for their source code. Additionally, some recipes feature an individual source download, listed both as a hyperlink for PDF users and as a QR-format barcode for downloading from the printed edition. These URLs are included at the end of each recipe. In each case the archive file is expected to contain a complete Eclipse project. The archives are also collected and published at the book's GitHub site, which can be found at *https://github.com/androidcook/Android-Cookbook-Examples*. Each directory in the repo contains one example program's project. As you will see if you visit this page, GitHub allows you to check out the source repository using the `git clone` command. As well, the web page offers the option to download the entire repository as a single (large) ZIP file as well as to browse portions of the repository in a web browser. Using git will allow you to receive corrections and updates, but the ZIP will download more quickly.

This book is here to help you get your job done. In general, you may use the code in this book in your programs and documentation. You do not need to contact us for permission unless you're reproducing a significant portion of the code. For example, writing a program that uses several chunks of code from this book does not require permission. Selling or distributing a CD-ROM of examples from O'Reilly books does require permission. Answering a question by citing this book and quoting example code does not require permission. Incorporating a significant amount of example code from this book into your product's documentation does require permission.

We appreciate, but do not require, attribution. An attribution usually includes the title, author, publisher, and ISBN. For example: "*Android Cookbook*, edited by Ian F. Darwin (O'Reilly). Copyright 2012 O'Reilly Media, Inc., 978-1-449-38841-6."

If you feel your use of code examples falls outside fair use or the permission given above, feel free to contact us at *permissions@oreilly.com*.

Safari® Books Online

Safari Safari Books Online is an on-demand digital library that lets you easily search over 7,500 technology and creative reference books and videos to find the answers you need quickly.

With a subscription, you can read any page and watch any video from our library online. Read books on your cell phone and mobile devices. Access new titles before they are available for print, and get exclusive access to manuscripts in development and post feedback for the authors. Copy and paste code samples, organize your favorites, download chapters, bookmark key sections, create notes, print out pages, and benefit from tons of other time-saving features.

O'Reilly Media has uploaded this book to the Safari Books Online service. To have full digital access to this book and others on similar topics from O'Reilly and other publishers, sign up for free at *http://my.safaribooksonline.com*.

How to Contact Us

Please address comments and questions concerning this book to the publisher:

O'Reilly Media, Inc.
1005 Gravenstein Highway North
Sebastopol, CA 95472
800-998-9938 (in the United States or Canada)
707-829-0515 (international or local)
707-829-0104 (fax)

We have a web page for this book, where we list errata, examples, and any additional information. You can access this page at:

http://shop.oreilly.com/product/0636920010241.do

To comment or ask technical questions about this book, send email to:

bookquestions@oreilly.com

For more information about our books, courses, conferences, and news, see our website at *http://www.oreilly.com*.

Find us on Facebook: *http://facebook.com/oreilly*

Follow us on Twitter: *http://twitter.com/oreillymedia*

Watch us on YouTube: *http://www.youtube.com/oreillymedia*

Acknowledgments

I would like to thank the dozens of people from the Android community at large who contributed so many of the recipes in this book: Amir Alagic, Jim Blackler, Luis Vitorio Cargnini, Rupesh Chavan, Adrian Cowham, Nidhin Jose Davis, Wagied Davids, David Dawes, Enrique Diaz, Marco Dinacci, Claudio Esperanca, Kurosh Fallahzadeh, Daniel Fowler, Jonathan Fuerth, Sunit Katkar, Roger Kind Kristiansen, Vladimir Kroz, Alex Leffelman, Ulysses Levy, Thomas Manthey, Emaad Manzoor, Keith Mendoza, Roberto Calvo Palomino, Federico Paolinelli, Johan Pelgrim, Catarina Reis, Mike Rowehl, Pratik Rupwal, Oscar Salguero, Ashwini Shahapurkar, Shraddha Shravagi, Rachee Singh, Saketkumar Srivastav, Corey Sunwold, Kailuo Wang, and Colin Wilcox.

I must also mention the many people at O'Reilly who have helped shape this book, including my editors Mike Loukides, Courtney Nash, and Meghan Blanchette; Adam Witwer and Sarah Schneider in production; production editor Teresa Elsey, who shepherded the whole production process; external copy editor Audrey Doyle, who painstakingly read every word and phrase; Stacie Arellano, who proofread it all again; Lucie Haskins, who added index terms to all those recipes; designers Karen Montgomery and David Futato; illustrators Robert Romano and Rebecca Demarest; and anyone whom I've neglected to mention—you know who you are!

My son Andrej Darwin helped with some administrative tasks late in the recipe editing phase. Thanks to all my family for their support.

Finally, a note of thanks to my two technical reviewers, Greg Ostravich and Zettie Chinfong, without whom there would be many more errors and omissions than the ones that doubtless remain.

To all of the above, *thank you*!

## CHAPTER 1

Getting Started

1.1 Introduction: Getting Started

Ian Darwin

Discussion

The famous "Hello, World" pattern came about when Kernighan and Plaugher wanted to write a "recipe" on how to get started in any new programming language and environment. This chapter is affectionately dedicated to these fine gentlemen, and to everyone who has ever struggled to get started in a new programming paradigm.

1.2 Learning the Java Language

Ian Darwin

Problem

Android apps are written in the Java programming language before they are converted into Android's own class file format, DEX. If you don't know how to program in Java you will find it hard to write Android apps.

Solution

Lots of resources are available for learning Java. Most of them will teach you what you need, but will also mention some API classes that are not available for Android development. *Avoid* any sections in any resource that talk about topics listed in the lefthand column of Table 1-1.

Table 1-1. Parts of the Java API to ignore

Java API	Android equivalent
Swing, applets	Android's GUI; see Chapter 7.
Application entry point main()	See Recipe 1.6.
J2ME/Java ME	Most of android.* replaces Java ME API.
Servlets/JSP, J2EE/Java EE	Designed for server-side use.

Discussion

Here are some books and resources on Java programming:

- *Java in a Nutshell* (*http://shop.oreilly.com/product/9780596007737.do*) by David Flanagan (O'Reilly) is a good introduction for programmers, particularly those who are coming from C/C++. This book has grown from an acorn to a coconut in size, to keep up with the growth of Java SE over its lifetime.

- *Head First Java* (*http://shop.oreilly.com/product/9780596009205.do*) by Kathy Sierra and Bert Bates (O'Reilly). This provides a great visual-learner-oriented introduction to the language.

- *Thinking in Java* (*http://www.mindview.net/Books/TIJ4*) by Bruce Eckel (Prentice-Hall).

- *Learning Java* (*http://shop.oreilly.com/product/9780596008734.do*) by Patrick Niemeyer and Jonathan Knudsen (O'Reilly).

- "Great Java: Level 1" (*http://shop.oreilly.com/product/9780596809393.do*), a video by Brett McLaughlin (O'Reilly). This provides a visual introduction to the language.

- *Java: The Good Parts* (*http://shop.oreilly.com/product/9780596803742.do*) by Jim Waldo (O'Reilly).

- *Java Cookbook* (*http://shop.oreilly.com/product/9780596007010.do*), which I wrote and which O'Reilly published. This is regarded as a good second book for Java developers. It has entire chapters on strings, regular expressions, numbers, dates and time, structuring data, I/O and directories, internationalization, threading, and networking, all of which apply to Android. It also has a number of chapters that are specific to Swing and to some EE-based technologies.

Please understand that this list will probably never be completely up-to-date. You should also refer to O'Reilly's freely downloadable (with registration) *Android Development Bibliography* (*http://shop.oreilly.com/product/0636920021896.do*), a compilation of all the books from the various publishers whose books are in the online Safari service. This book is also distributed without charge at relevant conferences where O'Reilly has a booth.

See Also

This book's primary author maintains a list of Java resources online at *http://www .darwinsys.com/java/*.

O'Reilly has many of the best Java books around; there's a complete list at *http://oreilly .com/pub/topic/java*.

1.3 Creating a "Hello, World" Application from the Command Line

Ian Darwin

Problem

You want to create a new Android project without using the Eclipse ADT plug-in.

Solution

Use the Android Development Kit (ADK) tool `android` with the `create project` argument and some additional arguments to configure your project.

Discussion

In addition to being the name of the platform, `android` is also the name of a command-line tool for creating, updating, and managing projects. You can either navigate into the *android-sdk-xxx* directory, or you can set your `PATH` variable to include its *tools* subdirectory.

Then, to create a new project, give the command `android create project` with some arguments. Example 1-1 is an example run under MS-DOS.

Example 1-1. Creating a new project

```
C:> PATH=%PATH%;"C:\Documents and Settings\Ian\My Documents\android-sdk-windows\tools"; \
        "C:\Documents and Settings\Ian\My Documents\android-sdk-windows\platform-tools"
C:> android create project --target android-7 --package com.example.foo
    --name Foo --activity FooActivity --path .\MyAndroid
Created project directory: C:\Documents and Settings\Ian\My Documents\MyAndroid
Created directory C:\Documents and Settings\Ian\My Documents\MyAndroid\src\com\example\foo
Added file C:\Documents and Settings\Ian\My
    Documents\MyAndroid\src\com\example\foo\FooActivity.java
Created directory C:\Documents and Settings\Ian\My Documents\MyAndroid\res
Created directory C:\Documents and Settings\Ian\My Documents\MyAndroid\bin
Created directory C:\Documents and Settings\Ian\My Documents\MyAndroid\libs
Created directory C:\Documents and Settings\Ian\My Documents\MyAndroid\res\values
Added file C:\Documents and Settings\Ian\My Documents\MyAndroid\res\values\strings.xml
Created directory C:\Documents and Settings\Ian\My Documents\MyAndroid\res\layout
Added file C:\Documents and Settings\Ian\My Documents\MyAndroid\res\layout\main.xml
Added file C:\Documents and Settings\Ian\My Documents\MyAndroid\AndroidManifest.xml
```

```
Added file C:\Documents and Settings\Ian\My Documents\MyAndroid\build.xml

C:>
```

Table 1-2 lists the arguments for the **create project** code.

Table 1-2. List of create project arguments

Name	Meaning	Example
`--activity`	Name of your "main class" and default name for the generated *.apk* file.	`--activity HelloActivity`
`--name`	Name of the project and the generated *.apk* file.	`--name MyProject`
`--package`	Name of the Java package for your classes.	`--package com.exam ple.hello`
`--path`	Path to create the project in (does not create a subdirectory under this, so don't use /home/*you*/workspace, but rather /home/*you*/workspace/ *NewProjectName*).	`--path /home/ian/ workspace/MyPro ject` (see above for Windows example)
`--target`	API level of the Android platform to target; use `android list tar gets` to see list of targets. A number is an "ID," not an API level; for that, use `android-` with the API level you want.	`--target android-10`

If it cannot complete the requested operation, the `android` command presents a volu-minous "command usage" message listing all the operations it can do and the arguments for them. If successful, the `android create project` command creates the files and directories listed in Table 1-3.

Table 1-3. Artifacts created by create project

Name	Meaning
AndroidManifest.xml	Config file that tells Android about your project
bin	Generated binaries (compiled class files)
build.properties	Editable properties file
build.xml	Standard Ant build control file
default.properties or *project.properties* (depending on tools version)	Stores SDK version and libraries used; maintained by plug-in
gen	Generated stuff
libs	Libraries, of course
res	Important resource files (*strings.xml*, layouts, etc.)
src	Source code for your application
src/packagename/ActivityName.java	Source of "main" starting activity
test	Copies of most of the above

It is a normal and recommended Android practice to create your user interface in XML using the layout file created under res/layout, but it is certainly possible to write all the code in Java. To keep this example self-contained, we'll do it the "wrong" way for now. Use your favorite text editor to replace the contents of the file *HelloWorld.java* with the contents of Example 1-2.

Example 1-2. HelloWorld.java

```java
import android.app.Activity;
import android.widget.*;

public class Hello extends Activity {

        /**
         * This method gets invoked when the activity is instantiated in
         * response to e.g., you clicked on the app's Icon in the Home Screen.
         */
        @Override
        public void onCreate(Bundle savedInstanceState) {
                super.onCreate(savedInstanceState);
                // Create a TextView for the current Activity
                TextView view = new TextView(this);
                // Make it say something
                view.setText("Hello World");
                // Put this newly created view into the Activity,
                // sort of like JFrame.getContentPane().add(view)
                setContentView(view);
        }
}
```

Assuming you have the Apache Software Foundation Ant Build Tool (*http://ant.apache .org/*) installed (and it is included with recent versions of the Android SDK), you can now (in a command-line window) change to the project directory (...MyDocuments \MyAndroid in Example 1-1) and issue the command:

```
ant debug
```

This will create an archive file named, for example, *MyAndroid.apk* (with "apk" standing for Android Package) in the *bin* directory.

If this is your first time here, you may need to create an Android Virtual Device (AVD), which is just a named configuration for the Android emulator specifying target resolution, API level, and so on. You can create an emulator using:

```
android create avd -n my_droid -t 7
```

For more details on creating an AVD, see Recipe 3.3.

You can then start the Android Debug Bridge (ADB) server and the emulator:

```
adb start-server
emulator -avd my_droid -t 5
```

Assuming you now have either the emulator running or your device plugged in and recognized via USB, you can then do:

```
adb -e install -r bin/MyAndroid.apk
```

The -e flag is for the emulator; use -d for a real device.

If you are handy with shell scripts or batch files, you'll want to create one called, say, *download*, to avoid typing the adb invocation on every build cycle.

Finally you can start your app! You can use the Application list: tap the little icon that looks like a 5×5 row of dots, scroll to your application by name, and tap its icon.

You will probably find it convenient to create an icon for your app on the home screen of the device or emulator; this icon will survive multiple install -r cycles, so it's the easiest way to test the running of your application.

See Also

Recipe 1.4. The blog "a little madness" has a more detailed formulation (*http://www.alittlemadness.com/2010/05/31/setting-up-an-android-project-build/*). The official Android reference site has a page on developing without Eclipse (*http://developer.android.com/guide/developing/other-ide.html*).

1.4 Creating a "Hello, World" Application in Eclipse

Ian Darwin

Problem

You want to use Eclipse to develop your Android application.

Solution

Install Eclipse (*http://www.eclipse.org/*), the Android SDK (*http://developer.android.com/sdk/*), and the ADT plug-in (*http://developer.android.com/sdk/eclipse-adt.html*). Create your project and start writing your app. Build it, and test it under the emulator, from within Eclipse.

Discussion

Once you have these items installed, you are ready to begin:

- Eclipse IDE (*http://www.eclipse.org/*)
- The Android SDK (*http://developer.android.com/sdk/*)
- The ADT plug-in (*http://developer.android.com/sdk/eclipse-adt.html*)

If you want a more detailed exposition of installing these three items, please refer to Recipe 1.5.

To get started, create a new project from the File→New menu (see Figure 1-1).

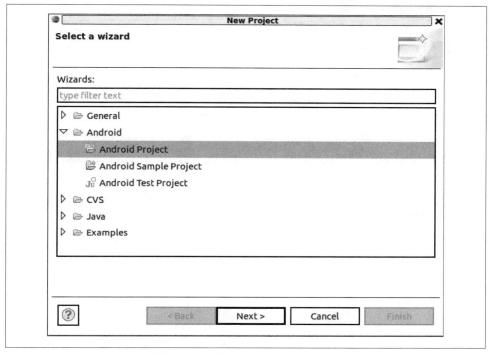

Figure 1-1. Starting to create an Eclipse project

Click Next. Give your new project a name, and click Next (see Figure 1-2).

Select an SDK version to target. Version 2.1 gives you almost all the devices in use today; version 3.x or 4.x gives you the latest features (see Figure 1-3). You decide.

Figure 1-4 shows the project structure expanded in the Project panel on the right. It also shows the extent to which you can use Eclipse auto-completion within Android— I added the **gravity** attribute for the label, and Eclipse is offering a full list of possible attribute values. I chose **center-horizontal**, so the label should be centered when we get the application running.

In fact, if you set **gravity** to **center_vertical** on the **LinearLayout** *and* set it to **cen ter_horizontal** on the **TextView**, the text will be centered both vertically and horizontally. Example 1-3 is the layout file *main.xml* (located under *res/layout*) which achieves this.

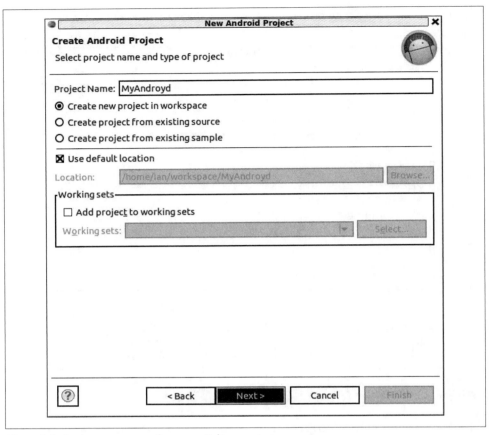

Figure 1-2. Setting parameters for a new Eclipse project

Example 1-3. The XML layout

```xml
<?xml version="1.0" encoding="utf-8"?>
<LinearLayout xmlns:android="http://schemas.android.com/apk/res/android"
    android:orientation="vertical"
    android:layout_width="fill_parent"
    android:layout_height="fill_parent"
    android:gravity="center_vertical"
    >
<TextView
    android:layout_width="fill_parent"
    android:layout_height="wrap_content"
    android:text="@string/hello"
    android:gravity="center_horizontal"
    />
</LinearLayout>
```

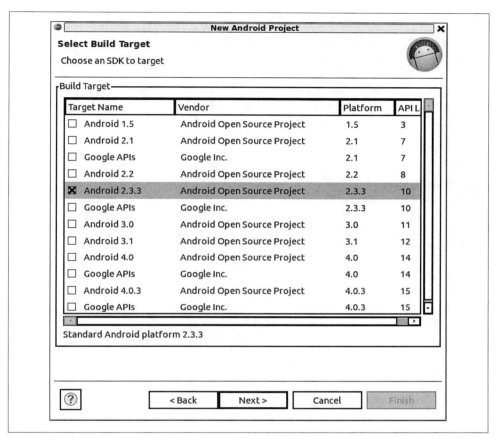

Figure 1-3. Setting SDK to target for a new Eclipse project

As always, Eclipse generates a compiled version whenever you save a source file. Also, in an Android project, it also runs an Ant build to create the compiled, packaged APK that is ready to run. So you only need to run it. Right-click on the project itself and select Run As → Android Project. (See Figure 1-5.)

This will start the Android emulator if it's not already running. The emulator will start with the word *Android* in typewriter text, then switch to the fancier Android font with a moving white patch over blue lettering—remember the Microsoft Windows 95 start-up? See Figure 1-6.

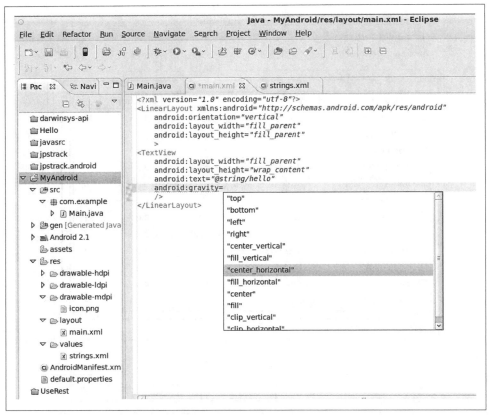

Figure 1-4. Using the Eclipse editor to set gravity on a TextView

After a little longer, your application should start up (Figure 1-5 only shows a screenshot of the application itself, since the rest of the emulator view is redundant). See Figure 1-7.

See Also

Recipe 1.3

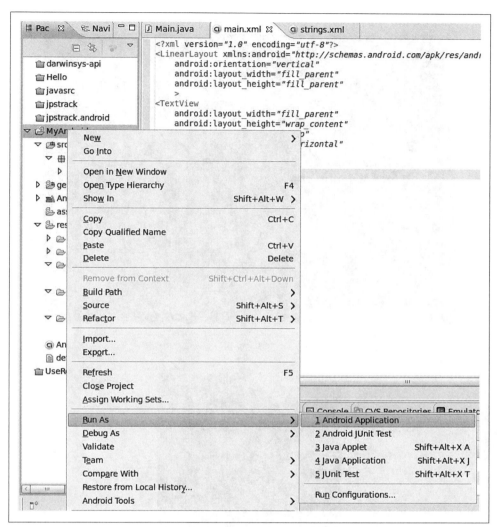

Figure 1-5. Running an Eclipse Android project

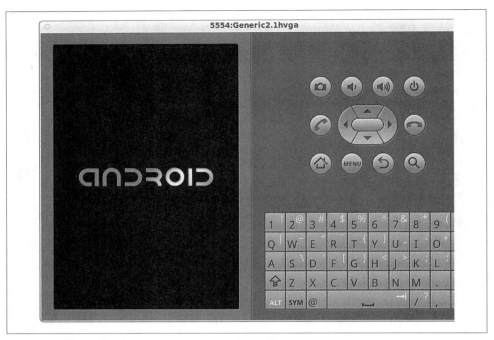

Figure 1-6. The Android project starting up in the emulator

Figure 1-7. The Eclipse project running in the emulator

1.5 Setting Up an IDE on Windows to Develop for Android

Daniel Fowler

Problem

You want to develop your Android applications using a Windows PC, so a concise guide to setting up an IDE for that platform is useful.

Solution

The use of the Eclipse IDE is recommended when developing Android apps. Configuring Eclipse on Windows is not a single-shot install; several stages need to be completed. This recipe provides details on those stages.

Discussion

To develop applications for Android, the Eclipse Integrated Development Environment (IDE) for Java is recommended. An Android Development Tools (ADT) plug-in is available to enhance Eclipse. The ADT plug-in uses the Android Software Development Kit (SDK) which provides essential programs for developing Android software. To set up a development system you will need to download and install the following:

- Java Standard Edition Development Kit
- Eclipse for Java Development
- Android Software Development Kit
- Android Development Tools plug-in (from within Eclipse)

In the subsections that follow, we will cover these stages in detail for a PC running Windows (tested on XP, Vista, and Windows 7).

Installing the JDK (Java Development Kit)

Go to the Java download page at *http://www.oracle.com/technetwork/java/javase/down loads/index.html*.

Select the Java icon to access the JDK downloads:

The list of JDK downloads will be shown. Click the Accept License Agreement radio button; otherwise, you will not be allowed to continue. Download and run the latest JDKs present; as of this writing, they are *jdk-7u2-windows-i586.exe* (or *jdk-7u2-windows-x64.exe* for 64-bit Windows). You may need to select the location of the download site. Accept any security warnings that appear, but only if you are downloading from the official Java download web page.

When the download has completed and is run you will need to go through the install screens, clicking Next until the JDK installer has finished. You should not need to change any options presented. When the JDK installer has completed, click the Finish button. A product registration web page may load; you can close this or you can choose to register your installation.

Installing Eclipse for Java development

The Eclipse Downloads web page is at *http://www.eclipse.org/downloads/*.

Windows needs to be selected in the Packages drop down; select the relevant Eclipse IDE for Java Developers download link (see Figure 1-8).

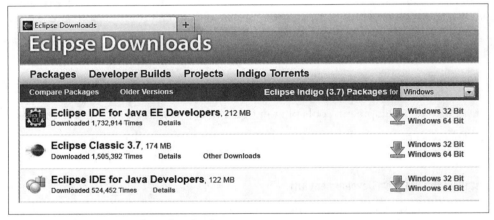

Figure 1-8. Choosing an Eclipse download

Download and open the ZIP file. In the file there will be an *eclipse* directory containing several files and subdirectories. Copy the *eclipse* directory and all its contents as it comes (Figure 1-9). The usual place to copy the files to is either the root of the C drive or under *C:\Program Files*. You may need to select Continue when Windows asks permission for the copy.

Make a desktop shortcut to *eclipse.exe*.

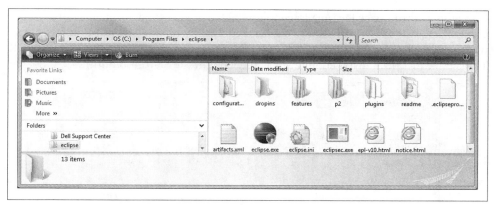

Figure 1-9. Contents of the Eclipse folder

Run Eclipse so that it sets up a workspace; this will also check that both Java and Eclipse were installed correctly. When you run Eclipse a security warning may be displayed; select Run to continue. Accept the default workspace location or use a different directory.

Installing the Android SDK (software development kit)

Go to the Android Software Development Kit download page at *http://developer.an droid.com/sdk/index.html*.

Choose the latest Windows EXE package (currently *installer_r16-windows.exe*) and select Run. Accept the security warning only if you are downloading from the official Android SDK website. The Android SDK Tools installer will show some screens. Select the Next button on each screen; you should not need to change any options. Since *C:\Program Files* is a protected directory, you can either get permission to install there or, as some developers do, install to your user folder or another directory—for example, *C:\Android\android-sdk*.

When the Install button is clicked, a progress screen will briefly display while the Android files are copied. Click the final Next button and the Finish button at the end of the installation. If you left the Start SDK Manager checkbox ticked the SDK Manager will run. Otherwise, select SDK Manager from the Android SDK Tools program group (Start→All Programs→Android SDK Tools→SDK Manager). When the SDK Manager starts the Android packages available to download are checked. Then a list of all available packages is shown with some preselected for download. A Status column shows whether a package is installed or not. In Figure 1-10, you can see that the Android SDK Tools have just been installed and this is reflected in the Status column.

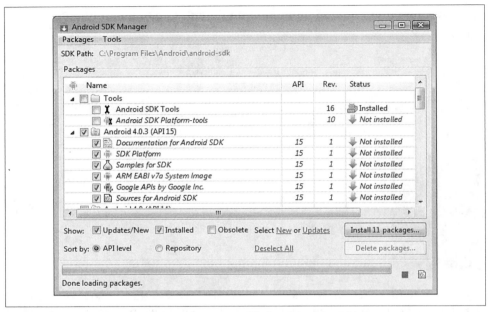

Figure 1-10. Android SDK Manager, showing installed and downloadable components

Check each package that needs to be installed. Multiple packages are available. These include SDK platform packages for each application programming interface (API) level, application samples for most API levels, Google Maps APIs, manufacturer-device-specific APIs, documentation, source code, and the following Google extra packages:

Android Support
    Used to support later Android APIs on older devices

AdMob Ads SDK
    For incorporating advertising into apps

Analytics SDK
    To support analysis of customers' purchases

Market Billing
    Adds support for in-app purchases

Market Licensing
    Helps protect apps from being illegally copied

USB Driver
    For debugging on physical devices (or using a manufacturer's driver)

Webdriver

Helps test a website's compatibility with the Android browser

It is recommended that you download several SDK platforms to allow testing of apps against various device configurations. It is worth noting that older computers will struggle to run the virtual device emulators for the later Android APIs; therefore, develop with the earlier SDK platforms on such computers. If in doubt about what to download, either accept the initial choices and rerun the SDK Manager to get other packages as and when required; or check all packages to download everything (the download may take a while). Click the "Install packages" button.

The selected packages will be shown in a list; if a package has licensing terms that require acceptance, it is shown with a question mark. Highlight each package that has a question mark to read the licensing terms. You can accept or reject the package using the radio buttons. Rejected packages are marked with a red ×. Alternatively, click Accept All to accept everything that is available. Click the Install button and a progress log will show the packages being installed, as well as any errors that occur. On Windows a common error occurs when the SDK Manager is unable to access or rename directories. Rerun the SDK Manager as administrator and check that the directory does not have any read-only flags or files; see Recipe 1.12 for further details. When complete close the SDK Manager by clicking the × button in the top corner of the window.

Installing the Android Development Tools (ADT) plug-in

You install the ADT plug-in via Eclipse, but to do so you must run Eclipse from the administrator account. Use the shortcut created earlier or *eclipse.exe* from the *eclipse* folder. In either case, bring up the context menu (usually via a right-click), select "Run as administrator," and accept any security warnings. When Eclipse has loaded open the Help menu item and select Install New Software....

On the Install screen enter the following address in the "Work with" box:

https://dl-ssl.google.com/android/eclipse/

Click the Add button. An Add Repository screen appears; in the Name box type something meaningful, such as "ADT plug-in" (the aforementioned web address will be displayed in the Location box); see Figure 1-11.

Click the OK button. The screen will update after briefly showing Pending in the Name column of the table.

Check the box next to Developer Tools. Then select the Next button at the bottom of the screen (see Figure 1-12).

A list of the items to be installed will be displayed. If you get an error message check that Eclipse has been run under the administrator account. Select Next again. A screen displays the licenses; ensure that each license has been accepted (select the "I accept the terms of the license agreements" radio button). Then click the Finish button. A

Figure 1-11. Adding the ADT plug-in repository

security warning will need to be accepted to complete the installation; select OK to this warning (the address entered earlier is a secure address). Eclipse will ask you for a restart. Select the Restart Now button and Eclipse will close and reload. A Welcome to Android Development dialog will appear. Set the SDK location in the Existing Location box (since the SDK Manager will have already run), browse to the Android SDK folder (by default, *C:\Program Files\Android\android-sdk*), and click Next (see Figure 1-13).

A Google Android SDK usage monitoring question will appear; change the option if required and click Finish. Eclipse is now configured to build and debug Android apps. See Recipe 3.3 to configure an Android emulator; then try Recipe 1.4 as a sanity check. Plug a physical device into the computer and use its settings to turn on USB Debugging (under Development in Applications).

See Also

Recipe 1.4; Recipe 1.12; Recipe 3.3; *http://developer.android.com/sdk/installing.html*, *http://www.eclipse.org/*; *http://www.oracle.com/technetwork/java/javase/downloads/index.html*

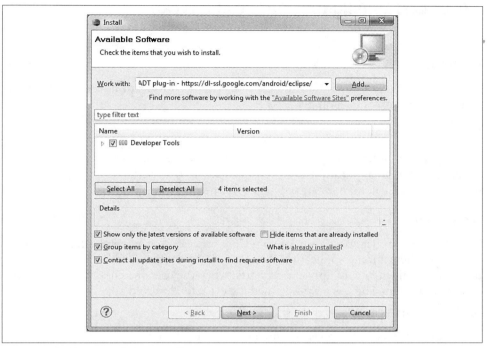

Figure 1-12. Choosing what to install

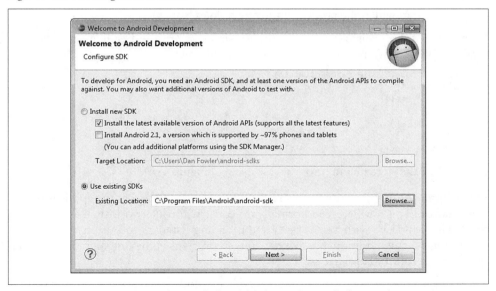

Figure 1-13. Connecting the newly installed SDK to the newly installed ADT plug-in

1.6 Understanding the Android Life Cycle

Ian Darwin

Problem

Android apps do not have a "main" method; you need to learn how they get started and how they stop or get stopped.

Solution

The class `android.Activity` provides a number of well-defined life-cycle methods that are called when an application is started, suspended, restarted, and so on, as well as a method you can call to mark an activity as finished.

Discussion

Your Android application runs in its own Unix process, so in general it cannot directly affect any other running application. The Dalvik VM interfaces with the operating system to call you when your application starts, when the user switches to another application, and so on. There is a well-defined life cycle for Android applications.

An Android application has three states it can be in:

- Active, in which the app is visible to the user and is running
- Paused, in which the app is partly obscured and has lost the input focus
- Stopped, in which the app is completely hidden from view

Your app will be transitioned among these states by Android calling the following methods on the current activity at the appropriate time:

```
void onCreate(Bundle savedInstanceState)
void onStart()
void onResume()
void onRestart()
void onPause()
void onStop()
void onDestroy()
```

You can see the state diagram for this life cycle in Figure 1-14.

For an application's first activity, `onCreate()` is how you know that the application has been started. This is where you normally do constructor-like work such as setting up the "main window" with `setContentView()`, adding listeners to buttons to do work (including starting additional activities), and so on. This is the one method that even the simplest Android app needs.

You can see the effects of the various life cycle methods by creating a dummy project in Eclipse and overriding all the methods with log "debug" statements.

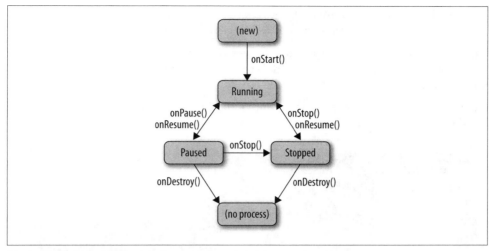

Figure 1-14. Android life-cycle states

1.7 Installing .apk Files onto an Emulator via the ADB

Rachee Singh

Problem

You have an application's *.apk* file, and you want to install it on the emulator to check out the application, or because an application you are developing requires it.

Solution

Use the ADB command-line tool to install the *.apk* file onto the running emulator; you can also use this tool to install an *.apk* file onto a connected Android device.

Discussion

To install the *.apk* file, follow these steps:

1. Find the location on your machine where you have installed the Android SDK. In the Android SDK directory, go to the *tools* directory.
2. Look for an executable named adb in the *tools* directory. If it is present that is the location of the adb file; otherwise, there should be a *.txt* file named "adb has moved." The contents of the file merely direct you to the location of the adb binary; the file states that adb is present in the *platform-tools* directory instead of the *tools* directory.
3. Once you have located the adb program, cd to that location in a terminal (Linux) or command prompt (Windows).

4. Use the command `adb install` *location of the .apk you want to install.* If you get "command not found" on Linux, try using "./adb" instead of just "adb".

This should start the installation on the device that is currently running (either an emulator that is running on your desktop, or a physical Android device that is connected).

After the installation finishes, in the menu of the Android device/emulator you should see the icon of the application you just installed (see Figure 1-15).

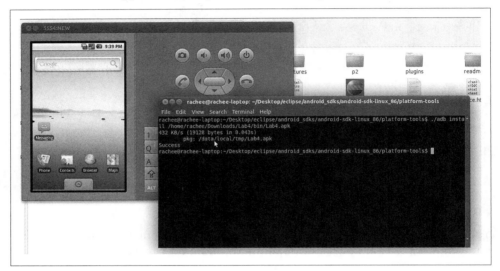

Figure 1-15. The installation command

1.8 Installing Apps onto an Emulator via SlideME

David Dawes

Problem

App stores are a huge element of the attraction of modern smartphones. Google's Android Market is the official app store, but you may want to use others as well.

Solution

SlideMe LLC (*http://slideme.org/*) offers an alternative app store. The SlideME app store allows you to install other apps (perhaps you want to integrate with other apps), as well as test the experience of publishing and downloading your own apps on your emulated Android device. SlideME also reaches many Android users who are locked out of the Google Android Market, including people with unsupported devices and those who don't live in a country that is supported by the Android Market.

Discussion

An alternative to the official Android Market is Slide ME, an alternative app store (*http: //slideme.org/*). SlideME may not have as many apps as Google's Android Market, but it has some advantages, including that it works easily on an emulated Android device.

Go to the SlideME website (*http://slideme.org/*) using your emulated Android device, browse or search through the apps, and click on a free one. After a pause to download the file, open the download (the little arrow on the top left), review the license, and launch the *.apk* file you've downloaded to install the app. During the installation, you will be asked to review and accept the license for the software.

Once the SlideME app is installed, you can go through the catalog and install more apps without using the browser. This is much easier than using a web browser to download the apps, since the presentation is designed for the Android device; simply choose a category, scroll through it, and choose an app to install. I have had some stability problems using the app on my emulator—it freezes on occasion—but I was able to install some basic free apps, like Grocery List.

I noticed in the Android Invasion discussion forum on Linkedin.com that some Android users are disappointed to find that many cell phone providers do *not* include the official Android Market in their Android cell phone offerings, and unless you're comfortable rooting and flashing your Android phone there's no way to get it. Most consumers are not comfortable rooting and flashing their phones, and for them SlideME offers an alternative way to find free and inexpensive apps for their phones.

See Also

SlideME also allows you to publish your apps to its app store; see the Applications page on the SlideME website (*http://slideme.org/applications*).

For information on developing apps for SlideME, see *http://slideme.org/developers*.

1.9 Sharing Java Classes from Another Eclipse Project

Ian Darwin

Problem

You want to use a class from another project, but you don't want to copy and paste.

Solution

Add the project as a "referenced project," and Eclipse (and DEX) will do the work.

Discussion

You often need to reuse classes from another project. In my JPSTrack GPS tracking program, the Android version borrows classes such as the file I/O module from the Java SE version. You surely do not want to copy and paste classes willy-nilly from one project into another, because this makes maintenance improbable.

In the simplest case, when the library project contains the source of the classes you want to import, all you have to do is declare the project containing the needed classes (the Java SE version in this case) as a referenced project on the build path. Select Project→Properties→Java Build Path, select Projects, and click Add. In Figure 1-16, I am adding the SE project "jpstrack" as a dependency on the Android project "jpstrack.android."

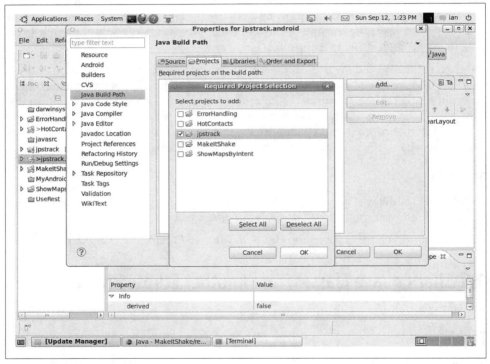

Figure 1-16. Making one project depend on another—using standard Eclipse

Mobile developers who create apps for other platforms as well should note that this technique does not work if you also have the current (late 2011) BlackBerry Java plug-in installed in your Eclipse installation. This is a bug in the BlackBerry Java plug-in; it incorrectly flags even non-BlackBerry projects as depending on non-BlackBerry-library projects, and marks the project as having an error, which will prevent correct code generation and execution. Remove the buggy plug-in, or put it in its own Eclipse installation.

Alternatively, create a JAR file using either Ant or the Eclipse wizard. Have the other project refer to it as an external JAR in the classpath settings. Or physically copy it into the *libs* directory and refer to it from there.

A newer method that is often more reliable and is now officially recommended, but is only useful if both projects are Android projects, is to declare the library one as a library project, under Project→Properties→Android→Library tab, and use the Add button on the other project on the same screen to list the library project as a dependency on the main project (see Figure 1-17).

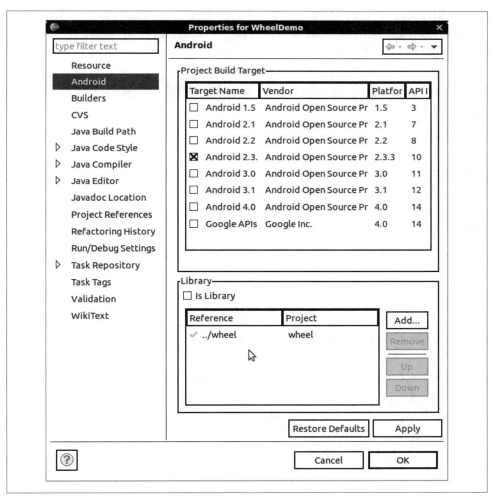

Figure 1-17. Making one project depend on another—using ADT

For command-line fans, the first method involves editing the *.classpath* file, while the second method simply creates entries in the *project.properties* file, for example:

```
# Project target
target=android-7
android.library=false
android.library.reference.1=../wheel
```

Since you are probably keeping both projects under source control (and if these are programs you ever intend to ship, you should!), remember to "tag" both projects when you release the Android project—one of the points in favor of source control is that you are able to re-create exactly what you shipped.

See Also

See the official documentation on Library Projects (*http://developer.android.com/guide/developing/projects/index.html#LibraryProjects*).

1.10 Referencing Libraries to Implement External Functionality

Rachee Singh

Problem

You need to reference an external library in your source code.

Solution

Obtain the JAR file for the library that you require and add it to your project.

Discussion

As an example, you might need to use AndroidPlot, a library for plotting charts and graphs in your application, or OpenStreetMap, a wiki project that creates and provides free geographic data and mapping. If so, your application needs to reference these libraries. You can do this in Eclipse in a few simple steps:

1. Download the JAR file corresponding to the library you wish to use.
2. After creating your Android project in Eclipse, right-click on the project name and select Properties in the menu (Figure 1-18).
3. From the list on the left side, select Java Build Path and click on the Libraries tab.
4. Click the Add External JARs button.
5. Provide the location where you downloaded the JAR file for the library you wish to use.

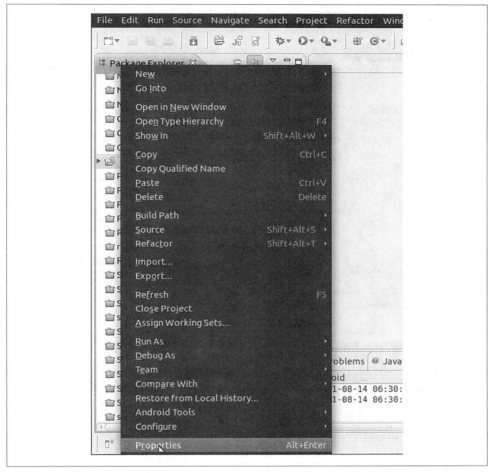

Figure 1-18. Selecting project properties

At this point you will see a *Referenced Libraries* directory in your project. The JARs you added will appear (see Figure 1-19).

An alternative approach is to create a *lib* folder in your project, physically copy the JAR files there, and add them individually as you did earlier, but instead clicking the Add JARs button. This keeps everything in one place (especially if your project is shared via a version control system with others who might use a different operating system and be unable to locate the external JARs in the same place). However, it does raise the burden of responsibility for licensing issues on the included JAR files. See Figure 1-20.

In either case, if you also build with Ant, be sure to update your *build.xml* file.

Whichever way you do it, it's pretty easy to add libraries to your project.

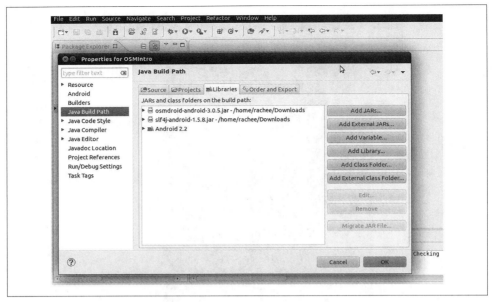

Figure 1-19. Adding libraries

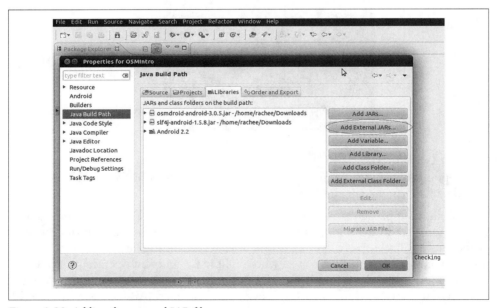

Figure 1-20. Adding the external JAR file

1.11 Using SDK Samples to Help Avoid Head Scratching

Daniel Fowler

Problem

Sometimes it is a struggle to code up some functionality, especially when the documentation is sketchy or does not provide any examples.

Solution

Looking at existing working code will help. The Android SDK has sample programs that you can pick apart to see how they work.

Discussion

The Android SDK comes with several sample applications that can be useful when trying to code up some functionality. Looking through the sample code can be insightful. Once you have installed the Android SDK, several samples become available:

- Accelerometer Play
- Accessibility Service
- API Demos
- Backup and Restore
- Bluetooth Chat
- Business Card
- Contact Manager
- Cube Live Wallpaper
- Home
- Honeycomb Gallery
- JetBoy
- Lunar Lander
- Multiple Resolutions
- Near Field Communication
- Note Pad
- RenderScript
- Sample Sync Adapter
- Searchable Dictionary
- Session Initiation Protocol
- Snake
- Soft Keyboard

- Spinner
- SpinnerTest
- StackView Widget
- TicTacToeLib
- TicTacToeMain
- USB
- Wiktionary
- Wiktionary (Simplified)
- Weather List Widget
- XML Adapters

To open a sample project from Eclipse open the File menu and then select Android Project. See Figure 1-21.

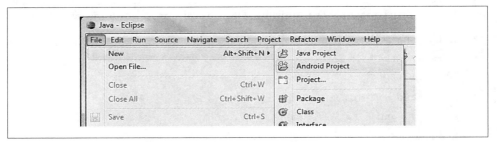

Figure 1-21. Starting a new Android project

On the New Android Project dialog, select the "Create project from existing sample" option. Click Next and select the Build Target. A list of available samples for the selected target is shown. If the required sample is not shown, go back and select another Build Target. (The sample may not be installed; the SDK Manager can be used to install additional samples if they were missed during the SDK setup.) Choose the sample to load, click Finish, and the sample is copied to the Workspace and built (with progress shown on the status bar).

After a short time, the sample will be ready to run and you will be able to browse the source code to see how it is all done.

If the samples have been moved from the SDK *samples* directory, use the "Create project from existing source" option on the New Android Project dialog to open the sample.

When the sample is first run select Android Application in the Run As dialog that may appear. It may also be necessary to configure an appropriate AVD to run the sample (see Recipe 3.3). See Figure 1-22.

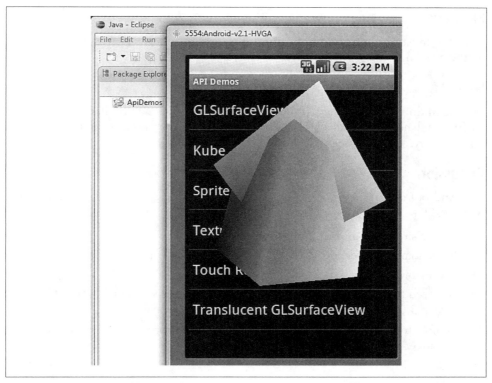

Figure 1-22. API demos in action

See Also

The Android Developers website at *http://developer.android.com/index.html*; this cookbook, of course.

You can also search the Web for additional programs or examples. If you still can't find what you need, you can seek help from Stack Overflow (*http://www.stackoverflow .com*; use "android" as the tag) or from the Internet Relay Chat (IRC) channel #android-dev on freenode.

1.12 Keeping the Android SDK Updated

Daniel Fowler

Problem

The SDK must be kept updated to allow app developers to work with the latest APIs on the evolving Android platform.

Solution

Use the Android SDK Manager program to update the existing installed SDK packages and to install new SDK packages. This includes third-party packages for device-specific functionality.

Discussion

The Android operating system (OS) is constantly evolving, and therefore, so is the Android SDK. The ongoing development of Android is driven by:

- Google's research and development
- Phone manufacturers developing new and improved handsets
- Addressing security issues and possible exploits
- The need to support new devices (e.g., support for tablet devices was added with version 3.0)
- Support for new hardware interfaces (e.g., support for near field communication was added in version 2.3).
- Fixing bugs
- Improvements in functionality (e.g., a new JavaScript engine)
- Changes in the underlying Linux kernel
- Deprecation of redundant programming interfaces
- New uses (e.g., Google TV)
- The wider Android development community

We covered Android SDK installation elsewhere (see Recipe 1.5 or *http://developer .android.com/sdk/installing.html*). After the SDK is installed on the development machine and the programming environment is running smoothly, once in a while developers will need to check for updates to the SDK.

You can keep the SDK up-to-date by running the SDK Manager program. (On a Windows machine run *SDK Manager.exe* in the folder *C:\Program Files\Android\android-sdk*, or use the Start button, then select All Programs→Android SDK Tools, and click SDK Manager). You can also run it from within Eclipse (using the Window menu and selecting Android SDK Manager). See Figure 1-23. The Android SDK is divided into

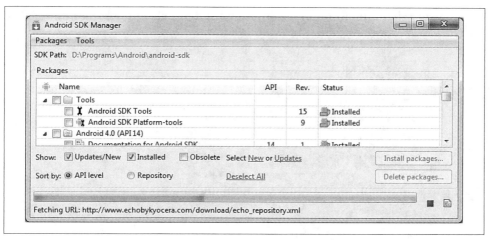

Figure 1-23. The Android SDK Manager

several packages. The SDK Manager automatically scans for updates to existing packages and will list new packages and those provided by device manufacturers.

Available updates will be shown in a list (as will available optional packages). If an update or package has licensing terms that require acceptance it is shown with a question mark. Highlight each package that has a question mark to read the licensing terms. You can accept or reject the package using the radio buttons. Rejected packages are marked with a red ×. See Figure 1-24.

Figure 1-24. Choosing SDK packages

Alternatively, click on Accept All to accept everything that is available. All packages and updates that are ready to download and install will be shown with a green tick.

Click the Install button to begin the download and installation; when complete click the Close button. See Figure 1-25.

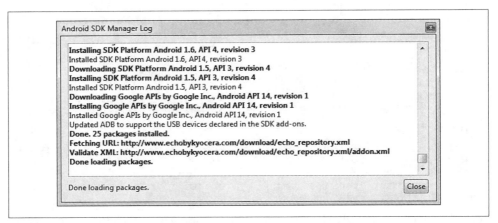

Figure 1-25. SDK Manager Log window

If the SDK Manager program has itself been updated, you will see a message asking you to restart the program (see Figure 1-26).

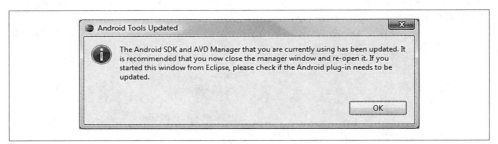

Figure 1-26. SDK Manager update notice

The SDK Manager is also used to download additional packages that are not part of the standard platform. This mechanism is used by device manufacturers to provide support for their own hardware. For example, LG Electronics provides a 3D device, and to support 3D capability in applications an additional package is provided. It is also used by Google to allow the download of optional APIs.

In the SDK Manager dialog, expand and tick the required packages in the left-hand list, and then click the Install button (see Figure 1-27). If a third-party package is not listed, the URL to a *respository.xml* file, provided by the package publisher, will need to be entered via the Tools menu.

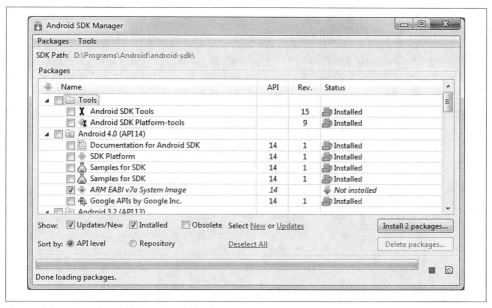

Figure 1-27. List of installed and installable components

Possible update errors on Windows

In a system this complex, there are many things that might go wrong. This section discusses some of these and their solutions.

Run SDK Manager as admin. On a Windows machine, the default location for the SDK is under the *C:\Program Files\Android\android-sdk* directory. This is a restricted directory and can cause the SDK installation to fail. A message dialog with the title "SDK Manager: failed to install" can appear (see Figure 1-28).

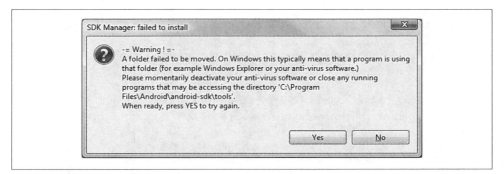

Figure 1-28. SDK Manager: Failed to install

To overcome this error there are a few things to check:

- Unplug any Android devices (this may prevent *adb.exe* from closing).

- Browse to *C:\Program Files\Android\Android-sdk* and bring up the Properties for the *tools* folder (select the context menu, and then Properties). Ensure that the "Read-only (Only applies to files in folder)" checkbox is cleared (see Figure 1-29).

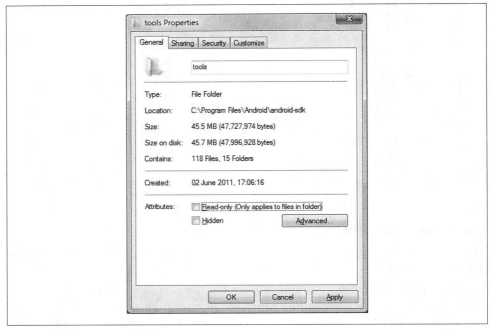

Figure 1-29. Setting read-write attribute under Microsoft Windows

You may need to give permission to change the attributes (see Figure 1-30).

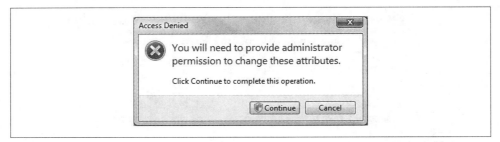

Figure 1-30. Permission required confirmation

A Confirm Attribute Changes dialog will appear; ensure the option "Apply changes to this folder, subfolders and files" is selected and click OK. Then do the following:

- Restart the computer.
- Ensure that all other programs are closed, especially any copies of File Explorer.
- Run *SDK Manager.exe* under the administrator account. Bring up the context menu and select "Run as administrator. (See Figure 1-31.)

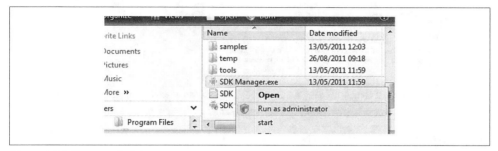

Figure 1-31. Run as administrator

Close ADB before updating. A message asking you to restart ADB (the Android Debugger) may appear (Figure 1-32).

Figure 1-32. Confirmation to restart ADB

Ideally, it is best to run the SDK Manager without ADB running, and it should not be running if Windows has just been started. Alternatively, you can use the Windows Task Manager to stop *adb.exe*. Answer No to this prompt if ADB was not running; otherwise, answer Yes.

SDK Manager cannot update itself. During the SDK update installation there may be an error related to the SDK Manager program (see Figure 1-33).

To resolve this error ensure that all programs are closed (including *adb.exe*). Then copy *SDK Manager.exe* from *C:\Program Files\Android\android-sdk\tools\lib* to *C:\Program Files\Android\android-sdk* (or wherever the SDK is installed). Then run the SDK Manager again. (See Figure 1-32.)

Updating Eclipse. After you update the SDK and open Eclipse a warning message may appear (see Figure 1-34).

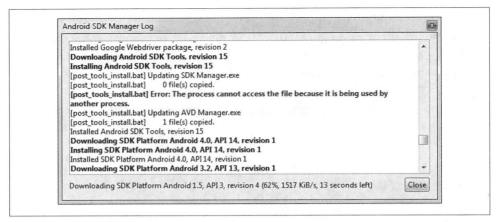

Figure 1-33. Android SDK Manager Log window

Figure 1-34. Android SDK version incorrect

In Eclipse, select Help and then select Check for Updates. Wait for the progress dialog to finish and the Android Eclipse updates will be shown. Click Next twice, and accept the licensing terms. Then click Finish to start the download and update process. A warning message about unsigned content may appear. Click OK to accept the warning (only do so if you are updating via Eclipse). Restart Eclipse once the update has completed (a message to do so will appear).

Further information on troubleshooting the SDK Manager and Android Eclipse plug-in is available on the Android Developers website.

See Also

Recipe 1.5; Installing the SDK (*http://developer.android.com/sdk/installing.html*); Adding SDK Components (*http://developer.android.com/sdk/adding-components.html*); ADT Plugin for Eclipse (*http://developer.android.com/sdk/eclipse-adt.html*)

1.13 Taking a Screenshot from the Emulator/Android Device

Rachee Singh

Problem

You want to take a screenshot of an application running on an Android device.

Solution

Use the Device Screen Capture feature of the Dalvik Debug Monitor Server (DDMS) view in Eclipse.

Discussion

To use the Device Screen Capture feature follow these steps:

1. Run the application in Eclipse and go to the DDMS view (Window menu→Open Perspective→Other→DDMS) or Window menu→Show View→Other→Android→Devices; the former is shown in Figure 1-36).

   Note that the line that reads "Resource...does not exist" appears in Figure 1-35 only because another Eclipse project has been closed, and does not affect the steps listed here.

Figure 1-35. Starting DDMS view

2. In the DDMS view, select the device or emulator whose screen you want to capture.

3. In the DDMS view, click the Screen Capture icon. See Figure 1-36.

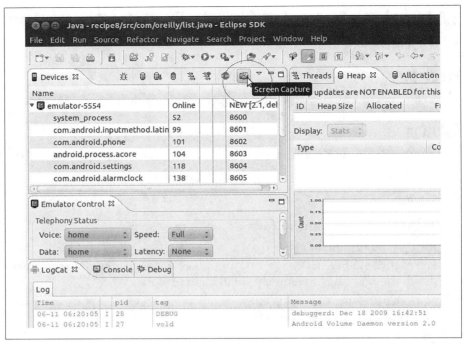

Figure 1-36. Device screen capture

4. A window showing the current screen of the emulator/Android device will pop up. It should look like Figure 1-37. You can save the screenshot and use it to describe the app!

Figure 1-37. The screenshot

See Also

Some distributions provide alternative ways of taking screenshots. CyanogenMod 7.x (*http://cyanogenmod.com/*) provides a screenshot in the menu you get when you long-press the power button. Some HTC tablets with pen support offer screen grabs in the Pen menu. Ice Cream Sandwich (Android 4.0) provides a built-in mechanism for taking screenshots on real devices: just press the Volume Down control at the same time as the Power button, and the image will be saved to your device and can be viewed in the Gallery application.

1.14 Program: A Simple CountDownTimer Example

Wagied Davids

Problem

You want a simple countdown timer, a program that will count down a given number of seconds until it reaches zero.

Solution

Android comes with a built-in class for constructing `CountDownTimer`s. It's easy to use, it's efficient, and it works (that goes without saying!).

Discussion

The steps to provide a countdown timer are as follows:

1. Create a subclass of `CountDownTimer`. This class's constructor takes two arguments, `CountDownTimer(long millisInFuture, long countDownInterval)`. The first is the number of milliseconds from now when the interval should be done; at this point the subclass's `onFinish()` method will be called. The second is the frequency in milliseconds of how often you want to get notified that the timer is still running, typically to update a progress monitor or otherwise communicate with the user. Your subclass's `onTick()` method will be called with each passage of this many milliseconds.

2. Override the `onTick()` and `onFinish()` methods.

3. Instantiate a new instance in your Android Activity.

4. Call the start() method on the new instance created!

The example Countdown Timer program consists of an XML Layout (shown in Example 1-4) and some Java code (shown in Example 1-5). When run, it should look something like Figure 1-38, though the times will probably be different.

Example 1-4. main.xml

```xml
<?xml version="1.0" encoding="utf-8"?>
<LinearLayout
    xmlns:android="http://schemas.android.com/apk/res/android"
    android:orientation="vertical"
    android:layout_width="fill_parent"
    android:layout_height="fill_parent">
    <Button
        android:id="@+id/button"
        android:text="Start"
        android:layout_width="fill_parent"
        android:layout_height="wrap_content" />
    <TableLayout
        android:padding="10dip"
        android:layout_gravity="center"
        android:layout_width="fill_parent"
        android:layout_height="wrap_content">
        <TableRow>
            <TextView
                android:id="@+id/timer"
                android:text="Time: "
                android:paddingRight="10dip"
                android:layout_width="wrap_content"
                android:layout_height="wrap_content" />

            <TextView
                android:id="@+id/timeElapsed"
                android:text="Time elapsed: "
                android:paddingRight="10dip"
                android:layout_width="wrap_content"
                android:layout_height="wrap_content" />
        </TableRow>
    </TableLayout>
</LinearLayout>
```

Example 1-5. Main.java

```java
package com.examples;

import android.app.Activity;
import android.os.Bundle;
import android.os.CountDownTimer;
import android.view.View;
import android.view.View.OnClickListener;
import android.widget.Button;
import android.widget.TextView;

public class Main extends Activity implements OnClickListener
    {
        private MalibuCountDownTimer countDownTimer;
        private long timeElapsed;
        private boolean timerHasStarted = false;
        private Button startB;
        private TextView text;
        private TextView timeElapsedView;
```

```
private final long startTime = 50 * 1000;
private final long interval = 1 * 1000;

/** Called when the activity is first created. */
@Override
public void onCreate(Bundle savedInstanceState)
    {
        super.onCreate(savedInstanceState);
        setContentView(R.layout.main);
        startB = (Button) this.findViewById(R.id.button);
        startB.setOnClickListener(this);

        text = (TextView) this.findViewById(R.id.timer);
        timeElapsedView = (TextView) this.findViewById(R.id.timeElapsed);
        countDownTimer = new MalibuCountDownTimer(startTime, interval);
        text.setText(text.getText() + String.valueOf(startTime));
    }

@Override
public void onClick(View v)
    {
        if (!timerHasStarted)
            {
                countDownTimer.start();
                timerHasStarted = true;
                startB.setText("Start");
            }
        else
            {

                countDownTimer.cancel();
                timerHasStarted = false;
                startB.setText("RESET");
            }
    }

// CountDownTimer class
public class MalibuCountDownTimer extends CountDownTimer
    {

        public MalibuCountDownTimer(long startTime, long interval)
            {
                super(startTime, interval);
            }

        @Override
        public void onFinish()
            {
                text.setText("Time's up!");
                timeElapsedView.setText("Time Elapsed: " +
                    String.valueOf(startTime));
            }

        @Override
```

```
        public void onTick(long millisUntilFinished)
            {
                text.setText("Time remain:" + millisUntilFinished);
                timeElapsed = startTime - millisUntilFinished;
                timeElapsedView.setText("Time Elapsed: " +
                    String.valueOf(timeElapsed));
            }
        }
    }
```

Figure 1-38. Timer reset

Source Download URL

The source code for this example is in the Android Cookbook repository at *http://github .com/AndroidCook/Android-Cookbook-Examples*, in the subdirectory CountDownTimerExample (see "Getting and Using the Code Examples" on page xvii).

1.15 Program: Tipster, a Tip Calculator for the Android OS

Sunit Katkar

Problem

When you go with friends to a restaurant and wish to divide the check and tip, you can get into a lot of manual calculations and disagreements. Instead, you want to use an app that lets you simply add the tip percentage to the total and divide by the number of diners. Tipster is an implementation of this in Android, to show a complete application.

Solution

This is a simple exercise that uses the basic GUI elements in Android and then pieces them together with some simple calculations and some event-driven UI code to tie it all together. We will use the following GUI components:

TableLayout
> This provides a good control over screen layout. This layout allows you to use the HTML Table tag paradigm to lay out widgets.

TableRow
> This defines a row in the TableLayout. It's like the HTML TR and TD tags combined.

TextView
> This View provides a label for displaying static text on the screen.

EditText
> This View provides a text field for entering values.

RadioGroup
> This groups together radio buttons.

RadioButton
> This provides a radio button.

Button
> This is the regular button.

View
> We will use a View to create a visual separator with certain height and color attributes.

Discussion

Android uses XML files for the layout of widgets. In our example project, the Android plug-in for Eclipse generates a *main.xml* file for the layout. This file has the XML-based definitions of the different widgets and their containers.

There is a *strings.xml* file which has all the string resources used in the application. A default *icon.png* file is provided for the application icon.

Then there is the *R.java* file which is automatically generated (and updated when any changes are made to *main.xml*). This file has the constants defined for each layout and widget. Do not edit this file manually; the plug-in does it for you when you make any changes to your XML files.

In our example we have *Tipster.java* as the main Java file for the Activity.

Recipe 1.4 as well as various Google tutorials highlight how to use the plug-in. Using the Eclipse plug-in, create an Android project named Tipster. The end result will be a project layout that looks like the one shown in Figure 1-39.

Creating the layout and placing the widgets

The end goal is to create a layout similar to the one shown in Figure 1-39.

For this screen layout we will use the following layouts and widgets:

TableLayout
> Provides good control over screen layout. This layout allows you to use the HTML Table tag paradigm to lay out widgets.

TableRow
> This defines a row in the TableLayout. It's like the HTML TR and TD tags combined.

TextView
> This View provides a label for displaying static text on the screen.

EditText
> This View provides a text field for entering values.

RadioGroup
> This groups together radio buttons.

RadioButton
> This provides a radio button.

Button
> This is the regular button.

View
> We will use a View to create a visual separator with certain height and color attributes.

Familiarize yourself with these widgets as you will be using these quite a lot in applications you build. When you go to the Javadocs for layout and widget, look up the XML attributes. This will help you correlate the usage in the *main.xml* layout file and the Java code (*Tipster.java* and *R.java*) where these are accessed.

Also available is a visual layout editor in the Eclipse ADT, as well as a standalone UI tool called DroidDraw (*http://www.droiddraw.org/*), both of which let you create a layout by dragging and dropping widgets from a palette, like any form designer tool. However, I recommend that you create the layout by hand in XML, at least in your initial stages of learning Android. Later on, as you learn all the nuances of the XML layout API, you can delegate the task to such tools.

The layout file, *main.xml*, has the layout information (see Example 1-6). A TableRow widget creates a single row inside the TableLayout. So you use as many TableRows as the number of rows you want. In this tutorial we will use eight TableRows—five for the widgets up to the visual separator below the buttons, and three for the results area below the buttons and separator.

Example 1-6. /res/layout/main.xml

```xml
<?xml version="1.0" encoding="utf-8"?>
<!-- Using table layout to have HTML table like control over layout -->
<TableLayout
        android:id="@+id/TableLayout01"
        android:layout_width="fill_parent"
        android:layout_height="fill_parent"
        android:stretchColumns="1"
        xmlns:android="http://schemas.android.com/apk/res/android">
    <!-- Row 1: Text label placed in column zero,
         text field placed in column two and allowed to
         span two columns. So a total of 4 columns in this row -->
        <TableRow>
        <TextView
                android:id="@+id/txtLbl1"
                android:layout_width="wrap_content"
                android:layout_height="wrap_content"
                android:layout_column="0"
                android:text="@string/textLbl1"/>
        <EditText❶
                android:id="@+id/txtAmount"
                android:layout_width="wrap_content"
                android:layout_height="wrap_content"
                android:numeric="decimal"
                android:layout_column="2"
                android:layout_span="2"
                />
        </TableRow>
    <!-- Row 2: Text label placed in column zero,
         text field placed in column two and allowed to
         span two columns. So a total of 4 columns in this row -->
        <TableRow>
        <TextView
                android:id="@+id/txtLbl2"
                android:layout_width="wrap_content"
                android:layout_height="wrap_content"
                android:layout_column="0"
                android:text="@string/textLbl2"/>
        <EditText
                android:id="@+id/txtPeople"
                android:layout_width="wrap_content"
                android:layout_height="wrap_content"
                android:numeric="integer"
                android:layout_column="2"
                android:layout_span="3"/>
        </TableRow>
    <!-- Row 3: This has just one text label placed in column zero  -->
        <TableRow>
        <TextView
                android:id="@+id/txtLbl3"
                android:layout_width="wrap_content"
```

```
                android:layout_height="wrap_content"
                android:text="@string/textLbl3"/>
        </TableRow>
<!-- Row 4: RadioGroup for RadioButtons placed at column zero
     with column span of three, thus creating one radio
     button per cell of the table row. Last cell number 4 has the
     textfield to enter a custom tip percentage -->
        <TableRow>
        <RadioGroup
                android:id="@+id/RadioGroupTips"
                android:orientation="horizontal"
                android:layout_width="wrap_content"
                android:layout_height="wrap_content"
                android:layout_column="0"
                android:layout_span="3"
                android:checkedButton="@+id/radioFifteen">
                <RadioButton android:id="@+id/radioFifteen"
                        android:layout_width="wrap_content"
                        android:layout_height="wrap_content"
                        android:text="@string/rdoTxt15"
                        android:textSize="15sp" />
                <RadioButton android:id="@+id/radioTwenty"
                        android:layout_width="wrap_content"
                        android:layout_height="wrap_content"
                        android:text="@string/rdoTxt20"
                        android:textSize="15sp" />
                <RadioButton android:id="@+id/radioOther"
                        android:layout_width="wrap_content"
                        android:layout_height="wrap_content"
                        android:text="@string/rdoTxtOther"
                        android:textSize="15sp" />
        </RadioGroup>
                <EditText
                        android:id="@+id/txtTipOther"
                        android:layout_width="fill_parent"
                        android:layout_height="wrap_content"
                        android:numeric="decimal"/>
        </TableRow>
<!--  Row for the Calculate and Rest buttons. The Calculate button
      is placed at column two, and Reset at column three -->
        <TableRow>
        <Button
                android:id="@+id/btnReset"
                android:layout_width="wrap_content"
                android:layout_height="wrap_content"
                android:layout_column="2"
                android:text="@string/btnReset"/>
        <Button
                android:id="@+id/btnCalculate"
                android:layout_width="wrap_content"
                android:layout_height="wrap_content"
                android:layout_column="3"
                android:text="@string/btnCalculate"/>
        </TableRow>
```

```xml
<!-- TableLayout allows any other views to be inserted between
     the TableRow elements. So insert a blank view to create a
     line separator. This separator view is used to separate
     the area below the buttons which will display the
     calculation results -->
<View
        android:layout_height="2px"
        android:background="#DDFFDD"
        android:layout_marginTop="5dip"
        android:layout_marginBottom="5dip"/>

<!-- Again table row is used to place the result textviews
     at column zero and the result in textviews at column two -->
<TableRow android:paddingBottom="10dip" android:paddingTop="5dip">
<TextView
        android:id="@+id/txtLbl4"
        android:layout_width="wrap_content"
        android:layout_height="wrap_content"
        android:layout_column="0"
        android:text="@string/textLbl4"/>
<TextView
        android:id="@+id/txtTipAmount"
        android:layout_width="wrap_content"
        android:layout_height="wrap_content"
        android:layout_column="2"
        android:layout_span="2"/>
</TableRow>

<TableRow android:paddingBottom="10dip" android:paddingTop="5dip">
<TextView
        android:id="@+id/txtLbl5"
        android:layout_width="wrap_content"
        android:layout_height="wrap_content"
        android:layout_column="0"
        android:text="@string/textLbl5"/>
<TextView
        android:id="@+id/txtTotalToPay"
        android:layout_width="wrap_content"
        android:layout_height="wrap_content"
        android:layout_column="2"
        android:layout_span="2"/>
</TableRow>

<TableRow android:paddingBottom="10dip" android:paddingTop="5dip">
<TextView
        android:id="@+id/txtLbl6"
        android:layout_width="wrap_content"
        android:layout_height="wrap_content"
        android:layout_column="0"
        android:text="@string/textLbl6"/>
<TextView
        android:id="@+id/txtTipPerPerson"
        android:layout_width="wrap_content"
        android:layout_height="wrap_content"
        android:layout_column="2"
```

```
                android:layout_span="2"/>
        </TableRow>
    <!--  End of all rows and widgets -->
</TableLayout>
```

TableLayout and TableRow

After examining *main.xml*, you can gather that the `TableLayout` and `TableRow` are straightforward to use. You create the `TableLayout` once, then insert a `TableRow`. Now you are free to insert any other widgets, such as `TextView`, `EditView`, and so on, inside this `TableRow`.

Do look at the attributes, especially `android:stretchColumns`, `android:layout_column`, and `android:layout_span`, which allow you to place widgets the same way you would use a regular HTML table. I recommend that you follow the links to these attributes and read up on how they work for a `TableLayout`.

Controlling input values

Controlling input values: Look at the `EditText` widget in the *main.xml* file at ❶. This is the first text field for entering the "Total Amount" of the check. We want only numbers here. We can accept decimal numbers because real restaurant checks can be for dollars and cents, and not just dollars. So we use the `android:numeric` attribute with a value of `decimal`. This will allow whole values like 10 and decimal values like 10.12, but will prevent any other type of entry.

This is a simple and concise way to control input values, thus saving us the trouble of writing validation code in the *Tipster.java* file, and ensuring that the user does not enter erroneous values. This XML-based constraints feature of Android is quite powerful and useful. You should explore all possible attributes that go with a particular widget to extract maximum benefits from this XML shorthand way of setting constraints. In a future release, unless I have missed it completely in this release, I hope that Android allows for entering ranges for the `android:numeric` attribute so that we can define what range of numbers we wish to accept.

Since ranges are not currently available (to the best of my knowledge), you will see later on that we do have to check for certain values like zero or empty values to ensure that our tip calculation arithmetic does not fail.

Examining Tipster.java

Now we will look at the *Tipster.java* file which controls our application. This is the main class that does the layout, the event handling, and the application logic.

The Android Eclipse plug-in creates the *Tipster.java* file in our project with the default code shown in Example 1-7.

Example 1-7. Code snippet 1 of /src/com/examples/tipcalc/Tipster.java

```
package com.examples.tipcalc;

import android.app.Activity;

public class Tipster extends Activity {
    /** Called when the activity is first created. */
    @Override
    public void onCreate(Bundle savedInstanceState) {
        super.onCreate(savedInstanceState);
        setContentView(R.layout.main);
    }
}
```

The `Tipster` class extends the `android.app.Activity` class. An activity is a single, focused thing that the user can do. The `Activity` class takes care of creating the window and then laying out the UI. You have to call the `setContentView(View view)` method to put your UI in the `Activity`. So think of `Activity` as an outer frame that is empty, and that you populate with your UI.

Now look at the snippet of the *Tipster.java* class shown in Example 1-8. First we define the widgets as class members. Look at ❶ through ❷ in particular for reference.

Then we use the `findViewById(int id)` method to locate the widgets. The ID of each widget, defined in your *main.xml* file, is automatically defined in the *R.java* file when you clean and build the project in Eclipse. (If you have set up Eclipse to build automatically, the *R.java* file is instantaneously updated when you update *main.xml*.)

Each widget is derived from the `View` class, and provides special GUI features. So a `TextView` provides a way to put labels on the UI, while the `EditText` provides a text field. Look at ❸ through ❻ in Example 1-8. You can see how `findViewById()` is used to locate the widgets.

Example 1-8. Code snippet 2 of /src/com/examples/tipcalc/Tipster.java

```
public class Tipster extends Activity {
    // Widgets in the application
    private EditText txtAmount;❶
    private EditText txtPeople;
    private EditText txtTipOther;
    private RadioGroup rdoGroupTips;
    private Button btnCalculate;
    private Button btnReset;

    private TextView txtTipAmount;
    private TextView txtTotalToPay;
    private TextView txtTipPerPerson;❷

    // For the id of radio button selected
    private int radioCheckedId = -1;

    /** Called when the activity is first created. */
```

```
@Override
public void onCreate(Bundle savedInstanceState) {
    super.onCreate(savedInstanceState);
    setContentView(R.layout.main);

    // Access the various widgets by their id in R.java
    txtAmount = (EditText) findViewById(R.id.txtAmount);❸
    //On app load, the cursor should be in the Amount field
    txtAmount.requestFocus();❹

    txtPeople = (EditText) findViewById(R.id.txtPeople);
    txtTipOther = (EditText) findViewById(R.id.txtTipOther);

    rdoGroupTips = (RadioGroup) findViewById(R.id.RadioGroupTips);

    btnCalculate = (Button) findViewById(R.id.btnCalculate);
    //On app load, the Calculate button is disabled
    btnCalculate.setEnabled(false);❺

    btnReset = (Button) findViewById(R.id.btnReset);

    txtTipAmount = (TextView) findViewById(R.id.txtTipAmount);
    txtTotalToPay = (TextView) findViewById(R.id.txtTotalToPay);
    txtTipPerPerson = (TextView) findViewById(R.id.txtTipPerPerson);❻

    // On app load, disable the Other Tip Percentage text field
    txtTipOther.setEnabled(false);❼
```

Addressing ease of use or usability concerns

Our application must try to be as usable as any other established application or web page. In short, adding usability features will result in a good user experience. To address these concerns look at Example 1-8 again.

Look at ❹ where we use the requestFocus() method of the View class. Since the Edit Text widget is derived from the View class, this method is applicable to it. This is done so that when our application loads the Total Amount text field will receive focus and the cursor will be placed in it. This is similar to popular web application login screens where the cursor is present in the username text field.

Now look at ❺ where the Calculate button is disabled by calling the setEnabled(boolean enabled) method on the Button widget. This is done so that the user cannot click on it before entering values in the required fields. If we allowed the user to click Calculate without entering values in the Total Amount and No. of People fields, we would have to write validation code to catch these conditions. This would entail showing an alert pop up warning the user about the empty values. This adds unnecessary code and user interaction. When the user sees the Calculate button disabled, it's quite obvious that unless all values are entered, the tip cannot be calculated.

Look at ❼ in Example 1-8. Here the Other Tip Percentage text field is disabled. This is done because the "15% tip" radio button is selected by default when the application loads. This default selection on application load is done via the *main.xml* file. Look at the line of *main.xml* where the following statement selects the "15% tip" radio button:

```
android:checkedButton="@+id/radioFifteen"
```

The `RadioGroup` attribute `android:checkedButton` allows you to select one of the `Radio Button` widgets in the group by default.

Most users who have used popular applications on the desktop as well as the Web are familiar with the "disabled widgets enabled on certain conditions" paradigm. Adding such small conveniences always makes an application more usable and the user experience richer.

Processing UI events

Like popular Windows, Java Swing, Flex, and other UI frameworks, Android also provides an event model which allows you to listen to certain events in the UI caused by user interaction. Let's see how we can use the Android event model in our application.

First let's focus on the radio buttons in the UI. We want to know which radio button the user selected, as this will allow us to determine the tip percentage in our calculations. To "listen" to radio buttons, we use the static interface `OnCheckedChangeListener()`. This will notify us when the selection state of a radio button changes.

In our application, we want to enable the Other Tip Percentage text field only when the Other radio button is selected. When the "15% tip" and "20% tip" buttons are selected we want to disable this text field. Besides this, we want to add some more logic for the sake of usability. As we discussed before, we should not enable the Calculate button until all the required fields have valid values. In terms of the three radio buttons, we want to ensure that the Calculate button gets enabled for the following two conditions:

- The Other radio button is selected and the Other Tip Percentage text field has valid values.

- The "15% tip" or "20% tip" radio button is selected and the Total Amount and No. of People text fields have valid values

Look at Example 1-9, which deals with the radio buttons. The source code comments are quite self-explanatory.

Example 1-9. Code snippet 3 of /src/com/examples/tipcalc/Tipster.java

```
/*
 * Attach an OnCheckedChangeListener to the
 * radio group to monitor radio buttons selected by user
 */
rdoGroupTips.setOnCheckedChangeListener(new OnCheckedChangeListener() {

@Override
public void onCheckedChanged(RadioGroup group, int checkedId) {
    // Enable/disable Other Tip Percentage field
```

```
    if (checkedId == R.id.radioFifteen
            || checkedId == R.id.radioTwenty) {
      txtTipOther.setEnabled(false);
      /*
       * Enable the calculate button if Total Amount and No. of
       * People fields have valid values.
       */
      btnCalculate.setEnabled(txtAmount.getText().length() > 0
              && txtPeople.getText().length() > 0);
    }
    if (checkedId == R.id.radioOther) {
      // enable the Other Tip Percentage field
      txtTipOther.setEnabled(true);
      // set the focus to this field
      txtTipOther.requestFocus();
      /*
       * Enable the calculate button if Total Amount and No. of
       * People fields have valid values. Also ensure that user
       * has entered an Other Tip Percentage value before enabling
       * the Calculate button.
       */
      btnCalculate.setEnabled(txtAmount.getText().length() > 0
              && txtPeople.getText().length() > 0
              && txtTipOther.getText().length() > 0);
    }
    // To determine the tip percentage choice made by user
    radioCheckedId = checkedId;
  }
});
```

Monitoring key activity in text fields

As I mentioned earlier, the Calculate button must not be enabled unless the text fields have valid values. So we have to ensure that the Calculate button will be enabled only if the Total Amount, No. of People, and Other Tip Percentage text fields have valid values. The Other Tip Percentage text field is enabled only if the Other Tip Percentage radio button is selected.

We do not have to worry about the type of values, that is, whether the user entered negative values or letters because the `android:numeric` attribute has been defined for the text fields, thus limiting the types of values that the user can enter. We have to just ensure that the values are present.

So we use the static interface `OnKeyListener()`. This will notify us when a key is pressed. The notification reaches us before the actual key pressed is sent to the `EditText` widget.

Look at the code in Examples 1-10 and 1-11 which deal with key events in the text fields. As in Example 1-9, the source code comments are quite self-explanatory.

Example 1-10. Code snippet 4 of /src/com/examples/tipcalc/Tipster.java

```
/*
 * Attach a KeyListener to the Tip Amount, No. of People and Other Tip
 * Percentage text fields
 */
txtAmount.setOnKeyListener(mKeyListener);
txtPeople.setOnKeyListener(mKeyListener);
txtTipOther.setOnKeyListener(mKeyListener);
```

Notice that we create just one listener instead of creating anonymous/inner listeners for each text field. I am not sure if my style is better or recommended, but I always write in this style if the listeners are going to perform some common actions. Here the common concern for all the text fields is that they should not be empty, and only when they have values should the Calculate button be enabled.

Example 1-11. Code snippet 5 from KeyListener.java

```
/*
 * KeyListener for the Total Amount, No of People and Other Tip Percentage
 * text fields. We need to apply this key listener to check for the following
 * conditions:
 *
 * 1) If the user selects Other Tip Percentage, then the Other Tip Percentage text field
 * should have a valid tip percentage entered by the user. Enable the
 * Calculate button only when the user enters a valid value.
 *
 * 2) If the user does not enter values in the Total Amount and No. of People fields,
 * we cannot perform the calculations. Hence we enable the Calculate button
 * only when the user enters valid values.
 */
private OnKeyListener mKeyListener = new OnKeyListener() {
    @Override
    public boolean onKey(View v, int keyCode, KeyEvent event) {

        switch (v.getId()) {❶
        case R.id.txtAmount:❷
        case R.id.txtPeople:❸
            btnCalculate.setEnabled(txtAmount.getText().length() > 0
                    && txtPeople.getText().length() > 0);
            break;
        case R.id.txtTipOther:❹
            btnCalculate.setEnabled(txtAmount.getText().length() > 0
                    && txtPeople.getText().length() > 0
                    && txtTipOther.getText().length() > 0);
            break;
        }
        return false;
    }

};
```

At ❶ in Example 1-11, we examine the ID of the View. Remember that each widget has a unique ID as we define it in the *main.xml* file. These values are then defined in the generated *R.java* class.

At ❷ and ❸, if the key event occurred in the Total Amount or No. of People fields, we check for the value entered in the field. We are ensuring that the user has not left both fields blank.

At ❹ we check if the user has selected the Other radio button, and then we ensure that the Other text field is not empty. We also check once again if the Total Amount and No. of People fields are empty.

So the purpose of our KeyListener is now clear: ensure that all text fields are not empty and only then enable the Calculate button.

Listening to button clicks

Now we will look at the Calculate and Reset buttons. When the user clicks these buttons, we use the static interface OnClickListener() which will let us know when a button is clicked.

As we did with the text fields, we create just one listener and within it we detect which button was clicked. Depending on the button that was clicked, the calculate() or reset() method is called.

Example 1-12 shows how the click listener is added to the buttons.

Example 1-12. Code snippet 6 of /src/com/examples/tipcalc/Tipster.java

```
/* Attach listener to the Calculate and Reset buttons */
btnCalculate.setOnClickListener(mClickListener);
btnReset.setOnClickListener(mClickListener);
```

Example 1-13 shows how to detect which button is clicked by checking for the ID of the View that receives the click event.

Example 1-13. Code snippet 7 of /src/com/examples/tipcalc/Tipster.java

```
/**
 * ClickListener for the Calculate and Reset buttons.
 * Depending on the button clicked, the corresponding
 * method is called.
 */
private OnClickListener mClickListener = new OnClickListener() {

    @Override
    public void onClick(View v) {
        if (v.getId() == R.id.btnCalculate) {
            calculate();
        } else {
            reset();
        }
```

```
    }
};
```

Resetting the application

When the user clicks the Reset button, the text fields should be cleared, the default "15% tip" radio button should be selected, and any results calculated should be cleared.

Example 1-14 shows the reset() method.

Example 1-14. Code snippet 8 of /src/com/examples/tipcalc/Tipster.java

```
/**
 * Resets the results text views at the bottom of the screen as well as
 * resets the text fields and radio buttons.
 */
private void reset() {
    txtTipAmount.setText("");
    txtTotalToPay.setText("");
    txtTipPerPerson.setText("");
    txtAmount.setText("");
    txtPeople.setText("");
    txtTipOther.setText("");
    rdoGroupTips.clearCheck();
    rdoGroupTips.check(R.id.radioFifteen);
    // set focus on the first field
    txtAmount.requestFocus();
}
```

Validating the input to calculate the tip

As I said before, we are limiting what type of values the user can enter in the text fields. However, the user could still enter a value of zero in the Total Amount, No. of People, and Other Tip Percentage text fields, thus causing error conditions like divide by zero in our tip calculations.

If the user enters zero we must show an alert pop up asking the user to enter non-zero values. We handle this with a method called showErrorAlert(String errorMessage, final int fieldId), but we will discuss this in more detail later.

First, look at Example 1-15 which shows the calculate() method. Notice how the values entered by the user are parsed as double values.

Now notice ❶ and ❷ where we check for zero values. If the user enters zero, we show an alert pop up to warn the user. Next, look at ❸, where the Other Tip Percentage text field is enabled because the user selected the Other radio button. Here, too, we must check for the tip percentage being zero.

When the application loads, the "15% tip" radio button is selected by default. If the user changes the selection, we assign the ID of the selected radio button to the member variable radioCheckedId, as we saw in Example 1-9, in OnCheckedChangeListener.

But if the user accepts the default selection, the radioCheckedId will have the default value of -1. In short, we will never know which radio button was selected. Of course, we know which one is selected by default and could have coded the logic slightly differently, to assume 15% if radioCheckedId has the value -1. But if you refer to the API, you will see that we can call the method getCheckedRadioButtonId() on the Radi oGroup and not on individual radio buttons. This is because OnCheckedChangeListener readily provides us with the ID of the radio button selected.

Showing the results

Calculating the tip is simple. If there are no validation errors, the boolean flag isEr ror will be false. Look at ❹ through ❺ in Example 1-15 for the simple tip calculations. Next, the calculated values are set to the TextView widgets from ❻ to ❼.

Example 1-15. Code snippet 9 of /src/com/examples/tipcalc/Tipster.java

```java
/**
 * Calculate the tip as per data entered by the user.
 */
private void calculate() {
    Double billAmount = Double.parseDouble(
        txtAmount.getText().toString());
    Double totalPeople = Double.parseDouble(
        txtPeople.getText().toString());
    Double percentage = null;
    boolean isError = false;
    if (billAmount < 1.0) {❶
        showErrorAlert("Enter a valid Total Amount.",
            txtAmount.getId());
        isError = true;
    }

    if (totalPeople < 1.0) {❷
        showErrorAlert("Enter a valid value for No. of People.",
            txtPeople.getId());
        isError = true;
    }

    /*
     * If the user never changes his radio selection, then it means
     * the default selection of 15% is in effect. But it's
     * safer to verify
     */
    if (radioCheckedId == -1) {
        radioCheckedId = rdoGroupTips.getCheckedRadioButtonId();
    }
    if (radioCheckedId == R.id.radioFifteen) {
        percentage = 15.00;
    } else if (radioCheckedId == R.id.radioTwenty) {
        percentage = 20.00;
    } else if (radioCheckedId == R.id.radioOther) {
        percentage = Double.parseDouble(
            txtTipOther.getText().toString());
```

```
        if (percentage < 1.0) {❸
            showErrorAlert("Enter a valid Tip percentage",
                txtTipOther.getId());
            isError = true;
        }
    }

    /*
     * If all fields are populated with valid values, then proceed to
     * calculate the tips
     */
    if (!isError) {
        Double tipAmount = ((billAmount * percentage) / 100);❹
        Double totalToPay = billAmount + tipAmount;
        Double perPersonPays = totalToPay / totalPeople;❺

        txtTipAmount.setText(tipAmount.toString());❻
        txtTotalToPay.setText(totalToPay.toString());
        txtTipPerPerson.setText(perPersonPays.toString());❼
    }
}
```

Showing the alerts

Showing the alerts Android provides the `AlertDialog` class to show alert pop ups. This lets us show a dialog with up to three buttons and a message.

Example 1-16 shows the `showErrorAlert` method which uses this `AlertDialog` to show the error messages. Notice that we pass two arguments to this method: `String error Message` and `int fieldId`. The first argument is the error message we want to show to the user. The `fieldId` is the ID of the field which caused the error condition. After the user dismisses the alert dialog, this `fieldId` will allow us to request the focus on that field, so the user knows which field has the error.

Example 1-16. Code snippet 10 of /src/com/examples/tipcalc/Tipster.java

```
/**
 * Shows the error message in an alert dialog
 *
 * @param errorMessage
 *            String for the error message to show
 * @param fieldId
 *            the Id of the field which caused the error.
 *            This is required so that the focus can be
 *            set on that field once the dialog is
 *            dismissed.
 */
private void showErrorAlert(String errorMessage,
    final int fieldId) {
    new AlertDialog.Builder(this).setTitle("Error")
    .setMessage(errorMessage).setNeutralButton("Close",
            new DialogInterface.OnClickListener() {
                @Override
                public void onClick(DialogInterface dialog,
```

```
                int which) {
            findViewById(fieldId).requestFocus();
        }
    }).show();
}
```

When all this is put together, it should look like Figure 1-39.

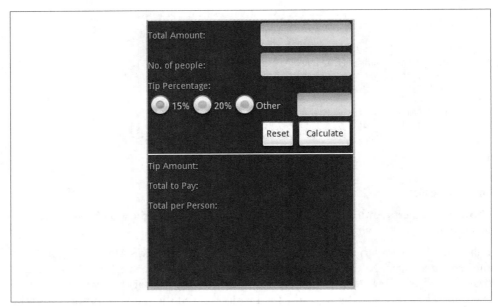

Figure 1-39. Tipster in action

Conclusion

Developing for the Android OS is not too different from developing for any other UI toolkit, including Microsoft Windows, X Windows, Java Swing, or Adobe Flex. Of course Android has its differences and, overall, a very good design. The XML layout paradigm is quite cool and useful for building complex UIs using simple XML. In addition, the event handling model is simple, feature-rich, and intuitive to use in code.

Source Download URL

You can download the source code for this example from *http://www.vidyut.com/sunit/android/tipster.zip*.

Binary Download URL

You can download the executable code for this example from *http://www.vidyut.com/sunit/android/tipster.zip*.

## CHAPTER 2

Designing a Successful Application

2.1 Introduction: Designing a Successful Android Application

Colin Wilcox

Discussion

This chapter is about design guidelines for writing imaginative and useful Android applications. Several recipes describe specific aspects of successful design. This section will list some others.

One purpose of this chapter is to explain the benefits of developing native Java Android applications over other methods of delivering rich content on mobile devices.

Requirements of a native handset application

There are a number of key requirements for successfully delivering any mobile handset application, regardless of the platform onto which it will be deployed:

- The application should be easy to install, remove, and update on a device.
- It should address the user's needs in a compelling, unique, and elegant way.
- It should be feature-rich while remaining usable by both novice and expert users.
- It should be familiar to users who have accessed the same information through other routes, such as a website.
- Key areas of functionality should be readily accessible.
- It should have a common look and feel with other native applications on the handset conforming to the target platform's standards and style guidelines.
- An application should be stable, scalable, usable, and responsive.
- It should use the platform's capabilities tastefully when it makes the user's experience more compelling.

Android application design

The Android application we will design in this chapter will exploit the features and functions unique to the Android OS platform. In general, the application will be an activity-based solution allowing independent and controlled access to data on a screen-by-screen basis. This approach helps to localize potential errors and allows sections of the flow to be readily replaced or enhanced independent of the rest of the application.

Navigation will use a similar approach to that of the Apple iPhone solution in that all key areas of functionality will be accessed from a single navigation bar control. The navigation bar will be accessible from anywhere within the application, allowing the user to freely move around the application.

The Android solution will exploit features inherent to Android devices, supporting the devices' touch-screen features, the hardware button that allows users to switch the application to the background, and application switching capability.

Android provides the ability to jump back into an application at the point where it was switched out. This will be supported, when possible, within this design.

The application will use only standard Android user interface controls to make it as portable as possible. The use of themes or custom controls is outside the scope of this chapter.

The application will be designed such that it interfaces to a thin layer of RESTful web services that provide data in a JSON format. This interface will be the same as the one used by the Apple iPhone, as well as applications written for other platforms.

The application will adopt the Android style and design guidelines wherever possible so that it fits in with other Android applications on the device.

Data that is local to each view will be saved when the view is exited and automatically restored with the corresponding user interface controls repopulated when the view is next loaded.

A number of important device characteristics should be considered, as discussed in the following subsections:

Screen size and density. In order to categorize devices by their screen type, Android defines two characteristics for each device: screen size (the physical dimensions of the screen) and screen density (the physical density of the pixels on the screen, or dpi [dots per inch]). To simplify all the different types of screen configurations, the Android system generalizes them into select groups that make them easier to target.

The designer should take into account the most appropriate choices for screen size and screen density when designing the application.

By default, your application is compatible with all screen sizes and densities, because the Android system makes the appropriate adjustments to your UI layout and image resources. However, you should create specialized layouts for certain screen sizes and provide specialized images for certain densities, by using alternative layout resources and by declaring in your manifest exactly which screen sizes your application supports.

Input configurations. Many devices provide a different type of user input mechanism, such as a hardware keyboard, a trackball, or a five-way navigation pad. If your application requires a particular kind of input hardware, you must declare it in the *AndroidManifest.xml* file, and be aware that the Android Market will not display your app on devices that lack this feature. However, it is rare that an application should require a certain input configuration.

Device features. There are many hardware and software features that may or may not exist on a given Android-powered device, such as a camera, a light sensor, Bluetooth capability, a certain version of OpenGL, or the fidelity of the touch screen. You should never assume that a certain feature is available on all Android-powered devices (other than the availability of the standard Android library).

The Android application will provide instances of the two types of menus provided by the Android framework, depending on the circumstances:

- Options menus contain primary functionality that applies globally to the current activity or starts a related activity. An options menu is typically invoked by a user pressing a hard button, often labeled Menu. An options menu is for any commands that are global to the current activity.
- Context menus contain secondary functionality for the currently selected item. A context menu is typically invoked by a user performing a long-press (press and hold) on an item. Like on the options menu, the operation can run in either the current or another activity.

A context menu is for any commands that apply to the current selection.

The commands on the context menu that appear when you long-press on an item should be duplicated on the activity you get to by a normal press on that item.

- Place the most frequently used operations first.
- Only the most important commands should appear as `Button`s on the screen; delegate the rest to the menu.

The system will automatically lay out the menus and provide standard ways for users to access them, ensuring that the application will conform to the Android user interface guidelines. In this sense, menus are familiar and dependable ways for users to access functionality across all applications.

The Android application will make extensive use of Google's Intent mechanism for passing data between `Activity` objects. Intents not only are used to pass data between views within a single application, but also allow data, or requests, to be passed to external modules. As such, much functionality can be adopted by the Android application by embedded functionality from other applications invoked by intent calls. This reduces the development process and maintains the common look and feel and functionality behavior across all applications.

Data feeds and feed formats. It is not a good idea to interface directly to any third-party data source; for example, it would be a bad idea to use a Type 3 JDBC driver in your mobile application to talk directly to a database on your server. The normal approach would be to mitigate the data, from several sources in potentially multiple data formats, through middleware which then passes data to an application through a series of RESTful web service APIs in the form of JSON data streams.

Typically, data is provided in such formats as XML, SOAP, or some other XML-derived representation. Representations such as SOAP are heavyweight, and as such, transferring data from the backend servers in this format increases development time significantly as the responsibility of converting this data into something more manageable falls on either the handset application or an object on the middleware server.

Mitigating the source data through a middleware server also helps to break the dependency between the application and the data. Such a dependency has the disadvantage that if, for some reason, the nature of the data changes or the data cannot be retrieved, the application may be broken and become unusable, and such changes may require the application to be republished. By mitigating the data on a middleware server, the application will continue to work, albeit possibly in a limited fashion, regardless of whether the source data exists or not. The link between the application and the mitigated data will remain.

2.2 Exception Handling

Ian Darwin

Problem

Java has a well-defined exception handling mechanism, but it takes some time to learn to use it effectively without frustrating either users or tech support people.

Solution

Java offers an Exception hierarchy that provides considerable flexibility when used correctly. Android offers several mechanisms, including dialogs and toasts, for notifying the user of error conditions. The Android developer should become acquainted with these mechanisms and learn to use them effectively.

Discussion

Java has had two categories of exceptions (actually of `Exception`'s parent, `Throwable`) since Java was introduced: checked and unchecked. In Java Standard Edition, apparently the intention was to force the programmer to face the fact that, while certain things could be detected at compile time, others could not. For example, if you were installing a desktop application on a large number of PCs, it's likely that the disk on some of those PCs would be near capacity, and trying to save data on them could fail; meanwhile, on other PCs some file the application depended upon would go missing, not due to programmer error but to user error, filesystem happenstance, gerbils chewing on the cables, or whatever. So the category of `IOException` was created as a "checked exception," meaning that the programmer would have to check for it, either by having a `try-catch` clause inside the file-using method or by having a `throws` clause on the method definition. The general rule, which all well-trained Java developers memorize, is the following:

> `Throwable` is the root of the throwable hierarchy. `Exception`, and all of its subclasses other than `RuntimeException` or any subclass thereof, is checked. All else is unchecked.

This means that `Error` and all of its subclasses are unchecked (see Figure 2-1). If you get a `VMError`, for example, it means there's a bug in the runtime. There's nothing you can do about this as an application programmer. And `RuntimeException` subclasses include things like the excessively long-named `ArrayIndexOutOfBoundsException`; this and friends are unchecked because it is your responsibility to catch them at development time, by testing for them (see Chapter 3).

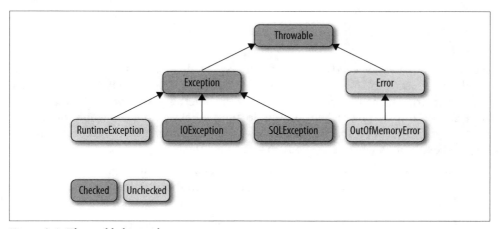

Figure 2-1. Throwable hierarchy

Where to catch exceptions

The early (over)use of checked exceptions led a lot of early Java developers to write code that was sprinkled with `try/catch` blocks, partly because the use of the `throws` clause was not emphasized early enough in some training programs and books. As Java itself has moved more to enterprise work, and newer frameworks such as Hibernate and Spring have come along and are emphasizing the use of unchecked exceptions, this early problem has been corrected. It is now generally accepted that you want to catch exceptions as close to the user as possible. Code that is meant for reuse—in libraries or even in multiple applications—should not try to do error handling. What it can do is what's called *exception translation*, that is, turning a technology-specific (and usually checked) exception into a generic, unchecked exception. Example 2-1 shows the basic pattern.

Example 2-1. Exception translation

```
public String readTheFile(String f) {
        BufferedReader is = null;
        try {
                is = new BufferedReader(new FileReader(f));
                String line = is.readLine();
                return line;
        } catch (FileNotFoundException fnf) {
                throw new RuntimeException("Could not open file " + f, fnf);
        } catch (IOException ex) {
                throw new RuntimeException("Could not read file " + f, ex);
        } finally {
                if (is != null) {
                        try {
                                is.close();
                        } catch(IOException grr) {
                                throw new RuntimeException("Error on close of " + f, grr);
                        }
                }
        }
}
```

Note how the use of checked exceptions clutters even this code: it is virtually impossible for the `is.close()` to fail, but since you want to have it in a `finally` block (to ensure that it gets tried if the file was opened but then something went wrong), you have to have an additional `try-catch` around it. So checked exceptions are (more often than not) a bad thing, should be avoided in new APIs, and should be paved over with unchecked exceptions when using code that requires them.

There is an opposing view, espoused by the official Oracle website and others. In a comment on the website from which this book was produced, Al Sutton points out the following:

> Checked exceptions exist to force developers to acknowledge that an error condition can occur and that they have thought about how they want to deal with it. In many cases there may be little that can be done beyond logging and recovery, but it is still an acknowledgment by the developer that they have considered what should happen with this type of error. The example shown ... stops callers of the method `from` differentiating between when a file doesn't exist (and thus may need to be re-fetched), and when there is a problem reading the file (and thus the file exists but is unreadable), which are two different types of error conditions.

Android, wishing to be faithful to the Java API, has a number of these checked exceptions (including the ones shown in the example), so they should be treated the same way.

What to do with exceptions

Exceptions should almost always be reported. When I see code that catches exceptions and does nothing at all about them, I despair. They should, however, be reported only once (do not both log and translate/rethrow!). The point of all normal exceptions is to indicate, as the name implies, an exceptional condition. Since on an Android device there is no system administrator or console operator, exceptional conditions need to be reported to the user.

You should think about whether to report exceptions via a dialog or a toast. The exception handling situation on a mobile device is different from that on a desktop computer. The user may be driving a car or operating other machinery, interacting with people, and so on so you should not assume you have her full attention. Remember that a toast will only appear on the screen for a few seconds; blink and you may miss it. If the user needs to do something to correct the problem, you should use a dialog. I know that most examples, even in this book, use a toast, because it involves less coding than a dialog (by contrast, the BlackBerry API makes it easy: `Dialog.alert("message");`). Toasts simply pop up and then obliviate. Dialogs require the user to acknowledge an exceptional condition, and either do, or give the app permission to do, something that might cost money (such as turning on Internet access in order to run an application that needs to download map tiles).

Use toasts to "pop up" unimportant information; use dialogs to display important information and to obtain confirmation.

2.3 Accessing Android's Application Object as a "Singleton"

Adrian Cowham

Problem

You need to access "global" data from within your Android app.

Solution

The best solution is to subclass `android.app.Application` and treat it as a singleton with static accessors. Every Android app is guaranteed to have exactly one `android.app.Application` instance for the lifetime of the app. If you choose to subclass `android.app.Application`, Android will create an instance of your class and invoke the `android.app.Application` life-cycle methods on it. Because there's nothing preventing you from creating another instance of your subclassed `android.app.Application`, it isn't a genuine singleton, but it's close enough.

Having globally accessible such objects as session handlers, web service gateways, or anything that your application only needs a single instance of, will dramatically simplify your code. Sometimes these objects can be implemented as singletons, and sometimes they cannot because they require a `Context` instance for proper initialization. In either case, it's still valuable to add static accessors to your subclassed `android.app.Application` instance so that you can consolidate all globally accessible data in one place, have guaranteed access to a `Context` instance, and easily write "correct" singleton code without having to worry about synchronization.

Discussion

When writing your Android app you may find it necessary to share data and services across multiple activities. For example, if your app has session data, such as the currently logged-in user, you will likely want to expose this information. When developing on the Android platform, the pattern for solving this problem is to have your `android.app.Application` instance own all global data, and then treat your `Application` instance as a singleton with static accessors to the various data and services.

When writing an Android app you're guaranteed to only have one instance of the `android.app.Application` class, so it's safe (and recommended by the Google Android team) to treat it as a singleton. That is, you can safely add a static `getInstance()` method to your `Application` implementation. Example 2-2 provides an example.

Example 2-2. The Application implementation

```java
public class AndroidApplication extends Application {

    private static AndroidApplication sInstance;

    private SessionHandler sessionHandler;

    public static AndroidApplication getInstance() {
      return sInstance;
    }

    public Session Handler getSessionHandler()
        return sessionHandler;
    }

    @Override
    public void onCreate() {
      super.onCreate();
      sInstance = this;
      sInstance.initializeInstance();
    }

    protected void initializeInstance() {
        // do all your initialization here
        sessionHandler = new SessionHandler(
            this.getSharedPreferences( "PREFS_PRIVATE", Context.MODE_PRIVATE ) );
```

```
        }
}
```

This isn't the classical singleton implementation, but given the constraints of the Android framework, this is the closest thing we have, it's safe, and it works.

Using this technique in this app has simplified and cleaned up the implementation. Also, it has made it much easier to develop tests. Using this technique in conjunction with the Robolectric testing framework, you can mock out the entire execution environment in a straightforward fashion.

Also, don't forget to add the application declaration to your *AndroidManifest.xml* file:

```
<application android:icon="@drawable/app_icon"
    android:label="@string/app_name"
    android:name="com.company.abc.AbcApplication">
```

See Also

http://mytensions.blogspot.com/2011/03/androids-application-object-as.html

2.4 Keeping Data When the User Rotates the Device

Ian Darwin

Problem

When the user rotates the device, Android will normally destroy and re-create the current activity. You want to keep some data across this cycle, but all the fields in your activity are lost during it.

Solution

There are several approaches. If all your data comprises primitive types, consists of `Strings`, or is `Serializable`, you can save it in `onSaveInstanceState()` in the `Bundle` that is passed in.

Another solution lets you return a single arbitrary object implement `onRetainNonConfigurationInstance()` in your activity to save some values; call `getLastNonConfigurationInstance()` near the end of your `onCreate()` to see if there is a previously saved value and, if so, assign your fields accordingly.

Discussion

Using onSaveInstanceState()

See Recipe 1.6.

Using onRetainNonConfigurationInstance()

The `getLastNonConfigurationInstance()` method's return type is `Object`, so you can return any value you want from it. You might want to create a `Map` or write an inner class in which to store the values, but it's often easier just to pass a reference to the current activity, for example, using this:

```
/** Returns arbitrary single token object to keep alive across
 * the destruction and re-creation of the entire Enterprise.
 */
@Override
public Object onRetainNonConfigurationInstance() {
        return this;
}
```

The preceding method will be called when Android destroys your main activity. Suppose you wanted to keep a reference to another object that was being updated by a running service, that is referred to by a field in your activity. There might also be a boolean to indicate whether the service is active. In the preceding code, we return a reference to the activity, from which all of its fields can be accessed (even private fields, of course, since the outgoing and incoming `Activity` objects are of the same class). In my geotracking app JPSTrack, for example, I have a `FileSaver` class which accepts data from the location service; I want it to keep getting the location, and saving it to disk, in spite of rotations, rather than having to restart it every time the screen rotates. Rotation is unlikely if your device is anchored in a car dash mount (we hope), but quite likely if a passenger, or a pedestrian, is taking pictures or other notes while geotracking.

After Android creates the new instance, it calls `onCreate()` to notify the new instance that it has been created. In `onCreate()` you typically do constructor-like actions such as initializing fields and assigning event listeners. Well, you still need to do those, so leave them alone. Near the end of `onCreate()`, however, you will add some code to get the old instance, if there is one, and get some of the important fields from it. The code should look something like Example 2-3.

Example 2-3. The onCreate method

```
@Override
public void onCreate(Bundle savedInstanceState) {
    super.onCreate(savedInstanceState);
    setContentView(R.layout.main);

    saving = false;
    paused = false;

    // lots of other initializations...

    // Now see if we just got interrupted by e.g., rotation
      Main old = (Main) getLastNonConfigurationInstance();
      if (old != null) {
          saving = old.saving;
          paused = old.paused;
```

```
        // this is the most important line: keep saving to same file!
        fileSaver = old.fileSaver;
        if (saving) {
                fileNameLabel.setText(fileSaver.getFileName());
        }
    return;
    }

    // I/O Helper
    fileSaver = new GPSFileSaver(...);
}
```

The fileSaver object is the big one, the one we want to keep running, and not re-create every time. If we don't have an old instance, we create the fileSaver only at the very end of onCreate(), since otherwise we'd be creating a new one just to replace it with the old one, which is at least bad for performance.

When the onCreate() method finishes, we hold no reference to the old instance, so it should be eligible for Java GC.

The net result is that the activity appears to keep running nicely across screen rotations, despite the re-creation.

An alternative possibility is to set android:configChanges="orientation" in your *AndroidManifest.xml*, but this is a bit riskier.

See Also

Recipe 2.3

Source Download URL

You can download the source code for this example from *http://projects.darwinsys.com/ jpstrack.android*. Note that you will also need the jpstrack project, from the same location.

2.5 Monitoring the Battery Level of an Android Device

Pratik Rupwal

Problem

You want to detect the battery level on an Android device so that you can notify the user when the battery level goes below a certain threshold, thereby avoiding unexpected surprises.

Solution

A broadcast receiver that receives the broadcast message sent when the battery status changes can identify the battery level and can be used to issue alerts to users.

Discussion

Sometimes we need to show an alert to the user when the battery level of an Android device goes below a certain limit. The code in Example 2-4 sets the broadcast message to be sent whenever the battery level changes, and creates a broadcast receiver to receive the broadcast message which can alert the user when the battery gets discharged below a certain level.

Example 2-4. The main activity

```
public class MainActivity extends Activity {

 /** Called when the activity is first created. */
 @Override
 public void onCreate(Bundle savedInstanceState) {
     super.onCreate(savedInstanceState);
     setContentView(R.layout.main);

 /**This registers the receiver for a broadcast message to be sent
    when the battery level is changed*/

     this.registerReceiver(this.myBatteryReceiver,
       new IntentFilter(Intent.ACTION_BATTERY_CHANGED));

     /** Intent.ACTION_BATTERY_CHANGED can be replaced with
      * Intent.ACTION_BATTERY_LOW for broadcasting
      * a message only when battery level is low rather than sending
      * a broadcast message every time battery level changes
      */
}

 private BroadcastReceiver myBatteryReceiver =
    new BroadcastReceiver(){

 @Override
 public void onReceive(Context arg0, Intent arg1) {
  int bLevel = arg1.getIntExtra("level", 0);// the battery level in integer
```

```
  Log.i("Level", ""+bLevel);
  }
  };
}
```

2.6 Creating Splash Screens in Android

Rachee Singh

Problem

You want to create a splash screen that will appear while an application is loading.

Solution

You can construct a splash screen as an activity or as a dialog. Since its purpose is accomplished within a few seconds, it can be dismissed after a short time interval has elapsed or upon the click of a button in the splash screen.

Discussion

The splash screen was invented in the PC era, initially as a cover-up for slow GUI construction when PCs were slow. Vendors have kept them for branding purposes. But in the mobile world, where the longest app start-up time is probably less than a second, people are starting to recognize that splash screens have become somewhat anachronistic. At eHealth Innovation, we have recognized this by making the splash screen for our BANT application disappear after a just one second. The question arises whether we still need splash screens at all, or whether it's time to retire the very idea of the splash screen. As with most mobile apps, the name and logo appear in the app launcher, and we have lots of other screens where the name and logo appear. Is it time to make it disappear altogether?

Nonetheless, for completeness, here are two methods of handling the application splash screen.

The first versions use an activity that is dedicated to displaying the splash screen. The splash screen displays for two seconds or until the user presses the Menu key, and then the main activity of the application appears. First we use a thread to wait for a fixed number of seconds, and then we use an intent to start the real main activity. The one downside to this method is that your "main" activity in your *AndroidManifest.xml* file is the splash activity, not your real main activity.

Example 2-5 shows the splash activity.

Example 2-5. The splash activity

```
public class SplashScreen extends Activity {
    private long ms=0;
    private long splashTime=2000;
```

```
private boolean splashActive = true;
private boolean paused=false;
@Override
protected void onCreate(Bundle savedInstanceState) {

    super.onCreate(savedInstanceState);
    setContentView(R.layout.splash);
     Thread mythread = new Thread() {
    public void run() {
        try {
            while (splashActive && ms < splashTime) {
                if(!paused)
                    ms=ms+100;
                sleep(100);
            }
        } catch(Exception e) {}
        finally {
            Intent intent = new Intent(SplashScreen.this, Main.class);
            startActivity(intent);
        }
        }
    };
    mythread.start();
    }

}
```

Example 2-6 shows the layout of the splash activity, *splash.xml*.

Example 2-6. The splash layout

```xml
<?xml version="1.0" encoding="utf-8"?>
<LinearLayout xmlns:android="http://schemas.android.com/apk/res/android"
    android:orientation="vertical" android:layout_width="fill_parent"
    android:layout_height="fill_parent">
    <ImageView android:src="@drawable/background"
    android:id="@+id/image"
    android:layout_width="wrap_content"
    android:layout_height="wrap_content" />
    <ProgressBar android:id="@+id/progressBar1"
    android:layout_width="wrap_content"
    android:layout_height="wrap_content"
    android:layout_below="@id/image"
    android:layout_gravity="center_horizontal">
    </ProgressBar>
</LinearLayout>
```

One additional requirement is to put the attribute `android:noHistory="true"` on the splash activity in your *AndroidManifest.xml* file so that this activity will not appear in the history stack, meaning if the user uses the Back button from the main app he will go to the expected home screen, not back into your splash screen! See Figure 2-2.

Figure 2-2. Splash screen

Two seconds later, this activity leads to the next activity, which is the standard "Hello, World" Android activity, as a proxy for your main application's main activity. See Figure 2-3.

Figure 2-3. "Main" activity

In this second version, the splash screen displays until the Menu button on the Android device is not pressed, and then the main activity of the application appears. For this, we add a Java class that displays the splash screen.

We check for the pressing of the Menu key by checking the KeyCode and then finishing the activity (see Example 2-7).

Example 2-7. Watching for KeyCodes

```java
public class SplashScreen extends Activity {
    private long ms=0;
    private long splashTime=2000;
    private boolean splashActive = true;
    private boolean paused=false;
    @Override
    protected void onCreate(Bundle savedInstanceState) {
        super.onCreate(savedInstanceState);
        setContentView(R.layout.splash);
    }

    public boolean onKeyDown(int keyCode, KeyEvent event) {
        super.onKeyDown(keyCode, event);
        if (KeyEvent.KEYCODE_MENU == keyCode) {
            Intent intent = new Intent(SplashScreen.this, Main.class);
            startActivity(intent);
        }
        if (KeyEvent.KEYCODE_BACK == keyCode) {
            finish();
        }
        return false;
    }
}
```

The layout of the splash activity, *splash.xml*, is unchanged from the earlier version.

As before, after the button press, this activity leads to the next activity, which represents the main activity.

The other major method involves use of a dialog, started from the onCreate() method in your main method. This has a number of advantages, including the simpler activity stack and the fact that you don't need an extra activity that's only used for the first few seconds. The disadvantage is that it takes a bit more code, as you can see in Example 2-8.

Example 2-8. The splash dialog

```java
public class SplashDialog extends Activity {
    private Dialog splashDialog;

    /** Called when the activity is first created. */
    @Override
    public void onCreate(Bundle savedInstanceState) {
        super.onCreate(savedInstanceState);

        StateSaver data = (StateSaver) getLastNonConfigurationInstance();
        if (data != null) { // "all this has happened before"
            if (data.showSplashScreen ) { // and we didn't already finish
                showSplashScreen();
            }
            setContentView(R.layout.main);
            // Do any UI rebuilding here using saved state
        } else {
            showSplashScreen();
```

```
        setContentView(R.layout.main);
        // Start any heavy-duty loading here, but on its own thread
    }
}
```

The full code is in the download, and a version is also listed on Ian Clifton's blog (see the "See Also" on page 79 section). The basic idea is to display the splash screen dialog at the beginning, but also to redisplay it if you get, for example, an orientation change while the splash screen is running, and to be careful to remove it at the correct time, if the user backs out or if the timer expires while the splash screen is running.

See Also

Ian Clifton's Android blog post titled "Splash Screens Done Right" (*http://blog.iangclif ton.com/2011/01/01/android-splash-screens-done-right/*) argues passionately for the dialog method.

Source Download URL

You can download the source code for the activity-based example from *https://docs.google.com/leaf?id=0B_rE SQKgad5LZGY1N2RjYzQtZGQxNC00Njk5LWIyM2ItNDdlN2IwZjg4MmVj&hl=en _US&authkey=COOL9NwM.*

The source code for this example is in the Android Cookbook repository at *http://github .com/AndroidCook/Android-Cookbook-Examples*, in the subdirectory SplashDialog (see "Getting and Using the Code Examples" on page xvii).

2.7 Designing a Conference/Camp/Hackathon/Institution App

Ian Darwin

Problem

You want to design an app for use at a conference, BarCamp, or hackathon, or inside a large institution such as a hospital.

Solution

Provide at least the required functions listed in the Discussion, and as many of the optional ones as you think make sense.

Discussion

A good app of this type needs some or most of the following functions, as appropriate:

- A map of the building, showing the locations of meetings, food service, washrooms, emergency exits, and so on. You get extra points if you provide a visual slider for moving up or down levels if your conference takes place on more than one floor or level in the building (think about a 3D fly-through of San Francisco's Moscone Center, including the huge escalators). Remember that some people may know the building, but others will not. Consider having a "where am I" function (the user will type in the name or number of a room he sees; you get extra points if you offer visual matching instead of making the user type) as well as a "where is" function (the user selects from a list and the application jumps to the map view with a pushpin showing the desired location).

- A map of the exhibit hall (if there is a show floor, have a map and an easy way to find a given exhibitor). Ditto for poster papers if your conference features these.

- A schedule view. Highlight changes in red as they happen, including additions, last-minute cancellations, and room changes.

- A sign-up button if your conference has Birds of a Feather (BOF) gatherings; you might even want a "Suggest a new BOF" activity.

- A local area map. This could be OpenStreetMap or Google Maps, or maybe something more detailed than the standard map functions. Add folklore, points of interest, navigation shortcuts, and other features. Limit it to a few blocks so that you can get the details right. A university campus is about the right size.

- An overview map of the city. Again, this is not the Google map, but an artistic, neighborhood/zone view with just the highlights.

- Tourist attractions within an hour of the site. Your mileage may vary.

- A food finder. People always get tired of convention food and set out on foot to find something better to eat.

- A friend finder. If Google's Latitude app were open to use by third-party apps, you could tie into Google's data. If it's a security conference, implement this functionality yourself.

- Private voice chat. If it's a small security gathering, provide a Session Initiation Protocol (SIP) server on a well-connected host, with carefully controlled access; it should be possible to have almost walkie-talkie-like service.

- Sign-ups for impromptu group formation for trips to tourist attractions or any other purpose.

- Functionality to post comments to Twitter, Facebook, and LinkedIn.

- Note taking! Many people will have Android on large-screen tablets, so a "Notepad" equivalent, ideally linked to the session the notes are taken in, will be useful.

- A way to signal your chosen friends that you want to eat (at a certain time, in so many minutes, *right now*) and including the type of food or restaurant name and seeing if they're also interested.

See Also

The rest of the book shows how to implement most of these functions.

At the time of this writing, Google Maps had recently started serving building maps; look at *http://googleblog.blogspot.com/2011/11/new-frontier-for-google-maps-mapping.html*. The article shows who to contact to get your building's internal locations added to the map data; if appropriate, consider getting the venue operators to give Google their building's data.

2.8 Using Google Analytics in an Android Application

Ashwini Shahapurkar

Problem

Often developers want to track their application in terms of features used by users. How can you determine which feature is most used by your app's users?

Solution

You can use Google Analytics to track the app based on defined criteria, similar to the website tracking mechanism.

Discussion

Before we use Google Analytics in our app, we need an analytics account and the Google Analytics SDK.

Download the Analytics SDK from *http://code.google.com/mobile/analytics/download.html*. Unzip the SDK and add *libGoogleAnalytics.jar* to your project's build path.

Add the following permissions in your project's *AndroidManifest.xml* file:

```
<uses-permission android:name="android.permission.INTERNET" />
<uses-permission android:name="android.permission.ACCESS_NETWORK_STATE" />
```

Now, sign in to your analytics account and create a website profile for the app. The website URL can be fake but should be descriptive. It is suggested that you use the reverse package name for this. For example, if the application package name is com.exam ple.analytics.test, the website URL for this app can be *http://test.analytics.example .com*. After the website profile has been created, a web property ID is generated for that profile. Jot it down as we will be using this in our app. This web property ID, also known as the UA number of your tracking code, uniquely identifies the website profile.

 You must mention in your app that you are collecting anonymous user data in your app to track your app.

Now we are ready to track our application. Obtain the singleton instance of the tracker by calling the GoogleAnalyticsTracker.getInstance() method. Then start tracking by calling its start() method. Usually, you will want to track more than activities in the app. In such a scenario, it is a good idea to have this tracker instance in the OnCreate() method of the Application class of the app (see Example 2-9).

Example 2-9. The application implementation for tracking

```
public class TestApp extends Application {

/*define your web property ID obtained after profile creation for the app*/
private String webId = "UA-NNNNNNNN-Y";

/*Analytics tracker instance*/
GoogleAnalyticsTracker tracker;

@Override
    public void onCreate() {
        super.onCreate();
                //get the singleton tracker instance
        tracker = GoogleAnalyticsTracker.getInstance();
                //start tracking app with your web property ID
        tracker.start(webId,getApplicationContext());
        //your app-specific code goes here
    }

        /* This is the getter for the tracker instance. This is called in
           the activity to get a reference to the tracker instance.*/
        public GoogleAnalyticsTracker getTracker() {
        return tracker;
    }

}
```

You can track page views and events in the activity by calling the trackPageView() and trackEvent() methods on the tracker instance (see Example 2-10).

Example 2-10. The main activity with tracking

```java
public class MainActivity extends Activity
{
    @Override
    protected void onCreate(Bundle savedInstanceState) {
        super.onCreate(savedInstanceState);

            //track the page view for the activity
        GoogleAnalyticsTracker tracker = ((TestApp)getApplication()).getTracker();
            tracker.trackPageView("/MainActivity");

            /*You can track events like button clicks*/
            findViewById(R.id.actionButton).setOnClickListener(
                new View.OnClickListener() {
                @Override
                public void onClick(View v) {
                    GoogleAnalyticsTracker tracker =
                        ((TestApp)getApplication()).getTracker();
                    tracker.trackEvent("Action Event",
                        "Action Button", "Button clicked",0);
                    tracker.dispatch();
                    }
            });
    // Your stuff goes here
    }
}
```

Remember, your events and page views will not be sent to the server until you call the `dispatch()` method on the tracker. In this way, you can track all the activities and events inside them.

2.9 A Simple Torch/Flashlight

Saketkumar Srivastav

Problem

You want to use your smartphone as a torch/flashlight when there is a power failure or other no-light situation.

Solution

Turn on the camera flash LED that is present in the smartphone or Android device, and keep it on, to serve as a torch. In a peculiar twist of terminology, what is known as a *torch* in the United Kingdom is called a *flashlight* in North America (this is reflected in the names of the `Parameter` constants used in the code), even though a flashlight doesn't usually flash, while a camera flash does. So, using the camera's flash as a flashlight is, well, brilliant!

Discussion

To begin the application, here are the design steps:

1. Access the `Camera` object of the phone.
2. Access the parameters of the `Camera` object.
3. Get the flash modes supported by the camera.
4. Set the flashlight parameter to `FLASH_MODE_TORCH` when in the `ON` state and to `FLASH_OFF` when in the `OFF` state.

The code in Example 2-11 implements the logic required for the application.

Example 2-11. Turning an Android device into a torch/flashlight

```
if (context.getPackageManager().hasSystemFeature(PackageManager.FEATURE_CAMERA_FLASH)) {
        mTorch = (ToggleButton) findViewById(R.id.toggleButton1);
        mTorch.setOnCheckedChangeListener(new OnCheckedChangeListener() {

            @Override
            public void onCheckedChanged(CompoundButton buttonView,
                boolean isChecked) {

                try{
                    if(cam != null){
                        cam = Camera.open();
                    }
                    camParams = cam.getParameters();
                    List<String> flashModes = camParams.getSupportedFlashModes();
                    if(isChecked){
                        if (flashModes.contains(Parameters.FLASH_MODE_TORCH)) {
                            camParams.setFlashMode(Parameters.FLASH_MODE_TORCH);
                        }else{
                            showDialog(MainActivity.this, FLASH_TORCH_NOT_SUPPORTED);
                        }
                    }else{
                        camParams.setFlashMode(Parameters.FLASH_MODE_OFF);
                    }
                    cam.setParameters(camParams);
                    cam.startPreview();
                }catch (Exception e) {
                    e.printStackTrace();
                    cam.stopPreview();
                    cam.release();
                }
            }
        });
    }else{
        showDialog(MainActivity.this, FLASH_NOT_SUPPORTED);
    }
```

The basic logic implemented in Example 2-12 is as follows:

1. Check for the existence of the flash in the device.

2. Get the Camera object and open it to access it.

3. Get the parameters of the captured Camera object.

4. Check the supported flash modes available from the current Camera object using getSupportedFlashModes().

5. If the toggle state is ON, set the flash mode of the camera to FLASH_MODE_TORCH; otherwise, set it to FLASH_MODE_OFF.

Example 2-12. Torch error handling

```
public void showDialog (Context context, int dialogId){
    switch(dialogId){
    case FLASH_NOT_SUPPORTED:
        builder = new AlertDialog.Builder(context);
        builder.setMessage("Sorry, Your phone does not support Torch Mode")
        .setCancelable(false)
        .setNeutralButton("Close", new OnClickListener() {
            @Override
            public void onClick(DialogInterface dialog, int which) {
                finish();
            }
        });
        alertDialog = builder.create();
        alertDialog.show();
        break;
    case FLASH_TORCH_NOT_SUPPORTED:
        builder = new AlertDialog.Builder(context);
        builder.setMessage("Sorry, Your camera flash does not support torch feature")
        .setCancelable(false)
        .setNeutralButton("Close", new OnClickListener() {

            @Override
            public void onClick(DialogInterface dialog, int which) {
                finish();
            }
        });
        alertDialog = builder.create();
        alertDialog.show();
    }

}
```

Source Download URL

You can download the source code for this example from *https://github.com/SaketSri vastav/SimpleTorchLight*.

2.10 Adapting an Android Phone Application to Be Used on a Tablet

Pratik Rupwal

Problem

You have developed an application for your smartphone, and you want a way to run it gracefully on a tablet without any significant changes to your code.

Solution

There are many considerations in making your application work as well on large-screen tablets as it does on medium- and small-screen phones. Some of these include screen resolution, orientation (tablets are more commonly used in landscape mode, except in "book reader" applications), and sizes of GUI components. Handling these in a portable fashion will help your phone-based app make the transition to tablets.

Discussion

If you haven't done so already, install the Android SDK on your computer. Then follow these steps:

1. Launch the Android SDK and AVD Manager and install the following:
   - SDK Platform Android 3.0
   - Android SDK Tools, revision 10
   - Android SDK Platform-tools, revision 3
   - Documentation for Android SDK, API 11
   - Samples for SDK API 11
2. Create an Android Virtual Device (AVD) for a tablet-type device, if you do not have (or want to use) an actual Honeycomb- or Ice Cream Sandwich-based tablet. Set the target to "Android 3.0" and the skin to "WXGA" (the default skin).

3. Open your manifest file and update the `uses-sdk` element to set `android:targetSdk Version` to "11". For example:

```
<manifest ... >
    <uses-sdk android:minSdkVersion="4"
              android:targetSdkVersion="11" />
    <application ... >
        ...
    <application>
</manifest>
```

By targeting the Android 3.0 platform, the system automatically applies the holographic theme to each activity when your application runs on an Android 3.0 device. The holographic theme provides a new design for widgets, such as buttons and text boxes, and new styles for other visual elements. This is the standard theme for applications built for Android 3.0, so your application will look and feel consistent with the system and other applications when it is enabled.

4. Build your application against the same version of the Android platform you have been using previously (such as the version declared in your `android:minSdkVer sion`), but install it on the Android 3.0 AVD. (You should not build against Android 3.0 unless you are using new APIs.) Repeat your tests to be sure that your user interface works well with the holographic theme.

Optional guidelines

The following guidelines are among the first things you should consider in moving your application to tablets:

1. Landscape layout: The "normal" orientation for tablet-type devices is usually landscape (wide), so you should be sure that your activities offer a layout that's optimized for a wide viewing area.

2. Button position and size: Consider whether the position and size of the most common buttons in your UI make them easily accessible while holding a tablet with two hands. In some cases, you might need to resize buttons, especially if they use `wrap_content` as the width value. To enlarge the buttons, if necessary, you should either add extra padding to the button; specify dimension values with dp units; or use `android:layout_weight` when the button is in a linear layout. Use your best judgment of proportions for each screen size—you don't want the buttons to be too big, either.

3. Font sizes: Be sure your application uses sp units when setting font sizes. This alone should ensure a readable experience on tablet-style devices, because it is a scale-independent pixel unit, which will resize as appropriate for the current screen configuration. In some cases, however, you still might want to consider larger font sizes for extra-large configurations.

2.11 Setting First-Run Preferences

Ashwini Shahapurkar

Problem

You have an application that collects app usage data anonymously, so you are obligated to make users aware of this the first time they run your application.

Solution

Use shared preferences as persistent storage to store a value, which gets updated only once. Each time the application launches, it will check for this value in the preferences. If the value has been set (is available), it is not the first run of the application; otherwise it is the first run.

Discussion

You can manage the application life cycle by using the `Application` class of the Android framework. We will use shared preferences as persistent storage to store the first-run value.

We will store a `boolean` flag if it is the first run in the preferences. When the application is installed and used for the first time, there are no preferences available for it. They will be created for us. In that case the flag will return a value of `true`. After getting the `true` flag, we can update this flag with a value of `false` as we no longer need it to be true. See Example 2-13.

Example 2-13. First-run preferences

```
public class MyApp extends Application {

    SharedPreferences mPrefs;

    @Override
    public void onCreate() {
        super.onCreate();

        Context mContext = this.getApplicationContext();
        // 0 = mode private. only this app can read these preferences
        mPrefs = mContext.getSharedPreferences("myAppPrefs", 0);


        // Your app initialization code goes here
    }

    public boolean getFirstRun() {
        return mPrefs.getBoolean("firstRun", true);
    }

    public void setRunned() {
```

```
        SharedPreferences.Editor edit = mPrefs.edit();
        edit.putBoolean("firstRun", false);
        edit.commit();
    }


}
```

This flag from the preferences will be tested in the launcher activity, as shown in Example 2-14.

Example 2-14. Checking whether this is the first run of this app

```
if(((MyApp) getApplication()).getFirstRun()){
    //This is the first run
    ((MyApp) getApplication()).setRunned();

    // your code for the first run goes here

    }
else{
    // this is not the first run on this device
}
```

Even if you publish updates for the app and the user installs the updates, these preferences will not be modified; therefore, the code will work for only the first run after installation. Consequent updates to the app will not bring the code into the picture, unless the user has manually uninstalled and reinstalled the app.

> You could use a similar technique for distributing shareware versions of an Android app (i.e., limit the number of trials of the application). In this case, you would use an integer count value in the preferences to indicate the number of trials. Each trial would update the preferences. After the desired value is reached, you would block the usage of the application until the user pays the usage fee.

2.12 Formatting the Time and Date for Display

Pratik Rupwal

Problem

You want to display the time and date in different standard formats.

Solution

The DateFormat class provides APIs for formatting time and date in a custom format. Using these APIs requires minimal effort.

Discussion

Example 2-15 adds five different `TextView`s for showing the time and date in different formats.

Example 2-15. The TextView layout

```xml
<?xml version="1.0" encoding="utf-8"?>
<LinearLayout xmlns:android="http://schemas.android.com/apk/res/android"
    android:orientation="vertical"
    android:layout_width="fill_parent"
    android:layout_height="fill_parent"
    >
<TextView
    android:layout_width="fill_parent"
    android:layout_height="wrap_content"
    android:id="@+id/textview1"
    />
<TextView
    android:layout_width="fill_parent"
    android:layout_height="wrap_content"
    android:id="@+id/textview2"
    />
    <TextView
    android:layout_width="fill_parent"
    android:layout_height="wrap_content"
    android:id="@+id/textview3"
    />
    <TextView
    android:layout_width="fill_parent"
    android:layout_height="wrap_content"
    android:id="@+id/textview4"
    />
    <TextView
    android:layout_width="fill_parent"
    android:layout_height="wrap_content"
    android:id="@+id/textview5"
    />

</LinearLayout>
```

Example 2-16 obtains the current time and date using the `java.util.Date` class and then displays it in different formats (please refer to the comments for sample output).

Example 2-16. The date formatter activity

```java
package com.sym.dateformatdemo;

import java.util.Calendar;
import android.app.Activity;
import android.os.Bundle;
import android.text.format.DateFormat;
import android.widget.TextView;

public class TestDateFormatterActivity extends Activity {
```

```
/** Called when the activity is first created. */
@Override
public void onCreate(Bundle savedInstanceState) {
    super.onCreate(savedInstanceState);
    setContentView(R.layout.main);
    TextView textView1 = (TextView) findViewById(R.id.textview1);
    TextView textView2 = (TextView) findViewById(R.id.textview2);
    TextView textView3 = (TextView) findViewById(R.id.textview3);
    TextView textView4 = (TextView) findViewById(R.id.textview4);
    TextView textView5 = (TextView) findViewById(R.id.textview5);

    String delegate = "MM/dd/yy hh:mm a"; // 09/21/2011 02:17 pm
    java.util.Date noteTS = Calendar.getInstance().getTime();
    textView1.setText("Found Time :: "+DateFormat.format(delegate,noteTS));

    delegate = "MMM dd, yyyy h:mm aa"; // Sep 21,2011 02:17 pm
    textView2.setText("Found Time :: "+DateFormat.format(delegate,noteTS));

    delegate = "MMMM dd, yyyy h:mmaa"; //September 21,2011 02:17pm
    textView3.setText("Found Time :: "+DateFormat.format(delegate,noteTS));

    delegate = "E, MMMM dd, yyyy h:mm:ss aa";//Wed, September 21,2011 02:17:48 pm
    textView4.setText("Found Time :: "+DateFormat.format(delegate,noteTS));

    delegate =
        "EEEE, MMMM dd, yyyy h:mm aa"; //Wednesday, September 21,2011 02:17:48 pm
    textView5.setText("Found Time :: "+DateFormat.format(delegate,noteTS));
    }
}
```

See Also

The classes shown in the following table, in package android.text.format, may be of use in this type of application.

Name	Usage
DateUtils	This class contains various date-related utilities for creating text for things like elapsed time and date ranges, strings for days of the week and months, and a.m./p.m. text.
Formatter	This is a utility class to aid in formatting common values that are not covered by java.util.Formatter.
Time	This class is a faster replacement for the java.util.Calendar and java.util.GregorianCalendar classes.

2.13 Controlling Input with KeyListeners

Pratik Rupwal

Problem

Your application contains a few text boxes in which you want to restrict users to entering only numbers; also, in some cases you want to allow only positive numbers, or integers, or dates.

Solution

Android provides `KeyListener` classes to help you restrict users to entering only numbers/positive numbers/integers/positive integers and much more.

Discussion

The `Android.text.method` package includes a `KeyListener` interface, along with some classes such as `DigitsKeyListener` and `DateKeyListener`, which implement this interface.

Example 2-17 is a sample application that demonstrates a few of these classes. This layout file creates five `TextView`s and five `EditView`s; the `TextView`s display the input type allowed for their respective `EditText`s.

Example 2-17. Layout with TextViews and EditTexts

```xml
<?xml version="1.0" encoding="utf-8"?>
<LinearLayout xmlns:android="http://schemas.android.com/apk/res/android"
    android:orientation="vertical"
    android:layout_width="fill_parent"
    android:layout_height="fill_parent"
    >

    <TextView
    android:layout_width="fill_parent"
    android:layout_height="wrap_content"
    android:id="@+id/textview1"
    android:text="digits listener with signs and decimal points"
    />
    <EditText
    android:layout_width="fill_parent"
    android:layout_height="wrap_content"
    android:id="@+id/editText1"
    />

    <TextView
    android:layout_width="fill_parent"
    android:layout_height="wrap_content"
    android:id="@+id/textview2"
    android:text="digits listener without signs and decimal points"
    />
    <EditText
    android:layout_width="fill_parent"
    android:layout_height="wrap_content"
    android:id="@+id/editText2"
    />
```

```
    <TextView
    android:layout_width="fill_parent"
    android:layout_height="wrap_content"
    android:id="@+id/textview3"
    android:text="date listener"
    />
    <EditText
    android:layout_width="fill_parent"
    android:layout_height="wrap_content"
    android:id="@+id/editText3"
    />

    <TextView
    android:layout_width="fill_parent"
    android:layout_height="wrap_content"
    android:id="@+id/textview4"
    android:text="multitap listener"
    />
    <EditText
    android:layout_width="fill_parent"
    android:layout_height="wrap_content"
    android:id="@+id/editText4"
    />

    <TextView
    android:layout_width="fill_parent"
    android:layout_height="wrap_content"
    android:id="@+id/textview5"
    android:text="qwerty listener"
    />
    <EditText
    android:layout_width="fill_parent"
    android:layout_height="wrap_content"
    android:id="@+id/editText5"
    />
</LinearLayout>
```

Example 2-18 is the code for the activity that restricts the EditText input to numbers, positive integers, and so on (refer to the comments for groups of keys allowed).

Example 2-18. The main activity

```
import android.app.Activity;
import android.os.Bundle;
import android.text.method.DateKeyListener;
import android.text.method.DigitsKeyListener;
import android.text.method.MultiTapKeyListener;
import android.text.method.QwertyKeyListener;
import android.text.method.TextKeyListener;
import android.widget.EditText;

public class KeyListenerDemo extends Activity {
    /** Called when the activity is first created. */
@Override
```

```
public void onCreate(Bundle savedInstanceState) {
super.onCreate(savedInstanceState);
    setContentView(R.layout.main);
        //allows digits with positive/negative signs and decimal points
        EditText editText1=(EditText)findViewById(R.id.editText1);
        DigitsKeyListenerdigkl1=DigitsKeyListener.getInstance(true,true);
        editText1.setKeyListener(digkl1);

        //allows positive integer only (no decimal values allowed)
        EditText editText2=(EditText)findViewById(R.id.editText2);
        DigitsKeyListener digkl2=DigitsKeyListener.getInstance();
        editText2.setKeyListener(digkl2);

        //allows date only
        EditText editText3=(EditText)findViewById(R.id.editText3);
        DateKeyListener dtkl=new DateKeyListener();
        editText3.setKeyListener(dtkl);

        //allows multitap with 12-key keypad layout
        EditText editText4=(EditText)findViewById(R.id.editText4);
        MultiTapKeyListener multitapkl =
            new MultiTapKeyListener(TextKeyListener.Capitalize.WORDS,true);
        editText4.setKeyListener(multitapkl);

        //allows qwerty layout for typing
        EditText editText5=(EditText)findViewById(R.id.editText5);
        QwertyKeyListener qkl =
            new QwertyKeyListener(TextKeyListener.Capitalize.SENTENCES,true);
        editText5.setKeyListener(qkl);
    }
}
```

To use MultiTapKeyListener, your phone should support the 12-key layout and it needs to be activated. To activate the 12-key layout, go to Settings→Language and Keyboard→On-screen Keyboard Layout and then select the "Phone layout" options.

See Also

The following Listener types will be of use in writing this type of application.

Name	Usage
BaseKeyListener	This is an abstract base class for key listeners.
DateTimeKey Listener	This is for entering dates and times in the same text field.
MetaKeyKeyListener	This base class encapsulates the behavior for tracking the state of meta keys such as SHIFT, ALT, and SYM as well as the pseudometa state of selecting text.
NumberKeyListener	This is for numeric text entry.
TextKeyListener	This is the key listener for typing normal text.
TimeKeyListener	This is for entering times in a text field.

2.14 Backing Up Android Application Data

Pratik Rupwal

Problem

When a user performs a factory reset or converts to a new Android-powered device, the application loses stored data or application settings.

Solution

Android's Backup Manager helps to automatically restore backup data or application settings when the application is reinstalled.

Discussion

Android's Backup Manager basically operates in two modes, backup and restore. During a backup operation, the Backup Manager (`BackupManager` class) queries your application for backup data, then hands it to a backup transport, which then delivers the data to cloud-based storage. During a restore operation, the Backup Manager retrieves the backup data from the backup transport and returns it to your application so that your application can restore the data to the device. It's possible for your application to request a restore, but not necessary as Android performs a restore operation when your application is installed and backup data exists associated with the user. The primary scenario in which backup data is restored happens when a user resets her device or upgrades to a new device and her previously installed applications are reinstalled.

Example 2-19 shows how to implement the Backup Manager for your application so that you can save the current state of your application.

Here is a basic description of the procedure in step-by-step form:

1. Create a `BackupManagerExample` project in Eclipse.
2. Open and insert the code in Example 2-19 into the *layout/backup_restore.xml* file.
3. Open the *values/string.xml* file and insert into it the code shown in Example 2-20.
4. Your manifest file will look like the code shown in Example 2-21.
5. The code in Example 2-22 completes the implementation of the Backup Manager for your application.

Example 2-19. The backup/restore layout

```
<LinearLayout xmlns:android="http://schemas.android.com/apk/res/android"
    android:orientation="vertical"
    android:layout_width="match_parent"
    android:layout_height="wrap_content">

    <ScrollView
        android:orientation="vertical"
```

```
        android:layout_width="fill_parent"
        android:layout_height="fill_parent"
        android:layout_weight="1">

    <LinearLayout
        android:orientation="vertical"
        android:layout_width="match_parent"
        android:layout_height="wrap_content">

        <TextView android:text="@string/filling_text"
            android:textSize="20dp"
            android:layout_marginTop="20dp"
            android:layout_marginBottom="10dp"
            android:layout_width="match_parent"
            android:layout_height="wrap_content"/>

        <RadioGroup android:id="@+id/filling_group"
            android:layout_width="match_parent"
            android:layout_height="wrap_content"
            android:layout_marginLeft="20dp"
            android:orientation="vertical">

            <RadioButton android:id="@+id/bacon"
                android:text="@string/bacon_label"/>
            <RadioButton android:id="@+id/pastrami"
                android:text="@string/pastrami_label"/>
            <RadioButton android:id="@+id/hummus"
                android:text="@string/hummus_label"/>

        </RadioGroup>

        <TextView android:text="@string/extras_text"
            android:textSize="20dp"
            android:layout_marginTop="20dp"
            android:layout_marginBottom="10dp"
            android:layout_width="match_parent"
            android:layout_height="wrap_content"/>

        <CheckBox android:id="@+id/mayo"
            android:text="@string/mayo_text"
            android:layout_marginLeft="20dp"
            android:layout_width="match_parent"
            android:layout_height="wrap_content"/>

        <CheckBox android:id="@+id/tomato"
            android:text="@string/tomato_text"
            android:layout_marginLeft="20dp"
            android:layout_width="match_parent"
            android:layout_height="wrap_content"/>

    </LinearLayout>

  </ScrollView>

</LinearLayout>
```

Example 2-20. Strings for the example

```xml
<resources>
  <string name="hello">Hello World, BackupManager!</string>
  <string name="app_name">BackupManager</string>
  <string name="filling_text">Choose Settings for your application:</string>
  <string name="bacon_label">Sound On</string>
  <string name="pastrami_label">Vibration On</string>
  <string name="hummus_label">Backlight On</string>
  <string name="extras_text">Extras:</string>
  <string name="mayo_text">Use Orientation?</string>
  <string name="tomato_text">Use Camera?</string>
</resources>
```

Example 2-21. AndroidManifest.xml

```xml
<?xml version="1.0" encoding="utf-8"?>
<manifest xmlns:android="http://schemas.android.com/apk/res/android"
      package="com.sym.backupmanager"
      android:versionCode="1"
      android:versionName="1.0">
    <uses-sdk android:minSdkVersion="9" />

    <application android:label="Backup/Restore" android:icon="@drawable/icon"
        android:backupAgent="ExampleAgent"> <!-- Here you specify the backup agent-->

        <!--Some backup transports may require API keys or other metadata-->
        <meta-data android:name="com.google.android.backup.api_key"
                android:value="INSERT YOUR API KEY HERE" />

        <activity android:name=".BackupManagerExample">
                <intent-filter>
                        <action android:name="android.intent.action.MAIN" />
                        <category android:name="android.intent.category.LAUNCHER" />
                </intent-filter>
        </activity> </application>

</manifest>
```

Example 2-22. The backup/restore activity

```java
package com.sym.backupmanager;

import android.app.Activity;
import android.app.backup.BackupManager;
import android.os.Bundle;
import android.util.Log;
import android.widget.CheckBox;
import android.widget.CompoundButton;
import android.widget.RadioGroup;
import java.io.File;
import java.io.IOException;
import java.io.RandomAccessFile;

public class BackupManagerExample extends Activity {
        static final String TAG = "BRActivity";
```

```
static final Object[] sDataLock = new Object[0];

static final String DATA_FILE_NAME = "saved_data";

RadioGroup mFillingGroup;
CheckBox mAddMayoCheckbox;
CheckBox mAddTomatoCheckbox;

File mDataFile;

BackupManager mBackupManager;

@Override
public void onCreate(Bundle savedInstanceState) {
    super.onCreate(savedInstanceState);

    setContentView(R.layout.backup_restore);

    mFillingGroup = (RadioGroup) findViewById(R.id.filling_group);
    mAddMayoCheckbox = (CheckBox) findViewById(R.id.mayo);
    mAddTomatoCheckbox = (CheckBox) findViewById(R.id.tomato);

    mDataFile = new File(getFilesDir(), BackupManagerExample.DATA_FILE_NAME);

    mBackupManager = new BackupManager(this);

    populateUI();
}

void populateUI() {
    RandomAccessFile file;

    int whichFilling = R.id.pastrami;
    boolean addMayo = false;
    boolean addTomato = false;

    synchronized (BackupManagerExample.sDataLock) {
        boolean exists = mDataFile.exists();
        try {
            file = new RandomAccessFile(mDataFile, "rw");
            if (exists) {
                Log.v(TAG, "datafile exists");
                whichFilling = file.readInt();
                addMayo = file.readBoolean();
                addTomato = file.readBoolean();
                Log.v(TAG, "   mayo=" + addMayo
                        + " tomato=" + addTomato
                        + " filling=" + whichFilling);
            } else {
                Log.v(TAG, "creating default datafile");
                writeDataToFileLocked(file,
                        addMayo, addTomato, whichFilling);

                mBackupManager.dataChanged();
```

```
            }
        } catch (IOException ioe) {
            // Do some error handling here!
        }
    }

    mFillingGroup.check(whichFilling);
    mAddMayoCheckbox.setChecked(addMayo);
    mAddTomatoCheckbox.setChecked(addTomato);

    mFillingGroup.setOnCheckedChangeListener(
            new RadioGroup.OnCheckedChangeListener() {
                public void onCheckedChanged(RadioGroup group,
                        int checkedId) {
                    Log.v(TAG, "New radio item selected: " + checkedId);
                    recordNewUIState();
                }
            });

    CompoundButton.OnCheckedChangeListener checkListener
            = new CompoundButton.OnCheckedChangeListener() {
        public void onCheckedChanged(CompoundButton buttonView,
                boolean isChecked) {
            Log.v(TAG, "Checkbox toggled: " + buttonView);
            recordNewUIState();
        }
    };
    mAddMayoCheckbox.setOnCheckedChangeListener(checkListener);
    mAddTomatoCheckbox.setOnCheckedChangeListener(checkListener);
}

void writeDataToFileLocked(RandomAccessFile file,
        boolean addMayo, boolean addTomato, int whichFilling)
    throws IOException {
        file.setLength(0L);
        file.writeInt(whichFilling);
        file.writeBoolean(addMayo);
        file.writeBoolean(addTomato);
        Log.v(TAG, "NEW STATE: mayo=" + addMayo
                + " tomato=" + addTomato
                + " filling=" + whichFilling);
}

void recordNewUIState() {
    boolean addMayo = mAddMayoCheckbox.isChecked();
    boolean addTomato = mAddTomatoCheckbox.isChecked();
    int whichFilling = mFillingGroup.getCheckedRadioButtonId();
    try {
        synchronized (BackupManagerExample.sDataLock) {
            RandomAccessFile file = new RandomAccessFile(mDataFile, "rw");
            writeDataToFileLocked(file, addMayo, addTomato, whichFilling);
        }
    } catch (IOException e) {
        Log.e(TAG, "Unable to record new UI state");
    }
```

```
        mBackupManager.dataChanged();
    }
}
```

Data backup is not guaranteed to be available on all Android-powered devices. However, your application is not adversely affected in the event that a device does not provide a backup transport. If you believe that users will benefit from data backup in your application, you can implement it as described in this document, test it, and then publish your application without any concern about which devices actually perform backups. When your application runs on a device that does not provide a backup transport, your application will operate normally, but will not receive callbacks from the Backup Manager to backup data.

Although you cannot know what the current transport is, you are always assured that your backup data cannot be read by other applications on the device. Only the Backup Manager and backup transport have access to the data you provide during a backup operation.

 Because the cloud storage and transport service can differ among devices, Android makes no guarantees about the security of your data while using backup. You should always be cautious about using backup to store sensitive data, such as usernames and passwords.

Testing your backup agent

Once you've implemented your backup agent, you can use the `bmgr` command to test the backup and restore functionality by following these steps:

1. Install your application on a suitable Android system image. If you are using the emulator, create and use an AVD with Android 2.2 (API Level 8). If you are using a device, the device must be running Android 2.2 or later and have the Android Market built in.

2. Ensure that backup capability is enabled. If you are using the emulator, you can enable backup with the following command from your SDK tools/path:

   ```
   adb shell bmgr enable true
   ```

   If you are using a device, open the system settings, select Privacy, and then enable "Back up my data" and "Automatic restore."

3. Open your application and initialize some data.

   If you've properly implemented backup capability in your application, it should request a backup each time the data changes. For example, each time the user changes some data, your app should call `dataChanged()`, which adds a backup request to the Backup Manager queue. For testing purposes, you can also make a request with the following `bmgr` command:

   ```
   adb shell bmgr backup your.package.name
   ```

4. Initiate a backup operation:

```
adb shell bmgr run
```

This forces the Backup Manager to perform all backup requests that are in its queue.

5. Uninstall your application:

```
adb uninstall your.package.name
```

6. Reinstall your application.

If your backup agent is successful, all the data you initialized in step 4 is restored.

2.15 Using Hints Instead of Tool Tips

Daniel Fowler

Problem

Android devices can have small screens, there may not be room for help text, and tool tips are not part of the platform.

Solution

Android provides the `hint` attribute for `Views`.

Discussion

Sometimes an input field needs clarification with regard to the value being entered. For example, a stock ordering application asking for item quantities may need to state the minimum order size. In desktop programs, with large screens and the use of a mouse, extra messages can be displayed in the form of tool tips (a pop-up label over a field when the mouse moves over it). Alternatively, long descriptive labels may be used. With Android devices the screen may be small and no mouse is generally used. The alternative here is to use the `android:hint` attribute on a `View`. This causes a "watermark" containing the hint text to be displayed in the input field when it is empty; this disappears when the user starts typing in the field. The corresponding function for `android:hint` is `setHint(int resourceId)`. The use of a hint is shown in Figure 2-4.

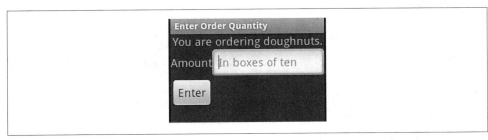

Figure 2-4. An example with hints

You can set the color of the hint text with `android:textColorHint`, with `setHintText Color(int color)` being the associated function.

Using these hints can also help with screen layouts when space is tight. It can allow labels to be removed to gain more space as the hints provide the necessary prompt for the user. In addition, a screen design can sometimes be improved by removing a label and using a hint, as shown in Figure 2-5.

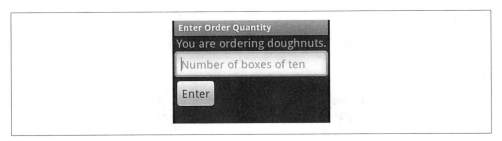

Figure 2-5. Hints and no label

The `EditText` definition in Figure 2-5 is shown in the following code so that you can see `android:hint` in use:

```
<EditText android:id="@+id/etQuantity"
    android:layout_width="fill_parent"
    android:layout_height="wrap_content"
    android:hint="Number of boxes of ten"
    android:textSize="18sp"/>
```

Hints can guide users as they are filling in app fields, though as with any feature overuse is possible. Hints should not be used when it is obvious what is required; a field with a label of "First Name" would not need a hint such as "Enter your first name here," for example. Figure 2-5 shows the ordering application improved somewhat by removing the redundant label.

## CHAPTER 3

Testing

3.1 Introduction: Testing

Ian Darwin

Discussion

"Test early and often" is a common cry among advocates of testing. As is the all-important question, "If you don't have a test, how do you know your code works?"

There are many types of testing. Unit testing checks out individual components in isolation (not hitting the network or the database). JUnit and TestNG are the leading frameworks here. Mock objects are used where interaction with other components is required; there are several good mocking frameworks for Java.

Android provides a number of specific testing techniques, many of which are discussed here.

The terms *NPE*, *ANR*, and *FC* are used without further explanation in this chapter. NPE is a "traditional Java" acronym for Null Pointer Exception. ANR is an Android-specific acronym; it stands for Application Not Responding, the first few words of a dialog you get when your application is judged to be taking too long to respond to a request. FC stands for Force Close, which occurs when Android requests that you close a failed application.

3.2 Doing Test-Driven Development (TDD) in Android

Kailuo Wang

Problem

The lack of mocking support makes test-driven development in Android apps cumbersome.

Solution

Set up two test projects: one created using the Android tool for the UI-related tests, and another standard unit test project for mock supported tests. Extract as much of your logic as possible to the classes that can be unit-tested.

Discussion

In the official documentation (at *http://developer.android.com*), the test-related articles are mostly about UI tests. An Android test project needs to be created so that it can be instrumented and deployed and the app can be tested in a simulator environment. It's very cool and necessary for testing the UI-related logic, but it also makes mocking very difficult. There are some workarounds, but they make things a bit ad hoc and potentially painful. If you step back and look at them from a higher level, these tests are more like integration tests than pure unit tests. They take longer to run, and they require that the entire environment be up and running. Without mocking, they might need to test a lot more than a unit of functionality. All of these limitations justify the need to make such tests a separate project/module from the normal unit test project/module. We can call this Android tool-created project/module the XYZ UI Test project, whose responsibility is to test only UI logic. Now you can set up another standard unit test project as you always do. Let's call it the XYZ Unit Test project. Here you can use your favorite tools, including mock frameworks. Also, it's testing only all the non-UI related logic which avoids all the less-than-test-friendly Android UI API. Now all you need to do is to extract as much logic as possible out of the nasty UI-dependent classes and have fun doing TDD.

See Also

http://developer.android.com/resources/tutorials/testing/helloandroid_test.html

3.3 Setting Up an Android Virtual Device (AVD) for App Testing

Daniel Fowler

Problem

Successful apps must run on a wide range of Android devices and versions, so you need to test them on a range of devices.

Solution

Use the Android SDK's device emulation toolkit to configure combinations of devices and operating systems. Testing on various combinations reduces issues related to hardware differences in devices.

Discussion

Android devices are manufactured to cover a wide market, from low cost to high specification and high value. Android has also been in the marketplace for more than a couple of years. For these reasons, a wide range of devices with a wide range of hardware options and operating system versions are being used. A successful application will be one that can run on such a range of devices. An app developer will only be able to test on a very small range of physical devices. Fortunately, a developer can boost the confidence he has in his app by using an Android Virtual Device (AVD).

A compiled app can be tested on a physical device or on a virtual device. An AVD is an emulation of an Android platform on a host machine, usually the development machine. AVDs simplify testing for these reasons:

- Multiple AVD configurations can be created to test an app on different versions of Android.
- Different (emulated) hardware configurations can be used—for example, GPS or no GPS.
- An AVD is automatically launched and your compiled app is installed onto it when the Run button is clicked in Eclipse.
- You can test your app on many more combinations of Android versions and hardware versions than physical devices you possess.
- Testing on AVDs greatly reduces the amount of testing required on physical devices.
- AVDs can be used alongside a physical device.
- You don't need to handicap your physical device to induce error conditions—for example, if you're testing on a device with no Secure Digital (SD) card, just set up an AVD with no SD card.
- An AVD can simulate network events without the costs involved in using a physical device; for example, you can simulate phone calls or send an SMS between two AVDs.
- You can simulate GPS data from an AVD from different physical locations without moving from your desk.
- When app users report bugs you can try to mimic their hardware configurations using AVDs.

Please note that on older development machines and when emulating larger Android devices the performance of an AVD will be less than that of a physical device.

You can configure an AVD using the SDK Manager program (opened directly from the filesystem or from within Eclipse). It is also possible to create AVDs from the command line.

To create an AVD with the SDK Manager, you must first load the program. When using Eclipse select Window from the menu bar and then select Android SDK and AVD Manager, as shown in Figure 3-1.

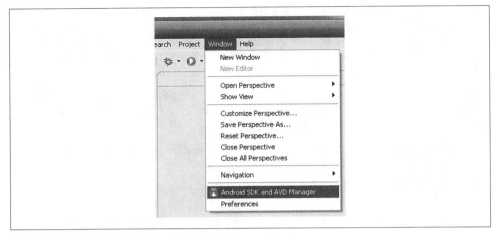

Figure 3-1. Selecting the SDK and AVD Manager

You can also start the program directly from the filesystem. For example, in Windows, open *C:\Program Files\Android\android-sdk\SDK Manager.exe*. If you started the program directly from the filesystem, the SDK Manager will check for SDK updates, in which case select Cancel to go to the main window, titled Android SDK and AVD Manager (see Figure 3-2). If you opened the program from Eclipse, the main window will show without the check for updates to the SDK.

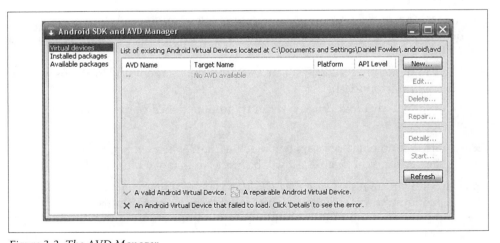

Figure 3-2. The AVD Manager

The lefthand side of the main window will list "Virtual Devices," "Installed packages," and "Available packages." "Virtual Devices" should already be selected; if not, select it and any existing defined AVDs will be listed in the table on the right. If the Android SDK has just been installed no AVDs may be listed.

To create an AVD, select the New button. The "Create new Android Virtual Device (AVD)" window will load (see Figure 3-3).

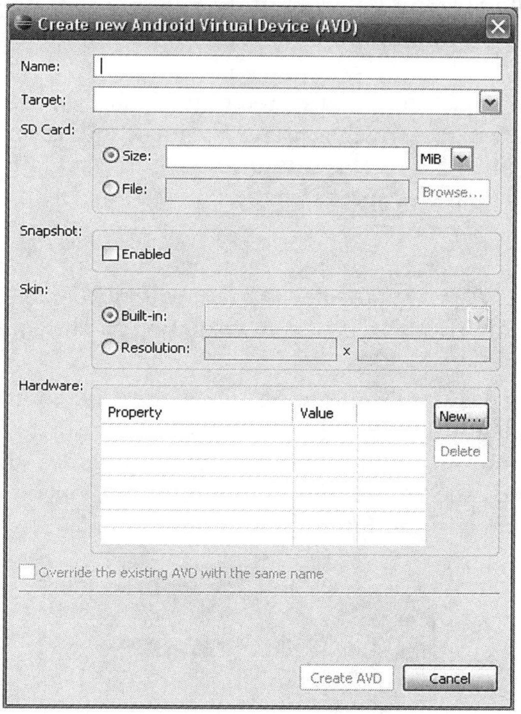

Figure 3-3. Creating a new AVD

The following fields are used to define an AVD:

Name
> Give a name to the new Android device that is to be emulated. Make the name descriptive—for example, if you're emulating a device with a version 2.1 operating system and medium resolution screen (HVGA) a name such as Android-v2.1-HVGA is better than AndroidDevice.

Target
> This is the version of the Android operating system that will be running on the emulated device. As an example for a device running version 2.1 this will be set to "Android 2.1-update1 - API Level 7".

SD Card

Here you specify the size of the device's emulated SD card, or select an existing SD card image (allowing the ability to share SD card data among different AVD emulations). To specify a new SD card enter the size in megabytes (MBs) for the card. Remember that the bigger the number the bigger the file created on the host computer system to mimic the SD card. Alternatively, select the File option and browse to an existing SD card image (on a Windows machine the *sdcard.img* files will be found in the subfolders of the *avd* directory under the *.android* directory in the logged-on user's folder).

Snapshot

Check the Enabled box if you want the runtime state of the emulated device to persist between sessions, which is useful if a long-running series of tests are being performed and when the AVD is closed you do not want to have to start the tests from the beginning. It also speeds up the start-up time of an AVD.

Skin

Here you select the screen size for the device; a list of common screen sizes is presented (e.g., HVGA, QVGA, etc.). The list will vary depending on the operating system version. Alternatively, a custom resolution can be entered.

Hardware

The table under the Hardware option allows the AVD to be configured with or without certain hardware features. To change features first add them to the table using the New button (a couple of features will be added and will default automatically based on the Target selected). A dialog will open to allow the selection of a hardware property (see Figure 3-4).

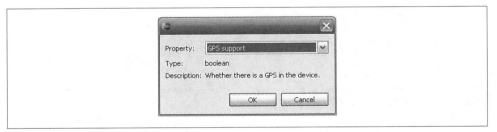

Figure 3-4. Setting a hardware property

For example, select "GPS support" and then "OK." Select "yes" next to "GPS support in the table" and change it to "no." The AVD will not support GPS (see Figure 3-5).

Table 3-1 lists the AVD supported properties.

Table 3-1. AVD supported properties

Name	Data type	Value	Description
Camera support	Boolean	Yes or no	Indicates whether the AVD supports the detection of a camera
Max VM application heap size	Integer	Size	The maximum size of the heap an app may allocate before being shut down by the system
Abstracted LCD density	Integer	120/160/240/320	Approximate density (dots per inch) of the AVD screen; 120 is low density, 160 is standard or normal density, 240 is high density, and 320 is extra-high density
Cache partition size	Integer mega-bytes	*Number*	Sets the size of the cache used by the browser
SD card support	Boolean	Yes or no	Indicates support for an SD card
Cache partition support	Boolean	Yes or no	Determines whether a browser uses a cache
Keyboard support	Boolean	Yes or no	Controls emulation of a physical keyboard (as opposed to an on-screen one)
Audio playback support	Boolean	Yes or no	Indicates support for audio playback
Keyboard lid support	Boolean	Yes or no	Indicates whether the emulated keyboard can be opened and closed
Audio recording support	Boolean	Yes or no	Indicates support for recording audio
DPad support	Boolean	Yes or no	Indicates emulation of a directional pad
Maximum vertical camera pixels	Integer	Pixels height	Determines the height of photos taken with the camera
Accelerometer	Boolean	Yes or no	Indicates whether a tilt and movement device can be detected
GPS support	Boolean	Yes or no	Indicates whether a Global Positioning System data can be provided
Device RAM size	Integer	Megabytes	Determines the size of the AVD's memory
Touch-screen support	Boolean	Yes or no	Determines whether the AVD supports operation via the screen
Proximity support	Boolean	Yes or no	Indicates support for a proximity sensor
Battery support	Boolean	Yes or no	Indicates support for simulated battery power
GSM modem support	Boolean	Yes or no	Determines emulation of telephony abilities
Trackball support	Boolean	Yes or no	Indicates support for a trackball
Maximum horizontal camera pixels	Integer	Pixel width	Determines the width of photos taken with the camera

When the required fields have been defined, click the Create AVD button to generate the AVD. The AVD will now be listed on the Android SDK and AVD Manager window (see Figure 3-6).

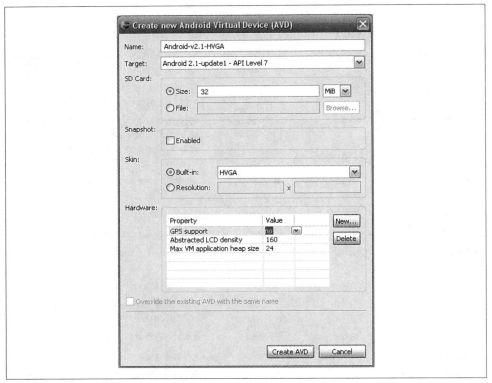

Figure 3-5. Creating an Android 2.1 AVD

The AVD is ready to be launched using the Start button. It is also ready to be selected in a project configuration to test an App under development. When the Start button is selected, the Launch Options window is shown (see Figure 3-7).

The options at launch are:

Scale the display to real size

On larger computer monitors you will not normally need to change the AVD scale. The dpi of the Android screen is greater than the standard dpi on computer monitors; therefore, the AVD screen will appear larger than the physical device. If necessary this can be scaled back to save screen space. Use this option to get the AVD to display at an approximate real size on the computer monitor. The values need to be set so that the AVD screen and keyboard are not too small to be used.

Wipe user data

When the AVD is started the user data file is reset and any user data generated from previous runs of the AVD is lost.

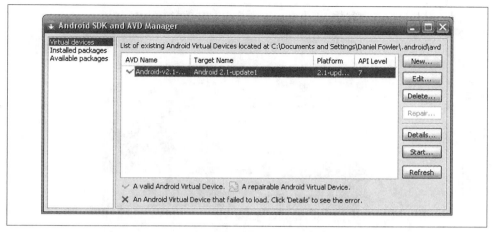

Figure 3-6. Starting the new AVD

Figure 3-7. Launch options for the AVD

Launch from snapshot

> If Snapshot has been Enabled for an AVD, after it has been first launched subsequent launches are quicker. The AVD is loaded from a snapshot and the Android operating system does not need to start up again. Although when the AVD is closed the shutdown takes longer because the snapshot has to be written to disk.

Save to snapshot

> When the AVD is closed the current state is saved for quicker launching next time; although it takes longer to close as the snapshot is written to disk. Once you have a snapshot you can uncheck this option so that closing an AVD is quick as well, though any changes since the last snapshot will be lost.

Use the Launch button to start the AVD. Once loaded it can be used like any other Android device and driven from the keyboard and mouse of the host computer. See Figure 3-8.

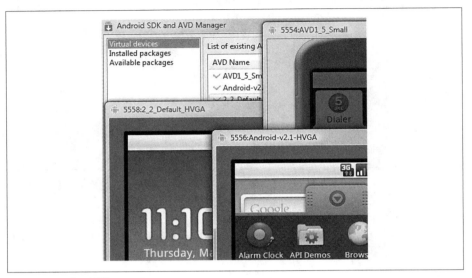

Figure 3-8. The AVD in action

Error message on Windows when launching

When trying to launch an AVD on a Windows installation, an error beginning with "invalid command-line parameter" may occur (see Figure 3-9).

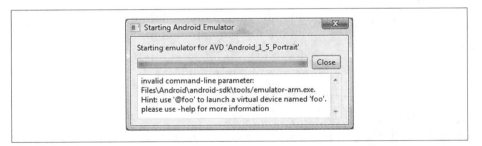

Figure 3-9. Error on Microsoft Windows

To fix this problem, change the path to the Android SDK directory so that it does not contain any spaces. The default installation path for the SDK is in *C:\Program Files\Android.* The space in *Program Files* needs to be removed. To do this and maintain a valid directory name *Program Files* needs to be converted to its Microsoft DOS format (also referred to as 8.3 format). This is usually the first six letters in uppercase followed by a tilde and the number 1, that is, *PROGRA~1*. If other directories start with *Program* followed by a space, the number may need to be increased. To see the DOS format for the *Program Files* directory on your machine open a command prompt (via Start→All Programs→Accessories). Change to root (type `cd\` and press Enter) and run `dir/x`, and the directory's DOS name will be displayed next to its full name (see Figure 3-10).

Figure 3-10. MS-DOS naming

In Eclipse, use the Windows→Preferences menu option and select Android; in the SDK Location field change Program Files to its DOS version (see Figure 3-11).

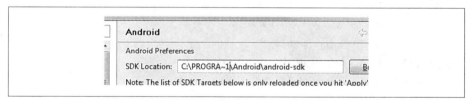

Figure 3-11. Setting the Android SDK Location

See Also

http://d.android.com/guide/developing/devices/emulator.html

3.4 Testing on a Huge Range of Devices with Cloud-based Testing

Ian Darwin

Problem

You need to test your app on a wide variety of devices.

Solution

Use one of several web-based or cloud-based app testing services.

Discussion

When Android was young, it was perhaps feasible to own one of each kind of device, to be able to say you had tested it on everything. I have half a dozen Android devices, most of them semiexpired, for this purpose. Yet today there are hundreds of different devices to test on, some with two or three different OS versions, different cell radios, and so on. It's just not practical for each developer to own enough devices to test on everything. That leaves two choices: either set up a hundred different AVDs as discussed elsewhere in this chapter, or use a "cloud-based" or web-based testing service.

The basic idea is that these companies buy lots of devices, and put them in server rooms with a webcam pointed at the screen and USB drivers that transfer keystrokes and touch gestures from your web-browser-based control program to the real devices. These devices are in cities around the world, so you can test while online with various mobile service providers, get GPS coordinates from the real location, and so on.

Here are some of the providers in this space, listed in alphabetical order. Some are Android-specific while some also cover iOS, BlackBerry, and other devices. Listing them here does not constitute an endorsement of their products or services; caveat emptor!

- Bitbar TestDroid (*http://bitbar.com*)
- Bsquare (*http://www.bsquare.com*)
- Experitest (*http://experitest.com*)
- Jamo Solutions (*http://www.jamosolutions.com*)
- Perfecto Mobile (*http://www.perfectomobile.com*)

3.5 Creating and Using a Test Project

Adrián Santalla

Problem

You need to create and use a new test project to test your Android application.

Solution

Here's how to create and use a test project:

1. Within your IDE create a new Android project associated with your Android application project.
2. Configure the *AndroidManifest.xml* file of your test project with the necessary lines to test your Android application.
3. And finally, write and run your tests.

Discussion

The following subsections describe the preceding steps in more detail.

Step 1: Create a new Android test project within your Android application project

First of all, you need to create a new Android project with the main application project to store your tests. This should be either a project, if you're using Eclipse, or a module, if you're using IntelliJ. IntelliJ IDEA allows you to nest the module inside your existing project; Eclipse does not allow projects to overlap, hence it requires the Android test project to be a top-level project. This new project should have an explicit dependency on your main application project. The Eclipse Android New Project Wizard will create this and set it up correctly when you create the original project, if you remember to click the checkbox.

Figure 3-12 shows the IDEA test project structure. As you can see, the new test project lies within the main application project.

Figure 3-13 is the corresponding Eclipse project structure: two projects.

Step 2: Configure the AndroidManifest.xml file of the test project

Once you have created your new test project, you should properly set all the values of the project's *AndroidManifest.xml* file. It's necessary to set the package name of the main source of the application that you would like to test.

Imagine that you are testing an application whose package name is `my.pkg.app`. You should create a test project, and your *AndroidManifest.xml* file should look like the code in Example 3-1.

Example 3-1. The AndroidManifest.xml file for testing

```xml
<?xml version="1.0" encoding="utf-8"?>

<manifest xmlns:android="http://schemas.android.com/apk/res/android"
    package="my.pkg.app.tests"
    android:versionCode="1"
    android:versionName="1.0">

    <application>
    <uses-library android:name="android.test.runner" />
    </application>

    <instrumentation android:name="android.test.InstrumentationTestRunner"
    android:targetPackage="my.pkg.app"
    android:label="Tests for my.pkg.app"/>
</manifest>
```

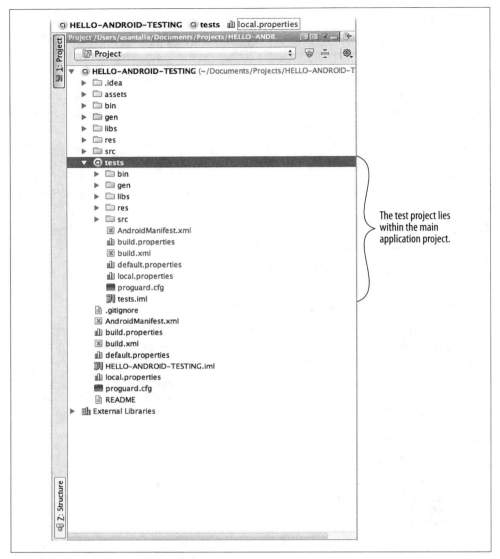

Figure 3-12. Test project in IntelliJ IDEA

The `package` attribute of the `manifest` tag stores the package name of the test project; more importantly, the `android:targetPackage` of the `instrumentation` tag stores the package name that you would like to test.

Again, the Eclipse wizard will set this up if you create the main and test projects at the same time. See Figure 3-13.

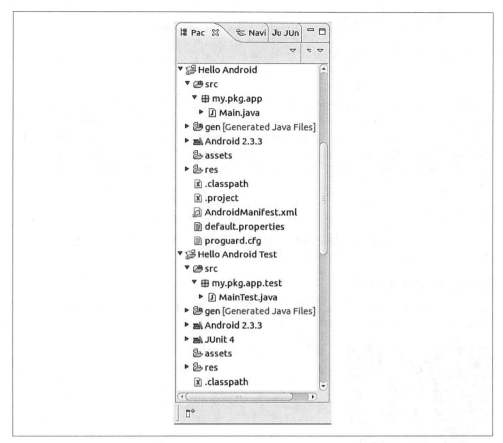

Figure 3-13. Test project in Eclipse

Step 3: Write and run your tests

Finally, you can start to write your own tests. The Android testing API is based on the JUnit API and provides several types of test classes, including `AndroidTestCase`, component-specific test case, `ApplicationTestCase`, and `InstrumentationTestCase`.

When you create your first test case with your IDE, it is very useful to create a test case that inherits from `ActivityInstrumentationTestCase2`. This kind of test class allows you to create functional tests. Example 3-2 shows a simple functional test.

Example 3-2. A test case

```
public class MainTest extends ActivityInstrumentationTestCase2<Main> {

        public MainTest() {
        super("my.pkg.app", Main.class);
        }
```

```
    public void test() {
    TextView textView = (TextView) getActivity().findViewById(R.id.textView);

    assertEquals("Hello World!", textView.getText());
    }
}
```

The Main class that appears in the test is the main activity of the main application project. The test constructor uses the main application package name and the class of the main activity. From now on, you can create test cases using the standard methods of the Android API to get references to the activity elements. In the preceding test we are testing that the main activity has a TextView with the text *"Hello World!"* associated with it.

See Also

Android documentation (*http://developer.android.com/guide/topics/testing/testing_an droid.html*)

Source Download URL

You can download the source code for this example from *https://github.com/asantalla/ Hello-Android-Testing*.

3.6 Troubleshooting Application Crashes

Ulysses Levy

Problem

Your app crashes and you are not sure why (see Figure 3-14).

Solution

Begin by viewing the log.

Figure 3-14. What an app crash looks like

Discussion

In terms of an app crash, we can use the `adb logcat` command or the Eclipse LogCat window to view our AVD's log. Example 3-3 shows how to find the failure location by looking in the stack trace using `adb logcat`.

Example 3-3. The permission denied stack trace

```
E/DatabaseUtils(   53): Writing exception to parcel
E/DatabaseUtils(   53): java.lang.SecurityException: Permission Denial: writing
    com.android.providers.settings.SettingsProvider uri content://settings/system
    from pid=430, uid=10030 requires android.permission.WRITE_SETTINGS
E/DatabaseUtils(   53): at android.content.ContentProvider$Transport.
    enforceWritePermission(ContentProvider.java:294)
E/DatabaseUtils(   53): at android.content.ContentProvider$Transport.
    insert(ContentProvider.java:149)
E/DatabaseUtils(   53): at android.content.ContentProviderNative.
    onTransact(ContentProviderNative.java:140)
E/DatabaseUtils(   53): at android.os.Binder.execTransact(Binder.java:287)
E/DatabaseUtils(   53): at com.android.server.SystemServer.init1(Native Method)
E/DatabaseUtils(   53): at com.android.server.SystemServer.main(SystemServer.java:497)
E/DatabaseUtils(   53): at java.lang.reflect.Method.invokeNative(Native Method)
E/DatabaseUtils(   53): at java.lang.reflect.Method.invoke(Method.java:521)
E/DatabaseUtils(   53): at com.android.internal.os.
    ZygoteInit$MethodAndArgsCaller.run(ZygoteInit.java:860)
```

```
E/DatabaseUtils(    53): at com.android.internal.os.ZygoteInit.main(ZygoteInit.java:618)
E/DatabaseUtils(    53): at dalvik.system.NativeStart.main(Native Method)
D/AndroidRuntime( 430): Shutting down VM
W/dalvikvm( 430): threadid=3: thread exiting with uncaught exception (group=0x4001b188)
...
```

In Example 3-3, we have a permission issue. So the solution in this particular instance is to add the WRITE_SETTINGS permission to our *AndroidManifest.xml* file.

```
<manifest ... >
    <application ... />
    <uses-permission android:name="android.permission.WRITE_SETTINGS" />
</manifest>
```

Another fairly common error is the Null Pointer Exception (NPE).

Example 3-4 shows the LogCat output.

Example 3-4. LogCat output

```
I/ActivityManager(    53): Displayed activity com.android.launcher/.Launcher:
    28640 ms (total 28640 ms)
I/ActivityManager(    53): Starting activity: Intent { act=android.intent.action.MAIN
    cat=[android.intent.category.LAUNCHER] flg=0x10200000 cmp=com.aschyiel.disp/.Disp }
I/ActivityManager(    53): Start proc com.aschyiel.disp for
    activity com.aschyiel.disp/.Disp: pid=214 uid=10030 gids={1015}
I/ARMAssembler(    53): generated scanline__00000177:03515104_00000001_00000000 [ 73 ipp]
    (95 ins) at [0x47c588:0x47c704] in 2087627 ns
I/ARMAssembler(    53): generated scanline__00000077:03545404_00000004_00000000 [ 47 ipp]
    (67 ins) at [0x47c708:0x47c814] in 1834173 ns
I/ARMAssembler(    53): generated scanline__00000077:03010104_00000004_00000000 [ 22 ipp]
    (41 ins) at [0x47c818:0x47c8bc] in 653016 ns
D/AndroidRuntime( 214): Shutting down VM
W/dalvikvm( 214): threadid=3: thread exiting with uncaught exception (group=0x4001b188)
E/AndroidRuntime( 214): Uncaught handler: thread main exiting due to uncaught exception
E/AndroidRuntime( 214): java.lang.RuntimeException: Unable to start activity
    ComponentInfo{com.aschyiel.disp/com.aschyiel.disp.Disp}:java.lang.NullPointerException
E/AndroidRuntime( 214): at android.app.ActivityThread.performLaunchActivity(
    ActivityThread.java:2496)
E/AndroidRuntime( 214): at android.app.ActivityThread.handleLaunchActivity(
    ActivityThread.java:2512)
E/AndroidRuntime( 214): at android.app.ActivityThread.access$2200(
    ActivityThread.java:119)
E/AndroidRuntime( 214): at android.app.ActivityThread$H.handleMessage(
    ActivityThread.java:1863)
E/AndroidRuntime( 214): at android.os.Handler.dispatchMessage(Handler.java:99)
E/AndroidRuntime( 214): at android.os.Looper.loop(Looper.java:123)
E/AndroidRuntime( 214): at android.app.ActivityThread.main(ActivityThread.java:4363)
E/AndroidRuntime( 214): at java.lang.reflect.Method.invokeNative(Native Method)
E/AndroidRuntime( 214): at java.lang.reflect.Method.invoke(Method.java:521)
E/AndroidRuntime( 214): at com.android.internal.os.ZygoteInit$MethodAndArgsCaller.run(
    ZygoteInit.java:860)
E/AndroidRuntime( 214): at com.android.internal.os.ZygoteInit.main(ZygoteInit.java:618)
E/AndroidRuntime( 214): at dalvik.system.NativeStart.main(Native Method)
E/AndroidRuntime( 214): Caused by: java.lang.NullPointerException
E/AndroidRuntime( 214): at com.aschyiel.disp.Disp.onCreate(Disp.java:66)
```

```
E/AndroidRuntime( 214): at android.app.Instrumentation.callActivityOnCreate(
    Instrumentation.java:1047)
E/AndroidRuntime( 214): at android.app.ActivityThread.performLaunchActivity(
    ActivityThread.java:2459)
E/AndroidRuntime( 214): ... 11 more
```

The example code with the error looks like this:

```
import ...

public class Disp extends Activity
{
    private TextView foo;
    @Override
    public void onCreate( Bundle savedInstanceState )
    {
        ...

        foo.setText("bar");
    }
}
```

The preceding code fails because we forgot to use findViewById().

Here is the example code with the fix:

```
import ...

public class Disp extends Activity
{
    private TextView foo;
    @Override
    public void onCreate( Bundle savedInstanceState )
    {
        ...

        foo = (TextView) findViewById( R.id.id_foo );
        foo.setText("bar");
    }
}
```

This code should make our error go away.

See Also

"Google I/O 2009-Debugging Arts of the Ninja Masters" (*http://developer.android .com/videos/index.html#v=Dgnx0E7m1GQ*); *http://groups.google.com/group/android -developers/browse_thread/thread/92ea776cfd42aa45*

3.7 Debugging Using Log.d and LogCat

Rachee Singh

Problem

Usually the Java code compiles without errors, but sometimes a running application crashes, giving a "Force Close" (or similar) error message.

Solution

Debugging the code using LogCat messages is a useful technique for developers who find themselves in such a situation.

Discussion

Those who are familiar with Java programming have probably used `System.out.println` statements while debugging their code. Similarly, debugging an Android application can be facilitated by using the `Log.d()` method. This enables you to print necessary values and messages in the LogCat window. Start by importing the `Log` class:

```
import android.util.Log;
```

Then, insert the following line at places in the code where you wish to check the status of the application:

```
Log.d("Testing", "Checkpoint 1");
```

`Testing` is the tag that appears in the "tag" column in the LogCat window, as shown in Figure 3-15; normally this would be defined as a constant in the main class to ensure consistent spelling. `Checkpoint 1` is the message that appears in the Message column in the LogCat window. `Log.d` takes these two arguments. Corresponding to these, an appropriate message is displayed in the LogCat window. So, if you have inserted this `Log.d` statement as a checkpoint and you get the `Checkpoint 1` message displayed in the LogCat window, it implies that the code works fine up to that point.

The `Log.d()` method does not accept variable arguments, so if you wish to format more than one item, use string concatenation or `String.format` (but omit the trailing `%n`):

```
Log.d("Testing", String.format("x0 = %5.2f, x1=%5.2f", x0, x1));
```

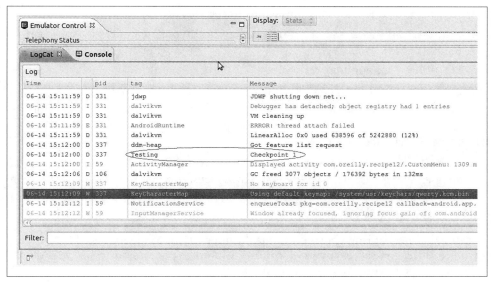

Figure 3-15. Debugging output

3.8 Getting Bug Reports from Users Automatically with BugSense

Ian Darwin

Problem

Users don't necessarily inform you every time your app crashes, and when they do, often important details are omitted. You'd like a service that catches every exception and reports it in detail.

Solution

Sign up with BugSense (Free or Premium edition), and add a JAR file and one call to your app. Then sit back and await notifications, or view the web dashboard for lists of errors and detail pages.

Discussion

There is no magic to the BugSense service, and it doesn't provide anything that you can't do yourself. But it's already done for you, so just use it! The basic steps are:

1. Create an account with BugSense Free or Premium, at *http://www.bugsense.com*.
2. Register your app and retrieve its unique key from the website.

3. Download and add a JAR file to your project.

4. Add one call (using the app's unique key) into your main activity's `onCreate()` method.

5. Distribute your app to users.

Steps 1 and 2 are straightforward, so we won't discuss them further. The remaining steps require a little more detail, and we discuss them in the following subsections.

Adding the JAR file to the project

The JAR file you need is *bugsense-trace.jar*; you can download it from *https://github .com/bugsense/bugsense-android/blob/master/bugsense-trace.jar?raw=true* or from *http://www.bugsense.com*.

You probably know how to add JARs to your project; if not, see Recipe 1.10.

Because this mechanism reports errors via the Internet, the following should go without saying (but let me say it anyway): you need Internet permission to use it! Add the following code to your *AndroidManifest.xml* file:

```
<uses-permission android:name="android.permission.INTERNET" />
```

Invoking BugSense at App Start

You really only need to make one call, in your `onCreate()` method, typically after invoking `setContentView()`.

Here, for example, is the first part of the `onCreate()` method of my JPSTrack program:

```java
private static final String OUR_BUGSENSE_API_KEY = "";

@Override
public void onCreate(Bundle savedInstanceState) {
    super.onCreate(savedInstanceState);
    setContentView(R.layout.main);

    // set up BugSense bug tracking
    BugSenseHandler.setup(this, OUR_BUGSENSE_API_KEY);
    ...
}
```

Of course, `BugSenseHandler` needs to be imported, but Eclipse will do that for you (if not, go to the Source menu→Organize Imports).

Distributing the App and Watching for Crash Reports

This also can only be done using the web reporting page, which is accessible after you log in.

See Also

Start at the BugSense website (*http://www.bugsense.com*). For more information on what BugSense can do, see the Features page (*http://www.bugsense.com/features*).

There is also a Google Code Project named ACRA (*http://code.google.com/p/acra/*) that provides similar data-capturing functionality but is not so strong on the reporting side, at least at the time of this writing.

3.9 Using a Local Runtime Application Log for Analysis of Field Errors or Situations

Atul Nene

Problem

Users reported something about your app that you don't think should happen, but now that the release mode app is on the market, you have no way to find out what's going on in the users' environment, and bug reports end up in a "cannot reproduce" scenario.

Solution

Design a built-in mechanism for your app that will give additional insight in such cases. You know the important events or state changes and resource needs of your app, and if you log them in a runtime application log from your app, the log becomes an additional much-needed resource that goes to the heart of the issue being reported and investigated. This simple preventive measure and mechanism goes a long way toward reducing low user ratings caused by unforeseen situations, and improves the quality of the overall user experience.

One solution is to use the standard `java.util.logging` package. This recipe provides an example `RuntimeLog` which uses `java.util.logging` to write to a logfile on the device, and gives the developer extensive control over what level of detail is recorded.

Discussion

You have designed, developed, and tested your application and released it on the Android Market, so now you think you can take a vacation. Not so fast! Apart from the simplest cases, one cannot take care of all possible scenarios during app testing, not that there is the luxury of time for this, and users are bound to report some unexpected app behavior. It doesn't have to be a bug; it might simply be a runtime situation you didn't encounter in your testing. Prepare for this in advance by designing a runtime application log mechanism into your app.

Log the most important events from your app into the log—for example, a state change, a resource timeout (Net access, thread wait), or a maxed-out retry count. It might even be worthwhile to defensively log an unexpected code path execution in a strange scenario, or some of the most important notifications that are sent to the user.

Only create log statements that will provide insight into how the app is working. Otherwise, the large size of the log itself may become a problem, and while Log.d() calls are ignored at runtime in signed apps, too many log statements may still slow down the app.

You may be wondering why you can't use LogCat or BugSense/ACRA to handle this task. These solutions do not suffice for the following reasons:

- The standard LogCat mechanism isn't useful in end-user runtime scenarios since the user is unlikely to have the ability to attach a debugger to his device. Too many Log.d and Log.i statements in your code may negatively impact app performance. In fact, for this reason, you shouldn't have Log.* statements compiled into the released app.
- ACRA/BugSense works well when the device is connected to the Internet. This may not always be true, and some class of applications may not require the Internet at all except for ACRA. Also, the ACRA stack trace provides only the details (in the stack trace) at the instant the Exception was thrown, while this recipe provides a longer-term view while the app is running.

The RuntimeLog class is shown in Example 3-5.

Example 3-5. The RuntimeLog class

```
// Use these built-in mechanisms
import java.util.logging.FileHandler;
import java.util.logging.Formatter;
import java.util.logging.Level;
import java.util.logging.LogRecord;
import java.util.logging.Logger;


public class RuntimeLog {
  public static final int MODE_DEBUG = 1;
  public static final int MODE_RELEASE = 2;
  public static final int ERROR = 3;
  public static final int WARNING = 4;
  public static final int INFO = 5;
  public static final int DEBUG = 6;
  public static final int VERBOSE = 7;

  // Change this to MODE_DEBUG to use for in-house debugging
  static boolean Mode = MODE_RELEASE;
  static logfileName = "/sdcard/YourAppName.log"
  static Logger logger;
```

```
static LogRecord record;

//initiate the log on first use of the class and
//create your custom formatter

static {
  try {
    FileHandler fh = new FileHandler(logfileName, true);
    fh.setFormatter(new Formatter() {
      public String format(LogRecord rec) {
        StringBuffer buf = new StringBuffer(1000);
        buf.append(new java.util.Date().getDate());
        buf.append('/');
        buf.append(new java.util.Date().getMonth());
        buf.append('/');
        buf.append((new java.util.Date().getYear())%100);
        buf.append(' ');
        buf.append(new java.util.Date().getHours());
        buf.append(':');
        buf.append(new java.util.Date().getMinutes());
        buf.append(':');
        buf.append(new java.util.Date().getSeconds());
        buf.append('\n');
        return buf.toString();
      }
    });
    logger = Logger.getLogger(logfileName);
    logger.addHandler(fh);
  }
  catch (IOException e) {
    e.printStackTrace();
  }
}

// the log method
public static void log(int logLevel,String msg) {
  //don't log DEBUG and VERBOSE statements in release mode
  if (Mode == MODE_RELEASE) && (logLevel >= DEBUG))
    return;
  record=new LogRecord(Level.ALL, msg);
  record.setLoggerName(logfileName);
  try {
    switch(logLevel) {
      case ERROR:
        record.setLevel(Level.SEVERE);
        logger.log(record);
        break;
      case WARNING:
        record.setLevel(Level.WARNING);
        logger.log(record);
        break;
      case INFO:
        record.setLevel(Level.INFO);
        logger.log(record);
        break;
```

```
      //FINE and FINEST levels may not work on some API versions
      //use INFO instead
      case DEBUG:
        record.setLevel(Level.INFO);
        logger.log(record);
        break;
      case VERBOSE:
        record.setLevel(Level.INFO);
        logger.log(record);
        break;
    }
  }
  catch(Exception exception) {
    exception.printStackTrace();
  }
 }
}
```

There are, of course, several variations that could be used:

- You can use the same mechanism to uncover complex runtime issues while you are developing the app. To do so, set the Mode variable to MODE_DEBUG.

- For a complex app with many modules, it might be useful to add the module name to the log call, as an additional parameter.

- You can also extract the ClassName and MethodName from the LogRecord and add them to the log statements; however, it is not recommended that you do this for runtime logs.

Example 3-6 shows that basic use of this facility is as simple as regular Log.d calls.

Example 3-6. Using the RuntimeLog class

```
RuntimeLog.log (RuntimeLog.ERROR, "Network resource access request failed");
RuntimeLog.log (RuntimeLog.WARNING, "App changed state to STRANGE_STATE");
...
```

If necessary, you can ask users to retrieve the logfile(s) from their SD cards and send them to your support team. Even better, you could write code to do that at the press of a button!

Here are a few additional considerations:

- This mechanism does not have to be in an "always on" state. You can log based on a user-settable configuration option and enable it only when actual end users are trying to reproduce certain scenarios.

- If it is always on, use a filename with the current date (determined on application start-up) for the log, and delete previous logfiles that are older than a certain date deemed no longer useful. This will help keep logfile sizes in check.

See Also

The ACRA website (*http://code.google.com/p/acra/*); Recipe 3.7; Recipe 3.8

3.10 Reproducing Activity Life-Cycle Scenarios for Testing

Daniel Fowler

Problem

Apps should be resilient to the activity life cycle. Developers need to know how to reproduce different life-cycle scenarios.

Solution

Use logging to get a good understanding of the activity life cycle. Life-cycle scenarios are then easier to reproduce for app testing.

Discussion

Android is designed for life on the go, where a user is engaged in multiple tasks: taking calls, checking email, sending SMS messages, engaging in social networking, taking pictures, accessing the Internet, running apps, and more, maybe even getting some work done! As such, a device can have multiple apps, and hence many Activities, loaded in memory. The foreground app and its current activity can be interrupted and paused at any moment. Apps, and hence activities, that are paused can be removed from memory to free up space for newly started apps. An app has a life cycle that it cannot control as it is the Android operating system that starts, monitors, pauses, resumes, and destroys the app's activities. Yet an activity does know what is going on, because as activities are instantiated, hidden, and destroyed various functions are called. This allows the activity to keep track of what the operating system is doing to the app, as we discussed in Recipe 1.6.

Because of all this, app developers become familiar with the functions invoked when an activity starts:

- `onCreate(Bundle savedInstanceState){...};`
- `onStart(){...};`
- `onResume(){...};`

and the functions called when an activity is paused and then removed from memory (destroyed):

- `onPause(){...};`
- `onStop(){...};`
- `onDestroy(){..};`

To see them in action, simply open the program from Recipe 1.4. Then, in the main activity class, override all six of the aforementioned functions, calling through to the superclass versions. Add a call to `Log.d()` to pass in the name of the app and the function being invoked. The code will look like Example 3-7.

Example 3-7. Life-cycle logging

```
public class Main extends Activity {
    @Override
    public void onCreate(Bundle savedInstanceState) {
        super.onCreate(savedInstanceState);
        setContentView(R.layout.main);
        Log.d("MyAndroid", "onCreate");
    }
    @Override
    public void onStart() {
        super.onStart();
        Log.d("MyAndroid", "onStart");
    }
    @Override
    public void onResume() {
        super.onResume();
        Log.d("MyAndroid","onResume");
    }
    @Override
    public void onPause() {
        super.onPause();
        Log.d("MyAndroid","onPause");
    }
    public void onStop() {
        super.onStop();
        Log.d("MyAndroid","onStop");
    }
    public void onDestroy() {
        super.onDestroy();
        Log.d("MyAndroid","onDestroy");
    }
}
```

Run the program. To see the debug messages, the LogCat view needs to be displayed. This is visible by default in the Dalvik Debug Monitor Server (DDMS) perspective, or you can open it via the Window menu option. Click Window→Show View→Other, expand Android, and select LogCat. The LogCat view appears on the bottom tabs.

To open the DDMS perspective click the DDMS button in the top-right corner of Eclipse. It should look something like Figure 3-16.

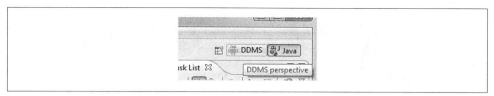

Figure 3-16. The DDMS perspective

The LogCat view will be on the bottom tabs. If it is not visible, use the Window method mentioned earlier or select Window→Reset Perspective. You can drag LogCat off into its own window by dragging the tab from Eclipse. After you start the program, you can see the three debug messages you added to the start-up functions (see Figure 3-17).

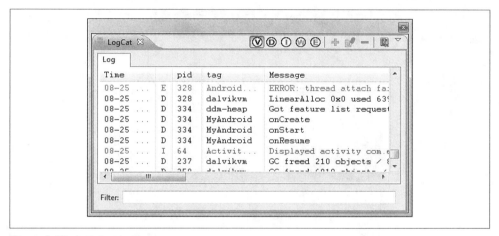

Figure 3-17. Activity start-up messages

When you press the Back key, you will see the three teardown messages (see Figure 3-18).

To see only the messages from the app add a LogCat filter. Click on the green plus sign in the top right of the LogCat screen. Give the filter a name and enter **MyAndroid** in the by Log Tagtag field (see Figure 3-19).

LogCat will now show a new tab with only the messages explicitly sent from the app (see Figure 3-20).

You can clear the LogCat output by clicking the top-right icon that shows a page with a small red ×. It can be useful to have a clean sheet before performing an action to watch for more messages.

To see the functions called when a program is paused, open an application over the MyAndroid program. First add the function for onRestart(), and the debug message.

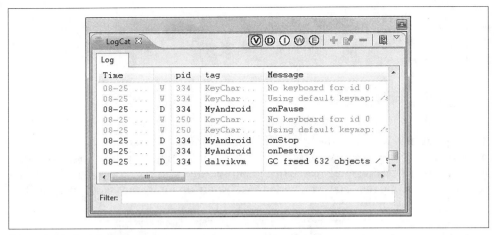

Figure 3-18. Activity tear-down messages

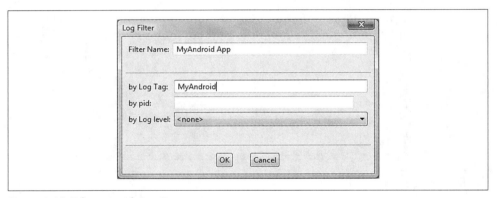

Figure 3-19. Filtering with LogCat

```
@Override
public void onRestart() {
    super.onRestart();
    Log.d("MyAndroid","onRestart");
}
```

Run the program, click the Home button, and then launch the program again from the device (or emulator).

LogCat shows the usual start-up function sequence; then, when the Home button is clicked, onPause() and onStop() run, but not onDestroy(). The program is not ending but effectively sleeping. When the program is run again it is not reloaded, so no onCreate() executes, and instead onRestart() is called.

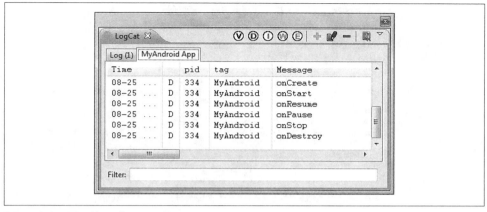

Figure 3-20. The filtered messages

Run the program again, on the device or emulator, and then go into Manage Applications (via Settings→Applications), select the program, and click the Force Close button. Then start the program again from the device (or emulator).

The usual start-up functions are invoked, and then the activity "sleeps." No onDest roy() is seen as the second instance is run.

In this recipe, we discussed the following different life-cycle scenarios:

- Normal start-up and then finish
- Start-up, pause, and then restart (see Figure 3-21)
- Start-up, pause, forced removal from memory, and then start-up again (see Figure 3-22)

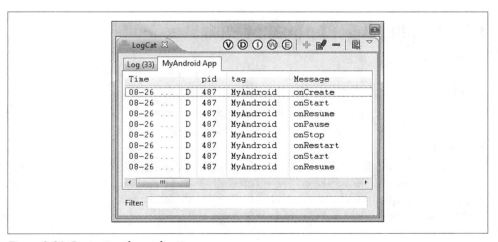

Figure 3-21. Restarting the application

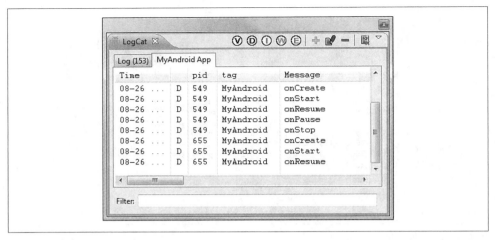

Figure 3-22. Force-stop messages

These scenarios result in different sequences of life-cycle functions being executed. Using these scenarios when testing ensures that an app performs correctly for a user. You can extend the techniques shown here when implementing additional overridden functions. The techniques also apply to using fragments in an activity and testing their life cycle.

See Also

Recipe 1.4; Recipe 1.6; *http://developer.android.com/reference/android/app/Activity .html*; *http://developer.android.com/reference/android/util/Log.html*; *http://developer.an droid.com/guide/topics/fundamentals/fragments.html*

3.11 Keeping Your App Snappy with StrictMode

Adrian Cowham

Problem

You want to make sure your app's GUI is as snappy as possible.

Solution

Android has a tool called StrictMode, which they introduced in the Gingerbread release that will detect all cases where an "Application Not Responding" (ANR) error might occur. For example, it will detect and log to LogCat all database reads and writes that happen on the main thread (i.e., the GUI thread).

Discussion

I wish I could've used a tool like StrictMode back when I was doing Java Swing desktop development. Making sure our Java Swing app was snappy was a constant challenge—green and seasoned engineers would invariably perform database operations on the UI thread that would cause the app to hiccup. Typically, we found these hiccups when QA (or customers) would use the app with a larger data set than the engineers were testing with. Having QA find these little defects was unacceptable and ultimately a waste of everyone's time (and the company's money). We eventually solved the problem by investing more heavily in peer reviews, but having a tool like StrictMode would have been comparatively cheaper.

The following example code illustrates how easy it is to turn on StrictMode in your app:

```
// make sure you import StrictMode
import android.os.StrictMode;

// In your app's android.app.Application instance, add the following
// lines to the onCreate(...) method.
if ( Build.VERSION.SDK_INT >= 9 && isDebug() ) {
  StrictMode.enableDefaults();
}
```

Please note that I have intentionally omitted the `isDebug()` implementation, as this will vary among developers. I recommend only enabling StrictMode when your app is in Debug mode; it's unwise to put your app in the Android Market with StrictMode running in the background and consuming resources unnecessarily.

StrictMode is highly configurable, allowing you to customize what problems to look for. For detailed information on customizing StrictMode policies, see *http://developer .android.com/reference/android/os/StrictMode.html*.

See Also

StrictMode is highly configurable, allowing you to customize what problems to look for. For detailed information on customizing StrictMode policies, see *http://developer .android.com/reference/android/os/StrictMode.html*.

3.12 Running the Monkey Program

Adrian Cowham

Problem

You want some good random usage testing of your application.

Solution

Use the Android Monkey command-line tool to test applications you are developing.

Discussion

Testing is so easy a monkey can do it, literally. Despite the lack of testing tools for Android, I have to admit that the Monkey is pretty cool. In case you're not familiar with the Android Monkey, it's a testing tool that comes with the Android SDK and simulates a monkey (or perhaps a child) using an Android device. Imagine a monkey sitting at a keyboard and flailing away—get the idea? What better way to flush out those hidden ANR messages?

Running the Monkey is as simple as starting the emulator (or connecting your development device to your development machine) and launching the Monkey script. I hate to admit this, but by running the Monkey on a daily basis, we've repeatedly found defects that probably would've escaped a normal QA pass and would've been very challenging to troubleshoot if found in the field—or, worse yet, caused users to stop using our app.

Here are a few best practices for using the Monkey in your development process:

- Create your own Monkey script that wraps Android's Monkey script. This is to ensure that all the developers on your team are running the Monkey with the same parameters. If you're a team of one, this helps with predictability (discussed shortly).

- Configure the Monkey so that it runs long enough to catch defects and not so long that it's a productivity killer. In our development process, we configured the Monkey to run for a total of 50,000 events. This took about 40 minutes to run on a Samsung Galaxy Tab. Not too bad, but I would've liked it to be in the 30-minute range. Obviously, faster tablets will have a higher throughput.

- The Monkey is random, so when we first started running it, every developer was getting different results and we were unable to reproduce defects. We then figured out that the Monkey allows you to set the seed for its random number generator. So, configure your wrapper script to set the Monkey's seed. This will ensure uniformity and predictability across Monkey runs in your development team.

- Once you gain confidence in your app with a specific seed value, change it, because you'll never know what the Monkey will find.

Here is a Monkey script wrapper, followed by a description of its arguments:

```bash
#!/bin/bash
# Utility script to run monkey
#
# See: http://developer.android.com/guide/developing/tools/monkey.html

rm tmp/monkey.log
adb shell monkey -p package.name.here --throttle 100 -s 43686 -v 50000 |
    tee tmp/monkey.log
```

- -p *package name* will ensure that the Monkey only targets the package specified.

- --throttle is the delay between events.

- `-s` is the seed value.
- `-v` is the VERBOSE option.
- `50000` is the number of events the Monkey will simulate.

Many more configuration options are available for the Monkey; we deliberately chose not to mess around with what types of events the Monkey generates because we appreciate the pain. For example, the seed value we chose causes the Monkey to disable Wi-Fi about halfway through the run. This was really frustrating at first because we felt like we weren't getting the coverage we wanted. It turns out that the Monkey did us a favor by disabling Wi-Fi and then relentlessly playing with our app. After discovering and fixing a few defects, we soon had complete confidence that our app operated as expected with no network connection.

Good monkey.

See Also

http://developer.android.com/guide/developing/tools/monkey.html

3.13 Sending Text Messages and Placing Calls Between AVDs

Johan Pelgrim

Problem

You have developed an app that needs to place or listen for calls or send or receive text messages and you want to test this.

Solution

Fire up two Android Virtual Devices (AVDs) and use the port number to send text messages and place calls.

Discussion

When you create an app that listens for incoming calls or text messages—similar to the one in Recipe 12.2—you can, of course, use the DDMS perspective in Eclipse to simulate placing calls or sending text messages, but you can also fire up another AVD!

If you look at the AVD window title you will see a number before your AVD's title. This is the port number which you can use to telnet to your AVD's shell (e.g., `telnet localhost 5554`). Fortunately, for testing purposes this number is your AVD's *phone number* as well. So you can use this number to place calls (see Figure 3-23) or to send text (Figure 3-24).

Figure 3-23. Calling from one AVD to another

Figure 3-24. Sending a text message (SMS) from one AVD to another

See Also

Recipe 12.2

## CHAPTER 4

Inter-/Intra-Process Communication

4.1 Introduction: Inter-/Intra-Process Communication

Ian Darwin

Discussion

Android offers a unique collection of mechanisms for inter- (and intra-) application communication. This chapter discusses the following:

Intents
> Specify what you intend to do next: either to invoke a particular class within your application, or to invoke whatever application the user has configured to process a particular request on a particular type of data

Broadcast receivers
> In conjunction with intent filters, allow you to define an application as able to process a particular request on a particular type of data (i.e., the target of an intent)

AsyncTask
> Allows you to specify long-running code that should not be on the "GUI thread" or "main event thread" to avoid slowing the app to the point that it gets ANR ("Application Not Responding") errors

Handlers
> Allow you to queue up messages from a background thread to be handled by another thread such as the main activity thread, usually to cause information to update the screen safely

4.2 Opening a Web Page, Phone Number, or Anything Else with an Intent

Ian Darwin

Problem

You want one application to have some entity processed by another application without knowing or caring what that application is.

Solution

Invoke the `Intent` constructor; then invoke `startActivity` on the constructed `Intent`.

Discussion

The `Intent` constructor takes two arguments: the action to take and the entity to act on. Think of the first as the verb and the second as the object of the verb. The most common action is `Intent.ACTION_VIEW`, for which the string representation is `android.intent.action.VIEW`. The second will typically be a URL or, as Android likes it less precisely (more generally), a URI. URIs can be created using the static `parse()` method in the `URI` class. Assuming that the string variable `data` contains the location we want to view, the code to create an `Intent` for it might be something like the following:

```
Intent intent = new Intent(Intent.ACTION_VIEW, Uri.parse(data));
```

That's all! The beauty of Android is shown here—we don't know or care if `data` contains a web page URL with `http:`, a phone number with `tel:`, or even something we've never seen. As long as there is an application registered to process this type of intent, Android will find it for us, after we invoke it. How do we invoke the intent? Remember that Android will start a new activity to run the intent. Assuming the code is in an activity, just call the inherited `startIntent` method, for example:

```
startActivity(intent);
```

If all goes well, the user will see the web browser, phone dialer, maps application, or whatever.

Google defines many other actions, such as `ACTION_OPEN` (which tries to open the named object). In some cases `VIEW` and `OPEN` will have the same effect, but in other cases the former may display data and the latter may allow the user to edit or update the data.

However, if things fail, the user will not see anything. Why not? We basically told Android that we don't care whether the intent succeeds or fails. To get feedback, we have to call `startActivityForResult`:

```
startActivityForResult(intent, requestCode);
```

The `requestCode` is an arbitrary number used to keep track of multiple `Intent` requests; you should generally pick a unique number for each `Intent` you start, and keep track of these numbers to track the results later (if you only have one `Intent` whose results you care about, just use the number 1).

Just making this change will have no effect, however, unless we also override an important method in `Activity`, that is:

```
@Override
public void onActivityResult(int requestCode, int resultCode, Intent data) {
    // do something with the results...
}
```

It may be obvious, but it is important to note that you cannot know the result of an `Intent` until the entire application that was processing it is finished, which may be an arbitrary time later. However, the `onActivityResult` will eventually be called.

The `resultCode` is, of course, used to indicate success or failure. There are defined constants for these, notably `Activity.RESULT_OK` and `Activity.RESULT_CANCELED`. Some `Intent`s provide their own, more specific result codes; for one example, see Recipe 10.9.

For information on use of the passed intent, please refer to recipes on passing extra data, such as Recipe 4.5.

Source Download URL

The source code for this example is in the Android Cookbook repository at *http://github .com/AndroidCook/Android-Cookbook-Examples*, in the subdirectory IntentsDemo (see "Getting and Using the Code Examples" on page xvii).

4.3 Emailing Text from a View

Wagied Davids

Problem

You want to send an email containing text or images from a view.

Solution

Pass the data to be emailed to the mail app as a parameter using an intent.

Discussion

The steps for emailing text from a view are pretty straightforward:

1. Modify the *AndroidManifest.xml* file to allow for an Internet connection so that email can be sent. This is shown in Example 4-1.

2. Create the visual presentation layer with an Email button that the user clicks. The layout is shown in Example 4-2, and the strings used to populate it are shown in Example 4-3.

3. Attach an `OnClickListener` to allow the email to be sent when the user clicks the Email button. The code for this is shown in Example 4-4.

Example 4-1. AndroidManifest.xml

```xml
<?xml version="1.0" encoding="utf-8"?>
<manifest
    xmlns:android="http://schemas.android.com/apk/res/android"
    package="com.examples"
    android:versionCode="1"
    android:versionName="1.0">
    <application
        android:icon="@drawable/icon"
        android:label="@string/app_name">
        <activity
            android:name=".Main"
            android:label="@string/app_name">
            <intent-filter>
                <action
                    android:name="android.intent.action.MAIN" />
                <category
                    android:name="android.intent.category.LAUNCHER" />
            </intent-filter>
        </activity>

        <!-- Required Permission  -->
        <uses-permission
            android:name="android.permission.INTERNET" />
        <uses-permission
            android:name="android.permission.ACCESS_NETWORK_STATE" />
        <uses-permission
            android:name="android.permission.ACCESS_COARSE_LOCATION"></uses-permission>
        <uses-permission
            android:name="android.permission.ACCESS_FINE_LOCATION"></uses-permission>
    </application>
</manifest>
```

Example 4-2. Main.xml

```xml
<?xml version="1.0" encoding="utf-8"?>
<LinearLayout
    xmlns:android="http://schemas.android.com/apk/res/android"
    android:orientation="vertical"
    android:layout_width="fill_parent"
    android:layout_height="fill_parent">

    <Button
        android:id="@+id/emailButton"
        android:text="Email Text!"
        android:layout_width="fill_parent"
        android:layout_height="wrap_content">
```

```
        </Button>

        <TextView
            android:id="@+id/text_to_email"
            android:layout_width="fill_parent"
            android:layout_height="wrap_content"
            android:text="@string/my_text" />

</LinearLayout>
```

Example 4-3. Strings.xml

```
<?xml version="1.0" encoding="utf-8"?>
<resources>
    <string
        name="hello">Hello World, Main!</string>
    <string
        name="app_name">EmailAndroid</string>
    <string
        name="my_text">
        Lorem Ipsum is simply dummy text of the printing and typesetting industry. Lorem
        Ipsum has been the industry's standard dummy text ever since the 1500s, when
        an unknown printer took a galley of type and scrambled it to make a type
        specimen book. It has survived not only five centuries, but also the leap into
        electronic typesetting, remaining essentially unchanged. It was popularised in
        the 1960s with the release of Letraset sheets containing Lorem Ipsum passages,
        and more recently with desktop publishing software like Aldus PageMaker
        including versions of Lorem Ipsum.
</string>
</resources>
```

Example 4-4. Main.java

```java
import android.app.Activity;
import android.content.Intent;
import android.os.Bundle;
import android.view.View;
import android.view.View.OnClickListener;
import android.widget.Button;

public class Main extends Activity implements OnClickListener
    {
        private static final String tag = "Main";
        private Button emailButton;

        /** Called when the activity is first created. */
        @Override
        public void onCreate(Bundle savedInstanceState)
            {
                super.onCreate(savedInstanceState);

                // Set the View Layer
                setContentView(R.layout.main);

                // Get reference to Email Button
                this.emailButton = (Button) this.findViewById(R.id.emailButton);
```

```
            // Sets the Event Listener onClick
            this.emailButton.setOnClickListener(this);

    }

    @Override
    public void onClick(View view) {
        if (view == this.emailButton) {
            Intent emailIntent = new Intent(android.content.Intent.ACTION_SEND);
            emailIntent.setType("text/html");
            emailIntent.putExtra(android.content.Intent.EXTRA_TITLE, "My Title");
            emailIntent.putExtra(android.content.Intent.EXTRA_SUBJECT, "My Subject");

            // Obtain reference to String and pass it to Intent
            emailIntent.putExtra(android.content.Intent.EXTRA_TEXT,
                getString(R.string.my_text));
            startActivity(emailIntent);
        }
    }
}
```

Source Download URL

The source code for this example is in the Android Cookbook repository at *http://github
.com/AndroidCook/Android-Cookbook-Examples*, in the subdirectory EmailAndroid
(see "Getting and Using the Code Examples" on page xvii).

4.4 Sending an Email with Attachments

Marco Dinacci

Problem

You want to send an email with attachments.

Solution

Create an Intent, add extended data to specify the file you want to include, and start
a new activity to allow the user to send the email.

Discussion

The easiest way to send an email is to create an Intent of type ACTION_SEND:

```
Intent intent = new Intent(Intent.ACTION_SEND);
intent.putExtra(Intent.EXTRA_SUBJECT, "Test single attachment");
intent.putExtra(Intent.EXTRA_EMAIL, new String[]{recipient_address});
intent.putExtra(Intent.EXTRA_TEXT, "Mail with an attachment");
```

To attach a single file, we add some extended data to our Intent:

```
intent.putExtra(Intent.EXTRA_STREAM, Uri.fromFile(new File("/path/to/file")));
intent.setType("text/plain");
```

The MIME type can always be set as text/plain, but you may want to be more specific so that applications parsing your message will work properly. For instance, if you're including a JPEG image you should write image/jpeg.

To send an email with multiple attachments, the procedure is slightly different, as shown in Example 4-5.

Example 4-5. Multiple attachments

```
Intent intent = new Intent(Intent.ACTION_SEND_MULTIPLE);
intent.setType("text/plain");
intent.putExtra(Intent.EXTRA_SUBJECT, "Test multiple attachments");
intent.putExtra(Intent.EXTRA_TEXT, "Mail with multiple attachments");
intent.putExtra(Intent.EXTRA_EMAIL, new String[]{recipient_address});

ArrayList<Uri> uris = new ArrayList<Uri>();
uris.add(Uri.fromFile(new File("/path/to/first/file")));
uris.add(Uri.fromFile(new File("/path/to/second/file")));

intent.putParcelableArrayListExtra(Intent.EXTRA_STREAM, uris);
```

First, you need to use Intent.ACTION_SEND_MULTIPLE, which has been available since Android 1.6. Second, you need to create an ArrayList with the URIs of the files you want to attach to the mail and call putParcelableArrayListExtra.

If you are sending different types of files you may want to use multipart/mixed as the MIME type.

Finally, in both cases, you can start a new Activity with the following code:

```
startActivity(Intent.createChooser(intent, "Send mail"));
```

Using Intent.createChooser is optional, but it will allow the user to select his favorite application to send the email.

4.5 Pushing String Values Using Intent.putExtra()

Ulysses Levy

Problem

You need to pass some parameters into an activity while launching it.

Solution

A quick solution is to use Intent.putExtra() to push the data. Then use getIntent().getExtras().getString() to retrieve it.

Discussion

Example 4-6 shows the code to push the data.

Example 4-6. The push data

```
import android.content.Intent;
    ...

    Intent intent =
        new Intent(
            this,
            MyActivity.class );
    intent.putExtra( "paramName", "paramValue" );
    startActivity( intent );
```

This code might be inside the main activity. `MyActivity.class` is the second activity we want to launch; it must be explicitly included in your *AndroidManifest.xml* file.

```
        <activity android:name=".MyActivity" />
```

Example 4-7 shows the code to pull the data.

Example 4-7. The pull data

```
import android.os.Bundle;

    ...

    Bundle extras = getIntent().getExtras();
    if (extras != null)
    {
        String myParam = extras.getString("paramName");
    }
    else
    {
        //..oops!
    }
```

In this example, the code would be inside your main *Activity.java* file.

There are a few limitations to this method. For example, it can only pass strings. Therefore, if, for example, you need to pass an `ArrayList` to your `ListActivity`, a possible workaround is to pass a comma-separated string and then split it on the other side.

Alternatively, you can use `SharedPreferences`.

See Also

http://mylifewithandroid.blogspot.com/2007/12/playing-with-intents.html; *http://devel oper.android.com/guide/appendix/faq/commontasks.html*

4.6 Retrieving Data from a Subactivity Back to Your Main Activity

Ulysses Levy

Problem

Your main activity needs to retrieve data from a subactivity.

Solution

Use `startActivityForResult()`, `onActivityResult()` in the main activity, and `setRe sult()` in the subactivity.

Discussion

In this example, we return a string from a subactivity (`MySubActivity`) back to the main activity (`MyMainActivity`).

The first step is to "push" data from `MyMainActivity` via the `Intent` mechanism (see Example 4-8).

Example 4-8. The push data from the activity

```
public class MyMainActivity extends Activity
{
    //..for logging..
    private static final String TAG = "MainActivity";

    //..The request code is supposed to be unique?..
    public static final int MY_REQUEST_CODE = 123;

    @Override
    public void onCreate( Bundle savedInstanceState )
    {
        ...
    }

    private void pushFxn()
    {
        Intent intent =
            new Intent(
                this,
                MySubActivity.class );

        startActivityForResult( intent, MY_REQUEST_CODE );
    }

    protected void onActivityResult(
            int requestCode,
            int resultCode,
            Intent pData)
```

```
{
    if ( requestCode == MY_REQUEST_CODE )
    {
        if (resultCode == Activity.RESULT_OK )
        {
            final String zData = pData.getExtras().getString
                ( MySubActivity.EXTRA_STRING_NAME );

            //..do something with our retrieved value..

            Log.v( TAG, "Retrieved Value zData is "+zData );
            //..logcats "Retrieved Value zData is returnValueAsString"

        }
    }

    }
}
```

In Example 4-8, the following occurs:

- The main activity's onActivityResult() gets called after MySubActivity.finish().
- The retrieved value is technically an Intent, and so we could use it for more complex data (such as a URI to a Google contact or something). However, in Example 4-8, we are only interested in a string value via Intent.getExtras().
- The requestCode (MY_REQUEST_CODE) is supposed to be unique, and might be useful later—for example, Activity.finishActivity(MY_REQUEST_CODE).

The second major step is to "pull" data back from MySubActivity to MyMainActivity (see Example 4-9).

Example 4-9. The pull data from the subactivity

```
public class MySubActivity extends Activity
{
    public static final String EXTRA_STRING_NAME = "extraStringName";

    @Override
    public void onCreate( Bundle savedInstanceState )
    {
        ...
    }


    private void pullFxn()
    {
        Intent iData = new Intent();
        iData.putExtra(
            EXTRA_STRING_NAME,
            "returnValueAsString" );

        setResult(
            android.app.Activity.RESULT_OK,
```

```
            iData );

        //..returns us to the parent "MyMainActivity"..
        finish();
    }
}
```

In Example 4-9, the following occurs:

- Once again, `Intent`s are used as data (i.e., `iData`).
- `setResult()` requires a result code such as `RESULT_OK`.
- `finish()` essentially pushes the result from `setResult()`.

In addition, note the following:

- Technically, the data from `MySubActivity` doesn't get "pull"-ed until we're back on the other side with `MyMainActivity`. So arguably it is more similar to a second "push."
- We don't have to use a public static final `String` variable for our "extra" field name, but I thought it was a good style.

Use case (informal)

In my app, I have a `ListActivity` with a `ContextMenu` (the user long-presses a selection to do something), and I wanted to let the `MainActivity` know which row the user had selected for the `ContextMenu` action (my app only has one action). I ended up using intent extras to pass the selected row's index as a string back to the parent activity; from there I could just convert the index back to an `int` and use it to identify the user row selection via `ArrayList.get(index)`. This worked for me; however, I am sure there is another/better way.

See Also

Recipe 4.5; `ResultCode` *"gotcha"* (*http://androidforums.com/application-development/ 102689-startactivityforresult.html*); `startActivityForResultExample` (under "Returning a Result from a Screen"); `Activity.startActivityForResult()` (*http://developer.an droid.com/reference/android/app/Activity.html#startActivityForResult(android.content .Intent, int)*)

4.7 Keeping a Service Running While Other Apps Are on Display

Ian Darwin

Problem

You want part of your application to continue running in the background while the user switches to interact with other apps.

Solution

Create a `Service` class to do the background work; start the service from your main application. Optionally provide a Notification icon to allow the user either to stop the running service or to resume the main application.

Discussion

A `Service` class (`android.app.Service`) runs as part of the same process as your main application, but has a property that allows it to keep running even if the user switches to another app or goes to the Home screen and starts up a new app.

As you know by now, `Activity` classes can be started either by an intent that matches their content provider, or by an intent that mentions them by class name. The same is true for services. This recipe focuses on starting a service directly; Recipe 4.2 covers starting a service implicitly. The example is taken from JPSTrack, a GPS tracking program for Android. Once you start tracking, you don't want the tracking to stop if you answer the phone or have to look at a map(!), so we made it into a service. As shown in Example 4-10, the service is started by the main activity when you click the Start Tracking button, and is stopped by the Stop button. Note that this is so common that `startService()` and `stopService()` are built into the `Activity` class.

Example 4-10. The onCreate method

```
@Override
public void onCreate(Bundle savedInstanceState) {
    ...
    Intent theIntent = new Intent(this, TrackService.class);
    Button startButton = (Button) findViewById(R.id.startButton);
    startButton.setOnClickListener(new OnClickListener() {
            @Override
            public void onClick(View v) {
                    startService(theIntent);
                    Toast.makeText(Main.this, "Starting", Toast.LENGTH_LONG).show();
            }
    });
    Button stopButton = (Button) findViewById(R.id.stopButton);
    stopButton.setOnClickListener(new OnClickListener() {
            @Override
            public void onClick(View v) {
                    stopService(theIntent);
                    Toast.makeText(Main.this, "Stopped", Toast.LENGTH_LONG).show();
            }
    });
    ...
}
```

The `TrackService` class directly extends `Service`, so it has to implement the abstract `onBind()` method. This is not used when the class is started directly, so it can be a stub method. You will typically override at least the `onStartCommand()` and `onUnbind()` methods, to begin and end some activity. Example 4-11 starts the GPS service sending us

notifications that we save to disk, and we do want that to keep running, hence this
Service class.

Example 4-11. The TrackService (GPS-using service) class

```java
public class TrackService extends Service {
        private LocationManager mgr;
        private String preferredProvider;

        @Override
        public IBinder onBind(Intent intent) {
                return null;
        }

        @Override
        public int onStartCommand(Intent intent, int flags, int startId) {
                initGPS();       // sets up the LocationManager mgr

                if (preferredProvider != null) {
                        mgr.requestLocationUpdates(preferredProvider, MIN_SECONDS * 1000,
                                        MIN_METRES, this);
                        return START_STICKY;
                }
                return START_NOT_STICKY;
        }

        @Override
        public boolean onUnbind(Intent intent) {
                mgr.removeUpdates(this);
                return super.onUnbind(intent);
        }
}
```

You may have noticed the different return values from **onStartCommand()**. If you return **START_STICKY**, Android will restart your service if it gets terminated. If you return
START_NOT_STICKY, the service will not be restarted automatically. These values are discussed in more detail in the online documentation for the **Service** class (see *http://
developer.android.com/reference/android/app/Service.html*).

Remember to declare the Service subclass in the Application part of your *Android-
Manifest.xml*:

```xml
<service android:enabled="true" android:name=".TrackService">
```

4.8 Sending/Receiving a Broadcast Message

Vladimir Kroz

Problem

You want to create an activity that receives a simple broadcast message sent by another
activity.

Solution

Set up a broadcast receiver, instantiate the message receiver object, and create an `IntentFilter`. Then register your receiver with an activity that must receive the broadcast message.

Discussion

The code in Example 4-12 sets up the broadcast receiver, instantiates the message receiver object, and creates the `IntentFilter`.

Example 4-12. Creating and registering the BroadcastReceiver

```
// Instantiate message receiver object. You should
// create this class by extending android.content.BroadcastReceiver
// The method onReceive() of this class will be called when broadcast is sent
MyBroadcastMessageReceiver _bcReceiver = new MyBroadcastMessageReceiver();

// Create IntentFilter
IntentFilter filter = new IntentFilter(
MyBroadcastMessageReceiver.class.getName());

// And register your receiver with your activity which must receive broadcast message
// Now whenever this type of message is generated somewhere in the system -
// _bcReceiver.onReceive() method will be called within main thread of myActivity
myActivity.registerReceiver(_bcReceiver, filter);
```

The code in Example 4-13 shows how to publish the broadcast event.

Example 4-13. Publishing the broadcast event

```
Intent intent = new Intent(
MyBroadcastMessageReceiver.class.getName());
intent.putExtra("some additional data", choice);
someActivity.sendBroadcast(intent);
```

4.9 Starting a Service After Device Reboot

Ashwini Shahapurkar

Problem

You have a service in your app and you want it to start after the phone reboots.

Solution

Listen to the intent for boot events and start the service when the event occurs.

Discussion

Whenever a platform boot is completed, an intent is broadcast with the `android.intent.action.BOOT_COMPLETED` action . You need to register your application to receive this intent. To do so, add the following code to your *AndroidManifest.xml* file:

```
<receiver android:name="ServiceManager">
        <intent-filter>
            <action android:name="android.intent.action.BOOT_COMPLETED" />
        </intent-filter>
</receiver>
```

For `ServiceManager` to be the broadcast receiver that receives the intent for the boot event, the `ServiceManager` class would have to be coded as shown in Example 4-14.

Example 4-14. The BroadcastReceiver implementation

```
public class ServiceManager extends BroadcastReceiver {

    Context mContext;
    private final String BOOT_ACTION = "android.intent.action.BOOT_COMPLETED";

    @Override
    public void onReceive(Context context, Intent intent) {
            //All registered broadcasts are received by this
        mContext = context;
        String action = intent.getAction();
        if (action.equalsIgnoreCase(BOOT_ACTION)) {
                    //check for boot complete event & start your service
            startService();
        }

    }


    private void startService() {
            //here, you will start your service
        Intent mServiceIntent = new Intent();
        mServiceIntent.setAction("com.bootservice.test.DataService");
        mContext.startService(mServiceIntent);
    }
}
```

4.10 Creating a Responsive Application Using Threads

Amir Alagic

Problem

You have an application that performs long tasks, and you don't want your application to appear nonresponsive while these are ongoing.

Solution

By using threads, you can create an application that is responsive even when it is handling time-consuming operations.

Discussion

To make your application responsive while time-consuming operations are running on the Android OS you have a few options. If you already know Java, you know you can create a class that extends the Thread class and overrides the `public void run()` method and then call `start()` method on that object to run the time-consuming process. If your class already extends another class, you can implement the Runnable interface. Another approach is to create your own class that extends Android's AsyncTask class, but we will talk about AsyncTask in Recipe 4.11.

First we will discuss usage of the Thread class. Example 4-15 shows the networked activity implementation of this class.

Example 4-15. The networked activity implementation

```
public class NetworkConnection extends Activity {
    /** Called when the activity is first created. */
    @Override
    public void onCreate(Bundle savedInstanceState) {
        super.onCreate(savedInstanceState);
        setContentView(R.layout.main);

        Thread thread = new Thread(new Runnable(){
        public void run() {
            getServerData();
        }
         });
        thread.start();
    }
}
```

As you can see, when we start our activity in the `onCreate()` method we create a thread object that is constructed with a Runnable object. The Runnable method `run()` will be executed after we call the `start()` method on the thread object. From here you can call another method or a few other methods and operations that are time-consuming and that would otherwise block the main thread and make your application look unresponsive.

Often when we are done with the thread we get results that we want to present to the application user. If you try to update the GUI from the thread that you started (not the main thread) your application will crash. You can read error messages and see that the problem is in fact a thread other than the main UI thread you tried to change UI on the main thread.

It is possible to change the UI with such data, with the help of a Handler class. If you need to do so, please refer to Recipe 4.12.

Threads created and started in this way will continue to run even if the user leaves your application. You can keep track of the threads and tell them to stop, typically by setting a "done" boolean. More simply, to be sure that your thread(s) stop when the user leaves your application, before you call the start() method on the thread object set the thread as a daemon thread:

```
thread.setDaemon(true);
```

In addition, sometimes it can be useful to name the thread.

You can give a name to your thread(s) when you create the thread object:

```
Thread thread = new Thread();
Thread thread = new Thread(runnable, "ThreadName1");
```

Or you can call the setName() method on the thread object:

```
thread.setName("ThreadName2");
```

These names will not be visible to the user, but will show up in various diagnostic logs, to help you find which thread is causing problems.

4.11 Using AsyncTask to Do Background Processing

Johan Pelgrim

Problem

You have to do some heavy processing, or load resources from the network, and you want to show the progress and results in the UI.

Solution

Use AsyncTask and ProgressDialog.

Discussion

Introduction

As explained in the Processes and Threads section of the Android Dev Guide (*http://developer.android.com/guide/topics/fundamentals/processes-and-threads.html*), you should *never* block the UI thread, or access the Android UI toolkit from outside the UI thread. Bad things will happen if you do.

You can run processes in the background and update the UI inside the UI thread (a.k.a. the main thread) in several ways, but using the AsyncTask class is very convenient and in every Android developer should know how to do it.

The steps boil down to creating a class that extends `AsyncTask`. `AsyncTask` itself is abstract and has one abstract method, `Result doInBackground(Params... params);`. The `AsyncTask` simply creates a callable working thread in which your implementation of `doInBackground` runs. `Result` and `Params` are two of the types we need to define in our class definition. The third is the `Progress` type which we will talk about later.

In Recipe 11.15, we will examine a potentially long-running document-parsing task, processing the content of a web page, which is an XML document, and returning the result as a list of `Datum` objects. Typically, this is something we want to do outside the UI thread.

Our first implementation will do everything in the background, showing the user a spinner in the title bar and updating the `ListView` once the processing is done. This is the typical use case, not interfering with the user's task at hand and updating the UI when you have retrieved the result.

The second implementation will use a *modal* dialog to show the processing progressing in the background. In some cases we want to prevent the user from doing anything else when some processing takes place, and this is a good way to do just that.

We will create a UI that contains three `Buttons` and a `Listview`. The first button is to start our first refresh process. The second is for the other refresh process and the third is to clear the results in the `ListView` (see Example 4-16).

Example 4-16. The main layout

```xml
<?xml version="1.0" encoding="utf-8"?>
<LinearLayout xmlns:android="http://schemas.android.com/apk/res/android"
    android:orientation="vertical" android:layout_width="fill_parent"
    android:layout_height="fill_parent">
    <LinearLayout xmlns:android="http://schemas.android.com/apk/res/android"
        android:orientation="horizontal" android:layout_width="fill_parent"
        android:layout_height="wrap_content">
        <Button android:text="Refresh 1" android:id="@+id/button1"
            android:layout_width="fill_parent" android:layout_height="wrap_content"
            android:layout_weight="1"></Button>
        <Button android:text="Refresh 2" android:id="@+id/button2"
            android:layout_width="fill_parent" android:layout_height="wrap_content"
            android:layout_weight="1"></Button>
        <Button android:text="Clear" android:id="@+id/button3"
            android:layout_width="fill_parent" android:layout_height="wrap_content"
            android:layout_weight="1"></Button>
    </LinearLayout>
    <ListView android:id="@+id/listView1" android:layout_height="fill_parent"
        android:layout_width="fill_parent"></ListView>
</LinearLayout>
```

We assign these UI elements to various fields in `onCreate` and add some click listeners (see Example 4-17).

Example 4-17. The onCreate() and onItemClick() methods

```
ListView mListView;
Button mClear;
Button mRefresh1;
Button mRefresh2;

@Override
public void onCreate(Bundle savedInstanceState) {
    super.onCreate(savedInstanceState);
    setContentView(R.layout.main);

    mListView = (ListView) findViewById(R.id.listView1);
    mListView.setTextFilterEnabled(true);
    mListView.setOnItemClickListener(this);

    mRefresh1 = (Button) findViewById(R.id.button1);

    mClear = (Button) findViewById(R.id.button3);
    mClear.setOnClickListener(new OnClickListener() {
        @Override
        public void onClick(View v) {
            mListView.setAdapter(null);
        }
    });

}

public void onItemClick(AdapterView<?> parent, View view, int position, long id) {
    Datum datum = (Datum) mListView.getItemAtPosition(position);
    Uri uri = Uri.parse("http://androidcookbook.com/Recipe.seam?recipeId=" +
        datum.getId());
    Intent intent = new Intent(Intent.ACTION_VIEW, uri);
    this.startActivity(intent);
}
```

The following two subsections describe two use cases: processing in the background and processing in the foreground.

Use case 1: Processing in the background

First we create an inner class that extends `AsyncTask`:

```
protected class LoadRecipesTask1 extends AsyncTask<String, Void, ArrayList<Datum>> {
...
}
```

As you can see, we must supply three types to the class definition. The first is the type of the parameter we will provide when starting this background task, in our case a `String`, containing a URL. The second type is used for progress updates (we will use this later). The third type is the type returned by our implementation of the `doInBack` `ground` method, and typically is something with which you can update a specific UI element (a `ListView` in our case).

Let's implement the doInBackground method:

```
@Override
protected ArrayList<Datum> doInBackground(String... urls) {
    ArrayList<Datum> datumList = new ArrayList<Datum>();
    try {
        datumList = parse(urls[0]);
    } catch (IOException e) {
        e.printStackTrace();
    } catch (XmlPullParserException e) {
        e.printStackTrace();
    }
    return datumList;
}
```

As you can see, this is pretty simple. The parse method—which creates a list of Datum objects—is described in Recipe 11.15. The result of the doInBackground method is then passed as an argument to the onPostExecute method in the same (inner) class. In this method we are allowed to update the UI elements in our layout, so we set the adapter of the ListView to show our result.

```
@Override
protected void onPostExecute(ArrayList<Datum> result) {
    mListView.setAdapter(new ArrayAdapter<Datum>(MainActivity.this,
        R.layout.list_item, result));
}
```

Now we need a way to start this task. We do this in the mRefresh1's onClickListener by calling the execute(Params... params) method of AsyncTask (execute(String... urls) in our case).

```
mRefresh1.setOnClickListener(new OnClickListener() {

    @Override
    public void onClick(View v) {
        LoadRecipesTask1 mLoadRecipesTask = new LoadRecipesTask1();
        mLoadRecipesTask.execute(
            "http://androidcookbook.com/seam/resource/rest/recipe/list");
    }
});
```

Now, when you start the app it indeed retrieves the recipes and fills the ListView, but the user has no idea that something is happening in the background. We can set the progress bar indeterminate window feature in this case, which displays a small progress animation in the top right of our app title bar.

To do this, we request this feature by calling the following method in onCreate: requestWindowFeature(Window.FEATURE_INDETERMINATE_PROGRESS);.

Then we can start the progress animation by calling the setProgressBarIndeterminateVisibility(Boolean visibility) method from within a new method in our inner class, the onPreExecute method.

```
protected void onPreExecute() {
    MainActivity.this.setProgressBarIndeterminateVisibility(true);
}
```

We stop the spinning progress bar in our window title by calling the same method from within our onPostExecute method, which will become:

```
protected void onPostExecute(ArrayList<Datum> result) {
    mListView.setAdapter(new ArrayAdapter<Datum>(MainActivity.this,
        R.layout.list_item, result));
    MainActivity.this.setProgressBarIndeterminateVisibility(false);
}
```

We're done! Take your app for a *spin* (pun intended).

As you can see, this is a nifty feature for creating a better user experience!

Use case 2: Processing in the foreground

In this example, we show a modal dialog to the user that displays the progress of loading the recipes in the background. Such a dialog is called a ProgressDialog. First we add it as a field to our activity.

```
ProgressDialog mProgressDialog;
```

Then we add the onCreateDialog method to be able to answer showDialog calls and create our dialog.

```
protected Dialog onCreateDialog(int id) {
    switch (id) {
    case DIALOG_KEY:                                                    ❶
        mProgressDialog = new ProgressDialog(this);
        mProgressDialog.setProgressStyle(ProgressDialog.STYLE_HORIZONTAL);  ❷
        mProgressDialog.setMessage("Retrieving recipes...");            ❸
        mProgressDialog.setCancelable(false);                          ❹
        return mProgressDialog;
    }
    return null;
}
```

❶ We should handle the request and creation of all dialogs here. The DIALOG_KEY is an int constant with an arbitrary value (we used 0) to identify this dialog.

❷ We set the progress style to STYLE_HORIZONTAL, which shows a horizontal progress bar. The default is STYLE_SPINNER.

❸ We set our custom message, which is displayed above the progress bar.

❹ By calling `setCancelable` with argument `false` we simply disable the Back button, making this dialog *modal*.

Our new implementation of `AsyncTask` is as shown in Example 4-18.

Example 4-18. The AsyncTask implementation

```
protected class LoadRecipesTask2 extends AsyncTask<String, Integer, ArrayList<Datum>>{

    @Override
    protected void onPreExecute() {
        mProgressDialog.show();                                              ❶
    }

    @Override
    protected ArrayList<Datum> doInBackground(String... urls) {
        ArrayList<Datum> datumList = new ArrayList<Datum>();
        for (int i = 0; i < urls.length; i++) {                             ❷
            try {
                datumList = parse(urls[i]);
                publishProgress((int) (((i+1) / (float) urls.length) * 100)); ❸
            } catch (IOException e) {
                e.printStackTrace();
            } catch (XmlPullParserException e) {
                e.printStackTrace();
            }
        }
        return datumList;
    }

    @Override
    protected void onProgressUpdate(Integer... values) {                    ❹
        mProgressDialog.setProgress(values[0]);                             ❺
    }

    @Override
    protected void onPostExecute(ArrayList<Datum> result) {
        mListView.setAdapter(new ArrayAdapter<Datum>(
            MainActivity.this, R.layout.list_item, result));
        mProgressDialog.dismiss();                                          ❻
    }
}
```

We see a couple of new things here.

❶ Before we start our background process we show the modal dialog.

❷ In our background process we loop through all the URLs, expecting to receive more than one. This will give us a good indication of our progress.

❸ We can update the progress by calling `publishProgress`. Notice that the argument is of type `int`, which will be auto-boxed to the second type defined in our class definition, `Integer`.

---

❹ The call to `publishProgress` will result in a call to `onProgressUpdate` which again has arguments of type `Integer`. You could, of course, use `String` or something else as the argument type by simply changing the second type in the inner class definition to `String` and, of course, in the call to `publishProgress`.

❺ We use the first `Integer` to set the new progress value in our `ProgressDialog`.

❻ We dismiss the dialog, which removes it.

Now we can bind this all together by implementing our `onClickListener` for our second refresh button.

```
mRefresh2.setOnClickListener(new OnClickListener() {

    @Override
    public void onClick(View v) {
        LoadRecipesTask2 mLoadRecipesTask = new LoadRecipesTask2();
        String url =
            "http://androidcookbook.com/seam/resource/rest/recipe/list";
        showDialog(DIALOG_KEY);                              ❶
        mLoadRecipesTask.execute(url, url, url, url, url);   ❷
    }
});
```

❶ We show the dialog by calling `showDialog` with the `DIALOG_KEY` argument, which will trigger our previously defined `onCreateDialog` method.

❷ We execute our new task with five URLs, simply to show a little bit of progress.

It will look something like Figure 4-1.

Conclusion

Implementing background tasks with `AsyncTask` is very simple and should be done for all long-running processes that also need to update your user interface.

See Also

Recipe 11.15; *http://developer.android.com/guide/topics/fundamentals/processes-and -threads.html*

Source Download URL

You can download the source code for this example from *https://github.com/downloads/ jpelgrim/androidcookbook/RecipeList.zip*.

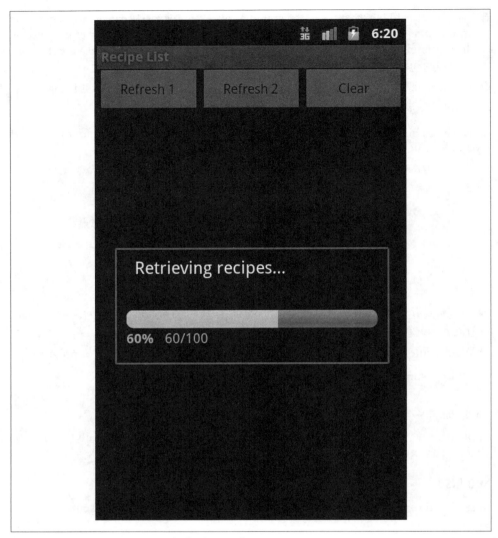

Figure 4-1. Retrieving recipes in the background

4.12 Sending Messages Between Threads Using an Activity Thread Queue and Handler

Vladimir Kroz

Problem

You need to pass information or data from a service or other background task to an activity. Because activities run on the UI thread, it is not safe to call them from a background thread. This will cause the Activity to be called at the handleMessage() method, but on the event thread so you can safely update the GUI.

Solution

You can write a nested class that extends Android's Handler class; then override the handleMessage() method that will read messages from the thread queue. Pass this Handler to the worker thread, usually via the worker class's constructor; in the worker thread, post messages using the various obtainMessage() and sendMessage() methods. This will cause the activity to be called at the handleMessage() method, but on the event thread so that you can safely update the GUI.

Discussion

There are many situations in which you must have a thread running in the background, and send information to the main activity's UI thread. At the architectural level, you can take one of the following two approaches:

- Use Android's AsyncTask class.
- Start a new thread.

Though using AsyncTask is very convenient, sometimes you really need to construct a worker thread by yourself. In such situations, you likely will need to send some information back to the activity thread. Keep in mind that Android doesn't allow other threads to modify any content of the main UI thread. Instead, you must wrap the data into messages and send the messages through the message queue.

To do this, you must first add an instance of the Handler class to, for example, your MapActivity instance (see Example 4-19).

Example 4-19. The handler

```
public class MyMap extends MapActivity {
    . . .
    public Handler _handler = new Handler() {
        @Override
        public void handleMessage(Message msg) {
            Log.d(TAG, String.format("Handler.handleMessage(): msg=%s", msg));
            // This is where the main activity thread receives messages
            // Put your handling of incoming messages posted by other threads here
            super.handleMessage(msg);
        }

    };
    . . .
}
```

Now, in the worker thread, post a message to the activity's main queue whenever you need to add the handler class instance to your main Activity instance (see Example 4-20).

Example 4-20. Posting a Runnable to the queue

```
/**
 * Performs background job
 */
class MyThreadRunner implements Runnable {
    // @Override
    public void run() {
        while (!Thread.currentThread().isInterrupted()) {
            // Dummy message -- real implementation
            // will put some meaningful data in it
            Message msg = Message.obtain();
            msg.what = 999;
            MyMap.this._handler.sendMessage(msg);
            // Dummy code to simulate delay while working with remote server
            try {
                Thread.sleep(5000);
            } catch (InterruptedException e) {
                Thread.currentThread().interrupt();
            }
        }
    }
}
```

4.13 Creating an Android Epoch HTML/JavaScript Calendar

Wagied Davids

Problem

You need a custom calendar written in JavaScript, and you want it to understand how to interact between JavaScript and Java.

Solution

Use a `WebView` component to load an HTML file containing the Epoch calendar Java-Script component. Briefly, here are the steps involved:

1. Download the Epoch DHTML/JavaScript calendar from *http://www.javascriptkit .com/script/script2/epoch/index.shtml*.

2. Create an assets directory under your Android Project folder (e.g., *TestCalendar/ assets/*).

3. Code your main HTML file for referencing the Epoch calendar.

4. Create an Android activity for launching the Epoch calendar.

Files placed in the Android assets directory are referenced as *file:///android_asset/* (note the triple leading slash and the singular spelling of *asset*).

Discussion

To enable interaction between the JavaScript-based view layer and the Java-based logic layer, a Java–JavaScript bridge interface is required: the `MyJavaScriptInterface` inner class. The `onDayClick()` function, shown in Example 4-21, shows how to call a Java-Script function from an Android activity—for example, `webview.loadUrl("javascript: popup();");`. The HTML/JavaScript component is shown in Example 4-21.

Example 4-21. calendarview.html

```html
<html>
    <head>
        <title>My Epoch DHTML JavaScript Calendar</title>
        <style type="text/css">
            dateheader {
                -background-color: #3399FF;
                -webkit-border-radius: 10px;
                -moz-border-radius: 10px;
                -border-radius: 10px;
                -padding: 5px;
            }
        </style>

        <style type="text/css">
        html {height:100%;}
        body {height:100%; margin:0; padding:0;}
```

```
#bg {position:fixed; top:0; left:0; width:100%; height:100%;}
#content {position:relative; z-index:1;}
</style>
<!--[if IE 6]>
<style type="text/css">
html {overflow-y:hidden;}
body {overflow-y:auto;}
#page-background {position:absolute; z-index:-1;}
#content {position:static;padding:10px;}
</style>
<![endif]-->

<link rel="stylesheet" type="text/css" href="epoch_v106/epoch_styles.css" />
<script type="text/javascript" src="epoch_v106/epoch_classes.js"></script>

<script type="text/javascript">
    /*You can also place this code in a separate
      file and link to it like epoch_classes.js*/
    var my_cal;

    window.onload = function () {
        my_cal = new Epoch('epoch_basic','flat',
            document.getElementById('basic_container'));
    };

    function popup()
        {
            var weekday=new Array("Sun","Mon","Tue","Wed","Thur","Fri","Sat");
            var monthname=new Array("Jan","Feb","Mar","Apr","May","Jun",
                "Jul","Aug","Sep","Oct","Nov","Dec");
            var date = my_cal.selectedDates.length > 0 ?
                my_cal.selectedDates[0] :
                null;
            if ( date != null )
                {
                    var day = date.getDate();
                    var dayOfWeek= date.getDay();
                    var month = date.getMonth();
                    var yy = date.getYear();
                    var year = (yy < 1000) ? yy + 1900 : yy;

                    /* Set the User selected date in HTML form */
                    var dateStr= weekday[dayOfWeek]  + ", " + day + " " +
                        monthname[month] + " " + year;
                    document.getElementById("selected_date").value= dateStr;

                    /* IMPORTANT:
                     * Call Android JavaScript->Java bridge setting a
                     * Java-field variable
                     */
                    window.android.setSelectedDate( date );
                    window.android.setCalendarButton( date );
                }
        }
</script>
```

```
        </head>
        <body>
        <div id="bg"><img src="bg.png" width="100%" height="100%" alt=""></div>
            <div id="content">
                <div class="dateheader" align="center">
                    <form name="form_selected_date">
                            <span style="color:white">Selected day:</span>
                            <input id="selected_date" name="selected_date" type="text"
                                readonly="true">
                    </form>
                </div>
                <div id="basic_container" onClick="popup()"></div>
            </div>
        </body>
</head>>
```

Example 4-22. CalendarView.java

```java
import java.util.Date;

import android.app.Activity;
import android.content.Intent;
import android.os.Bundle;
import android.os.Handler;
import android.util.Log;
import android.view.View;
import android.view.View.OnClickListener;
import android.webkit.JsResult;
import android.webkit.WebChromeClient;
import android.webkit.WebSettings;
import android.webkit.WebView;
import android.widget.Button;
import android.widget.ImageView;
import android.widget.Toast;

import com.pfizer.android.R;
import com.pfizer.android.utils.DateUtils;
import com.pfizer.android.view.screens.journal.CreateEntryScreen;

public class CalendarViewActivity extends Activity
    {
        private static final String tag = "CalendarViewActivity";
        private ImageView calendarToJournalButton;
        private Button calendarDateButton;
        private WebView webview;
        private Date selectedCalDate;

        private final Handler jsHandler = new Handler();

        /** Called when the activity is first created. */
        @Override
        public void onCreate(Bundle savedInstanceState)
            {
                Log.d(tag, "Creating View ...");
                super.onCreate(savedInstanceState);
```

```java
        // Set the View Layer
        Log.d(tag, "Setting-up the View Layer");
        setContentView(R.layout.calendar_view);

        // Go to CreateJournalEntry
        calendarToJournalButton = (ImageView) this.findViewById
            (R.id.calendarToJournalButton);
        calendarToJournalButton.setOnClickListener(new OnClickListener()
            {
                @Override
                public void onClick(View v)
                    {
                        Log.d(tag, "Re-directing -> CreateEntryScreen ...");
                        Intent intent = intent =
                            new Intent(getApplicationContext(),
                                CreateEntryScreen.class);
                        startActivity(intent);
                    }
            });

        // User-Selected Calendar Date
        calendarDateButton = (Button) this.findViewById(R.id.calendarDateButton);

        // Get access to the WebView holder
        webview = (WebView) this.findViewById(R.id.webview);

        // Get the settings
        WebSettings settings = webview.getSettings();

        // Enable JavaScript
        settings.setJavaScriptEnabled(true);

        // Enable ZoomControls visibility
        settings.setSupportZoom(true);

        // Add JavaScript Interface
        webview.addJavaScriptInterface(new MyJavaScriptInterface(), "android");

        // Set the Chrome Client
        webview.setWebChromeClient(new MyWebChromeClient());

        // Load the URL of the HTML file
        webview.loadUrl("file:///android_asset/calendarview.html");

    }

public void setCalendarButton(Date selectedCalDate)
    {
        Log.d(tag, jsHandler.obtainMessage().toString());
        calendarDateButton.setText(
            DateUtils.convertDateToSectionHeaderFormat(
                selectedCalDate.getTime()));
    }

/**
```

```java
 *
 * @param selectedCalDate
 */
public void setSelectedCalDate(Date selectedCalDate)
    {
        this.selectedCalDate = selectedCalDate;
    }

/**
 *
 * @return
 */
public Date getSelectedCalDate()
    {
        return selectedCalDate;
    }

/**
 * JAVA->JAVASCRIPT INTERFACE
 *
 * @author wagied
 *
 */
final class MyJavaScriptInterface
    {
        private Date jsSelectedDate;
        MyJavaScriptInterface()
            {
                // EMPTY;
            }

        public void onDayClick()
            {
                jsHandler.post(new Runnable()
                    {
                        public void run()
                            {
                                // Java telling JavaScript to do things
                                webview.loadUrl("javascript: popup();");
                            }
                    });
            }

        /**
         * NOTE: THIS FUNCTION IS BEING SET IN JAVASCRIPT User-selected Date in
         * WebView
         *
         * @param dateStr
         */
        public void setSelectedDate(String dateStr)
            {
                Toast.makeText(getApplicationContext(), dateStr,
                    Toast.LENGTH_SHORT).show();
                Log.d(tag, "User Selected Date: JavaScript -> Java : " + dateStr);
```

```java
                // Set the User Selected Calendar date
                setJsSelectedDate(new Date(Date.parse(dateStr)));
                Log.d(tag, "java.util.Date Object: " +
                    Date.parse(dateStr).toString());
            }
            private void setJsSelectedDate(Date userSelectedDate)
                {
                    jsSelectedDate = userSelectedDate;
                }
            public Date getJsSelectedDate()
                {
                    return jsSelectedDate;
                }
        }

    /**
     * Alert pop-up for debugging purposes
     *
     * @author wdavid01
     *
     */
    final class MyWebChromeClient extends WebChromeClient
        {
            @Override
            public boolean onJsAlert(WebView view, String url,
                String message, JsResult result)
                {
                    Log.d(tag, message);
                    result.confirm();
                    return true;
                }
        }

    @Override
    public void onDestroy()
        {
            Log.d(tag, "Destroying View!");
            super.onDestroy();
        }
}
```

For debugging purposes, a `MyWebChromeClient` is created—this is the final inner class extending `WebChromeClient` defined near the end of the main class—and in particular the `onJsAlert()` method is overridden.

## CHAPTER 5

Content Providers

5.1 Introduction: Content Providers

Ian Darwin

Discussion

The content provider is one of Android's more clever ideas. It allows totally unrelated applications to share data, which is usually stored in an SQLite database, without prior arrangement, knowing only the names of the tables and fields in the data.

One widely used content provider is the Android Contacts provider. The first recipe in this chapter shows how easy it is to make an initial selection of data (this is done using an intent, as you might guess, but it returns a URI, not the actual data). You then drill down using an SQLite cursor or two.

Then we have a recipe that shows you how to create your own content provider. Again as you might expect, "there's an interface for that."

Finally, while it's not directly related to content providers, Android also offers a more general remote procedure mechanism layered on AIDL (the Android Interface Definition Language), and the recipe for that is at the end of this chapter because it's a similar topic.

5.2 Retrieving Data from a Content Provider

Ian Darwin

Problem

You want to read from a content provider such as Contacts.

Solution

Create a PICK URI, open it in an intent using startActivityForResult, extract the URI from the returned intent, use Activity.getContentProvider(), and process the data using SQLite Cursor methods.

Discussion

This is part of the contact selection code from TabbyText, my SMS text message sender for WiFi-Only Honeycomb tablets (the rest of the code is in Recipe 11.17).

First, the main program sets up an OnClickListener to launch the Contacts app from a Find Contact button:

```
b.setOnClickListener(new View.OnClickListener() {
    @Override
    public void onClick(View arg0) {
        Uri uri = ContactsContract.Contacts.CONTENT_URI;
        System.out.println(uri);
        Intent intent = new Intent(Intent.ACTION_PICK, uri);
        startActivityForResult(intent, REQ_GET_CONTACT);
    }
});
```

The URI is predefined for us; it actually has the value content://com.android.contacts/contacts. The constant REQ_GET_CONTACT is arbitrary; it's just there to associate this intent start-up with the handler code, since more complex apps will often start more than one intent and they need to handle the results differently. Once this button is pressed, control passes from our app, out to the Contacts app. The user can then select a contact he wishes to SMS. The Contacts app then is backgrounded and control returns to our app at the onActivityResult() method, to indicate that the activity we started has completed and delivered a result.

The next bit of code shows how the onActivityResult() method converts the response from the activity into an SQLite cursor (see Example 5-1).

Example 5-1. OnActivityResult

```
@Override
protected void onActivityResult(int requestCode, int resultCode, Intent data) {
    if (requestCode == REQ_GET_CONTACT) {
        switch(resultCode) {
        case Activity.RESULT_OK:
            // The Contacts API is about the most complex to use.
            // First retrieve the Contact, as we only get its URI from the Intent
            Uri resultUri = data.getData(); // e.g., content://contacts/people/123
            Cursor cont = getContentResolver().query(resultUri, null, null, null, null);
            if (!cont.moveToNext()) {    // expect 001 row(s)
                Toast.makeText(this, "Cursor contains no data", Toast.LENGTH_LONG).show();
                return;
            }
            ...
```

There are a few key things to note here. First, make sure the request code is the one you started, and the `resultCode` is `RESULT_OK` or `RESULT_CANCELED` (if not, pop up a warning dialog). Then, extract the URL for the response you picked—the intent data from the returned intent—and use that to create a query, using the inherited activity method `getContentResolver()` to get the `ContentResolver` and its `query()` method to make up an SQLite cursor.

We expect the user to have selected one contact, so if that's not the case we error out. Otherwise, we'd go ahead and use the SQLite cursor to read the data. The exact formatting of the Contact database is a bit out of scope for this recipe, so it's been deferred to Recipe 11.17.

5.3 Writing a Content Provider

Ashwini Shahapurkar

Problem

Often your application generates data, which can be processed and analyzed by another application. You want to ensure that the app is doing this in the safest way possible without giving direct access to your application's database.

Solution

Write a custom content provider that will allow other applications to access data generated by your app.

Discussion

Content providers allow other applications to access the data generated by your app. A custom content provider requires that we build up the app database and provide the wrapper over it for other applications. To make other apps aware that a content provider is available, we need to declare it in *AndroidManifest.xml* as follows:

```
<provider android:authorities="com.example.android.contentprovider"
          android:name="MyContentProvider" />
```

Here the name refers to the class `MyContentProvider`, which extends the `ContentProvider` class. We need to override the following methods in this class:

```
onCreate();
delete(Uri, String, String[]);
getType(Uri);
insert(Uri, ContentValues);
query(Uri, String[], String, String[], String);
update(Uri, ContentValues, String, String[]);
```

Usually these are wrapper functions for SQL queries on the SQLite database. We parse the input parameters and perform the queries on the database, as shown in Example 5-2.

Example 5-2. The content provider

```
public class MyContentProvider extends ContentProvider {

    DatabaseHelper mDatabase;
        private static final int RECORDS = 1;
    public static final Uri CONTENT_URI = Uri
            .parse("content://com.example.android.contentprovider");

    public static final String AUTHORITY = "com.example.android.contentprovider";
    private static final UriMatcher matcher = new UriMatcher(
            UriMatcher.NO_MATCH);

    static {
        matcher.addURI(AUTHORITY, "records", RECORDS);
    }

    @Override
    public int delete(Uri uri, String selection, String[] selectionArgs) {
        // the app-specific code for deleting records from the database goes here
        return 0;
    }

    @Override
    public String getType(Uri uri) {
        int matchType = matcher.match(uri);
        switch (matchType) {
        case RECORDS:
            return ContentResolver.CURSOR_DIR_BASE_TYPE + "/records";
        default:
            throw new IllegalArgumentException("Unknown or Invalid URI " + uri);
        }
    }

    @Override
    public Uri insert(Uri uri, ContentValues values) {
                //your app specific insertion code goes here
                // it can be as simple as follows; inserting all values
                // in database and returning the record id
        long id = mDatabase.getWritableDatabase().insert(Helper.TABLE_NAME,
                null, values);
        uri = Uri.withAppendedPath(uri, "/" + id);
        return uri;
    }

    @Override
    public boolean onCreate() {
                //initialize your database constructs
        return true;
    }
```

```
        @Override
        public Cursor query(Uri uri, String[] projection, String selection,
                String[] selectionArgs, String sortOrder) {
                    //build your query with SQLiteQueryBuilder
            SQLiteQueryBuilder qBuilder = new SQLiteQueryBuilder();
            qBuilder.setTables(Helper.TABLE_NAME);
            int uriType = matcher.match(uri);

                    //query the database and get result in cursor
            Cursor resultCursor = qBuilder.query(mDatabase.getWritableDatabase(),
                    projection, selection, selectionArgs, null, null, sortOrder,
                    null);
            resultCursor.setNotificationUri(getContext().getContentResolver(), uri);
            return resultCursor;

        }

        @Override
        public int update(Uri uri, ContentValues values, String selection,
                String[] selectionArgs) {
            // to be implemented
            return 0;
        }

}
```

By providing a content provider, you avoid giving access to your database to other developers and also reduce the chances of database inconsistency.

5.4 Writing an Android Remote Service

Rupesh Chavan

Problem

You want to know how to write a remote service and access it from another application.

Solution

Android has provided an AIDL-based programming interface that both the client and the service agree upon in order to communicate with each other using inter-process communication (IPC).

Discussion

Inter-process communication (IPC) is a key feature of the Android programming model. IPC provides the following two mechanisms:

- Intent-based communication
- Remote-service-based communication

In this recipe we will be concentrating on the remote-service-based communication approach. This Android feature allows you to make method calls that look "local" but are executed in another process. They involve use of the Android Interface Definition Language (AIDL). The service has to declare a service interface in an AIDL file and the AIDL tool will automatically create a Java interface corresponding to the AIDL file. The AIDL tool also generates a stub class that provides an abstract implementation of the service interface methods. The actual service class will have to extend this stub class to provide the real implementation of the methods exposed through the interface.

The service clients will have to invoke the onBind() method on the service to be able to connect to the service. The onBind() method returns an object of the stub class to the client. Example 5-3 shows the code-related snippets.

Example 5-3. The AIDL file

```
package com.demoapp.service;

interface IMyRemoteService {
  String getMessage();
}
```

If you are using Eclipse it will automatically generate the remote interface corresponding to your AIDL file. The remote interface will also provide a stub inner class that has to have an implementation provided by the RemoteService class. The stub class implementation within the service class is as shown in Example 5-4.

Example 5-4. Remote service stub

```
private IMyRemoteService.Stub myRemoteServiceStub = new IMyRemoteService.Stub() {
    public int getMessage() throws RemoteException {
        return "Hello World!";
    }
};
// The onBind() method in the service class:
public IBinder onBind(Intent arg0) {
    Log.d(getClass().getSimpleName(), "onBind()");
    return myRemoteServiceStub;
}
```

Now, let us quickly look at the meat of the service class before we move on to how the client connects to this service class. My RemoteService class is just returning a string. Here are the overridden onCreate(), onStart(), and onDestroy() methods. The onCreate() method of the service will be called only once in a service life cycle. The onStart() method will be called every time the service is started. Note that the resources are all released in the onDestroy() method (see Example 5-5).

Example 5-5. onCreate() and onDestroy()

```
public void onCreate() {
    super.onCreate();
    Log.d(getClass().getSimpleName(),"onCreate()");
```

```
    }
    public void onStart(Intent intent, int startId) {
        super.onStart(intent, startId);
        Log.d(getClass().getSimpleName(), "onStart()");
    }
    public void onDestroy() {
        super.onDestroy();
        Log.d(getClass().getSimpleName(),"onDestroy()");
    }
```

Let's discuss the client class. Here, for simplicity, I have put the start, stop, bind, release, and invoke methods all in the same client. In reality, though, one client may start and another can bind to the already started service.

There are five buttons: one each for the start, stop, bind, release, and invoke actions. A client needs to bind to a service before it can invoke any method on the service. Example 5-6 shows the start method.

Example 5-6. The startService() method

```
    private void startService(){
        if (started) {
            Toast.makeText(RemoteServiceClient.this, "Service already started",
                Toast.LENGTH_SHORT).show();
        } else {
            Intent i = new Intent();
            i.setClassName("com.demoapp.service", "com.demoapp.service.RemoteService");
            startService(i);
            started = true;
            updateServiceStatus();
            Log.d( getClass().getSimpleName(), "startService()" );
        }
    }
```

An explicit intent is created and the service is started with the `Context.startSer vice(i)` method. The rest of the code updates some status on the UI. There is nothing specific to a remote service invocation here. It is on the `bindService()` method that we see the difference from a local service (see Example 5-7).

Example 5-7. The bindService() method

```
    private void bindService() {
        if(conn == null) {
            conn = new RemoteServiceConnection();
            Intent i = new Intent();
            i.setClassName("com.demoapp.service", "com.demoapp.service.RemoteService");
            bindService(i, conn, Context.BIND_AUTO_CREATE);
            updateServiceStatus();
            Log.d( getClass().getSimpleName(), "bindService()" );
        } else {
            Toast.makeText(RemoteServiceClient.this,
                "Cannot bind - service already bound", Toast.LENGTH_SHORT).show();
        }
    }
```

Here we get a connection to the remote service through the `RemoteServiceConnection` class which implements the `ServiceConnection` interface. The connection object is required by the `bindService()` method—an intent, a connection object, and the type of binding are to be specified. So, how do we create a connection to the `RemoteService`? Example 5-8 shows the implementation.

Example 5-8. The ServiceConnection implementation

```
class RemoteServiceConnection implements ServiceConnection {
    public void onServiceConnected(ComponentName className,
    IBinder boundService ) {
        remoteService = IMyRemoteService.Stub.asInterface((IBinder)boundService);
        Log.d( getClass().getSimpleName(), "onServiceConnected()" );
    }

    public void onServiceDisconnected(ComponentName className) {
        remoteService = null;
        updateServiceStatus();
        Log.d( getClass().getSimpleName(), "onServiceDisconnected" );
    }
};
```

The `Context.BIND_AUTO_CREATE` ensures that a service is created if one did not exist, although the `onstart()` will be called only on explicit start of the service.

Once the client is bound to the service and the service has already started, we can invoke any of the methods that are exposed by the service. Here we have only one method and that is `getMessage()`. In this example, the invocation is done by clicking the Invoke button. That would return the text message and update it below the button.

Example 5-9 shows the invoke method.

Example 5-9. The invokeService() method

```
private void invokeService() {
    if(conn == null) {
        Toast.makeText(RemoteServiceClient.this,
            "Cannot invoke - service not bound", Toast.LENGTH_SHORT).show();
    } else {
        try {
            String message = remoteService.getCounter();
            TextView t = (TextView)findViewById(R.id.notApplicable);
            t.setText( "Message: "+message );
            Log.d( getClass().getSimpleName(), "invokeService()" );
        } catch (RemoteException re) {
            Log.e( getClass().getSimpleName(), "RemoteException" );
        }
    }
}
```

Once we use the service methods, we can release the service. This is done as shown in Example 5-10 (by clicking the Release button).

Example 5-10. The releaseService() method

```
private void releaseService() {
    if(conn != null) {
        unbindService(conn);
        conn = null;
        updateServiceStatus();
        Log.d( getClass().getSimpleName(), "releaseService()" );
    } else {
        Toast.makeText(RemoteServiceClient.this,
            "Cannot unbind - service not bound",
            Toast.LENGTH_SHORT).show();
    }
}
```

Finally, we can stop the service by clicking the Stop button. After this point, no client can invoke this service. Example 5-11 shows the relevant code.

Example 5-11. The stopService() method

```
private void stopService() {
    if (!started) {
        Toast.makeText(RemoteServiceClient.this, "Service not yet started",
            Toast.LENGTH_SHORT).show();
    } else {
        Intent i = new Intent();
        i.setClassName("com.demoapp.service", "com.demoapp.service.RemoteService");
        stopService(i);
        started = false;
        updateServiceStatus();
        Log.d( getClass().getSimpleName(), "stopService()" );
    }
}
```

 If the client and the service are using different package structures, the client has to include the AIDL file along with the package structure, just like the service does.

These are the basics of working with a remote service on the Android platform. All the best!

## CHAPTER 6

Graphics

6.1 Introduction: Graphics

Ian Darwin

Discussion

Computer graphics are any kind of display for which there isn't a GUI component: charting, displaying pictures, and so on. Android is well provisioned for graphics, including a full implementation of OpenGL EL, a subset of OpenGL intended for smaller devices.

The chapter starts with a recipe for using a custom font for special text effects, then some recipes on GL graphics proper, and a note on graphical "touch" input. From there we continue the input theme with various image capture techniques. Then we have some recipes on graphics files, and one to round out the chapter discussing "pinch to zoom," using user touch input to scale graphical output.

6.2 Using a Custom Font

Ian Darwin

Problem

The range of fonts that comes with Android 2.x is amazingly minuscule—three variants of the "Droid" font. You want something better.

Solution

Install a TTF or OTF version of your font in *assets/fonts* (creating this directory if necessary). In your code, create a typeface from the "asset" and call the `View`'s `setTypeface()` method. You're done!

Discussion

You can provide one or more fonts with your application. We have not yet discovered a documented way to install system-wide fonts. Beware of huge fonts, as they will be downloaded with your application, increasing its size.

Your custom font's format should be TTF or OTF (TrueType or OpenTypeFace, a TTF extension). You need to create the *fonts* subdirectory under *assets* in your project, and install the font there.

While you can refer to the pre-defined fonts just using XML, you cannot refer to your own fonts using XML. This may change someday, but for now the content model of the `android:typeface` attribute is an XML enumeration containing only `normal`, `sans`, `serif`, and `monospace`—that's it! Therefore, you have to use code.

There are several `Typeface.create()` methods, including:

- `create(String familyName, int style);`
- `create(TypeFace family, inst style);`
- `createFromAsset(AssetManager mgr, String path);`
- `createFromFile(File path);`
- `createFromFile(String path);`

You can easily see how most of these should work. The parameter "style" is, as in Java, one of several constants defined on the class representing fonts, here `Typeface`. Our code example uses the `createFromAsset()` method, so we don't have to worry about font locations. You could probably provide a font shared by several locations using an absolute path into `/sdcard` using the latter two forms; remember to request permission in the *AndroidManifest.xml* file to read the SD card! You can create representations of the built-in fonts, and variations on them, using the first two forms.

The font I used is the nice Iceberg font, from SoftMaker Software GmbH (*http://www.softmaker.de*). This font is copyrighted and I do not have permission to redistribute it, so when you download the project and want to run it, you will need to install a True-Type font file at *assets/fonts/fontdemo.ttf*. Note that if the font is invalid, Android will *silently ignore it* and use the built-in Droid font.

In this demo we provide two text areas, one using the built-in serif font and one using a custom font. They are defined, and various attributes added, in *main.xml* (see Example 6-1).

Example 6-1. XML layout with font specification

```
<?xml version="1.0" encoding="utf-8"?>
<LinearLayout
    xmlns:android="http://schemas.android.com/apk/res/android"
    android:orientation="vertical"
    android:layout_width="fill_parent"
    android:layout_height="fill_parent"
```

```
        >
<TextView
    android:id="@+id/PlainTextView"
    android:layout_width="fill_parent"
    android:layout_height="wrap_content"
    android:text="@string/plain"
    android:textSize="36sp"
    android:typeface="serif"
    android:padding="10sp"
    android:gravity="center"
    />
<TextView
    android:id="@+id/FontView"
    android:layout_width="fill_parent"
    android:layout_height="wrap_content"
    android:text="@string/nicer"
    android:textSize="36sp"
    android:typeface="normal"
    android:padding="10sp"
    android:gravity="center"
    />
</LinearLayout>
```

Example 6-2 shows the source code.

Example 6-2. Setting a custom font

```
public class FontDemo extends Activity {

    @Override
    public void onCreate(Bundle savedInstanceState) {
        super.onCreate(savedInstanceState);
        setContentView(R.layout.main);

        TextView v = (TextView) findViewById(R.id.FontView);    ❶
        Typeface t = Typeface.createFromAsset(getAssets(),      ❷
                "fonts/fontdemo.ttf");
        v.setTypeface(t, Typeface.BOLD_ITALIC);                 ❸
    }
}
```

❶ Find the View you want to use your font in.

❷ Create a Typeface object from one of the Typeface class's static create() methods.

❸ Message the Typeface into the View's setTypeface method.

If all is well, running the app should look like Figure 6-1.

Figure 6-1. Custom font

Source Download URL

The source code for this example is in the Android Cookbook repository at *http://github .com/AndroidCook/Android-Cookbook-Examples*, in the subdirectory FontDemo (see "Getting and Using the Code Examples" on page xvii).

6.3 Drawing a Spinning Cube with OpenGL ES

Marco Dinacci

Problem

You want to create a basic OpenGL ES application.

Solution

Create a `GLSurfaceView` and a custom `Renderer` that will draw a spinning cube.

Discussion

Android supports 3D graphics via the OpenGL ES API, a flavor of OpenGL specifically designed for embedded devices.

The recipe is not an OpenGL tutorial; it assumes the reader already has basic OpenGL knowledge.

The final result will look like Figure 6-2.

Figure 6-2. GL graphics sample

First we write a new `Activity` and in the `onCreate` method we create the two funda-
mental objects we need to use the OpenGL API: a `GLSurfaceView` and a `Renderer` (see
Example 6-3).

Example 6-3. OpenGL demo activity

```
public class OpenGLDemoActivity extends Activity {

    @Override
    public void onCreate(Bundle savedInstanceState) {
        super.onCreate(savedInstanceState);

        // Go fullscreen
        requestWindowFeature(Window.FEATURE_NO_TITLE);
        getWindow().setFlags(WindowManager.LayoutParams.FLAG_FULLSCREEN,
                        WindowManager.LayoutParams.FLAG_FULLSCREEN);

        GLSurfaceView view = new GLSurfaceView(this);
        view.setRenderer(new OpenGLRenderer());
        setContentView(view);
    }
}
```

Example 6-4 is the code for our `Renderer` that uses a simple `Cube` object we'll describe
later to display a spinning cube.

Example 6-4. The rendered implementation

```
class OpenGLRenderer implements Renderer {

        private Cube mCube = new Cube();
        private float mCubeRotation;

        @Override
        public void onSurfaceCreated(GL10 gl, EGLConfig config) {
            gl.glClearColor(0.0f, 0.0f, 0.0f, 0.5f);

            gl.glClearDepthf(1.0f);
            gl.glEnable(GL10.GL_DEPTH_TEST);
```

```
        gl.glDepthFunc(GL10.GL_LEQUAL);

        gl.glHint(GL10.GL_PERSPECTIVE_CORRECTION_HINT,
                GL10.GL_NICEST);

    }

    @Override
    public void onDrawFrame(GL10 gl) {
        gl.glClear(GL10.GL_COLOR_BUFFER_BIT | GL10.GL_DEPTH_BUFFER_BIT);
        gl.glLoadIdentity();

        gl.glTranslatef(0.0f, 0.0f, -10.0f);
        gl.glRotatef(mCubeRotation, 1.0f, 1.0f, 1.0f);

        mCube.draw(gl);

        gl.glLoadIdentity();

        mCubeRotation -= 0.15f;
    }

    @Override
    public void onSurfaceChanged(GL10 gl, int width, int height) {
        gl.glViewport(0, 0, width, height);
        gl.glMatrixMode(GL10.GL_PROJECTION);
        gl.glLoadIdentity();
        GLU.gluPerspective(gl, 45.0f, (float)width / (float)height, 0.1f, 100.0f);
        gl.glViewport(0, 0, width, height);

        gl.glMatrixMode(GL10.GL_MODELVIEW);
        gl.glLoadIdentity();
    }
}
```

Our onSurfaceChanged and onDrawFrame methods are basically the equivalent of the GLUT glutReshapeFunc and glutDisplayFunc. The first is called when the surface is resized—for instance, when the phone switches between landscape and portrait modes. The second is called at every frame, and that's where we put the code to draw our cube (see Example 6-5).

Example 6-5. The Cube class

```
class Cube {

    private FloatBuffer mVertexBuffer;
    private FloatBuffer mColorBuffer;
    private ByteBuffer  mIndexBuffer;

    private float vertices[] = {
                            -1.0f, -1.0f, -1.0f,
                            1.0f, -1.0f, -1.0f,
                            1.0f,  1.0f, -1.0f,
                            -1.0f, 1.0f, -1.0f,
                            -1.0f, -1.0f,  1.0f,
```

```
                                   1.0f,  -1.0f,   1.0f,
                                   1.0f,   1.0f,   1.0f,
                                  -1.0f,   1.0f,   1.0f
                                   };
private float colors[] = {
                                   0.0f,   1.0f,   0.0f,   1.0f,
                                   0.0f,   1.0f,   0.0f,   1.0f,
                                   1.0f,   0.5f,   0.0f,   1.0f,
                                   1.0f,   0.5f,   0.0f,   1.0f,
                                   1.0f,   0.0f,   0.0f,   1.0f,
                                   1.0f,   0.0f,   0.0f,   1.0f,
                                   0.0f,   0.0f,   1.0f,   1.0f,
                                   1.0f,   0.0f,   1.0f,   1.0f
                               };

private byte indices[] = {
                                   0, 4, 5, 0, 5, 1,
                                   1, 5, 6, 1, 6, 2,
                                   2, 6, 7, 2, 7, 3,
                                   3, 7, 4, 3, 4, 0,
                                   4, 7, 6, 4, 6, 5,
                                   3, 0, 1, 3, 1, 2
                                   };

public Cube() {
        ByteBuffer byteBuf = ByteBuffer.allocateDirect(vertices.length * 4);
        byteBuf.order(ByteOrder.nativeOrder());
        mVertexBuffer = byteBuf.asFloatBuffer();
        mVertexBuffer.put(vertices);
        mVertexBuffer.position(0);

        byteBuf = ByteBuffer.allocateDirect(colors.length * 4);
        byteBuf.order(ByteOrder.nativeOrder());
        mColorBuffer = byteBuf.asFloatBuffer();
        mColorBuffer.put(colors);
        mColorBuffer.position(0);

        mIndexBuffer = ByteBuffer.allocateDirect(indices.length);
        mIndexBuffer.put(indices);
        mIndexBuffer.position(0);
}

public void draw(GL10 gl) {
        gl.glFrontFace(GL10.GL_CW);

        gl.glVertexPointer(3, GL10.GL_FLOAT, 0, mVertexBuffer);
        gl.glColorPointer(4, GL10.GL_FLOAT, 0, mColorBuffer);

        gl.glEnableClientState(GL10.GL_VERTEX_ARRAY);
        gl.glEnableClientState(GL10.GL_COLOR_ARRAY);

        gl.glDrawElements(GL10.GL_TRIANGLES, 36, GL10.GL_UNSIGNED_BYTE,
                        mIndexBuffer);

        gl.glDisableClientState(GL10.GL_VERTEX_ARRAY);
```

```
            gl.glDisableClientState(GL10.GL_COLOR_ARRAY);
        }
    }
```

The `Cube` uses two `FloatBuffer` objects to store vertex and color information and a `ByteBuffer` to store the face indexes. In order for the buffers to work it is important to set their order according to the endianness of the platform, using the `order` method. Once the buffers have been filled with the values from the arrays, the internal cursor must be restored to the beginning of the data using `buffer.position(0)`.

See Also

http://www.khronos.org/opengles

6.4 Adding Controls to the OpenGL Spinning Cube

Marco Dinacci

Problem

You want to interact with an OpenGL polygon using your device's keyboard.

Solution

Create a custom `GLSurfaceView` and override the `onKeyUp` method to listen to the `KeyEvent` created from a directional pad (D-pad).

Discussion

This recipe extends on Recipe 6.3 to show how to control the cube using a D-pad. We're going to increment the speed rotation along the x-axis and y-axis using the D-pad's directional keys.

The biggest change is that we now have our custom class that extends the `Surface View`. We do this so that we can override the `onKeyUp` method and be notified when the user uses the D-pad.

The `onCreate` of our `Activity` looks like Example 6-6.

Example 6-6. The spinning cube activity

```
public class SpinningCubeActivity2 extends Activity {
    @Override
    public void onCreate(Bundle savedInstanceState) {
        super.onCreate(savedInstanceState);

        // go fullscreen
        requestWindowFeature(Window.FEATURE_NO_TITLE);
        getWindow().setFlags(WindowManager.LayoutParams.FLAG_FULLSCREEN,
                    WindowManager.LayoutParams.FLAG_FULLSCREEN);
```

```
    // create our custom view
    GLSurfaceView view = new OpenGLSurfaceView(this);
    view.setRenderer((Renderer)view);
    setContentView(view);
    }
}
```

Our new `GLSurfaceView` also implements the `Renderer` interface. The `onSurfaceCre`
`ated` and `onSurfaceChanged` methods are exactly the same as in the preceding recipe;
most of the changes occur in the `onDrawFrame` as we introduce four new parameters:
`mXrot` and `mYrot` to control the rotation of the cube along the x-axis and y-axis, and
`mXspeed` and `mYSpeed` to store the speed of the rotation along the x-axis and y-axis.

Each time the user clicks on a D-pad button we alter the speed of the cube by modifying
these parameters.

Example 6-7 shows the full code of our new class.

Example 6-7. The GLSurfaceView implementation

```java
class OpenGLSurfaceView extends GLSurfaceView implements Renderer {

    private Cube mCube;
    private float mXrot;
    private float mYrot;
    private float mXspeed;
    private float mYspeed;

    public OpenGLSurfaceView(Context context) {
        super(context);

        // give focus to the GLSurfaceView
        requestFocus();
        setFocusableInTouchMode(true);

        mCube = new Cube();
    }

    @Override
    public void onDrawFrame(GL10 gl) {
        gl.glClear(GL10.GL_COLOR_BUFFER_BIT | GL10.GL_DEPTH_BUFFER_BIT);
        gl.glLoadIdentity();

        gl.glTranslatef(0.0f, 0.0f, -10.0f);

        gl.glRotatef(mXrot, 1.0f, 0.0f, 0.0f);
        gl.glRotatef(mYrot, 0.0f, 1.0f, 0.0f);

        mCube.draw(gl);

        gl.glLoadIdentity();

        mXrot += mXspeed;
```

```
        mYrot += mYspeed;
    }

    @Override
    public boolean onKeyUp(int keyCode, KeyEvent event) {
        if(keyCode == KeyEvent.KEYCODE_DPAD_LEFT)
            mYspeed -= 0.1f;
        else if(keyCode == KeyEvent.KEYCODE_DPAD_RIGHT)
            mYspeed += 0.1f;
        else if(keyCode == KeyEvent.KEYCODE_DPAD_UP)
            mXspeed -= 0.1f;
        else if(keyCode == KeyEvent.KEYCODE_DPAD_DOWN)
            mXspeed += 0.1f;

        return true;
    }

    // unchanged
    @Override
    public void onSurfaceCreated(GL10 gl, EGLConfig config) {
        gl.glClearColor(0.0f, 0.0f, 0.0f, 0.5f);

        gl.glClearDepthf(1.0f);
        gl.glEnable(GL10.GL_DEPTH_TEST);
        gl.glDepthFunc(GL10.GL_LEQUAL);

        gl.glHint(GL10.GL_PERSPECTIVE_CORRECTION_HINT,
                GL10.GL_NICEST);
    }


    // unchanged
    @Override
    public void onSurfaceChanged(GL10 gl, int width, int height) {
        gl.glViewport(0, 0, width, height);
        gl.glMatrixMode(GL10.GL_PROJECTION);
        gl.glLoadIdentity();
        GLU.gluPerspective(gl, 45.0f, (float)width / (float)height, 0.1f, 100.0f);
        gl.glViewport(0, 0, width, height);

        gl.glMatrixMode(GL10.GL_MODELVIEW);
        gl.glLoadIdentity();
    }
}
```

The Cube is inherited from the preceding recipe. Don't forget to call the requestFo
cus() and setFocusableInTouchMode(true) in the constructor of the view or else the key
events will not be received.

See Also

Recipe 6.3

Source Download URL

You can download the source code for this example from *http://www.intransitione.com/ intransitione.com/code/android/spinning_cube_controllable.zip*.

6.5 Freehand Drawing Smooth Curves

Ian Darwin

Problem

You want to allow the user to draw smooth curves, such as freehand bezier curves, legal signatures, and so on.

Solution

Create a custom `View` with a carefully written `OnTouchListener` that handles the case where input arrives faster than your code can process it; save the results in an array, and draw them in `onDraw()`.

Discussion

This code was originally written by Eric Burke of Square Inc., to capture signatures when people use the Square app to capture credit card purchases. To be legally acceptable as proof of purchase intent, the captured signatures have to be of good quality. Square has graciously placed this code under the Apache Software License 2.0, but was not able to provide it as part of this recipe.

I have since adapted the signature code for use in JabaGator, my very simple drawing program that I hope to get into the Android Market in 2012. JabaGator is a general-purpose drawing program for the Java desktop and for Android, but the fact that the name rhymes with a well-known illustration program from Adobe is, of course, purely coincidental.

Eric's initial, "by the book" drawing code worked but was very jerky and very slow. Upon investigation, Square learned that Android's graphics layer sends touch events in "batches" when it cannot deliver them quickly enough individually. Each MotionEvent delivered to onTouchEvent() may contain a number of touch coordinates, as many as were captured since the last onTouchEvent() call. To draw a smooth curve, you must get all of the points. You do this using the number of coordinates from the TouchEvent method getHistorySize(), iterating over that count, and calling getHistor icalX(int) and getHistoricalY(int) to get the point locations (see Example 6-8).

Example 6-8. Drawing all the points

```
// in onTouchEvent(TouchEvent):
for (int i=0; i < event.getHistorySize(); i++) {
    float historicalX = event.getHistoricalX(i);
    float historicalY = event.getHistoricalY(i);
    ... add point (historicalX, historicalY) to your path ...
}
... add point (eventX, eventY) to your path ...
```

This provides significant improvements, but it still is too slow for people to draw with—many non-geeks will wait for the drawing code to catch up with their finger if it doesn't draw quickly enough! The problem was that a simple solution calls invalidate() after each line segment, which is correct but very slow as it forces Android to redraw the entire screen. The solution to this problem is to call invalidate() with just the region that you drew the line segment into, and involves a bit of arithmetic to get the region correct; see the expandDirtyRect() method in Example 6-9. The dirty-region algorithm is, in Eric's own words:

1. "Create a rectangle representing the dirty region."
2. "Set the points for the four corners to the X and Y coordinates from the ACTION_DOWN event."
3. "For ACTION_MOVE and ACTION_UP, expand the rectangle to encompass the new points. (Don't forget the historical coordinates!)"
4. "Pass just the dirty rectangle to invalidate(). Android won't redraw the rest."

This makes the drawing code responsive, and the application usable.

Example 6-9 shows my version of the final code. I have several OnTouchListeners, one for drawing curves, one for selecting objects, one for drawing rectangles, and so on. That code is not complete at present, but the curve drawing part works nicely.

Example 6-9. DrawingView.java

```
// This code is dual-licensed under Creative Commons and Apache Software License 2.0
public class DrawingView extends View {

    private static final float STROKE_WIDTH = 5f;

    /** Need to track this so the dirty region can accommodate the stroke. **/
    private static final float HALF_STROKE_WIDTH = STROKE_WIDTH / 2;

    private Paint paint = new Paint();
```

```java
private Path path = new Path();

/**
 * Optimizes painting by invalidating the smallest possible area.
 */
private float lastTouchX;
private float lastTouchY;
private final RectF dirtyRect = new RectF();

final OnTouchListener selectionAndMoveListener = // not shown;

final OnTouchListener drawRectangleListener = // not shown;

final OnTouchListener drawOvalListener = // not shown;

final OnTouchListener drawPolyLineListener = new OnTouchListener() {

  @Override
  public boolean onTouch(View v, MotionEvent event) {
      // Log.d("jabagator", "onTouch: " + event);
      float eventX = event.getX();
      float eventY = event.getY();

      switch (event.getAction()) {
        case MotionEvent.ACTION_DOWN:
          path.moveTo(eventX, eventY);
          lastTouchX = eventX;
          lastTouchY = eventY;
          // No end point yet, so don't waste cycles invalidating.
          return true;

        case MotionEvent.ACTION_MOVE:
        case MotionEvent.ACTION_UP:
          // Start tracking the dirty region.
          resetDirtyRect(eventX, eventY);

          // When the hardware tracks events faster than
          // they can be delivered to the app, the
          // event will contain a history of those skipped points.
          int historySize = event.getHistorySize();
          for (int i = 0; i < historySize; i++) {
            float historicalX = event.getHistoricalX(i);
            float historicalY = event.getHistoricalY(i);
            expandDirtyRect(historicalX, historicalY);
            path.lineTo(historicalX, historicalY);
          }

          // After replaying history, connect the line to the touch point.
          path.lineTo(eventX, eventY);
          break;

        default:
          Log.d("jabagator", "Unknown touch event  " + event.toString());
          return false;
      }
```

```
        // Include half the stroke width to avoid clipping.
        invalidate(
            (int) (dirtyRect.left - HALF_STROKE_WIDTH),
            (int) (dirtyRect.top - HALF_STROKE_WIDTH),
            (int) (dirtyRect.right + HALF_STROKE_WIDTH),
            (int) (dirtyRect.bottom + HALF_STROKE_WIDTH));

        lastTouchX = eventX;
        lastTouchY = eventY;

        return true;
    }

    /**
     * Called when replaying history to ensure the dirty region
     * includes all points.
     */
    private void expandDirtyRect(float historicalX, float historicalY) {
        if (historicalX < dirtyRect.left) {
            dirtyRect.left = historicalX;
        } else if (historicalX > dirtyRect.right) {
            dirtyRect.right = historicalX;
        }
        if (historicalY < dirtyRect.top) {
            dirtyRect.top = historicalY;
        } else if (historicalY > dirtyRect.bottom) {
            dirtyRect.bottom = historicalY;
        }
    }

    /**
     * Resets the dirty region when the motion event occurs.
     */
    private void resetDirtyRect(float eventX, float eventY) {

        // The lastTouchX and lastTouchY were set when the ACTION_DOWN
        // motion event occurred.
        dirtyRect.left = Math.min(lastTouchX, eventX);
        dirtyRect.right = Math.max(lastTouchX, eventX);
        dirtyRect.top = Math.min(lastTouchY, eventY);
        dirtyRect.bottom = Math.max(lastTouchY, eventY);
    }
};

/** DrawingView Constructor */
public DrawingView(Context context, AttributeSet attrs) {
    super(context, attrs);

    paint.setAntiAlias(true);
    paint.setColor(Color.WHITE);
    paint.setStyle(Paint.Style.STROKE);
    paint.setStrokeJoin(Paint.Join.ROUND);
    paint.setStrokeWidth(STROKE_WIDTH);
```

```
        setMode(MotionMode.DRAW_POLY);
    }

    public void clear() {
        path.reset();

        // Repaints the entire view.
        invalidate();
    }

    @Override
    protected void onDraw(Canvas canvas) {
        canvas.drawPath(path, paint);
    }

    /**
     * Sets the DrawingView into one of several modes, such
     * as "select" mode (e.g., for moving or resizing objects),
     * or "Draw polyline" (smooth curve), "draw rectangle", etc.
     */
    private void setMode(MotionMode motionMode) {
        switch(motionMode) {
        case SELECT_AND_MOVE:
            setOnTouchListener(selectionAndMoveListener);
            break;
        case DRAW_POLY:
            setOnTouchListener(drawPolyLineListener);
            break;
        case DRAW_RECTANGLE:
            setOnTouchListener(drawRectangleListener);
            break;
        case DRAW_OVAL:
            setOnTouchListener(drawOvalListener);
            break;
        default:
            throw new IllegalStateException("Unknown MotionMode " + motionMode);
        }
    }
}
```

Figure 6-3 shows JabaGator running, showing my attempt at legible handwriting (don't worry, that's not my legal signature).

Figure 6-3. Touch drawing sample

This gives good drawing performance and smooth curves. The code to capture the curves into the drawing data model is not shown as it is application-specific.

See Also

You can find the original code and Eric's description online at *http://corner.squareup .com/2010/07/smooth-signatures.html*.

Source Download URL

You can download the source code for this example from *http://projects.darwinsys.com/ jabagator.android-src.zip*.

6.6 Taking a Picture Using an Intent

Ian Darwin

Problem

You want to take a picture from within your app and don't want to write a lot of code.

Solution

Create an `Intent` for `MediaStore.ACTION_IMAGE_CAPTURE`, tailor it a little, and call `star tActivityForResult` on this `Intent`. Provide an `onActivityResult()` callback to get notified when the user is done with the camera.

Discussion

Example 6-10 shows the complete camera activity from my JPSTrack application.

Assuming that you want to save the image with your application's data (instead of in the Media Gallery location), you want to provide a file-based URI referring to the target location, using `intent.putExtra(MediaStore.EXTRA_OUTPUT, uri);`. Note that, according to discussions on various forum sites, the intent handler may give significantly different results on different vendors' platforms. On the Motorola Milestone, using the Android 2.1 load from Telus Canada, with the code in Example 6-10, the defined directory gets a preview-scale image and the Media Gallery gets a copy that is one-fourth the full resolution (1280 × 960). Hopefully this will be cleaned up and standardized in version 2.2.

Example 6-10. The camera capture activity

```
import jpstrack.android.MainActivity;
import jpstrack.android.FileNameUtils;

public class CameraNoteActivity extends Activity {

    private File imageFile;

    @Override
    protected void onCreate(Bundle savedInstanceState) {
        super.onCreate(savedInstanceState);
        // Use an Intent to get the Camera app going.
        Intent intent = new Intent(MediaStore.ACTION_IMAGE_CAPTURE);
        // Set up file to save image into.
        imageFile = new File(MainActivity.getDataDir(),
            FileNameUtils.getNextFilename("jpg"));
        Uri uri = Uri.fromFile(imageFile);
        intent.putExtra(MediaStore.EXTRA_OUTPUT, uri);
        intent.putExtra(MediaStore.EXTRA_VIDEO_QUALITY, 1);
        // And away we go!
        startActivityForResult(intent, 0);
    }
```

```
@Override
public void onActivityResult(int requestCode,
        int resultCode, Intent data) {
    switch(requestCode) {
    case 0: // take picture
        switch(resultCode) {
        case Activity.RESULT_OK:
            if (imageFile.exists())
                Toast.makeText(this,
            "Bitmap saved as " + imageFile.getAbsoluteFile(),
                Toast.LENGTH_LONG).show();
            else {
                AlertDialog.Builder alert =
                new AlertDialog.Builder(this);
                alert.setTitle("Error").setMessage(
                "Returned OK but image not created!").show();
            }
            break;
        case Activity.RESULT_CANCELED:
            //  no blather required!
            break;
        default:
            Toast.makeText(this,
            "Unexpected resultCode: " + resultCode,
                Toast.LENGTH_LONG).show();
        }
        break;
    default:
        Toast.makeText(this,
        "UNEXPECTED ACTIVITY COMPLETION",
            Toast.LENGTH_LONG).show();
    }
    finish();    // back to main app
    }
}
```

See Also

Taking a pictures as shown in Recipe 6.7 requires more code but gives you more control over the process.

Source Download URL

You can download the source code for this example from *http://www.darwinsys.com/jpstrack/*.

6.7 Taking a Picture Using android.media.Camera

Marco Dinacci

Problem

You want to have more control of the various stages involved when taking a picture.

Solution

Create a `SurfaceView` and implement the callbacks fired when the user takes a picture in order to have control over the image capture process.

Discussion

Sometimes you may want more control over the stages involved when taking a picture, or you may want to access and modify the raw image data acquired by the camera. In these cases, using a simple `Intent` to take a picture is not enough.

We're going to create a new `Activity` and customize the view to make it full-screen inside the `onCreate` method (Example 6-11).

Example 6-11. The take picture activity

```
public class TakePictureActivity extends Activity {
    private Preview mCameraView;

    @Override
    public void onCreate(Bundle savedInstanceState) {
        super.onCreate(savedInstanceState);

        // Force screen in landscape mode as showing a video in
        // portrait mode is not easily doable on all devices
        setRequestedOrientation(ActivityInfo.SCREEN_ORIENTATION_LANDSCAPE);

        // Hide window title and go fullscreen
        requestWindowFeature(Window.FEATURE_NO_TITLE);
        getWindow().addFlags(WindowManager.LayoutParams.FLAG_FULLSCREEN);
```

```
    mCameraView= new Preview(this);
    setContentView(mCameraView);
  }
}
```

The **Preview** class is the bulk of the recipe. It handles the **Surface** where the pixels are drawn, and the **Camera** object.

We define a **ClickListener** in the constructor so that the user can take a picture by just tapping once on the screen. Once we get the notification of the click, we take a picture, passing as parameters four (all optional) callbacks (see Example 6-12).

Example 6-12. The SurfaceView implementation

```
class Preview extends SurfaceView implements SurfaceHolder.Callback, PictureCallback  {

    private SurfaceHolder mHolder;
    private Camera mCamera;
    private RawCallback mRawCallback;

    public Preview(Context context) {
        super(context);

        mHolder = getHolder();
        mHolder.addCallback(this);
        mHolder.setType(SurfaceHolder.SURFACE_TYPE_PUSH_BUFFERS);
        mRawCallback = new RawCallback();

        setOnClickListener(new OnClickListener() {

            @Override
            public void onClick(View v) {
                mCamera.takePicture(mRawCallback, mRawCallback, null,
                            Preview.this);
            }
        });
    }
```

The **Preview** class implements the **SurfaceHolder.Callback** interface in order to be notified when the underlying surface is created, changed, and destroyed. We'll use these callbacks to properly handle the **Camera** object (see Example 6-13).

Example 6-13. The surfaceChanged() method

```
    @Override
    public void surfaceChanged(SurfaceHolder holder, int format, int width,
            int height) {

        Camera.Parameters parameters = mCamera.getParameters();
        parameters.setPreviewSize(width, height);
        mCamera.setParameters(parameters);

        mCamera.startPreview();
    }
```

```
@Override
public void surfaceCreated(SurfaceHolder holder) {
    mCamera = Camera.open();

    configure(mCamera);

    try {
        mCamera.setPreviewDisplay(holder);
    } catch (IOException exception) {
        closeCamera();
    }
}

@Override
public void surfaceDestroyed(SurfaceHolder holder) {
    closeCamera();
}
```

As soon as the camera is created we call configure in order to set the parameters the camera will use to take a picture—things like flash mode, effects, picture format, picture size, scene mode and so on (Example 6-14). Since not all devices support all kinds of features, always ask which features are supported before setting them.

Example 6-14. The configure() method

```
private void configure(Camera camera) {
    Camera.Parameters params = camera.getParameters();

    // Configure image format. RGB_565 is the most common format.
    List<Integer> formats = params.getSupportedPictureFormats();
    if (formats.contains(PixelFormat.RGB_565))
        params.setPictureFormat(PixelFormat.RGB_565);
    else
        params.setPictureFormat(PixelFormat.JPEG);

    // Choose the biggest picture size supported by the hardware
    List<Size> sizes = params.getSupportedPictureSizes();
    Camera.Size size = sizes.get(sizes.size()-1);
    params.setPictureSize(size.width, size.height);

    List<String> flashModes = params.getSupportedFlashModes();
    if (flashModes.size() > 0)
        params.setFlashMode(Camera.Parameters.FLASH_MODE_AUTO);

    // Action mode takes pictures of fast moving objects
    List<String> sceneModes = params.getSupportedSceneModes();
    if (sceneModes.contains(Camera.Parameters.SCENE_MODE_ACTION))
        params.setSceneMode(Camera.Parameters.SCENE_MODE_ACTION);
    else
        params.setSceneMode(Camera.Parameters.SCENE_MODE_AUTO);

    // if you choose FOCUS_MODE_AUTO remember to call autoFocus() on
    // the Camera object before taking a picture
    params.setFocusMode(Camera.Parameters.FOCUS_MODE_FIXED);
```

```
    camera.setParameters(params);
}
```

When the surface is destroyed we close the camera and free its resources:

```
private void closeCamera() {
    if (mCamera != null) {
        mCamera.stopPreview();
        mCamera.release();
        mCamera = null;
    }
}
```

The **jpeg** callback is the last one called; this is where we restart the preview and save the file on disk.

```
@Override
public void onPictureTaken(byte[] jpeg, Camera camera) {
    // now that all the callbacks have been called it is safe to resume preview
    mCamera.startPreview();

    saveFile(jpeg);
}
}
```

Finally, we implement the **ShutterCallback** and we again implement the **PictureCall back** to receive the uncompressed raw image data (see Example 6-15).

Example 6-15. The ShutterCallback implementation

```
class RawCallback implements ShutterCallback, PictureCallback {

    @Override
    public void onShutter() {
        // notify the user, normally with a sound, that the picture has
        // been taken
    }

    @Override
    public void onPictureTaken(byte[] data, Camera camera) {
        // manipulate uncompressed image data
    }
}
```

See Also

Recipe 6.6

6.8 Scanning a Barcode or QR Code with the Google ZXing Barcode Scanner

Daniel Fowler

Problem

You want your app to be able to scan a barcode or QR (Quick Response) Code.

Solution

Use an `Intent` to access the scanning functionality exposed by the Google ZXing barcode scanner.

Discussion

One of the great features of Android is how easy it is to tap into existing functionality. Scanning barcodes and QR codes is a good example. Google has a free scanning app that you can access via an `Intent`; thus an app can easily add scanning functionality, opening up new interface, communication, and feature possibilities.

The program in this recipe is an example of how to access the Google barcode scanner via an `Intent`. Make sure the Google barcode scanner is installed (*https://market.android .com/details?id=com.google.zxing.client.android*). In Example 6-16 there are three buttons to choose to scan either a QR code, a product barcode, or something else. There are two `TextView`s to display the type of barcode scanned and the data it contains.

Example 6-16. Scan program layout

```xml
<?xml version="1.0" encoding="utf-8"?>
<LinearLayout xmlns:android="http://schemas.android.com/apk/res/android"
    android:orientation="vertical"
    android:layout_width="fill_parent"
    android:layout_height="fill_parent">
  <LinearLayout android:orientation="horizontal"
    android:layout_width="fill_parent"
    android:layout_height="wrap_content">
    <Button android:layout_width="wrap_content"
        android:layout_height="wrap_content"
        android:id="@+id/butQR"
        android:text="QR Code"
        android:textSize="18sp"/>
    <Button android:layout_width="wrap_content"
        android:layout_height="wrap_content"
        android:id="@+id/butProd"
        android:text="Product"
        android:textSize="18sp"/>
    <Button android:layout_width="wrap_content"
        android:layout_height="wrap_content"
        android:id="@+id/butOther"
        android:text="Other"
        android:textSize="18sp"/>
  </LinearLayout>
  <TextView android:layout_width="fill_parent"
    android:layout_height="wrap_content"
    android:id="@+id/tvStatus"
    android:text="Press a button to start a scan."
```

```
        android:textSize="18sp" />
    <TextView android:layout_width="fill_parent"
        android:layout_height="fill_parent"
        android:id="@+id/tvResult"
        android:text="Ready"
        android:textSize="18sp"
        android:background="@android:color/white"
        android:textColor="@android:color/black"/>
</LinearLayout>
```

Depending on which button is pressed, the program puts the relevant parameters into the Intent before starting the ZXing activity and waiting for the result (see Example 6-17).

Example 6-17. Scan program main activity

```java
public class Main extends Activity {
    @Override
    public void onCreate(Bundle savedInstanceState) {
        super.onCreate(savedInstanceState);
        setContentView(R.layout.main);
        HandleClick hc = new HandleClick();
        findViewById(R.id.butQR).setOnClickListener(hc);
        findViewById(R.id.butProd).setOnClickListener(hc);
        findViewById(R.id.butOther).setOnClickListener(hc);
    }
    private class HandleClick implements OnClickListener{
        public void onClick(View arg0) {
            Intent intent = new Intent("com.google.zxing.client.android.SCAN");
            switch(arg0.getId()){
                case R.id.butQR:
                    intent.putExtra("SCAN_MODE", "QR_CODE_MODE");
                    break;
                case R.id.butProd:
                    intent.putExtra("SCAN_MODE", "PRODUCT_MODE");
                    break;
                case R.id.butOther:
                    intent.putExtra("SCAN_FORMATS",
                        "CODE_39,CODE_93,CODE_128,DATA_MATRIX,ITF");
                    break;
            }
            startActivityForResult(intent, 0);    //barcode scanner to scan for us
        }
    }
    public void onActivityResult(int requestCode, int resultCode, Intent intent) {
        if (requestCode == 0) {
            TextView tvStatus=(TextView)findViewById(R.id.tvStatus);
            TextView tvResult=(TextView)findViewById(R.id.tvResult);
            if (resultCode == RESULT_OK) {
                tvStatus.setText(intent.getStringExtra("SCAN_RESULT_FORMAT"));
                tvResult.setText(intent.getStringExtra("SCAN_RESULT"));
            } else if (resultCode == RESULT_CANCELED) {
                tvStatus.setText("Press a button to start a scan.");
                tvResult.setText("Scan cancelled.");
            }
```

```
            }
        }
}
```

Notice, in the table that follows, how it is possible to scan for a family of barcodes (using SCAN_MODE) or a specific type of barcode (using SCAN_FORMATS). If you know what type of barcode is being decoded, setting a scan format to that one particular type may result in faster decoding (it will not be trying to run through all the barcode decoding algorithms), as in `intent.putExtra("SCAN_FORMATS", "CODE_39")`. For multiple SCAN_FOR MATS pass a comma-separated list, refer back to Example 6-17.

SCAN_MODE	SCAN_FORMATS
QR_CODE_MODE	QR_CODE
PRODUCT_MODE	EAN_13
	EAN_8
	RSS_14
	UPC_A
	UPC_E
ONE_D_MODE	As for product mode plus...
	CODE_39
	CODE_93
	CODE_128
	ITF
DATA_MATRIX_MODE	DATA_MATRIX

The ZXing team is also working to support SCAN_FORMATS of CODABAR, RSS_EXPANDED, AZTEC, and PDF_417.

Now go and make that scanning inventory control or grocery list app you've been thinking of!

See Also

http://code.google.com/p/zxing/ and *http://developer.android.com/guide/topics/intents/intents-filters.html*

6.9 Using AndroidPlot to Display Charts and Graphs

Rachee Singh

Problem

You want to display data graphically in an Android application.

Solution

Use one of the many third-party graph libraries available for Android. In this example we will use AndroidPlot, an open source library, to depict a simple graph.

Discussion

If you don't have it already, download AndroidPlot library from *http://androidplot.com/wiki/Download* (any version).

Now you need to create a new Android project and add the AndroidPlot library to the new project. To do this, create a new folder in the project folder and name it *lib*. To this folder add the downloaded AndroidPlot JAR file; it should be named *Androidplot-core-0.4a-release.jar* or something similar. (At this stage, you should have directories such as *src*, *res*, *gen*, and *lib*.)

To use the library, you must add it to the build path. In Eclipse, right-click the *.jar* file you added and select the Build Path–Add to Build Path option. This will show another directory called *Referenced Libraries* in the Eclipse project.

In our sample application, we are hardcoding some data and showing the plot corresponding to the data in the application. So we need to add an (x,y) plot to our XML layout (*main.xml*). Example 6-18 shows what *main.xml* looks like with an XYPlot component in a linear layout.

Example 6-18. The XML layout with XYPlot

```
<?xml version="1.0" encoding="utf-8"?>
<LinearLayout xmlns:android="http://schemas.android.com/apk/res/android"
    android:orientation="vertical"
    android:layout_width="fill_parent"
    android:layout_height="fill_parent"
    >
  <com.androidplot.xy.XYPlot
    android:id="@+id/mySimpleXYPlot"
    android:layout_width="fill_parent"
    android:layout_height="wrap_content"
```

```
        title="Stats"/>
</LinearLayout>
```

Get a reference to the XYPlot defined in the XML:

```
        mySimpleXYPlot = (XYPlot) findViewById(R.id.mySimpleXYPlot);
```

Initialize two arrays of numbers for which the plot will be displayed:

```
    // Create two arrays of y-values to plot:
    Number[] series1Numbers = {1, 8, 5, 2, 7, 4};
    Number[] series2Numbers = {4, 6, 3, 8, 2, 10};
```

Turn the arrays into XYSeries:

```
    XYSeries series1 = new SimpleXYSeries(
        // SimpleXYSeries takes a List so turn our array into a List
        Arrays.asList(series1Numbers),
        // Y_VALS_ONLY means use the element index as the x value
        SimpleXYSeries.ArrayFormat.Y_VALS_ONLY,
        // Set the display title of the series
        "Series1");
```

Create a formatter to use for drawing a series using LineAndPointRenderer:

```
    LineAndPointFormatter series1Format = new LineAndPointFormatter(
        Color.rgb(0, 200, 0),              // line color
        Color.rgb(0, 100, 0),              // point color
        Color.rgb(150, 190, 150));         // fill color (optional)
```

Add series1 and series2 to the XYPlot:

```
    mySimpleXYPlot.addSeries(series1, series1Format);
    mySimpleXYPlot.addSeries(series2, new LineAndPointFormatter(Color.rgb(0, 0, 200),
        Color.rgb(0, 0, 100), Color.rgb(150, 150, 190)));
```

Make it look cleaner:

```
    // Reduce the number of range labels
    mySimpleXYPlot.setTicksPerRangeLabel(3);

    // By default, AndroidPlot displays developer guides to aid in laying out
    // your plot. To get rid of them call disableAllMarkup():
    mySimpleXYPlot.disableAllMarkup();

    mySimpleXYPlot.getBackgroundPaint().setAlpha(0);
    mySimpleXYPlot.getGraphWidget().getBackgroundPaint().setAlpha(0);
    mySimpleXYPlot.getGraphWidget().getGridBackgroundPaint().setAlpha(0);
```

Run the application! It should look like Figure 6-4.

Source Download URL

You can download the source code for this example from *https://docs.google.com/leaf ?id=0B_rESQKgad5LNTJjMDQ2MTktZjAzMi00ZjBkLWFhOTktZ jA5OWY4YjE2MTRh&hl=en_US*.

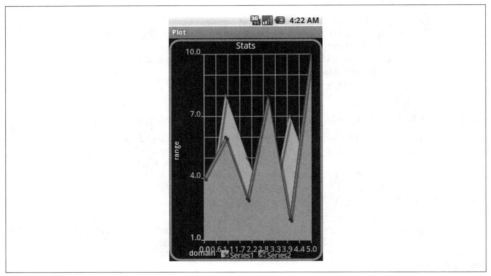

Figure 6-4. AndroidPlot display

6.10 Using Inkscape to Create an Android Launcher Icon

Daniel Fowler

Problem

You want a custom launcher icon for your Android app.

Solution

Inkscape is a free and feature-rich graphics program that supports the ability to export to a bitmap file; you can use it to create the variously sized icons needed for an app.

Discussion

A graphics program is used to design the graphical resources used in an Android application. Inkscape is a free multiplatform graphics program with some very powerful features. You can use it to generate high-quality vector graphic images that can then be exported to any required resolution. This is ideal for generating Android launcher icons (and other graphical resources). See the Inkscape website at *http://inkscape.org/* for more information on the program and to download the latest version.

When a project is created in Eclipse a default icon is generated in the *res/drawable* folder. This default icon is 48 × 48 pixels. Icons are stored in the Portable Network Graphics (PNG) file format. Android supports different screen densities, measured in dots per inch (dpi). Screen densities are grouped into low density (120 dpi), medium density (160 dpi), high density (240 dpi), and extra-high density (320 dpi). The 48 × 48 pixel icon is suitable for medium-density screens; for all other densities, the 48 × 48 pixel icon is scaled up or down as required. Ideally, for best results (sharp images with no pixelation) a project will include an icon for all the possible screen densities that an app will encounter. To do this, four drawable folders are created under the *res* folder, one for each possible screen density; icon files of the correct size are placed into these directories:

- 36 × 36 pixel icon in *res/drawable-ldpi* for low-density screens
- 48 × 48 pixel icon in *res/drawable-mdpi* for medium-density screens
- 72 × 72 pixel icon in *res/drawable-hdpi* for high-density screens
- 96 × 96 pixel icon in *res/drawable-xhdpi* for extra-high-density screens

Each icon must include a border around the central image, used for on-screen spacing and minor image protrusions (see Figure 6-5). The recommended border is one-twelfth of the icon size. This means the space the actual icon image occupies is smaller than the icon pixel size:

- For a 36 × 36 icon, the image size is 30 × 30 pixels.
- For a 48 × 48 icon, the image size is 40 × 40 pixels.
- For a 72 × 72 icon, the image size is 60 × 60 pixels.
- For a 96 × 96 icon, the image size is 80 × 80 pixels.

Figure 6-5. Icon with border

When designing an icon it is better to work with images that are larger than the required size. A larger image is easier to work with in a graphics package and easily scaled down when completed. An image that is 576 × 576 pixels is divisible equally by all the icon sizes and is a reasonable size in which to design. For a vector-based graphics package, such as Inkscape, the image size is irrelevant; it can be scaled up and down without losing quality. Inkscape uses the open Scalable Vector Graphics (SVG) format. Image detail is only lost when the final bitmap images are produced from the vector image.

Those wanting to learn to design images in Inkscape can use the many tutorials that are available both via the Help menu and online; *http://inkscapetutorials.wordpress .com/* is a good tutorial reference.

Once you have designed an image in Inkscape, you can export it to a PNG file for use as an app icon. In the following example the image to be converted to icons came from the tutorial at *http://vector.tutsplus.com/tutorials/illustration/creating-a-coffee-cup-with -inkscape/*. If you follow the tutorial, the image shown in Figure 6-6 is produced.

Figure 6-6. A cup of java

You can convert the image to an icon for a coffee ordering/coffee break timer/coffee break game or whatever coffee-related app is currently in the pipeline. Those who do not want to follow the tutorial can obtain the image from *http://openclipart.org*, a great source (more than 33,000) of free images (see Figure 6-7). Search for "coffee" and you will see various coffee-related images, including the one shown in Figure 6-6, uploaded by this recipe's author. Click on the image, select the View SVG button, and use the browser's File→Save Page As (Firefox) or File→Save As (Internet Explorer) menu.

Figure 6-7. Searching for the perfect cup

The four required icon sizes are generated from the image using the Inkscape Export Bitmap option. The image is opened and correctly proportioned for the export. This can be done for any image designed or opened in Inkscape. Remember that images should not be overly detailed or have too many colors (detail is reduced during resizing), and that they should try to fill (or fit) a square area. Android icon guidelines also suggest images that are face on with minor drop shadows and a little top lighting; see *http://developer.android.com/guide/practices/ui_guidelines/icon_design_launcher.html*.

With the image open, resize the document to 576 × 576 pixels. To do this, use the Document Properties option under the File menu (see Figure 6-8). In "Custom size" set Width and Height to 576 and check that Units is set to "px" (for pixels). Ensure that the "Show page border" checkbox is ticked.

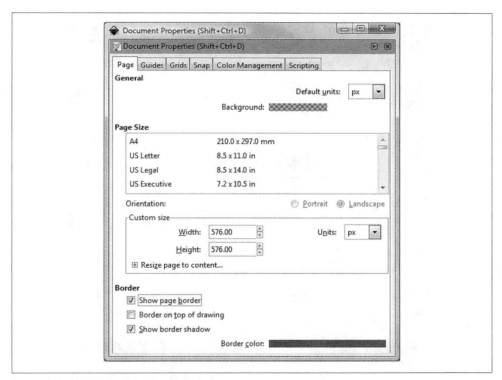

Figure 6-8. The Document Properties dialog

Drag two vertical and two horizontal guides from the rulers (click and drag from any part of the page ruler). Drag them inside each page border approximately one-twelfth of the width and height of the visible page border. The accurate position of the guides will be set using the guide properties. If the rulers are not visible use the View→Show/Hide→Rulers menu option to display them. Double-click each guide and set the following positions accurately:

Guide	x	y
Top horizontal	0	528
Bottom horizontal	0	48
Left vertical	48	0
Right vertical	528	0

At this point, you should be able to easily adjust the image to fit within the guides. Minor protrusions into the border area are allowed if required for image balance. Use the menu Edit→Select All or press Ctrl-A to select the image, drag the image into position, and resize as appropriate to fit within the box outlined by the guides (Figure 6-9).

Figure 6-9. Resizing in Inkscape

With the image created and correctly proportioned, you can now create the bitmaps for an Android project. Using Eclipse, open the project in which the icons are required. Select the *res* folder and create four new folders (menu option File→New→Folder or context menu New→Folder):

- *res/drawable-ldpi*
- *res/drawable-mdpi*
- *res/drawable-hdpi*
- *res/drawable-xhdpi*

The existing *drawable* folder is used as fallback if an icon cannot be found or for apps that can run on Android 1.5.

Back in Inkscape, ensure that the image is not selected (click outside the image). Use the File→Export Bitmap menu option to bring up the Export Bitmap dialog (see Figure 6-10). Select Page, then under Bitmap Size set Width and Height to 96; you do not need to change the dpi setting (it will change as Width and Height are changed). Under Filename, browse to the project directory for the xhdpi icon (*res/drawable-xhdpi*) and enter "icon.png" for the filename. Click the Export button to generate the icon.

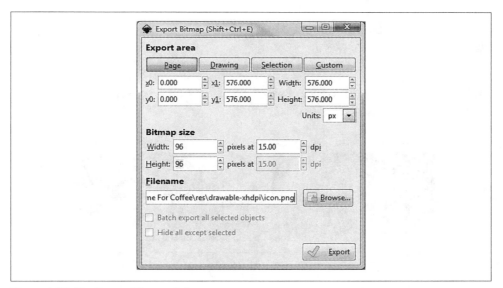

Figure 6-10. The Export Bitmap dialog

For the other three icon resolutions set Width and Height appropriately (72, then 48, and finally 36), and browse to the correct folder to export each icon. Finally, copy the icon from the *res/drawable-mdpi* folder into the *drawable* folder to replace the default icon. This process will have generated the variously sized icons required to support different device screens (see Figure 6-11).

If Eclipse was open when the icons are generated, you will need to refresh the open project to see the new icons in the folders; select File→Refresh or press F5 (see Figure 6-12).

Figure 6-11. Coffee cup in various sizes

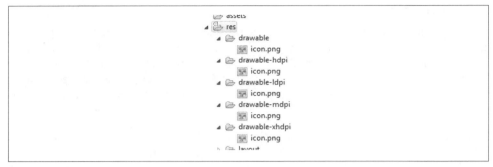

Figure 6-12. Icon placement in the project

You should test the application on physical and virtual devices to ensure that the icons appear as expected (see Figure 6-13).

Figure 6-13. Icon in use

The icon files do not need to be called icon.png; see Recipe 6.11 for information on changing the launcher icon filename.

See Also

Recipe 6.11; *http://inkscape.org/*; *http://inkscapetutorials.wordpress.com/*; *http://vector .tutsplus.com/tutorials/illustration/creating-a-coffee-cup-with-inkscape/*; *http://opencli part.org*; *http://developer.android.com/guide/practices/ui_guidelines/icon_design _launcher.html*

6.11 Creating Easy Launcher Icons from OpenClipArt.org Using Paint.NET

Daniel Fowler

Problem

You want to set your app apart from others and make it look more professional.

Solution

OpenClipArt.org is a good source of free graphics that you can adapt for use as an icon for your app.

Discussion

When a developer is getting ready to release his app, he must determine what he needs to do to get the app ready for the Android Market. One thing he must do is provide a good icon. The icon will usually be the most common graphical representation of the app that a user encounters. It will represent the app on the Applications screen, in Manage Applications, and as a shortcut if added to the Home screen. A good icon helps to foster a positive first impression of the app, and helps the app stand out in the crowd. Developers with access to a graphic artist, either professionally or through friends, or who are good artists themselves will have finer control of the graphics within their application. However, many developers find that creating the graphics in an app is a chore. This recipe shows how to generate a good icon quickly, though compromising the fine control provided by a dedicated artist.

The Open Clipart Library at *http://www.openclipart.org* provides more than 33,000 free graphics. The graphics provided are in vector format, which makes them great for scaling to icon size. Icons are in raster format, so once you have chosen a suitable graphic, you need to convert it into the Android icon format, which is Portable Network Graphics (PNG).

For this recipe, we will add an icon to the example "Hello, World" app created in Recipe 1.4.

First, find a suitable free graphic as a starting point. Go to *http://www.openclipart.org* and use the Search box. The search results may include graphics that do not always appear logical. This is because the search not only includes the name of the graphic, but also includes tags and descriptions, as well as partial words; therefore, graphics unrelated to the major search term will appear, as will contributions with misspellings or whose names are in a different language. However, this also means that occasionally an unexpected but suitable graphic will be found. Page through the search results, which are provided as thumbnails with title, contributor name, and date of submission, and number of downloads.

When looking for a graphic to use as an icon there are some pointers to keep in mind:

- There is a recommended color palette to fit in with the Android theme; this is only a recommendation, but it is a useful guide (see Figure 6-14). Avoid any color that is too extreme.

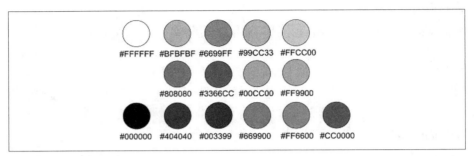

Figure 6-14. Color palette

- The graphic will be scaled down dramatically, so do not choose one with too much detail. The search result thumbnail itself is a good indicator.
- Clear and simple designs with smooth lines and bright, neutral colors will scale well and look good on a device screen.
- Keep in mind the Android design guidelines at *http://developer.android.com/guide/practices/ui_guidelines/icon_design_launcher.html*; graphical representations should be face on, with a small drop shadow and top lighting.
- Icons are square, so look for an image that, if bounded by a square, would fill most of that square.

For the *Hello, World* app I used the search term *earth* (see Figure 6-15).

I chose the graphic titled "A simple globe" as the basis for the icon from the second page of search results. Click on the graphic to bring up its details. You can save the graphic to the local machine by clicking on it (or click on the View SVG button) and using the browser's File menu. In Firefox, select Save Page As and select its location. In Internet Explorer, select "Save as..."; alternatively, both browsers support Ctrl-S. This will save the file as a vector file, which, as we discussed earlier, is not a good format for an icon. Fortunately, the image's Open Clip Art page also has an option to obtain the file as a PNG file.

SVG filesize: 36030 bytes

Figure 6-15. Clip art search results

Android icons need to be provided in four different sizes so that Android can display the best possible icon for the device's screen density. It is recommended that an app supply all the icon sizes required to prevent poor icons from being displayed on some devices. The four icon sizes are:

- 36 × 36 pixels for low-density displays (120 dpi)
- 48 × 48 pixels for medium-density displays (160 dpi)
- 72 × 72 pixels for high-density displays (240 dpi)
- 96 × 96 pixels for extra-high-density displays (320 dpi)

There is also a border to take into consideration; the border area allows for spacing and image overrun and is recommended to be one-twelfth of the icon width (see Figure 6-16).

Figure 6-16. Icon border area

This means the practical image size for the icon graphic is smaller than the stated icon size:

- 30 × 30 pixels for low density
- 40 × 40 pixels for medium density
- 60 × 60 pixels for high density
- 80 × 80 pixels for extra-high density

On the Open Clip Art page for the required graphic, we can use the PNG button to obtain a PNG in the four image sizes required. In the box next to the PNG button type in the first image size required, 80 (for the extra-high-density icon; see Figure 6-17). We cannot put in the icon size, 96, because that would not leave any border.

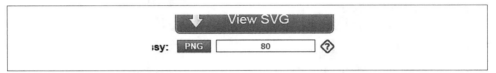

Figure 6-17. Convert to PNG with size 80

Click on the PNG button and then use the browser's File menu (or Ctrl-S) to save the generated PNG file. Press the browser's Back button to return to the image's web page. Clear the box next to the PNG button and enter the size of the next icon graphic required, in this case 60 for the high-density icon. Again click the PNG button and save the generated file. Do the same with the values 40 and 30 to generate the other two graphics.

A couple of problems may occur. Sometimes the conversion will still produce the previously sized graphic. If this happens, reload the image's Open Clip Art page (click on the address bar, and with the cursor at the end of the address, press Enter; using F5 will not clear the problem). A graphic may also fail to convert to PNG. In Mozilla a message will be displayed stating that the graphic contained errors; in Internet Explorer a small box with an X in it will be displayed. If the graphic fails to convert, either select another image or download the SVG file and use a graphics application that supports SVG. Alternatively, on the image's Open Clip Art page bring up the context menu on the graphic itself and save it as a full-size PNG (you can resize it in a graphics application and reset the transparency).

After you use the PNG button on the selected graphic, there will be four files, each containing the same image at four resolutions (Figure 6-18). The graphics files may not be perfectly square—for example, they may be 39 × 40 instead of 40 × 40—but the small difference does not matter.

Figure 6-18. Icons of Earth in various sizes

You need to resize the files to the correct icon size by adding the empty border. You can do this in a graphics application, such as GIMP (*http://www.gimp.org*), Inkscape (*http://www.inkscape.org*), or Paint.NET (*http://www.getpaint.net*; Windows only). For this recipe, we will use Paint.NET.

In Paint.NET, open the first graphics file. Set the secondary (background) color to transparency by selecting the Window menu option, and then selecting Colors (or press F8); on the Colors dialog ensure that Secondary is selected in the drop down, and then click the More button to see the advanced options. Set the Transparency option in the bottom right of the Colors dialog to zero (see Figure 6-19).

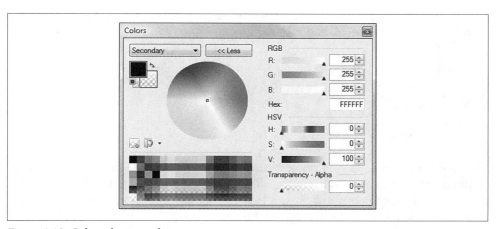

Figure 6-19. Color selection palette

Next, open the Canvas Size dialog by using the Image menu option and selecting Canvas Size (or press Ctrl-Shift-R). Select the "By absolute size" radio button but ignore the "Maintain aspect ratio" checkbox; if the graphic is square it can be checked, and if not it should be unchecked. In the "Pixel size" options set the correct Width and Height for the icon for the given graphic—both 36 for the 30 × 30 graphic, both 48 for the 40 × 40 graphic, both 72 for the 60 × 60 graphic, and both 96 for the 80 × 80 graphic. Set the Anchor option to Middle. Select OK.

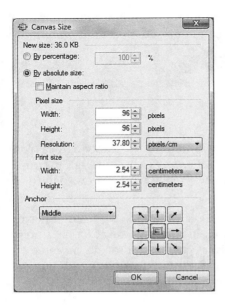

Save the resized image and repeat for the other three graphics, to finish with four PNG icon files at sizes 36, 48, 72, and 96 (see Figure 6-18).

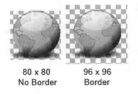

80 x 80   96 x 96
No Border   Border

The four files now need to be copied into the project where the icons are to be used. In the project directories each icon is placed into a folder under the *res* folder for each dpi setting. If the project is in Eclipse it is likely that the *res* folder already contains the folders *drawable-hdpi*, *drawable-ldpi*, and *drawable-mdpi*, all with the default icon.

The existing icons are replaced with the newly created ones; in the process the folder for **xhdpi** is added; it is called *drawable-xhdpi*. If the app supports Android version 1.5, a folder simply called *drawable* containing the 48 × 48 icon is also required (see Figure 6-20). Table 6-1 provides a summary.

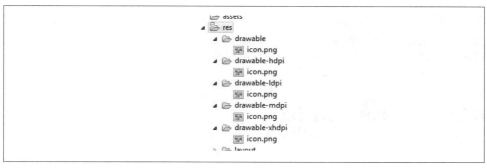

Figure 6-20. Icon Folders

Table 6-1. Icon formatting summary

Folder	Icon size	Image size	dpi	Android density	Example screen	Notes
drawable-ldpi	36 × 36	30 × 30	120	ldpi	Small QVGA	
drawable-mdpi	48 × 48	40 × 40	160	mdpi	Normal HVGA	Default icon in absence of anything else
drawable-hdpi	72 × 72	60 × 60	240	hdpi	Normal WVGA800	
drawable-xhdpi	96 × 96	80 × 80	320	xhdpi	Custom	
drawable	48 × 48	40 × 40	160	mdpi	Normal HVGA	Default icon in absence of anything else

The icon file does not need to be called *icon.png*. As long as all the filenames in all the "drawable" folders are valid and the same, they can be named something else. For example, the icon files could be called *globe.png*. If the filename is changed from the default, the `android:icon` attribute in the `application` element in the manifest file will also need to change from `icon` to `globe`. Open the *AndroidManifest.xml* file. Locate the `application` element and change `android:icon="@drawable/icon"` to `android:icon="@drawable/globe"`.

Remember to give thanks for free stuff; in this case I thank Open Clipart Library contributor "jhnri4."

See Also

Recipe 1.4; *http://developer.android.com/guide/practices/ui_guidelines/icon_design _launcher.html*; *http://www.openclipart.org*; *http://www.getpaint.net*; *http://www.ink scape.org*; *http://www.gimp.org*

6.12 Using Nine Patch Files

Daniel Fowler

Problem

When designing a user interface you want to change the default view backgrounds to fit in with an app's overall style. The backgrounds must be able to scale correctly for variously sized views.

Solution

Use Android's Nine Patch files to provide support for scaling of backgrounds as view sizes change.

Discussion

In the following picture the word Text has a background that is a rounded rectangle (a black border with a gray background). The rectangle has then been uniformly scaled to fit in Longer Text. As a result of scaling, the corners and vertical edges have been distorted to give the rounded rectangle an unbalanced look. Compare that to the second Longer Text where the background has maintained its balance.

To correctly scale the background, selected parts of the image are scaled in a particular direction or not scaled at all. Which parts are scaled and in which direction are shown in this diagram.

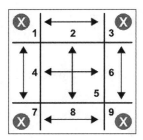

The X indicates that corners are not scaled, the vertical edges are scaled vertically, the horizontal edges are scaled horizontally, and the central area is scaled in both directions. Hence the name Nine Patch:

```
4 corners +
2 vertical edges +
2 horizontal edges +
1 central area
---------------------
9 areas (patches) in total
```

In the following example, the default black border and gray gradient background of an `EditText` is replaced with a solid turquoise background with a black border. The required rounded rectangle is drawn in a graphics program (such as GIMP, *http://www .gimp.org*, or Paint.NET, *http://www.getpaint.net/*). The rectangle is drawn as small as possible (resembling a circle) to support small views. There is a 1-pixel border and transparent background. A version of the rectangle with an orange border is drawn to support focus indication used with keypad navigation.

Android needs to know which proportion of the vertical and horizontal edges need to be scaled, as well as where the view content sits in relation to the background. These factors are determined from indicators drawn within the image. To apply these indicators the draw9patch program supplied in the Android SDK tools folder is used. Start the program and open the background image (drag and drop it onto the draw9patch dialog). The program will expand the image by one pixel all around. It is on this extra 1-pixel edging that indicator lines are drawn. Enlarge the image using the Zoom slider. In the lefthand and top edges, draw the indicator lines to mark which of the vertical and horizontal pixels can be duplicated for scaling. In the righthand and bottom edges, draw the indicator lines to show where content can be positioned.

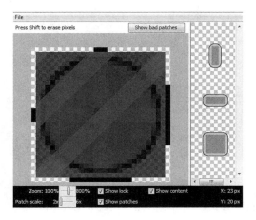

The following diagram shows the right and bottom markers for content placement. If content does not fit in the indicated rectangle, the background image is stretched using the area shown by the left and top markers.

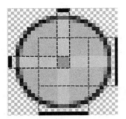

Save the marked-up file in the *res/drawable* folder for a project. Android determines if an image is scaled using Nine Patch scaling instead of uniform scaling via the filename; it must have *.9* before the *.png* file extension. For example, an image file named *turquoise.png* would be named *turquoise.9.png*. To use the background image, reference it in a layout, `android:background="@drawable/turquoise"`. If you are also using another image to indicate view focus, use a selector file—for example, save this XML file in the *drawable* folder as *selector.xml*:

```xml
<?xml version="1.0" encoding="utf-8"?>
    <selector xmlns:android="http://schemas.android.com/apk/res/android">
        <item android:state_focused="true"
          android:drawable="@drawable/turqfocus" />
        <item android:drawable="@drawable/turquoise" />
    </selector>
```

Reference this as `android:background="@drawable/selector"`.

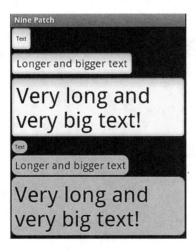

Notice that the new view background is using a little less space than the default (this is useful to know if a project needs a little bit more screen area).

Nine Patch files are not restricted to simple view backgrounds. This Nine Patch file is used to frame a photograph.

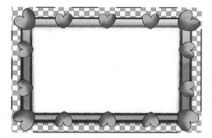

Notice how the left and top scaling indicators are split where detail that must not be scaled (because it would distort) is located.

See Also

http://developer.android.com/guide/topics/graphics/2d-graphics.html#nine-patch

6.13 Creating HTML5 Charts with Android RGraph

Wagied Davids

Problem

You need to visualize data in a chart and be able to interact with the plot/chart via JavaScript.

Solution

As an alternative to creating Android charts in pure Java, create charts using RGraph, an HTML5 JavaScript charts library.

 RGraph uses the HTML5 Canvas component, which is not accommodated in the webkit packaged with Android 1.5. RGraph works nicely and has been tested with Android 2.1 and later.

Discussion

To create a chart with RGraph, follow these steps:

1. Create an assets directory for HTML files; Android internally maps it to *file:/// android_asset/* (note the triple slash and singular spelling of "asset").

2. Copy *rgraphview.html* (see Example 6-19) into it: *res/assets/rgraphview.html*.

3. Create a JavaScript directory: *res/assets/RGraph*.

4. Create the layout (Example 6-20) and the activity (Example 6-21) as in any other Android project.

Example 6-19 shows the HTML using the RGraph library. Figure 6-21 shows the RGraph output.

Example 6-19. HTML using the RGraph library

```
<html>
<head>
<title>RGraph: HTML5 canvas graph library - pie chart</title>

    <script src="RGraph/libraries/RGraph.common.core.js" ></script>
    <script src="RGraph/libraries/RGraph.common.annotate.js" ></script>
    <script src="RGraph/libraries/RGraph.common.context.js" ></script>
    <script src="RGraph/libraries/RGraph.common.tooltips.js" ></script>
    <script src="RGraph/libraries/RGraph.common.zoom.js" ></script>
    <script src="RGraph/libraries/RGraph.common.resizing.js" ></script>
    <script src="RGraph/libraries/RGraph.pie.js" ></script>

  <script>
    window.onload = function ()
    {
        /**
         * These are not angles - these are values.
         * The appropriate angles are calculated
         */
        var pie1 = new RGraph.Pie('pie1', [41,37,16,3,3]); // Create the pie object
        pie1.Set('chart.labels', ['MSIE 7 (41%)', 'MSIE 6 (37%)',
                                  'Firefox (16%)', 'Safari (3%)', 'Other (3%)']);
        pie1.Set('chart.gutter', 30);
        pie1.Set('chart.title', "Browsers (tooltips, context, zoom)");
```

```
                pie1.Set('chart.shadow', false);
                pie1.Set('chart.tooltips.effect', 'contract');
                pie1.Set('chart.tooltips', [
                                            'Internet Explorer 7 (41%)',
                                            'Internet Explorer 6 (37%)',
                                            'Mozilla Firefox (16%)',
                                            'Apple Safari (3%)',
                                            'Other (3%)'
                                          ]
                                         );
                pie1.Set('chart.highlight.style', '3d'); // 2d or 3d; defaults to 3d anyway

                if (!RGraph.isIE8()) {
                    pie1.Set('chart.zoom.hdir', 'center');
                    pie1.Set('chart.zoom.vdir', 'up');
                    pie1.Set('chart.labels.sticks', true);
                    pie1.Set('chart.labels.sticks.color', '#aaa');
                    pie1.Set('chart.contextmenu', [['Zoom in', RGraph.Zoom]]);
                }

                pie1.Set('chart.linewidth', 5);
                pie1.Set('chart.labels.sticks', true);
                pie1.Set('chart.strokestyle', 'white');
                pie1.Draw();

                var pie2 = new RGraph.Pie('pie2', [2,29,45,17,7]); // Create the pie object
                pie2.Set('chart.gutter', 45);
                pie2.Set('chart.title', "Some data (context, annotatable)");
                pie2.Set('chart.linewidth', 1);
                pie2.Set('chart.strokestyle', '#333');
                pie2.Set('chart.shadow', true);
                pie2.Set('chart.shadow.blur', 3);
                pie2.Set('chart.shadow.offsetx', 3);
                pie2.Set('chart.shadow.offsety', 3);
                pie2.Set('chart.shadow.color', 'rgba(0,0,0,0.5)');
                pie2.Set('chart.colors', ['red', 'pink', '#6f6', 'blue', 'yellow']);
                pie2.Set('chart.contextmenu', [['Clear',
                    function () {RGraph.Clear(pie2.canvas); pie2.Draw();}]]);
                pie2.Set('chart.key', ['John (2%)', 'Richard (29%)',
                    'Fred (45%)', 'Brian (17%)', 'Peter (7%)']);
                pie2.Set('chart.key.background', 'white');
                pie2.Set('chart.key.shadow', true);
                pie2.Set('chart.annotatable', true);
                pie2.Set('chart.align', 'left');
                pie2.Draw();
            }
        </script>
    </head>
    <body>

        <div style="text-align: center">
            <canvas id="pie1" width="420" height="300">[No canvas support]</canvas>
            <canvas id="pie2" width="440" height="300">[No canvas support]</canvas>
        </div>
```

```
</body>
</html>
```

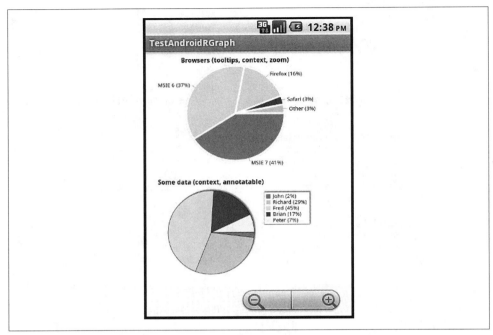

Figure 6-21. RGraph output

Example 6-20. The main.xml file

```xml
<?xml version="1.0" encoding="utf-8"?>
<LinearLayout
    xmlns:android="http://schemas.android.com/apk/res/android"
    android:orientation="horizontal"
    android:layout_width="fill_parent"
    android:layout_height="fill_parent"
    android:background="#FFFFFF">

    <WebView
        android:id="@+id/webview"
        android:layout_width="fill_parent"
        android:layout_height="fill_parent">
    </WebView>
</LinearLayout>
```

Example 6-21. The main activity

```java
import android.app.Activity;
import android.os.Bundle;
import android.webkit.WebChromeClient;
import android.webkit.WebSettings;
import android.webkit.WebView;
```

```
import android.webkit.WebViewClient;

public class Main extends Activity
    {

        /** Called when the activity is first created. */
        @Override
        public void onCreate(Bundle savedInstanceState)
            {
                super.onCreate(savedInstanceState);
                setContentView(R.layout.main);

                // Obtain reference to the WebView holder
                WebView webview = (WebView) this.findViewById(R.id.webview);

                // Get the settings
                WebSettings webSettings = webview.getSettings();

                // Enable JavaScript for user interaction clicks
                webSettings.setJavaScriptEnabled(true);

                // Display Zoom Controls
                webSettings.setBuiltInZoomControls(true);
                webview.requestFocusFromTouch();

                // Set the client
                webview.setWebViewClient(new WebViewClient());
                webview.setWebChromeClient(new WebChromeClient());

                // Load the URL
                webview.loadUrl("file:///android_asset/rgraphview.html");
            }

    }
```

Source Download URL

The source code for this example is in the Android Cookbook repository at *http://github .com/AndroidCook/Android-Cookbook-Examples*, in the subdirectory RGraphDemo (see "Getting and Using the Code Examples" on page xvii).

6.14 Adding a Simple Raster Animation

Daniel Fowler

Problem

You need to add an animated image to a screen.

Solution

Android has good support for user interface animation; it is easy to sequence images using the `AnimationDrawable` class.

Discussion

To create the animation, first the images to be sequenced are generated using a graphics program. Each image represents one frame of the animation; the images will usually be the same size, with changes between each frame as required.

This animation recipe will sequence some traffic light images. The images can be generated using the open source vector graphics program Inkscape (see *http://inkscape .org*). A copy of the image used is available from the Open Clipart Library (*http://www .openclipart.org/*); search for "Traffic Lights Turned Off," select the image, click on the View SVG button, and save the file from your browser. Open the file in Inkscape.

The animation will comprise four images showing the sequence of traffic lights as used in the United Kingdom: red, red and yellow, green, yellow, and back to red. The SVG image has all the lights available—they are just hidden behind a translucent circle. To generate the first image select the circle covering the red light and delete it. Then from the Edit menu use Select All to highlight the whole image. Using the File menu, select Export Bitmap. In the Export Bitmap dialog, under "Bitmap size," enter 150 in the Height box, and choose a directory and filename for the file to be generated—for example, *red.png*. Click the Export button to export the bitmap. Delete the circle covering the yellow light, click Select All again, and export as before to a file; for example, *red_yellow.png*. Use the Edit menu and choose Undo (twice) to cover the red light and yellow light, and then delete the circle covering the green light. Export to *green.png*. Again use undo to cover the green light and delete the circle covering the yellow light. Export the bitmap to *yellow.png* (see Figure 6-22).

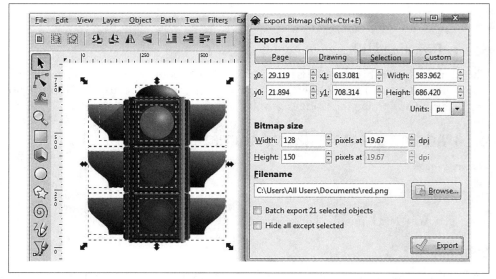

Figure 6-22. The Export Bitmap dialog

Four files are now ready for the animation.

Start an Android project. Copy the four generated files into the *res/drawable* directory. An `animation-list` needs to be defined in the same directory. Create a new file in *res/drawable* called *uktrafficlights.xml*. In this new file add the following:

```xml
<?xml version="1.0" encoding="utf-8"?>
<animation-list xmlns:android="http://schemas.android.com/apk/res/android"
    android:oneshot="false">
    <item android:drawable="@drawable/red" android:duration="2000" />
    <item android:drawable="@drawable/red_yellow" android:duration="2000" />
    <item android:drawable="@drawable/green" android:duration="2000" />
    <item android:drawable="@drawable/yellow" android:duration="2000" />
</animation-list>
```

This lists the images to be animated in the order of the animation and how long each one needs to be displayed (in milliseconds). If the animation needs to stop after running through the images, the attribute `android:oneshot` is set to `true`.

In the layout file for the program an `ImageView` is added whose source is given as *@drawable/uktrafficlights* (i.e., pointing to the created file):

```xml
<?xml version="1.0" encoding="utf-8"?>
<LinearLayout xmlns:android="http://schemas.android.com/apk/res/android"
    android:orientation="vertical"
    android:layout_width="fill_parent"
    android:layout_height="fill_parent">
    <ImageView android:id="@+id/imageView1"
        android:src="@drawable/uktrafficlights"
        android:layout_height="wrap_content"
        android:layout_width="wrap_content"/>
</LinearLayout>
```

In the `Activity` class an `AnimationDrawable` (the Android class that performs the animation) is declared. In `onCreate` it is assigned to the `Drawable` that the `ImageView` uses. Finally, the animation is started by calling the `AnimationDrawable start()` method (there is a `stop()` method available to end the animation if required). The start method is called in `onWindowFocusChanged` to ensure that everything has loaded before the animation starts (it could easily have been started with a button or other type of input). Example 6-22 shows the code for the main activity.

Example 6-22. The main activity

```java
public class main extends Activity {
    AnimationDrawable lightsAnimation;
    @Override
    public void onCreate(Bundle savedInstanceState) {
        super.onCreate(savedInstanceState);
```

```
        setContentView(R.layout.main);
        ImageView lights = (ImageView) findViewById(R.id.imageView1);
        lightsAnimation=(AnimationDrawable) lights.getDrawable();
    }
    @Override
    public void onWindowFocusChanged(boolean hasFocus) {
        super.onWindowFocusChanged(hasFocus);
        lightsAnimation.start();
    }
}
```

Image animations can be useful to add interest to screens and can be used in games or cartoons.

See Also

http://inkscape.org; *http://www.openclipart.org*

6.15 Using Pinch to Zoom

Pratik Rupwal

Problem

You want to use touch capability to change the position of an image viewed on the screen, and use pinch-in and pinch-out movements for zoom-in and zoom-out operations.

Solution

Scale the image as a matrix to apply transformations to it, to show different visual effects.

Discussion

First, a simple ImageView is added inside a FrameLayout in *main.xml*, as shown in the following code:

```
<?xml version="1.0" encoding="utf-8"?>
<FrameLayout
```

```
    xmlns:android="http://schemas.android.com/apk/res/android"
    android:layout_width="fill_parent"
    android:layout_height="fill_parent" >
<ImageView android:id="@+id/imageView"
    android:layout_width="fill_parent"
    android:layout_height="fill_parent"
    android:src="@drawable/nature"
    android:scaleType="matrix" >
</ImageView>
</FrameLayout>
```

Example 6-23 scales the ImageView as a matrix to apply transformations on it.

Example 6-23. Touch listener with scaling

```java
import android.app.Activity;
import android.graphics.Bitmap;
import android.graphics.Matrix;
import android.graphics.PointF;
import android.os.Bundle;
import android.util.FloatMath;
import android.util.Log;
import android.view.MotionEvent;
import android.view.View;
import android.view.View.OnTouchListener;
import android.widget.GridView;
import android.widget.ImageView;

public class Touch extends Activity implements OnTouchListener {
private static final String TAG = "Touch";

// These matrixes will be used to move and zoom image
Matrix matrix = new Matrix();
Matrix savedMatrix = new Matrix();

// We can be in one of these 3 states
static final int NONE = 0;
static final int DRAG = 1;
static final int ZOOM = 2;
int mode = NONE;

// Remember some things for zooming
PointF start = new PointF();
PointF mid = new PointF();
float oldDist = 1f;

@Override
public void onCreate(Bundle savedInstanceState) {
    super.onCreate(savedInstanceState);
    setContentView(R.layout.main);
    ImageView view = (ImageView) findViewById(R.id.imageView);
    view.setScaleType(ImageView.ScaleType.FIT_CENTER); // make the image fit to the center.
    view.setOnTouchListener(this);
}

public boolean onTouch(View v, MotionEvent event) {
```

```java
ImageView view = (ImageView) v;
// make the image scalable as a matrix
view.setScaleType(ImageView.ScaleType.MATRIX);
float scale;

// Handle touch events here...
switch (event.getAction() & MotionEvent.ACTION_MASK) {

case MotionEvent.ACTION_DOWN: //first finger down only
    savedMatrix.set(matrix);
    start.set(event.getX(), event.getY());
    Log.d(TAG, "mode=DRAG" );
    mode = DRAG;
    break;
case MotionEvent.ACTION_UP: //first finger lifted
case MotionEvent.ACTION_POINTER_UP: //second finger lifted
    mode = NONE;
    Log.d(TAG, "mode=NONE" );
    break;
case MotionEvent.ACTION_POINTER_DOWN: //second finger down
    // calculates the distance between two points where user touched.
    oldDist = spacing(event);
    Log.d(TAG, "oldDist=" + oldDist);
    // minimal distance between both the fingers
    if (oldDist > 5f) {
        savedMatrix.set(matrix);
        // sets the mid-point of the straight line between two points where user touched.
        midPoint(mid, event);
        mode = ZOOM;
        Log.d(TAG, "mode=ZOOM" );
    }
    break;

case MotionEvent.ACTION_MOVE:
    if (mode == DRAG)
    { //movement of first finger
        matrix.set(savedMatrix);
        if (view.getLeft() >= -392)
        {
            matrix.postTranslate(event.getX() - start.x, event.getY() - start.y);
        }
    }
    else if (mode == ZOOM) { //pinch zooming
        float newDist = spacing(event);
        Log.d(TAG, "newDist=" + newDist);
        if (newDist > 5f) {
            matrix.set(savedMatrix);
            //thinking I need to play around with this value to limit it**
            scale = newDist/oldDist;
            matrix.postScale(scale, scale, mid.x, mid.y);
        }
    }
    break;
}
```

```
    // Perform the transformation
    view.setImageMatrix(matrix);

    return true; // indicate event was handled
}

private float spacing(MotionEvent event) {
    float x = event.getX(0) - event.getX(1);
    float y = event.getY(0) - event.getY(1);
    return FloatMath.sqrt(x * x + y * y);
}

private void midPoint(PointF point, MotionEvent event) {
    float x = event.getX(0) + event.getX(1);
    float y = event.getY(0) + event.getY(1);
    point.set(x / 2, y / 2);
}
}
```

## CHAPTER 7

Graphical User Interface

7.1 Introduction: GUI

Ian Darwin

Discussion

When Android was being invented, its designers faced many choices whose outcome would determine the success or failure of their project. Once they had rejected all the other smartphone operating systems, both closed and open source, and decided to build their own atop the Linux kernel, they were faced with somewhat of a blank canvas. One important choice was which user interface technology to deploy: Java ME, Swing, SWT, or none of the above.

JavaME (*http://www.oracle.com/technetwork/java/javame/*) is the Java Micro Edition, Sun/Oracle's official standard API for cell phones and other small devices. Java ME is actually a pretty big success story: tens or hundreds of millions of cell phones have a Java Micro Edition runtime inside. And every BlackBerry made since around 2000, and all BlackBerry smartphone applications in the world (before BBX), are based on Java ME. But the Java ME GUI was regarded as too limiting, having been designed for the days when cell phones had really tiny screens.

Swing (*http://java.sun.com/javase/6/docs/technotes/guides/swing/index.html*) is the Java Standard Edition (Desktop Java, Java SE, a.k.a. JDK or JRE) GUI. It is based atop Java's earlier widget toolkit (AWT). It can make some beautiful GUI music in the right hands (*http://filthyrichclients.org/*), but is just too large and uses too much overhead for Android.

SWT is the GUI layer developed for use in the Eclipse IDE (*http://www.eclipse.org/*) itself and in Eclipse rich clients. It is an abstraction layer, and depends on the underlying operating system–specific toolkit (e.g., Win32 in the Microsoft arena, GTK under Unix/Linux, etc.).

The final option, and the one ultimately chosen, was to go it alone. The Android designers thus built their own GUI toolkit designed specifically for smartphones. But they took many good ideas from the other toolkits, and learned from the mistakes that had been made along the way.

To learn any new GUI framework is, necessarily, a lot of work. Making your apps work well in the community of apps for that UI is even more work. Recognizing this, Google has set up the Android Design site (*http://developer.android.com/design/index.html*), mainly aimed at Android 4 (Ice Cream Sandwich). Another set of guidelines that can help is the Android Patterns site (*http://androidpatterns.com*), which is not about coding but about showing designers *how* the Android visual experience is supposed to work. Illustrated, crowd-sourced, and recommended!

One word of terminological warning: the term *widget* has two distinct meanings. All GUI controls such as buttons, labels, and the like are widgets and appear in the `android.widget` package. This package also contains the "layout containers" which are like a combination of `JPanel` and `LayoutManager` in Swing. Simple widgets and layouts are subclassed from `View`, so collectively they are often referred to a view. The other kind of widget is one that can appear on an Android Home screen; these are now called "app widgets" to distinguish them from the basic ones, and are in their own package, `android.appwidget`. This type of widget is commonly used for status displays such as news, weather, friends/social streams, and the like. We have one recipe on app widgets, at the end of this chapter. While we'll try to use the terms *widget* and *app widget* correctly, you sometimes have to infer from the context which meaning is meant.

This chapter covers the main GUI elements in Android. Two following chapters cover the all-important `ListView` component and the "things that go bump in your device": menus, dialogs, toasts, and notifications.

7.2 Understanding and Following User Interface Guidelines

Ian Darwin

Problem

Lots of developers, even good ones, are very bad at user interface design.

Solution

Use the user interface guidelines. But which ones?

Discussion

UI guidelines have been around almost since Xerox PARC invented GUIs in the 1980s and showed them to Microsoft and Apple. A given set of guidelines must be appropriate to the platform. General guidelines for mobile devices are available from several sources. Android.com publishes advice too.

The official Android UI Guidelines (*http://developer.android.com/guide/practices/ui _guidelines/index.html*) are probably as good a starting place as any, especially if you already have some background in UI design. If not, some of the other works discussed in this recipe may help with your background understanding of UI design issues.

For some thoughtful UI pattern notes, see *http://android-developers.blogspot.com/2010/ 05/twitter-for-android-closer-look-at.html*.

There is an article from Research in Motion that is somewhat specific to the BlackBerry platform but may be useful to any mobile designer: see *http://na.blackberry.com/eng/ developers/resources/Newsletter/2010/Featured_Story_Jan_2010.jsp?html*.

One of the oldest GUI guides is Microsoft's *The Gui Guide: International Terminology for the Windows Interface* (*http://www.amazon.com/dp/1556155387*). This was less about UI design than about internationalization; it came with a floppy disk (remember those?) containing recommended translations for common Microsoft Windows GUI element names into a dozen or so common languages. This book is rather dated today.

In the 1980s and 1990s Sun's user interface development was heavily influenced by Xerox PARC, in its Unix OPEN LOOK user interface (long defunct) and in the "Java Look and Feel," respectively. A classic but technology-specific work from this time and place is the *Java Look and Feel Design Guidelines* (*http://www.amazon.com/dp/ 0201775824/*).

A more general work from Sun is *Designing Visual Interfaces: Communication-Oriented Techniques* (*http://www.amazon.com/dp/0133033899*) by Muller and Sano. This is a thorough discussion of the design issues, mostly from a desktop perspective (Mac, Unix, Windows), but the principles spelled out here will be useful in dealing with human-computer interaction issues.

Concluding the desktop front is Microsoft's more recent book *About Face: The Essentials of Interaction Design* (*http://www.amazon.com/dp/0470084111/*). Now in its third edition, this book was originally written by Alan Cooper, known as the "Father of Visual Basic."

7.3 Handling Configuration Changes by Decoupling the View from the Model

Alex Leffelman

Problem

When your device's configuration changes (most frequently due to an orientation change), your `Activity` is destroyed and re-created, making state information difficult to maintain.

Solution

Decouple your user interface from your data model so that the destruction of your `Activity` doesn't affect your state data.

Discussion

It's a situation that every Android developer (except those who read this part of this book in time) runs into with their very first application: "My application works great, but when I change my phone's orientation everything resets!"

By design, when a device's configuration (read: orientation) changes, the Android UI framework destroys the current `Activity` and re-creates it for the new configuration. This enables the designer to optimize the layout for different screen orientations and sizes. However, this causes a problem for the developer who wishes to maintain the state of the `Activity` as it was before the orientation change destroyed the screen. Attempting to solve this problem can lead to many complicated solutions, some more graceful than others. But if we take a step back and design our application wisely, we can write cleaner, more robust code that makes life easier for everyone.

A graphical user interface (GUI) is exactly what its name describes. It is a graphical representation of an underlying data model that allows the user to interface with and manipulate the data. It is *not* the data model itself. Let's talk our way through an example to illustrate why that is an important point to make.

Consider a tic-tac-toe application. A simple main `Activity` for this would most likely include *at bare minimum* a `GridView` (with appropriate `Adapter`) to display the board and a `TextView` to tell the user whose turn it is. When the user clicks a square in the grid, an appropriate X or O is placed in that grid cell. As new Android developers, we find it logical to also include a two-dimensional array containing a representation of the board to store its data so that we can determine if the game is over, and if so, who won (see Example 7-1).

Example 7-1. First version of the TicTacToe activity class

```
public class TicTacToeActivity extends Activity {

    private TicTacToeState[][] mBoardState;

    private GridView mBoard;
    private TextView mTurnText;

    @Override
    public void onCreate(Bundle savedInstanceState) {

        setContentView(R.layout.main);

        mBoardState = new TicTacToeState[3][3];

        mBoard = (GridView)findViewById(R.id.board);
        mTurnText = (TextView)findViewById(R.id.turn_text);

        // ... Set up Adapter, OnClickListeners, etc., for mBoard.
    }
}
```

This is easy enough to imagine and implement, and everything works great. Except that when you turn your phone sideways in the middle of an intense round of tic-tac-toe, you have a fresh board staring you in the face and your inevitable victory is postponed. As described earlier, the UI framework just destroyed your `Activity` and re-created it, calling `onCreate()` and resetting the board data.

While reading the code in Example 7-1, you might have said to yourself, "Hey, that `Bundle savedInstanceState` looks promising!" And you'd be right. For this painfully, almost criminally simple example, you could stick your board data into a `Bundle` and use it to reload your screen. There's even a pair of methods, `onRetainNonConfiguratio nInstance()` and `getLastNonConfigurationInstance()`, that let you pass any `Object` you want from your old, destroyed `Activity`, to your newly created one. For this example you could just pass your `mBoardState` array to your new `Activity` and you'd be all set. But we're going to write big, successful, amazing apps any day now, and that just doesn't scale well with complicated interfaces. We can do better!

This is why separating your GUI from your data model is so handy. Your GUI can be destroyed, re-created, and changed, but the underlying data can survive unharmed through as many UI changes as you can throw at it. Let's separate our game state out into a separate data class (see Example 7-2).

Example 7-2. The TicTacToe class divided

```
public class TicTacToeGame {

    private TicTacToeState[][] mBoardState;

    public TicTacToeGame() {
        mBoardState = new TicTacToeState[3][3];
```

```
        // ... Initialize
    }

    public TicTacToeState getCellState(int row, int col) {
        return mBoardState[row][col];
    }
    public void setCellState(int row, int col, TicTacToeState state) {
        mBoardState[row][col] = state;
    }

    // ... Other utility methods to determine whose turn it is, if the game is over, etc.
}
```

This will not only help us maintain our application state, but it's generally just good object-oriented design.

Now that we have our data safely outside of the volatile `Activity`, how do we access it to build our interface? There are two common approaches: 1) declare all variables in `TicTacToeGame` as `static`, and access them through static methods; 2) design `TicTacToe Game` as a singleton, allowing access to one global instance to be used throughout our application.

I prefer the second option purely from a design preference perspective. We can turn `TicTacToeGame` into a singleton by making the constructor `private` and adding the following lines to the top of the class:

```
private static TicTacToeGame instance = new TicTacToeGame();
public static TicTacToeGame getInstance() {
    return instance;
};
```

Now all we have to do is to obtain the game data, and set our UI elements to appropriately display the data. It's most useful to wrap this in its own function—refre shUI(), perhaps—so that it can be used whenever your `Activity` makes a change to the data. For example, when a user clicks a cell of the board, there need only be two lines of code in the listener: one call to modify the data model (via our `TicTacToeGame` singleton), and one call to refresh the UI.

It may be obvious, but it is worth mentioning that your data classes survive only as long as your application's process is running. If it is killed by the user or the system, naturally the data is lost. That situation necessitates more persistent storage through the filesystem or databases and is outside the scope of this recipe.

This approach very effectively decouples your visual representation of the data from the data itself, and makes orientation changes trivial. Simply calling refreshUI() in your onCreate(Bundle) method is enough to ensure that whenever your `Activity` is destroyed and re-created, it can access the data model and display itself correctly. And as an added bonus, you're now practicing better object-oriented design and will see your code base become cleaner, more scalable, and easier to maintain.

7.4 Creating a Button and Its Click Event Listener

Ian Darwin

Problem

You need to do something when the user presses a button.

Solution

Create a button in your layout. In onCreate(), find it by ViewID. Call its setOnClickListener(). In the OnClickListener implementation, check for the ViewID (if the listener might be used for more than one event source) and perform the relevant action.

Discussion

Creating a button in your layout is simple. Assuming an XML layout:

```
<Button android:id="@+id/start_button"
    android:text="@string/start_button_label"
    android:layout_width="wrap_content"
    android:layout_height="wrap_content"/>
```

In your activity's onCreate() method, find the button by its ViewID (in this example, R.id.start_button). Call its onClickListener() method with an OnClickListener.

In the OnClickListener implementation, check for the ViewID and perform the relevant action:

```
public class Main extends Activity implements OnClickListener {
    public void onCreate() {
        startButton = findViewById(R.id.start_button);
        startButton.setOnClickListener(this);
        ...
    }

    @Override
    public void onClick(View v) {
        switch (v.getId()) {
        case R.id.start_button:
            // Start whatever it is the start button starts...
            ...
        case R.id.some_other_button:
            // etc.
        }
    }
}
```

Any experienced Java programmer would expect to use an anonymous inner class for the onClickListener, as has been done in AWT and Swing since Java 1.1. Due to efficiency, early Android documentation recommended against this, simply having the Activity implement OnClickListener and checking the ViewID (i.e., the Java 1.0 way of doing things). As with Swing, however, the power of devices has gotten much faster, and such old-style ways of doing things are becoming less popular, though you will still see both styles in use for some time.

7.5 Wiring Up an Event Listener in Five Different Ways

Daniel Fowler

Problem

You need to be familiar with the different ways to code event handlers, both to know when to use which approach and because you will come across the various methods in this Cookbook and elsewhere.

Solution

When writing software, very rarely is there only one way to do things. This is true when wiring up `View` events; five methods are shown in this recipe.

Discussion

When a `View` fires an event an application will not respond to it unless it is listening for it. To detect the event a class that implements a listener is instantiated and assigned to the `View`. Take, for example, the `onClick` event, the most widely used event in Android apps. Nearly every `View` that can be added to an app screen will fire the event when the user presses it with her finger (on touch screens) or presses the trackpad/trackball when the `View` has focus. This event is listened to by a class implementing the `OnClickLis` `tener` interface. The class instance is then assigned to the required `View` using the `View`'s `setOnClickListener` method. In the `HandleClick` inner class in "Method 1. The Member class" on page 246 an `Activity` sets the text of a `TextView` (`textview1`) when a `Button` (`button1`) is pressed.

Method 1. The Member class

A nested class called `HandleClick` implementing `OnClickListener` is declared as a member of the `Activity` (`main`). This is useful when several listeners require similar processing that can be handled by a single class.

Example 7-3. The Member class

```
public class Main extends Activity {
    @Override
    public void onCreate(Bundle savedInstanceState) {
        super.onCreate(savedInstanceState);
        setContentView(R.layout.main);
        //attach an instance of HandleClick to the Button
        findViewById(R.id.button1).setOnClickListener(new HandleClick());
    }
```

```
    private class HandleClick implements OnClickListener{
        public void onClick(View arg0) {
        Button btn = (Button)arg0;      //cast view to a button
        // get a reference to the TextView
        TextView tv = (TextView) findViewById(R.id.textview1);
        // update the TextView text
        tv.setText("You pressed " + btn.getText());
    }
    }
}
```

Method 2. The Interface type

In Java an `Interface` can be used as a type. A variable is declared as an `OnClickLis` `tener` and assigned using `new OnClickListener(){...}`, while behind the scenes Java is creating an object (an anonymous class) that implements `OnClickListener`. This has similar benefits to the first method (see Example 7-4).

Example 7-4. The Interface type

```
public class Main extends Activity {
    @Override
    public void onCreate(Bundle savedInstanceState) {
        super.onCreate(savedInstanceState);
        setContentView(R.layout.main);
        //use the handleClick variable to attach the event listener
        findViewById(R.id.button1).setOnClickListener(handleClick);
    }
    private OnClickListener handleClick = new OnClickListener(){
        public void onClick(View arg0) {
        Button btn = (Button)arg0;
        TextView tv = (TextView) findViewById(R.id.textview1);
        tv.setText("You pressed " + btn.getText());
    }
    };
}
```

Method 3. The anonymous inner class

Declaring the `OnClickListener` within the call to the `setOnClickListener` method is common. This method is useful when each listener does not have functionality that could be shared with other listeners. Some novice developers find this type of code difficult to understand. Again, behind the scenes for `new OnClickListener(){...}` Java is creating an object that implements the interface (see Example 7-5).

Example 7-5. The anonymous inner class

```
public class Main extends Activity {
    @Override
    public void onCreate(Bundle savedInstanceState) {
        super.onCreate(savedInstanceState);
        setContentView(R.layout.main);
        findViewById(R.id.button1).setOnClickListener(new OnClickListener(){
```

```
        public void onClick(View arg0) {
        Button btn = (Button)arg0;
        TextView tv = (TextView) findViewById(R.id.textview1);
        tv.setText("You pressed " + btn.getText());
        }
    });
    }
}
```

Method 4. Implementation in Activity

The `Activity` itself can implement the `OnClickListener`. Since the `Activity` object (`main`) already exists, this saves a small amount of memory by not requiring another object to host the `onClick` method. It does make public a method that is unlikely to be used elsewhere. Implementing multiple events will make the declaration of `main` long (see Example 7-6).

Example 7-6. Implementation in Activity

```
public class main extends Activity implements OnClickListener{
    @Override
    public void onCreate(Bundle savedInstanceState) {
        super.onCreate(savedInstanceState);
        setContentView(R.layout.main);
        findViewById(R.id.button1).setOnClickListener(this);
    }
    public void onClick(View arg0) {
    Button btn = (Button)arg0;
    TextView tv = (TextView) findViewById(R.id.textview1);
    tv.setText("You pressed " + btn.getText());
    }
}
```

Method 5. Attribute in View layout for OnClick events

In Android 1.6 and later (API level 4 and upward) the name of a method defined in the `Activity` can be assigned to the `android:onClick` attribute in a layout file (see Example 7-7). This can save you from having to write a lot of boilerplate code.

Example 7-7. Class named in manifest

```
public class Main extends Activity {
    @Override
    public void onCreate(Bundle savedInstanceState) {
        super.onCreate(savedInstanceState);
        setContentView(R.layout.main);
    }
    public void HandleClick(View arg0) {
    Button btn = (Button)arg0;
        TextView tv = (TextView) findViewById(R.id.textview1);
    tv.setText("You pressed " + btn.getText());
    }
}
```

In the layout file the `Button` would be declared with the `android:onClick` attribute.

```
<Button android:id="@+id/button1"
        android:layout_width="wrap_content"
        android:layout_height="wrap_content"
        android:text="Button 1"
        android:onClick="HandleClick"/>
```

The first four methods of handling events can be used with other event types (`onLong Click`, `onKey`, `onTouch`, `onCreateContextMenu`, `onFocusChange`). The fifth method, described in this subsection, only applies to the `onClick` event. The layout file in Example 7-8 declares an additional two buttons; using the `android:onClick` attribute, no additional code is required than that defined earlier; that is, no additional `findView ById` and `setOnClickListener` for each button is required. This should appear as in Figure 7-1.

Example 7-8. Multiple uses of android:onClick

```
<?xml version="1.0" encoding="utf-8"?>
<LinearLayout xmlns:android="http://schemas.android.com/apk/res/android"
    android:orientation="vertical"
    android:layout_width="fill_parent"
    android:layout_height="fill_parent">
  <TextView android:id="@+id/textview1"
            android:layout_width="fill_parent"
            android:layout_height="wrap_content"
            android:text="Click a button."
            android:textSize="20dp"/>
  <LinearLayout android:orientation="horizontal"
                android:layout_width="fill_parent"
                android:layout_height="wrap_content">
    <Button android:id="@+id/button1"
            android:layout_width="wrap_content"
            android:layout_height="wrap_content"
            android:text="Button 1"
            android:onClick="HandleClick"/>
    <Button android:id="@+id/button2"
            android:layout_width="wrap_content"
            android:layout_height="wrap_content"
            android:text="Button 2"
            android:onClick="HandleClick"/>
    <Button android:id="@+id/button3"
            android:layout_width="wrap_content"
            android:layout_height="wrap_content"
            android:text="Button 3"
            android:onClick="HandleClick"/>
  </LinearLayout>
</LinearLayout>
```

Deciding which technique to use to wire up a listener will depend on the functionality required, how much code is reusable across `Views` and how easy the code would be to understand by future maintainers. Ideally the code should be succinct and easy to view.

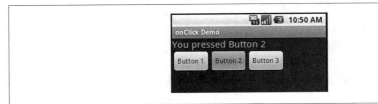

Figure 7-1. OnClick event from android:onClick

One method not shown here is similar to the first method. In the first method it would be possible to save the listener class in a different class file as a public class. Then instances of that public class could be used by other activities, passing the activity's context in via the constructor. However, activities should try to stay self-contained in case they are killed by Android. Sharing listeners across activities is against the ideals of the Android platform and could lead to unnecessary complexity passing references between the public classes.

7.6 Using CheckBoxes and RadioButtons

Blake Meike

Problem

You want to offer the user a set of choices that is more limited than a list.

Solution

Use CheckBoxes, RadioButtons, or Spinners as appropriate.

Discussion

These views are probably familiar to you from other user interfaces. They allow the user to choose from multiple options. Checkboxes are typically used when you want to offer multiple selections with a yes/no or true/false choice for each. Radio buttons are used when only one choice is allowed at a time.

Spinners are similar to combo boxes in some GUI frameworks, and are covered in Recipe 7.8. Android has adapted these familiar components to make them more useful in a touch-screen environment. Figure 7-2 shows the three types of multiple-choice views laid out on an Android application, with the spinner pulled down to show the options. The layout XML file that created the screen in the figure looks like this:

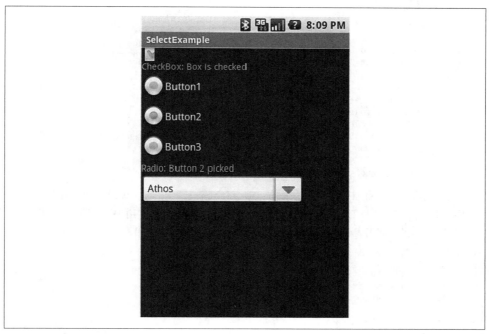

Figure 7-2. A checkbox and three radio buttons

```xml
<?xml version="1.0" encoding="utf-8"?>
<LinearLayout xmlns:android="http://schemas.android.com/apk/res/android"
    android:orientation="vertical"
    android:layout_width="fill_parent"
    android:layout_height="fill_parent"
    >
<CheckBox
  android:id="@+id/cbxBox1"
  android:layout_width="20dp"
  android:layout_height="20dp"
  android:checked="false"
  />
<TextView
  android:id="@+id/txtCheckBox"
    android:layout_width="fill_parent"
    android:layout_height="wrap_content"
    android:text="CheckBox: Not checked"
    />
<RadioGroup
  android:id="@+id/rgGroup1"
  android:layout_width="fill_parent"
  android:layout_height="wrap_content"
  android:orientation="vertical">
  <RadioButton android:id="@+id/RB1" android:text="Button1" />
  <RadioButton android:id="@+id/RB2" android:text="Button2" />
  <RadioButton android:id="@+id/RB3" android:text="Button3" />
```

```
        </RadioGroup>
    <TextView
      android:id="@+id/txtRadio"
      android:layout_width="fill_parent"
      android:layout_height="wrap_content"
      android:text="RadioGroup: Nothing picked"
      />
    <Spinner
      android:id="@+id/spnMusketeers"
      android:layout_width="250dp"
      android:layout_height="wrap_content"
      android:layout_centerHorizontal="true"
      android:layout_marginTop="2dp"
      />
  </LinearLayout>
```

The XML file just lists each view we want on the screen along with the attributes we want. A RadioGroup is really a ViewGroup, so it contains the appropriate RadioButton Views. Example 7-9 is the Java file that responds to user clicks.

Example 7-9. The Chooser examples

```java
package com.oreilly.select;
import java.util.ArrayList;
import java.util.HashMap;
import java.util.List;
import com.google.android.maps.GeoPoint;
import android.app.Activity;
import android.os.Bundle;
import android.util.Log;
import android.view.View;
import android.widget.AdapterView;
import android.widget.ArrayAdapter;
import android.widget.CheckBox;
import android.widget.RadioButton;
import android.widget.RadioGroup;
import android.widget.Spinner;
import android.widget.TextView;
import android.widget.AdapterView.OnItemSelectedListener;

public class SelectExample extends Activity {
  private CheckBox checkBox;
  private TextView txtCheckBox, txtRadio;
  private RadioButton rb1, rb2, rb3;
  private Spinner spnMusketeers;

    /** Called when the activity is first created. */
    @Override
    public void onCreate(Bundle savedInstanceState) {
        super.onCreate(savedInstanceState);
        setContentView(R.layout.main);
        checkBox = (CheckBox) findViewById(R.id.cbxBox1);
        txtCheckBox = (TextView) findViewById(R.id.txtCheckBox);
        txtRadio = (TextView) findViewById(R.id.txtRadio);
        rb1 = (RadioButton) findViewById(R.id.RB1);
```

```
            rb2 = (RadioButton) findViewById(R.id.RB2);
            rb3 = (RadioButton) findViewById(R.id.RB3);
            spnMusketeers = (Spinner) findViewById(R.id.spnMusketeers);
            // React to events from the CheckBox
            checkBox.setOnClickListener(new CheckBox.OnClickListener() {
              public void onClick(View v){
                    if (checkBox.isChecked()) {
                        txtCheckBox.setText("CheckBox: Box is checked");
                    }
                    else
                    {
                        txtCheckBox.setText("CheckBox: Not checked");
                    }
              }
            });
            // React to events from the RadioGroup
            rb1.setOnClickListener(new RadioGroup.OnClickListener() {
              public void onClick(View v){
                  txtRadio.setText("Radio: Button 1 picked");
              }
            });
            rb2.setOnClickListener(new RadioGroup.OnClickListener() {
              public void onClick(View v){
                  txtRadio.setText("Radio: Button 2 picked");
              }
            });
            rb3.setOnClickListener(new RadioGroup.OnClickListener() {
              public void onClick(View v){
                  txtRadio.setText("Radio: Button 3 picked");
              }
            });
            // Set up the Spinner entries
            List<String> lsMusketeers = new ArrayList<String>();
            lsMusketeers.add("Athos");
            lsMusketeers.add("Porthos");
            lsMusketeers.add("Aramis");
            ArrayAdapter<String> aspnMusketeers =
              new ArrayAdapter<String>(this, android.R.layout.simple_spinner_item,
                lsMusketeers);
            aspnMusketeers.setDropDownViewResource
                (android.R.layout.simple_spinner_dropdown_item);
            spnMusketeers.setAdapter(aspnMusketeers);
    // Set up a callback for the spinner
    spnMusketeers.setOnItemSelectedListener(
        new OnItemSelectedListener() {
            public void onNothingSelected(AdapterView<?> arg0) { }
            public void onItemSelected(AdapterView<?> parent, View v,
              int position, long id) {
                // Code that does something when the Spinner value changes
            }
        });
    }
}
```

These Views work as follows:

CheckBox
> The CheckBox View takes care of flipping its state back and forth and displaying the appropriate check mark when the state is true. All you have to do is to create an OnClickListener to catch click events, and you can add whatever code you want to react.

RadioGroup
> As mentioned earlier, the RadioGroup View is really a ViewGroup that contains any number of RadioButton Views. The user can select only one of the buttons at a time, and you capture the selections by setting OnClickListeners for each RadioButton. Note that clicking on one of the RadioButtons does not fire a click event for the RadioGroup.

Taken together, these three Views let you provide a short set of choices and have the user select one or multiple choices from those offered.

7.7 Enhancing UI Design Using Image Buttons

Rachee Singh

Problem

You want to enhance your UI design, but without adding a lot of descriptive text.

Solution

Use an image button. This requires less effort than a text view with descriptive text, since an image can explain the scenario much better than a lot of words can.

Discussion

Making your own image buttons requires defining the characteristics of the button as an XML file that should be placed in */res/drawable*. This XML specifies the three states of an image button:

- Pressed state
- Focused state
- Some other state

For instance:

```
<?xml version="1.0" encoding="utf-8"?>
<selector xmlns:android="http://schemas.android.com/apk/res/android">
    <item android:drawable="@drawable/play_pressed"
          android:state_checked="true" />
    <item android:drawable="@drawable/play" />
</selector>
```

So, for each of these states, the ID of an image is specified (the image present in */res/ drawable* as a *.png* file). When the button is pressed, the `play_pressed` image is displayed. There are two such buttons in the application: the play button and the settings button. In the *.java* file of the application, `onClick` aspect of the buttons can be taken care of. In this recipe, merely a toast is displayed with some appropriate text. Programmers can start a new activity from here or broadcast an intent and many other things based on their requirements.

Figure 7-3 shows the Play button not pressed, and Figure 7-4 shows the Play button pressed.

Figure 7-3. Play button not pressed

Figure 7-4. Play button pressed

Source Download URL

You can download the source code for this example from *https://docs.google.com/leaf ?id=0B_rESQKgad5LYTVjZGMzZmItNDYzNC00YmRmLTlkMTktO TIzNTM0NzVmMDQ2&hl=en_US*.

7.8 Offering a Drop-Down Chooser via the Spinner Class

Ian Darwin

Problem

You want to offer a drop-down choice item.

Solution

Use a `Spinner` object; you can pass the list of selections as an `Adapter`.

Discussion

Generally known as a combo box, the `Spinner` is the analog of the HTML `SELECT` or the Swing `JComboBox`. It provides a drop-down chooser whose values appear to float over the screen when the spinner is clicked. One item can be selected and the floating version will pop down, displaying the selection in the spinner (see Figure 7-5).

Like all standard components, the spinner can be created and customized in XML. In this example, the term *context* is used to indicate when a patient's blood pressure reading was taken (after breakfast, after lunch, etc.), so that the health care practitioner can understand the value *in context* of the patient's day. Here is an excerpt from *res/layout/ main.xml*:

```
<Spinner  android:id="@+id/contextChooser"
          android:layout_height="wrap_content"
          android:layout_width="wrap_content"
          android:prompt="@string/context_choice"/>
```

Ideally the list of values won't be hardcoded but will come from a resource file, so as to be internationalizable. Here is the file *res/values/contexts.xml* containing the XML values for the list of times to choose:

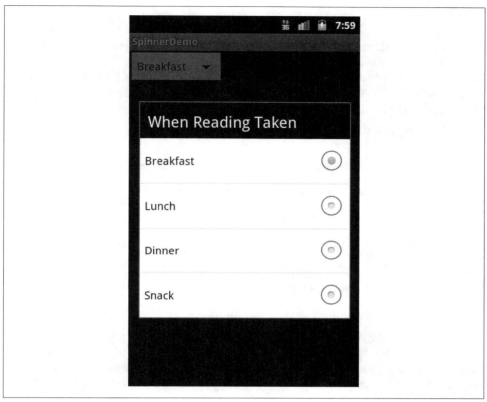

Figure 7-5. Spinner (drop-down) demonstration

```
<?xml version="1.0" encoding="utf-8"?>
<resources>
        <string name="context_choice">When Reading Taken</string>
    <string-array name="context_names">
        <item>Breakfast</item>
        <item>Lunch</item>
        <item>Dinner</item>
        <item>Snack</item>
    </string-array>
</resources>
```

To tie the list of strings to the Spinner at runtime, just locate the Spinner and set the values, as shown here:

```
Spinner contextChooser = (Spinner) findViewById(R.id.contextChooser);
ArrayAdapter<CharSequence> adapter = ArrayAdapter.createFromResource(
        this, R.array.context_names, android.R.layout.simple_spinner_item);
    adapter.setDropDownViewResource(
        android.R.layout.simple_spinner_dropdown_item);
    contextChooser.setAdapter(adapter);
```

That is all you need in order for the spinner to appear, and to allow the user to select items (see Figure 7-5). If you want to know the chosen value right away, you can send an instance of OnItemSelectedListener to the Spinner's setOnItemSelectedListener. This interface has two callback methods, setItemSelected and setNothingSelected. Both are called with the Spinner (but the argument is declared as a ViewAdapter); the former method is called with two integer arguments, the list position and the identity of the selected item.

```
contextChooser.setOnItemSelectedListener(new OnItemSelectedListener() {

    @Override
    public void onItemSelected(AdapterView<?> spinner, View arg1,
            int pos, long id) {
        Toast.makeText(SpinnerDemoActivity.this,
            "You selected " + contextChooser.getSelectedItem(),
            Toast.LENGTH_LONG).show();
    }

    @Override
    public void onNothingSelected(AdapterView<?> spinner) {
        Toast.makeText(SpinnerDemoActivity.this,
            "Nothing selected.", Toast.LENGTH_LONG).show();
    }
});
```

On the other hand, you may not need the value from the Spinner until the user fills in multiple items and clicks a button. In this case, you can simply call the Spinner's getSelectedItem() method, which returns the item placed in that position by the Adapter. Assuming you placed strings in the list, you can just call toString() to get back the given String value.

7.9 Handling Long-Press/Long-Click Events

Ian Darwin

Problem

You want to listen for long-press/long-click events and react to them, without having to manually check for multiple events.

Solution

In Android 3.0 and later, you can use the View class's setLongClickable() and setOnLongClickListener() methods, and provide an OnLongClickListener.

Discussion

Handling long-press events was problematic before the Android Honeycomb release. Recipe 16.15 shows how to handle a long-press by collapsing multiple events into a single event. This method is a bit dodgy, so in version 3.0 explicit support was added; the `View` class now has `setLongClickable(boolean)` to enable/disable long-click support, and the corresponding `setOnLongClickListener(OnLongClickListener)` methods. In this example we listen for long clicks on a `View`, and respond by popping up a `Popup Menu`, which will be modal, and will appear in front of the `ListView`.

```
final View myView = findViewById(R.id.myView);
...
myView.setOnLongClickListener(new OnLongClickListener() {
        @Override
        public boolean onLongClick(View view) {
            PopupMenu p = new PopupMenu(Main.this, view);
            p.getMenuInflater().inflate(
                R.layout.main_popup_menu, p.getMenu());
            p.show();
            return true;
        }
});
```

The pop-up menu will be dismissed when you click one of its items; the list of menu items comes from the XML file *res/menu/main_popup_menu.xml*, which just contains a series of `item` elements with the text for the menu items.

Note that calling `setOnLongClickListener()` has the side effect of calling `setLongClick Enabled(true)`.

Note also that adding an `onClickListener` to a `ListView` (or other multi-item view) does not work as you might expect; the list items simply get dispatched as per a normal click. Instead, you must use the `setOnItemLongClickListener` method which takes, unsurprisingly, an instance of `OnItemLongClickListener()`, which will be invoked when you long-press on an item in the list.

In fact, you can even simplify this for a `ListView` by preinflating your menu and passing it to the `Activity`'s `setContextMenu(view, menu)` method.

Source Download URL

The source code for this example is in the Android Cookbook repository at *http://github .com/AndroidCook/Android-Cookbook-Examples*, in the subdirectory ListViewDemos (see "Getting and Using the Code Examples" on page xvii).

7.10 Displaying Text Fields with TextView and EditText

Ian Darwin

Problem

You want to display text on the screen, either read-only or editable.

Solution

Use a `TextView` when you want the user to have read-only access to text; this includes what most other GUI API packages call a `Label`, there being no explicit `Label` class in `android.widget`. Use an `EditText` when you want the user to have read-write access to text; this includes what other packages may call a `TextField` or a `TextArea`.

Discussion

`EditText` is a direct subclass of `TextView`. Note that `EditText` has many direct and indirect subclasses, many of which are GUI controls in their own right, such as `Check Box`, `RadioButton`, and the like. A further subclass is the `AutoCompleteTextView` which, as the name implies, allows for auto-completion when the user types the first few letters of some data item. As with the recipes in Chapter 9, there is an Adapter to provide the completable text items.

Placing an `EditText` or `TextView` is trivial using the XML layout. Assigning the initial values to be displayed is also simple using XML. It is possible to set the value directly using the following:

```
<TextView android:text="Welcome!"/>
```

However, it is preferable to use a value like "@+string/welcome_text" and define the string in *strings.xml* so that it can be changed and internationalized more readily.

Since `TextView` and `EditText` are used throughout this book, we do not have a sample application that uses them. One is provided with the Android API Examples, called `LabelView`, if you need it.

7.11 Constraining EditText Values with Attributes and the TextWatcher Interface

Daniel Fowler

Problem

You need to limit the range and type of values being input.

Solution

Use appropriate attributes on the `EditText` Views in the layout XML and enhance them by implementing the `TextWatcher` interface.

Discussion

When an application needs input from a user, sometimes only a specific type of value is required; maybe a whole number, a decimal number, a number between two values, or words that are capitalized. When defining an `EditText` in a layout, attributes such as `android:inputType` can be used to constrain what the user is able to type. This automatically reduces the amount of code required later on because there are fewer checks to perform on the data that was entered. The `TextWatcher` interface is also useful for restricting values. In the following example an `EditText` only allows a value between 0 and 100—for example, to represent a percentage. There is no need to check the value because it is all done as the user types.

Here a simple layout has one `EditText`:

```xml
<?xml version="1.0" encoding="utf-8"?>
<LinearLayout xmlns:android="http://schemas.android.com/apk/res/android"
              android:orientation="vertical"
              android:layout_width="fill_parent"
              android:layout_height="fill_parent">
    <EditText android:layout_width="fill_parent"
              android:layout_height="wrap_content"
              android:id="@+id/percent"
              android:text="0"
              android:maxLength="3"
              android:inputType="number"/>
</LinearLayout>
```

The `EditText` is given a starting value of zero with `android:text="0"`, and the number of characters that can be typed has been limited to three with `android:maxLength="3"` because the largest number we need, 100, only has three digits. Finally, the user is restricted to only positive numbers with `android:inputType="number"`.

Within Example 7-10's `Activity` class, an inner class is used to implement the `Text Watcher` interface (the `Activity` itself could be used to implement the interface). The `afterTextChanged()` method is overridden and will be called when the text changes as the user types. In this method the value being typed is checked to see if it is greater than 100. If so, it is set to 100. There is no need to check for values less than zero because they cannot be entered, because of the XML attributes. The `try catch` is need for when all the numbers are deleted, in which case the test for values greater than 100 would cause an exception (trying to parse an empty string).

`TextWatcher` also has a `beforeTextChanged()` and `onTextChanged()` method to be overridden, but they are not used in this example.

Example 7-10. The TextWatcher implementation

```java
class CheckPercentage implements TextWatcher{
    @Override
    public void afterTextChanged(Editable s) {
        try {
            Log.d("Percentage", "input: " + s);
            if(Integer.parseInt(s.toString())>100)
                s.replace(0, s.length(), "100");
        }
        catch(NumberFormatException nfe){}
    }
```

```
@Override
public void beforeTextChanged(CharSequence s, int start, int count, int after) {
    // Not used, details on text just before it changed
// used to track in detail changes made to text, e.g. implement an undo
}
@Override
public void onTextChanged(CharSequence s, int start, int before, int count) {
    // Not used, details on text at the point change made
}
}
```

Finally, in the onCreate() method for the Activity, the class implementing Text Watcher is connected to the EditText using its addTextChangedListener() method:

```
@Override
public void onCreate(Bundle savedInstanceState) {
    super.onCreate(savedInstanceState);
    setContentView(R.layout.main);
    EditText percentage=(EditText) findViewById(R.id.percent);
    percentage.addTextChangedListener(new CheckPercentage());
}
```

Note that it is fine to change the EditText value in afterTextChanged() as its internal Editable class is passed in. However, you cannot change it by altering the CharSequence passed into beforeTextChanged() and onTextChanged().

Running this example, with LogCat running, should show the values being set, as shown in Figure 7-6.

For further details on the attributes supported by EditText see the Android documentation on the TextView, from which EditText is subclassed.

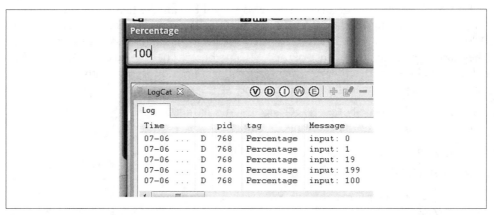

Figure 7-6. TextWatcher in action

Also remember that if you change the value in the EditText, it will cause the afterTextChanged() method to be called again. Care must be taken to ensure that the code using a TextWatcher does not result in endless looping.

It is a good idea to review the attributes that Android views support, as defining them in the XML layout can reduce the amount of code to write.

See Also

http://developer.android.com/reference/android/widget/TextView.html; *http://developer*
.android.com/reference/android/widget/EditText.html; *http://developer.android.com/ref*
erence/android/text/TextWatcher.html

7.12 Implementing AutoCompleteTextView

Rachee Singh

Problem

You want to save the user from typing entire words, and instead auto-complete the entries based on the first few characters the user enters.

Solution

Use the `AutoCompleteTextView` widget that acts as a cross between an `EditText` and a `Spinner`, enabling auto-completion.

Discussion

This layout includes a `TextView` which supports auto-completion. Auto-completion is done using an `AutoTextCompleteTextView` widget. Example 7-11 shows the layout XML code.

Example 7-11. The auto-completion layout

```
<LinearLayout xmlns:android="http://schemas.android.com/apk/res/android"
    android:orientation="vertical"
    android:layout_width="fill_parent"
    android:layout_height="fill_parent"
    >
    <TextView
    android:id="@+id/field"
    android:layout_width="fill_parent"
    android:layout_height="wrap_content"
    />
    <AutoCompleteTextView
    android:id="@+id/autocomplete"
    android:layout_width="fill_parent"
    android:layout_height="wrap_content"
    android:completionThreshold="2"/>

</LinearLayout>
```

The completionThreshold field in the AutoCompleteTextView sets the minimum number of characters that the user has to enter in the TextView so that auto-completion options corresponding to his input to show up.

The Activity (in which we are implementing auto-completion) should implement TextWatcher so that we can override the onTextChanged() method:

```
public class AutoComplete extends Activity implements TextWatcher {
```

We would need to override the unimplemented methods: onTextChanged, beforeTextChanged, and afterTextChanged.

We also require three fields:

- A handle onto the TextView
- A handle onto the AutoCompleteTextView
- A list of String items within which the auto-completion would happen

```
private TextView field;
private AutoCompleteTextView autocomplete;
String autocompleteItems [] = {"apple", "banana", "mango", "pineapple","apricot",
    "orange", "pear", "grapes"};
```

Our onTextChanged() method simply copies the current value of the text field into another text field; this is not mandatory, but in this demo it will show you what values are being set in the auto-completion component.

```
@Override
    public void onTextChanged(CharSequence arg0, int arg1, int arg2, int arg3) {
        field.setText(autocomplete.getText());
    }
```

In the onCreate method of the same activity, we get a handle on the TextView and the AutoCompleteTextView components of the layout. To the AutoCompleteTextView we will set a String adapter:

```
setContentView(R.layout.main);
field = (TextView) findViewById(R.id.field);
autocomplete = (AutoCompleteTextView)findViewById(R.id.autocomplete);
autocomplete.addTextChangedListener(this);
autocomplete.setAdapter(new ArrayAdapter<String>(this,
    android.R.layout.simple_dropdown_item_1line, autocompleteItems));
```

Source Download URL

You can download the source code for this example from *https://docs.google.com/leaf?id=0B_rESQKgad5LYzVkOTdlOGUtODg5My00ZTRmLWIyNTYtMDdiMzA0NjhiNGRk&hl=en_US*i.

7.13 Feeding AutoCompleteTextView Using an SQLite Database Query

Jonathan Fuerth

Problem

Although the Android documentation contains a complete working example of using `AutoCompleteTextView` with an `ArrayAdapter`, just substituting a `SimpleCursorAdapter` into the example does not work.

Solution

There are two extra twists to using `SimpleCursorAdapter` instead of `ArrayAdapter`:

- You need to tell the adapter which column to use to fill the text view after the user selects a completion.
- You need to tell the adapter how to requery based on the user's latest input in the text field. Otherwise, it shows all rows returned by the cursor and the list never shrinks to include the items of actual interest.

Discussion

The following example code would typically be found in the `onCreate()` method of the activity that contains the `AutoCompleteTextView`. It retrieves the `AutoCompleteTextView` from its activity's layout, creates a `SimpleCursorAdapter`, configures that `SimpleCursor Adapter` to work with the `AutoCompleteTextView`, and then assigns the adapter to the view.

The two important differences from the `ArrayAdapter` example in the Android Dev Guide are marked in Example 7-12. They are each covered by a short discussion following the example.

Example 7-12. The onCreate() code

```
final AutoCompleteTextView itemName =
    (AutoCompleteTextView) findViewById(R.id.item_name_view);

SimpleCursorAdapter itemNameAdapter = new SimpleCursorAdapter(
        this, R.layout.completion_item, itemNameCursor, fromCol, toView);

        itemNameAdapter.setStringConversionColumn(                    ❶
        itemNameCursor.getColumnIndexOrThrow(GroceryDBAdapter.ITEM_NAME_COL));

        itemNameAdapter.setFilterQueryProvider(new FilterQueryProvider() { ❷

        public Cursor runQuery(CharSequence constraint) {
            String partialItemName = null;
            if (constraint != null) {
                partialItemName = constraint.toString();
            }
            return groceryDb.suggestItemCompletions(partialItemName);
        }
    });

itemName.setAdapter(itemNameAdapter);
```

❶ With `ArrayAdapter`, there is no need to specify how to convert the user's selection into a `String`. However, `SimpleCursorAdapter` supports using one column for the text of the suggestion, and a different column for the text that's fed into the text field after the user selects a suggestion. Although the most common case is to use the same text for the suggestion as you get in the text field after picking it, this is *not* the default. The default is to fill the text view with the `toString()` representation of your cursor—something like `android.database.sqlite.SQLiteCursor@f00f00d0`.

❷ With `ArrayAdapter`, the system takes care of filtering the alternatives to display only those strings that start with what the user has typed into the text field so far. The `SimpleCursorAdapter` is more flexible, but again, the default behavior is not useful. If you fail to write a `FilterQueryProvider` for your adapter, the `AutoCompleteText View` will simply show the initial set of suggestions no matter what the user types. With the `FilterQueryProvider`, the suggestions work as expected.

7.14 Turning Edit Fields into Password Fields

Rachee Singh

Problem

You need to designate an `EditText` as a password field so that characters the user types will not be visible to "shoulder surfers."

Solution

Android provides the `password` attribute on the `EditText` class, which provides the needed behavior.

Discussion

If your application requires the user to enter a password, the `EditText` being used should be special. It should hide the characters entered. This can be done by adding this property to the `EditText` in XML:

```
android:password="True"
```

Figure 7-7 shows how the password `EditText` would look.

Figure 7-7. EditText with password

7.15 Changing the Enter Key to "Next" on the Soft Keyboard

Jonathan Fuerth

Problem

Several apps, including the Web Browser and the Contacts apps, replace the Enter key on the on-screen keyboard with a Next key that gives focus to the next data entry view. You want to add this kind of polish to your own apps.

Solution

Set the appropriate Input Method Editor (IME) attribute on the views in question.

Discussion

Figure 7-8 shows a simple layout with three text fields (`EditText` views) and a Submit button.

Figure 7-8. Three text fields and a submit button

Note the Enter key in the bottom right. Pressing it causes the currently focused text field to expand vertically to accommodate another line of text. This is not what you normally want!

Here is the code for that layout:

```
<?xml version="1.0" encoding="utf-8"?>
<LinearLayout xmlns:android="http://schemas.android.com/apk/res/android"
```

```
    android:orientation="vertical"
    android:layout_width="fill_parent"
    android:layout_height="fill_parent">
<EditText
    android:layout_width="fill_parent"
    android:layout_height="wrap_content"
    android:text="Field 1" />
<EditText
    android:layout_width="fill_parent"
    android:layout_height="wrap_content"
    android:text="Field 2" />
<EditText
    android:layout_width="fill_parent"
    android:layout_height="wrap_content"
    android:text="Field 3" />
<Button
    android:layout_width="wrap_content"
    android:layout_height="wrap_content"
    android:layout_gravity="center_horizontal"
    android:text="Submit" />
</LinearLayout>
```

Figure 7-9 shows a better version of the same UI, with a Next key where Enter was.

Figure 7-9. Improved UI: Next key

Besides being more convenient for users, this also prevents people from entering multiple lines of text into a field that was only intended to hold a single line.

Here's how to tell Android to display a Next button on your keyboard. Note the `android:imeOptions` attributes on each of the three `EditText` views:

```xml
<?xml version="1.0" encoding="utf-8"?>
<LinearLayout xmlns:android="http://schemas.android.com/apk/res/android"
    android:orientation="vertical"
    android:layout_width="fill_parent"
    android:layout_height="fill_parent">
<EditText
    android:layout_width="fill_parent"
    android:layout_height="wrap_content"
    android:text="Field 1"
    android:imeOptions="actionNext" />
<EditText
    android:layout_width="fill_parent"
    android:layout_height="wrap_content"
    android:text="Field 2"
    android:imeOptions="actionNext" />
<EditText
    android:layout_width="fill_parent"
    android:layout_height="wrap_content"
    android:text="Field 3"
    android:imeOptions="actionDone" />
<Button
    android:layout_width="wrap_content"
    android:layout_height="wrap_content"
    android:layout_gravity="center_horizontal"
    android:text="Submit" />
</LinearLayout>
```

Finally, notice the `actionDone` on the third text field: the button that follows is not focusable in touch mode, and if it was, it wouldn't display a keyboard anyway. As you might guess, `actionDone` puts a Done button where the Enter key normally goes. Pressing the Done button simply hides the keyboard.

There are a number of refinements you can make to the appearance of the software keyboard, including hints about the input type, suggested capitalization, and even select-all-on-focus behavior. They are all worth investigating. Every little touch can make your app more pleasurable to use.

See Also

The Android API documentation for TextView (*http://developer.android.com/reference/android/widget/TextView.html*), especially the section on ImeOptions (*http://developer.android.com/reference/android/widget/TextView.html#attr_android:imeOptions*).

7.16 Processing Key-Press Events in an Activity

Rachee Singh

Problem

You want to intercept the keys pressed by the user and perform actions corresponding to them.

Solution

Override the onKeyDown method in an `Activity`.

Discussion

If the application must react differently at different key presses, you need to override the onKeyDown method in the `Activity`'s Java code. This method takes the `KeyCode` as an argument so that within a `switch-case` block different actions can be carried out (see Example 7-13).

Example 7-13. The onKeyDown method

```
public boolean onKeyDown(int keyCode, KeyEvent service) {
    switch(keyCode) {
        case KeyEvent.KEYCODE_HOME:
            keyType.setText("Home Key Pressed!");
            break;
        case KeyEvent.KEYCODE_DPAD_CENTER :
            keyType.setText("Center Key Pressed!");
            break;
        case KeyEvent.KEYCODE_DPAD_DOWN :
            keyType.setText("Down Key Pressed!");
            break;
        //and so on..
    }
}
```

Source Download URL

You can download the source code for this example from *https://docs.google.com/leaf ?id=0B_rESQKgad5LMDdhMDllYmYtOWE5Mi00MDU0LWE4YWEtODkwN GYwMWVkOTNl&hl=en_US.*

7.17 Let Them See Stars: Using RatingBar

Ian Darwin

Problem

You want the user to choose from a number of identical GUI elements in a group to indicate a value such as a "rating" or "evaluation."

Solution

Use the `RatingBar` widget; it lets you specify the number of stars to appear and the default rating, notifies you when the user changes the value, and lets you retrieve the rating.

Discussion

`RatingBar` provides the newly familiar "rating" user interface experience, where a user is asked to rank or rate something using star classification (the `RatingBar` doesn't display the thing to be rated; that's up to the rest of your app). `RatingBar` is a subclass of `ProgressBar`, extended to display a whole number of icons ("the star") in the bar. Its primary properties are:

numStars
> The number of stars to display (`int`)

rating
> The user's chosen rating (`float`, because of `stepSize`)

stepSize
> The increment for selection (`float`, common values are 1.0 and 0.5, depending on how fine-grained you want the rating to be)

isIndicator
> A `boolean`, set to `true` to make this read-only

These are normally set in the XML:

```
<RatingBar
    android:id="@+id/serviceBar"
    android:gravity="center"
    android:layout_width="wrap_content"
    android:layout_height="wrap_content"
    android:numStars="5"
    android:rating="3"
    android:stepSize="1.0"
    android:isIndicator='false'
    />
```

The RatingBar maintains its rating value internally. You can find out how the user has rated the item in two ways:

- Invoke the getRating() method.
- Provide a change notification listener of type OnRatingBarChangeListener.

The OnRatingBarChangeListener has a single method, onRatingChanged, called with three arguments:

RatingBar rBar
> The event source, a reference to the particular RatingBar

float fRating
> The rating that was set

boolean fromUser
> Is true if set by a user, false if set programmatically

Example 7-14 simulates a customer survey; it creates two RatingBars, one to rate service and another to rate price (the XML for both is identical except for the android:id). In the main program, an OnRatingBarChangeListener is created, to display touchy-feely-sounding feedback for the given rating (the rating is converted to an int and a switch statement is used to generate a message for Toast).

Example 7-14. The RatingBar demo app

```
public class Main extends Activity {
    /** Called when the activity is first created. */
    @Override
    public void onCreate(Bundle savedInstanceState) {
        super.onCreate(savedInstanceState);
        setContentView(R.layout.main);
        OnRatingBarChangeListener barChangeListener = new OnRatingBarChangeListener() {
            @Override
            public void onRatingChanged(RatingBar rBar, float fRating, boolean fromUser) {
                int rating = (int) fRating;
                String message = null;
                switch(rating) {
                case 1: message = "Sorry you're really upset with us"; break;
                case 2: message = "Sorry you're not happy"; break;
                case 3: message = "Good enough is not good enough"; break;
                case 4: message = "Thanks, we're glad you liked it."; break;
                case 5: message = "Awesome - thanks!"; break;
                }
                Toast.makeText(Main.this,
                    message,
                    Toast.LENGTH_LONG).show();
            }
        };
```

```
        final RatingBar sBar = (RatingBar) findViewById(R.id.serviceBar);
        sBar.setOnRatingBarChangeListener(barChangeListener);
        final RatingBar pBar = (RatingBar) findViewById(R.id.priceBar);
        pBar.setOnRatingBarChangeListener(barChangeListener);

        Button doneButton = (Button) findViewById(R.id.doneButton);
        doneButton.setOnClickListener(new OnClickListener() {

            @Override
            public void onClick(View arg0) {
                String message = String.format(
                        "Final Answer: Price %.0f/%d, Service %.0f/%d%nThank you!",
                        sBar.getRating(), sBar.getNumStars(),
                        pBar.getRating(), pBar.getNumStars()
                        );
                // Thank the user
                Toast.makeText(Main.this,
                        message,
                        Toast.LENGTH_LONG).show();
                // And upload the numbers to a database, hopefully...

                // That's all for this Activity, hence this App.
                finish();
            }
        });
    }
}
```

There is more than one RatingBar, so we don't save the value in the listener, because an incomplete survey is not useful; in the Done button action listener, we fetch both values and display them, and this would be the place to save them. Your mileage may vary: it may make more sense to save them in the OnRatingBarChangeListener.

If you're not used to printf-like formatting, the String.format call uses %.0f to format the float as an int, instead of casting it (since we have to do nice formatting anyway). Ideally the format message should be from the XML strings, but it's only a demo program.

The main UI is shown in Figure 7-10.

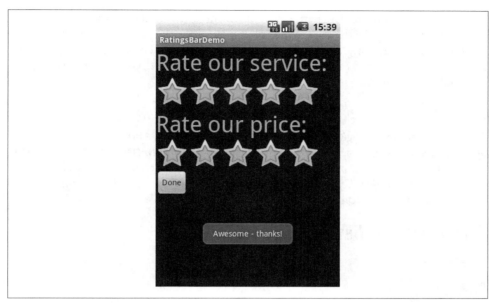

Figure 7-10. Displaying a feedback rating

When the user clicks the Done button, she will see the Farewell message displayed on the desktop window (see Figure 7-11).

Figure 7-11. Completion of the rating/survey

When you wish both to display the current "average" or similar measure ratings from a community *and* allow the user to enter her own rating, it is customary to display the current ratings read-only, and to create a pop-up dialog to enter the user's particular rating. This is described on the Android Patterns website (*http://www.androidpatterns .com/uap_pattern/rating-stars*).

See Also

The discussion on `RatingBar` in the "Form Stuff" tutorial on Android.com (*http://devel oper.android.com/resources/tutorials/views/hello-formstuff.html#RatingBar*); an MVC tutorial that also shows how to construct your own `RatingBar`-like `View` component (*http://www.wiseandroid.com/post/2010/07/19/Use-MVC-and-develop-a-simple-Star -Rating-widget-on-Android.aspx*)

7.18 Making a View Shake

Ian Darwin

Problem

You want a `View` component to shake for a few seconds to catch the user's attention.

Solution

Create an animation in the XML, then call the `View` object's `startAnimation()` method, using the convenience routing `loadAnimation()` method to load the XML.

Discussion

The animation specification is created in XML files in the *anim* directory. In this example, we want the text entry field to be able to shake either left-to-right (to emulate a person shaking his head from side to side, meaning "no" or "I disagree" in many parts of the world) or up and down (a person nodding in agreement). So we create two animations, *horizontal.xml* and *vertical.xml*. Here is *horizontal.xml*:

```xml
<?xml version="1.0" encoding="utf-8"?>
<translate
    xmlns:android="http://schemas.android.com/apk/res/android"
    android:fromXDelta="0"
    android:toXDelta="10"
    android:duration="1000"
    android:interpolator="@anim/cycler"
    />
```

The file *vertical.xml* is identical except it uses `fromYDelta` and `toYDelta`.

The `Interpolator`—the function that drives the animation—is contained in another file, *cycler.xml*, shown here:

```xml
<?xml version="1.0"?>
<cycleInterpolator
    xmlns:android="http://schemas.android.com/apk/res/android"
    android:cycles="5"/>
```

To apply one of the two animations to a `View` component, you need a reference to it. You can, of course, use the common `findViewById(R.id.*)`. You can also use the `Activity` method `getCurrentFocus()` if you are dealing with the current input (focus) view component; this avoids coupling to the name of a particular component, if you know that your animation will always apply to the current input object. In my code I know this is true because the animation start-up is done in an `onClick()` method. Alternatively, you could use the `View` that is passed into the `onClick()` method, but that would make the button shake, not the text field.

I won't show the whole application, but here is the `onClick()` method that contains all the animation code (see Example 7-15):

Example 7-15. The animation code

```java
@Override
public void onClick(View v) {
    String answer = answerEdit.getText().toString();
    if ("yes".equalsIgnoreCase(answer)) {
        getCurrentFocus().startAnimation(
        AnimationUtils.loadAnimation(getApplicationContext(),
        R.anim.vertical));
        return;
    }
    if ("no".equalsIgnoreCase(answer)) {
        getCurrentFocus().startAnimation(
        AnimationUtils.loadAnimation(getApplicationContext(),
        R.anim.horizontal));
        return;
    }
    Toast.makeText(this, "Try to be more definite, OK?",
        Toast.LENGTH_SHORT).show();
}
```

The shaking effect is convenient for drawing the user's attention to an input that is incorrect, but it can easily be overdone. Use judiciously!

7.19 Providing Haptic Feedback

Adrian Cowham

Problem

You want to provide haptic feedback with your application.

Solution

Use Android's haptic controls to provide instant physical feedback.

Discussion

Building confidence among users that their actions had an effect is a requirement for any app on any platform. The canonical example is displaying a progress bar to let users know their action took effect and it's being processed. For touch interfaces this technique still applies, but the advantage of a touch interface is that developers have the opportunity to provide physical feedback, as users are capable of actually feeling the device react to their actions.

I've played with many apps on Android phones and tablets, and the thing I appreciate most is knowing that touching the screen had an effect. I like to know immediately that the app recognized and is reacting to my touch. This reaction comes in three forms: visual, audio, or physical. This recipe discusses how to increase user confidence in your app by providing instant physical feedback through the use of Android's haptic controls.

Android has some stock haptic controls, but if these don't satisfy your needs you can gain control of the device's vibrator for custom feedback.

Custom control of the device's vibrator requires permission. This is something you'll have to explicitly list in your *AndroidManifest.xml* file. If you're paranoid about asking for permission or if you already have a long list of permissions, you may want to use the stock Android haptic feedback options.

 Some devices, such as the Motorola Xoom, don't have a vibrator; therefore, the examples in this recipe will compile and run, but you will not receive haptic feedback.

I'll start by showing the more complicated example first, custom haptic feedback.

Custom haptic feedback using the device's vibrator

Your first step is to request the necessary permission. Add the following line to your *AndroidManifest.xml* file:

```
<uses-permission android:name="android.permission.VIBRATE" />
```

Now define a listener to respond to touch events. It's not shown in Example 7-16, but the `CustomHapticListener` class is actually a private nonstatic inner class of my `Activity`. This is because it needs access to the `Context.getSystemService(...)` method.

Example 7-16. The haptic feedback OnTouchListener implementation

```
private class CustomHapticListener implements OnTouchListener {

  // Duration in milliseconds to vibrate
  private final int durationMs;

  public CustomHapticListener( int ms ) {
    durationMs = ms;
  }

  @Override
  public boolean onTouch( View v, MotionEvent event ) {
    if( event.getAction() == MotionEvent.ACTION_DOWN ){
      Vibrator vibe = ( Vibrator ) getSystemService( VIBRATOR_SERVICE );❶
      vibe.vibrate( durationMs );                                        ❷
    }
    return true;
  }
}
```

❶ and ❷ are the important lines. ❶ gets a reference to the Vibrator service and ❷ vibrates the device. If you have not requested the vibrate permission, ❷ will throw an exception.

Now register the listener. In your `Activity`'s `onCreate(...)` method, you'll need to get a reference to the GUI element you want to attach haptic feedback to and then register the `OnTouchListener` we defined earlier:

```
@Override
public void onCreate( Bundle savedInstance ) {
  Button customBtn = ( Button ) findViewById( R.id.btn_custom );
  customBtn.setOnTouchListener( new CustomHapticListener( 100 ) );
}
```

That's it; you're in control of the haptic feedback. Now we'll move on to using stock Android haptic feedback.

Stock haptic feedback events

First things first: to use stock Android haptic feedback events you must enable this on `View`-by-`View` basis. That is, you must explicitly enable haptic feedback for each `View`. You can enable haptic feedback declaratively in your layout file or programmatically in Java. To enable haptic feedback in your layout, simply add the `android:hapticFeed` `backEnabled="true"` attribute to your `View`(s). Here's an abbreviated example:

```
<button android:hapticFeedbackEnabled="true">
</button>
```

Here's how you do the same thing in code:

```
Button keyboardTapBtn = ( Button ) findViewById( btnId );
keyboardTapBtn.setHapticFeedbackEnabled( true );
```

Now that haptic feedback has been enabled, the next step is to register an `OnTouchLis`
`tener` and then perform the actual feedback. Example 7-17 is an example of registering
an `OnTouchListener` and performing haptic feedback when a user touches the view.

Example 7-17. Haptic feedback demo app

```
// Initialize some buttons with the stock Android haptic feedback values
private void initializeButtons() {
    // initialize the buttons with the standard haptic feedback options
    initializeButton( R.id.btn_keyboardTap, HapticFeedbackConstants.KEYBOARD_TAP );❶
    initializeButton( R.id.btn_longPress,   HapticFeedbackConstants.LONG_PRESS );  ❷
    initializeButton( R.id.btn_virtualKey,  HapticFeedbackConstants.VIRTUAL_KEY ); ❸
}

// helper method to initialize single buttons and register an OnTouchListener
// to perform the haptic feedback
private void initializeButton( int btnId, int hapticId ) {
    Button btn = ( Button ) findViewById( btnId );
    btn.setOnTouchListener( new HapticTouchListener( hapticId ) );
}

// Class to handle touch events and respond with haptic feedback
private class HapticTouchListener implements OnTouchListener {

    private final int feedbackType;

    public HapticTouchListener( int type ) { feedbackType = type; }

    public int feedbackType() { return feedbackType; }

    @Override
    public boolean onTouch(View v, MotionEvent event) {
        // only perform feedback when the user touches the view, as opposed
        // to lifting a finger off the view
        if( event.getAction() == MotionEvent.ACTION_DOWN ){
            // perform the feedback
            v.performHapticFeedback( feedbackType() );❹
        }
        return true;
    }
}
```

You'll notice on lines ❶ through ❸ I'm initializing three different buttons with three
different haptic feedback constants. These are Android's stock values; two of the three
seem to provide exactly the same feedback. Example 7-17 is part of a test app I wrote
to demonstrate haptic feedback and I could not tell the difference between `HapticFeed`
`backConstants.LONG_PRESS` and `HapticFeedbackConstants.KeyboardTap`. Also, `Haptic`
`FeedbackConstants.VIRTUAL_KEY` does not appear to provide any feedback when tested.

❹ is where the haptic feedback is performed. All in all, providing haptic feedback is
pretty simple, but remember that if you want control of the device's vibrator you must
request permission in your *AndroidManifest.xml* file. If you choose to use the stock

Android haptic feedback options, make sure you enable haptic feedback for your views either in the layout or programmatically.

See Also

http://mytensions.blogspot.com/2011/03/androids-haptic-feedback.html

Source Download URL

You can download the source code for this example from *https://docs.google.com/leaf ?id=0BwH86cQEzwiZZjZiMThmM2EtZDk3Zi00NTViLTk0NjYtN DU2YzI5MjVmMzYw&hl=en&authkey=CJu58JcL.*

7.20 Navigating Different Activities Within a TabView

Pratik Rupwal

Problem

You want to change from an activity within a tab view to another activity within the same tab.

Solution

Replace the content view of the tab by the new activity you want to move to.

Discussion

When a "calling" activity within a TabView calls another activity through an intent the TabView gets replaced by the view of the called activity. To show the called activity within the TabView we can replace the view of the calling activity with the view of the called activity so that the TabView remains stable. To achieve this we need to extend the calling activity from ActivityGroup rather than Activity.

In Example 7-18 the Calling activity extended from ActivityGroup has been set within a TabView.

Example 7-18. Replacing the activity within a tab

```
//'Calling' activity.
public class Calling extends ActivityGroup implements OnClickListener
{
    Button b1;
    Intent i1;
    /** Called when the activity is first created.*/
        @Override
        public void onCreate(Bundle savedInstanceState)
        {
        super.onCreate(savedInstanceState);
            setContentView(R.layout.calling);
        b1=(Button)findViewById(R.id.changeactivity);
        b1.setOnClickListener();
    }
    public void onClick(View view)
    {
        // This creates an intent to call the 'Called' activity
        i1=new Intent(this.getBaseContext(),Called.class);
        // calls the method to replace View.
        replaceContentView("Called", i1);
    }
    // This method is used to replace the view of 'Calling' activity by 'Called' activity.
    public void replaceContentView(String id, Intent newIntent)
    {
        // Obtain the view of 'Called' activity using its Intent 'newIntent'
        View view = getLocalActivityManager().startActivity(id,
            newIntent.addFlags(Intent.FLAG_ACTIVITY_CLEAR_TOP)) .getDecorView();
        //set the above view to the content of 'Calling' activity.
        this.setContentView(view);
    }
}
```

The "called activity" can also call another activity (say CalledSecond), as below:

```
//'Called activity'
public class Called extends Activity implements OnClickListener
{
    Button b1;
    Intent i1;
    Calling caller;
    /** Called when the activity is first created.*/
        @Override
        public void onCreate(Bundle savedInstanceState)
        {
        super.onCreate(savedInstanceState);
            setContentView(R.layout.called);
        b1=(Button)findViewById(R.id.changeactivity);
        b1.setOnClickListener();
    }
    public void onClick(View view)
    {
        // This creates an intent to call the 'CalledSecond' activity
        i1=new Intent(this.getBaseContext(),CalledSecond.class);
        /* 'CalledSecond' can be any activity, even the
```

```
        * 'Calling'(In case backward navigation is required)
        */

       // Initialize the object of the 'Calling' class.
       caller=(Calling)getParent();
       // calls the method to replace View.
       caller.replaceContentView("CalledSecond", i1);
    }
}
```

7.21 Creating a Custom Title Bar

Shraddha Shravagi

Problem

You cannot have any buttons or custom text in the standard title bar, the part that normally contains your application name at the top of your window.

Solution

Implement your own title bar by following these steps:

1. Create an XML file for the title bar.
2. Create a class that uses the title bar and implements the button functionality.
3. Change your layout files.
4. Extend your activities from the custom class that you created in step 2.

Discussion

Example 7-19 shows the *maintitlebar.xml* file, which has one text view and three image buttons, with orientation set to horizontal.

Example 7-19. The maintitlebar.xml file

```
    <RelativeLayout xmlns:android=
       "http://schemas.android.com/apk/res/android"
  android:layout_width="fill_parent" android:layout_height="40dp"
  android:orientation="horizontal" android:paddingLeft="5dp"
  >

  <TextView android:id="@+id/title" android:layout_width="wrap_content"
     android:layout_height="wrap_content"
     android:text="Symphony's GHealth Demo"
     />
     <View android:id="@+id/View01" android:layout_width="1dp"
      android:layout_height="500dip"
      android:background="#2B497B"  android:layout_toLeftOf="@+id/facebookBtn">
   </View>
  <!-- Facebook button -->
   <ImageView android:src="@drawable/icon_facebook"
```

```
        android:layout_toLeftOf="@+id/twitterBtn" android:layout_width="28dp"
        android:layout_height="28dp" android:id="@id/facebookBtn"
        android:clickable="true" />
    <!-- Twitter button -->
    <ImageView android:src="@drawable/icon_twitter"
        android:clickable="true"
        android:layout_width="28dp" android:layout_height="28dp"
        android:id="@id/twitterBtn"
        android:layout_marginLeft="3dp" android:layout_marginRight="3dp"
        android:layout_toLeftOf="@+id/linkedinBtn" />
    <!-- Linkedin button -->
    <ImageView android:src="@drawable/icon_linkedin"
        android:layout_width="28dp"
        android:layout_height="28dp" android:clickable="true"
        android:layout_alignParentRight="true"
        android:id="@id/linkedinBtn" />
</RelativeLayout>
```

Example 7-20 shows the most important class: the window activity. As you can see in the code, first we have to request the custom title bar, then set the layout file, and finally set the title bar.

Example 7-20. The window activity

```
    public class CustomWindow extends Activity {
    protected TextView title;
    protected ImageView icon;
    protected void onCreate(Bundle savedInstanceState) {
        super.onCreate(savedInstanceState);
        // Request for custom title bar
        requestWindowFeature(Window.FEATURE_CUSTOM_TITLE);
        //set to your layout file
        setContentView(R.layout.main);
        //Set the titlebar layout
        getWindow().setFeatureInt(Window.FEATURE_CUSTOM_TITLE, R.layout.maintitlebar);
    }
    public void facebookBtnClicked(View v)
    {
            // Handle the button click event
    }
    public void twitterBtnClicked(View v)
    {
            // Handle the button click event
    }
    public void linkedinBtnClicked(View v)
    {
            // Handle the button click event
    }
}
```

For every layout file where you want to implement the custom title bar use match_par
ent in layout_height and layout_width, like so:

```
        <LinearLayout android:id="@+id/LinearLayout01"
        android:layout_width="match_parent" android:layout_height="match_parent"
```

```
xmlns:android="http://schemas.android.com/apk/res/android"
android:orientation="vertical" android:background="#E5E5E5">
```

Once you've extended your activity from the custom class, here's how your activity should look:

```
//CustomWindow will take care of loading the title bar
public class Credentials extends CustomWindow
{
//set the layout file
setContentView(R.layout.login);
}
```

Figure 7-12 shows how your activity should look.

Figure 7-12. Custom title bar

You do not have to use a separate class to implement the title bar, but it is a good coding practice.

7.22 Formatting Numbers

Ian Darwin

Problem

You need to format numbers, because the default formatting of `Double.toString()` and friends does not give you enough control over how the results are displayed.

Solution

Use `String.format()` or one of the `NumberFormat` subclasses.

Discussion

The `printf()` function was included in the C programming language in the 1970s, and it has been used in many other languages since, including Java. Here's a simple `printf` example in Java SE:

```
System.out.printf("Hello %s at %s%n", userName, time);
```

The preceding example could be expected to print something like this:

```
Hello Robin at Wed Jun 16 08:38:46 EDT 2010
```

Since we don't use `System.out` in Android, you'll be relieved to note that you can get the same string that would be printed, for putting it into a view, by using:

```
String msg = String.format("Hello %s at %s%n", userName, time);
```

If you haven't seen `printf` before, the first argument is obviously the format code string, and any number of other arguments (`userName` and `time`) are values to be formatted. The format codes begin with a percent sign (%) and have at least one "type" code; Table 7-1 shows common type codes.

Table 7-1. Some common format codes

Character	Meaning
s	String (convert primitive values using defaults; convert objects by `toString`)
d	Decimal integer (`int`, `long`)
f	Floating point (`float`, `double`)
n	Newline
t	Time/date formats, Java-specific; see the discussion referred to in the "See Also" section at the end of the recipe

The default date formatting is pretty ugly, so we often need to expand on it. The `printf` formatting capabilities are actually housed in the `java.util.Formatter` class, to which reference should be made for the full details of its formatting language.

Unlike `printf` in other languages you may have used, all these format routines optionally allow you to refer to arguments by their number, by putting a number plus a dollar sign after the % lead-in but before the formatting code proper; for example, `%2$3.1f` means to format the second argument as a decimal number with three characters and one digit after the decimal place. This numbering can be used for two purposes: to change the order in which arguments print (often useful with internationalization), and to refer to a given argument more than once. The date/time format character t requires a second character after it, such as Y for the year, m for the month, and so on. Here we take the `time` argument and extract several fields from it:

```
msg = String.format("Hello at %1$tB %1$td, %1$tY%n", time);
```

This might format as July 4, 2010.

To print numbers with a specific precision, you can use f with a width and a precision, such as:

```
msg = String.format("Latitude: %10.6f", latitude);
```

This might yield:

```
Latitude: -79.281818
```

While such formatting is OK for specific uses such as latitudes and longitudes, for general use such as currencies, it may give you too much control.

General formatters

Java has an entire package, `java.text`, that is full of formatting routines as general and flexible as anything you might imagine. As with `printf`, it has an involved formatting language, described in the online documentation page. Consider the presentation of numbers. In North America, the number "one thousand twenty-four and a quarter" is written 1,024.25; in most of Europe it is 1 024,25, and in some other part of the world it might be written 1.024,25. The formatting of currencies and percentages is equally varied. Trying to keep track of this yourself would drive the average software developer around the bend rather quickly.

Fortunately, the `java.text` package includes a `Locale` class. Furthermore, the Java or Android runtime automatically sets a default `Locale` object based on the user's environment; this code works the same on desktop Java as it does in Android. To provide formatters customized for numbers, currencies, and percentages, the `NumberFormat` class has static factory methods that normally return a `DecimalFormat` with the correct pattern already instantiated. A `DecimalFormat` object appropriate to the user's locale can be obtained from the factory method `NumberFormat.getInstance()` and manipulated using set methods. Surprisingly, the method `setMinimumIntegerDigits()` turns out to be the easy way to generate a number format with leading zeros. Example 7-21 is an example.

Example 7-21. Number formatting demo

```java
import java.text.NumberFormat;

/*
 * Format a number our way and the default way.
 */
public class NumFormat2 {
    /** A number to format */
    public static final double data[] = {
```

```
       0, 1, 22d/7, 100.2345678
};

public static void main(String[] av) {
    // Get a format instance
    NumberFormat form = NumberFormat.getInstance();

    // Tailor it to look like 999.99[99]
    form.setMinimumIntegerDigits(3);
    form.setMinimumFractionDigits(2);
    form.setMaximumFractionDigits(4);

    // Now print using it.
    for (int i=0; i<data.length; i++)
        System.out.println(data[i] + "\tformats as " +
            form.format(data[i]));
    }
}
```

This prints the contents of the array using the NumberFormat instance form. We show running it as a main program instead of in an Android application just to isolate the effects of the NumberFormat.

For example, $ java NumFormat2 0.0 formats as 000.00; with argument 1.0 it formats as 001.00; 3.142857142857143 formats as 003.1429; and 100.2345678 formats as 100.2346.

You can also construct a DecimalFormat with a particular pattern or change the pattern dynamically using applyPattern(). Table 7-2 shows some of the more common pattern characters.

Table 7-2. DecimalFormat pattern characters

Character	Explanation
#	Numeric digit (leading zeros suppressed)
0	Numeric digit (leading zeros provided)
.	Locale-specific decimal separator (decimal point)
,	Locale-specific grouping separator (comma in English)
-	Locale-specific negative indicator (minus sign)
%	Shows the value as a percentage
;	Separates two formats: the first for positive and the second for negative values
'	Escapes one of the above characters so that it appears as itself
Anything else	Appears as itself

The NumFormatTest program uses one DecimalFormat to print a number with only two decimal places and a second to format the number according to the default locale, as shown in Example 7-22.

Example 7-22. NumberFormat demo Java SE program

```java
import java.text.DecimalFormat;
import java.text.NumberFormat;

public class NumFormatDemo {
    /** A number to format */
    public static final double intlNumber = 1024.25;
    /** Another number to format */
    public static final double ourNumber = 100.2345678;

    public static void main(String[] av) {

        NumberFormat defForm = NumberFormat.getInstance();
        NumberFormat ourForm = new DecimalFormat("##0.##");
        // toPattern() will reveal the combination of #0., etc.
        // that this particular Locale uses to format with
        System.out.println("defForm's pattern is " +
            ((DecimalFormat)defForm).toPattern());
        System.out.println(intlNumber + " formats as " +
            defForm.format(intlNumber));
        System.out.println(ourNumber + " formats as " +
            ourForm.format(ourNumber));
        System.out.println(ourNumber + " formats as " +
            defForm.format(ourNumber) + " using the default format");
    }
}
```

This program prints the given pattern and then formats the same number using several formats:

```
$ java NumFormatTest
defForm's pattern is #,##0.###
1024.25 formats as 1,024.25
100.2345678 formats as 100.23
100.2345678 formats as 100.235 using the default format
```

See Also

Chapter 10 of *Java Cookbook* by Ian F. Darwin (O'Reilly); Part VI of *Java I/O* by Elliotte Rusty Harold (O'Reilly)

7.23 Formatting with Correct Plurals

Ian Darwin

Problem

You're displaying something like "Found "+ n + " items", but in English, "Found 1 reviews" is ungrammatical. You want "Found 1 review" for the case n==1.

Solution

For simple, English-only results, use a conditional statement. For better results, that can be internationalized, use a `ChoiceFormat`. On Android, you can use `<plural>` in an XML resources file.

Discussion

The "quick and dirty" method is to use Java's ternary operator (`cond ? trueval : falseval`) in a string concatenation. Since in English, for most nouns, both zero and plurals get an *s* appended to the noun in English ("no books, one book, two books"), we need only test for `n==1`.

```
// FormatPlurals.java
public static void main(String argv[]) {
  report(0);
  report(1);
  report(2);
}
/** report -- using conditional operator */
public static void report(int n) {
  System.out.println("Found " + n + " item" + (n==1?"":"s"));
}
```

Running this on Java SE as a main program shows the following output:

```
$ java FormatPlurals
Found 0 items
Found 1 item
Found 2 items
$
```

The final `println()` statement is short for:

```
if (n==1)
  System.out.println("Found " + n + " item");
else
  System.out.println("Found " + n + " items");
```

This is a lot longer, in fact, so Java's ternary conditional operator is worth learning.

Of course, you can't use this arbitrarily, because English is a strange and somewhat idiosyncratic language. Some nouns, such as *bus*, require "es" at the end, while others, such as *cash*, are collective nouns with no plural (you can have two flocks of geese or two stacks of cash, but you cannot have "two geeses" or "two cashes"). Some nouns, such as *fish*, can be considered plural as is, although *fishes* is also a correct plural.

A better way

The `ChoiceFormat` class from `java.text` is ideal for handling plurals; it lets you specify singular and plural (or, more generally, range) variations on the noun. It is capable of more, but in Example 7-23 I'll show only a couple of the simpler uses. I specify the values 0, 1, and 2 (or more), and the string values to print corresponding to each number. The numbers are then formatted according to the range they fall into.

Example 7-23. Formatting plurals using ChoiceFormat

```java
import java.text.*;

/**
 * Format a plural correctly, using a ChoiceFormat.
 */
public class FormatPluralsChoice extends FormatPlurals {

    // ChoiceFormat to just give pluralized word
    static double[] limits = { 0, 1, 2 };
    static String[] formats = { "reviews", "review", "reviews"};
    static ChoiceFormat pluralizedFormat =
        new ChoiceFormat(limits, formats);

    // ChoiceFormat to give English text version, quantified
    static ChoiceFormat quantizedFormat = new ChoiceFormat(
        "0#no reviews|1#one review|1<many reviews");

    // Test data
    static int[] data = { -1, 0, 1, 2, 3 };

    public static void main(String[] argv) {
        System.out.println("Pluralized Format");
        for (int i : data) {
            System.out.println("Found " + i + " " +
                pluralizedFormat.format(i));
        }

        System.out.println("Quantized Format");
        for (int i : data) {
            System.out.println("Found " +
                quantizedFormat.format(i));
        }
    }
}
```

Either of these loops generates similar output to the basic version. The code using the `ChoiceFormat` is slightly longer, but more general, and lends itself better to internationalization. Put the string for the "quantized" form constructor into *strings.xml* and it will be part of your localization actions.

Best way of all (Android-only)

Create a file in */res/values/<somefilename>.xml* containing something like this:

```xml
<?xml version="1.0" encoding="utf-8"?>
<resources>
<plurals name="numberOfSongsAvailable">
<item quantity="one">One item found.</item>
<item quantity="other">%d items found.</item>
```

```
    </plurals>
    </resources>
```

In your code you then use the following:

```
    int count = getNumberOfsongsAvailable();
    Resources res = getResources();
    String songsFound = res.getQuantityString(R.plurals.numberOfSongsAvailable, count);
```

This part was suggested by Tomas Persson.

See Also

For the Android-only way, see *http://developer.android.com/guide/topics/resources/ string-resource.html#Plurals*.

Source Download URL

You can download the source code for this example from *http://javacook.darwinsys .com/javasrc/numbers/FormatPluralsChoice.java*i.

7.24 Starting a Second Screen from the First

Daniel Fowler

Problem

New app developers need a simple example on how to open another screen, thus understanding how Android handles UI creation.

Solution

Building upon the "Hello, World" Eclipse example, load another screen from a new button to demonstrate the principles of starting a new UI screen.

Discussion

An Android application will interact with a user through one or more screens. Each screen presents information and UI elements, such as buttons, lists, sliders, edit boxes, and many others. The number of screens depends upon the required functionality of the app and the type of Android device. A low-cost Android phone may have a 2.5-inch display, an expensive phone may have a 4.5-inch display, and a tablet may have a 7-inch or 10-inch display. An app may only need one screen for functionality on a tablet, two or three screens on a high-end phone, or four or five on a low-cost phone.

Each screen presented to the user is controlled by an `Activity`. The `Activity` is responsible for creating and displaying the screen and managing the UI elements. The Android `View` is the basic building block for UIs. Each screen element, such as a `Button` or `EditText`, is provided in the package `android.widget`. Screen elements are derived from `View`. They are placed onto the screen within containers derived from a `ViewGroup`—for example, a `LinearLayout` (`ViewGroup`s are also derived from `View`). A variety of `View Group` layouts can be used, including horizontal, vertical, table, grid, and others (see Figure 7-13).

The Home screens can hold special `View` types commonly referred to as *widgets*; these are small UI gadgets that can be used to provide feedback from an app to the user without the need for a full app to be open. These *app widgets* should not be confused with the package `android.widget`. The latter holds the various types of screen elements, while the former is the commonly used name for Home screen gadgets. App widgets are defined using `RemoteViews` which are also part of the `android.widget` package.

You can see the many types of `View`s and `ViewGroup`s available in Android by opening or creating an Android layout resource file in Eclipse (in the project folder *res/layout*). When the resource file is open click on the Graphical Layout tab at the bottom of the editor. A toolbar of all available UI elements will be shown on the left of the editor. It is possible to filter by API level using the drop down toward the top right of the editor pane.

You can define a `Fragment`, which is a reusable piece of screen. You can also lay out a `Fragment` using `ViewGroup`s and `View`s. You can then use the `Fragment` on more than one screen, thus defining a section of UI once when the same section needs to be used on several screens.

As soon as an app has more than one screen defined there will be a need to load the second screen from the first. In other operating systems a second screen is often loaded directly by the first screen. Due to the design of Android an app can never directly start a new screen; it has to ask the Android operating system to start it. This is because Android was designed for mobility from the start. Android needs full control of an app to enable efficient handling of events outside of the app. Such events can include those that must interrupt the user, such as a telephone call or low-battery condition; and those that notify the user, such as incoming mail or a reminder firing, causing the user to leave the app to deal with the notification. The user may also open another app. A

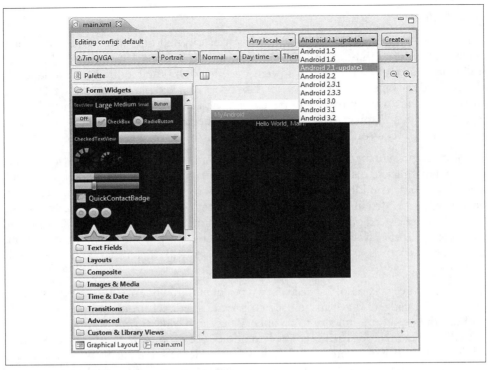

Figure 7-13. Available views in the visual palette

variety of things can happen that will need Android to have fine control of how an app executes and responds. When Android starts a screen it knows what is running and their state. Android can dispatch messages to the activities and they can react to unexpected events accordingly. This is also why an app does not have a main method for programs as on other systems (as mentioned in Recipe 1.6). A main method is not required because Android itself is controlling the start-up.

To get a screen up and running in an app the following is required:

1. The definition of the screen must be composed in a layout.
2. An `Activity` must be defined in a Java class file to handle the screen.
3. Android must be notified that the `Activity` exists, via the app's manifest file.
4. The app must tell Android when it is required to start the new screen.

As an example, we can add another screen to the MyAndroid app in Recipe 1.4. The new screen will also contain a simple message and will be started when a button is pressed on the opening screen. Open Eclipse and open the `MyAndroid` project as created in the *Hello World* recipe. First we will add three strings: one for the new screen's title, one for the message on the new screen, and one for the caption for the button that will be used to start the new screen. In the project tree in the Package Explorer open the *strings.xml* file in the *res/values* folder. Add three strings, one with the name `screen2Title` with value `Screen 2`, one named `hello2` with the value `Hello! Again.`, and one named `next` with the value `Next`. The *strings.xml* file will look like this:

```xml
<?xml version="1.0" encoding="utf-8"?>
<resources>
    <string name="hello">Hello World, Main!</string>
    <string name="app_name">MyAndroid</string>
    <string name="screen2Title">Screen 2</string>
    <string name="hello2">Hello! Again.</string>
    <string name="next">Next</string>
</resources>
```

From the File menu (or using the context menu on the project tree) select New and then *Android XML File*. Set the following fields in the dialog that opens, keeping all others at their defaults (see Figure 7-14):

File	secondscreen.xml
Type of resource	Layout
Folder	/res/layout

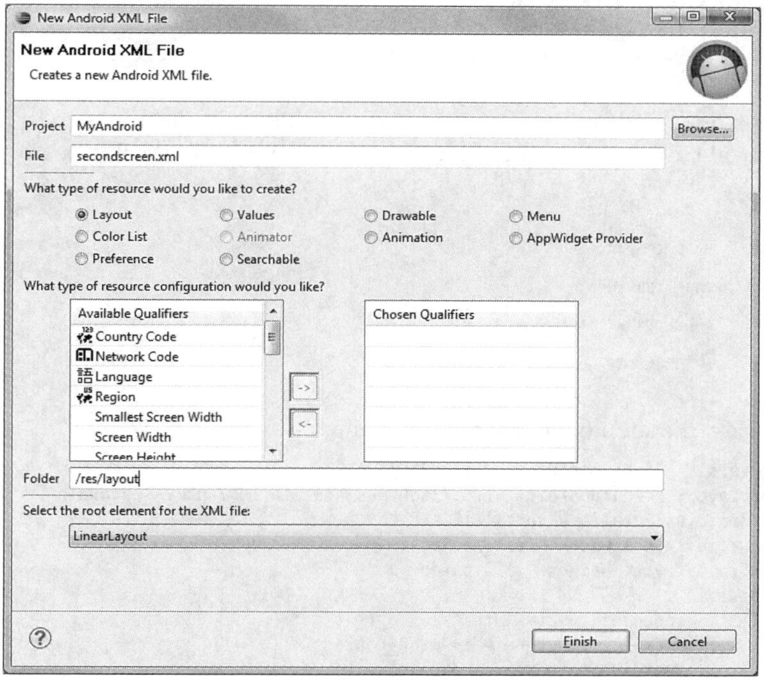

Figure 7-14. New Android XML file, part two

Select Finish.

With *secondscreen.xml* open either drag a `TextView` onto the screen in the Graphical Layout pane, or in the XML pane enter the `TextView` code. Set the `TextView` properties as follows:

Layout width	fill_parent
Layout height	wrap_content
Text	@string/hello2
Text size	10pt

The *secondscreen.xml* file should contain the following:

```xml
<?xml version="1.0" encoding="utf-8"?>
<LinearLayout
  xmlns:android="http://schemas.android.com/apk/res/android"
  android:layout_width="fill_parent"
  android:layout_height="fill_parent">
    <TextView
        android:layout_width="fill_parent"
      android:layout_height="wrap_content"
      android:text="@string/hello2"
      android:gravity="center_horizontal"
      android:textSize="10pt"></TextView>
</LinearLayout>
```

Open the *main.xml* file in the *res/layout* folder. Either drag a `Button` onto the screen in the Graphical Layout or add the `Button` in the XML view. Set the `Button` properties as follows:

Layout width	wrap_content
Layout height	wrap_content
Id	@+id/nextButton
Text	@string/next

The *Main.xml* file should contain the following:

```xml
<?xml version="1.0" encoding="utf-8"?>
<LinearLayout xmlns:android="http://schemas.android.com/apk/res/android"
    android:orientation="vertical"
    android:layout_width="fill_parent"
    android:layout_height="fill_parent">
    <TextView
        android:layout_width="fill_parent"
        android:layout_height="wrap_content"
        android:text="@string/hello"
        android:gravity="center_horizontal" />
    <Button
        android:id="@+id/nextButton"
        android:layout_width="wrap_content"
```

```
        android:layout_height="wrap_content"
        android:text="@string/next" />
</LinearLayout>
```

From the File menu (or using the context menu on the project tree) select New and then Class. Set the following fields in the dialog that opens, keeping all others at their defaults (see Figure 7-15):

Source folder	MyAndroid/src
Package	com.example
Name	Screen2

Figure 7-15. Defining a new Java class

Select Finish.

Within the *Screen2.java* file we extend the class to be a subclass of `Activity` and override the `onCreate` method, the same way as in the `Main` class. We then call `setContentView` passing the new *secondscreen* layout. All resource references are accessed via a generated

Java class named R, hence the reference to the new screen's layout is via R.layout.sec ondscreen (the R class is generated from the files and folders under the *res* folder). With the required imports the *Screen2.java* file will look like this:

```
package com.example;

import android.app.Activity;
import android.os.Bundle;

public class Screen2 extends Activity {
    @Override
    public void onCreate(Bundle savedInstanceState) {
        super.onCreate(savedInstanceState);
        setContentView(R.layout.secondscreen);
    }
}
```

The button needs code to tell Android of our intention to start the activity that contains the new screen. This can be achieved by passing the name of the required activity in an Intent object to the startActivity method when the button is pressed. The startAc tivity method is available on the Context object; Context has a host of useful methods that provide access to the environment in which the app is executing. Activity is a subclass of Context, so the startActivity method is always available within an Activ ity. By using startActivity Android gets the opportunity to perform any required housekeeping and then fire up the Activity class that was defined in the app.

Recipe 7.4 shows how to add a handler for button presses. Here, instead of getting the Main class to implement the onClick method, it will be done with an inner class.

Within onClick the code is needed to start the Screen2 activity. An intent declaration requires a context and activity (Screen2). Since Main is an Activity, which is derived from Context, we can use this (in this case Main.this because of the inner class for the onClick handler). With all the imports the *Main.java* code will be:

```
package com.example;

import android.app.Activity;
import android.content.Intent;
import android.os.Bundle;
import android.view.View;
import android.view.View.OnClickListener;

public class Main extends Activity {
    @Override
    public void onCreate(Bundle savedInstanceState) {
        super.onCreate(savedInstanceState);
        setContentView(R.layout.main);
        findViewById(R.id.nextButton).setOnClickListener(new OnClickListener() {
        public void onClick(View v) {
        Intent intent = new Intent(Main.this, Screen2.class);
        startActivity(intent);
        }});
```

```
        }
    }
```

Alternatively, to make the code easier to understand, the object to handle the button presses can be declared separately:

```
    public class Main extends Activity {
        @Override
        public void onCreate(Bundle savedInstanceState) {
            super.onCreate(savedInstanceState);
            setContentView(R.layout.main);
            findViewById(R.id.nextButton).setOnClickListener(new handleButton());
        }
        class handleButton implements OnClickListener {
            public void onClick(View v) {
            Intent intent = new Intent(Main.this, Screen2.class);
            startActivity(intent);
        }
        }
    }
```

(The handler example in Recipe 7.4 can also be adapted for this example.)

Finally, to register the new screen with Android an **activity** definition is added to the *AndroidManifest.xml* file in the project, after the activity declaration for **Main**. The activity section will be:

```
    <application android:icon="@drawable/globe" android:label="@string/app_name">
        <activity android:name=".Main"
            android:label="@string/app_name">
            <intent-filter>
                <action android:name="android.intent.action.MAIN" />
                <category android:name="android.intent.category.LAUNCHER" />
            </intent-filter>
        </activity>
        <activity android:name=".Screen2"
                android:label="@string/screen2Title">
            </activity>
    </application>
```

The dot in front of **Main** and **Screen2** signifies that the activity is within the application package. If the activity was defined in another package the activity name would include the full package name.

When the app runs the first screen will look like Figure 7-16.

Figure 7-16. First screen with Next button

Figure 7-17 shows the screen after the Next button is pressed.

Figure 7-17. Next app window

A button is not required to go back to the first screen. Android manages a stack of activities, as well as a Back button either on the device or on the bottom of the screen below the application's window.

See Also

Recipe 1.4, Recipe 7.4

7.25 Creating a Loading Screen That Will Appear Between Two Activities

Shraddha Shravagi

Problem

You are getting a black screen before loading an activity.

Solution

Create a simple activity that shows a loading image instead of a black screen.

Discussion

Sometimes it takes time for an activity to fetch user-requested data from a database or the Internet, and then to load the data onto the user's screen. In such cases, usually the screen goes black while the user waits for the data to load. The following scenario illustrates this:

ProfileList (the user selects one profile)→Black screen→ProfileData

Instead of showing the user a black screen while he waits for the data to load, you can show an image, as illustrated in the following scenario:

ProfileList (the user selects one profile)→LoadingScreenActivity→ProfileData

In this recipe we will create a simple loading screen that appears for 2.5 seconds while the next activity loads.

To do this, you need to start by creating a LoadingScreen layout file. This layout creates a screen which displays a "loading text" message and a progress bar:

```
<LinearLayout
  xmlns:android="http://schemas.android.com/apk/res/android"
  android:layout_width="fill_parent"
  android:gravity="center" android:orientation="vertical"
  android:layout_height="fill_parent" android:background="#E5E5E5">

  <TextView android:text="Please wait while your data is being loaded..."
      android:layout_width="wrap_content" android:layout_height="wrap_content"
      android:textColor="#000000">
```

```
    </TextView>
    <ProgressBar android:id="@+id/mainSpinner1" android:layout_gravity="center"
            android:layout_width="wrap_content" android:layout_height="wrap_content"
            android:indeterminate="true"
            style="?android:attr/progressBarStyleInverse">
    </ProgressBar>

</LinearLayout>
```

Next, create a `LoadingScreen` class file (see Example 7-24).

Example 7-24. The LoadingScreen class

```java
public class LoadingScreenActivity extends Activity {

    //Introduce a delay
    private final int WAIT_TIME = 2500;
    @Override
    protected void onCreate(Bundle savedInstanceState) {

        super.onCreate(savedInstanceState);
        System.out.println("LoadingScreenActivity  screen started");
        setContentView(R.layout.loading_screen);
        findViewById(R.id.mainSpinner1).setVisibility(View.VISIBLE);

        new Handler().postDelayed(new Runnable() {
            @Override
            public void run() {
                //Simulating a long running task
                try {
                    Thread.sleep(1000);
                } catch (InterruptedException e) {
                    // canthappen
                }
                System.out.println("Going to Profile Data");
                /* Create an Intent that will start the ProfileData Activity. */
                Intent mainIntent =
                    new Intent(LoadingScreenActivity.this, ProfileData.class);
                LoadingScreenActivity.this.startActivity(mainIntent);
                LoadingScreenActivity.this.finish();
            }
        }, WAIT_TIME);
    }
}
```

This will load the next activity once `WAIT_TIME` has elapsed.

Now all you need to do is to create an intent to launch the loading screen activity:

```java
protected void onListItemClick(ListView l, View v, int position, long id) {
        super.onListItemClick(l, v, position, id);

Intent intent = new Intent(ProfileList.this, LoadingScreenActivity.class);
        startActivity(intent);
}
```

7.26 Using SlidingDrawer to Overlap Other Components

Mike Rowehl

Problem

The SlidingDrawer component allows the user to "open" a GUI container holding a different set of components than is initially in a View. The Android 2.x Application Drawer is a good example of this. However, the proper layout of SlidingDrawer isn't covered too well in the SDK documentation. You need to know how to use the control to overlay other components in a layout, as well as how to position elements in the underlying layout to avoid colliding with the drawer handle.

Solution

Place the SlidingDrawer inside a FrameLayout or a RelativeLayout. (Using it in a LinearLayout makes it difficult to get the drawer to overlay the rest of the controls on the screen.) To prevent the SlidingDrawer from overlaying data when positioning it over a ListView, use a spacer in the underlying layout to get everything to line up.

Discussion

First let's take a look at the layout, including the SlidingDrawer itself. Note in Example 7-25 that there's a spacer TextView aligned with the bottom of the RelativeLayout using the DrawerButton style. The drawer handle itself is also a TextView using the same style. Positioning the main ListView for the layout above the spacer ensures that none of the list items are hidden by the handle when the drawer is closed.

Example 7-25. SlidingDrawer layout

```xml
<?xml version="1.0" encoding="utf-8"?>
<RelativeLayout xmlns:android="http://schemas.android.com/apk/res/android"
    android:layout_width="fill_parent"
    android:layout_height="fill_parent">

    <TextView style="@style/DrawerButton" android:layout_alignParentBottom="true"
            android:id="@+id/spacer" android:text="Spacer" />
    <ListView
        android:orientation="vertical"
        android:layout_width="fill_parent"
        android:layout_height="fill_parent"
        android:id="@+id/contact_list"
        android:layout_alignParentTop="true"
        android:layout_above="@id/spacer"
        >
    </ListView>
```

```
    <SlidingDrawer android:layout_width="fill_parent"
        android:id="@+id/drawer" android:handle="@+id/drawer_button"
        android:content="@+id/drawer_content"
        android:layout_height="wrap_content" android:layout_alignParentBottom="true">
        <TextView android:id="@id/drawer_button" style="@style/DrawerButton"
            android:gravity="right|center_vertical" android:text="Handle"
            ></TextView>
        <ListView
            android:layout_width="fill_parent"
            android:layout_height="fill_parent"
            android:id="@+id/drawer_content"
            android:background="#000000"
            >
        </ListView>
    </SlidingDrawer>
</RelativeLayout>
```

In Example 7-26 we extract the DrawerButton settings out into a style file (*xml/ styles.xml*) so that we don't have to change them on both the spacer and the handle item to keep them in sync.

Example 7-26. DrawerButton settings

```
<?xml version="1.0" encoding="utf-8"?>
<resources>
    <style name="DrawerButton" parent="@android:style/TextAppearance.Medium">
        <item name="android:layout_width">fill_parent</item>
        <item name="android:layout_height">wrap_content</item>
        <item name="android:background">#EEEEEE</item>
        <item name="android:textColor">#111111</item>
        <item name="android:gravity">right|center_vertical</item>
        <item name="android:paddingRight">3pt</item>
        <item name="android:paddingTop">2pt</item>
        <item name="android:paddingBottom">2pt</item>
    </style>
</resources>
```

Now the drawer should slide up over the ListView on the main screen without hiding any of the content when closed. Figure 7-18 shows three views: the initial view (Contacts), dragging the drawer up, and the drawer fully open (showing a phonetic example alphabet).

Figure 7-18. SlidingDrawer in motion

See Also

The `SlidingDrawer` can be activated programmatically using its `open()`, `close()`, `tog gle()`, and `animateOpen()` methods. See the documentation at *http://developer.android .com*.

The `animateOpen()` method normally opens the drawer from the bottom up. You can animate it from the top down; see Recipe 7.27.

7.27 Customizing the SlidingDrawer Component to Animate/ Transition from the Top Down

Wagied Davids

Problem

When the user drags the `SlidingDrawer` to open it, or you request that it be open by calling the `open()` method, it slides up from the bottom of the container. You want the `SlidingDrawer` component to instead animate/transition from the top down.

Solution

Use the open source `org.panel` package to create the top-down animation/transition.

Discussion

The steps are as follows:

1. Include the `org.panel` easing interpolator package.

---

2. Include as a new namespace, such as panel, in your Android view XML.

3. Use the tag set instead of the Android SlidingDrawer component.

Example 7-27 shows the *Main.xml* layout file.

Example 7-27. The layout file main.xml

```xml
<?xml version="1.0" encoding="utf-8"?>
<FrameLayout
    xmlns:android="http://schemas.android.com/apk/res/android"
    xmlns:panel="http://schemas.android.com/apk/res/org.panel"
    android:layout_width="fill_parent"
    android:layout_height="fill_parent">

    <LinearLayout
        android:orientation="vertical"
        android:layout_width="fill_parent"
        android:layout_height="fill_parent">
        <org.panel.Panel
            android:layout_width="fill_parent"
            android:layout_height="wrap_content"
            android:id="@+id/topPanel"
            android:paddingBottom="20dip"
            panel:position="top"
            panel:animationDuration="1000"
            panel:linearFlying="true"
            panel:openedHandle="@drawable/top_switcher_expanded_background"
            panel:closedHandle="@drawable/top_switcher_collapsed_background">
            <Button
                android:id="@id/panelHandle"
                android:layout_width="fill_parent"
                android:layout_height="33dip" />
            <LinearLayout
                android:id="@id/panelContent"
                android:orientation="vertical"
                android:layout_width="fill_parent"
                android:layout_height="wrap_content">
                <TextView
                    android:layout_width="fill_parent"
                    android:layout_height="wrap_content"
                    android:gravity="center"
                    android:text="From the Top -> Down"
                    android:textSize="16dip"
                    android:padding="4dip"
                    android:textStyle="bold" />

                <ImageView
                    android:src="@drawable/android_skateboard"
                    android:layout_gravity="center"
                    android:layout_width="wrap_content"
                    android:layout_height="wrap_content" />

            </LinearLayout>
        </org.panel.Panel>
```

```
        </LinearLayout>
    </FrameLayout>
```

Example 7-28 shows the main activity.

Example 7-28. The main activity

```java
import android.app.Activity;
import android.os.Bundle;

public class Test extends Activity {
        /** Called when the activity is first created. */
        @Override
        public void onCreate(Bundle savedInstanceState)
            {
                super.onCreate(savedInstanceState);
                setContentView(R.layout.main);
            }
    }
```

Source Download URL

The source code for this example is in the Android Cookbook repository at *http://github .com/AndroidCook/Android-Cookbook-Examples*, in the subdirectory SlidingDrawer-TopDown (see "Getting and Using the Code Examples" on page xvii).

7.28 Adding a Border with Rounded Corners to a Layout

Daniel Fowler

Problem

You need to put a border around an area of the screen or add interest to a user interface.

Solution

Define an Android shape in an XML file and assign it to a layout's background attribute.

Discussion

The *drawable* folder, under *res*, in an Android project is not restricted to bitmaps (PNG or JPG files) but can also hold shapes defined in XML files. These shapes can then be reused in the project. A shape can be used to put a border around a layout. This example shows a rectangular border with curved corners.

A new file called *customborder.xml* is created in the *drawable* folder (in Eclipse, use the File menu and select New and then File; with the *drawable* folder selected, type in the filename and click Finish).

The XML defining the border shape is entered:

```
<?xml version="1.0" encoding="UTF-8"?>
<shape xmlns:android="http://schemas.android.com/apk/res/android"
android:shape="rectangle">
    <corners android:radius="20dp"/>
    <padding android:left="10dp" android:right="10dp"
    android:top="10dp" android:bottom="10dp"/>
    <solid android:color="#CCCCCC"/>
</shape>
```

The attribute android:shape is set to rectangle (shape files also support oval, line, and ring). Rectangle is the default value, so this attribute could be left out if it is a rectangle being defined. For detailed information on shape files, refer to the URL for the Android documentation on shapes, provided in the "See Also" section.

The element corners sets the rectangle corners to be rounded; it is possible to set a different radius on each corner (see the Android reference).

The padding attributes are used to move the contents of the View to which the shape is applied, to prevent the contents from overlapping the border.

The border color here is set to a light gray (CCCCCC hexadecimal RGB value).

Shapes also support gradients, but that is not being used here; again, see the Android resources to see how a gradient is defined.

The shape is applied using android:background="@drawable/customborder".

Within the layout other views can be added as normal. In this example a single Text View has been added, and the text is white (FFFFFF hexadecimal RGB). The background is set to blue, plus some transparency to reduce the brightness (A00000FF hexadecimal alpha RGB value).

Finally, the layout is offset from the screen edge by placing it into another layout with a small amount of padding. The full layout file is thus:

```
<?xml version="1.0" encoding="utf-8"?>
<LinearLayout xmlns:android="http://schemas.android.com/apk/res/android"
            android:orientation="vertical"
            android:layout_width="fill_parent"
            android:layout_height="fill_parent"
            android:padding="5dp">
    <LinearLayout android:orientation="vertical"
            android:layout_width="fill_parent"
            android:layout_height="fill_parent"
            android:background="@drawable/customborder">
      <TextView android:layout_width="fill_parent"
            android:layout_height="fill_parent"
            android:text="Text View"
            android:textSize="20dp"
            android:textColor="#FFFFFF"
            android:gravity="center_horizontal"
            android:background="#A00000FF" />
```

```
    </LinearLayout>
  </LinearLayout>
```

This produces the result shown in Figure 7-19.

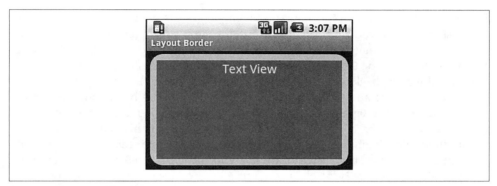

Figure 7-19. Curved border

See Also

http://developer.android.com/guide/topics/resources/drawable-resource.html#Shape

7.29 Detecting Gestures in Android

Pratik Rupwal

Problem

You want to traverse through different screens using simple gestures, such as flipping/ scrolling the page.

Solution

Use the `GestureDetector` class to detect simple gestures such as tapping, scrolling, swiping, or flipping.

Discussion

The sample application has four views, each a different color. It also has two modes: SCROLL and FLIP. The application starts in FLIP mode. In this mode, when you perform the swipe/fling gesture in a left-to-right or top-to-bottom direction, the view changes back and forth. When a long-press is detected, the application changes to SCROLL mode, in which you can scroll the displayed view. While in this mode, you can double-tap on the screen to bring the screen back to its original position. When a long-press is detected again, the application changes to FLIP mode.

This recipe focuses on gesture detection, hence the animation applied is not discussed. Refer to Recipe 7.18 for an example of shaking a view using an animation, as well as the Android docs for "android.view.animation*" (see *http://developer.android.com/ref erence/android/view/animation/package-summary.html*).

Example 7-29 provides an introduction to simple gesture detection in Android. Our GestureDetector class detects gestures using the supplied MotionEvent class. We use this class along with the onTouchEvent. Inside this method we call GestureDetec tor.onTouchEvent. The GestureDetector class identifies the gestures or events that occurred and reports back to us using the GestureDetector.OnGestureListener callback interface. We create an instance of the GestureDetector class by passing the Context and GestureDetector.OnGestureListener listener. The double-tap event is not present in the GestureDetector.onGestureListener callback interface; this event is reported using another callback interface, GestureDetector.onDoubleTapListener. To use this call-back interface we have to register for these events using GestureDetector.setOnDouble TapListener. The MotionEvent class contains all the values corresponding to a movement and touch event. This class holds values such as the X and Y positions at which the event occurred, the timestamp at which the event occurred, and the mouse pointer index.

Example 7-29. Gesture detection

```
...
import android.view.GestureDetector;
...
import android.view.animation.OvershootInterpolator;
import android.view.animation.TranslateAnimation;

public class FlipperActivity extends Activity
        implements GestureDetector.OnGestureListener,
            GestureDetector.OnDoubleTapListener{

        final private int SWIPE_MIN_DISTANCE = 100;
        final private int SWIPE_MIN_VELOCITY = 100;

        private ViewFlipper flipper = null;
        private ArrayList<TextView> views = null;
        private GestureDetector gesturedetector = null;
        private Vibrator vibrator = null;
        int colors[] = { Color.rgb(255,128,128),
            Color.rgb(128,255,128),
            Color.rgb(128,128,255),
            Color.rgb(128,128,128) };

        private Animation animleftin = null;
        private Animation animleftout = null;

        private Animation animrightin = null;
        private Animation animrightout = null;

        private Animation animupin = null;
```

```
        private Animation animupout = null;

        private Animation animdownin = null;
        private Animation animdownout = null;

        private boolean isDragMode = false;
        private int currentview = 0;

/** Initializes the first screen and animation to be applied to the screen
after detecting the gesture */

    @Override
    public void onCreate(Bundle savedInstanceState) {
        super.onCreate(savedInstanceState);

        flipper = new ViewFlipper(this);
        gesturedetector = new GestureDetector(this, this);
        vibrator = (Vibrator)getSystemService(VIBRATOR_SERVICE);
        gesturedetector.setOnDoubleTapListener(this);

        flipper.setInAnimation(animleftin);
        flipper.setOutAnimation(animleftout);
        flipper.setFlipInterval(3000);
        flipper.setAnimateFirstView(true);

        prepareAnimations();
        prepareViews();
        addViews();
        setViewText();

        setContentView(flipper);
    }

        private void prepareAnimations() {
        animleftin = new TranslateAnimation(
            Animation.RELATIVE_TO_PARENT, +1.0f, Animation.RELATIVE_TO_PARENT,  0.0f,
            Animation.RELATIVE_TO_PARENT,  0.0f, Animation.RELATIVE_TO_PARENT,  0.0f);

        animleftout = new TranslateAnimation(
            Animation.RELATIVE_TO_PARENT,  0.0f, Animation.RELATIVE_TO_PARENT, -1.0f,
            Animation.RELATIVE_TO_PARENT,  0.0f, Animation.RELATIVE_TO_PARENT,  0.0f);

        animrightin = new TranslateAnimation(
            Animation.RELATIVE_TO_PARENT, -1.0f, Animation.RELATIVE_TO_PARENT,  0.0f,
            Animation.RELATIVE_TO_PARENT,  0.0f, Animation.RELATIVE_TO_PARENT,  0.0f);

        animrightout = new TranslateAnimation(
            Animation.RELATIVE_TO_PARENT,  0.0f, Animation.RELATIVE_TO_PARENT, +1.0f,
            Animation.RELATIVE_TO_PARENT,  0.0f, Animation.RELATIVE_TO_PARENT,  0.0f);

        animupin = new TranslateAnimation(
            Animation.RELATIVE_TO_PARENT,  0.0f, Animation.RELATIVE_TO_PARENT,  0.0f,
            Animation.RELATIVE_TO_PARENT, +1.0f, Animation.RELATIVE_TO_PARENT,  0.0f);

        animupout = new TranslateAnimation(
```

```
                    Animation.RELATIVE_TO_PARENT,  0.0f, Animation.RELATIVE_TO_PARENT,  0.0f,
                    Animation.RELATIVE_TO_PARENT,  0.0f, Animation.RELATIVE_TO_PARENT,  -1.0f);

        animdownin = new TranslateAnimation(
                    Animation.RELATIVE_TO_PARENT,  0.0f, Animation.RELATIVE_TO_PARENT,  0.0f,
                    Animation.RELATIVE_TO_PARENT,  -1.0f, Animation.RELATIVE_TO_PARENT,   0.0f);

        animdownout = new TranslateAnimation(
                    Animation.RELATIVE_TO_PARENT,  0.0f, Animation.RELATIVE_TO_PARENT,  0.0f,
                    Animation.RELATIVE_TO_PARENT,  0.0f, Animation.RELATIVE_TO_PARENT,  +1.0f);

        animleftin.setDuration(1000);
        animleftin.setInterpolator(new OvershootInterpolator());
        animleftout.setDuration(1000);
        animleftout.setInterpolator(new OvershootInterpolator());

        animrightin.setDuration(1000);
        animrightin.setInterpolator(new OvershootInterpolator());
        animrightout.setDuration(1000);
        animrightout.setInterpolator(new OvershootInterpolator());

        animupin.setDuration(1000);
        animupin.setInterpolator(new OvershootInterpolator());
        animupout.setDuration(1000);
        animupout.setInterpolator(new OvershootInterpolator());

        animdownin.setDuration(1000);
        animdownin.setInterpolator(new OvershootInterpolator());
        animdownout.setDuration(1000);
        animdownout.setInterpolator(new OvershootInterpolator());
    }

    private void prepareViews() {
            TextView view = null;

            views = new ArrayList<TextView>();

            for (int color: colors) {
                    view = new TextView(this);

                    view.setBackgroundColor(color);
                    view.setTextColor(Color.BLACK);
                    view.setGravity(
                        Gravity.CENTER_HORIZONTAL | Gravity.CENTER_VERTICAL);

                    views.add(view);
            }
    }

    private void addViews() {
            for (int index=0; index<views.size(); ++index) {
                    flipper.addView(views.get(index),index,
                                    new LayoutParams(LayoutParams.FILL_PARENT,
                                    LayoutParams.FILL_PARENT));
            }
```

```
        }

        private void setViewText(){
                String text = getString(isDragMode ? R.string.app_info_drag :
                R.string.app_info_flip);
                for (int index=0; index<views.size(); ++index) {
                        views.get(index).setText(text);
                }
        }

        /**Gets invoked when a screen touch is detected*/
        @Override
        public boolean onTouchEvent(MotionEvent event) {
                return gesturedetector.onTouchEvent(event);
        }

        /** The onDown method is called when the user first touches the screen;
         * the MotionEvent parameter represents the event that corresponds to
         * the touch event. */
        @Override
        public boolean onDown(MotionEvent e) {
                return false;
        }

        /** The onFling method is called whenever the user swipes the screen
         * in any direction, i.e., the user touches the screen and immediately
         * moves the finger in any direction. */
        @Override
        public boolean onFling(MotionEvent event1, MotionEvent event2,
        float velocityX,float velocityY) {
                if(isDragMode)
                        return false;

                final float ev1x = event1.getX();
                final float ev1y = event1.getY();
                final float ev2x = event2.getX();
                final float ev2y = event2.getY();
                final float xdiff = Math.abs(ev1x - ev2x);
                final float ydiff = Math.abs(ev1y - ev2y);
                final float xvelocity = Math.abs(velocityX);
                final float yvelocity = Math.abs(velocityY);

                if(xvelocity > this.SWIPE_MIN_VELOCITY && xdiff > this.SWIPE_MIN_DISTANCE)
                {
                        if(ev1x > ev2x) //Swipe Left
                        {
                                --currentview;

                                if(currentview < 0)
                                {
                                        currentview = views.size() - 1;
                                }

                                flipper.setInAnimation(animleftin);
                                flipper.setOutAnimation(animleftout);
```

```
                }
                else //Swipe Right
                {
                        ++currentview;

                        if(currentview >= views.size())
                        {
                                currentview = 0;
                        }

                        flipper.setInAnimation(animrightin);
                        flipper.setOutAnimation(animrightout);
                }

                flipper.scrollTo(0,0);
                flipper.setDisplayedChild(currentview);
        }
        else if (yvelocity > this.SWIPE_MIN_VELOCITY &&
            ydiff > this.SWIPE_MIN_DISTANCE) {
                if(ev1y > ev2y) //Swipe Up
                {
                        --currentview;

                        if(currentview < 0)
                        {
                                currentview = views.size() - 1;
                        }

                        flipper.setInAnimation(animupin);
                        flipper.setOutAnimation(animupout);
                }
                else //Swipe Down
                {
                        ++currentview;

                        if(currentview >= views.size())
                        {
                                currentview = 0;
                        }
                        flipper.setInAnimation(animdownin);
                        flipper.setOutAnimation(animdownout);
                }

                flipper.scrollTo(0,0);
                flipper.setDisplayedChild(currentview);
        }

        return false;
}

/** The onLongPress method is called when user touches the screen
and holds it for a period of time. The MotionEvent parameter represents
the event that corresponds to the touch event. */
@Override
public void onLongPress(MotionEvent e) {
```

```
            vibrator.vibrate(200);
            flipper.scrollTo(0,0);

            isDragMode = !isDragMode;

            setViewText();
    }

    /**The onScroll method is called when the user touches the screen
    and moves to another location on the screen.*/
    @Override
    public boolean onScroll(MotionEvent e1, MotionEvent e2,
            float distanceX,float distanceY) {
            if(isDragMode)
                    flipper.scrollBy((int)distanceX, (int)distanceY);

            return false;
    }

    /**The onShowPress method is called when the user touches the screen
     * and has not moved yet. This event is mostly used for giving visual
     * feedback to the user to show their action.*/
    @Override
    public void onShowPress(MotionEvent e) {
    }

    /** onSingleTapUp() is called when a tap occurred, i.e., user taps the screen.*/
    @Override
    public boolean onSingleTapUp(MotionEvent e) {
            return false;
    }

    /** The onDoubleTap method is called when a double-tap event has occurred.
     * The only parameter, MotionEvent, corresponds to the double-tap
     * event that occurred. */
    @Override
    public boolean onDoubleTap(MotionEvent e) {
            flipper.scrollTo(0,0);

            return false;
    }

    /** The onDoubleTapEvent is called for all events that occurred within
     * the double-tap, i.e., down, move and up events.*/

    @Override
    public boolean onDoubleTapEvent(MotionEvent e) {
            return false;
    }

    /** The onSingleTapConfirmed method is called when a single tap
    has occurred and been confirmed, but this is not same as the
    single-tap event in the GestureDetector.onGestureListener.  This
    is called when the GestureDetector detects and confirms that
    this tap does not lead to a double-tap.
```

```
    */
    @Override
    public boolean onSingleTapConfirmed(MotionEvent e) {
            return false;
    }
}
```

When the mode of the application changes the user is notified with a vibration. To use the vibrator set the following permission in your application's *AndroidManifest.xml* file:

```
<uses-permission android:name="android.permission.VIBRATE"></uses-permission>
```

The application uses some strings, which are declared under *res/values/string.xml*:

```
<?xml version="1.0" encoding="utf-8"?>
<resources>
    <string name="app_info_drag">
    GestureDetector sample.\n\nCurrent Mode:
        SCROLL\n\nDrag the view using finger.\nLong press to change
    the mode to FLIP.\nDouble tap to reposition the view to normal.</string>
    <string name="app_name">Gesture Detector Sample</string>
    <string name="app_info_flip">
    GestureDetector sample.\n\nCurrent Mode: FLIP\n\nSwipe left, right, up, down
        to change the views\nLong
    press to change to mode to SCROLL</string>
</resources>
```

See Also

Check the `GestureOverlayView` class (*http://developer.android.com/reference/android/gesture/GestureOverlayView.html*) for handling complex gestures in Android.

7.30 Building a UI Using Android 3.0 Fragments in Android 1.6 and Later

Saketkumar Srivastav

Problem

Fragments are small chunks of the UI that constitute a single activity. Fragments were originally only available in Android 3.0 and later. You want to add fragments to the UI in Android version 1.6 and later.

Solution

Use Google's Android Compatibility package to build applications using the Fragments API in Android 2.0 and later versions.

Discussion

A fragment can be treated as an individual portlet of a portal page. It is very similar to an activity in terms of its look, life cycle, and so on, but it is different from an activity in the sense that a fragment should always reside in an activity; fragments cannot exist independently as activities.

To create a fragment, we need to extend one of the Fragment classes. Different kinds of fragments are available, including ListFragment (ListActivity), DialogFragment (DialogInterface), and PreferenceFragment (PreferenceActivity).

Let's start with the FragmentTestActivity class (see Example 7-30). In the onCreate() method we set the list adapter to hold a string array of magazine titles of the EFY Group. We also set the listener on the list items so that we can perform some action when an item from the list is clicked.

In the onItemClickListener() method we perform the main task of managing the fragment. We obtain the instance of the fragment passing the position of the clicked item. Now we need to replace the fragment element that we have in *main.xml* with the new fragment TestFragment, which has a meaningful UI associated with it. To accomplish this we get the instance of the FragmentTransaction class; this API allows us to add, remove, and replace a fragment programmatically. We replace the R.id.the_frag which corresponds to the <fragment> element of *main.xml* with the newly created fragment f. The setTransition() method signifies the kind of transition that happens with the fragment. The addToBackStack() method adds the fragment transaction to the back of the fragment stack so that when the Back button is pressed on the device, we go to the last transaction of the fragment and do not exit the application. After all the transactions have been made, we commit the transaction.

Now let's set up the TestFragment class (see Example 7-31). We initialize the position of the clicked item from the list to the variable magznumber. As we discussed earlier, if a fragment is being associated with a UI the onCreateView() method is used to inflate the view to the fragment. Here, we create a linear layout for the fragment and then load it with the appropriate image of the magazine in an ImageView, and this ImageView is added to the linear layout.

Example 7-30. FragmentTestActivity.java

```
public class FragmentTestActivity
    extends FragmentActivity implements OnItemClickListener {

    /** Called when the activity is first created. */
    @Override
    public void onCreate(Bundle savedInstanceState) {
        super.onCreate(savedInstanceState);
        setContentView(R.layout.main);

        ListView l = (ListView) findViewById(R.id.number_list);
        ArrayAdapter<String> magzTitles =
```

```
            new ArrayAdapter<String>(getApplicationContext(),
            android.R.layout.simple_list_item_1, new String[]{"Electronics For You",
                                                  "Linux For You",
                                                  "Facts For you"});
        // It would be better to move the array of titles into XML and use
        // R.array.magz_titles);
    l.setAdapter(magzTitles);
    l.setOnItemClickListener(this);
}

/**
 * Called when a number gets clicked
 */
public void onItemClick(AdapterView<?> parent, View view, int position, long id) {

    Fragment f = new TestFragment(position+1);

    FragmentTransaction ft = getSupportFragmentManager().beginTransaction();
    ft.replace(R.id.the_frag, f);
    ft.setTransition(FragmentTransaction.TRANSIT_FRAGMENT_FADE);
    ft.addToBackStack(null);
    ft.commit();
    }
}
```

Example 7-31. TestFragment.java

```
public class TestFragment extends Fragment {

    private int magznumber;

    public TestFragment() {

    }

    /**
     * Constructor for being created explicitly
     */
    public TestFragment(int position) {
            this.magznumber = position;
    }

    /**
     * If we are being created with saved state, restore our state
     */
    @Override
    public void onCreate(Bundle saved) {
        super.onCreate(saved);
        if (null != saved) {
            magznumber = saved.getInt("magznumber");
        }
    }

    /**
     * Save the number of Androids to be displayed
     */
```

```
@Override
public void onSaveInstanceState(Bundle toSave) {
    toSave.putInt("magznumber", magznumber);
}

/**
 * Make a grid to view the magazines
 */
@Override
public View onCreateView(LayoutInflater inflater, ViewGroup container, Bundle saved) {

    Context c = getActivity().getApplicationContext();

    LinearLayout l = new LinearLayout(c);
    LayoutParams params = new LayoutParams(LayoutParams.WRAP_CONTENT,
    LayoutParams.MATCH_PARENT, 0);

    l.setLayoutParams(params);

    ImageView i = new ImageView(c);

    switch(magznumber){
    case 1:
        i.setImageResource(R.drawable.efymag);
        break;
    case 2:
        i.setImageResource(R.drawable.lfymag);
        break;
    case 3:
        i.setImageResource(R.drawable.ffymag);
        break;
    }

    l.addView(i);

    return l;
    }
}
```

Figure 7-20 shows the results of running this code.

Figure 7-20. Fragments API example

See Also

See these official Android articles on the fragments API (*http://developer.android.com/guide/topics/fundamentals/fragments.html*) and on the compatibility package (*http://android-developers.blogspot.com/2011/03/fragments-for-all.html*).

Source Download URL

You can download the source code for this example from *https://github.com/SaketSri vastav/AndroidFragmentDemo*.

7.31 Using the Android 3.0 Photo Gallery

Wagied Davids

Problem

You have a number of static images, and you want to display them in a photo gallery so that the user can act on them in some way.

Solution

Use the Android 3.0 Photo Gallery to display images that users can interact with.

Discussion

To use the Android 3.0 Photo Gallery follow these steps:

1. Download the Android 3.x SDK either by using the SDK download manager or from within the Eclipse IDE by using the Android SDK Manager.
2. Create an AVD to run the emulator.
3. Create an Android project (*Important*: set Min. SDK Version to "Honeycomb") and click Finish.
4. Create a main entry point Java file—for example, *Main.java*.
5. Create an *ImageAdapter.java* file.
6. Create an XML layout file (see Example 7-32).
7. Package and run the Android app.

Example 7-32. The main layout file main.xml

```xml
<?xml version="1.0" encoding="utf-8"?>
<LinearLayout
    xmlns:android="http://schemas.android.com/apk/res/android"
    android:orientation="vertical"
    android:layout_width="fill_parent"
    android:layout_height="fill_parent"
```

```
            android:gravity="center"
            >

    <Gallery
        android:id="@+id/gallery1"
        android:layout_height="wrap_content"
        android:layout_width="match_parent"
        android:spacing="10dip"
        >
    </Gallery>
</LinearLayout>
```

Example 7-33 shows the code for the main activity.

Example 7-33. The main activity

```
import android.app.Activity;
import android.graphics.Bitmap;
import android.graphics.BitmapFactory;
import android.graphics.drawable.Drawable;
import android.os.Bundle;
import android.view.View;
import android.widget.AdapterView;
import android.widget.AdapterView.OnItemClickListener;
import android.widget.Gallery;
import android.widget.Toast;

public class Main extends Activity implements OnItemClickListener
    {
        private static final String tag = "Main";
        private Gallery _gallery;
        private ImageAdapter _imageAdapter;

        /** Called when the activity is first created. */
        @Override
        public void onCreate(Bundle savedInstanceState)
            {
                super.onCreate(savedInstanceState);
                setContentView(R.layout.main);
                setTitle("Android Honeycomb Photo Gallery Example");

                _gallery = (Gallery) this.findViewById(R.id.gallery1);
                _imageAdapter = new ImageAdapter(this);
                _gallery.setAdapter(_imageAdapter);
                _gallery.setOnItemClickListener(this);
            }

        @Override
        public void onItemClick(AdapterView<?> arg0, View view,
            int position, long duration) {
                int resourcId = (Integer) _imageAdapter.getItem(position);
                Drawable drawable = getResources().getDrawable(resourcId);
                Bitmap bitmap = BitmapFactory.decodeResource(getResources(), resourcId);

                Toast.makeText(this,
```

```
                "Selected Image: " + getResources().getText(resourcId) + "\n" +
                "Height: " + bitmap.getHeight() + "\nWidth: " + bitmap.getWidth(),
                Toast.LENGTH_SHORT).show();
        }
    }
```

Example 7-34 shows the code for the ImageAdapter class.

Example 7-34. The ImageAdapter class

```
public class ImageAdapter extends BaseAdapter {
        private Context _context = null;
        private final int[] imageIds = { R.drawable.formula, R.drawable.hollywood,
        R.drawable.mode1, R.drawable.mode2, R.drawable.mother1, R.drawable.mother2,
        R.drawable.nights, R.drawable.ontwerpje1,R.drawable.ontwerpje2,
        R.drawable.relation1,
        R.drawable.relation2, R.drawable.renaissance, R.drawable.renaissance_zoom };
        public ImageAdapter(Context context) {
                this._context = context;
        }

        @Override
        public int getCount()
            {
                return imageIds.length;
            }

        @Override
        public Object getItem(int index)
            {
                return imageIds[index];
            }

        @Override
        public long getItemId(int index)
            {
                return index;
            }

        @Override
        public View getView(int postion, View view, ViewGroup group)
            {
                ImageView imageView = new ImageView(_context);
                imageView.setImageResource(imageIds[postion]);
                imageView.setScaleType(ScaleType.FIT_XY);
                imageView.setLayoutParams(new Gallery.LayoutParams(400, 400));
                return imageView;
            }
    }
```

Figure 7-21 shows the result.

Figure 7-21. Photo gallery example

Source Download URL

The source code for this example is in the Android Cookbook repository at *http://github*
.com/AndroidCook/Android-Cookbook-Examples, in the subdirectory HoneycombGal-
lery (see "Getting and Using the Code Examples" on page xvii).

7.32 Creating a Simple App Widget

Catarina Reis

Problem

You want to enable users to more easily interact with your application.

Solution

Create an Application widget, which is a simple GUI control that appears on the Home
screen and allows users to easily interact with an existing application (activity and/or
service).

Discussion

In this recipe we will create a widget that starts a service that updates its visual components. The widget, called `CurrentMoodWidget`, presents the user's current mood in the form of a "smiley text" in a widget. The current mood smiley changes to a random mood smiley whenever the user clicks the "smiley image" button. Figure 7-22 shows the initial view, and Figure 7-23 shows the view after a random change.

Figure 7-22. Initial mood widget

Figure 7-23. Current mood widget

1. Start by creating a new Android project (`CurrentMoodWidgetProject`). Use "Current Mood" as the application name and "oreillymedia.cookbook.android.spikes" as the package name. Do not create an activity. Set the minimum SDK version to 8 (for Android 2.2, the version that introduced App Widgets).

2. Add the text support required for the widget. Place this under the resources file folder (*res/values/string.xml*), according to the following name-value pairs:

- widgettext - "current mood:"
- widgetmoodtext - ":)"

3. Add the images that will appear in the widget's button. Place these under the *res/drawable* structure (*smile_icon.png*).

4. Create a new layout file inside *res/layout*, under the project structure, that will define the widget layout (*widgetlayout.xml*) according to the following structure:

```
<TextView android:text="@string/widgettext"
          android:layout_width="0dp"
          android:layout_height="wrap_content"
          android:layout_weight="0.8"
          android:layout_gravity="center_vertical"
```

```
                    android:textColor="#000000"></TextView>
    <TextView android:text="@string/widgetmoodtext"
                    android:id="@+id/widgetMood" android:layout_width="0dp"
                    android:layout_height="wrap_content"
                    android:layout_weight="0.3"
                    android:layout_gravity="center_vertical"
                    android:textColor="#000000"></TextView>
    <ImageButton android:id="@+id/widgetBtn" android:layout_width="0dp"
                    android:layout_height="wrap_content"
                    android:layout_weight="0.5" android:src="@drawable/smile_icon"
                    android:layout_gravity="center_vertical"></ImageButton>
```

5. Provide the widget provider setup configuration by first creating the *res/xml* folder under the project structure and then creating an XML file (*widgetproviderinfo.xml*) with the following parameters:

```
<appwidget-provider
    xmlns:android="http://schemas.android.com/apk/res/android"
    android:minWidth="220dp"
    android:minHeight="72dp"
    android:updatePeriodMillis="86400000"
    android:initialLayout="@layout/widgetlayout">
</appwidget-provider>
```

6. Create the service that reacts to the user interaction with the smiley image button (`CurrentMoodService.java`); see Example 7-35.

Example 7-35. Widget's service implementation

```
@Override
public int onStartCommand(Intent intent, int flags, int startId) {
    super.onStart(intent, startId);
            updateMood(intent);
    stopSelf(startId);
    return START_STICKY;
}

private void updateMood(Intent intent) {
        if (intent != null){
         String requestedAction = intent.getAction();
         if (requestedAction != null &&  requestedAction.equals(UPDATEMOOD)){
            this.currentMood = getRandomMood();
            int widgetId = intent.getIntExtra(AppWidgetManager.EXTRA_APPWIDGET_ID, 0);
            AppWidgetManager appWidgetMan = AppWidgetManager.getInstance(this);
            RemoteViews views =
                new RemoteViews(this.getPackageName(),R.layout.widgetlayout);
            views.setTextViewText(R.id.widgetMood, currentMood);
            appWidgetMan.updateAppWidget(widgetId, views);
        }
        }
    }
```

7. Implement the widget provider class (`CurrentMoodWidgetProvider.java`); see Example 7-36.

Example 7-36. Widget provider class

```
    @Override
public void onUpdate(Context context, AppWidgetManager appWidgetManager,
        int[] appWidgetIds) {
    super.onUpdate(context, appWidgetManager, appWidgetIds);

    for (int i=0; i<appWidgetIds.length; i++) {
        int appWidgetId = appWidgetIds[i];
        RemoteViews views = new RemoteViews(context.getPackageName(),
            R.layout.widgetlayout);
        Intent intent = new Intent(context, CurrentMoodService.class);
        intent.setAction(CurrentMoodService.UPDATEMOOD);
        intent.putExtra(AppWidgetManager.EXTRA_APPWIDGET_ID, appWidgetId);
        PendingIntent pendingIntent = PendingIntent.getService(context, 0, intent, 0);
        views.setOnClickPendingIntent(R.id.widgetBtn, pendingIntent);
        appWidgetManager.updateAppWidget(appWidgetId, views);
    }
}
```

8. Finally, declare the service and the app widget provider in the manifest file (*AndroidManifest.xml*).

```
            <service android:name=".CurrentMoodService">
            </service>
        <receiver android:name=".CurrentMoodWidgetProvider">
            <intent-filter>
                <action android:name="android.appwidget.action.APPWIDGET_UPDATE" />
            </intent-filter>
            <meta-data android:name="android.appwidget.provider"
                    android:resource="@xml/widgetproviderinfo" />
        </receiver>
```

Source Download URL

You can download the source code for this example from *http://sites.google.com/site/androidsourcecode/src/CurrentMoodWidgetProject.rar*.

## CHAPTER 8

GUI Alerts: Menus, Dialogs, Toasts, and Notifications

8.1 Introduction: GUI Alerts

Ian Darwin

Discussion

User interface toolkits as diverse as Java Swing, Apple Macintosh, Microsoft Windows, and browser JavaScript all feature the ubiquitous "pop-up menu," usually in the window-frame version and the context (in-window) form. Android follows this, with some variations to be expected due to the smaller screens used on many devices (e.g., pop-up or context menus cover a large portion of the screen). As well, frame-anchored menus appear at the bottom of the screen rather than the top.

Those other window systems also feature the ubiquitous "dialog," a window smaller than the main screen that pops up to notify you of some condition or occurrence, and asks you to confirm your acceptance, or asks you to make one of several choices, provide some information, and so on.

Android provides a fairly standard dialog mechanism. But it doesn't stop there. It provides a smaller, lighter "pop up" called a toast. This only appears on screen for a few seconds, and fades away on its own. Intended for passive notification of low-importance events, it is often incorrectly used for error notification, although I advise against this usage.

And it doesn't stop there. Android also provides a "notification" mechanism, which allows you to put text and/or an icon in the notifications bar (top right of the screen in Gingerbread, bottom right in Honeycomb). A notification can optionally be accompanied by any combination of LED flashing, audio sounds, and device vibration.

Each of these interactive mechanisms is discussed in this chapter. The chapter proceeds in the same order as this introduction, from menus, to dialogs and toasts, to notifications.

8.2 Creating and Displaying a Menu

Rachee Singh

Problem

You want to show a menu when the user presses the Menu button on the Android device.

Solution

Implement a menu by setting it up in the XML and attaching it to your `Activity` by overriding onCreateOptionsMenu().

Discussion

First, create a directory named *menu* in the *res* directory of the project. In the *menu* directory create a *Menu.xml* file. Example 8-1 shows the code for *Menu.xml*.

Example 8-1. The menu definition

```
<menu xmlns:android="http://schemas.android.com/apk/res/android">
    <item android:id="@+id/icon1"
        android:title="One"
        android:icon="@drawable/first" />
    <item android:id="@+id/icon2"
        android:title="Two"
        android:icon="@drawable/second" />
    <item android:id="@+id/icon3"
        android:title="Three"
        android:icon="@drawable/three" />
    <item android:id="@+id/icon4"
        android:title="Four"
        android:icon="@drawable/four" />
</menu>
```

In this XML code we add a menu and to it we add as many items as our application requires. We can also provide an image for each menu item (in this example, default images have been used).

In the Java code for the `Activity`, override the onCreateOptionsMenu.

```
@Override
public boolean onCreateOptionsMenu(Menu menu) {
    MenuInflater inflater = getMenuInflater();
    inflater.inflate(R.menu.menu, menu);
```

```
        return true;
    }
```

Figure 8-1 shows how the menu should look.

Figure 8-1. Custom menu

8.3 Handling Choice Selection in a Menu

Rachee Singh

Problem

After creating a custom menu, you want to react when the user clicks a menu item.

Solution

Override the onOptionsItemSelected method.

Discussion

In the Java Activity we need to override onOptionsItemSelected. This method takes in a MenuItem and checks for its ID. Based on the ID of the item that is clicked, a switch-case can be used. Depending on the case selected, appropriate action can be taken. The custom menu would look something like Figure 8-2.

For this example, the cases just display toasts.

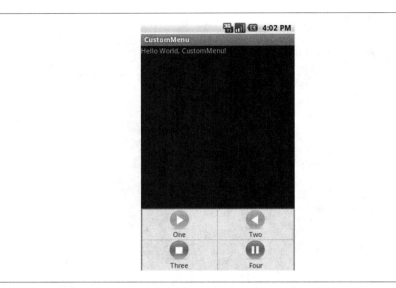

Figure 8-2. Custom menu

Here's the source code:

```
@Override
    public boolean onOptionsItemSelected(MenuItem item) {
        switch (item.getItemId()) {
            case R.id.icon1:
                Toast.makeText(this, "Icon 1 Beep Bop!", Toast.LENGTH_LONG).show();
                break;
            case R.id.icon2:
                Toast.makeText(this, "Icon 2 Beep Bop!", Toast.LENGTH_LONG).show();
                break;
            case R.id.icon3:
                Toast.makeText(this, "Icon 3 Beep Bop!", Toast.LENGTH_LONG).show();
                break;
            case R.id.icon4 :
                Toast.makeText(this, "Icon 4 Beep Bop!", Toast.LENGTH_LONG).show();
                break;
        }
        return true;
    }
```

Figure 8-3 shows the result.

Source Download URL

You can download the source code from *https://docs.google.com/leaf?id=0B_rE SQKgad5LZWM0ODRiNjAtNzJhOS00MGRjLTkwMjMtMjNlOTQwZDU0OGE2& hl=en_US&authkey=CJKD4IoH*.

Figure 8-3. Menu choice confirmed

8.4 Creating a Submenu

Rachee Singh

Problem

You want to display options to the user from within an existing menu.

Solution

Use a submenu implementation to provide options to the user.

Discussion

A submenu is a part of a menu that displays options in a hierarchical manner. On desktop operating systems, submenus appear to "cascade" down and to the side, usually the right side. Android devices may not have room for that, so submenus appear like dialogs in that they float over the main screen of the application, rather like a spinner (see Recipe 7.8). You can create the menus in the following ways:

1. By inflating an XML layout
2. By creating the menu items in the Java code

In this recipe we will follow the second approach, and we will create the menu/submenu items in the onCreateOptionsMenu() method.

First we add the submenu to the menu using the addSubMenu() method. In order to prevent conflicts with other items in the menu, we explicitly provide the group ID and item ID to the submenu we are creating (constants for the item ID and group ID are specified). Then we set an icon for the submenu with the setIcon method and an icon for the header of the submenu (see Example 8-2).

To add items to the submenu we use the add() method. As arguments to the method, the group ID, item ID, position of the item in the submenu, and text associated with each item are specified:

```
private static final int OPTION_1 = 0;
private static final int OPTION_2 = 1;
private int GROUP_ID = 4;
private int ITEM_ID =3;
```

Example 8-2. The menu listener methods

```
@Override
public boolean onCreateOptionsMenu(Menu menu) {

    SubMenu sub1 = menu.addSubMenu(GROUP_ID, ITEM_ID , Menu.NONE, R.string.submenu_1);
    sub1.setHeaderIcon(R.drawable.icon);
    sub1.setIcon(R.drawable.icon);

    sub1.add(GROUP_ID , OPTION_1, 0, "Submenu Option 1");
    sub1.add(GROUP_ID, OPTION_2, 1, "Submenu Option 2");

    return super.onCreateOptionsMenu(menu);
}
@Override
public boolean onOptionsItemSelected(MenuItem item) {
    switch (item.getItemId()) {
      case OPTION_1:
        Toast.makeText(this, "Submenu 1, Option 1", Toast.LENGTH_LONG).show();
            break;
        case OPTION_2:
            Toast.makeText(this, "Submenu 1, Option 2", Toast.LENGTH_LONG).show();
            break;
    }
```

```
        return true;
}
```

The onOptionItemSelected() method is called when an item of the menu/submenu is selected. In this method, using a switch-case we check for the item that is clicked and an appropriate message is displayed.

Figure 8-4 shows the initial menu that appears when you press the Menu button; Figure 8-5 shows the submenu that appears when you click on the main menu item.

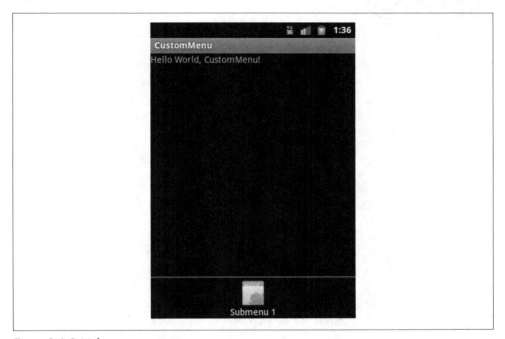

Figure 8-4. Initial menu

Source Download URL

You can download the source code for this example from *https://docs.google.com/leaf ?id=0B_rESQKgad5LN2I5ZmIxNjEtYzc3Zi00MjczLTk5NzEtYmZjNzRlNjM1ZTc2& hl=en_US&authkey=CN-BsekI.*

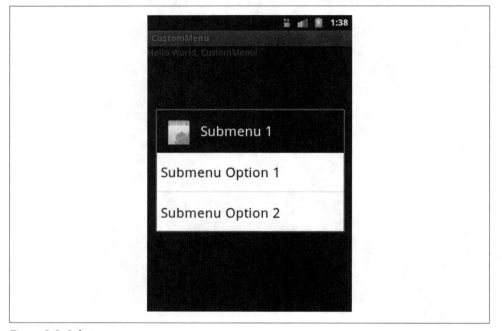

Figure 8-5. Submenu

8.5 Creating a Pop-up/Alert Dialog

Rachee Singh

Problem

You would like a way to prompt the user about things such as unsaved changes in the application through an alerting mechanism.

Solution

Use `AlertDialog`, a class that enables you to provides suitable options to the user. In the case of an "unsaved changes" scenario, the options would be:

- Save
- Discard Changes
- Cancel

Discussion

Through the `AlertDialog` class, you can provide the user with up to three options that can be used in any scenario:

- Positive reaction
- Neutral reaction
- Negative reaction

If the user has entered some data in an `EditText` and is then attempting to cancel that `Activity`, the application should prompt the user to either save his changes, discard them, or cancel the alert dialog, which should also cancel the cancellation of the `Activity` as well.

Here is the code that would implement this kind of `AlertDialog` along with appropriate click listeners on each button on the dialog:

```
alertDialog = new AlertDialog.Builder(this)
.setTitle(R.string.unsaved)
.setMessage(R.string.unsaved_changes_message)
.setPositiveButton(R.string.save_changes, new AlertDialog.OnClickListener() {
    public void onClick(DialogInterface dialog, int which) {
        saveInformation();
    }
})
.setNeutralButton(R.string.discard_changes, new AlertDialog.OnClickListener() {
    public void onClick(DialogInterface dialog, int which) {
            finish();
    }
})
.setNegativeButton(android.R.string.cancel_dialog, new AlertDialog.OnClickListener() {
    public void onClick(DialogInterface dialog, int which) {
            alertDialog.cancel();
    }
})
.create();
alertDialog.show();
```

8.6 Using a Timepicker Widget

Pratik Rupwal

Problem

You need to ask the user to enter the time for processing some element in the application. Accepting time in text boxes is not graceful, and requires validation.

Solution

You can use the standard `Timepicker` widget to accept time from the user. It makes the app appear graceful and reduces the requirement of validation. The `Datepicker` works in a similar fashion for choosing dates.

Discussion

The code in Example 8-3 shows how to reveal the current time on the screen, and gives a button which, when clicked, produces the `Timepicker` widget through which the user can accept the time.

Example 8-3. The main activity

```
public class Main extends Activity {

private TextView mTimeDisplay;
private Button mPickTime;

private int mHour;
private int mMinute;

static final int TIME_DIALOG_ID = 0;

    /** Called when the activity is first created. */
    @Override
    public void onCreate(Bundle savedInstanceState) {
        super.onCreate(savedInstanceState);
        setContentView(R.layout.main);

        // capture our View elements
        mTimeDisplay = (TextView) findViewById(R.id.timeDisplay);
        mPickTime = (Button) findViewById(R.id.pickTime);

        // add a click listener to the button
        mPickTime.setOnClickListener(new View.OnClickListener() {
            public void onClick(View v) {
                showDialog(TIME_DIALOG_ID);
            }
        });

        // get the current time
        final Calendar c = Calendar.getInstance();
```

```
        mHour = c.get(Calendar.HOUR_OF_DAY);
        mMinute = c.get(Calendar.MINUTE);

        // display the current date
        updateDisplay();
    }

    // The overridden method shown below gets invoked when
    //'showDialog()' is called inside the 'onClick()' method defined
    // for handling the click event of the button 'change the time'

    @Override
    protected Dialog onCreateDialog(int id) {
        switch (id) {
        case TIME_DIALOG_ID:
            return new TimePickerDialog(this,
                    mTimeSetListener, mHour, mMinute, false);
        }
        return null;
    }

// updates the time we display in the TextView
    private void updateDisplay() {
        mTimeDisplay.setText(
            new StringBuilder()
                    .append(pad(mHour)).append(":")
                    .append(pad(mMinute)));
    }

// the callback received when the user "sets" the time in the dialog
    private TimePickerDialog.OnTimeSetListener mTimeSetListener =
        new TimePickerDialog.OnTimeSetListener() {
     public void onTimeSet(android.widget.TimePicker view, int hourOfDay, int minute) {
                mHour = hourOfDay;
                mMinute = minute;
                updateDisplay();
            }
        };

        private static String pad(int c)
        {
            if (c >= 10)
                return String.valueOf(c);
            else
                return "0" + String.valueOf(c);
        }
}
```

Figure 8-6 shows the timepicker that appears on the screen after the user clicks the "Change the time" button.

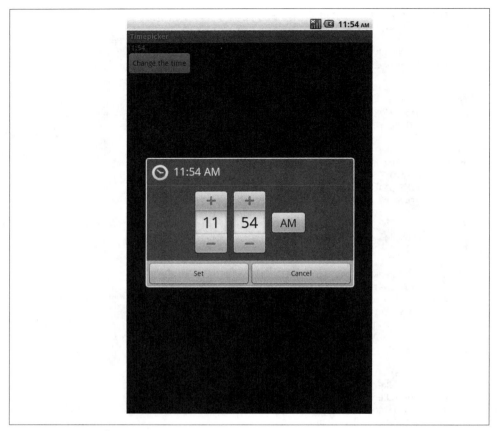

Figure 8-6. Setting the time

8.7 Creating an iPhone-like Wheel Picker for Selection

Wagied Davids

Problem

You want a selection UI component similar to the iPhone's wheel picker.

Solution

Create a scroll-wheel picker with the third-party widget Android-Wheel, the iPhone-like WheelPicker for Android.

Discussion

You can download Android-Wheel from *http://code.google.com/p/android-wheel/*. Unfortunately, installation requires more than installing a JAR file in your *libs* directory.

Because resources needed for drawing must be in the *res* directory, you can extract the *android-wheel-xx.zip* file, and copy the *wheel/src* and *wheel/res* folders into your project. Alternatively, create a new Android project from the *wheel* subdirectory (Android will automatically make it an Android Library project) and make your main project depend on that (see Recipe 1.9). Then you can add one or more `WheelView` objects to your `Layout`, using the full class name. This class and its friends are found in the `kan kan.wheel.widget` package; the `adapters` subpackage provides the `WheelViewAdapter` interface and some implementations. The widget package provides two interfaces that follow the standard `setListener` pattern on the `WheelView` component: these are `wheel.addChangingListener(OnWheelChangedListener)` and `wheel.addScrollingListener(OnWheelScrollListener)`.

The code in Example 8-4, from a medical app, lets you choose a body part and location (R or L for Right or Left). The choices are hardcoded here; in a real-world app they would come from an XML file to allow for internationalization. The app should appear as shown in Figure 8-7.

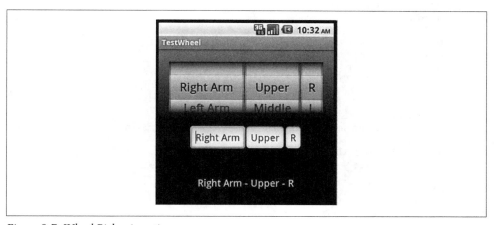

Figure 8-7. Wheel Picker in action

Example 8-4. The ScrollWheel example code

```
import kankan.wheel.widget.OnWheelChangedListener;
import kankan.wheel.widget.OnWheelScrollListener;
import kankan.wheel.widget.WheelView;
import kankan.wheel.widget.adapters.ArrayWheelAdapter;
import android.app.Activity;
import android.os.Bundle;
import android.util.Log;
import android.widget.EditText;
import android.widget.TextView;

public class WheelDemoActivity extends Activity {

    private final static String TAG = "WheelDemo";
```

```
String wheelMenu1[] = new String[]{
    "Right Arm", "Left Arm", "R-Abdomen", "L-Abdomen", "Right Thigh", "Left Thigh"};
String wheelMenu2[] = new String[]{"Upper", "Middle", "Lower"};
String wheelMenu3[] = new String[]{"R", "L"};

// Wheel scrolled flag
private boolean wheelScrolled = false;

private TextView text;
private EditText text1;
private EditText text2;
private EditText text3;

@Override
public void onCreate(Bundle savedInstanceState) {
    super.onCreate(savedInstanceState);
    setContentView(R.layout.empty_layout);

    initWheel(R.id.p1, wheelMenu1);
    initWheel(R.id.p2, wheelMenu2);
    initWheel(R.id.p3, wheelMenu3);

    text1 = (EditText) this.findViewById(R.id.r1);
    text2 = (EditText) this.findViewById(R.id.r2);
    text3 = (EditText) this.findViewById(R.id.r3);
    resultText = (TextView) this.findViewById(R.id.result);
}

// Wheel scrolled listener
OnWheelScrollListener scrolledListener = new OnWheelScrollListener()  {
    @Override
    public void onScrollingStarted(WheelView wheel) {
        wheelScrolled = true;
    }
    @Override
    public void onScrollingFinished(WheelView wheel) {
        wheelScrolled = false;
        updateStatus();
    }
};

// Wheel changed listener
private final OnWheelChangedListener changedListener = new OnWheelChangedListener() {
    @Override
    public void onChanged(WheelView wheel, int oldValue, int newValue) {
        Log.d(TAG, "onChanged, wheelScrolled = " + wheelScrolled);
        if (!wheelScrolled) {
            updateStatus();
        }
    }
};

/**
 * Updates entered PIN status
```

```
      */
    private void updateStatus() {
        text1.setText(wheelMenu1[getWheel(R.id.p1).getCurrentItem()]);
        text2.setText(wheelMenu2[getWheel(R.id.p2).getCurrentItem()]);
        text3.setText(wheelMenu3[getWheel(R.id.p3).getCurrentItem()]);

        resultText.setText(
            wheelMenu1[getWheel(R.id.p1).getCurrentItem()] + " - " +
            wheelMenu2[getWheel(R.id.p2).getCurrentItem()] + " - " +
            wheelMenu3[getWheel(R.id.p3).getCurrentItem()]);
    }

    /**
     * Initializes wheel
     *
     * @param id
     *          the wheel widget Id
     */
    private void initWheel(int id, String[] wheelMenu1) {
        WheelView wheel = (WheelView) findViewById(id);
        wheel.setViewAdapter(new ArrayWheelAdapter<String>(this, wheelMenu1));
        wheel.setVisibleItems(2);
        wheel.setCurrentItem(0);
        wheel.addChangingListener(changedListener);
        wheel.addScrollingListener(scrolledListener);
    }

    /**
     * Returns wheel by Id
     *
     * @param id
     *          the wheel Id
     * @return the wheel with passed Id
     */
    private WheelView getWheel(int id) {
        return (WheelView) findViewById(id);
    }
}
```

8.8 Creating a Tabbed Dialog

Rachee Singh

Problem

You want to categorize the display of information in a custom dialog.

Solution

Use a tabbed layout within a custom dialog.

Discussion

The custom dialog class implements the `Dialog` class:

```
public class CustomDialog extends Dialog
```

The constructor of the class has to be initialized:

```
public CustomDialog(final Context context) {
        super(context);

        setTitle("My First Custom Tabbed Dialog");
        setContentView(R.layout.custom_dialog_layout);
```

To create the two tabs, insert the Example 8-5 code within the constructor: place `tab_image1` and `tab_image2` in */res/drawable*. These images are placed on the tabs of the tabbed custom dialog.

Example 8-5. Constructor code to create and add the tabs

```
// get our tabHost from the xml
TabHost tabHost = (TabHost)findViewById(R.id.TabHost01);
tabHost.setup();

// create tab 1
TabHost.TabSpec spec1 = tabHost.newTabSpec("tab1");
spec1.setIndicator("Profile",
    context.getResources().getDrawable(R.drawable.tab_image1));
spec1.setContent(R.id.TextView01);
tabHost.addTab(spec1);
//create tab2
TabHost.TabSpec spec2 = tabHost.newTabSpec("tab2");
spec2.setIndicator("Profile",
    context.getResources().getDrawable(R.drawable.tab_image2));
spec2.setContent(R.id.TextView02);
tabHost.addTab(spec2);
```

This is a simple tabbed dialog. It required the addition of just a few lines into the constructor's code. To implement something like a list view, a list view adapter would be required. A variety of tabs can be inserted based on the application's requirements.

As shown in Example 8-6, the XML code for a tabbed dialog would require <tab host> tags enclosing the entire layout. Within these tags you would place the location of various parts of the tabbed dialog. You must use a frame layout to place the content of the different tabs. In this case, we are creating two tabs, both with a scroll view containing text (stored in *Strings.xml* and named *lorem_ipsum*).

Example 8-6. The custom_dialog_layout.xml file

```
<TabHost
    xmlns:android="http://schemas.android.com/apk/res/android"
    android:id="@+id/TabHost01"
    android:layout_width="fill_parent"
    android:layout_height="500dip">
```

```xml
<LinearLayout
    android:orientation="vertical"
    android:layout_width="fill_parent"
    android:layout_height="wrap_content"
    android:padding="5dp">

        <TabWidget
    android:id="@android:id/tabs"
    android:layout_width="fill_parent"
    android:layout_height="wrap_content"/>

        <FrameLayout
    android:id="@android:id/tabcontent"
    android:layout_width="fill_parent"
    android:layout_height="wrap_content"
    android:padding="5dp">

        <ScrollView android:id="@+id/ScrollView01"
            android:layout_width="wrap_content"
            android:layout_height="200px">

        <TextView
            android:id="@+id/TextView01"
            android:text="@string/lorem_ipsum"
            android:layout_width="wrap_content"
            android:layout_height="wrap_content"
            android:gravity="center_horizontal"
            android:paddingLeft="15dip"
            android:paddingTop="15dip"
            android:paddingRight="20dip"
            android:paddingBottom="15dip"/>

        </ScrollView>

        <ScrollView android:id="@+id/ScrollView02"
            android:layout_width="wrap_content"
            android:layout_height="200px">

        <TextView
            android:id="@+id/TextView02"
            android:text="@string/lorem_ipsum"
            android:layout_width="wrap_content"
            android:layout_height="wrap_content"
            android:gravity="center_horizontal"
            android:paddingLeft="15dip"
            android:paddingTop="15dip"
            android:paddingRight="20dip"
            android:paddingBottom="15dip"/>

        </ScrollView>
    </FrameLayout>
    </LinearLayout>
</TabHost>
```

8.9 Creating a ProgressDialog

Rachee Singh

Problem

You want to be able to alert the user of background processing occurring in the application.

Solution

Show a `ProgressDialog` while the processing is being carried out.

Discussion

In this recipe we will provide a button that shows a `ProgressDialog` when clicked. In the `ProgressDialog` we set the title as "Please Wait" and the content as "Processing Information...". After this we create a new thread and start the thread's execution. In the `run()` method (which gets executed once the thread gets started) we call the sleep method for four seconds. After these four seconds expire the `ProgressDialog` is dismissed and the text in the `TextView` gets changed:

```
complete = (TextView) this.findViewById(R.id.complete);
complete.setText("Press the Button to start Processing");
processing = (Button)findViewById(R.id.processing);
processing.setOnClickListener(new View.OnClickListener() {

    @Override
    public void onClick(View arg0) {
        progressDialog = ProgressDialog.show(ProgressDialogExp.this,
            "Please Wait", "Processing Information..", true,false);
        Thread thread = new Thread(ProgressDialogExp.this);
        thread.start();
    }
});
```

We use a `Handler` to update the UI once thread execution finishes. We send an empty message to the `Handler` after thread execution completes, and then in the `Handler` we dismiss the `ProgressDialog` and update the text of the `TextView`.

```
public void run() {
    try {
        Thread.sleep(4000);
    } catch (InterruptedException e) {
        e.printStackTrace();
    }
        handler.sendEmptyMessage(0);
}

private Handler handler = new Handler() {
        @Override
        public void handleMessage(Message msg) {
```

```
        progressDialog.dismiss();
        complete.setText("Processing Finished");
    }
};
```

Source Download URL

You can download the source code for this example from *https://docs.google.com/leaf ?id=0B_rESQKgad5LMTE2NDcyMDEtNGMzMS00MzI4LTgyNGUtNzliZ mY4ZjhhOWE2&hl=en_US.*

8.10 Creating a Custom Dialog with Buttons, Images, and Text

Rachee Singh

Problem

Your application requires a dialog-like structure in place of a full-fledged **Activity** to show some information. Text, images, and a button are required on this custom dialog.

Solution

Create a custom dialog with tabs. Since everything can be squeezed into a dialog in place of an entire **Activity**, the application will seem more compact.

Discussion

The **CustomDialog** class can directly extend **Dialog**:

```
public class CustomDialog extends Dialog
```

The following lines of code in the **CustomDialog** class's **onCreate()** method add a title and get handles for the buttons in the dialog:

```
setTitle("Dialog Title");
setContentView(R.layout.custom_dialog_layout);
//OnClickListeners for the buttons present in the Dialog
Button button1 = (Button) findViewById(R.id.button1);
Button button2 = (Button) findViewById(R.id.button2);
```

For the two buttons that are added, `OnClickListeners` are defined in the following lines of code. On being clicked, `button1` dismisses the dialog and `button2` starts a new activity:

```java
button1.setOnClickListener(new View.OnClickListener() {

    @Override
    public void onClick(View v) {
        dismiss(); //to dismiss the Dialog
    }
});

button2.setOnClickListener(new View.OnClickListener() {

    @Override
    public void onClick(View v) {
        // Fire an intent on click of this button
        Intent showQuickInfo = new Intent("com.android.oreilly.QuickInfo");
        showQuickInfo.setFlags(Intent.FLAG_ACTIVITY_NEW_TASK);
        context.startActivity(showQuickInfo);
    }
});
```

Here is the XML layout of the dialog, present in */res/layout custom_dialog_layout*. The entire code is enclosed in a `LinearLayout`. Within the `LinearLayout`, a `RelativeLayout` is used to position two buttons. Then, below the `RelativeLayout`, another `RelativeLay out` containing a scroll view is present. *android_button* and *thumbsup* are the names of the images in */res/drawable*.

```xml
<LinearLayout
        android:orientation="vertical"
        android:layout_width="fill_parent"
        android:layout_height="wrap_content"
        android:padding="5dp">

    <RelativeLayout
        android:layout_width="fill_parent"
        android:layout_height="wrap_content"
        android:paddingBottom="10dip">
            <Button
                android:id="@+id/button1"
                android:background="@drawable/android_button"
                android:layout_height="80dip"
                android:layout_width="80dip"
                android:layout_alignParentLeft="true"
                android:layout_marginLeft="10dip"
                android:gravity="center"/>

            <Button
                android:id="@+id/button2"
                android:background="@drawable/thumbsup"
                android:layout_height="80dip"
                android:layout_width="80dip"
                android:layout_alignParentRight="true"
                android:layout_marginRight="10dip"
                android:gravity="center"/>
```

```
        </RelativeLayout>

        <RelativeLayout
        android:layout_width="fill_parent"
        android:layout_height="wrap_content"
        android:paddingBottom="10dip">

                <ScrollView android:id="@+id/ScrollView01"
                    android:layout_width="wrap_content"
                    android:layout_height="200px">

                <TextView
                    android:id="@+id/TextView01"
                    android:text="@string/lorem"
                    android:layout_width="wrap_content"
                    android:layout_height="wrap_content"
                    android:gravity="center_horizontal"
                    android:paddingLeft="15dip"
                    android:paddingTop="15dip"
                    android:paddingRight="20dip"
                    android:paddingBottom="15dip"/>

                </ScrollView>
        </RelativeLayout>
    </LinearLayout>
```

8.11 Creating a Reusable About Box Class

Daniel Fowler

Problem

About boxes are common in applications; it is useful not to have to recode them for each new app.

Solution

Write an `AboutBox` class that can be installed into any new app.

Discussion

Whatever the operating system, whatever the program, chances are it has an About option. There is a Wikipedia entry for it, *http://en.wikipedia.org/wiki/About_box*, and it is useful for support:

"Hello, there is a problem with my application."

"Hi, can you press About and tell me the version number?"

Since it is likely to be required again and again, it is worth having a ready-made About Box class that you can easily add to any new app that you develop. At a minimum, the About option should display a dialog with a title, such as About My App, the version name from the manifest, some descriptive text (loaded from a string resource), and an OK button.

The version name can be read from the `PackageInfo` class. (`PackageInfo` is obtained from `PackageManager` which itself is available from the app's `Context`). Here is a method to read an app's version name string:

```
static String VersionName(Context context) {
    try {
        return context.getPackageManager().getPackageInfo(
            context.getPackageName(),0).versionName;
    }
    catch (NameNotFoundException e) {
    return "Unknown";
    }
}
```

`PageInfo` can throw a `NameNotFoundException` (for when the class is used to find information on other packages). The exception is unlikely to occur; here it is just consumed by returning an error string. (To return the version code, the app's internal version number, swap `versionName` for `versionCode` and return an integer.)

With an `AlertDialog.Builder` and the `setTitle()`, `setMessage()`, and `show()` methods, you will soon have an About option up and running; but you can improve the About option by using the Android `Linkify` class and a custom layout. In the About text any web addresses (such as app help pages on the Web) and email addresses (useful for a support email link) can be made clickable. Save the layout shown in Example 8-7 into the *res/layout* folder as *aboutbox.xml*.

Example 8-7. The aboutbox.xml file

```xml
<?xml version="1.0" encoding="utf-8"?>
<ScrollView xmlns:android="http://schemas.android.com/apk/res/android"
    android:id="@+id/aboutView"
    android:layout_width="fill_parent"
    android:layout_height="fill_parent">
    <LinearLayout android:id="@+id/aboutLayout"
    android:orientation="horizontal"
    android:layout_width="fill_parent"
    android:layout_height="fill_parent"
    android:padding="5dp">
    <TextView android:id="@+id/aboutText"
        android:layout_width="wrap_content"
        android:layout_height="fill_parent"
        android:textColor="#FFF"/>
    </LinearLayout>
</ScrollView>
```

A `ScrollView` is required for when the About text is long and the screens are small (QVGA). Another advantage of the custom layout for the About box text is that the look of the text can be modified (this recipe sets it to white with a little padding).

The `AboutBox` class uses a `Spannable` to hold the text which can then be passed to `Linkify` via the `TextView` in the custom layout. The layout is inflated, the About text is set, and then `AlertBuilder.Builder` is used to create the dialog. Example 8-8 shows the full code for the class.

Example 8-8. The AboutBox class

```java
public class AboutBox {
    static String VersionName(Context context) {
    try {
        return context.getPackageManager().getPackageInfo(
            context.getPackageName(),0).versionName;
    }
    catch (NameNotFoundException e) {
        return "Unknown";
    }
    }
    public static void Show(Activity callingActivity) {
    //Use a Spannable to allow for links highlighting
    SpannableString aboutText = new SpannableString("Version " +
        VersionName(callingActivity)+ "\n\n" +
        callingActivity.getString(R.string.about));
    //Generate views to pass to AlertDialog.Builder and to set the text
    View about;
    TextView tvAbout;
    try {
        //Inflate the custom view
        LayoutInflater inflater = callingActivity.getLayoutInflater();
        about = inflater.inflate(R.layout.aboutbox,
            (ViewGroup) callingActivity.findViewById(R.id.aboutView));
        tvAbout = (TextView) about.findViewById(R.id.aboutText);
    }
    catch(InflateException e) {
        //Inflater can throw exception, unlikely but default to TextView if it occurs
        about = tvAbout = new TextView(callingActivity);
    }
    //Set the about text
    tvAbout.setText(aboutText);
    // Now Linkify the text
    Linkify.addLinks(tvAbout, Linkify.ALL);
    //Build and show the dialog
    new AlertDialog.Builder(callingActivity)
        .setTitle("About " + callingActivity.getString(R.string.app_name))
        .setCancelable(true)
        .setIcon(R.drawable.icon)
        .setPositiveButton("OK", null)
        .setView(about)
        .show();    //Builder method returns allow for method chaining
    }
}
```

Notice that the app's icon can be shown in the About box title using `setIcon(R.drawable.icon)`. String resources for the app's name and About text are required in the usual *res/values/strings.xml*:

```xml
<?xml version="1.0" encoding="utf-8"?>
<resources>
    <string name="app_name">My App</string>
    <string name="about">This is our App, please see
    http://www.example.com. Email support at support@example.com.</string>
</resources>
```

Showing the About box requires only one line of code, shown here on a button click:

```java
public class Main extends Activity {
    @Override
    public void onCreate(Bundle savedInstanceState) {
    super.onCreate(savedInstanceState);
    setContentView(R.layout.main);
    findViewById(R.id.button1).setOnClickListener(new OnClickListener(){
        public void onClick(View arg0) {
        AboutBox.Show(Main.this);
        }
    });
    }
}
```

The result should look like Figure 8-8.

Figure 8-8. The About box in action

To reuse this About box, just drop the *aboutbox.xml* file into a project's *res/layout* folder, add a new class called AboutBox, and replace the class code with the AboutBox class code just shown. Then just call AboutBox.Show() from a button or menu click. Web addresses and email addresses highlighted in the text can be clicked and invoke the browser or email client, which can be very useful.

See Also

http://developer.android.com/reference/android/text/util/Linkify.html;   *http://developer .android.com/guide/topics/ui/dialogs.html*

8.12 Customizing the Appearance of a Toast

Rachee Singh

Problem

You want to customize the look of toast notifications.

Solution

Define an XML layout for the toast and then inflate the view in Java.

Discussion

First, we will define the layout of the custom toast in an XML file, *toast_layout.xml*. It contains an `ImageView` and a `TextView`, as shown in Example 8-9.

Example 8-9. Toast layout in XML

```xml
<LinearLayout xmlns:android="http://schemas.android.com/apk/res/android"
              android:id="@+id/toast_layout_root"
              android:orientation="horizontal"
              android:layout_width="fill_parent"
              android:layout_height="fill_parent"
              android:padding="10dp"
              android:background="#f0ffef"
              >
    <ImageView android:id="@+id/image"
               android:layout_width="wrap_content"
               android:layout_height="fill_parent"
               android:layout_marginRight="10dp"
               />
    <TextView android:id="@+id/text"
              android:layout_width="wrap_content"
              android:layout_height="fill_parent"
              android:textColor="#000000"
              />
</LinearLayout>
```

Then, in the Java code, we inflate this view using `LayoutInflater`. We set the gravity and duration of the toast. The `setGravity` method modifies the position at which the toast will be displayed. On the click of the `customToast` button, we show the toast (see Example 8-10).

Example 8-10. Inflating the view

```java
customToast = (Button)findViewById(R.id.customToast);

LayoutInflater inflater = getLayoutInflater();
View layout = inflater.inflate(R.layout.toast_layout,
    (ViewGroup) findViewById(R.id.toast_layout_root));

ImageView image = (ImageView) layout.findViewById(R.id.image);
```

```
image.setImageResource(R.drawable.icon);
TextView text = (TextView) layout.findViewById(R.id.text);
text.setText("Hello! This is a custom toast!");

final Toast toast = new Toast(getApplicationContext());
toast.setGravity(Gravity.CENTER_VERTICAL, 0, 0);
toast.setDuration(Toast.LENGTH_LONG);
toast.setView(layout);
customToast.setOnClickListener(new View.OnClickListener() {
    @Override
        public void onClick(View arg0) {
        toast.show();
    }
});
```

Source Download URL

You can download the source code for this example from *https://docs.google.com/leaf ?id=0B_rESQKgad5LYTFjYjY4NWEtM2YzZC00NzEzLTg5ZGEtMzFhM2Ux OWM2MmFk&hl=en_US*.

8.13 Creating a Notification in the Status Bar

Ian Darwin

Problem

You want to place a notification icon in the status bar to call the user's attention to an event that occurred *or* to remind her of a service that is running in the background.

Solution

Create a Notification object, and provide it with a PendingIntent that wraps a real Intent for what to do when the user selects the notification. At the same time you pass in the PendingIntent you also pass a title and text to be displayed in the notification area. You should set the AUTO_CANCEL flag unless you want to remove the notification from the status bar manually. Finally, you find and ask the NotificationManager to display (notify) your notification, associating with it an ID so that you can refer to it later (e.g., to remove it).

Discussion

Notifications are normally used from a running `Service` class to notify (hence the name) the user of some fact. Either an event has occurred (receipt of a message, loss of contact with a server, or whatever), or, you just want to remind the user that a long-running service is still running. The notification is commonly used to start an activity and is, in fact, the only recommended way for a background service to start an activity (services should never start activities directly!).

Create a `Notification` object; the constructor takes an `Icon` ID, the text to display briefly in the status bar, and the time at which the event occurred (timestamp in milliseconds). Before you can show the notification, you have to provide it with a `PendingIntent` for what to do when the user selects the notification, and ask the `NotificationManager` to display your notification. Example 8-11 shows the notification code.

 The following code shows doing the right thing in the wrong place; notifications are normally shown from services. This recipe is just focusing on the Notification API.

Example 8-11. The notification code

```java
public class Main extends Activity {

        private static final int NOTIFICATION_ID = 1;

        /** Called when the activity is first created. */
        @Override
        public void onCreate(Bundle savedInstanceState) {
                super.onCreate(savedInstanceState);
                setContentView(R.layout.main);

                int icon = R.drawable.icon;  // Preferably a distinct icon

                // Create the notification itself
                String noticeMeText = getString(R.string.noticeMe);
                Notification n =
                        new Notification(
                        icon, noticeMeText, System.currentTimeMillis());

                // And the Intent of what to do when user selects notification
                Context applicationContext = getApplicationContext();
                Intent notifyIntent = new Intent(this, NotificationTarget.class);
                PendingIntent wrappedIntent =
                        PendingIntent.getActivity(this, 0,
                        notifyIntent, Intent.FLAG_ACTIVITY_NEW_TASK);

                // Condition the Notification
                String title = getString(R.string.title);
```

```
            String message = getString(R.string.message);
            n.setLatestEventInfo(applicationContext, title,
                    message, wrappedIntent);
            n.flags |= Notification.FLAG_AUTO_CANCEL;

            // Now invoke the Notification Service
            String notifService = Context.NOTIFICATION_SERVICE;
            NotificationManager mgr =
                    (NotificationManager) getSystemService(notifService);
            mgr.notify(NOTIFICATION_ID, n);
        }
}
```

The following is the file *strings.xml*:

```
<resources>
    <string name="app_name">NotificationDemo</string>
    <string name="hello">Hello World, Main!</string>
    <string name="noticeMe">Lookie Here!!</string>
    <string name="title">My Notification</string>
    <string name="message">This is my message</string>
    <string name="target_name">Notification Target</string>
    <string name="thanks">Thank you for selecting the notification.</string>
</resources>
```

The noticeMe string appears briefly (only a few seconds) in the status bar. Notification text and icons appear in the very upper left of the screen in Gingerbread (2.x) and in the lower right in Honeycomb (3.x), as shown in Figure 8-9.

Then the main view will appear, as seen in Figure 8-10.

When the user drags the status bar down, it expands to show the details, which include the icons and the title and message strings (see Figure 8-11). You can also use a custom view here; see the official Android documentation, cited in "See Also" on page 360.

If you have auto-clear set, the notification will no longer appear in the status bar. If the user selects the notification box, the PendingIntent becomes current. Ours simply shows a basic Thank You notification (Figure 8-12). If the user clicks the Clear button, however, the Intent does not get run (even with auto-clear, which can leave you in a bit of a lurch).

Sounds and other irritants

If the user's attention is needed at once, you can specify a sound to be played when the notification is first displayed (or, to really annoy the user, repeatedly). Or you can make the device vibrate, where supported.

The user's default notification sound can be played as follows:

```
notification.defaults |= Notification.DEFAULT_SOUND;
```

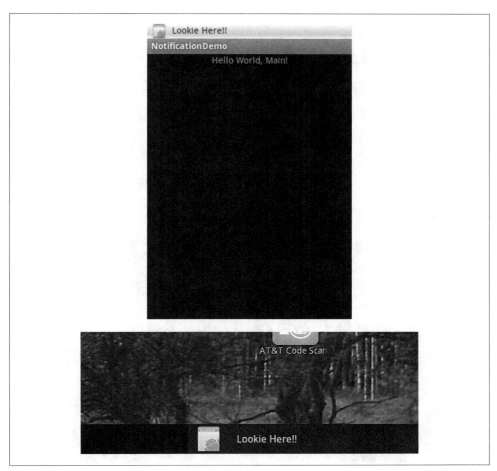

Figure 8-9. Notification demo (Gingerbread and Honeycomb)

Alternatively, you can provide a URI to a sound file, either on the SD card or in your application:

```
notification.sound = Uri.parse("file:///sdcard/mydata/annoy_the_user.mp3");
```

Note that if you both set `DEFAULT_SOUND` and provide a "sound" URI, only the default will be used.

To really annoy the user, you can make the sound play repeatedly; just add the flag `FLAG_INSISTENT` to the `flags` field.

```
notification.defaults |= Notification.FLAG_INSISTENT;
```

Invoking device vibration when your notification is displayed is as simple as:

```
notification.defaults |= Notification.DEFAULT_VIBRATE;
```

Figure 8-10. Notification demo continued

Lighting the LED

As a final flourish, you can make the LED flash in various colors and patterns, on devices with a signaling LED (on most phones it's near the bottom of the physical screen or otherwise in the controls area). At a bare minimum, you need:

```
notification.ledARGB = color;
notification.defaults |= Notification.FLAGS_SHOW_LIGHTS;
```

The color is an integer with four bytes containing, as the name hints, Alpha (transparency), Red, Green, and Blue. These are similar to traditional web color syntax but for the transparency part. Thus 0xff0000ff is bright blue (full opacity/no transparency; no red or green).

Figure 8-11. Notification "pulled down"

Figure 8-12. Response to choosing a notification

You can also specify a flashing pattern using `notification.ledOnMS` and `notifica tion.ledOffMS`, which are the times in milliseconds for the LED to be on and off as it flashes. Again, if you set any of these values but don't specify `FLAGS_SHOW_LIGHTS`, nothing will happen.

See Also

The official tutorial is at *http://developer.android.com/guide/topics/ui/notifiers/notifica tions.html*.

Source Download URL

The source code for this example is in the Android Cookbook repository at *http://github .com/AndroidCook/Android-Cookbook-Examples*, in the subdirectory NotificationDemo (see "Getting and Using the Code Examples" on page xvii).

## CHAPTER 9

GUI: ListView

9.1 Introduction: ListView

Ian Darwin

Discussion

It may seem odd to have a separate chapter for the `ListView` component. But it is, in fact, one of the most important components, being used in probably 80% of all Android applications. And it is very flexible; you can do a lot with it, but figuring out how to do it is sometimes not as intuitive as it could be.

In this chapter we cover topics from basic `ListView` uses through to advanced uses.

See the official doc at *http://developer.android.com/reference/android/widget/ListView .html*.

Another good overview of `ListView` can be found in a Google I/O 2010 presentation, which can be found on Google's YouTube channel, at *http://www.youtube.com/watch ?v=wDBM6wVEO70*; this was presented by Google employees Romain Guy and Adam Powell who work on the code for `ListView` itself.

9.2 Building List-Based Applications with ListView

Jim Blackler

Problem

Many mobile applications follow a similar pattern, allowing users to browse and interact with multiple items in a list. How can developers use standard Android UI classes to quickly build an app that works the way users will expect, providing them a list-based view onto their data?

Solution

Use a ListView, an extremely versatile control that is well suited to the screen size and control constraints of a mobile application, displaying information in a vertical stack of rows. This recipe shows how to set up a ListView, including rows that contain any combination of standard UI views.

Discussion

Many Android applications are based on the ListView control. It solves the problem of how to present a lot of information in a way that's quick for the user to browse. It displays information in a vertical stack of rows that the user can scroll through. As the user reaches the results toward the end of the list, more results can be generated and added. This allows results paging in a natural and intuitive manner.

Android's ListView helps organize your code by separating browsing and editing operations into separate activities. A ListView simply requires the user to press somewhere in the row, which works well on a small, finger-operated screen. When the row is clicked, a new Activity can be launched that can contain further options to manipulate the data shown in the row.

Another advantage of the ListView format is that it allows paging in an uncomplicated way. Paging is where all the information requested by a user cannot feasibly be shown at once. For instance, the user may be browsing his email inbox, which contains 2,000 emails; it would not be feasible to download all 2,000 messages from the email server. Nor would it be required, as the user will probably only scan the first 10 or so entries.

Most web applications handle this problem by segmenting the results into pages, and having controls at the footer to allow the user to navigate through these pages. With a ListView, the application can retrieve an initial batch of the first results, which are shown to the user in a list. When the user reaches the end of the list, a final row is seen, containing an indeterminate progress bar. As this comes into view, the application can fetch the next batch of results in the background. When they are ready to be shown, the last progress bar row is replaced with rows containing the new data. The user's view of the list is not interrupted, and new data is fetched purely on demand.

To implement a ListView in your Android application, you require an activity layout to host it. This should contain a ListView control configured to take up most of the screen layout. This allows other elements such as progress bars or extra overlaid indicators to be included in the layout.

While many Android experts recommend using the ListActivity, I personally do not recommend using ListActivity to host the view. It supplies little extra logic over a plain Activity, but using it restricts the form of the inheritance tree your application's activities can take. For instance, it is very common that all activities will inherit from a single common activity, such as ApplicationActivity, supplying common functionality such as About or Help menus. This pattern won't be possible if some activities are inherited from ListActivity and some are directly inherited from Activity.

An application controls the data added to a ListView by supplying a ListAdapter using the setListAdapter() method. There are 13 functions that a ListAdapter is expected to supply. However, if a BaseAdapter is used, this reduces the number of functions supplied to four, representing the minimum functionality that must be supplied. The adapter specifies the number of item rows in the list, and is expected to supply a View object to represent any item given its row number. It is also expected to return both an object and an object ID to represent any given row number. This is to aid advanced list features such as row selection (not covered in this recipe).

I suggest starting with the most versatile type of ListAdapter, the BaseAdapter (android.widget.BaseAdapter). This allows any layout to be specified for a row (multiple layouts can be matched to multiple row types). These layouts can contain any View elements that a layout would normally contain.

Rows are created on demand by the adapter as they come onto the screen. The adapter is expected to either inflate a view of the appropriate type, or recycle the existing view, and then customize it to display a row of data.

This "recycling" is a technique employed by the Android OS to improve performance. When new rows come onto the screen, the OS will pass the View of a row that has moved off the screen into the adapter method $. It is up to the method to decide whether it is appropriate to reuse that View to create the new row. For this to be the case the View has to represent the layout of the new row. One way to check this is to write the layout ID into the Tag of each View inflated with setTag(). When checking to see if it is appropriate to reuse a given View, use getTag() to see if the View was inflated with the correct type. If an application is able to recycle a view the scrolling appears to be smoother for the user because CPU time is saved inflating the view.

Another way to make scrolling smoother is to do as little as possible on the UI thread. This is the default thread that your $ method will be invoked on. If time-intensive operations need to be invoked, these can be done by creating a new background thread especially for the operation ($example). Then when the UI thread is required again so that controls can be updated, operations can be invoked on it with $. Care must be taken to ensure that the View to be modified has not been recycled for another row. This can happen if the row has moved off the screen in the time it took the operation to complete. This is quite feasible if the operation was a lengthy download operation.

Setting up a basic ListView

Use the Eclipse Android New Project Wizard to create a new Android project with a starting activity called MainActivity. In the *main.xml* layout replace the existing Text View section with the following:

```
<ListView android:id="@+id/ListView01"
    android:layout_width="wrap_content"
    android:layout_height="fill_parent"/>
```

In `MainActivity.onCreate()` insert the following snippet at the bottom of the method (see Example 9-1). This will declare a dummy anonymous class extending `BaseAdapter`, and apply an instance of it to the `ListView`. The code illustrates the methods that need to be supplied in order to populate the `ListView` with data.

Example 9-1. The adapter implementation

```
ListView listView = (ListView) findViewById(R.id.ListView01);
listView.setAdapter(new BaseAdapter(){

    public int getCount() {
      return 0;
    }

    public Object getItem(int position) {
      return null;
    }

    public long getItemId(int position) {
      return 0;
    }

    public View getView(int position, View convertView, ViewGroup parent) {
      return null;
    }});
```

By customizing the anonymous class members, you can modify the data shown by the control. However, before any data can be shown, a layout must be supplied to present the data in rows. Add a file *list_row.xml* to your project's *res/layout* directory with the following content:

```
<LinearLayout xmlns:android="http://schemas.android.com/apk/res/android"
  android:layout_width="wrap_content" android:layout_height="wrap_content">
  <TextView android:text="@+id/TextView01" android:id="@+id/TextView01"
    android:layout_width="fill_parent" android:layout_height="wrap_content"/>
</LinearLayout>
```

In your `MainActivity`, add the following static array field containing just three strings:

```
static String[] words = {"one", "two", "three"};
```

Now customize your existing anonymous `BaseAdapter` as follows, in order to display the contents of the `words` array in the `ListView` (see Example 9-2).

Example 9-2. The adapter implementation

```
listView.setAdapter(new BaseAdapter(){

        public int getCount() {
          return words.length;
        }

        public Object getItem(int position) {
          return words[position];
        }

        public long getItemId(int position) {
          return position;
        }

        public View getView(int position, View convertView, ViewGroup parent) {
          LayoutInflater inflater =
              (LayoutInflater) getSystemService(LAYOUT_INFLATER_SERVICE);
          View view = inflater.inflate(R.layout.list_row, null);
          TextView textView = (TextView) view.findViewById(R.id.TextView01);
          textView.setText(words[position]);
          return view;
        }});
```

The getCount() method is customized to return the number of items in the list. Both getItem() and getItemId() supply the ListView with unique objects and IDs to identify the data in the rows. Finally, getView() creates and customizes an Android View to represent the row. This is the most complex step, so let's break down what's done.

```
          LayoutInflater inflater =
          (LayoutInflater) getSystemService(LAYOUT_INFLATER_SERVICE);
```

The system LayoutInflater is obtained. This is the service that creates views.

```
          View view = inflater.inflate(R.layout.list_row, null)
```

The new layout we created earlier is inflated.

```
          TextView textView = (TextView) view.findViewById(R.id.TextView01)
```

The TextView is located.

```
          textView.setText(words[position])
```

The TextView is customized with the appropriate item in the words array.

```
          return view;
```

This allows the user to view elements from the words array in a ListView. Other recipes will discuss more details on ListView usage.

9.3 Creating a "No Data" View for ListViews

Rachee Singh

Problem

When a `ListView` has no items to show, the screen on an Android device is blank. You want to show an appropriate message on the screen, indicating the absence of data in the `ListView`.

Solution

Use the "No Data" view from the XML layout.

Discussion

Often we need to use a `ListView` in an Android app. Before a user has loaded any data into the application, the list of data that the `ListView` shows is empty, generally resulting in a blank screen. In order to make the user feel more comfortable with the application, we might want to display an appropriate message (or even an image) stating that the list is empty. For this purpose, we can use a No Data view. This is a simple process involving the addition of a few lines of code in the XML layout of the activity that contains the `ListView`:

```xml
<?xml version="1.0" encoding="utf-8"?>
<RelativeLayout xmlns:android="http://schemas.android.com/apk/res/android"
    android:layout_width="fill_parent"
    android:layout_height="fill_parent"
    >

<ListView
    android:id="@id/android:list"
    android:layout_width="fill_parent"
    android:layout_height="wrap_content"
    android:layout_below="@id/textView1"/>
    <TextView
        android:id="@id/android:empty"adapter
        android:text = "@string/list_is_empty"
            android:layout_width="fill_parent"
        android:layout_height="fill_parent"
        android:layout_below = "@id/textView1"
        android:textSize="25sp"
        android:gravity="center_vertical|center_horizontal"/>
</RelativeLayout>
```

The important line is `android:id="@id/android:empty"`. This line ensures that when the list is empty, the `TextView` with this ID will be displayed on the screen. In this `Text View` the string `List is Empty` is displayed (see Figure 9-1).

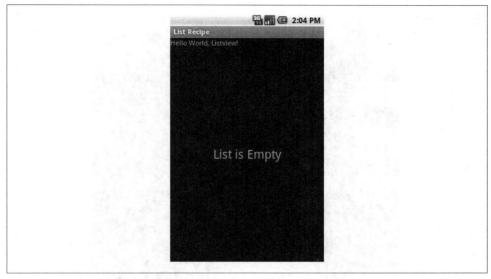

Figure 9-1. Empty list

9.4 Creating an Advanced ListView with Images and Text

Marco Dinacci

Problem

You want to write a `ListView` that shows an image next to a string.

Solution

Create an `Activity` that extends from `ListActivity`, prepare the XML resource files, and create a custom view adapter to load the resources onto the view.

Discussion

The Android documentation says that the `ListView` widget is easy to use. This is true if you just want to display a simple list of strings, but as soon as you want to customize your list things become more complicated.

This recipe shows you how to write a `ListView` that displays a static list of images and strings, similar to the settings list on your phone.

Figure 9-2 shows the final result.

Let's start with the `Activity` code. First of all, we extend from `ListActivity` instead of `Activity` so that we can easily supply our custom adapter (see Example 9-3).

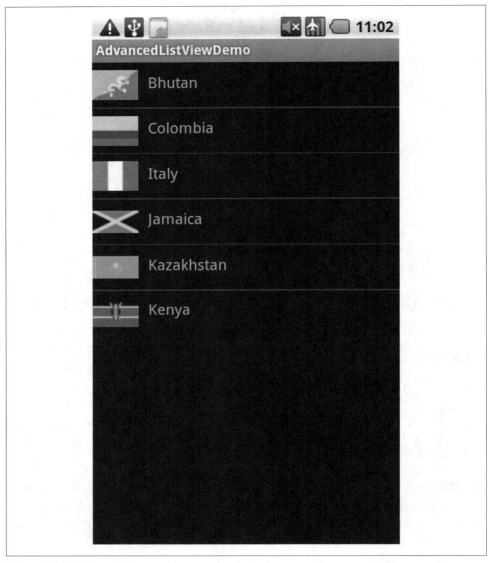

Figure 9-2. ListView with icons

Example 9-3. The ListActivity implementation

```
public class AdvancedListViewActivity extends ListActivity {

    @Override
    public void onCreate(Bundle savedInstanceState) {
        super.onCreate(savedInstanceState);
        setContentView(R.layout.main);
```

```
        Context ctx = getApplicationContext();
    Resources res = ctx.getResources();

    String[] options = res.getStringArray(R.array.country_names);
    TypedArray icons = res.obtainTypedArray(R.array.country_icons);

    setListAdapter(new ImageAndTextAdapter(ctx, R.layout.main_list_item, options, icons));
    }
}
```

In the onCreate we also create an array of strings, which contains the country names, and a TypedArray, which will contain our Drawable flags.

The arrays are created from an XML file. Here is the content of the *countries.xml* file:

```
<?xml version="1.0" encoding="utf-8"?>
<resources>
    <string-array name="country_names">
        <item>Bhutan</item>
        <item>Colombia</item>
        <item>Italy</item>
        <item>Jamaica</item>
        <item>Kazakhstan</item>
        <item>Kenya</item>
    </string-array>
    <array name="country_icons">
        <item>@drawable/bhutan</item>
        <item>@drawable/colombia</item>
        <item>@drawable/italy</item>
        <item>@drawable/jamaica</item>
        <item>@drawable/kazakhstan</item>
        <item>@drawable/kenya</item>
    </array>
</resources>
```

Now we're ready to create the adapter. The official documentation (at *http://developer .android.com/reference/android/widget/Adapter.html*) for Adapter says:

> An Adapter object acts as a bridge between an AdapterView and the underlying data for that view. The Adapter provides access to the data items. The Adapter is also responsible for making a View for each item in the data set.

There are several subclasses of Adapter; we're going to extend on ArrayAdapter, which is a concrete BaseAdapter that is backed by an array of arbitrary objects (see Example 9-4).

Example 9-4. The ImageAndTextAdapter class

```
public class ImageAndTextAdapter extends ArrayAdapter<String> {

    private LayoutInflater mInflater;

    private String[] mStrings;
    private TypedArray mIcons;
```

```
        private int mViewResourceId;

        public ImageAndTextAdapter(Context ctx, int viewResourceId,
                String[] strings, TypedArray icons) {
            super(ctx, viewResourceId, strings);

            mInflater = (LayoutInflater)ctx.getSystemService(
                    Context.LAYOUT_INFLATER_SERVICE);

            mStrings = strings;
            mIcons = icons;

            mViewResourceId = viewResourceId;
        }

        @Override
        public int getCount() {
            return mStrings.length;
        }

        @Override
        public String getItem(int position) {
            return mStrings[position];
        }

        @Override
        public long getItemId(int position) {
            return 0;
        }

        @Override
        public View getView(int position, View convertView, ViewGroup parent) {
            convertView = mInflater.inflate(mViewResourceId, null);

            ImageView iv = (ImageView)convertView.findViewById(R.id.option_icon);
            iv.setImageDrawable(mIcons.getDrawable(position));

            TextView tv = (TextView)convertView.findViewById(R.id.option_text);
            tv.setText(mStrings[position]);

            return convertView;
        }
    }
}
```

The constructor accepts a Context, the id of the layout that will be used for every row (more on this soon), an array of strings (the country names), and a TypedArray (our flags).

The getView method is where we build a row for the list. We first use a LayoutIn flater to create a View from XML, and then we retrieve the country flag as a Drawable and the country name as a String and we use them to populate the ImageView and TextView that we've declared in the layout.

Here is the layout for the list rows:

```xml
<?xml version="1.0" encoding="utf-8"?>
<LinearLayout xmlns:android="http://schemas.android.com/apk/res/android">
    <ImageView
    android:id="@+id/option_icon"
    android:layout_width="48dp"
    android:layout_height="fill_parent"/>
    <TextView
        android:id="@+id/option_text"
        android:layout_width="fill_parent"
        android:layout_height="fill_parent"
        android:padding="10dp"
        android:textSize="16dp" >
    </TextView>
</LinearLayout>
```

And this is the content of the main layout:

```xml
<?xml version="1.0" encoding="utf-8"?>
<LinearLayout xmlns:android="http://schemas.android.com/apk/res/android"
    android:orientation="vertical"
    android:layout_width="fill_parent"
    android:layout_height="fill_parent"
    >
<ListView android:id="@android:id/list"
    android:layout_height="wrap_content"
    android:layout_width="fill_parent"
    />
</LinearLayout>
```

Note that the `ListView` ID must be exactly `@android:id/list` or you'll get a `RuntimeException`.

Source Download URL

You can download the source code for this example from *http://www.intransitione.com/ intransitione.com/code/android/adv_listview_demo.zip*.

9.5 Using Section Headers in ListViews

Wagied Davids

Problem

You want to display categorized items—for example, by time/day, by product category, or by sales/price.

Solution

Use Jeff Sharkey's idea of "section headers" to display journal entries by day.

Discussion

Jeff Sharkey implemented the original section headers (*http://jsharkey.org/blog/2008/08/18/separating-lists-with-headers-in-android-09/*) very early on in Android—in the days of the 0.9 release, in fact. The intention was to duplicate the look of the standard "Settings" app, which at the time featured a look similar to the image below, which we will develop in this recipe. The reusable part of this application is Jeff's `SeparatedListAdapter` class, which implements the Composite design pattern (*http://en.wikipedia.org/wiki/Composite_pattern*) by holding multiple `Adapter`s inside it, and figuring out the correct one in its `getItem()` method.

We start with four XML files, one for the main layout (see Example 9-5) and three for the list entries. Figuring out the built-in but rather occult styles used was credited by Jeff to Romain Guy of Google.

Example 9-5. main.xml

```
<?xml version="1.0" encoding="utf-8"?>
<LinearLayout
    xmlns:android="http://schemas.android.com/apk/res/android"
    android:orientation="vertical"
```

```
    android:layout_width="fill_parent"
    android:layout_height="fill_parent">

    <ListView
        android:id="@+id/add_journalentry_menuitem"
        android:layout_width="fill_parent"
        android:layout_height="wrap_content" />
    <ListView
        android:id="@+id/list_journal"
        android:layout_width="fill_parent"
        android:layout_height="wrap_content" />
</LinearLayout>
```

The `list_header` (see Example 9-6) is used for the smaller list separators (e.g., "Security").

Example 9-6. list_header.xml

```
<TextView
    xmlns:android="http://schemas.android.com/apk/res/android"
    android:id="@+id/list_header_title"
    android:layout_width="fill_parent"
    android:layout_height="wrap_content"
    android:paddingTop="2dip"
    android:paddingBottom="2dip"
    android:paddingLeft="5dip"
    style="?android:attr/listSeparatorTextViewStyle" />
```

The `list_item` and `list_complex` layouts are, of course, used for individual items (see Examples 9-7 and 9-8).

Example 9-7. list_item.xml

```
<?xml version="1.0" encoding="utf-8"?>
<TextView
    xmlns:android="http://schemas.android.com/apk/res/android"
    android:id="@+id/list_item_title"
    android:layout_width="fill_parent"
    android:layout_height="fill_parent"
    android:paddingTop="10dip"
    android:paddingBottom="10dip"
    android:paddingLeft="15dip"
    android:textAppearance="?android:attr/textAppearanceLarge"
    />
```

Example 9-8. list_complex.xml

```
<?xml version="1.0" encoding="utf-8"?>
<LinearLayout
    xmlns:android="http://schemas.android.com/apk/res/android"
    android:layout_width="fill_parent"
    android:layout_height="wrap_content"
    android:orientation="vertical"
    android:paddingTop="10dip"
    android:paddingBottom="10dip"
```

```
        android:paddingLeft="15dip"
        >
    <TextView
        android:id="@+id/list_complex_title"
        android:layout_width="fill_parent"
        android:layout_height="wrap_content"
        android:textAppearance="?android:attr/textAppearanceLarge"
        />
    <TextView
        android:id="@+id/list_complex_caption"
        android:layout_width="fill_parent"
        android:layout_height="wrap_content"
        android:textAppearance="?android:attr/textAppearanceSmall"
        />
</LinearLayout>
```

The add_journalentry_menuitem layout is used to add new entries, and is not shown in
action here (Example 9-9).

Example 9-9. add_journalentry_menuitem.xml

```
<?xml version="1.0" encoding="utf-8"?>
<!-- list_item.xml -->
<TextView
    xmlns:android="http://schemas.android.com/apk/res/android"
    android:id="@+id/list_item_title"
    android:gravity="right"
    android:drawableRight="@drawable/ic_menu_add"
    android:layout_width="fill_parent"
    android:layout_height="fill_parent"
    android:paddingTop="0dip"
    android:paddingBottom="0dip"
    android:paddingLeft="10dip"
    android:textAppearance="?android:attr/textAppearanceLarge" />
```

Finally, Example 9-10 contains the Java activity code.

Example 9-10. ListSample.java

```
import java.util.HashMap;
import java.util.Map;
import android.app.Activity;
import android.os.Bundle;
import android.view.View;
import android.widget.AdapterView;
import android.widget.ArrayAdapter;
import android.widget.ListView;
import android.widget.Toast;
import android.widget.AdapterView.OnItemClickListener;

public class ListSample extends Activity
    {

        public final static String ITEM_TITLE = "title";
        public final static String ITEM_CAPTION = "caption";
```

```java
// SectionHeaders
private final static String[] days =
    new String[]{"Mon", "Tue", "Wed", "Thur", "Fri"};

// Section Contents
private final static String[] notes = new String[]
    {"Ate Breakfast", "Ran a Marathon ...yah really", "Slept all day"};

// Menu - ListView
private ListView addJournalEntryItem;

// Adapter for ListView Contents
private SeparatedListAdapter adapter;

// ListView Contents
private ListView journalListView;

public Map<String, ?> createItem(String title, String caption)
    {
        Map<String, String> item = new HashMap<String, String>();
        item.put(ITEM_TITLE, title);
        item.put(ITEM_CAPTION, caption);
        return item;
    }

@Override
public void onCreate(Bundle icicle)
    {
        super.onCreate(icicle);

        // Sets the View Layer
        setContentView(R.layout.main);

        // Interactive Tools
        final ArrayAdapter<String> journalEntryAdapter =
            new ArrayAdapter<String>(this, R.layout.add_journalentry_menuitem,
            new String[]{"Add Journal Entry"});

        // AddJournalEntryItem
        addJournalEntryItem = (ListView) this.findViewById(
            R.id.add_journalentry_menuitem);
        addJournalEntryItem.setAdapter(journalEntryAdapter);
        addJournalEntryItem.setOnItemClickListener(new OnItemClickListener()
            {
                @Override
                public void onItemClick(AdapterView<?> parent, View view,
                    int position, long duration)
                    {
                        String item = journalEntryAdapter.getItem(position);
                        Toast.makeText(getApplicationContext(), item,
                            Toast.LENGTH_SHORT).show();
                    }
            });
```

```
// Create the ListView Adapter
adapter = new SeparatedListAdapter(this);
ArrayAdapter<String> listadapter = new ArrayAdapter<String>(this,
    R.layout.list_item, notes);

// Add Sections
for (int i = 0; i < days.length; i++)
    {
        adapter.addSection(days[i], listadapter);
    }

// Get a reference to the ListView holder
journalListView = (ListView) this.findViewById(R.id.list_journal);

// Set the adapter on the ListView holder
journalListView.setAdapter(adapter);

// Listen for Click events
journalListView.setOnItemClickListener(new OnItemClickListener()
    {
        @Override
        public void onItemClick(AdapterView<?> parent, View view,
            int position, long duration)
            {
                String item = (String) adapter.getItem(position);
                Toast.makeText(getApplicationContext(), item,
                    Toast.LENGTH_SHORT).show();
            }
    });
}

}
```

Unfortunately, we could not get copyright clearance from Jeff Sharkey to include the code, so you will have to download his SeparatedListAdapter, which ties all the pieces together; the link appears in the See Also section below.

See Also

Jeff's original article on section headers (*http://jsharkey.org/blog/2008/08/18/separating -lists-with-headers-in-android-09/*).

Source Download URL

The source code for this example is in the Android Cookbook repository at *http://github .com/AndroidCook/Android-Cookbook-Examples*, in the subdirectory SectionedHeaderListView (see "Getting and Using the Code Examples" on page xvii).

9.6 Keeping the ListView with the User's Focus

Ian Darwin

Problem

You don't want to distract the user by moving the `ListView` to its beginning, away from what the user just did.

Solution

Keep track of the last thing you did in the `List`, and move the view there in `onCreate()`.

Discussion

One of my biggest peeves is list-based applications that are always going back to the top of the list. Here are a few examples:

- The standard Contacts manager, when you edit an item, forgets about it and goes back to the top of the list.
- The OpenIntents File Manager, when you delete an item from the bottom of a long list, goes back to the top of the list to redisplay it, ignoring the fact that if I deleted an item, I may be cleaning up, and would like to keep working in the same area.
- The HTC SenseUI for Tablets mail program, when you select a large number of emails using the per-message checkboxes and then delete them as one, leaves the scrolling list in its previous position, which is now typically occupied by mail from yesterday or the day before!

It's actually pretty simple to set the focus where you want it. Just find the item's index in the `Adapter` (possibly using `theList.getAdapter()` if needed), and then call:

```
theList.setSelection(index);
```

This will scroll to the given item, and also select it so that it becomes the default to act upon, though it doesn't invoke the action associated with the item.

You can calculate this anyplace in your action code, and pass it back to the main list view with `Intent.putExtra()`, or set it as a field in your main class, and scroll the list in your `onCreate()` method or elsewhere.

9.7 Writing a Custom List Adapter

Alex Leffelman

Problem

You want to customize the content of a `ListView`.

Solution

In the `Activity` that will host your `ListView`, define a private class that extends Android's `BaseAdapter` class. Then override the base class's methods to display custom views that you define in an XML layout file.

Discussion

It's no secret that the best way to explain something is through an example, so let's dive in. This is code lifted out of a media application I wrote that allowed the user to build playlists from the songs on his SD card. As promised, we'll be extending the `BaseAdapter` class inside my `MediaListActivity`:

```
private class MediaAdapter extends BaseAdapter {
...
}
```

Querying the phone for the media info is outside the scope of this recipe, but the data to populate the list was stored in a `MediaItem` class that kept standard artist, title, album, and track number information, as well as a Boolean field indicating if the item was selected for the current playlist. In certain cases you may want to continually add items to your list—for example, if you're downloading information and displaying it as it comes in—but for this purpose we're going to supply all the required data to the `Adapter` at once in the constructor.

```
public MediaAdapter(ArrayList<MediaItem> items) {
    mMediaList = items;
    ...
}
```

If you're developing in Eclipse you'll notice that it wants us to override `BaseAdapter`'s abstract methods; if you're not, you'll find out as soon as you try to compile the code without them. Let's take a look at those.

```
public int getCount() {
    return mMediaList.size();
}
```

The framework needs to know how many `Views` it needs to create in your list. It finds out by asking your `Adapter` how many items you're managing. In our case we'll have a `View` for every item in the media list.

```
public Object getItem(int position) {
    return mMediaList.get(position);
}
public long getItemId(int position) {
    return position;
}
```

We won't really be using these methods, but for completeness, `getItem(int)` is what gets returned when the `ListView` hosting this adapter calls `getItemAtPosition(int)`, which won't happen in our case. `getItemId(int)` is what gets passed to the List

View.onListItemClick(ListView, View, int, int) callback when you select an item. It gives you the position of the view in the list and the ID supplied by your adapter. In our case they're the same.

The real work of your custom adapter will be done in the getView() method. This method is called every time the ListView brings a new item into view. When an item goes out of view, it is recycled by the system to be used later. This is a powerful mechanism for providing potentially thousands of View objects to our ListView while using only as many Views as can be displayed on the screen. The getView() method provides the position of the item it is creating, a View that may be not-null which the system is recycling for you to use, and the ViewGroup parent. You'll return either a new View for the list to display, or a modified copy of the supplied convertView parameter to conserve system resources. Example 9-11 shows the code.

Example 9-11. The getView method

```
public View getView(int position, View convertView, ViewGroup parent) {
    View V = convertView;

    if(V == null) {
        LayoutInflater vi =
            (LayoutInflater)getSystemService(Context.LAYOUT_INFLATER_SERVICE);
        V = vi.inflate(R.layout.media_row, null);
    }

    MediaItem mi = mMediaList.get(position);
    ImageView icon = (ImageView)V.findViewById(R.id.media_image);
    TextView title = (TextView)V.findViewById(R.id.media_title);
    TextView artist = (TextView)V.findViewById(R.id.media_artist);

    if(mi.isSelected()) {
        icon.setImageResource(R.drawable.item_selected);
    }
    else {
        icon.setImageResource(R.drawable.item_unselected);
    }

    title.setText(mi.getTitle());
    artist.setText("by " + mi.getArtist());

    return V;
}
```

We start by checking whether we'll be recycling a View (which is a good practice), or whether we need to generate a new View from scratch. If we weren't given a convert View, we'll call the LayoutInflater service to build a View that we've defined in an XML layout file.

Using the View which we've ensured was built with our desired layout resource (or is a recycled copy of one we previously built), it's simply a matter of updating its UI elements. In our case we want to display the song title, the artist, and an indication of whether or not the song is in our current playlist. (I've removed the error checking, but it's a good practice to make sure any UI elements you're updating are not null—you don't want to crash the whole ListView if there was a small mistake in one item.) This method gets called for every (visible) item in the ListView, so in this example we have a list of identical View objects with different data being displayed in each one. If you wanted to get really creative, you could populate the list with different view layouts based on the list item's position or content.

That takes care of the required BaseAdapter overrides. However, you can add any functionality to your Adapter to work on the data set it represents. In my example, I want the user to be able to click a list item and toggle it on/off for the current playlist. This is easily accomplished with a simple callback on the ListView and a short function in the Adapter.

This function belongs to ListActivity:

```
protected void onListItemClick(ListView l, View v, int position, long id) {
    super.onListItemClick(l, v, position, id);

    mAdapter.toggleItem(position);
}
```

This is a member function in our MediaAdapter:

```
public void toggleItem(int position) {
    MediaItem mi = mMediaList.get(position);

    mi.setSelected(!mi.getSelected());
    mMediaList.set(position, mi);

    this.notifyDataSetChanged();
}
```

First we simply register a callback for when the user clicks an item in our list. We're given the ListView, the View, the position, and the ID of the item that was clicked, but we'll only need the position, which we simply pass to the MediaAdapter.toggleItem(int) method. In that method we update the state of the corresponding MediaItem and make an important call to notifyDataSetChanged(). This method lets the framework know that it needs to redraw the ListView. If we don't call it, we can do whatever we want to the data, but we won't see anything change until the next redraw (e.g., when we scroll the list).

When all is said and done, we need to tell the parent ListView to use our Adapter to populate the list. That's done with a simple call in the ListActivity's onCreate(Bundle) method:

```
MediaAdapter mAdapter = new MediaAdapter(getSongsFromSD());
this.setListAdapter(mAdapter);
```

First we instantiate a new Adapter with data generated from a private function that queries the phone for the song data, and then we tell the ListActivity to use that adapter to draw the list. And there it is—your own list adapter with a custom view and extensible functionality.

9.8 Handling Orientation Changes: From ListView Data Values to Landscape Charting

Wagied Davids

Problem

You want to react to orientation changes in layout-appropriate ways. For example, data values to be plotted are contained in a portrait list view, and upon device rotation to landscape, a graph of the data values in a chart/plot is displayed.

Solution

Do something in reaction to physical device orientation changes. A new `View` object is created on orientation changes. The `Activity` method `onConfigurationChanged(Config uration newConfig)` can be overriden to accommodate orientation changes.

Discussion

In this recipe, data values to be plotted are contained in a portrait list view. When the device/emulator is changed to counterclockwise, a new `Intent` is launched to change to a plot/charting `View` to graphically display the data values. Charting is accomplished using the excellent DroidCharts package (*http://code.google.com/p/droidcharts/*).

Note that for testing this in the Android emulator, the Ctrl-F11 key combination will result in a portrait to landscape (or vice versa) orientation change.

The most important trick is to modify the *AndroidManifest.xml* (shown in Example 9-12) to allow for the following:

```
android:configChanges="orientation|keyboardHidden"
        android:screenOrientation="portrait"
```

Example 9-12. AndroidManifest.xml

```
<?xml version="1.0" encoding="utf-8"?>
<manifest
    xmlns:android="http://schemas.android.com/apk/res/android"
    package="com.examples"
    android:versionCode="1"
    android:versionName="1.0">
    <application
        android:icon="@drawable/icon"
        android:label="@string/app_name"
        android:debuggable="true">
        <activity
            android:name=".DemoList"
```

```
                android:label="@string/app_name"
                android:configChanges="orientation|keyboardHidden"
                android:screenOrientation="portrait">
                <intent-filter>
                    <action
                        android:name="android.intent.action.MAIN" />
                    <category
                        android:name="android.intent.category.LAUNCHER" />
                </intent-filter>
            </activity>
            <activity
                android:name=".DemoCharts"
                android:configChanges="orientation|keyboardHidden"></activity>
        </application>
</manifest>
```

The main activity in this example is DemoCharts, shown in Example 9-13. It does the usual onCreate() stuff, but also, if a parameter was passed, it assumes we were restarted from the DemoList class shown in Example 9-14 and sets up the data accordingly. A number of methods have been elided as they aren't relevant to the core issue, that of configuration changes. These are in the online source for this recipe.

Example 9-13. DemoCharts.java

```
...
import net.droidsolutions.droidcharts.core.data.XYDataset;
import net.droidsolutions.droidcharts.core.data.xy.XYSeries;
import net.droidsolutions.droidcharts.core.data.xy.XYSeriesCollection;

public class DemoCharts extends Activity {
        private static final String tag = "DemoCharts";
        private final String chartTitle = "My Daily Starbucks Allowance";
        private final String xLabel = "Week Day";
        private final String yLabel = "Allowance";

        /** Called when the activity is first created. */
        @Override
        public void onCreate(Bundle savedInstanceState) {
                super.onCreate(savedInstanceState);

                // Access the Extras from the Intent
                Bundle params = getIntent().getExtras();

                // If we get no parameters, we do nothing
                if (params == null) { return; }

                // Get the passed parameter values
                String paramVals = params.getString("param");

                Log.d(tag, "Data Param:= " + paramVals);
                Toast.makeText(getApplicationContext(), "Data Param:= " +
                        paramVals, Toast.LENGTH_LONG).show();

                ArrayList<ArrayList<Double>> dataVals = stringArrayToDouble(paramVals);
```

```
            XYDataset dataset =
                createDataset("My Daily Starbucks Allowance", dataVals);
            XYLineChartView graphView = new XYLineChartView(this, chartTitle,
                xLabel, yLabel, dataset);
            setContentView(graphView);
    }

    private String arrayToString(String[] data) {
            ...
    }


    private ArrayList<ArrayList<Double>> stringArrayToDouble(String paramVals) {
            ...
    }

    /**
     * Creates a sample dataset.
     */
    private XYDataset createDataset(String title,
            ArrayList<ArrayList<Double>> dataVals) {

            final XYSeries series1 = new XYSeries(title);
            for (ArrayList<Double> tuple : dataVals)
                {
                    double x = tuple.get(0).doubleValue();
                    double y = tuple.get(1).doubleValue();

                    series1.add(x, y);
                }

            // Create a collection to hold various data sets
            final XYSeriesCollection dataset = new XYSeriesCollection();
            dataset.addSeries(series1);
            return dataset;
        }


    @Override
    public void onConfigurationChanged(Configuration newConfig)
        {
            super.onConfigurationChanged(newConfig);
            Toast.makeText(this, "Orientation Change", Toast.LENGTH_SHORT);

            // Let's go to our DemoList view
            Intent intent = new Intent(this, DemoList.class);
            startActivity(intent);

            // Finish current Activity
            this.finish();
        }
}
```

The DemoList view is the portrait view. Its onConfigure() passes control back to the landscape DemoCharts class if a configuration change occurs.

Example 9-14. DemoList.java

```java
public class DemoList extends ListActivity implements OnItemClickListener {
        private static final String tag = "DemoList";
        private ListView listview;
        private ArrayAdapter<String> listAdapter;

        // Want to pass data values as parameters to next Activity/View/Page
        private String params;

        // Our data for plotting
        private final double[][] data = {
            { 1, 1.0 }, { 2.0, 4.0 }, { 3.0, 10.0 }, { 4, 2.0 },
            { 5.0, 20 }, { 6.0, 4.0 }, { 7.0, 1.0 },
        };

        @Override
        public void onCreate(Bundle savedInstanceState)
            {
                super.onCreate(savedInstanceState);

                // Set the View Layer
                setContentView(R.layout.data_listview);

                // Get the Default declared ListView @android:list
                listview = getListView();

                // List for click events to the ListView items
                listview.setOnItemClickListener(this);

                // Get the data
                ArrayList<String> dataList = getDataStringList(data);

                // Create an Adapter for viewing the ListView
                listAdapter = new ArrayAdapter<String>(this,
                    android.R.layout.simple_list_item_1, dataList);

                // Bind the adapter to the ListView
                listview.setAdapter(listAdapter);

                // Set the parameters to pass to the next view/ page
                setParameters(data);
        }

        private String doubleArrayToString(double[][] dataVals) {
                ...
        }

        /**
         * Sets parameters for the Bundle
         *
         * @param dataList
         */
        private void setParameters(double[][] dataVals) {
                params = toJSON(dataVals);
        }
```

```java
public String getParameters() {
        return this.params;
}

/**
 *
 * @param dataVals
 * @return
 */
private String toJSON(double[][] dataVals) {
        ...
}

private ArrayList<String> getDataStringList(double[][] dataVals) {
        ...
}

@Override
public void onConfigurationChanged(Configuration newConfig) {
        super.onConfigurationChanged(newConfig);

        // Create an Intent to switch view to the next page view
        Intent intent = new Intent(this, DemoCharts.class);

        // Pass parameters along to the next page
        intent.putExtra("param", getParameters());

        // Start the activity
        startActivity(intent);

        Log.d(tag, "Orientation Change...");
        Log.d(tag, "Params: " + getParameters());
}

@Override
public void onItemClick(AdapterView<?> parent, View view,
        int position, long duration) {

        // Upon clicking item in list, pop up a toast
        String msg = "#Item: " + String.valueOf(position) +
            " - " + listAdapter.getItem(position);
        Toast.makeText(getApplicationContext(), msg, Toast.LENGTH_LONG).show();
    }
}
```

The XYLineChartView class is not included here as it relates only to the plotting. It is included in the online version of the code, which you can download as per the following section.

Source Download URL

The source code for this example is in the Android Cookbook repository at *http://github .com/AndroidCook/Android-Cookbook-Examples*, in the subdirectory Orientation-Changes (see "Getting and Using the Code Examples" on page xvii).

## CHAPTER 10

Multimedia

10.1 Introduction: Multimedia

Ian Darwin

Discussion

Android is a rich multimedia environment. The standard Android load includes music and video players, and most commercial devices ship with these or fancier versions as well as YouTube players and more. The recipes in this chapter show you how to control some aspects of the multimedia world that Android provides.

10.2 Playing a YouTube Video

Marco Dinacci

Problem

You want to play a video from YouTube on your device.

Solution

Given a URI to play the video, create an `ACTION_VIEW Intent` with it and start a new `Activity`.

Discussion

Example 10-1 shows the code required to start a YouTube video with an `Intent`.

 For this recipe to work, the user needs the standard YouTube application installed on the device.

Example 10-1. Starting a YouTube video with an Intent

```
public void onCreate(Bundle savedInstanceState) {
    super.onCreate(savedInstanceState);
    setContentView(R.layout.main);

    String video_path = "http://www.youtube.com/watch?v=opZ69P-OJbc";
    Uri uri = Uri.parse(video_path);

    // With this line the YouTube application, if installed, will launch immediately.
    // Without it you will be prompted with a list of the application to choose.
    uri = Uri.parse("vnd.youtube:" + uri.getQueryParameter("v"));

    Intent intent = new Intent(Intent.ACTION_VIEW, uri);
    startActivity(intent);
}
```

The example uses a standard YouTube.com URL. The `uri.getQueryParameter("v")` is used to extract the video ID from the URI itself; in our example the ID is `opZ69P-OJbc`.

10.3 Using the Gallery with the ImageSwitcher View

Nidhin Jose Davis

Problem

You want to create a user interface for browsing through a collection of images.

Solution

Use the `Gallery` with the `ImageSwitcher` view to achieve this.

Discussion

You can use the `Gallery` (`android.widget.Gallery`) alongside the `ImageSwitcher` (`android.widget.ImageSwitcher`) to create a nice image browser for your application. Example 10-2 shows the layout for the `Gallery`.

Example 10-2. The layout for the Gallery

```
<?xml version="1.0" encoding="utf-8"?>
<RelativeLayout xmlns:android="http://schemas.android.com/apk/res/android"
    android:orientation="vertical"
    android:layout_width="fill_parent"
    android:layout_height="fill_parent"
    >

    <ImageSwitcher
        android:id="@+id/switcher"
        android:layout_width="fill_parent"
        android:layout_height="wrap_content"
        android:layout_alignParentLeft="true"
```

```
            android:layout_alignParentRight="true"
            android:layout_alignParentBottom="true"
                />

    <Gallery
            android:id="@+id/gallery"
            android:background="#55000000"
            android:layout_width="fill_parent"
            android:layout_height="60dip"
            android:spacing="16px"
            android:layout_alignParentBottom="true"
            android:layout_alignParentLeft="true"
            android:gravity="center_vertical"
            />

</RelativeLayout>
```

Example 10-3 shows how to use this layout.

Example 10-3. The Gallery example ImageBrowser main activity

```
public class ImageBrowser extends Activity
        implements AdapterView.OnItemSelectedListener, ViewSwitcher.ViewFactory {
    private ImageSwitcher mISwitcher;
    private ArrayList<Drawable> allimages = new ArrayList<Drawable>();

    @Override
    public void onCreate(Bundle savedInstanceState) {
        super.onCreate(savedInstanceState);
                // let's remove the title bar
        requestWindowFeature(Window.FEATURE_NO_TITLE);
        setContentView(R.layout.main);

        getImages();

        mISwitcher = (ImageSwitcher)findViewById(R.id.switcher);
        mISwitcher.setFactory(this);
                // some animation when image changes
        mISwitcher.setInAnimation(AnimationUtils.loadAnimation(this,
                android.R.anim.fade_in));
        mISwitcher.setOutAnimation(AnimationUtils.loadAnimation(this,
                android.R.anim.fade_out));

        Gallery gallery = (Gallery) findViewById(R.id.gallery);
        gallery.setAdapter(new ImageAdapter(this));
        gallery.setOnItemSelectedListener(this);
    }


    private void getImages() {
        allimages.add(this.getResources().getDrawable(R.drawable.image1));
        allimages.add(this.getResources().getDrawable(R.drawable.image2));
        allimages.add(this.getResources().getDrawable(R.drawable.image3));
        allimages.add(this.getResources().getDrawable(R.drawable.image4));
        allimages.add(this.getResources().getDrawable(R.drawable.image5));
```

```
        allimages.add(this.getResources().getDrawable(R.drawable.image6));
        allimages.add(this.getResources().getDrawable(R.drawable.image7));
        allimages.add(this.getResources().getDrawable(R.drawable.image8));
        allimages.add(this.getResources().getDrawable(R.drawable.image9));

    }


    @Override
    public void onItemSelected(AdapterView<?> arg0, View v, int position, long id) {
        try{
            mISwitcher.setImageDrawable(allimages.get(position));
        }catch(Exception e){}
    }


    @Override
    public void onNothingSelected(AdapterView<?> arg0) {
        // empty
    }


    @Override
    public View makeView() {
        ImageView i = new ImageView(this);
        i.setBackgroundColor(0xFF000000);
        i.setScaleType(ImageView.ScaleType.FIT_CENTER);
        i.setLayoutParams(new ImageSwitcher.LayoutParams(
            ImageSwitcher.LayoutParams.FILL_PARENT,
            ImageSwitcher.LayoutParams.FILL_PARENT));
        return i;
    }


    public class ImageAdapter extends BaseAdapter {
        private Context mContext;

        public ImageAdapter(Context c) {
            mContext = c;
        }

        public int getCount() {
            return allimages.size();
        }

        public Object getItem(int position) {
            return position;
        }

        public long getItemId(int position) {
            return position;
        }

        public View getView(int position, View convertView, ViewGroup parent) {
                ImageView galleryview = new ImageView(mContext);
```

```
galleryview.setImageDrawable(allimages.get(position));
galleryview.setAdjustViewBounds(true);
galleryview.setLayoutParams(new LayoutParams(LayoutParams.WRAP_CONTENT,
    LayoutParams.WRAP_CONTENT));
galleryview.setPadding(5, 0, 5, 0);
galleryview.setBackgroundResource(android.R.drawable.picture_frame);
return galleryview;
        }
    }
}
```

10.4 Capturing Video Using MediaRecorder

Marco Dinacci

Problem

You want to capture video using the built-in device camera and save it to disk.

Solution

Capture a video and record it on the phone by using the `MediaRecorder` class provided by the Android framework.

Discussion

The `MediaRecorder` is normally used to perform audio and/or video recording. The class has a straightforward API, but as it's based on a simple state machine, the methods must be called in the proper order in order to avoid `IllegalStateException`s from popping up.

Create a new `Activity` and override the `onCreate` method with the code shown in Example 10-4.

Example 10-4. The onCreate() method of the main activity

```
@Override
public void onCreate(Bundle savedInstanceState) {
    super.onCreate(savedInstanceState);
    setContentView(R.layout.media_recorder_recipe);

    // we shall take the video in landscape orientation
    setRequestedOrientation(ActivityInfo.SCREEN_ORIENTATION_LANDSCAPE);

    mSurfaceView = (SurfaceView) findViewById(R.id.surfaceView);
    mHolder = mSurfaceView.getHolder();
    mHolder.addCallback(this);
    mHolder.setType(SurfaceHolder.SURFACE_TYPE_PUSH_BUFFERS);

    mToggleButton = (ToggleButton) findViewById(R.id.toggleRecordingButton);
    mToggleButton.setOnClickListener(new OnClickListener() {
            @Override
```

```
            // toggle video recording
            public void onClick(View v) {
                    if (((ToggleButton)v).isChecked())
                        mMediaRecorder.start();
                    else {
                        mMediaRecorder.stop();
                        mMediaRecorder.reset();
                        try {
                                initRecorder(mHolder.getSurface());
                        } catch (IOException e) {
                                e.printStackTrace();
                        }
                    }
                }
        });
}
```

The preview frames from the camera will be displayed on a SurfaceView. Recording is controlled by a toggle button. After the recording is over, we stop the MediaRecorder. Since the stop method resets all the state machine variables in order to be able to grab another video, we reset the state machine and call our initRecorder once more.

initRecorder is where we configure the MediaRecorder and the camera, as shown in Example 10-5.

Example 10-5. Setting up the MediaRecorder

```
/* Init the MediaRecorder, the order the methods are called is vital to
 * its correct functioning.
 */
private void initRecorder(Surface surface) throws IOException {
    // It is very important to unlock the camera before doing setCamera
    // or it will result in a black preview
    if(mCamera == null) {
        mCamera = Camera.open();
        mCamera.unlock();
    }

    if(mMediaRecorder == null)
        mMediaRecorder = new MediaRecorder();

    mMediaRecorder.setPreviewDisplay(surface);
    mMediaRecorder.setCamera(mCamera);

    mMediaRecorder.setVideoSource(MediaRecorder.VideoSource.CAMERA);
    mMediaRecorder.setOutputFormat(MediaRecorder.OutputFormat.DEFAULT);
    File file = createFile();

    mMediaRecorder.setOutputFile(file.getAbsolutePath());

    // No limit. Don't forget to check the space on disk.
    mMediaRecorder.setMaxDuration(-1);
    mMediaRecorder.setVideoFrameRate(15);

    mMediaRecorder.setVideoEncoder(MediaRecorder.VideoEncoder.DEFAULT);
```

```
    try {
        mMediaRecorder.prepare();
    } catch (IllegalStateException e) {
        // This is thrown if the previous calls are not called with the
        // proper order
        e.printStackTrace();
    }

    mInitSuccesful = true;
}
```

It is important to create and unlock a `Camera` object before the creation of a `MediaRecor` der. `setPreviewDisplay` and `setCamera` must be called immediately after the creation of the `MediaRecorder`. The choice of the format and the output file is obligatory. Other options, if present, must be called in the order outlined in Example 10-5.

The `MediaRecorder` is best initialized when the surface has been created. We register our `Activity` as a `SurfaceHolder.Callback` listener in order to be notified of this and override the `surfaceCreated` method to call our initialization code:

```
@Override
public void surfaceCreated(SurfaceHolder holder) {
    try {
        if(!mInitSuccessful)
            initRecorder(mHolder.getSurface());
    } catch (IOException e) {
        e.printStackTrace();      // better error handling?
    }
}
```

When you're done with the surface, don't forget to release the resources, as the camera is a shared object and may be used by other applications as well:

```
private void shutdown() {
    // Release MediaRecorder and especially the Camera as it's a shared
    // object that can be used by other applications
    mMediaRecorder.reset();
    mMediaRecorder.release();
    mCamera.release();

    // once the objects have been released they can't be reused
    mMediaRecorder = null;
    mCamera = null;
}
```

Override the `surfaceDestroyed` method so that the preceding code can be called automatically when the user is done with the `Activity`:

```
@Override
public void surfaceDestroyed(SurfaceHolder holder) {
    shutdown();
}
```

Source Download URL

You can download the source code for this example from *http://www.intransitione.com/intransitione.com/code/android/media_recorder_recipe_code.zip.*

10.5 Using Android's Face Detection Capability

Wagied Davids

Problem

You want to find out whether a given photograph contains any human faces and, if so, where.

Solution

Use Android's built-in face detection capability.

Face detection is a cool and fun hidden API feature of Android, and has been around since Android 1.5. In essence, face detection is the act of recognizing the parts of an image that appear to be human faces. It is part of a machine learning technique of recognizing objects using a set of features. Note that this is not face recognition; it detects the parts of the image that are faces, but does not tell you whose face they belong to. Ice Cream Sandwich (Android API 4.0) features face recognition for unlocking the phone.

Discussion

The main activity (see Example 10-6) creates an instance of our `FaceDetectionView`. In this example, we hardcode the file to be scanned, but in real life you would probably want to capture the image using the camera, or choose the image from a `Gallery`.

Example 10-6. The main activity

```
import android.app.Activity;
import android.os.Bundle;

public class Main extends Activity
{
/** Called when the activity is first created. */
@Override
public void onCreate(Bundle savedInstanceState)
{
super.onCreate(savedInstanceState);
setContentView(new FaceDetectionView(this, "face5.JPG"));
}
}
```

`FaceDetectionView` is our custom class used to manage the face detection code using
`android.media.FaceDetector`. The `init()` method conditions some graphics used to
mark the faces—in this example we know where the faces are, and hope that Android
will find them. The real work is done in `detectFaces()`, where we call the `FaceDetec`
`tor`'s `findFaces` method, passing in our image and an array to contain the results. We
then iterate over the found faces. Example 10-7 shows the code. Figure 10-1 shows the
result.

Figure 10-1. Face detection in action

Example 10-7. FaceDetectionView.java

```
...
import android.media.FaceDetector;

public class FaceDetectionView extends View {
    private static final String tag = FaceDetectionView.class.getName();
    private static final int NUM_FACES = 10;
    private FaceDetector arrayFaces;
    private final FaceDetector.Face getAllFaces[] = new FaceDetector.Face[NUM_FACES];
    private FaceDetector.Face getFace = null;

    private final PointF eyesMidPts[] = new PointF[NUM_FACES];
    private final float eyesDistance[] = new float[NUM_FACES];

    private Bitmap sourceImage;

    private final Paint tmpPaint = new Paint(Paint.ANTI_ALIAS_FLAG);
    private final Paint pOuterBullsEye = new Paint(Paint.ANTI_ALIAS_FLAG);
    private final Paint pInnerBullsEye = new Paint(Paint.ANTI_ALIAS_FLAG);

    private int picWidth, picHeight;
    private float xRatio, yRatio;
    private ImageLoader mImageLoader = null;

    public FaceDetectionView(Context context, String imagePath) {
        super(context);
        init();
        mImageLoader = ImageLoader.getInstance(context);
        sourceImage = mImageLoader.loadFromFile(imagePath);
        detectFaces();
    }

    private void init() {
        Log.d(tag, "Init()...");
        pInnerBullsEye.setStyle(Paint.Style.FILL);
        pInnerBullsEye.setColor(Color.RED);
        pOuterBullsEye.setStyle(Paint.Style.STROKE);
        pOuterBullsEye.setColor(Color.RED);
        tmpPaint.setStyle(Paint.Style.STROKE);
        tmpPaint.setTextAlign(Paint.Align.CENTER);
        BitmapFactory.Options bfo = new BitmapFactory.Options();
        bfo.inPreferredConfig = Bitmap.Config.RGB_565;
    }

    private void loadImage(String imagePath) {
        sourceImage = mImageLoader.loadFromFile(imagePath);
    }

    @Override
    protected void onDraw(Canvas canvas) {
        Log.d(tag, "onDraw()...");

        xRatio = getWidth() * 1.0f / picWidth;
        yRatio = getHeight() * 1.0f / picHeight;
        canvas.drawBitmap(
```

```
            sourceImage, null, new Rect(0, 0, getWidth(), getHeight()), tmpPaint);
        for (int i = 0; i < eyesMidPts.length; i++) {
            if (eyesMidPts[i] != null) {
                pOuterBullsEye.setStrokeWidth(eyesDistance[i] / 6);
                canvas.drawCircle(eyesMidPts[i].x * xRatio,
                    eyesMidPts[i].y * yRatio, eyesDistance[i] / 2, pOuterBullsEye);
                canvas.drawCircle(eyesMidPts[i].x * xRatio,
                    eyesMidPts[i].y * yRatio, eyesDistance[i] / 6, pInnerBullsEye);
            }
        }
    }

    private void detectFaces() {
        Log.d(tag, "detectFaces()...");

        picWidth = sourceImage.getWidth();
        picHeight = sourceImage.getHeight();

        arrayFaces = new FaceDetector(picWidth, picHeight, NUM_FACES);
        arrayFaces.findFaces(sourceImage, getAllFaces);

        for (int i = 0; i < getAllFaces.length; i++) {
            getFace = getAllFaces[i];
            try {
                PointF eyesMP = new PointF();
                getFace.getMidPoint(eyesMP);
                eyesDistance[i] = getFace.eyesDistance();
                eyesMidPts[i] = eyesMP;

                Log.i("Face",
                    i + " " + getFace.confidence() + " " + getFace.eyesDistance() + " " +
                    "Pose: (" + getFace.pose(FaceDetector.Face.EULER_X) + "," +
                    getFace.pose(FaceDetector.Face.EULER_Y) + "," +
                    getFace.pose(FaceDetector.Face.EULER_Z) + ")" +
                    "Eyes Midpoint: (" + eyesMidPts[i].x + "," + eyesMidPts[i].y + ")");
            } catch (Exception e) {
                Log.e("Face", i + " is null");
            }
        }
    }
}
```

Source Download URL

The source code for this example is in the Android Cookbook repository at *http://github
.com/AndroidCook/Android-Cookbook-Examples*, in the subdirectory FaceFinder (see
"Getting and Using the Code Examples" on page xvii).

10.6 Playing Audio from a File

Marco Dinacci

Problem

You want to play an audio file stored on the device.

Solution

Create and properly configure a `MediaPlayer` and a `MediaController`, provide the path of the audio file to play, and enjoy the music.

Discussion

Playing an audio file is as easy as setting up a `MediaPlayer` and a `MediaController`.

First create a new activity that implements the `MediaPlayerControl` interface (see Example 10-8).

Example 10-8. The MediaPlayerControl class header

```
public class PlayAudioActivity extends Activity implements MediaPlayerControl {
        private MediaController mMediaController;
        private MediaPlayer mMediaPlayer;
        private Handler mHandler = new Handler();
```

In the `onCreate` method, we create and configure a `MediaPlayer` and a `MediaControl ler`. The first is the object that performs the typical operations on an audio file, such as playing, pausing, and seeking. The second is a view containing the buttons that launch the aforementioned operations through our `MediaPlayerControl` class.

Example 10-9 shows the `onCreate` code.

Example 10-9. The AudioPlayer's onCreate() method

```
    @Override
    public void onCreate(Bundle savedInstanceState) {
        super.onCreate(savedInstanceState);
        setContentView(R.layout.main);

        mMediaPlayer = new MediaPlayer();
        mMediaController = new MediaController(this);
        mMediaController.setMediaPlayer(PlayAudioActivity.this);
        mMediaController.setAnchorView(findViewById(R.id.audioView));

        String audioFile = "" ;
        try {
            mMediaPlayer.setDataSource(audioFile);
            mMediaPlayer.prepare();
        } catch (IOException e) {
            Log.e("PlayAudioDemo",
                "Could not open file " + audioFile + " for playback.", e);
```

```
        }

    mMediaPlayer.setOnPreparedListener(new OnPreparedListener() {
        @Override
        public void onPrepared(MediaPlayer mp) {
                mHandler.post(new Runnable() {
                        public void run() {
                                mMediaController.show(10000);
                                mMediaPlayer.start();
                        }
                });
        }
    });
}
```

In addition to configuring our `MediaController` and `MediaPlayer` we create an anonymous `OnPreparedListener` in order to start the player only when the media source is ready for playback.

Remember to clean up the `MediaPlayer` when the `Activity` is destroyed (see Example 10-10).

Example 10-10. The AudioPlayer clean up

```
@Override
protected void onDestroy() {
    super.onDestroy();
    mMediaPlayer.stop();
    mMediaPlayer.release();
}
```

At last we implement the `MediaPlayerControl` interface. The code is very straightforward, as shown in Example 10-11.

Example 10-11. The MediaPlayerControl implementation

```
@Override
public boolean canPause() {
    return true;
}

@Override
public boolean canSeekBackward() {
    return false;
}

@Override
public boolean canSeekForward() {
    return false;
}

@Override
public int getBufferPercentage() {
    return (mMediaPlayer.getCurrentPosition() * 100) / mMediaPlayer.getDuration();
}
```

```
    // Remaining methods just delegate to the MediaPlayer
}
```

As a final touch we override the onTouchEvent in order to show the MediaController buttons when the user clicks on the screen.

Since we create our MediaController programmatically, the layout is very simple:

```xml
<?xml version="1.0" encoding="utf-8"?>
<LinearLayout xmlns:android="http://schemas.android.com/apk/res/android"
    android:orientation="vertical"
    android:layout_width="fill_parent"
    android:layout_height="fill_parent"
    android:id="@+id/audioView"
    >
</LinearLayout>
```

Source Download URL

You can download the source code for this example from *http://www.intransitione.com/intransitione.com/code/android/play_audio_demo.zip*.

10.7 Playing Audio Without Interaction

Ian Darwin

Problem

You want to play an audio file with no interaction.

Solution

All you need to do to play a file with no interaction (e.g., not user-settable volume, pause, etc. controls) is to create a MediaPlayer for the file, and call its start() method.

Discussion

This is the simplest way to play a sound file. In contrast with Recipe 10.6, this version offers the user no controls to interact with the sound. You should therefore usually offer at least a "stop" or "cancel" button, especially if the audio file is or might be long. If you're just playing a short sound effect within your application, no such control is needed.

You must have a `MediaPlayer` created for your file. The audio file may be on the SD card or it may be in your application's *res/raw* directory. If the sound file is part of your application, store it under *res/raw*. Suppose it is in *res/raw/alarm_sound.3gp*. Then the reference to it is `R.raw.alarm_sound`, and you can play it as follows:

```
MediaPlayer player = MediaPlayer.create(this, R.raw.alarm_sound);
player.start();
```

In the SD card case, use the following invocation:

```
MediaPlayer player = new MediaPlayer();
player.setDataSource(fileName);
player.prepare();
player.start();
```

There is also a convenience routine, `MediaPlayer.create(Context, URI)`, that you can use; in all cases, `create()` calls `prepare()` for you.

To control the player from within your application, you can call the relevant methods such as `player.stop()`, `player.pause()`, and so on. If you want to reuse a player after stopping it, you must call `prepare()` again.

To be notified when the audio is finished, use an `OnCompletionListener`:

```
player.setOnCompletionListener(new OnCompletionListener() {
        @Override
        public void onCompletion(MediaPlayer mp) {
                Toast.makeText(Main.this,
                        "Media Play Complete", Toast.LENGTH_SHORT).show();
        }
});
```

When you are truly done with any `MediaPlayer` instance, you should call its `release()` method to free up memory, or you will run out of resources if you are creating a lot of `MediaPlayer` objects.

See Also

To really use the `MediaPlayer` effectively you should understand its various states and transitions, as this will help you to understand what methods are valid. There is a complete state diagram for the `MediaPlayer` at *http://developer.android.com/reference/android/media/MediaPlayer.html*.

Source Download URL

The source code for this example is in the Android Cookbook repository at *http://github .com/AndroidCook/Android-Cookbook-Examples*, in the subdirectory MediaPlayerDemo (see "Getting and Using the Code Examples" on page xvii).

10.8 Using Speech to Text

Corey Sunwold

Problem

You want to accept speech input and process it as text.

Solution

One of Android's unique features is native speech to text processing. This provides an alternative form of text input for the user, who in some situations might not have her hands readily available to type in information.

Discussion

Android provides an easy API for using its built-in voice recognition through the `Rec ognizerIntent`.

The example layout will be very simple (see Example 10-12). I've only included a `TextView` called `speechText` and a `Button` called `getSpeechButton`. The `Button` will be used to launch the voice recognizer, and when results are returned they will be displayed in the `TextView`.

Example 10-12. The speech recognizer demo program

```
public class Main extends Activity {

    private static final int RECOGNIZER_RESULT = 1234;

    /** Called when the activity is first created. */
    @Override
    public void onCreate(Bundle savedInstanceState) {
        super.onCreate(savedInstanceState);
        setContentView(R.layout.main);

        Button startSpeech = (Button)findViewById(R.id.getSpeechButton);
        startSpeech.setOnClickListener(new OnClickListener() {

            @Override
            public void onClick(View v) {
            Intent intent = new Intent(RecognizerIntent.ACTION_RECOGNIZE_SPEECH);
            intent.putExtra(RecognizerIntent.EXTRA_LANGUAGE_MODEL,
                        RecognizerIntent.LANGUAGE_MODEL_FREE_FORM);
```

```
            intent.putExtra(RecognizerIntent.EXTRA_PROMPT, "Speech to text");
             startActivityForResult(intent, RECOGNIZER_RESULT);
        }

    });
}

/**
 * Handle the results from the recognition activity.
 */
@Override
protected void onActivityResult(int requestCode, int resultCode, Intent data) {
    if (requestCode == RECOGNIZER_RESULT && resultCode == RESULT_OK) {
        ArrayList<String> matches = data.getStringArrayListExtra(
                RecognizerIntent.EXTRA_RESULTS);

        TextView speechText = (TextView)findViewById(R.id.speechText);
        speechText.setText(matches.get(0).toString());
    }

    super.onActivityResult(requestCode, resultCode, data);
    }
}
```

See Also

http://developer.android.com/reference/android/speech/RecognizerIntent.html

10.9 Making the Device Speak with Text-to-Speech

Ian Darwin

Problem

You want your application to pronounce words of text so that the user can perceive them without watching the screen (e.g., when driving).

Solution

Use the TextToSpeech API.

Discussion

The TextToSpeech API is built into Android (though you may have to install the voice files, depending on the version you are using).

To get started you just need a **TextToSpeech** object. In theory, you could just do this:

```
private TextToSpeech myTTS = new TextToSpeech(this, this);
myTTS.setLanguage(Locale.US);
myTTS.speak(textToBeSpoken, TextToSpeech.QUEUE_FLUSH, null);
myTTS.shutdown();
```

However, to ensure success, you actually have to use a couple of intents, one to check that the TTS data is available and/or install it if not, and another to start the TTS mechanism. So, in practice, the code needs to look something like Example 10-13. This quaint little application chooses one of half a dozen banal phrases to utter each time the Speak button is pressed.

Example 10-13. The text-to-speech demo program

```
public class Main extends Activity implements OnInitListener {

    private TextToSpeech myTTS;
    private List<String> phrases = new ArrayList<String>();

    public void onCreate(Bundle savedInstanceState) {

        phrases.add("Hello Android, Goodbye iPhone");
        phrases.add("The quick brown fox jumped over the lazy dog");
        phrases.add("What is your mother's maiden name?");
        phrases.add("Etaoin Shrdlu for Prime Minister");
        phrases.add("The letter 'Q' does not appear in 'antidisestablishmentarianism')");
        super.onCreate(savedInstanceState);
        setContentView(R.layout.main);

        Button startButton = (Button) findViewById(R.id.start_button);
        startButton.setOnClickListener(new View.OnClickListener() {
            @Override
            public void onClick(View arg0) {
                Intent checkIntent = new Intent();
                checkIntent.setAction(TextToSpeech.Engine.ACTION_CHECK_TTS_DATA);
                startActivityForResult(checkIntent, 1);
            }
        });
    }

    protected void onActivityResult(int requestCode, int resultCode, Intent data) {
        if (requestCode == 1) {

            if (resultCode == TextToSpeech.Engine.CHECK_VOICE_DATA_PASS) {
                myTTS = new TextToSpeech(this, this);  ❶
                myTTS.setLanguage(Locale.US);
            } else {
                // TTS data not yet loaded, try to install it
                Intent ttsLoadIntent = new Intent();
                ttsLoadIntent.setAction(TextToSpeech.Engine.ACTION_INSTALL_TTS_DATA);
                startActivity(ttsLoadIntent);
            }
        }
    }

    public void onInit(int status) {
        if (status == TextToSpeech.SUCCESS) {

            int n = (int)(Math.random() * phrases.size());
            myTTS.speak(phrases.get(n), TextToSpeech.QUEUE_FLUSH, null);
```

```
        } else if (status == TextToSpeech.ERROR) {
            myTTS.shutdown();
        }
    }
```

❶ The first argument is a `Context` (the `Activity`) and the second is an `OnInitLis`
`tener`, also implemented by the main activity in this case. When the initialization of
the `TextToSpeech` object is done, it calls the listener, whose `onInit()` method is meant
to notify that the TTS is ready. In our trivial Speaker program here, we simply do
the speaking. In a longer example you would probably want to start a thread or
service to do the speaking operation.

Source Download URL

The source code for this example is in the Android Cookbook repository at *http://github*
.com/AndroidCook/Android-Cookbook-Examples, in the subdirectory Speaker (see
"Getting and Using the Code Examples" on page xvii).

## CHAPTER 11

Data Persistence

11.1 Introduction: Data Persistence

Ian Darwin

Discussion

Data persistence is a wide topic. In this chapter we focus on selected topics, including:

- Filesystem topics relating to the app-accessible parts of the filesystems (*/sdcard* and friends)—but we assume you know the basics of reading/writing text files
- Persisting data in a database, commonly but not exclusively SQLite.
- More specifically, reading and writing the Contacts database
- Some data format conversions (e.g., JSON and XML conversions) that don't fit naturally into any of the other chapters

11.2 Getting File Information

Ian Darwin

Problem

You need to know all you can about a given file "on disk," typically on internal memory or on the SD card.

Solution

Use a `java.io.File` object.

Discussion

The `File` class has a number of "informational" methods. To use any of these, you must construct a `File` object containing the name of the file on which it is to operate. It should be noted up front that creating a `File` object has no effect on the permanent filesystem; it is only an object in Java's memory. You must call methods on the File object in order to change the filesystem; as we'll see, there are numerous "change" methods, such as one for creating a new (but empty) file, one for renaming a file, and so on, as well as many informational methods. Table 11-1 lists some of the informational methods.

Table 11-1. File class informational methods

Return type	Method name	Meaning
boolean	exists()	True if something of that name exists
String	getCanonicalPath()	Full name
String	getName()	Relative filename
String	getParent()	Parent directory
boolean	canRead()	True if file is readable
boolean	canWrite()	True if file is writable
long	lastModified()	File modification time
long	length()	File size
boolean	isFile()	True if it's a file
boolean	isDirectory()	True if it's a directory (note: might be neither file nor directory)

You cannot change the name stored in a `File` object; you simply create a new `File` object each time you need to refer to a different file.

Example 11-1 is drawn from Desktop Java, but the `File` object operates the same in Android as in Java SE.

Example 11-1. A file information program

```java
import java.io.*;
import java.util.*;

/**
 * Report on a file's status in Java
 */

public class FileStatus {

    public static void main(String[] argv) throws IOException {
        // Ensure that a filename (or something) was given in argv[0]
        if (argv.length == 0) {
            System.err.println("Usage: FileStatus filename");
            System.exit(1);
        }

        for (int i = 0; i< argv.length; i++) {
            status(argv[i]);
        }
    }
```

```java
public static void status(String fileName) throws IOException {
    System.out.println("---" + fileName + "---");

    // Construct a File object for the given file.
    File f = new File(fileName);

    // See if it actually exists
    if (!f.exists()) {
        System.out.println("file not found");
        System.out.println(); // Blank line
        return;
    }

    // Print full name
    System.out.println("Canonical name " + f.getCanonicalPath());

    // Print parent directory if possible
    String p = f.getParent();
    if (p != null) {
        System.out.println("Parent directory: " + p);
    }

    // Check our permissions on this file
    if (f.canRead()) {
        System.out.println("File is readable by us.");
    }
    // Check if the file is writable
    if (f.canWrite()) {
        System.out.println("File is writable by us.");
    }

    // Report on the modification time.
    Date d = new Date();
    d.setTime(f.lastModified());
    System.out.println("Last modified " + d);

    // See if file, directory, or other. If file, print size.
    if (f.isFile()) {
        // Report on the file's size
        System.out.println("File size is " + f.length() + " bytes.");
    } else if (f.isDirectory()) {
        System.out.println("It's a directory");
    } else {
        System.out.println("So weird, man! Neither a file nor a directory!");
    }

    System.out.println(); // blank line between entries
}
}
```

When run with the three command-line arguments shown, it produces the output shown in Example 11-2.

Example 11-2. The file information program in action on Microsoft Windows

```
C:\javasrc\dir_file>java FileStatus / /tmp/id /autoexec.bat
---/---
Canonical name C:\
File is readable.
File is writable.
Last modified Thu Jan 01 00:00:00 GMT 1970
It's a directory

---/tmp/id---
file not found

---/autoexec.bat---
Canonical name C:\AUTOEXEC.BAT
Parent directory: \
File is readable.
File is writable.
Last modified Fri Sep 10 15:40:32 GMT 1999
File size is 308 bytes.
```

As you can see, the so-called *canonical name* not only includes a leading directory root of C:\ , but also has had the name converted to uppercase. You can tell I ran that on an older version of Microsoft Windows. On Unix, it behaves differently, as you can see in Example 11-3:

Example 11-3. The file information program in action on Unix

```
$ java FileStatus / /tmp/id /autoexec.bat
---/---
Canonical name /
File is readable.
Last modified October 4, 1999 6:29:14 AM PDT
It's a directory

---/tmp/id---
Canonical name /tmp/id
Parent directory: /tmp
File is readable.
File is writable.
Last modified October 8, 1999 1:01:54 PM PDT
File size is 0 bytes.

---/autoexec.bat---

file not found

$
```

This is because a typical Unix system has no *autoexec.bat* file. And Unix filenames (like those on the filesystem inside your Android device, and those on a Mac) can consist of upper- and lowercase characters: what you type is what you get.

11.3 Reading a File Shipped with the App Rather Than in the Filesystem

Rachee Singh

Problem

You need to access data stored in a file in the */res/raw* directory rather than in the filesystem (*/data*, */sdcard*, or */mnt*). The standard file-oriented Java I/O classes can only open files stored on "disk" (e.g., the */data* directory or the */sdcard* directory).

Solution

Using the getResources() and openRawResource() methods to open the sample file, and then read it normally.

Discussion

We wish to read information from a file packaged with the Android application. So we will need to put the relevant file in the *res/raw* directory (and need to create the directory since it is not present by default). Since it is in *res/*, the generated R class will have an ID for it, which we pass into openRawResource(). Then we will read the file using the returned InputStreamReader wrapped in a BufferedReader. Finally, we extract the string from the BufferedReader using the readLine method. Eclipse asks us to enclose the readLine function within a try-catch block since there is a possibility of it throwing an IOException.

The example file included in */res/raw* is named *samplefile* and is shown in Example 11-4.

Example 11-4. The reading code

```
InputStreamReader is =
    new InputStreamReader(this.getResources().openRawResource(R.raw.samplefile));
BufferedReader reader = new BufferedReader(is);
StringBuilder finalText = new StringBuilder();
String line;
try {
    while ((line = reader.readLine()) != null) {
        finalText.append(line);
    }
} catch (IOException e) {
    e.printStackTrace();
}
fileTextView = (TextView)findViewById(R.id.fileText);
fileTextView.setText(finalText.toString());
```

After reading the entire string, we set it to the TextView in the activity. Figure 11-1 shows the result.

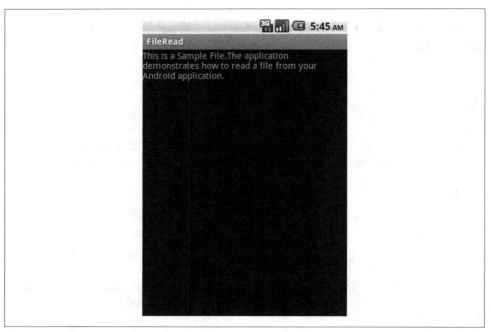

Figure 11-1. File read from application resource

Source Download URL

You can download the source code for this example from *https://docs.google.com/leaf ?id=0B_rESQKgad5LMWJjYjQwMjYtNDVlMi00Y2M5LTk1MmItMTc3OGNhNW ZiNjNh&hl=en_US*.

11.4 Listing a Directory

Ian Darwin

Problem

You need to list the filesystem entries named in a directory.

Solution

Use a `java.io.File` object's `list()` or `listFiles()` method.

Discussion

The `java.io.File` class contains several methods for working with directories. For example, to list the filesystem entities named in the current directory, just write:

```
String[] list = new File(".").list()
```

To get an array of already constructed `File` objects rather than strings, use:

```
File[] list = new File(".").listFiles();
```

You can display the result in a `ListView` (see Recipe 9.2).

Of course, there's lots of room for elaboration. You could print the names in multiple columns across or down the screen in a `TextView` in a monospace font, since you know the number of items in the list before you print. You could omit filenames with leading periods, as does the Unix `ls` program. Or print the directory names first; as some "file manager" type programs do. By using `listFiles()`, which constructs a new `File` object for each name, you could print the size of each, as per the MS-DOS `dir` command or the Unix `ls -l` command (see Recipe 11.2, available on this book's website at *http://androidcookbook.com/r/3220*). Or you could figure out whether each is a file, a directory, or neither. Having done that, you could pass each directory to your top-level function, and you would have directory recursion (the Unix find command, or `ls -R`, or the DOS `DIR /S` command). Quite the makings of a file manager application of your own.

A more flexible way to list filesystem entries is with `list(FilenameFilter ff)`. `FilenameFilter` is a tiny interface with only one method: `boolean accept(File inDir, String fileName)`. Suppose you want a listing of only Java-related files (*.java*, *.class*, *.jar*, etc.). Just write the `accept()` method so that it returns true for these files and false for any others. Example 11-5 shows the `Ls` class warmed over to use a `FilenameFilter` instance.

Example 11-5. Directory Lister with FilenameFilter

```
import java.io.*;

/**
```

```
 * FNFilter - directory lister modified to use FilenameFilter
 */
public class FNFilter {
 public static String[] getListing(String startingDir) {
 // Generate the selective list, with a one-use File object.
 String[] dir = new java.io.File(startingDir).list(new OnlyJava());
 java.util.Arrays.sort(dir); // Sorts by name
 return dir;
}

/** FilenameFilter implementation:
 * The Accept method only returns true for .java , .jar and class files.
 */
class OnlyJava implements FilenameFilter {
 public boolean accept(File dir, String s) {
 if (s.endsWith(".java") || s.endsWith(".jar") || s.endsWith(".dex"))
 return true;
 // others: projects, ... ?
 return false;
 }
}
```

The FilenameFilter could be more flexible; in a full-scale application, the list of files returned by the FilenameFilter would be chosen dynamically, possibly automatically, based on what you were working on. File Chooser dialogs implement this as well, allowing the user to select interactively from one of several sets of files to be listed. This is a great convenience in finding files, just as it is here in reducing the number of files that must be examined.

For the listFiles() method, there is an additional overload that accepts a FileFilter. The only difference is that FileFilter's accept() method is called with a File object, whereas FileNameFilter's is called with a filename string.

See Also

See Recipe 9.2 to display the results in your GUI. Chapter 11 of *Java Cookbook* (*http://shop.oreilly.com/product/9780596007010.do*), written by me and published by O'Reilly, has more information on file and directory operations.

11.5 Getting Total and Free Space Information About the SD Card

Amir Alagic

Problem

You want to find out the amount of total and available space on the SD card.

Solution

Use `StatFs` and `Environment` classes from the `android.os` package to find total and available space on the SD card.

Discussion

Here is some code that obtains the information:

```
StatFs statFs = new StatFs(Environment.getExternalStorageDirectory().getPath());
double bytesTotal = (long) statFs.getBlockSize() * (long) statFs.getBlockCount();
double megTotal = bytesTotal / 1048576;
```

To get total space on the SD card use `StatFs` in the `android.os` package; and as a constructor parameter use `Environment.getExternalStorageDirectory().getPath()`.

Then, multiply the block size by the number of blocks on the SD card:

```
(long) statFs.getBlockSize() * (long) statFs.getBlockCount();
```

To get size in megabytes, divide the result by 1048576. To get the amount of available space on the SD card, replace `statFs.getBlockCount()` with `statFs.getAvailable Blocks()`:

```
(long) statFs.getBlockSize() * (long) statFs.getAvailableBlocks();
```

If you want to display the value with two decimal places you can use a `DecimalFormat` object from `java.text`:

```
DecimalFormat twoDecimalForm = new DecimalFormat("#.##");
```

11.6 Providing User Preference Activity with Minimal Effort

Ian Darwin

Problem

You want to let the user specify one or more preferences values, and have them persisted across runs of the program.

Solution

Have your Preferences or Settings menu item or button load an activity that subclasses `PreferenceActivity`; in its `onCreate()`, load the XML `PreferenceScreen`.

Discussion

Android will happily maintain a `SharedPreferences` object for you in semipermanent storage. To retrieve settings from it, use:

```
sharedPreferences = PreferenceManager.getDefaultSharedPreferences(this);
```

This should be called in your main activity's onCreate() method, or in the onCreate() of any activity that needs to view the user's chosen preferences.

You do need to tell Android what values you want the user to be able to specify, such as name, Twitter account, favorite color, or whatever. You don't use the traditional view items such as ListView or Spinner, but instead use the special Preference items. A reasonable set of choices are available, such as Lists, TextEdits, CheckBoxes, and so on. Example 11-6 uses a List, a TextEdit, and a CheckBox.

Example 11-6. XML PreferenceScreen

```xml
<PreferenceScreen xmlns:android="http://schemas.android.com/apk/res/android">

    <ListPreference
        android:key="listChoice"
        android:title="List Choice"
        android:entries="@array/choices"
        android:entryValues="@array/choices"
        />

    <PreferenceCategory
        android:title="Personal">

        <EditTextPreference
            android:key="nameChoice"
            android:title="Name"
            android:hint="Name"
        />

        <CheckBoxPreference
            android:key="booleanChoice"
            android:title="Binary Choice"
        />

    </PreferenceCategory>

</PreferenceScreen>
```

The PreferenceCategory in the XML allows you to subdivide your panel into labelled sections. It is also possible to have more than one PreferenceScreen if you have a large number of settings and want to divide it into "pages." Several additional kinds of UI elements can be used in the XML PreferenceScreen; see the official documentation for details.

The PreferenceActivity subclass consists of nothing more than this onCreate() method:

```java
@Override
protected void onCreate(Bundle savedInstanceState) {
    super.onCreate(savedInstanceState);
    addPreferencesFromResource(R.layout.prefs);
}
```

When activated, the `PreferenceActivity` looks like Figure 11-2.

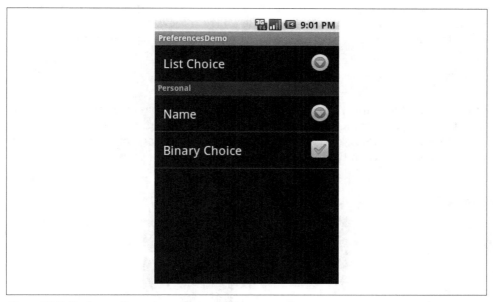

Figure 11-2. PreferenceScreen

When the user clicks on, say, Name, an Edit dialog opens, as in Figure 11-3.

Figure 11-3. String edit dialog

In the XML layout for the Preferences screen, each preference setting is assigned a name or "key," as in a Java Map or Properties. The supported value types are the obvious string, integer, float, and boolean. You use this to retrieve the user's values, and you provide a default value in case the settings screen hasn't been put up yet or in case the user didn't bother to specify a particular setting.

```
String preferredName =
    sharedPreferences.getString("nameChoice", "No name");
```

Like many Android apps, this demo has no Back button from its preferences; the user simply presses the system's Back button. When the user returns to the main activity, a real app would operate based on the user's choices. My demo app simply displays the values. This is shown in Figure 11-4.

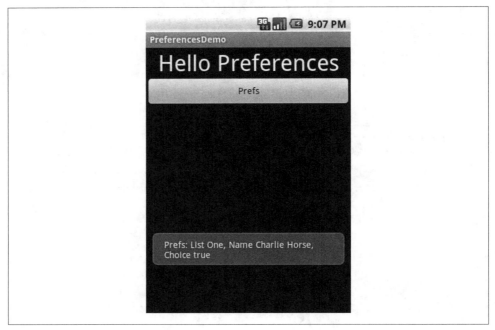

Figure 11-4. Values the main activity uses

Basically that's all you need: an XML PreferenceScreen to define the properties and how the user sets them, a call to getDefaultSharedPrefences(), and calls to get String(), getBoolean(), and so on, on the returned SharedPreferences object. It's easy to handle preferences this way, and it gives the Android system a feel of uniformity, consistency, and predictability that is important to the overall user experience.

11.7 Checking the Consistency of Default Shared Preferences

Federico Paolinelli

Problem

Android provides a very easy way to set up default preferences by defining a `PreferenceActivity` and providing it a resource file, as discussed in Recipe 11.6. What is not clear is how to perform checks on preferences given by the user.

Solution

You can implement the `PreferenceActivity` method `onSharedPreferenceChanged`:

```
public void onSharedPreferenceChanged(SharedPreferences prefs, String key)
```

You perform your checks in this method's body. If the check fails you can restore a default value in the preference. You must be aware that even if the `SharedPreferences` will contain the right value, you won't see it displayed correctly. For this reason, you need to reload the preferences activity.

Discussion

If you have a default preference activity that implements `OnSharedPreferenceChangeListener`, as shown in Example 11-7, your `PreferenceActivity` can implement the `onSharedPreferenceChanged` method.

Example 11-7. PreferenceActivity implementation

```
public class MyPreferenceActivity extends PreferenceActivity
implements OnSharedPreferenceChangeListener {

public void onCreate(Bundle savedInstanceState) {
    super.onCreate(savedInstanceState);
    Context context = getApplicationContext();
    prefs = PreferenceManager.getDefaultSharedPreferences(context);
    addPreferencesFromResource(R.xml.userprefs);
}
```

The `onSharedPreferenceChanged()` method will be called after the change is committed, so every other change you perform will be permanent.

The idea is to check whether you like the value, and otherwise to put a default value/disable it.

To get the method notified, you have to register your activity as a valid listener. A good way to do so is to register in `onResume` and unregister in `onPause`:

```
@Override
protected void onResume() {
    super.onResume();
        prefs.registerOnSharedPreferenceChangeListener(this);
```

```
        }

        @Override
        protected void onPause() {
            super.onPause();
            prefs.unregisterOnSharedPreferenceChangeListener(this);
        }
```

Now it's time to perform the consistency check. For example, if you have an option whose key is MY_OPTION_KEY, you can use the code in Example 11-8 to check and allow/disallow the value.

Example 11-8. Checking and allowing/disallowing the value

```
public void onSharedPreferenceChanged(SharedPreferences prefs, String key) {
    SharedPreferences.Editor prefEditor = prefs.edit();


    if(key.equals(MY_OPTION_KEY)){
        String optionValue = prefs.getString(MY_OPTION_KEY, "");
        if(dontLikeTheValue(optionValue)){
            prefEditor.putString(MY_OPTION_KEY, "Default value");
            prefEditor.commit();
            reload();
        }
    }
    return;
}
```

Of course in this way the user will be surprised and will not know why you refused his option. You can then show an error dialog and perform the reload action after the user confirms the dialog (see Example 11-9).

Example 11-9. Explaining rejection

```
private void showErrorDialog(String errorString){
    String okButtonString = context.getString(R.string.ok_name);
    AlertDialog.Builder ad = new AlertDialog.Builder(context);
    ad.setTitle(context.getString(R.string.error_name));
    ad.setMessage(errorString);
    ad.setPositiveButton(okButtonString,new OnClickListener() {
            public void onClick(DialogInterface dialog, int arg1) {
                reload();
            } } );
    ad.show();
    return;
}
```

In this way, the dontLikeTheValue "if" becomes:

```
        if(dontLikeTheValue(optionValue)){
            if(!GeneralUtils.isPhoneNumber(smsNumber)){
                showErrorDialog("I dont like the option");
                prefEditor.putString(MY_OPTION_KEY, "Default value");
                prefEditor.commit();
```

```
        }
    }
```

What's still missing is the `reload()` function, but it's pretty obvious. It relaunches the activity using the same intent that fired it:

```
private void reload(){
        startActivity(getIntent());
        finish();
    }
```

11.8 Performing Advanced Text Searches

Claudio Esperanca

Problem

You want to implement an advanced "search" capability, and you need to know how to build a data layer to store and search text data using SQLite's Full Text Search.

Solution

Using an SQLite Full Text Search 3 (FTS3) virtual table and match function from SQLite it's possible to build such a mechanism.

Discussion

By following these steps, you will be able to create an example Android project with a data layer where you will be able to store and retrieve some data using an SQLite database.

1. Create a new Android project (`AdvancedSearchProject`).
2. Select an API level equal to or greater than 8.
3. Specify `AdvancedSearch` as the application name.
4. Use `com.androidcookbook.example.advancedsearch` as the package name.
5. Create an activity with the name `AdvancedSearchActivity`.
6. The Min SDK version should be 8 (for Android 2.2, codenamed Froyo).
7. Create a new Java class `DbAdapter` within the package `com.androidcookbook.example.advancedsearch` on the *src* folder.

To create the data layer for the example application, enter the Example 11-10 source code in the created file.

Example 11-10. The DbAdapter class

```
package com.androidcookbook.example.advancedsearch;

import java.util.LinkedList;
```

```
import android.content.ContentValues;
import android.content.Context;
import android.database.Cursor;
import android.database.SQLException;
import android.database.sqlite.SQLiteDatabase;
import android.database.sqlite.SQLiteOpenHelper;
import android.util.Log;

public class DbAdapter {
    public static final String APP_NAME = "AdvancedSearch";
    private static final String DATABASE_NAME = "AdvancedSearch_db";
    private static final int DATABASE_VERSION = 1;
    // Our internal database version (e.g. to control upgrades)
    private static final String TABLE_NAME = "example_tbl";
    public static final String KEY_USERNAME = "username";
    public static final String KEY_FULLNAME = "fullname";
    public static final String KEY_EMAIL = "email";
    public static long GENERIC_ERROR = -1;
    public static long GENERIC_NO_RESULTS = -2;
    public static long ROW_INSERT_FAILED = -3;
    private final Context context;
    private DbHelper dbHelper;
    private SQLiteDatabase sqlDatabase;

    public DbAdapter(Context context) {
        this.context = context;
    }

    private static class DbHelper extends SQLiteOpenHelper {
        private boolean databaseCreated=false;
        DbHelper(Context context) {
            super(context, DATABASE_NAME, null, DATABASE_VERSION);
        }
        @Override
        public void onCreate(SQLiteDatabase db) {
            Log.d(APP_NAME, "Creating the application database");

            try{
                // Create the full text search 3 virtual table
                db.execSQL(
                    "CREATE VIRTUAL TABLE ["+TABLE_NAME+"] USING FTS3 (" +
                        "["+KEY_USERNAME+"] TEXT," +
                        "["+KEY_FULLNAME+"] TEXT," +
                        "["+KEY_EMAIL+"] TEXT" +
                    ");"
                );
                this.databaseCreated = true;
            } catch (Exception e) {
                Log.e(APP_NAME,
                    "An error occurred while creating the database: " + e.toString(), e);
                this.deleteDatabaseStructure(db);
            }
        }
        @Override
```

```java
    public void onUpgrade(SQLiteDatabase db, int oldVersion, int newVersion) {
        Log.d(APP_NAME, "Updating the database from the version " +
    oldVersion + " to " + newVersion + "...");
        this.deleteDatabaseStructure(db); // toy example: purge prev. data on upgrade
        this.onCreate(db);
    }
    public boolean databaseCreated(){
        return this.databaseCreated;
    }
    private boolean deleteDatabaseStructure(SQLiteDatabase db){
        try{
            db.execSQL("DROP TABLE IF EXISTS ["+TABLE_NAME+"];");

            return true;
        }catch (Exception e) {
            Log.e(APP_NAME,
                "An error occurred while deleting the database: " + e.toString(), e);
        }
        return false;
    }
}

/**
 * Open the database; if the database can't be opened, try to create it
 *
 * @return {@link Boolean} true if database opened/created OK, false otherwise
 * @throws {@link SQLException] if an error occurred
 */
public boolean open() throws SQLException {
    try{
        this.dbHelper = new DbHelper(this.context);
        this.sqlDatabase = this.dbHelper.getWritableDatabase();
        return this.sqlDatabase.isOpen();
    }catch (SQLException e) {
        throw e;
    }
}

/**
 * Close the database connection
 * @return {@link Boolean} true if the connection was terminated, false otherwise
 */
public boolean close() {
    this.dbHelper.close();
    return !this.sqlDatabase.isOpen();
}

/**
 * Check if the database is opened
 *
 * @return {@link Boolean} true if it was, false otherwise
 */
public boolean isOpen(){
    return this.sqlDatabase.isOpen();
}
```

```
/**
 * Check if the database was created
 *
 * @return {@link Boolean} true if it was, false otherwise
 */
public boolean databaseCreated(){
    return this.dbHelper.databaseCreated();
}


/**
 * Insert a new row on the table
 *
 * @param username {@link String} with the username
 * @param fullname {@link String} with the fullname
 * @param email {@link String} with the email
 * @return {@link Long} with the row id or ROW_INSERT_FAILED (bellow 0 value) on error
 */
public long insertRow(String username, String fullname, String email) {
    try{
        // Prepare the values
        ContentValues values = new ContentValues();
        values.put(KEY_USERNAME, username);
        values.put(KEY_FULLNAME, fullname);
        values.put(KEY_EMAIL, email);

        // Try to insert the row
        return this.sqlDatabase.insert(TABLE_NAME, null, values);
    }catch (Exception e) {
        Log.e(APP_NAME,
            "An error occurred while inserting the row: "+e.toString(), e);
    }
    return ROW_INSERT_FAILED;
}

/**
 * The search method Uses the full text search 3 virtual table and
 * the MATCH function from SQLite to search for data.
 * @see http://www.sqlite.org/fts3.html to know more about the syntax
 * @param search {@link String} with the search expression
 * @return {@link LinkedList} with the {@link String} search results
 */
public LinkedList<String> search(String search) {

    LinkedList<String> results = new LinkedList<String>();
    Cursor cursor = null;
    try{
        cursor = this.sqlDatabase.query(true, TABLE_NAME, new String[] {
            KEY_USERNAME, KEY_FULLNAME, KEY_EMAIL }, TABLE_NAME + " MATCH ?",
            new String[] { search }, null, null, null, null);

        if(cursor!=null && cursor.getCount()>0 && cursor.moveToFirst()){
            int iUsername = cursor.getColumnIndex(KEY_USERNAME);
            int iFullname = cursor.getColumnIndex(KEY_FULLNAME);
```

```
                    int iEmail = cursor.getColumnIndex(KEY_EMAIL);

                    do {
                        results.add(
                            new String(
                                "Username: "+cursor.getString(iUsername) +
                                ", Fullname: "+cursor.getString(iFullname) +
                                ", Email: "+cursor.getString(iEmail)
                            )
                        );
                    }while(cursor.moveToNext());
                }
            }catch(Exception e){
                Log.e(APP_NAME,
                    "An error occurred while searching for "+search+": "+e.toString(), e);
            }finally{
                if(cursor!=null && !cursor.isClosed()){
                    cursor.close();
                }
            }

            return results;
        }
}
```

Now that the data layer is usable, the activity `AdvancedSearchActivity` can be used to test it.

To define the application strings, replace the contents of the *res/values/strings.xml* file:

```xml
<?xml version="1.0" encoding="utf-8"?>
<resources>
    <string name="label_search">Search</string>
    <string name="app_name">AdvancedSearch</string>
</resources>
```

The application layout can be set within the file *res/layout/main.xml*. This contains the expected `EditText` (named `etSearch`), a `Button` (named `btnSearch`), and a `TextView` (named `tvResults`) to display the results, all in a `LinearLayout`.

Finally, Example 11-11 shows the *AdvancedSearchActivity.java* code.

Example 11-11. AdvancedSearchActivity

```java
package com.androidcookbook.example.advancedsearch;

import java.util.Iterator;
import java.util.LinkedList;

import android.app.Activity;
import android.os.Bundle;
import android.view.View;
import android.widget.Button;
import android.widget.EditText;
import android.widget.TextView;
```

```java
public class AdvancedSearchActivity extends Activity {
    private DbAdapter dbAdapter;
    @Override
    public void onCreate(Bundle savedInstanceState) {
        super.onCreate(savedInstanceState);
        setContentView(R.layout.main);

        dbAdapter = new DbAdapter(this);
        dbAdapter.open();

        if(dbAdapter.databaseCreated()){
            dbAdapter.insertRow("test", "test example", "example_test@example.com");
            dbAdapter.insertRow("lorem", "lorem ipsum", "lorem.ipsum@example2.com");
            dbAdapter.insertRow("jdoe", "Jonh Doe", "j.doe@example.com");
        }

        Button button = (Button) findViewById(R.id.btnSearch);
        final EditText etSearch = (EditText) findViewById(R.id.etSearch);
        final TextView tvResults = (TextView) findViewById(R.id.tvResults);
        button.setOnClickListener(new View.OnClickListener() {
            public void onClick(View v) {
                LinkedList<String> results =
                    dbAdapter.search(etSearch.getText().toString());

                if(results.isEmpty()){
                    tvResults.setText("No results found");
                }else{
                    Iterator<String> i = results.iterator();
                    tvResults.setText("");
                    while(i.hasNext()){
                        tvResults.setText(tvResults.getText()+i.next()+"\n");
                    }
                }
            }
        });
    }
    @Override
    protected void onDestroy() {
        dbAdapter.close();
        super.onDestroy();
    }
}
```

See Also

http://www.sqlite.org/fts3.html to know more about the Full Text Search 3 capability, including the search syntax; (*http://code.google.com/p/localizeandroid/*) to learn about a project with an implementation of this search mechanism

11.9 Creating an SQLite Database in an Android Application

Rachee Singh

Problem

You want data you save to last longer than the application's run, and you want easy access to the data.

Solution

SQLite is a popular relational database using the SQL model that you can use to store application data. The normal way to use it is to extend the `SQLiteOpenHelper` class.

Discussion

In order to use SQLite databases in an Android application, it is necessary to inherit from the `SQLiteOpenHelper` class. This is a standard Android class that helps open the database file. It checks for the existence of the database file and if it exists, it opens it; otherwise, it creates one.

```
public class SqlOpenHelper extends SQLiteOpenHelper {
```

The constructor for the `SQLiteOpenHelper` class takes in a few arguments: the context, database name, `CursorFactory` object, and version number.

```
    public static final String DBNAME = "tasksdb.sqlite";
    public static final int VERSION =1;
    public static final String TABLE_NAME = "tasks";
    public static final String ID= "id";
    public static final String NAME="name";

    public SqlOpenHelper(Context context) {
        super(context, DBNAME, null, VERSION);

}
```

To create a database in SQL you use the "create" statement:

```
CREATE TABLE <table-name> (column1 INTEGER PRIMARY KEY AUTOINCREMENT NOT NULL,
column2 TEXT);
```

The `SQLiteOpenHelper` method `onCreate()` is called to allow you to create (and possibly populate) the database.

```
    public void onCreate(SQLiteDatabase db) {
        createDatabase(db);
    }

    private void createDatabase(SQLiteDatabase db) {
        db.execSQL("create table " + TABLE_NAME + "(" +
            ID + " integer primary key autoincrement not null, " +
            NAME + " text "
            + ");"
```

```
                    );
            }
```

To get a handle on the SQL database you created, instantiate the class inheriting `SQLiteOpenHelper`:

```
        SqlOpenHelper helper = new SqlOpenHelper(this);
        SQLiteDatabase database= helper.getWritableDatabase();
```

Now, the `SQLiteDatabase` database can be used to load elements stored in the database, as well as update and insert elements to it.

11.10 Inserting Values into an SQLite Database

Rachee Singh

Problem

You want to save data values into an SQLite database.

Solution

Use the `insert()` method and pass an object of type `ContentValues`.

Discussion

`ContentValues` provides something similar to a key-value pair, so, for example, `NAME` would be a final string containing the key, and `Mangoes` could be the value. This would insert a row in the database with the value `Mangoes` in it.

```
        ContentValues values = new ContentValues();
        values.put(NAME, "Mangoes");
```

After creating the values, we insert them into the table using the `insert()` method. SQLite returns the ID for that row in the database.

```
        Long id = (database.insert(TABLE_NAME, null, values));
        tasks.add(t);
```

`id` is the ID for the row that we inserted into the database.

11.11 Loading Values from an Existing SQLite Database

Rachee Singh

Problem

Previous runs of your application have created and populated an SQLite database. Now you need to retrieve application data from the existing database.

Solution

Use the `query()` method of the database, and use the returned `Cursor` object to iterate over the database and process the date.

Discussion

In order to iterate over items in a database, we require an object of the `Cursor` class. To query the database, we use the query method along with appropriate arguments, most importantly the table name and the column names for which we are extracting values (see Example 11-12).

Example 11-12. Querying and iterating over results

```
ArrayList<Food> foods = new ArrayList(this);
Cursor listCursor = database.query(TABLE_NAME, new String [] {
ID, NAME}, null, null, null, null, String.format("%s", NAME));
listCursor.moveToFirst();
Food t;
if(! listCursor.isAfterLast()) {
    do {
        Long id = listCursor.getLong(0);
        String name= listCursor.getString(1);
        t = new Food(name);
        foods.add(t);
    } while (listCursor.moveToNext());
}
    listCursor.close();
```

The `moveToFirst()` method starts from the first item in the database and `moveToNext()` moves the cursor to the next item. We keep checking until we have reached the end of the database. Each item of the database is added to an `ArrayList`.

11.12 Working with Dates in SQLite

Jonathan Fuerth

Problem

Android's embedded SQLite3 database supports date and time data directly, including some useful date and time arithmetic. However, getting these dates out of the database is troublesome: there is no `Cursor.getDate()` in the Android API.

Solution

Use SQLite's `strftime()` function to convert between SQLite timestamp format and the Java API's "milliseconds since the epoch" representation.

Discussion

This recipe demonstrates the advantages of using SQLite timestamps over storing raw milliseconds values in your database, and shows how to retrieve those timestamps from your database as `java.util.Date` objects.

Background

The usual representation for an absolute timestamp in Unix is `time_t`, which historically was just an alias for a 32-bit integer. This integer represented the date as the number of seconds elapsed since UTC 00:00 on January 1, 1970 (the Unix time *epoch*). On systems where `time_t` is still a 32-bit integer, the clock will roll over partway through the year 2038.

Java adopted a similar convention, but with a few twists. The epoch remains the same, but the count is always stored in a 64-bit signed integer (the native Java `long` type) and the units are milliseconds rather than seconds. This method of timekeeping will not roll over for another 292 million years.

Android example code that deals with persisting dates and times tends to simply store and retrieve the raw *milliseconds since the epoch* values in the database. However, by doing this, it misses out on some useful features built into SQLite.

The advantages

There are several advantages to storing proper SQLite timestamps in your data: you can default timestamp columns to the current time using no Java code at all; you can perform calendar-sensitive arithmetic such as selecting the first day of a week or month, or adding a week to the value stored in the database; and you can extract just the date or time components and return those from your data provider.

All of these code-saving advantages come with two added bonuses: first, your data provider's API can stick to the Android convention of passing timestamps around as `long` values; second, all of this date manipulation is done in the natively compiled SQLite code, so the manipulations don't incur the garbage collection overhead of creating multiple `java.util.Date` or `java.util.Calendar` objects.

The code

Without further ado, here's how to do it.

First, create a table that defines a column of type `timestamp`.

```
CREATE TABLE current_list (
        item_id INTEGER NOT NULL,
        added_on TIMESTAMP NOT NULL DEFAULT current_timestamp,
        added_by VARCHAR(50) NOT NULL,
        quantity INTEGER NOT NULL,
        units VARCHAR(50) NOT NULL,
```

```
                CONSTRAINT current_list_pk PRIMARY KEY (item_id)
        );
```

Note the default value for the added_on column. Whenever you insert a row into this table, SQLite will automatically fill in the current time (accurate to the second) for the new record (we show this using the command-line SQLite program running on a desktop; we'll show later in this recipe how to get these into a database under Android).

```
sqlite> insert into current_list (item_id, added_by, quantity, units)
    ...> values (1, 'fuerth', 1, 'EA');
sqlite> select * from current_list where item_id = 1;
1|2010-05-14 23:10:26|fuerth|1|EA
sqlite>
```

See how the current date was inserted automatically? This is one of the advantages you get from working with SQLite timestamps.

How about the other advantages?

Select just the date part, forcing the time back to midnight:

```
sqlite> select item_id, date(added_on,'start of day')
    ...> from current_list where item_id = 1;
1|2010-05-14
sqlite>
```

Or adjust the date to the Monday of the following week:

```
sqlite> select item_id, date(added_on,'weekday 1')
    ...> from current_list where item_id = 1;
1|2010-05-17
sqlite>
```

Or the Monday before:

```
sqlite> select item_id, date(added_on,'weekday 1','-7 days')
    ...> from current_list where item_id = 1;
1|2010-05-10
sqlite>
```

These examples are just the tip of the iceberg. You can do a lot of useful things with your timestamps once SQLite recognizes them as such.

Last, but not least, you must be wondering how to get these dates back into your Java code. The trick is to press another of SQLite's date functions into service—this time strftime(). Here is a Java method that fetches a row from the current_list table we've been working with:

```
Cursor cursor = database.rawQuery(
        "SELECT item_id AS _id," +
        " (strftime('%s', added_on) * 1000) AS added_on," +
        " added_by, quantity, units" +
        " FROM current_list", new String[0]);
long millis = cursor.getLong(cursor.getColumnIndexOrThrow("added_on"));
Date addedOn = new Date(millis);
```

That's it: using strftime's %s format, you can select timestamps directly into your Cursor as Java *milliseconds since the epoch* values. Client code will be none the wiser, except that your content provider will be able to do date manipulations for free that would take significant amounts of Java code and extra object allocations.

See Also

SQLite's documentation for its date and time functions (*http://www.sqlite.org/lang_da tefunc.html*)

11.13 Parsing JSON Using JSONObject

Rachee Singh

Problem

JSON stands for JavaScript Object Notation and is a simpler format than XML for data interchange. Many websites provide data in JSON, and many applications need to parse JSON and provide that data in the application.

Solution

Using built-in classes such as JSONObject simplifies the process of parsing JSON and retrieving the data values contained in it.

Discussion

For this recipe, we will use a method to generate JSON code. In a real application you would likely obtain the JSON data from some web service. In this method we make use of a JSONObject class object to put in values and then to return the corresponding string (using the toString() method). Creating an object of type JSONObject can throw a JSONException, so we enclose the code in a try-catch block (see Example 11-13).

Example 11-13. Generating mock data in JSON format

```
private String getJsonString() {
    JSONObject string = new JSONObject();
    try {
        string.put("name", "John Doe");
        string.put("age", new Integer(25));
        string.put("address", "75 Ninth Avenue 2nd and 4th Floors New York, NY 10011");
        string.put("phone", "8367667829");
    } catch (JSONException e) {
        e.printStackTrace();
    }
    return string.toString();
}
```

We need to instantiate an object of class `JSONObject` that takes the JSON string as an argument. In this case, the JSON string is being obtained from the `getJsonString` method. From the `JSONObject` we extract the information and print it in a `TextView`.

Example 11-14. Parsing the JSON string and retrieving values

```
try {
    String jsonString = getJsonString();
    JSONObject jsonObject = new JSONObject(jsonString);
    String name = jsonObject.getString("name");
    String age = jsonObject.getString("age");
    String address = jsonObject.getString("address");
    String phone = jsonObject.getString("phone");
    String jsonText=name + "\n" + age + "\n" + address + "\n" + phone;
        json= (TextView)findViewById(R.id.json);
        json.setText(jsonText);
} catch (JSONException e) {
    // Display the Exception...
}
```

Source Download URL

You can download the source code for this example from *https://docs.google.com/leaf?id=0B_rE SQKgad5LZDYxN2E3NTItMjE3Yy00YjE2LThjY2UtMGE2MTIyM2I0YjUx&hl=en _US.*

11.14 Parsing an XML Document Using the DOM API

Ian Darwin

Problem

You have data in XML, and you want to transform it into something useful in your application.

Solution

Android provides a fairly good clone of the standard DOM API used in the Java Standard Edition. Using the DOM API instead of writing your own parsing code just makes sense.

Discussion

This is the code that parses the XML document containing the list of recipes in this book, as discussed in Recipe 13.2. The input file has a single recipes root element, followed by a sequence of recipe elements, each with an id and a title with textual content.

The code creates a DOM DocumentBuilderFactory, which can be tailored, for example, to make schema-aware parsers. In real code you could create this in a static initializer instead of re-creating it each time. The DocumentBuilderFactory is used to create a Document Builder, a.k.a. parser. The parser expects to be reading from an Input Stream, so we convert the data which we have in string form into an array of bytes and construct a ByteArrayInputStream. Again, in real life you would probably want to combine this code with the web service consumer so that you could simply get the input stream from the network connection and read the XML directly into the parser, instead of saving it as a string and then wrapping that in a converter as we do here.

Once the elements are parsed, we convert the document into an array of data (the singular of data is datum, so the class is called Datum) by calling the DOM API methods such as getDocumentElement(), getChildNodes(), and getNodeValue(). Since the DOM API was not invented by Java people, it doesn't use the standard Collections API but has its own collections, like NodeList. In DOM's defense, the same or similar APIs are used in a really wide variety of programming languages, so it can be said to be as much a standard as Java's Collections.

Example 11-15 shows the code.

Example 11-15. Parsing XML code

```
/** Convert the list of Recipes in the String result from the
 * web service into an ArrayList of Datum.
 * @throws ParserConfigurationException
 * @throws IOException
 * @throws SAXException
 */
public static ArrayList<Datum> parse(String input) throws Exception {

    final ArrayList<Datum> results = new ArrayList<Datum>(1000);
    final DocumentBuilderFactory dbFactory =
        DocumentBuilderFactory.newInstance();
    final DocumentBuilder parser = dbFactory.newDocumentBuilder();

    final Document document =
    parser.parse(new ByteArrayInputStream(input.getBytes()));
```

```
    Element root = document.getDocumentElement();
    NodeList recipesList = root.getChildNodes();
    for (int i = 0; i < recipesList.getLength(); i++) {
        Node recipe = recipesList.item(i);
        NodeList fields = recipe.getChildNodes();
        String id = ((Element) fields.item(0)).getNodeValue();
        String title =
            ((Element) fields.item(1)).getNodeValue();
        Datum d = new Datum(Integer.parseInt(id), title);
        results.add(d);
    }
    return results;
}
```

In converting this code from Java SE to Android, the only change we had to make was to use getNodeValue() in the retrieval of id and title instead of Java SE's getTextContent(); so the API really is very close.

See Also

The web service is discussed in Recipe 13.2. There is much more in the XML chapter of my *Java Cookbook* (*http://shop.oreilly.com/product/9780596007010.do*).

11.15 Parsing an XML Document Using an XmlPullParser

Johan Pelgrim

Problem

You have data in XML, and you want to transform it into something useful in your application.

Solution

Apart from allowing you to process XML using DOM or SAX, the Android framework also provides an implementation of the XmlPullParser interface provided in the XML Pull v1 API.

Discussion

The XmlPull v1 API is an easy-to-use XML pull parsing API that was designed for simplicity and very good performance both in constrained environments such as those defined by Java Micro Edition and on the server side when used in J2EE application servers. XML pull parsing allows incremental (sometimes called *streaming*) parsing of XML where the application is in control—the parsing can be interrupted at any given moment and resumed when the application is ready to consume more input.

Parsing XML with the XmlPullParser

The code in Example 11-16 parses the XML document containing the list of recipes in this book, as discussed in Recipe 13.2 and Recipe 11.14. The input file has a single recipes root element, followed by a sequence of recipe elements, each with an id and a title with textual content.

First we get an instance of an XmlPullParserFactory by calling its static newInstance() method. Basically this scans the classpath for instances of XmlPullParserFactory and XmlPullParser. If it cannot find any instances, this method throws an XmlPullParserEx ception. We get an instance of an XmlPullParser by calling the newPullParser() factory method. We then pass the recipe list URL via the setInput(InputStream inputStream, String inputEncoding) method. The call to setInput resets the parser state and sets the event type to the initial value START_DOCUMENT. Also note that we don't need to first retrieve the URL's content with the converse method, as is done in Recipe 13.2 and Recipe 11.14.

Parsing XML input with an XmlPullParser means we are processing parser *events*. Simple events can be of the following type: START_DOCUMENT, END_DOCUMENT, START_TAG, END_TAG, and TEXT. (You might notice that these closely mimic the SAX callback event handler methods.) Once we have passed our URL to the setInput() method we are ready to process these events.

The first event is of type START_DOCUMENT. We process the input until we encounter the END_DOCUMENT tag. We advance to the next event by calling the next() method. (Note: you can even process more events by calling the nextToken() method, but that is out of scope here.)

The code simply keeps on advancing to the next event until it encounters a START_TAG. In this case we retrieve the element's local name by calling the getName() method. When namespace processing is disabled, the raw name is returned. We store the tag name in a local variable currentTag, as a bread crumb. (Note: when a start element contains attributes you can extract them via the getAttributeValue(String namespace, String name) method, again out of scope here.) Now we simply fall through the loop and advance to the next event.

Once we encounter a TEXT event we check whether the currentTag is id or title. If this is the case we retrieve the text contents by calling the getText() method and assign it to the appropriate local variable. We keep on doing this until we encounter a recipe END_TAG event. In this case we simply create a new Datum object with the previously created id and title variables.

Example 11-16. Using the pull parser

```
public static ArrayList<Datum> parse(String url) throws IOException,
XmlPullParserException {
    final ArrayList<Datum> results = new ArrayList<Datum>(1000);

    XmlPullParserFactory factory = XmlPullParserFactory.newInstance();
```

```
    factory.setNamespaceAware(true);
    XmlPullParser xpp = factory.newPullParser();

    URL input = new URL(url);
    xpp.setInput(input.openStream(), null);

    int eventType = xpp.getEventType();
    String currentTag = null;
    Integer id = null;
    String title = null;
    while (eventType != XmlPullParser.END_DOCUMENT) {
        if (eventType == XmlPullParser.START_TAG) {
            currentTag = xpp.getName();
        } else if (eventType == XmlPullParser.TEXT) {
            if ("id".equals(currentTag)) {
                id = Integer.valueOf(xpp.getText());
            }
            if ("title".equals(currentTag)) {
                title = xpp.getText();
            }
        } else if (eventType == XmlPullParser.END_TAG) {
            if ("recipe".equals(xpp.getName())) {
                results.add(new Datum(id, title));
            }
        }
        eventType = xpp.next();
    }
    return results;
}
```

Making it stricter

We can rewrite the parse method to make it a bit stricter. In this Example 11-17 we use the `require()` method to verify the expected XML structure. Once we are on the `id` or `title` START_TAG event we call `nextText()` to retrieve the element's text content and advance to the END_TAG event immediately after.

Example 11-17. Stricter parsing

```
public static ArrayList<Datum> parse(String url)
throws IOException, XmlPullParserException {
    final ArrayList<Datum> results = new ArrayList<Datum>(1000);

    XmlPullParserFactory factory = XmlPullParserFactory.newInstance();
    factory.setNamespaceAware(true);
    XmlPullParser xpp = factory.newPullParser();

    URL input = new URL(url);
    xpp.setInput(input.openStream(), null);

    xpp.nextTag();
    xpp.require(XmlPullParser.START_TAG, null, "recipes");
    while (xpp.nextTag() == XmlPullParser.START_TAG) {
        xpp.require(XmlPullParser.START_TAG, null, "recipe");
```

```
        xpp.nextTag();
        xpp.require(XmlPullParser.START_TAG, null, "id");
        Integer id = Integer.valueOf(xpp.nextText());
        xpp.require(XmlPullParser.END_TAG, null, "id");

        xpp.nextTag();
        xpp.require(XmlPullParser.START_TAG, null, "title");
        String title = xpp.nextText();
        xpp.require(XmlPullParser.END_TAG, null, "title");

        xpp.nextTag();
        xpp.require(XmlPullParser.END_TAG, null, "recipe");

        results.add(new Datum(id, title));
    }
    xpp.require(XmlPullParser.END_TAG, null, "recipes");

    return results;
}
```

Both methods return the same results. The recipe's downloadable source code uses the retrieved list of `Datum` objects to fill a `ListActivity`. When you click on a list item your are redirected to the corresponding recipe's web page.

Processing static XML resources

You can easily process static XML resources with an `XmlPullParser`. Simply call the `getXml()` method via your context's `getResources()` method and you will receive an instance of `XmlResourceParser`. This basically is an implementation of `XmlPullParser` with an extra convenience method to close the input resource, so you can use the techniques described in this recipe to process your static XML resources as well!

Conclusion

The `XmlPullParser` is the parser of choice for many developers, basically because of its simplicity. If you want speed you should pick SAX. DOM is about twice as slow as SAX. Parsing XML with the `XmlPullParser` is somewhere in the middle between SAX and DOM.

 Don't forget to add the `android.permission.INTERNET` permission to your *AndroidManifest.xml* file or you will not be able to access any web connections.

See Also

Recipe 13.2; Recipe 11.14; Recipe 4.11; *http://developer.android.com/reference/org/ xmlpull/v1/XmlPullParser.html*; *http://developer.android.com/reference/org/xmlpull/v1/*

XmlPullParserFactory.html; *http://developer.android.com/reference/android/content/*
res/XmlResourceParser.html

Source Download URL

You can download the source code for this example from *https://github.com/downloads/*
jpelgrim/androidcookbook/RecipeList.zip.

11.16 Adding a Contact

Ian Darwin

Problem

You have a person's contact information that you want to save for use by the Contacts
application and other apps on your device.

Solution

Set up a list of operations for batch insert, and tell the persistence manager to run it.

Discussion

The Contacts database is, to be sure, "flexible." It has to adapt to many different kinds
of accounts and contact management uses, with different types of data. And it is, as a
result, somewhat complicated.

In current versions, the classes named `Contacts` (and, by extension, all
their inner classes and interfaces) are deprecated, meaning "don't use
them in new development." The classes and interfaces that take their
place have names beginning with (the somewhat cumbersome and
somewhat tongue-twisting) `ContactsContract`.

We'll start with the simplest case of adding a person's contact information. We want to insert the following information—which we either got from the user or found on the network someplace:

Name	Jon Smith
Home Phone	416-555-5555
Work Phone	416-555-6666
Email	jon@jonsmith.domain

First we have to determine which Android account to associate the data with. For now we will use a fake account name (*darwinian* is both an adjective and my name, so we'll use that).

For each of the four fields, we'll need to create an account operation.

We add all five operations to a List, and pass that into getContentResolver().apply Batch().

Example 11-18 shows the code for the addContact() method.

Example 11-18. The addContact() method

```
private void addContact() {
    final String ACCOUNT_NAME = "darwinian"
    String name = "Jon Smith";
    String homePhone = "416-555-5555";
    String workPhone = "416-555-6666";
    String email = "jon@jonsmith.domain";

    // Use new-style batch operations: Build List of ops then call applyBatch
    try {
        ArrayList<ContentProviderOperation> ops =
            new ArrayList<ContentProviderOperation>();
        AuthenticatorDescription[] types = accountManager.getAuthenticatorTypes();
        ops.add(ContentProviderOperation.newInsert(
                ContactsContract.RawContacts.CONTENT_URI).withValue(
                    ContactsContract.RawContacts.ACCOUNT_TYPE, types[0].type)
                    .withValue(ContactsContract.RawContacts.ACCOUNT_NAME, ACCOUNT_NAME)
                    .build());
        ops.add(ContentProviderOperation
                .newInsert(ContactsContract.Data.CONTENT_URI)
                .withValueBackReference(ContactsContract.Data.RAW_CONTACT_ID, 0)
                .withValue(ContactsContract.Data.MIMETYPE,
                    ContactsContract.CommonDataKinds.StructuredName.CONTENT_ITEM_TYPE)
                .withValue
                (ContactsContract.CommonDataKinds.StructuredName.DISPLAY_NAME,name)
                .build());
        ops.add(ContentProviderOperation.newInsert(
                ContactsContract.Data.CONTENT_URI).withValueBackReference(
                    ContactsContract.Data.RAW_CONTACT_ID, 0).withValue(
                        ContactsContract.Data.MIMETYPE,
                        ContactsContract.CommonDataKinds.Phone.CONTENT_ITEM_TYPE)
```

```
                    .withValue(ContactsContract.CommonDataKinds.Phone.NUMBER,
                        homePhone).withValue(
                            ContactsContract.CommonDataKinds.Phone.TYPE,
                            ContactsContract.CommonDataKinds.Phone.TYPE_HOME)
                    .build());
        ops.add(ContentProviderOperation.newInsert(
                ContactsContract.Data.CONTENT_URI).withValueBackReference(
                    ContactsContract.Data.RAW_CONTACT_ID, 0).withValue(
                        ContactsContract.Data.MIMETYPE,
                        ContactsContract.CommonDataKinds.Phone.CONTENT_ITEM_TYPE)
                    .withValue(ContactsContract.CommonDataKinds.Phone.NUMBER,
                            workPhone).withValue(
                                ContactsContract.CommonDataKinds.Phone.TYPE,
                                ContactsContract.CommonDataKinds.Phone.TYPE_WORK)
                    .build());
        ops.add(ContentProviderOperation.newInsert(
                ContactsContract.Data.CONTENT_URI).withValueBackReference(
                    ContactsContract.Data.RAW_CONTACT_ID, 0).withValue(
                        ContactsContract.Data.MIMETYPE,
                        ContactsContract.CommonDataKinds.Email.CONTENT_ITEM_TYPE)
                    .withValue(ContactsContract.CommonDataKinds.Email.DATA, email)
                    .withValue(ContactsContract.CommonDataKinds.Email.TYPE,
                            ContactsContract.CommonDataKinds.Email.TYPE_HOME)
                    .build());

        getContentResolver().applyBatch(ContactsContract.AUTHORITY, ops);

        Toast.makeText(this, getString(R.string.addContactSuccess),
                Toast.LENGTH_LONG).show();
    } catch (Exception e) {

        Toast.makeText(this, getString(R.string.addContactFailure),
                Toast.LENGTH_LONG).show();
        Log.e(LOG_TAG, getString(R.string.addContactFailure), e);
    }
}
```

The resultant contact shows up in the Contact Manager or People app, as shown in Figure 11-5. If it is not initially visible, go to the main Contacts list page, press Menu, select Display Options, and select groups until it does appear. Alternatively, you can Search in All Contacts and it will show up.

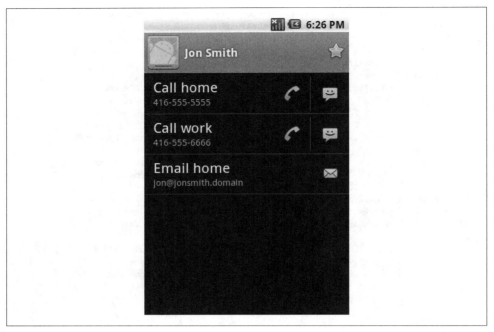

Figure 11-5. Contact added

11.17 Reading Contact Data

Ian Darwin

Problem

You need to extract details, such as a phone number or email address, from the Contacts database.

Solution

Use an intent to let the user pick one contact. Use a `ContentResolver` to create an SQLite query for the chosen contact. Use SQLite and predefined constants in the confusingly named `ContactContract` class to retrieve the parts you want. Be aware that the Contacts database was designed for generality, not for simplicity.

Discussion

The code in Example 11-18 is from TabbyText, my SMS Text Message sender for tablets. The user has already picked the given contact (using the Contact app; see Recipe 5.2). In this code we want to extract the mobile number and save it in a text field in the current activity, so the user can post-edit it if need be, or even reject it, before actually sending the SMS, so we just set the text in an `EditText` once we find it.

Finding it turns out to be the hard part. We start with a query that we get from the content provider, to extract the ID field for the given contact. Information such as phone numbers and emails are in their own tables, so we need a second query, to feed in the ID as part of the "select" part of the query. This query gives a list of the contact's phone numbers. We iterate through this, taking each valid phone number and setting it on the EditText.

A further elaboration would restrict this to only selecting the mobile number (Contacts allows both home fax and work fax, but only one mobile number, at least as of Honeycomb 3.2).

Example 11-19. Getting the contact from the intent query's ContentResolver

```
@Override
protected void onActivityResult(int requestCode, int resultCode, Intent data) {
    if (requestCode == REQ_GET_CONTACT) {
        switch(resultCode) {
        case Activity.RESULT_OK:
            // The Contacts API is about the most complex to use.
            // First we have to retrieve the Contact, since
            // we only get its URI from the Intent
            Uri resultUri = data.getData(); // e.g., content://contacts/people/123
            Cursor cont =
                getContentResolver().query(resultUri, null, null, null, null);
            if (!cont.moveToNext()) {     // expect 001 row(s)
                Toast.makeText(this,
                    "Cursor contains no data", Toast.LENGTH_LONG).show();
                return;
            }
            int columnIndexForId = cont.getColumnIndex(ContactsContract.Contacts._ID);
            String contactId =
            cont.getString(columnIndexForId);
            int columnIndexForHasPhone =
                cont.getColumnIndex(ContactsContract.Contacts.HAS_PHONE_NUMBER);
            boolean hasAnyPhone =
                Boolean.parseBoolean(cont.getString(columnIndexForHasPhone));
            if (!hasAnyPhone) {
                Toast.makeText(this,
                    "Selected contact seems to have no phone numbers ",
                    Toast.LENGTH_LONG).show();
            }

            // Now we have to do another query to actually get the numbers!
            Cursor numbers = getContentResolver().query(
                    ContactsContract.CommonDataKinds.Phone.CONTENT_URI,
                    null,
                    ContactsContract.CommonDataKinds.Phone.CONTACT_ID +
                    "=" + contactId, // "selection",
                    null, null);
            // Could further restrict to Mobile number...
            while (numbers.moveToNext()) {
                String aNumber = numbers.getString(numbers.getColumnIndex(
                ContactsContract.CommonDataKinds.Phone.NUMBER));
                System.out.println(aNumber);
```

```
                    number.setText(aNumber);
                }
                if (cont.moveToNext()) {
                    System.out.println("WARNING: More than 1 contact returned by picker!");
                }
                numbers.close();
                cont.close();
                break;
            case Activity.RESULT_CANCELED:
                // nothing to do here
                break;
            default:
                Toast.makeText(this, "Unexpected resultCode: " + resultCode,
                Toast.LENGTH_LONG).show();
                break;
        }
    }
    super.onActivityResult(requestCode, resultCode, data);
}
```

Source Download URL

You can download the source code for this example from *http://projects.darwinsys.com/ TabbyText-src.zip*.

Telephone Applications

12.1 Introduction: Telephone Applications

Ian Darwin

Discussion

Android began as a platform for cellular telephone handsets, so it is no surprise that Android apps are very capable of dealing with the phone. You can write apps that dial the phone, or that guide the user to do so. You can write apps that verify or modify the number the user is calling (e.g., to add a long-distance dialing prefix). You can also send and receive SMS (Short Message Service) messages, a.k.a. text messages, assuming your device is telephony-equipped. Nowadays, a great many Android tablets are WiFi-only, and do not have 3G or even 2G telephone/SMS capabilities. For these devices, other capabilities such as SMS via the Internet and VoIP (Voice over IP, usually SIP) have to be used.

This chapter covers most of these topics; a few are discussed elsewhere in this book.

12.2 Doing Something When the Phone Rings

Johan Pelgrim

Problem

You want to act on an incoming phone call and do something with the incoming number.

Solution

You can implement a broadcast receiver and then listen for a `TelephonyManager.ACTION_PHONE_STATE_CHANGED` action.

Discussion

If you want to do something when the phone rings you have to implement a *broadcast receiver*, which listens for the `TelephonyManager.ACTION_PHONE_STATE_CHANGED` intent action. This is a broadcast intent action indicating that the call state (cellular) on the device has changed. Example 12-1 shows the code for the incoming call interceptor, and Example 12-2 shows the incoming call interceptor's layout file.

Example 12-1. The incoming call interceptor

```
package nl.codestone.cookbook.incomingcallinterceptor;

import android.content.BroadcastReceiver;
import android.content.Context;
import android.content.Intent;
import android.telephony.TelephonyManager;
import android.widget.Toast;

public class IncomingCallInterceptor extends BroadcastReceiver {        ❶

    @Override
    public void onReceive(Context context, Intent intent) {             ❷
        String state = intent.getStringExtra(TelephonyManager.EXTRA_STATE);❸
        String msg = "Phone state changed to " + state;

        if (TelephonyManager.EXTRA_STATE_RINGING.equals(state)) {       ❹
            String incomingNumber = intent.getStringExtra
            (TelephonyManager.EXTRA_INCOMING_NUMBER);❺
            msg += ". Incoming number is " + incomingNumber;

            // This is where you have to "Do something when the phone rings" ;-)

        }

        Toast.makeText(context, msg, Toast.LENGTH_LONG).show();

    }

}
```

❶ Create an `IncomingCallInterceptor` class that extends `BroadcastReceiver`.

❷ Override the `onReceive` method to handle incoming broadcast messages.

❸ The `EXTRA_STATE` intent extra in this case indicates the new call state.

❹ If (and only if) the new state is `RINGING`, a second intent extra, `EXTRA_INCOMING_NUMBER`, provides the incoming phone number as a string.

❺ We extract the number information from the `EXTRA_INCOMING_NUMBER` intent extra.

Additionally, you can act on a state change to OFFHOOK or IDLE when the user picks up the phone or ends/rejects the phone call, respectively.

Example 12-2. The incoming call interceptor's layout file

```xml
<?xml version="1.0" encoding="utf-8"?>
<manifest xmlns:android="http://schemas.android.com/apk/res/android"
    package="nl.codestone.cookbook.incomingcallinterceptor"
    android:versionCode="1"
    android:versionName="1.0">
    <uses-sdk android:minSdkVersion="3" />

    <application android:icon="@drawable/icon" android:label="Incoming Call Interceptor">

        <receiver android:name="IncomingCallInterceptor">          ❶
            <intent-filter>                                         ❷
                <action android:name="android.intent.action.PHONE_STATE"/>❸
            </intent-filter>
        </receiver>

    </application>

    <uses-permission android:name="android.permission.READ_PHONE_STATE"/>  ❹

</manifest>
```

❶ We have to register our IncomingCallInterceptor as a <receiver> within the <application> element in the *AndroidManifest.xml* file.

❷ We register an <intent-filter> ...

❸ And an <action value that registers our receiver to listen for TelephonyManager.ACTION_PHONE_STATE_CHANGED broadcast messages.

❹ Finally, we have to register a <uses-permission> so that we are allowed to listen to phone state changes.

If all is well, you should see something like Figure 12-1 when the phone rings.

What happens if two receivers listen for phone state changes?

In general, a *broadcast message* is just that, a message that is sent out to many receivers at the same time. This is the case for a *normal broadcast*, which is used to send out the ACTION_PHONE_STATE_CHANGED intent as well. All receivers of the broadcast are run in an undefined order, often at the same time, and for that reason *order* is not applicable.

In other cases the system sends out an *ordered broadcast*, which is described in more detail in Recipe 12.3.

Figure 12-1. Incoming call intercepted

Final notes

When your `BroadcastReceiver` does not finish within 10 seconds the Android framework will show the infamous Application Not Responding (ANR) dialog, giving your users the ability to kill your program. If you need to do some processing that takes longer than 10 seconds, implement a `Service` and call the service method.

It is also not advisable to start an activity from a `BroadcastReceiver`, as it will spawn a new screen that will steal focus from whatever application the user is currently running. If your application has something to show the user in response to an intent broadcast, it should do so using the Notification Manager.

See Also

Recipe 12.3; *http://developer.android.com/reference/android/content/BroadcastReceiver .html*; *http://developer.android.com/reference/android/telephony/TelephonyManager .html#ACTION_PHONE_STATE_CHANGED*

Source Download URL

You can download the source code for this example from *https://github.com/downloads/ jpelgrim/androidcookbook/IncomingCallInterceptor.zip*.

12.3 Processing Outgoing Phone Calls

Johan Pelgrim

Problem

You want to block certain calls, or alter the phone number about to be called.

Solution

Listen for the `Intent.ACTION_NEW_OUTGOING_CALL` broadcast action and set the result data of the broadcast receiver to the new number.

Discussion

If you want to intercept a call before it is about to be placed you can implement a broadcast receiver and listen for the `Intent.ACTION_NEW_OUTGOING_CALL` action. This recipe is, in essence, similar to Recipe 12.2, but it is more interesting since we can actually manipulate the phone number in this case!

Here are the steps. Example 12-3 shows the code.

❶ Create an `OutgoingCallInterceptor` class that extends the `BroadcastReceiver`.

❷ Override the `onReceive` method.

❸ Extract the phone number that the user originally intended to call via the `Intent.EXTRA_PHONE_NUMBER` intent extra.

❹ Replace this number by calling `setResultData` with the new number as the `String` argument.

Once the broadcast is finished, the result data is used as the actual number to call. If the result data is `null`, no call will be placed at all!

Example 12-3. The outgoing call interceptor (a BroadcastReceiver)

```
package nl.codestone.cookbook.outgoingcallinterceptor;

import android.content.BroadcastReceiver;
import android.content.Context;
import android.content.Intent;
import android.widget.Toast;

public class OutgoingCallInterceptor extends BroadcastReceiver {          ❶

    @Override
    public void onReceive(Context context, Intent intent) {              ❷
        final String oldNumber = intent.getStringExtra(Intent.EXTRA_PHONE_NUMBER);  ❸
        this.setResultData("0123456789");                                ❹
        final String newNumber = this.getResultData();
        String msg = "Intercepted outgoing call. Old number " +
                        oldNumber + ", new number " + newNumber;
        Toast.makeText(context, msg, Toast.LENGTH_LONG).show();
    }

}
```

Example 12-4 shows the code in the outgoing call interceptor's *AndroidManifest.xml* file.

❶ We have to register our `OutgoingCallInterceptor` as a `<receiver>` within the `<application>` element in the *AndroidManifest.xml* file.

❷ We add an `<intent-filter>` element within this `<receiver>` declaration and add an `android:priority` of 1.

❸ We add an `<action>` element within the `<intent-filter>` to only receive `Intent.ACTION_NEW_OUTGOING_CALL` intent actions.

❹ We have to hold the `PROCESS_OUTGOING_CALLS` permission to receive this intent, so we register a `<uses-permission>` to `PROCESS_OUTGOING_CALLS` right below the `<application>` element.

Example 12-4. The outgoing call interceptor's AndroidManifest.xml file

```
<?xml version="1.0" encoding="utf-8"?>
<manifest xmlns:android="http://schemas.android.com/apk/res/android"
    package="nl.codestone.cookbook.outgoingcallinterceptor"
    android:versionCode="1" android:versionName="1.0">
    <uses-sdk android:minSdkVersion="3" />

    <application android:icon="@drawable/icon" android:label="Outgoing Call Interceptor">

        <receiver android:name="OutgoingCallInterceptor">                ❶
            <intent-filter android:priority="1">                        ❷
                <action android:name="android.intent.action.NEW_OUTGOING_CALL" />  ❸
            </intent-filter>
        </receiver>
```

```
    </application>

    <uses-permission android:name="android.permission.PROCESS_OUTGOING_CALLS" />   ❹
```

</manifest>

Now, when you try to dial the number 11111 you will actually be forwarded to
0123456789 instead! (See Figure 12-2.)

Figure 12-2. Outgoing call intercepted

What happens if two receivers process outgoing calls?

As was stated before, the Intent.ACTION_NEW_OUTGOING_CALL is an *ordered broadcast* and
is a protected intent that can only be sent by the system. *Ordered broadcast* messages
come with three additional features compared to *normal broadcast* messages:

- You can use the <intent-filter> element's android:priority attribute to influence
  your position in the sending mechanism. The android:priority is an integer indicating which parent (receiver) has higher priority in processing the incoming
  broadcast message. The higher the number, the higher the priority and the sooner
  that receiver can process the broadcast message.
- You can propagate a *result* to the next receiver by calling the setResultData method.
- You can completely abort the broadcast by calling the abortBroadcast() method
  so that it won't be passed to other receivers.

Note that according to the API, any `BroadcastReceiver` receiving the `Intent.ACTION_NEW_OUTGOING_CALL` must *not abort* the broadcast by calling the `abort Broadcast()` method. Doing so does not present any errors, but apparently some system receivers still want to have a go at the broadcast message. Emergency calls *cannot* be intercepted using this mechanism, and other calls cannot be modified to call emergency numbers using this mechanism.

It is perfectly acceptable for multiple receivers to process the outgoing call in turn: for example, a parental control application might verify that the user is authorized to place the call at that time, and then a number-rewriting application might add an area code if one was not specified.

If two receivers are defined with an equal `android:priority` attribute they will be run in an arbitrary order (according to the API). However, in practice, when they both reside in the same *AndroidManifest.xml* file, it *looks* like the order in which the receivers are defined determines the order in which they will receive the broadcast message.

Furthermore, if two receivers are defined with an equal `android:priority` attribute but they are defined in a different *AndroidManifest.xml* file (i.e., they belong to a different application) it *looks* like the broadcast receiver, which was *installed* first, is *registered* first and thus will be the one that is allowed to process the message first. But again, don't count on it!

If you want to have a shot at being the very first to process a message, you can use the maximum integer value (2147483647). Even though the API this still does not guarantee you will be first, you will have a pretty good chance!

Other applications could have intercepted the phone number before us. If you are pretty sure you want to take action on the original number, you can use the `EXTRA_PHONE_NUM BER` intent extra as described earlier and completely ignore the result from the receiver before you. If you simply want to fall in line and pick up where another broadcast receiver has left off, you can retrieve the intermediary phone number via the `getResult Data()` method.

For consistency, any receiver whose purpose is to prohibit phone calls should have a priority of `0`, to ensure that it will see the final phone number to be dialed. Any receiver whose purpose is to rewrite phone numbers to be called should have a *positive* priority. Negative priorities are reserved for the system for this broadcast; using them may cause problems.

See Also

Recipe 12.2; *http://developer.android.com/reference/android/content/Intent.html#AC TION_NEW_OUTGOING_CALL*

Source Download URL

You can download the source code for this example from *https://github.com/downloads/jpelgrim/androidcookbook/OutgoingCallInterceptor.zip*.

12.4 Dialing the Phone

Ian Darwin

Problem

You want to dial the phone from within an application, without worrying about details of telephony.

Solution

Start an Intent to dial the phone.

Discussion

One of the beauties of Android is the ease with which applications can reuse other applications, without being tightly coupled to the details (or even name) of the other program, using the Intent mechanism. For example, to dial the phone, you only need to create and start an Intent with an action of DIAL and a URI of "tel" + the number you want to dial. Thus, a basic dialer can be as simple as Example 12-5:

Example 12-5. Simple dialer activity

```
public class Main extends Activity {
    String phoneNumber = "555-1212";
    String intentStr = "tel:" + phoneNumber;

    /** Standard creational callback.
     * Just dial the phone
     */
    @Override
    public void onCreate(Bundle savedInstanceState) {
        super.onCreate(savedInstanceState);
```

```
        setContentView(R.layout.main);

        Intent intent = new Intent("android.intent.action.DIAL",
                Uri.parse(intentStr));

        startActivity(intent);
    }
}
```

You need to have the permission `android.permission.CALL_PHONE` to use this code. The user will see the screen shown in Figure 12-3; users know to press the green phone button to let the call proceed.

Figure 12-3. Simple dialer

Typically, in real life you would not hardcode the number. In other circumstances you might want the user to call a number from the phone's Contacts list.

12.5 Sending Single-Part or Multipart SMS Messages

Colin Wilcox

Problem

You want a simple way to send either a single-part or a multipart SMS/text message from a single entry point.

Solution

Use `SmsManager`.

Discussion

SMS (Short Message Service) messages, also called text messages, have been part of cellular technology for years. The Android API allows you to send an SMS message either by an Intent or in code; we're only covering the code approach here.

SMS messages are limited to about 160 characters, depending on the carrier (in case you ever wondered where Twitter got the idea for 140-character messages). Text messages above this size must be broken into chunks. To give you control over this, the `SmsManager` class allows you to break a message into "parts", and returns a list of them.

If there is only one part, the message is short enough to send directly, so we use the `sendTextMessage()` method. Otherwise, we have to send the list of parts, so we pass the list back into the `sentMultipartTextMessage()` method. The actual sending code is shown in Example 12-6. The downloadable code features a trivial `Activity` to invoke the sending code. Although sent as three parts, the message arrives at the sender as a single message, as shown in Figure 12-4.

Figure 12-4. The multipart message arrived

As you might expect, the application needs the `android.permission.SEND_SMS` permission in its *AndroidManifest.xml* file.

Example 12-6. The SMS sender

```
package com.example.sendsms;
import java.util.ArrayList;

import android.telephony.SmsManager;
import android.util.Log;

/** The code for dealing with the SMS manager;
 * called from the GUI code.
 */
public class SendSMS {
    static String TAG = "SendSMS";
    SmsManager mSMSManager = null;
    /* The list of message parts our message
     * gets broken up into by SmsManager */
    ArrayList<String> mFragmentList = null;
    /* Service Center - not used */
    String mServiceCentreAddr = null;

    SendSMS() {
        mSMSManager = SmsManager.getDefault();
    }

    /* Called from the GUI to send one message to one destination */
    public boolean sendSMSMessage(
            String aDestinationAddress,
            String aMessageText) {

        if (mSMSManager == null) {
            return (false);
        }

        mFragmentList = mSMSManager.divideMessage(aMessageText);
        int fragmentCount = mFragmentList.size();
        if (fragmentCount > 1) {
            Log.d(TAG, "Sending " + fragmentCount + " parts");
            mSMSManager.sendMultipartTextMessage(aDestinationAddress,
                    mServiceCentreAddr,
                    mFragmentList, null, null);
        } else {
            Log.d(TAG, "Sending one part");
            mSMSManager.sendTextMessage(aDestinationAddress,
                    mServiceCentreAddr,
                    aMessageText, null, null);
        }

        return true;
    }
}
```

See Also

For information on the SmsManager, see *http://developer.android.com/reference/an droid/telephony/SmsManager.html*. For information about how the division of longer messages into parts works "under the hood," see *http://en.wikipedia.org/wiki/Concaten ated_SMS*.

Source Download URL

The source code for this example is in the Android Cookbook repository at *http://github .com/AndroidCook/Android-Cookbook-Examples*, in the subdirectory SendSMS (see "Getting and Using the Code Examples" on page xvii).

12.6 Receiving an SMS Message in an Android Application

Rachee Singh

Problem

You wish to enable your application to receive incoming SMS messages.

Solution

Use a broadcast receiver to listen for incoming SMS messages and then extract the messages.

Discussion

When an Android device receives a message, a broadcast intent is fired (the intent also includes the SMS message that is sent). The application can register to receive these intents. The intent has an action, `android.provider.Telephony.SMS_RECEIVED`. The application designed to receive SMS messages should include the `RECEIVE_SMS` permission in the manifest:

```
<uses-permission android:name="android.permission.RECEIVE_SMS"/>
```

When a message is received, the `onReceive()` method (overridden) is called. Within this method, the message can be processed. From the intent that is received, the SMS message has to be extracted using the `get()` method. The `BroadcastReceiver` with the code for extracting the message part looks like Example 12-7.

Example 12-7. The SMS BroadcastReceiver

```
public class InvitationSmsReceiver extends BroadcastReceiver {

    public void onReceive(Context context, Intent intent) {

        Bundle bundle = intent.getExtras();
        SmsMessage[] msgs = null;
        String message = "";
        if(bundle != null) {
            Object[] pdus = (Object[]) bundle.get("pdus");
            msgs = new SmsMessage[pdus.length];

            for(int i=0; i<msgs.length;i++) {
```

```
                msgs[i] = SmsMessage.createFromPdu((byte[]) pdus[i]);
                message = msgs[i].getMessageBody();
                Toast.makeText(context,message,Toast.LENGTH_SHORT).show();
            }

        }

    }

}
```

The code makes a toast with the contents of the SMS message sent.

To register the `InvitationSmsReceiver` class for receiving the SMS messages, add the following code in the manifest:

```
<receiver android:name=".InvitationSmsReceiver"
    android:enabled="true">
        <intent-filter>
            <action android:name="android.provider.Telephony.SMS_RECEIVED"/>
            <category android:name="android.intent.category.DEFAULT"/>
        </intent-filter>
</receiver>
```

Source Download URL

You can download the source code for this example from *https://docs.google.com/leaf ?id=0B_rESQKgad5LMjk0YjJiZTgtZGI5ZC00Mjk3LTk2MGUtMjhkOGYzNmF mYWMz&hl=en_US&authkey=CMWZvskL.*

12.7 Using Emulator Controls to Send SMS Messages to the Emulator

Rachee Singh

Problem

To interactively test an SMS-message-based application before loading it onto a device, you need to be able to send an SMS message to the emulator.

Solution

Emulator control in the DDMS perspective of Eclipse allows the functionality of sending SMS messages to the emulator.

Discussion

To test whether your application responds to incoming SMS messages, you need to send an SMS message to the emulator. The DDMS perspective of Eclipse provides this function. You may wish to maximize the Emulator Control window as otherwise the important parts of it may be hidden and need both vertical and horizontal scrolling to access. In the Emulator Control tab, go to Telephony Actions and provide a phone number. This number can be any random number to which you would want the message to appear to come from. Select the SMS radio button. In the Message box, type in the message you wish to send. Finally, press the Send button below the message text. See Figure 12-5.

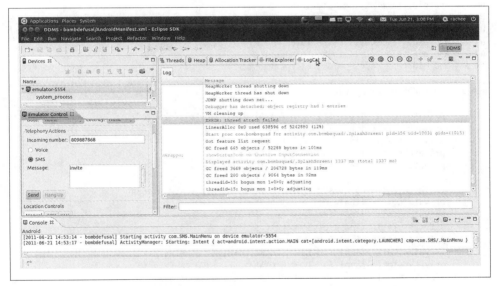

Figure 12-5. Emulator control sending SMS message

12.8 Using Android's TelephonyManager to Obtain Device Information

Pratik Rupwal

Problem

You want to obtain network-related and telephony information on the device.

Solution

Use Android's standard `TelephonyManager` to obtain different statistics regarding network status and telephony information.

Discussion

Android's `TelephonyManager` provides information about the Android telephony system. It assists in collecting different information such as cell location, International Mobile Equipment Identity (IMEI) number, network provider, and more.

The program in Example 12-8 is a long one that covers most of the facilities provided by the Android `TelephonyManager`. It is unlikely you would need all of these in one real application, but they are consolidated here for a comprehensive example program.

Example 12-8. The phone state sample activity

```
...
import android.telephony.CellLocation;
import android.telephony.NeighboringCellInfo;
import android.telephony.PhoneStateListener;
import android.telephony.ServiceState;
import android.telephony.TelephonyManager;
import android.telephony.gsm.GsmCellLocation;

public class PhoneStateSample extends Activity {

        private static final String APP_NAME = "SignalLevelSample";
        private static final int EXCELLENT_LEVEL = 75;
        private static final int GOOD_LEVEL = 50;
        private static final int MODERATE_LEVEL = 25;
        private static final int WEAK_LEVEL = 0;

        // These are used to store Strings into an array for display.
        private static final int INFO_SERVICE_STATE_INDEX = 0;
        private static final int INFO_CELL_LOCATION_INDEX = 1;
        private static final int INFO_CALL_STATE_INDEX = 2;
        private static final int INFO_CONNECTION_STATE_INDEX = 3;
        private static final int INFO_SIGNAL_LEVEL_INDEX = 4;
        private static final int INFO_SIGNAL_LEVEL_INFO_INDEX = 5;
        private static final int INFO_DATA_DIRECTION_INDEX = 6;
        private static final int INFO_DEVICE_INFO_INDEX = 7;

        // These are the IDs of the displays; must keep in sync with above constants
        private static final int[] info_ids= {
                R.id.serviceState_info,
                R.id.cellLocation_info,
                R.id.callState_info,
                R.id.connectionState_info,
                R.id.signalLevel,
                R.id.signalLevelInfo,
                R.id.dataDirection,
                R.id.device_info
        };
```

```java
@Override
public void onCreate(Bundle savedInstanceState) {
    super.onCreate(savedInstanceState);
    setContentView(R.layout.main);
    startSignalLevelListener();
    displayTelephonyInfo();
}

@Override
protected void onPause()
{
        super.onPause();
        stopListening();
}

@Override
protected void onResume()
{
        super.onResume();
        startSignalLevelListener();
}

@Override
protected void onDestroy()
{
        stopListening();
        super.onDestroy();
}

private void setTextViewText(int id,String text) {
        ((TextView)findViewById(id)).setText(text);
}
private void setSignalLevel(int id,int infoid,int level){
        int progress = (int) ((((float)level)/31.0) * 100);
        String signalLevelString =getSignalLevelString(progress);
        ((ProgressBar)findViewById(id)).setProgress(progress);
        ((TextView)findViewById(infoid)).setText(signalLevelString);
        Log.i("signalLevel ","" + progress);
}

private String getSignalLevelString(int level) {
        String signalLevelString = "Weak";
        if(level > EXCELLENT_LEVEL)      signalLevelString = "Excellent";
        else if(level > GOOD_LEVEL)      signalLevelString = "Good";
        else if(level > MODERATE_LEVEL) signalLevelString = "Moderate";
        else if(level > WEAK_LEVEL)      signalLevelString= "Weak";
        return signalLevelString;
}

private void stopListening(){
        TelephonyManager tm =
            (TelephonyManager) getSystemService(TELEPHONY_SERVICE);
        tm.listen(phoneStateListener, PhoneStateListener.LISTEN_NONE);
}
```

```
private void setDataDirection(int id, int direction){
        int resid = getDataDirectionRes(direction);
        ((ImageView)findViewById(id)).setImageResource(resid);
}
private int getDataDirectionRes(int direction){
        int resid = R.drawable.data_none;

        switch(direction)
        {
                case TelephonyManager.DATA_ACTIVITY_IN:
                    resid = R.drawable.data_in; break;
                case TelephonyManager.DATA_ACTIVITY_OUT:
                    resid = R.drawable.data_out; break;
                case TelephonyManager.DATA_ACTIVITY_INOUT:
                    resid = R.drawable.data_both; break;
                case TelephonyManager.DATA_ACTIVITY_NONE:
                    resid = R.drawable.data_none; break;
                default: resid = R.drawable.data_none; break;
        }
        return resid;
}
private void startSignalLevelListener() {
TelephonyManager tm =
    (TelephonyManager) getSystemService(TELEPHONY_SERVICE);
int events = PhoneStateListener.LISTEN_SIGNAL_STRENGTH |
                PhoneStateListener.LISTEN_DATA_ACTIVITY |
                PhoneStateListener.LISTEN_CELL_LOCATION|
                PhoneStateListener.LISTEN_CALL_STATE |
                PhoneStateListener.LISTEN_CALL_FORWARDING_INDICATOR |
                PhoneStateListener.LISTEN_DATA_CONNECTION_STATE |
                PhoneStateListener.LISTEN_MESSAGE_WAITING_INDICATOR |
                PhoneStateListener.LISTEN_SERVICE_STATE;
    tm.listen(phoneStateListener, events);
}
...
```

Much of the information gathering in this program is done by the various listeners. One exception is the method displayTelephonyInfo(), shown in Example 12-9, which simply gathers a large number of information bits directly from the TelephonyManager and adds them to a long string, which is displayed in the TextView.

Example 12-9. The phone state activity (continued)

```
    ...

private void displayTelephonyInfo(){
        TelephonyManager tm = (TelephonyManager)getSystemService(TELEPHONY_SERVICE);
        GsmCellLocation loc = (GsmCellLocation)tm.getCellLocation();
        int cellid = loc.getCid();
        int lac = loc.getLac();
        String deviceid = tm.getDeviceId();
        String phonenumber = tm.getLine1Number();
        String softwareversion = tm.getDeviceSoftwareVersion();
        String operatorname = tm.getNetworkOperatorName();
```

```
        String simcountrycode = tm.getSimCountryIso();
        String simoperator = tm.getSimOperatorName();
        String simserialno = tm.getSimSerialNumber();
        String subscriberid = tm.getSubscriberId();
        String networktype = getNetworkTypeString(tm.getNetworkType());
        String phonetype = getPhoneTypeString(tm.getPhoneType());
        logString("CellID: " + cellid);
        logString("LAC: " + lac);
        logString("Device ID: " + deviceid);
        logString("Phone Number: " + phonenumber);
        logString("Software Version: " + softwareversion);
        logString("Operator Name: " + operatorname);
        logString("SIM Country Code: " + simcountrycode);
        logString("SIM Operator: " + simoperator);
        logString("SIM Serial No.: " + simserialno);
        logString("Sibscriber ID: " + subscriberid);
        String deviceinfo = "";
        deviceinfo += ("CellID: " + cellid + "\n");
        deviceinfo += ("LAC: " + lac + "\n");
        deviceinfo += ("Device ID: " + deviceid + "\n");
        deviceinfo += ("Phone Number: " + phonenumber + "\n");
        deviceinfo += ("Software Version: " + softwareversion + "\n");
        deviceinfo += ("Operator Name: " + operatorname + "\n");
        deviceinfo += ("SIM Country Code: " + simcountrycode + "\n");
        deviceinfo += ("SIM Operator: " + simoperator + "\n");
        deviceinfo += ("SIM Serial No.: " + simserialno + "\n");
        deviceinfo += ("Subscriber ID: " + subscriberid + "\n");
        deviceinfo += ("Network Type: " + networktype + "\n");
        deviceinfo += ("Phone Type: " + phonetype + "\n");
        List<NeighboringCellInfo> cellinfo =tm.getNeighboringCellInfo();
        if(null != cellinfo){
                for(NeighboringCellInfo info: cellinfo){
                        deviceinfo += ("\tCellID: " +
                        info.getCid() +", RSSI: " + info.getRssi() + "\n");
                }
        }
        setTextViewText(info_ids[INFO_DEVICE_INFO_INDEX],deviceinfo);
}

private String getNetworkTypeString(int type) {
        String typeString = "Unknown";
        switch(type)
        {
                case TelephonyManager.NETWORK_TYPE_EDGE:
                    typeString = "EDGE"; break;
                case TelephonyManager.NETWORK_TYPE_GPRS:
                    typeString = "GPRS"; break;
                case TelephonyManager.NETWORK_TYPE_UMTS:
                    typeString = "UMTS"; break;
                default:
                    typeString = "UNKOWN"; break;
        }
        return typeString;
}
```

```java
private String getPhoneTypeString(int type){
        String typeString = "Unknown";
        switch(type)
        {
                case TelephonyManager.PHONE_TYPE_GSM:
                    typeString = GSM"; break;
                case TelephonyManager.PHONE_TYPE_NONE:
                    typeString = UNKNOWN"; break;
                default:typeString = "UNKNOWN"; break;
        }
        return typeString;
}

private int logString(String message) {
        return Log.i(APP_NAME,message);
}

private final PhoneStateListener phoneStateListener = new PhoneStateListener(){

        @Override
        public void onCallForwardingIndicatorChanged(boolean cfi)
        {
                Log.i(APP_NAME, "onCallForwardingIndicatorChanged " +cfi);
                super.onCallForwardingIndicatorChanged(cfi);
        }

        @Override
        public void onCallStateChanged(int state, String incomingNumber)
        {
                String callState = "UNKNOWN";
                switch(state)
                {
                        case TelephonyManager.CALL_STATE_IDLE:
                            callState = "IDLE"; break;
                        case TelephonyManager.CALL_STATE_RINGING:
                            callState = "Ringing (" + incomingNumber + ")"; break;
                        case TelephonyManager.CALL_STATE_OFFHOOK:
                            callState = "Offhook"; break;
                }
                setTextViewText(info_ids[INFO_CALL_STATE_INDEX],callState);
                Log.i(APP_NAME, "onCallStateChanged " + callState);
                super.onCallStateChanged(state, incomingNumber);
        }
        @Override
        public void onCellLocationChanged(CellLocation location)
        {
                String locationString = location.toString();
                setTextViewText(
                    info_ids[INFO_CELL_LOCATION_INDEX],locationString);

                Log.i(APP_NAME, "onCellLocationChanged " + locationString);
                super.onCellLocationChanged(location);
        }

        @Override
```

```java
public void onDataActivity(int direction)
{
        String directionString = "none";
        switch (direction) {
                case TelephonyManager.DATA_ACTIVITY_IN:
                    directionString = "IN"; break;
                case TelephonyManager.DATA_ACTIVITY_OUT:
                    directionString = "OUT"; break;
                case TelephonyManager.DATA_ACTIVITY_INOUT:
                    directionString = "INOUT"; break;
                case TelephonyManager.DATA_ACTIVITY_NONE:
                    directionString = "NONE"; break;
                default: directionString = "UNKNOWN: " + direction; break;
        }
        setDataDirection(info_ids[INFO_DATA_DIRECTION_INDEX],direction);
        Log.i(APP_NAME, "onDataActivity " + directionString);
        super.onDataActivity(direction);
}

@Override
public void onDataConnectionStateChanged(int state)
{
        String connectionState = "Unknown";
        switch(state) {
                case TelephonyManager.DATA_CONNECTED:
                    connectionState = "Connected"; break;
                case TelephonyManager.DATA_CONNECTING:
                    connectionState = "Connecting"; break;
                case TelephonyManager.DATA_DISCONNECTED:
                    connectionState = "Disconnected"; break;
                case TelephonyManager.DATA_SUSPENDED:
                    connectionState = "Suspended"; break;
                default:
                    connectionState = "Unknown: " + state; break;
        }

        setTextViewText(
            info_ids[INFO_CONNECTION_STATE_INDEX], connectionState);

        Log.i(APP_NAME,
            "onDataConnectionStateChanged " + connectionState);

        super.onDataConnectionStateChanged(state);
}

@Override
public void onMessageWaitingIndicatorChanged(boolean mwi) {
        Log.i(APP_NAME, "onMessageWaitingIndicatorChanged " + mwi);
        super.onMessageWaitingIndicatorChanged(mwi);
}

@Override
public void onServiceStateChanged(ServiceState serviceState) {
        String serviceStateString = "UNKNOWN";
        switch(serviceState.getState()) {
```

```
                        case ServiceState.STATE_IN_SERVICE:
                            serviceStateString = "IN SERVICE"; break;
                        case ServiceState.STATE_EMERGENCY_ONLY:
                            serviceStateString = "EMERGENCY ONLY"; break;
                        case ServiceState.STATE_OUT_OF_SERVICE:
                            serviceStateString = "OUT OF SERVICE"; break;
                        case ServiceState.STATE_POWER_OFF:
                            serviceStateString = "POWER OFF"; break;
                        default:
                            serviceStateString = "UNKNOWN"; break;
                }

                setTextViewText(
                    info_ids[INFO_SERVICE_STATE_INDEX], serviceStateString);

                Log.i(APP_NAME, "onServiceStateChanged " + serviceStateString);

                super.onServiceStateChanged(serviceState);
            }

            @Override
            public void onSignalStrengthChanged(int asu)
            {
                Log.i(APP_NAME, "onSignalStrengthChanged " + asu);
                setSignalLevel(info_ids[INFO_SIGNAL_LEVEL_INDEX],
                    info_ids[INFO_SIGNAL_LEVEL_INFO_INDEX],asu);
                super.onSignalStrengthChanged(asu);
            }
    };
}
```

The *main.xml* layout shown next consists of a variety of nested linear layouts so that all the information gathered in the preceding code can be displayed neatly.

```xml
<?xml version="1.0" encoding="utf-8"?>
<ScrollView xmlns:android="http://schemas.android.com/apk/res/android"
        android:layout_width="fill_parent"
        android:layout_height="wrap_content"
        android:orientation="vertical"
        android:scrollbarStyle="insideOverlay"
        android:scrollbarAlwaysDrawVerticalTrack="false">
        <LinearLayout
        android:orientation="vertical"
        android:layout_width="fill_parent"
        android:layout_height="fill_parent">
                <LinearLayout
                        android:layout_width="fill_parent"
                        android:layout_height="wrap_content"
                        android:orientation="horizontal">
                        <TextView android:text="Service State"
style="@style/labelStyleRight"/>
                        <TextView android:id="@+id/serviceState_info"
style="@style/textStyle"/>
                </LinearLayout>
                <LinearLayout
```

```
                    android:layout_width="fill_parent"
                    android:layout_height="wrap_content"
                    android:orientation="horizontal">
                    <TextView android:text="Cell Location"
style="@style/labelStyleRight"/>
                        <TextView android:id="@+id/cellLocation_info"
style="@style/textStyle"/>
                </LinearLayout>
                <LinearLayout
                    android:layout_width="fill_parent"
                    android:layout_height="wrap_content"
                    android:orientation="horizontal">
                    <TextView android:text="Call State"
style="@style/labelStyleRight"/>
                        <TextView android:id="@+id/callState_info"
style="@style/textStyle"/>
                </LinearLayout>
                <LinearLayout
                    android:layout_width="fill_parent"
                    android:layout_height="wrap_content"
                    android:orientation="horizontal">
                    <TextView android:text="Connection State"
style="@style/labelStyleRight"/>
                        <TextView android:id="@+id/connectionState_info"
style="@style/textStyle"/>
                </LinearLayout>
                <LinearLayout
                    android:layout_width="fill_parent"
                    android:layout_height="wrap_content"
                    android:orientation="horizontal">
                    <TextView android:text="Signal Level"
style="@style/labelStyleRight"/>
                        <LinearLayout
                            android:layout_width="fill_parent"
                            android:layout_height="wrap_content"
                            android:layout_weight="0.5"
                            android:orientation="horizontal">
                            <ProgressBar
android:id="@+id/signalLevel" style="@style/progressStyle"/>
                            <TextView
android:id="@+id/signalLevelInfo" style="@style/textSmallStyle"/>
                        </LinearLayout>
                </LinearLayout>
                <LinearLayout
                    android:layout_width="fill_parent"
                    android:layout_height="wrap_content"
                    android:orientation="horizontal">
                    <TextView android:text="Data"
style="@style/labelStyleRight"/>
                        <ImageView android:id="@+id/dataDirection"
style="@style/imageStyle"/>
                </LinearLayout>
                <TextView android:id="@+id/device_info"
style="@style/labelStyleLeft"/>
```

```
            </LinearLayout>
    </ScrollView>
```

Our code uses some UI styles, which are declared in this file, named *styles.xml*:

```xml
<?xml version="1.0" encoding="utf-8"?>
<resources>
        <style name="labelStyleRight">
                <item name="android:layout_width">fill_parent</item>
                <item name="android:layout_height">wrap_content</item>
                <item name="android:layout_weight">0.5</item>
                <item name="android:textSize">15dip</item>
                <item name="android:textStyle">bold</item>
                <item name="android:layout_margin">10dip</item>
                <item name="android:gravity">center_vertical|right</item>
        </style>

        <style name="labelStyleLeft">
                <item name="android:layout_width">fill_parent</item>
                <item name="android:layout_height">wrap_content</item>
                <item name="android:layout_weight">0.5</item>
                <item name="android:textSize">15dip</item>
                <item name="android:textStyle">bold</item>
                <item name="android:layout_margin">10dip</item>
                <item name="android:gravity">center_vertical|left</item>
        </style>

        <style name="textStyle">
                <item name="android:layout_width">fill_parent</item>
                <item name="android:layout_height">wrap_content</item>
                <item name="android:layout_weight">0.5</item>
                <item name="android:textSize">15dip</item>
                <item name="android:textStyle">bold</item>
                <item name="android:layout_margin">10dip</item>
                <item name="android:gravity">center_vertical|left</item>
        </style>

        <style name="textSmallStyle">
                <item name="android:layout_width">fill_parent</item>
                <item name="android:layout_height">fill_parent</item>
                <item name="android:layout_weight">0.5</item>
                <item name="android:textSize">10dip</item>
                <item name="android:layout_margin">10dip</item>
                <item name="android:gravity">center_vertical|left</item>
        </style>

        <style name="progressStyle">
                <item name="android:layout_width">fill_parent</item>
                <item name="android:layout_height">wrap_content</item>
                <item name="android:layout_margin">10dip</item>
                <item name="android:layout_weight">0.5</item>
                <item name="android:indeterminateOnly">false</item>
                <item name="android:minHeight">20dip</item>
                <item name="android:maxHeight">20dip</item>
                <item name="android:progress">15</item>
                <item name="android:max">100</item>
```

```
                    <item name="android:gravity">center_vertical|left</item>
                    <item name="android:progressDrawable">
                        @android:drawable/progress_horizontal</item>
                    <item name="android:indeterminateDrawable">
                        @android:drawable/progress_indeterminate_horizontal</item>
        </style>

        <style name="imageStyle">
                    <item name="android:layout_width">fill_parent</item>
                    <item name="android:layout_height">wrap_content</item>
                    <item name="android:layout_weight">0.5</item>
                    <item name="android:src">@drawable/icon</item>
                    <item name="android:scaleType">fitStart</item>
                    <item name="android:layout_margin">10dip</item>
                    <item name="android:gravity">center_vertical|left</item>
        </style>
</resources>
```

The application uses *coarse location* permission (get approximate location from the cell radio service) which needs to be added in the *AndroidManifest.xml* file of your project:

```
<uses-permission android:name="android.permission.ACCESS_COARSE_LOCATION" />
```

The application also uses some images for indicating the data communication state as no data communication, incoming data communication, outgoing data communication, and both ways data communication. These images are respectively named as *data_none.png*, *data_in.png*, *data_out.png*, and *data_both.png*. Please add some icons with the aforementioned names in the *res/drawable* folder of your project structure.

Source Download URL

The source code for this example is in the Android Cookbook repository at *http://github.com/AndroidCook/Android-Cookbook-Examples*, in the subdirectory TelephonyManager (see "Getting and Using the Code Examples" on page xvii).

Networked Applications

13.1 Introduction: Networking

Ian Darwin

Discussion

Networking. One could talk about it for hours. In the Android context it is primarily about web services, which are services accessed by another program (your Android app) over the HTTP ("web") protocol. Web services come in two flavors: XML/SOAP and RESTful. XML/SOAP web services are more formal and thus have significantly more overhead, both at development time and at runtime, but offer more capability. RESTful services are much lighter weight, and are not tied to XML: we have recipes on using JSON (JavaScript Object Notation) and other formats with web services.

Choose your protocol wisely

While Java makes it easy to create network connections on any protocol, experience shows that HTTP (and HTTPS) are the most universal. If you use a custom protocol talking to your own server, there are some users who will not be able to access your server. Bear in mind that in some countries, high-speed data (a.k.a. 3G) is either not yet available or very expensive, whereas GPRS/EDGE is less expensive and more widely available. Most GPRS service providers only allow HTTP/HTTPS connections, often through a WAP proxy. That being said, there may be things you need to do that can't be done via HTTP—for example, because the protocol demands a different port number (e.g., SIP over port 5000). But do try to make HTTP your first choice when you can—you'll include more customers.

13.2 Using a RESTful Web Service

Ian Darwin

Problem

You need to access a RESTful web service.

Solution

You can use either the "standard" Java URL and `URLConnection` objects, or the Android-provided Apache HttpClient library to code at a slightly higher level or to use HTTP methods other than `GET` and `POST`.

Discussion

REST was originally intended as an architectural description of the early Web, in which `GET` requests were used and in which the URL fully specified (represented) the state of the request. Today RESTful web services are those that eschew the overhead of XML SOAP, WSDL, and (usually) XML Schema, and simply send URLs that contain all the information needed to perform the request (or almost all of it, as there is often a `POST` body sent for some types of requests). For example, to support an Android client that allows offline editing of recipes for this book, there is a (draft) web service that allows you to view the list of recipes (you send an HTTP `GET` request ending in `/recipe/list`), to view the details of one recipe (HTTP `GET` ending in */recipe/NNN* where *NNN* is the primary key of the entry, gotten from the requested list of recipes), and later to upload your revised version of the recipe using an HTTP `POST` to */recipe/NNN* with the `POST` body containing the revised recipe in the same XML document format as the "get recipe" operation downloads it.

By the way, the RESTful service used by these examples is implemented in server-side Java using the JAX-RS APII, provided by JBoss Seam (*http://seamframework.org/*) using RestEasy (*http://www.jboss.org/resteasy*).

Using URL and URLConnection

Android's developers wisely preserved a lot of the Java standard API, including some widely used classes for networking, so as to make it easy to port existing code. The `converse()` method shown in Example 13-1 uses a URL and `URLConnection` from `java.net` to do a `GET`, and is extracted from an example in the networking chapter of my *Java Cookbook* (*http://shop.oreilly.com/product/9780596007010.do*), published by O'Reilly. Comments in this version show what you'd need to change to do a `POST`.

Example 13-1. The RESTful web service client—URLConnection Version

```
public static String converse(String host, int port, String path) throws IOException {
URL url = new URL("http", host, port, path);
    URLConnection conn = url.openConnection();
```

```
// This does a GET; to do a POST, add conn.setDoOutput(true);
conn.setDoInput(true);
conn.setAllowUserInteraction(true); // useless but harmless

conn.connect();

// To do a POST, you'd write to conn.getOutputStream());

StringBuilder sb = new StringBuilder();
BufferedReader in = new BufferedReader(
    new InputStreamReader(conn.getInputStream()));
String line;
while ((line = in.readLine()) != null) {
    sb.append(line);
}
in.close();
return sb.toString();
}
```

The invocation of this method in, say, your onResume() or onCreate() method, can be as simple as the following, which gets the list of recipes from this book:

```
String host = "androidcookbook.net";
String path = "/seam/resource/rest/recipe/list";
String ret = converse(host, 80, path);
```

Using HttpClient

Android supports the Apache HttpClient library, which is widely used for communicating at a slightly higher level than the URLConnection. I've used it in my PageUnit web test framework (*http://www.darwinsys.com/pageunit/*). HttpClient also lets you use other HTTP methods that are common in RESTful services, such as PUT and DELETE. (The URLConnection object used earlier, by contrast, only supports GET and POST). Example 13-2 shows the same converse method coded for a GET using HttpClient.

Example 13-2. The RESTful web service client—HttpClient version

```
public static String converse(String host, int port, String path,
    String postBody) throws IOException {
    HttpHost target = new HttpHost(host, port);
    HttpClient client = new DefaultHttpClient();
    HttpGet get = new HttpGet(path);
    HttpEntity results = null;
    try {
        HttpResponse response=client.execute(target, get);
        results = response.getEntity();
        return EntityUtils.toString(results);
    } catch (Exception e) {
        throw new RuntimeException("Web Service Failure");
    } finally {
        if (results!=null)
            try {
                results.consumeContent();
            } catch (IOException e) {
```

```
                    // empty, Checked exception but don't care
            }
        }
    }
```

Usage will be exactly the same as for the URLConnection-based version.

The results

In the present version of the web service, the return value comes back as an XML document, which you'd need to parse to display in a List. If there is enough interest, we might add a JSON version as well.

 Don't forget to add the android.permission.INTERNET permission to your *AndroidManifest.xml* file or you will not be able to access any web connections.

See Also

Recipe 11.14; Recipe 9.1

13.3 Extracting Information from Unstructured Text Using Regular Expressions

Ian Darwin

Problem

You want to get information from another organization, but the organization doesn't make it available as information, only as a viewable web page.

Solution

Use java.net to download the HTML page, and use regular expressions to extract the information from the page.

Discussion

If you aren't already a big fan of regular expressions, well, you should be. And maybe this recipe will help interest you in learning regex technology.

Suppose that I, as a published author, want to track how my book is selling in comparison to others. I can obtain this information for free just by clicking on the page for my book on any of the major bookseller sites, reading the sales rank number off the screen, and typing the number into a file—but that's too tedious. As I wrote in one of my earlier books, "computers get paid to extract relevant information from files; people should not have to do such mundane tasks." This program uses the Regular Expressions API and, in particular, newline matching to extract a value from an HTML page on the Amazon.com website. It also reads from a URL object (see Recipe 13.2). The pattern to look for is something like this (bear in mind that the HTML may change at any time, so I want to keep the pattern fairly general):

```
(bookstore name here) Sales Rank:
# 26,252
```

As the pattern may extend over more than one line, I read the entire web page from the URL into a single long string using a private convenience routine, `readerToString()`, instead of the more traditional line-at-a-time paradigm. The value is extracted from the regular expression, converted to an integer value, and returned. The longer version of this code in *Java Cookbook* would also plot a graph using an external program. The complete program is shown in Example 13-3.

Example 13-3. Part of class BookRank

```java
public static int getBookRank(String isbn) throws IOException {
    // The RE pattern - digits and commas allowed
    final String pattern = "Rank:</b> #([\\d,]+)";
    final Pattern r = Pattern.compile(pattern);

    // The url -- must have the "isbn=" at the very end, or otherwise
    // be amenable to being appended to.
    final String url = "http://www.amazon.com/exec/obidos/ASIN/" + isbn;

    // Open the URL and get a Reader from it.
    final BufferedReader is = new BufferedReader(new InputStreamReader(
        new URL(url).openStream()));
    // Read the URL looking for the rank information, as
    // a single long string, so can match RE across multi-lines.
    final String input = readerToString(is);

    // If found, append to sales data file.
    Matcher m = r.matcher(input);
    if (m.find()) {
        // Group 1 is digits (and maybe ','s) that matched; remove comma
        return Integer.parseInt(m.group(1).replace(",",""));
    } else {
        throw new RuntimeException(
            "Pattern not matched in `" + url + "'!");
    }
}
```

See Also

As mentioned, using the regex API is vital to being able to deal with semistructured data that you will meet in real life. Chapter 4 of *Java Cookbook* (*http://shop.oreilly.com/product/9780596007010.do*), written by me and published by O'Reilly, is all about regex, as is Jeffrey Friedl's comprehensive *Mastering Regular Expressions* (*http://shop.oreilly.com/product/9780596528126.do*), also published by O'Reilly.

Source Download URL

You can download the source code for this example from *http://javacook.darwinsys* *.com/javasrc/regex/BookRank.java*.

13.4 Parsing RSS/Atom Feeds Using ROME

Wagied Davids

Problem

You want to parse RSS/Atom feeds, which are commonly used to provide an updated list of news articles on websites, often identified by the "news" icon:

Solution

This recipe shows an RSS/Atom feed parser based on ROME (*https://rome.dev.java* *.net/*), a Java-based RSS syndication feed parser. It has some nifty features such as HTTP conditional GETs, ETags, and Gzip compression. It also covers a wide range of formats, including RSS 0.90, RSS 2.0, and Atom 0.3 and 1.0.

> Due to an administrative error made by Oracle, as of this writing the java.net project sites present an intimidating "Invalid Security Certificate" warning. As long as the site is actually rome.dev.java.net, you should be OK to proceed.

Discussion

The basic steps are as follows:

1. Modify your *AndroidManifest.xml* file to allow for Internet browsing:

   ```
   <uses-permission android:name="android.permission.INTERNET"/>
   ```

2. Download the appropriate JAR files, *rome-0.9.jar* and *jdom-1.0.jar*.

3. Create an Android project. Set the layout file to be the contents of Example 13-4.

---

4. Create the `Activity` code shown in Example 13-5. In particular, the `getRSS()` method demonstrates the use of the ROME API to parse the XML RSS feed and display the results.

When run with the given feed URL (*http://rss.cbc.ca/lineup/topstories.xml*), the output should look like Figure 13-1, except with newer news items.

Example 13-4. main.xml

```xml
<?xml version="1.0" encoding="utf-8"?>
<LinearLayout
    xmlns:android="http://schemas.android.com/apk/res/android"
    android:orientation="vertical"
    android:layout_width="fill_parent"
    android:layout_height="fill_parent">

    <TableLayout
        android:id="@+id/table"
        android:layout_width="fill_parent"
        android:layout_height="wrap_content"
        android:stretchColumns="0">
        <TableRow
            android:id="@+id/top_add_entry_row"
            android:layout_height="wrap_content"
            android:layout_width="fill_parent">

            <EditText
                android:id="@+id/rssURL"
                android:hint="Enter RSS URL"
                android:singleLine="true"
                android:maxLines="1"
                android:maxWidth="220dp"
                android:layout_width="wrap_content"
                android:layout_height="wrap_content">
            </EditText>
            <Button
                android:id="@+id/goButton"
                android:text="Go"
                android:layout_width="fill_parent"
                android:layout_height="wrap_content">
            </Button>
        </TableRow>
    </TableLayout>

    <!-- Mid Panel -->
    <ListView
        android:id="@+id/ListView"
        android:layout_weight="1"
        android:layout_width="fill_parent"
        android:layout_height="wrap_content">
    </ListView>

    <Button
        android:id="@+id/clearButton"
        android:text="Clear"
```

```
                android:layout_width="fill_parent"
                android:layout_height="wrap_content">
        </Button>
</LinearLayout>
```

Example 13-5. AndroidRss.java

```java
import java.io.IOException;
import java.net.MalformedURLException;
import java.net.URL;
import java.util.ArrayList;
import java.util.Iterator;
import java.util.List;

import android.app.Activity;
import android.os.Bundle;
import android.util.Log;
import android.view.View;
import android.view.View.OnClickListener;
import android.widget.AdapterView;
import android.widget.ArrayAdapter;
import android.widget.Button;
import android.widget.EditText;
import android.widget.ListView;
import android.widget.Toast;
import android.widget.AdapterView.OnItemClickListener;

import com.sun.syndication.feed.synd.SyndEntry;
import com.sun.syndication.feed.synd.SyndFeed;
import com.sun.syndication.io.FeedException;
import com.sun.syndication.io.SyndFeedInput;
import com.sun.syndication.io.XmlReader;

public class AndroidRss extends Activity
    {
        private static final String tag="AndroidRss ";
        private int selectedItemIndex = 0;
        private final ArrayList list = new ArrayList();
        private EditText text;
        private ListView listView;
        private Button goButton;
        private Button clearButton;
        private ArrayAdapter adapter = null;

        @Override
        public void onCreate(Bundle savedInstanceState)
            {
                super.onCreate(savedInstanceState);
                setContentView(R.layout.main);

                text = (EditText) this.findViewById(R.id.rssURL);
                goButton = (Button) this.findViewById(R.id.goButton);
                goButton.setOnClickListener(new OnClickListener()
                    {
                        @Override
                        public void onClick(View v)
```

```
                  {
                        String rss = text.getText().toString().trim();
                        getRSS(rss);
                  }
            });

      clearButton = (Button) this.findViewById(R.id.clearButton);
      clearButton.setOnClickListener(new OnClickListener()
            {
                  @Override
                  public void onClick(View v)
                        {
                              adapter.clear();
                              adapter.notifyDataSetChanged();
                        }
            });

      listView = (ListView) this.findViewById(R.id.ListView);
      listView.setOnItemClickListener(new OnItemClickListener() {
                  @Override
                  public void onItemClick(AdapterView parent, View view,
                  int position, long duration)
                        {
                              selectedItemIndex = position;
                              Toast.makeText(getApplicationContext(),
                                  "Selected " + adapter.getItem(position) +
                                  " @ " + position, Toast.LENGTH_SHORT).show();
                        }
            });

      adapter = new ArrayAdapter(this, R.layout.dataview, R.id.ListItemView);
      listView.setAdapter(adapter);

}

private void getRSS(String rss) {

      URL feedUrl;
      try
            {
                  Log.d("DEBUG", "Entered:" + rss);
                  feedUrl = new URL(rss);

                  SyndFeedInput input = new SyndFeedInput();
                  SyndFeed feed = input.build(new XmlReader(feedUrl));
                  List entries = feed.getEntries();
                  Toast.makeText(this,
                  "#Feeds retrieved: " + entries.size(), Toast.LENGTH_SHORT).show();

                  Iterator iterator = entries.listIterator();
                  while (iterator.hasNext())
                        {
                              SyndEntry ent = (SyndEntry) iterator.next();
                              String title = ent.getTitle();
                              adapter.add(title);
```

```
                }
                adapter.notifyDataSetChanged();

            }
        catch (MalformedURLException e)
            {
                e.printStackTrace();
            }
        catch (IllegalArgumentException e)
            {
                e.printStackTrace();
            }
        catch (FeedException e)
            {
                e.printStackTrace();
            }
        catch (IOException e)
            {
                e.printStackTrace();
            }
        }

    private void clearTextFields()
        {
            Log.d(tag, "clearTextFields()");
            this.text.setText("");
        }
    }
```

Figure 13-1. RSS feed in ListView

Source Download URL

The source code for this example is in the Android Cookbook repository at *http://github
.com/AndroidCook/Android-Cookbook-Examples*, in the subdirectory AndroidRss (see
"Getting and Using the Code Examples" on page xvii).

13.5 Using MD5 to Digest Clear Text

Colin Wilcox

Problem

Sometimes it is necessary to convert clear text to a nonreadable form before saving or transmitting it.

Solution

Android provides a standard Java MD5 class to allow plain text to be replaced with an MD5 digest of the original text. This is a one-way digest that is not believed to be easily reversible (if you need that, use Java Cryptography).

Discussion

Example 13-6 is a simple function that takes a clear-text string and digests it using MD5, returning the encrypted string as a return value.

Example 13-6. MD5 hash

```
public static String md5(String s) {
      try {
          // Create MD5 Hasher
          MessageDigest digest = java.security.MessageDigest.getInstance("MD5");
          digest.update(s.getBytes());
          byte messageDigest[] = digest.digest();
          // Create Hex String
          StringBuffer hexString = new StringBuffer();
          for (int i = 0; i < messageDigest.length; i++)
          {
              hexString.append(Integer.toHexString(0xFF & messageDigest[i]));
          }
          return hexString.toString();
      }
      catch (NoSuchAlgorithmException e) {
          e.printStackTrace();
      }
      return "";    // or give the user an Exception...
  }
```

13.6 Converting Text into Hyperlinks

Rachee Singh

Problem

You need to turn web page URLs into hyperlinks in a `TextView` of your Android app.

Solution

Use the `autoLink` property for a `TextView`.

Discussion

Say you are setting the URL *www.google.com* as part of the text in a `TextView`, but you want this text to be a hyperlink so that the user can open the web page in a browser by clicking on it. To achieve this, add the `autoLink` property to the `TextView`:

```
android:autoLink = "all"
```

Now, in the activity's code, you can set any text to the `TextView` and all the URLs will be converted to hyperlinks!

```
linkText = (TextView)findViewById(R.id.link);
linkText.setText("The link is: www.google.com");
```

13.7 Accessing a Web Page Using WebView

Rachee Singh

Problem

You want to download and display a web page within your application.

Solution

Embed the standard `WebView` component in the layout and invoke its `loadUrl()` method to load and display the web page.

Discussion

`WebView` is a `View` component that can be placed in an activity. Its primary use is, as its name implies, to handle web pages for you.

Since `WebView` usually needs to access remote web page(s), don't forget to add the Internet permission into the manifest file:

```
<uses-permission android:name="android.permission.INTERNET" />
```

Then you can add the `WebView` to your XML layout:

```
<WebView
android:id="@+id/webview"
android:layout_height="fill_parent"
android:layout_width="fill_parent"/>
```

In the Java code for the activity that displays the web page, we obtain a handle onto the `WebView` using the `findViewById()` method. On the `WebView` we use the `loadUrl()` method to provide it the URL of the website we wish to open in the application.

```
WebView webview = (WebView)findViewById(R.id.webview);
webview.loadUrl("http://google.com");
```

Source Download URL

You can download the source code for this example from *https://docs.google.com/leaf ?id=0B_rESQKgad5LN2JhMDFjZTUtY2IwZS00NzkyLWFlNjItMzhiZWR lYTQxMWNm&hl=en_US*.

13.8 Customizing a WebView

Rachee Singh

Problem

You need to customize the WebView opened by your application.

Solution

Use the WebSettings class to access built-in functions for customizing the browser.

Discussion

As discussed in Recipe 13.7, to open a web page in an Android application we use a WebView component. Then, to load a URL in the WebView we use, for example:

```
webview.loadUrl("http://www.google.com/");
```

We can do many things to customize the browser to suit users' needs. To customize the view, we need an instance of the WebSettings class, which we can get from the WebView component:

```
WebSettings webSettings = webView.getSettings();
```

Here are some of the things we can do using WebSettings:

- Tell the WebView to block network images:

  ```
  webSettings.setBlockNetworkImage(true);
  ```
- Set the default font size in the browser:

  ```
  webSettings.setDefaultFontSize(25);
  ```
- Set whether the WebView supports zoom:

  ```
  webSettings.setSupportZoom(true);
  ```
- Tell the WebView to enable JavaScript execution:

  ```
  webSettings.setJavaScriptEnabled(true);
  ```

- Control whether the WebView will save passwords:

  ```
  webSettings.setSavePassword(false);
  ```
- Control whether the WebView will saving form data:

  ```
  webSettings.setSaveFormData(false);
  ```

Many more methods of this kind are available. For more information, see the Android Developers page on the topic.

Gaming and Animation

14.1 Introduction: Gaming and Animation

Ian Darwin

Discussion

Gaming is obviously an important application for which people used to use "computers" and now use mobile devices, and Android is a perfectly capable contender in the graphics arena, providing support for OpenGL ES.

If you want to use some advanced gaming features without having to write a lot of code, you're in luck, as there are many game development frameworks in existence today. Many of them are primarily or exclusively for desktops. The ones shown in Table 14-1 are known to be usable on Android; if you find others, please add a comment to the online version of this web page, at *http://androidcookbook.com/r/1816*, and we will incorporate it into the online version and eventually into a future revision of the published book.

Table 14-1. Android game frameworks

Name	Open source?	Cost	URL
AndEngine	Y	Free	*http://www.andengine.org/*
Box2D	Y	Free	*http://code.google.com/p/box2d/*
Corona SDK	?	$199+/year	*http://www.anscamobile.com/corona/*
Flixel	Y	Free	*http://flixel.org/index.html*
libgdx	Y	Free	*http://code.google.com/p/libgdx/*
PlayN	Y	Free	*http://code.google.com/p/playn*
rokon	Y	Free	*http://code.google.com/p/rokon/*
ShiVa 3D	N	€169.00+ each for editor and server	*http://www.stonetrip.com/*
Unity	N	$400+	*http://unity3d.com/unity/publishing/android.html*

You will need to compare the functions that each offers before committing to using one over another in your project.

14.2 Building an Android Game Using flixel-android

Wagied Davids

Problem

You want to build an Android game using a high-level framework.

Solution

Use Flixel (*http://flixel.org/index.html*), an ActionScript-based game framework developed by Adam ("Atomic") Saltsman.

Discussion

Thanks to the tremendous work of Wing Eraser, a Java-based port has been created (*http://code.google.com/p/flixel-android/*), which closely resembles the AS3-based Flixel in terms of programming paradigm.

In this recipe, we will create a simple jumper game, containing a few entities, a droid, a pusher, and a few elevators. Each entity is declared as a separate class containing its own asset resources, and listeners for digital touchpad events.

Example 14-1 shows the code for the Flixel-based game activity.

Example 14-1. The Flixel-based game activity

```
import android.app.Activity;
import android.content.pm.ActivityInfo;
import android.os.Bundle;
import android.view.Window;
import android.view.WindowManager;

public class Main extends Activity
  {
    @Override
    public void onCreate(Bundle savedInstanceState)
      {
        super.onCreate(savedInstanceState);

        requestWindowFeature(Window.FEATURE_NO_TITLE);
        getWindow().setFlags(WindowManager.LayoutParams.FLAG_FULLSCREEN,
        WindowManager.LayoutParams.FLAG_FULLSCREEN);

        // ORIENTATION
        // setRequestedOrientation(ActivityInfo.SCREEN_ORIENTATION_PORTRAIT);
        setRequestedOrientation(ActivityInfo.SCREEN_ORIENTATION_LANDSCAPE);
```

```
      setContentView(new GameView(this, R.class));
    }
}
```

Example 14-2 shows the code for the Flixel-based game view.

Example 14-2. The Flixel-based game view

```
import org.flixel.FlxGame;
import org.flixel.FlxGameView;
import android.content.Context;

public class GameView extends FlxGameView
  {
    public GameView(Context context, Class<? extends Object> resource)
      {
        super(new FlxGame(400, 240, SimpleJumper.class, context, resource), context);
      }
  }
```

A sprite is a small graphic that moves around in a graphics application; for example, a player in a video game. Example 14-3 shows the code for the Flixel-based **Sprite** class.

Example 14-3. Droid.java, a FlxSprite implementation

```
import org.flixel.FlxG;
import org.flixel.FlxSound;
import org.flixel.FlxSprite;

public class Droid extends FlxSprite
  {
    private final FlxSound sound = new FlxSound();

    public Droid(int X, int Y)
      {
        super(X, Y);
        loadGraphic(R.drawable.player, true, true);
        maxVelocity.x = 100; // walking speed
        acceleration.y = 400; // gravity
        drag.x = maxVelocity.x * 4; // deceleration (sliding to a stop)

        // tweak the bounding box for better feel
        width = 8;
        height = 10;

        offset.x = 3;
        offset.y = 3;

        addAnimation("idle", new int[] { 0 }, 0, false);
        addAnimation("walk", new int[] { 1, 2, 3, 0 }, 12);
        addAnimation("walk_back", new int[] { 3, 2, 1, 0 }, 10, true);
        addAnimation("flail", new int[] { 1, 2, 3, 0 }, 18, true);
        addAnimation("jump", new int[] { 4 }, 0, false);
      }
```

```
@Override
public void update()
  {
    // Smooth slidey walking controls
    acceleration.x = 0;
    if (FlxG.dpad.pressed("LEFT")) acceleration.x -= drag.x;
    if (FlxG.dpad.pressed("RIGHT")) acceleration.x += drag.x;

    if (onFloor)
      {
        // Jump controls
        if (FlxG.dpad.justTouched("UP"))
          {
            sound.loadEmbedded(R.raw.jump);
            sound.play();

            velocity.y = -acceleration.y * 0.51f;
            play("jump");

          }// Animations
        else if (velocity.x > 0)
          {
            play("walk");
          }
        else if (velocity.x < 0)
          {
            play("walk_back");
          }
        else play("idle");
      }
    else if (velocity.y < 0) play("jump");
    else play("flail");

    // Default object physics update
    super.update();
  }

}
```

Source Download URL

The source code for this example is in the Android Cookbook repository at *http://github .com/AndroidCook/Android-Cookbook-Examples*, in the subdirectory SimpleJumper (see "Getting and Using the Code Examples" on page xvii).

14.3 Building an Android Game Using AndEngine (Android-Engine)

Wagied Davids

Problem

You want to design an Android game using the AndEngine game framework.

Solution

AndEngine (*http://www.andengine.org/*) is a game engine framework designed for producing games on Android. Originally developed by Nicholas Gramlich, it has some advanced features for producing awesome games.

Discussion

For this recipe, I have designed a simple pool game with physics capabilities, such that the effects of the accelerometer are taken into account, as are touch events. As a result, touching a specific billiard ball and pulling down on it will cause it to shoot into other balls, with the collision detection taken care of. Example 14-4 shows the code for the AndDev-based game activity.

Example 14-4. The AndDev-based game activity

```
import org.anddev.andengine.engine.Engine;
import org.anddev.andengine.engine.camera.Camera;
import org.anddev.andengine.engine.options.EngineOptions;
import org.anddev.andengine.engine.options.EngineOptions.ScreenOrientation;
import org.anddev.andengine.engine.options.resolutionpolicy.RatioResolutionPolicy;
import org.anddev.andengine.entity.Entity;
import org.anddev.andengine.entity.primitive.Rectangle;
import org.anddev.andengine.entity.scene.Scene;
import org.anddev.andengine.entity.scene.Scene.IOnAreaTouchListener;
import org.anddev.andengine.entity.scene.Scene.IOnSceneTouchListener;
import org.anddev.andengine.entity.scene.Scene.ITouchArea;
import org.anddev.andengine.entity.shape.Shape;
import org.anddev.andengine.entity.sprite.AnimatedSprite;
import org.anddev.andengine.entity.sprite.Sprite;
import org.anddev.andengine.entity.util.FPSLogger;
import org.anddev.andengine.extension.physics.box2d.PhysicsConnector;
import org.anddev.andengine.extension.physics.box2d.PhysicsFactory;
import org.anddev.andengine.extension.physics.box2d.PhysicsWorld;
import org.anddev.andengine.extension.physics.box2d.util.Vector2Pool;
import org.anddev.andengine.input.touch.TouchEvent;
import org.anddev.andengine.opengl.texture.Texture;
import org.anddev.andengine.opengl.texture.TextureOptions;
import org.anddev.andengine.opengl.texture.region.TextureRegion;
import org.anddev.andengine.opengl.texture.region.TextureRegionFactory;
import org.anddev.andengine.opengl.texture.region.TiledTextureRegion;
import org.anddev.andengine.sensor.accelerometer.AccelerometerData;
```

```
import org.anddev.andengine.sensor.accelerometer.IAccelerometerListener;
import org.anddev.andengine.ui.activity.BaseGameActivity;

import android.hardware.SensorManager;
import android.util.DisplayMetrics;

import com.badlogic.gdx.math.Vector2;
import com.badlogic.gdx.physics.box2d.Body;
import com.badlogic.gdx.physics.box2d.BodyDef.BodyType;
import com.badlogic.gdx.physics.box2d.FixtureDef;

public class SimplePool extends BaseGameActivity implements IAccelerometerListener,
IOnSceneTouchListener, IOnAreaTouchListener
  {

    private Camera mCamera;
    private Texture mTexture;
    private Texture mBallYellowTexture;
    private Texture mBallRedTexture;
    private Texture mBallBlackTexture;
    private Texture mBallBlueTexture;
    private Texture mBallGreenTexture;
    private Texture mBallOrangeTexture;
    private Texture mBallPinkTexture;
    private Texture mBallPurpleTexture;
    private Texture mBallWhiteTexture;

    private TiledTextureRegion mBallYellowTextureRegion;
    private TiledTextureRegion mBallRedTextureRegion;
    private TiledTextureRegion mBallBlackTextureRegion;
    private TiledTextureRegion mBallBlueTextureRegion;
    private TiledTextureRegion mBallGreenTextureRegion;
    private TiledTextureRegion mBallOrangeTextureRegion;
    private TiledTextureRegion mBallPinkTextureRegion;
    private TiledTextureRegion mBallPurpleTextureRegion;
    private TiledTextureRegion mBallWhiteTextureRegion;

    private Texture mBackgroundTexture;
    private TextureRegion mBackgroundTextureRegion;

    private PhysicsWorld mPhysicsWorld;

    private float mGravityX;
    private float mGravityY;
    private Scene mScene;

    private final int mFaceCount = 0;

    private final int CAMERA_WIDTH = 720;
    private final int CAMERA_HEIGHT = 480;

    @Override
    public Engine onLoadEngine()
      {
        DisplayMetrics dm = new DisplayMetrics();
```

```
      getWindowManager().getDefaultDisplay().getMetrics(dm);

      this.mCamera = new Camera(0, 0, CAMERA_WIDTH, CAMERA_HEIGHT);
      return new Engine(new EngineOptions(true, ScreenOrientation.LANDSCAPE,
      new RatioResolutionPolicy(CAMERA_WIDTH, CAMERA_HEIGHT), this.mCamera));
   }

@Override
public void onLoadResources()
   {
      this.mTexture =
         new Texture(64, 64, TextureOptions.BILINEAR_PREMULTIPLYALPHA);
      this.mBallBlackTexture =
         new Texture(64, 64, TextureOptions.BILINEAR_PREMULTIPLYALPHA);
      this.mBallBlueTexture =
         new Texture(64, 64, TextureOptions.BILINEAR_PREMULTIPLYALPHA);
      this.mBallGreenTexture =
         new Texture(64, 64, TextureOptions.BILINEAR_PREMULTIPLYALPHA);
      this.mBallOrangeTexture =
         new Texture(64, 64, TextureOptions.BILINEAR_PREMULTIPLYALPHA);
      this.mBallPinkTexture =
         new Texture(64, 64, TextureOptions.BILINEAR_PREMULTIPLYALPHA);
      this.mBallPurpleTexture =
         new Texture(64, 64, TextureOptions.BILINEAR_PREMULTIPLYALPHA);
      this.mBallYellowTexture =
         new Texture(64, 64, TextureOptions.BILINEAR_PREMULTIPLYALPHA);
      this.mBallRedTexture =
         new Texture(64, 64, TextureOptions.BILINEAR_PREMULTIPLYALPHA);
      this.mBallWhiteTexture =
         new Texture(64, 64, TextureOptions.BILINEAR_PREMULTIPLYALPHA);

      TextureRegionFactory.setAssetBasePath("gfx/");
      mBallYellowTextureRegion =
         TextureRegionFactory.createTiledFromAsset(this.mBallYellowTexture, this,
         "ball_yellow.png", 0, 0, 1, 1); // 64x32
      mBallRedTextureRegion =
         TextureRegionFactory.createTiledFromAsset(this.mBallRedTexture, this,
         "ball_red.png", 0, 0, 1, 1); // 64x32
      mBallBlackTextureRegion =
         TextureRegionFactory.createTiledFromAsset(this.mBallBlackTexture, this,
         "ball_black.png", 0, 0, 1, 1); // 64x32
      mBallBlueTextureRegion =
         TextureRegionFactory.createTiledFromAsset(this.mBallBlueTexture, this,
         "ball_blue.png", 0, 0, 1, 1); // 64x32
      mBallGreenTextureRegion =
         TextureRegionFactory.createTiledFromAsset(this.mBallGreenTexture, this,
         "ball_green.png", 0, 0, 1, 1); // 64x32
      mBallOrangeTextureRegion =
         TextureRegionFactory.createTiledFromAsset(this.mBallOrangeTexture, this,
         "ball_orange.png", 0, 0, 1, 1); // 64x32
      mBallPinkTextureRegion =
         TextureRegionFactory.createTiledFromAsset(this.mBallPinkTexture, this,
         "ball_pink.png", 0, 0, 1, 1); // 64x32
      mBallPurpleTextureRegion =
         TextureRegionFactory.createTiledFromAsset(this.mBallPurpleTexture, this,
```

```
      "ball_purple.png", 0, 0, 1, 1); // 64x32
    mBallWhiteTextureRegion =
      TextureRegionFactory.createTiledFromAsset(this.mBallWhiteTexture, this,
      "ball_white.png", 0, 0, 1, 1); // 64x32

    this.mBackgroundTexture = new Texture(512, 1024,
      TextureOptions.BILINEAR_PREMULTIPLYALPHA);
    this.mBackgroundTextureRegion =
      TextureRegionFactory.createFromAsset(this.mBackgroundTexture, this,
      "table_bkg.png", 0, 0);

    this.enableAccelerometerSensor(this);

    mEngine.getTextureManager().loadTextures(mBackgroundTexture, mBallYellowTexture,
      mBallRedTexture, mBallBlackTexture, mBallBlueTexture,
      mBallGreenTexture, mBallOrangeTexture,
      mBallPinkTexture, mBallPurpleTexture);
  }

@Override
public Scene onLoadScene()
  {
    this.mEngine.registerUpdateHandler(new FPSLogger());

    this.mPhysicsWorld = new PhysicsWorld(
        new Vector2(0, SensorManager.GRAVITY_EARTH), false);

    this.mScene = new Scene();
    this.mScene.attachChild(new Entity());

    this.mScene.setBackgroundEnabled(false);
    this.mScene.setOnSceneTouchListener(this);
    Sprite background = new Sprite(0, 0, this.mBackgroundTextureRegion);
    background.setWidth(CAMERA_WIDTH);
    background.setHeight(CAMERA_HEIGHT);
    background.setPosition(0, 0);
    this.mScene.getChild(0).attachChild(background);

    final Shape ground = new Rectangle(0, CAMERA_HEIGHT, CAMERA_WIDTH, 0);
    final Shape roof = new Rectangle(0, 0, CAMERA_WIDTH, 0);
    final Shape left = new Rectangle(0, 0, 0, CAMERA_HEIGHT);
    final Shape right = new Rectangle(CAMERA_WIDTH, 0, 0, CAMERA_HEIGHT);

    final FixtureDef wallFixtureDef = PhysicsFactory.createFixtureDef(0, 0.5f, 0.5f);
    PhysicsFactory.createBoxBody(
        mPhysicsWorld, ground, BodyType.StaticBody, wallFixtureDef);
    PhysicsFactory.createBoxBody(
        mPhysicsWorld, roof, BodyType.StaticBody, wallFixtureDef);
    PhysicsFactory.createBoxBody(
        mPhysicsWorld, left, BodyType.StaticBody, wallFixtureDef);
    PhysicsFactory.createBoxBody(
        mPhysicsWorld, right, BodyType.StaticBody, wallFixtureDef);

    this.mScene.attachChild(ground);
    this.mScene.attachChild(roof);
```

```
      this.mScene.attachChild(left);
      this.mScene.attachChild(right);

      this.mScene.registerUpdateHandler(this.mPhysicsWorld);
      this.mScene.setOnAreaTouchListener(this);

      return this.mScene;
   }

@Override
public void onLoadComplete()
   {
      setupBalls();

   }

@Override
public boolean onAreaTouched(
   final TouchEvent pSceneTouchEvent, final ITouchArea pTouchArea,
   final float pTouchAreaLocalX, final float pTouchAreaLocalY)
   {
      if (pSceneTouchEvent.isActionDown())
         {
            final AnimatedSprite face = (AnimatedSprite) pTouchArea;
            this.jumpFace(face);
            return true;
         }

      return false;
   }

@Override
public boolean onSceneTouchEvent(
   final Scene pScene, final TouchEvent pSceneTouchEvent)
   {
      if (this.mPhysicsWorld != null)
         {
            if (pSceneTouchEvent.isActionDown())
               {
                  // this.addFace(pSceneTouchEvent.getX(),
                  // pSceneTouchEvent.getY());
                  return true;
               }
         }
      return false;
   }

@Override
public void onAccelerometerChanged(final AccelerometerData pAccelerometerData)
   {
      this.mGravityX = pAccelerometerData.getX();
      this.mGravityY = pAccelerometerData.getY();

      final Vector2 gravity = Vector2Pool.obtain(this.mGravityX, this.mGravityY);
      this.mPhysicsWorld.setGravity(gravity);
```

```
            Vector2Pool.recycle(gravity);
    }

    private void setupBalls()
      {
        final AnimatedSprite[] balls = new AnimatedSprite[9];

        final FixtureDef objectFixtureDef = PhysicsFactory.createFixtureDef(1, 0.5f, 0.5f);

        AnimatedSprite redBall =
            new AnimatedSprite(10, 10, this.mBallRedTextureRegion);
        AnimatedSprite yellowBall =
            new AnimatedSprite(20, 20, this.mBallYellowTextureRegion);
        AnimatedSprite blueBall =
            new AnimatedSprite(30, 30, this.mBallBlueTextureRegion);
        AnimatedSprite greenBall =
            new AnimatedSprite(40, 40, this.mBallGreenTextureRegion);
        AnimatedSprite orangeBall =
            new AnimatedSprite(50, 50, this.mBallOrangeTextureRegion);
        AnimatedSprite pinkBall =
            new AnimatedSprite(60, 60, this.mBallPinkTextureRegion);
        AnimatedSprite purpleBall =
            new AnimatedSprite(70, 70, this.mBallPurpleTextureRegion);
        AnimatedSprite blackBall =
            new AnimatedSprite(70, 70, this.mBallBlackTextureRegion);
        AnimatedSprite whiteBall =
            new AnimatedSprite(70, 70, this.mBallWhiteTextureRegion);

        balls[0] = redBall;
        balls[1] = yellowBall;
        balls[2] = blueBall;
        balls[3] = greenBall;
        balls[4] = orangeBall;
        balls[5] = pinkBall;
        balls[6] = purpleBall;
        balls[7] = blackBall;
        balls[8] = whiteBall;

        for (int i = 0; i < 9; i++)
          {
            Body body = PhysicsFactory.createBoxBody(this.mPhysicsWorld, balls[i],
            BodyType.DynamicBody, objectFixtureDef);
            this.mPhysicsWorld.registerPhysicsConnector(new PhysicsConnector(balls[i],
            body, true, true));

            balls[i].animate(new long[] { 200, 200 }, 0, 1, true);
            balls[i].setUserData(body);
            this.mScene.registerTouchArea(balls[i]);
            this.mScene.attachChild(balls[i]);
          }
    }

    private void jumpFace(final AnimatedSprite face)
      {
        final Body faceBody = (Body) face.getUserData();
```

```
        final Vector2 velocity =
            Vector2Pool.obtain(this.mGravityX * -50, this.mGravityY * -50);
        faceBody.setLinearVelocity(velocity);
        Vector2Pool.recycle(velocity);
        }
    }
}
```

Source Download URL

The source code for this example is in the Android Cookbook repository at *http://github .com/AndroidCook/Android-Cookbook-Examples*, in the subdirectory SimplePool (see "Getting and Using the Code Examples" on page xvii).

14.4 Processing Timed Keyboard Input

Kurosh Fallahzadeh

Problem

You want to determine whether a user-generated action, such as a key press/release, has occurred within a certain time interval. This can be useful in game input handling and elsewhere.

Solution

Put the thread to sleep for the time interval and use a handler to determine if a key press/release has occurred.

Discussion

The interval is a long integer that represents time in milliseconds. In Example 14-5, we override the onKeyUp method so that when the user releases a key, Android will invoke our taskHandler methods, which basically continue to repeatedly execute task A as long as the user continues to press/release any key within the one-second interval; otherwise, they execute task B.

Example 14-5. The keyboard input timing code

```
// In the main class...

private long interval = 1000; // 1 second time interval

private taskHandler myTaskHandler = new TaskHandler();

class TaskHandler extends Handler {

    @Override
    public void handleMessage(Message msg) {
        MyMainClass.this.executeTaskB();
    }
```

```java
    public void sleep(long timeInterval) {
      //remove previous keyboard message in queue
        this.removeMessages(0);
        //enqueue current keyboard message to execute after timeInterval
        sendMessageDelayed(obtainMessage(0), timeInterval);
    }
}


@Override
public boolean onKeyUp(int keyCode, KeyEvent event) {

//execute TaskA and call handler to execute TaskB if
// key release message arrives after 'interval' has elapsed
    executeTaskA();
    myTaskHandler.sleep(interval);

 return true;
}

public void executeTaskA() {
...
}

public void executeTaskB() {
...
}
```

Social Networking

15.1 Introduction: Social Networking

Ian Darwin

Discussion

In the second decade of this century, nobody writing about the Internet would under-estimate the importance of social networking. Dominated as it is by a few major sites—Facebook and Twitter being the biggest of the big—social networking provides both an opportunity for developers and a missed opportunity for the developer community as a whole. Certainly there are still opportunities for creative use of social networking. But what is missing (despite valiant efforts) is a single "open social networking" API that includes authorization, messaging, and media interchange.

This chapter provides a few how-tos on accessing Facebook and Twitter, using plain HTTP (they all originated as web-based sites just before the explosion of mobile apps) and using more comprehensive but more-specific APIs.

15.2 Integrating Social Networking Using HTTP

Shraddha Shravagi

Problem

You need a basic level of social networking support in your app.

Solution

Instead of diving into the API, you can simply add social networking support.

For Facebook, Twitter, and LinkedIn integration, just follow three simple steps to get started:

1. Download the logos for Facebook, Twitter, and LinkedIn.
2. Create image buttons for each of them.
3. Implement an event handler that, when the user presses the button, passes control to the relevant site and displays the results in a browser window.

Discussion

Here is a simple approach to adding basic social networking.

Step 1: Get the logos

Just download the logos from their respective websites, or use a web search engine.

Step 2: Create image buttons for each logo

The layout shown in Example 15-1 provides image buttons for each of the social networking sites. Figure 15-1 shows the buttons.

Example 15-1. The main layout

```
<!-- Facebook button -->
<ImageView android:src="@drawable/icon_facebook"
    android:layout_width="28dip"
    android:layout_height="28dip" android:id="@+id/facebookBtn"
    android:clickable="true"
    android:onClick="facebookBtnClicked" />

<!-- Twitter button -->
<ImageView android:src="@drawable/icon_twitter"
    android:clickable="true"
    android:layout_width="30dip" android:layout_height="28dip"
    android:id="@+id/twitterBtn" android:layout_marginLeft="3dp"
    android:layout_marginRight="3dp" android:onClick="twitterBtnClicked"
    />

<!-- Linkedin button -->
<ImageView android:src="@drawable/icon_linkedin"
    android:layout_width="28dip"
    android:layout_height="30dip" android:clickable="true"
    android:id="@+id/linkedinBtn"
    android:onClick="linkedinBtnClicked"
    />
```

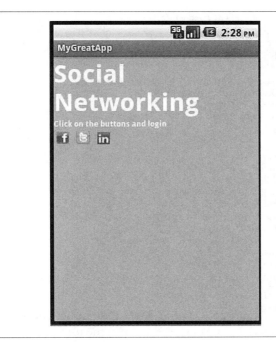

Figure 15-1. Social networking buttons

Step 3: Implement the click event

The code in Example 15-2 provides a series of listeners, each of which will open an Intent to the respective social networking website. These are added as OnClickLis teners by use of android:onClick attributes in the layout in Example 15-1, so the main activity code is fairly short.

Example 15-2. The social networking action handling code

```
/* The URL used here is for the application I want the user to redirect to,
 * and a comment about, for example, here I am
 * using http://goo.gl/eRAD9 as the URL. But you can use the URL of your app.
 * Take the URL from Google Play and shorten with bit.ly or Google URL shortener
 * */

public void facebookBtnClicked(View v) {
    Toast.makeText(this,
        "Facebook Loading...\n Please make sure you are connected to the internet.",
        Toast.LENGTH_SHORT).show();
    String url="http://m.facebook.com/sharer.php?u=http%3A%2F%2Fgoo.gl%2FeRAD9";
    Intent i = new Intent(Intent.ACTION_VIEW);
    i.setData(Uri.parse(url));
    startActivity(i);
}
```

```
public void twitterBtnClicked(View v) {
    Toast.makeText(this,
    "Twitter Loading... \n Please make sure you are connected to the internet.",
    Toast.LENGTH_SHORT).show();
    /**/
    String url = "http://www.twitter.com/share?text=
    Checkout+This+Demo+http://goo.gl/eRAD9+";
    Intent i = new Intent(Intent.ACTION_VIEW);
    i.setData(Uri.parse(url));
    startActivity(i);
}

public void linkedinBtnClicked(View v) {
    Toast.makeText(this,
    "LinkedIn Loading... \n Please make sure you are connected to the internet",
    Toast.LENGTH_SHORT).show();
    String url="http://www.linkedin.com/shareArticle?url=
    http%3A%2F%2Fgoo.gl%2FeRAD9&mini=
    true&source=SampleApp&title=App+on+your+mobile";
    Intent intent=new Intent(Intent.ACTION_VIEW);
    intent.setData(Uri.parse(url));
    startActivity(intent);
}
```

This is how, in three simple steps, you can get a social networking feature for your application. Here we used intents to start the site in the user's browser; you could also use a `WebView` as shown in Recipe 13.7.

15.3 Loading a User's Twitter Timeline Using JSON

Rachee Singh

Problem

You want to load a user's Twitter timeline (his list of tweets) into an Android application.

Solution

Since timeline information is public, you don't need to deal with Twitter's authentication. You can just use an `HttpGet` request to obtain the data from the user's Twitter page in JSON format. Then the user can process the JSON to obtain the tweets.

Discussion

In Example 15-3, `HttpGet` is used to obtain data from the Twitter page, in this example for the *Times of India* (a newspaper). The response obtained after executing the request should contain data from the Twitter page in JSON format. We check for the status code; and unless the code is 200, the request could not fetch the data. From the response, we obtain the JSON and put it into a `StringBuilder` object. The `getTwitterTimeline()` method returns the string that contains the data in JSON format.

Example 15-3. The getTwitterTimeline() method

```java
public String getTwitterTimeline() {
    StringBuilder builder = new StringBuilder();
    HttpClient client = new DefaultHttpClient();
    HttpGet httpGet = new HttpGet(
        "http://twitter.com/statuses/user_timeline/timesofindia.json");
    try {
        HttpResponse response = client.execute(httpGet);
        StatusLine statusLine = response.getStatusLine();
        int statusCode = statusLine.getStatusCode();
        if (statusCode == 200) {
            HttpEntity entity = response.getEntity();
            InputStream content = entity.getContent();
            BufferedReader reader = new BufferedReader(new InputStreamReader(content));
            String line;
            while ((line = reader.readLine()) != null) {
                builder.append(line);
            }
        } else {
            //Couldn't obtain the data
        }
    } catch (ClientProtocolException e) {
    e.printStackTrace();
    } catch (IOException e) {
        e.printStackTrace();
    }
    return builder.toString();
    }
}
```

Now we process the JSON returned from the `getTwitterTimeline()` method in the standard way, using the `getString()` method. We then insert the tweets into a `Text View`. The result should look like Example 15-4 and Figure 15-2.

Example 15-4. Loading the timeline from JSON into ListView

```java
String twitterTimeline = getTwitterTimeline();
    try {
        String tweets = "";
        JSONArray jsonArray = new JSONArray(twitterTimeline);
        for (int i = 0; i < jsonArray.length(); i++) {
            JSONObject jsonObject = jsonArray.getJSONObject(i);
            int j = i+1;
            tweets +="*** " + j + " ***\n";
            tweets += "Date:" + jsonObject.getString("created_at") + "\n";
            tweets += "Post:" + jsonObject.getString("text") + "\n\n";
        }
        json= (TextView)findViewById(R.id.json);
        json.setText(tweets);
    } catch (JSONException e) {
```

```
        e.printStackTrace();
}
```

Figure 15-2. Twitter data parsed by JSON

Source Download URL

You can download the source code for this example from *https://docs.google.com/leaf ?id=0B_rESQKgad5LZDE3MzIxNmYtMDU3Yy00OTZjLTk2NTgtMDBiNTZiYj dlYzlm&hl=en_US.*

Location and Map Applications

16.1 Introduction: Location-Aware Applications

Ian Darwin

Discussion

Not that long ago, GPS devices were either unavailable, expensive, or cumbersome. Today, almost every smartphone has a GPS receiver, and many digital cameras do too. GPS is well on its way to becoming truly ubiquitous in devices. The organizations that provide map data have not been unaware of this trend. Indeed, OpenStreetMap (*http: //openstreetmap.org/*) exists and provides its "free, editable map of the world" in part because of the rise of consumer GPS devices—most of its map data was provided by enthusiasts. Google gets much of its data from commercial mapping services, but in Android, Google has been very driven by the availability of GPS receivers in Android devices. This chapter thus concentrates on the ins and outs of using Google Maps and OpenStreetMap in Android devices.

16.2 Getting Location Information

Ian Darwin

Problem

You just want to know where you are.

Solution

Use Android's built-in location providers.

Android provides two levels of locational position. If you need to know fairly precisely where you are, you can use the FINE resolution, which is GPS-based. If you only need to know roughly where you are, you can use the COARSE resolution, which is based on the location of the cell phone tower(s) your phone is talking to or in range of. The fine resolution is usually accurate to a few meters; the coarse resolution may be accurate down to the building or city block in densely built-up areas, or as inaccurate as five or 10 kilometers in very lightly populated areas with cell towers maximally spaced out.

Discussion

Example 16-1 shows the setup portion of the code. This is part of JPStrack (*http://www .darwinsys.com/jpstrack/*), a mapping application for OpenStreetMap (*http://www.open streetmap.org/*). For mapping purposes the GPS is a must, so I only ask for the FINE resolution.

Example 16-1. Getting location data

```
// Part of jpstrack Main.java
LocationManager mgr =
    (LocationManager) getSystemService(LOCATION_SERVICE);
for (String prov : mgr.getAllProviders()) {
    Log.i(LOG_TAG, getString(R.string.provider_found) + prov);
}

// GPS setup
Criteria criteria = new Criteria();
criteria.setAccuracy(Criteria.ACCURACY_FINE);
List<String> providers = mgr.getProviders(criteria, true);
if (providers == null || providers.size() == 0) {
    Log.e(JPSTRACK, getString(R.string.cannot_get_gps_service));
    Toast.makeText(this, "Could not open GPS service",
        Toast.LENGTH_LONG).show();
    return;
}
String preferred = providers.get(0); // first == preferred
```

After this setup, when you actually want to start the GPS sending you location data, you have to call LocationManager.requestLocationUpdates with the name of the provider you looked up previously, the minimum time between updates (in milliseconds), the minimum distance between updates (in meters), and an instance of the Location Listener interface. You should stop updates by calling removeUpdates with the previously passed-in LocationListener; doing so will reduce overhead and save battery life. In JPStrack the code looks like Example 16-2.

Example 16-2. Suspend and resume location updates

```
@Override
protected void onResume() {
    super.onResume();
    if (preferred != null) {
        mgr.requestLocationUpdates(preferred,
            MIN_SECONDS * 1000,
            MIN_METRES, this);
    }
}
```

```
@Override
protected void onPause() {
    super.onPause();
    if (preferred != null) {
        mgr.removeUpdates(this);
    }
}
```

Finally, the LocationListener's onLocationChanged() method is called when the location changes, and this is where you do something with the location information.

```
@Override
public void onLocationChanged(Location location) {
    long time = location.getTime();
    double latitude = location.getLatitude();
    double longitude = location.getLongitude();
    // do something with latitude and longitude (and time?)...
}
```

The remaining few methods in LocationListener can be stub methods.

What you do with the location data depends on your application, of course. In JPStrack I save it into a track file with handwritten XML-writing code. Commonly you would use it to update your position on a map, or upload it to a location service. There's no limit to what you can do with it.

Source Download URL

You can download the source code for this example from *http://www.darwinsys.com/jpstrack/*.

16.3 Accessing GPS Information in Your Application

Pratik Rupwal

Problem

You need access to the GPS location in a class of your application.

Solution

Add a class that implements the `LocationListener` interface. Create an instance of this class where you want to access the GPS information and retrieve the data.

Discussion

In Example 16-3 the `MyLocationListener` class implements `LocationListener`.

Example 16-3. LocationListener implementation

```
public class MyLocationListener implements LocationListener
    {

        @Override
        public void onLocationChanged(Location loc)
        {
            loc.getLatitude();
            loc.getLongitude();

        }

        @Override
        public void onProviderDisabled(String provider)
        {

        }
        @Override
        public void onProviderEnabled(String provider)
        {

        }
        @Override
        public void onStatusChanged(String provider, int status, Bundle extras)
        {

        }
    }// End of Class MyLocationListener.
```

Add the class file in Example 16-3 in the package of your application; you can use its instance as shown in Example 16-4 to access GPS information in any class.

You can use the `Location` object `loc` in `onLocationChanged` to access GPS information; however, it is not always possible in an application to perform all the GPS information-related tasks in this overridden method due to reasons such as data accessibility. For example, in an application providing information on shopping malls near the user's current location, the app accesses the names of malls according to the user's location and displays them to the user; when the user chooses a mall, the app displays the different stores in that mall. In this example, the application uses the user's location to determine which mall name to fetch from the database through a database handler that is a private member of the class hosting the view to the display list of malls; hence that database handler cannot be accessible in this overridden method, and therefore this operation cannot be carried out.

Example 16-4. Class that uses the LocationListener

```
public class AccessGPS extends Activity
{
//declaration of required objects

LocationManager mlocManager;
LocationListener mlocListener;
Location lastKnownLocation;
Double latitude,longitude;
...
...

protected void onCreate(Bundle savedInstanceState)
{
    ...
    ...
//instantiating objects for accessing GPS information.

mlocListener = new MyLocationListener();

//request for location updates

mlocManager.requestLocationUpdates( LocationManager.GPS_PROVIDER, 0, 0, mlocListener);
locationProvider=LocationManager.GPS_PROVIDER;
...
...

// Access the last identified location

lastKnownLocation = mlocManager.getLastKnownLocation(locationProvider);

// The above object can be used for accessing GPS data as below

latitude=lastKnownLocation.getLatitude();
longitude=lastKnownLocation.getLongitude();

// The above GPS data can be used to carry out the operations specific to the location.
...
...

}
}
```

16.4 Mocking GPS Coordinates on a Device

Emaad Manzoor

Problem

You need to demonstrate your application, but you are scared it might choke when trying to triangulate your GPS coordinates. Or you'd like to simulate being in a place you're not.

Solution

Attach a mock location provider to your `LocationManager` object, and then attach mock coordinates to the mock location provider.

Discussion

Writing the setMockLocation method

The function in Example 16-5 is what you will eventually use in your application to set mock GPS coordinates on the device.

Example 16-5. Setting mock GPS coordinates

```
private void setMockLocation(double latitude, double longitude, float accuracy) {
    lm.addTestProvider (LocationManager.GPS_PROVIDER,
                        "requiresNetwork" == "",
                        "requiresSatellite" == "",
                        "requiresCell" == "",
                        "hasMonetaryCost" == "",
                        "supportsAltitude" == "",
                        "supportsSpeed" == "",
                        "supportsBearing" == "",
                         android.location.Criteria.POWER_LOW,
                         android.location.Criteria.ACCURACY_FINE);

    Location newLocation = new Location(LocationManager.GPS_PROVIDER);

    newLocation.setLatitude(latitude);
    newLocation.setLongitude(longitude);
    newLocation.setAccuracy(accuracy);

    lm.setTestProviderEnabled(LocationManager.GPS_PROVIDER, true);

    lm.setTestProviderStatus(LocationManager.GPS_PROVIDER,
                             LocationProvider.AVAILABLE,
                             null,System.currentTimeMillis());

    lm.setTestProviderLocation(LocationManager.GPS_PROVIDER, newLocation);

}
```

What's happening? In Example 16-5, we add a mock provider using the `addTestPro`
`vider` method of the `LocationManager` class. Then we create a new location using the
`Location` object, which allows us to set latitude, longitude, and accuracy.

We activate the mock provider by first setting a mock-enabled `value` for the `Location`
`Manager` using its `setTestProviderEnabled()` method; then we set a mock `status`, and
finally a mock `location`.

Using the setMockLocation method

To use the method, you must create a `LocationManager` object as you usually would,
and then invoke the method with your coordinates (see Example 16-6).

Example 16-6. Mocking location

```
LocationManager lm = (LocationManager)getSystemService(Context.LOCATION_SERVICE);

lm.requestLocationUpdates(LocationManager.GPS_PROVIDER, 0, 0, new LocationListener() {
        @Override
        public void onStatusChanged(String provider, int status, Bundle extras) {}
        @Override
        public void onProviderEnabled(String provider) {}
        @Override
        public void onProviderDisabled(String provider) {}
        @Override
        public void onLocationChanged(Location location) {}
});

/* Set a mock location for debugging purposes */
setMockLocation(15.387653, 73.872585, 500);
```

You may need to restart the device after using the mock GPS to reenable
the real GPS.

Example application usage

Find Me X (*https://github.com/emaadmanzoor/findmex*) is an Android application that
takes in a search query of the form *place_type* in *locality, city* and returns results aug-
mented with their distance from the user. The location in this application is mocked
to be BITS–Pilani Goa Campus, Goa, India.

See Also

Recipe 16.2; *http://developer.android.com/reference/android/location/LocationManager*
.html; *http://developer.android.com/reference/android/location/Location.html*

Source Download URL

You can download the source code for this example from *https://github.com/emaad manzoor/findmex*.

16.5 Using Geocoding and Reverse Geocoding

Nidhin Jose Davis

Problem

You want to geocode (convert an address to its coordinates) and reverse geocode (convert coordinates to an address).

Solution

Use the built-in Geocoder class.

Discussion

Geocoding is the process of finding the geographical coordinates (latitude and longitude) of a given address or location.

Reverse geocoding, as you might have guessed, is the opposite of geocoding. In this case a latitude and longitude pair is converted into an address or location.

In order to geocode or reverse geocode the first thing to do is to import the Geocoder class:

```
import android.location.Geocoder;
```

The geocoding or reverse geocoding should not be done on the UI thread as it may involve server access, and thus might cause the system to display an Application Not Responding (ANR) dialog to the user. The work has to be done in a separate thread. Example 16-7 shows the code for geocoding and Example 16-8 shows the code for reverse geocoding.

Example 16-7. To geocode

```
Geocoder gc = new Geocoder(context);

if(gc.isPresent()){
  List<Address> list =
    gc.getFromLocationName("1600 Amphitheatre Parkway, Mountain View, CA", 1);

  Address address = list.get(0);

  double lat = address.getLatitude();
  double lng = address.getLongitude();
}
```

Example 16-8. To reverse geocode

```
Geocoder gc = new Geocoder(context);

if(gc.isPresent()){
  List<Address> list = gc.getFromLocation(37.42279, -122.08506,1);

  Address address = list.get(0);

  StringBuffer str = new StringBuffer();
  str.append("Name: " + address.getLocality() + "\n");
  str.append("Sub-Admin Areas: " + address.getSubAdminArea() + "\n");
  str.append("Admin Area: " + address.getAdminArea() + "\n");
  str.append("Country: " + address.getCountryName() + "\n");
  str.append("Country Code: " + address.getCountryCode() + "\n");

  String strAddress = str.toString();
}
```

16.6 Getting Ready for Google Maps Development

Johan Pelgrim

Problem

You want to get set up to use Google MapView layout elements in your Android app.

Solution

Use the Google Maps API library, a MapView layout element, and a MapActivity.

Discussion

Let's start by creating an Android project that displays a default map.

Setting up an AVD that makes use of the Google API SDK libraries

When you create a new Android project you have to indicate which minimum SDK version your app needs and which SDK version you are targeting. Since we will be using the Google Maps API we have to make sure we have an Android Virtual Device (AVD) with those libraries pre-installed.

Make sure you have an AVD with a build target of "Google APIs - 1.5 - API level 3" or higher. See Figure 16-1.

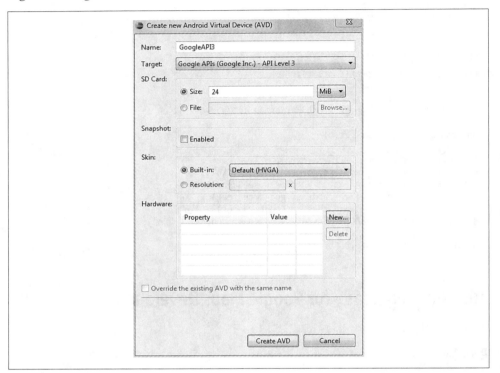

Figure 16-1. Creating an AVD with Google API support

Creating a new Android project that targets "Google APIs - 1.5 - API level 3"

Now you need to create a `MapTest` project that targets "Google APIs - 1.5 - API level 3" or higher, and uses minSDKversion 3 (see Figure 16-2). Let the Android New Project Wizard create a `MapTest` activity for you. Click Finish.

The `MapView` element can only live inside a `MapActivity`, so make sure the `MapTest` activity extends that class. A `MapActivity` must implement the `isRouteDisplayed()` method. This method is required for some accounting from the Maps service to see if you're currently displaying any route information. In this example, we are not. We still have to implement the method, but it's OK to simply return `false` for now. To be able to zoom in the map we can set the built-in zoom controls to true by calling the set BuiltInZoomControls method on the MapView object. Example 16-9 shows the code.

Example 16-9. The MapTest class

```
package nl.codestone.cookbook.maptest;

import android.os.Bundle;

import com.google.android.maps.MapActivity;

public class MapTest extends <tt>MapActivity</tt> {

    @Override
    public void onCreate(Bundle savedInstanceState) {
        super.onCreate(savedInstanceState);
        setContentView(R.layout.main);

        MapView mapview = (MapView) findViewById(R.id.mapview);
        mapview.setBuiltInZoomControls(true);

    }

    @Override
    protected boolean isRouteDisplayed() {
        return false;
    }
}
```

Adding the MapView element to your layout file

Open the *res/layout/main.xml* file. Delete the TextView element and replace it with a MapView element:

```
<com.google.android.maps.MapView
    android:id="@+id/mapview"
    android:layout_width="fill_parent"
    android:layout_height="fill_parent"
    android:apiKey="your_api_key_here"
    android:clickable="true"
    />
```

Some highlights here:

- The MapView is not part of the standard com.android.view package, so we have to include the full package name in this element.
- We have to set the android:clickable attribute to true to be able to drag the map and zoom in and out.
- Your MapView object has to be configured with a personalized Google Maps API key in a special attribute android:apiKey, on the MapView definition. You can obtain this key by registering your MD5 hash from the keystore you sign your apps with (or the debug.keystore during your development cycle).

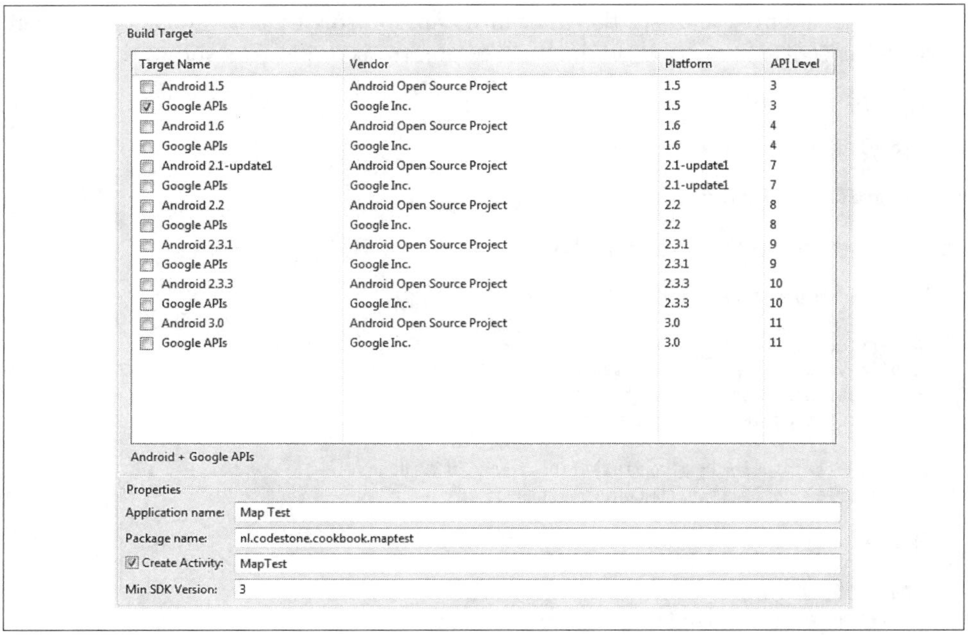

Figure 16-2. Creating the project with Google API support

Registering the Google Maps API key

A full description of how to register a Google Maps API key is available at *http://code .google.com/android/add-ons/google-apis/mapkey.html*.

This section extracts the minimal steps to get such a key. If you get stuck please refer to the full description provided by Google.

Android applications have to be signed with a certificate. These certificates are kept in a keystore. For your commercial apps you have to work with a private (self-signed) certificate that is imported in a `keystore`. When you create and deploy Android applications in your development environment a `debug.keystore` is used to sign your applications. This `debug.keystore` is located in an *.android* directory in your user directory. You need your private `androiddebugkey` key entry's fingerprint (MD5 hash) to register for a Google Maps API key.

Open a command shell and change to the *.android* directory located in your user directory (e.g., `cd ~/.android` in Unix-like environments).

Issue the following command:

```
keytool -list -alias androiddebugkey -keystore debug.keystore -storepass android
```

You will be presented with something like this:

```
androiddebugkey, 29-mrt-2011, PrivateKeyEntry,
Certificate fingerprint (MD5): 2E:54:39:DB:33:E7:D6:3A:9E:18:3D:7F:FB:6D:BC:8D
```

Copy the bit after `Certificate fingerprint (MD5):` to your clipboard and go to *http://code.google.com/android/maps-api-signup.html* to sign up for a Google Maps API key.

You'll receive a key like this:

`18Qcs3h-Sq5l8A7L56bjLwY1gwxgeMYF9Rp_OCg`

Copy and paste this key in the `android:apiKey` attribute in the `MapView` element in your *res/main.xml* layout file. If you are instantiating a `MapView` directly from code, you should pass the Maps API key in the `MapView` constructor.

 You can always regenerate the key as described in the preceding steps, so there's no need to keep this key somewhere safe. On the other hand, you'd better make a copy of the `keystore` you use for signing your personal apps!

Make the following changes in the *AndroidManifest.xml* file, as shown in Example 16-10:

- You have to register a `<uses-permission android:name="android.permission.INTER NET"/>` in your *AndroidManifest.xml* file to be able to get map tile information from the Internet. These map tiles are automatically cached in your *apps-data* directory, so you don't have to do anything extra for that.
- The Google Maps classes are not standard, so you have to indicate that you use the com.google.android.maps library in your *AndroidManifest.xml* file.

Example 16-10. Example AndroidManifest.xml file

```xml
<?xml version="1.0" encoding="utf-8"?>
<manifest xmlns:android="http://schemas.android.com/apk/res/android"
    package="nl.codestone.cookbook.maptest"
    android:versionCode="1"
    android:versionName="1.0">
  <uses-sdk android:minSdkVersion="3" />

  <uses-permission android:name="android.permission.INTERNET" />

  <application android:icon="@drawable/icon" android:label="@string/app_name">

    <activity android:name=".MapTest"
            android:label="@string/app_name">
      <intent-filter>
        <action android:name="android.intent.action.MAIN" />
        <category android:name="android.intent.category.LAUNCHER" />
      </intent-filter>
    </activity>

    <uses-library android:name="com.google.android.maps" />

  </application>
</manifest>
```

There's another file called *default.properties* (or *project.properties* depending on which version of the Android SDK you are using), which contains the build target (level) of your app. This file is automatically generated when you created this project, so there is no need to change anything. It is good to know that the build target level is defined here if you decide to increase or decrease it at some point. You can either change the level in this file or do it via the project properties dialog in Eclipse.

```
target=Google Inc.:Google APIs:3
```

That's it! Start your AVD and run your Android application. If all's well you should see a map of North and South America which you can drag around and zoom into! (See Figure 16-3.)

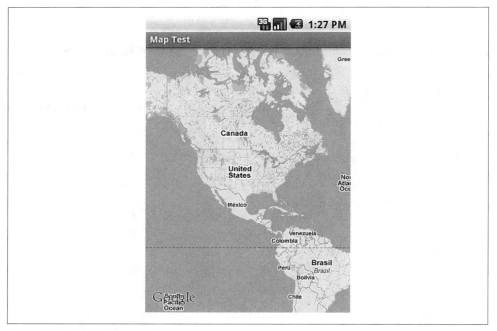

Figure 16-3. Map of the Americas

Checklist

We end this recipe with a checklist that you can use to quickly set up projects for the other Google Maps recipes:

- Use an AVD that makes use of the Google API SDK libraries.
- Your `Activity` should extend the `MapActivity` class.
- You must implement the `isRouteDisplayed()` method. The default—let it return `false`—is fine in most cases.

- Set the built-in zoom controls to `true` by calling the `setBuiltInZoomControls` method on the `MapView` object.
- Add the full package name to the `MapView` element in your layout file (i.e., `com.google.android.maps.MapView`).
- Add your Google Maps API key to the `android:apiKey` attribute on the `MapView` element.
- If you are instantiating a `MapView` directly from code, you should pass the Google Maps API key directly in the `MapView` constructor.
- Set the `android:clickable` attribute on the `MapView` element to `true` to be able to drag the map and zoom in and out.
- Register a `<uses-permission android:name="android.permission.INTERNET "/>` as a child of the `manifest` element in your *AndroidManifest.xml* file.
- Register a `<uses-library android:name="com.google.android.maps" />` as a child of the `application` element in your *AndroidManifest.xml* file.

See Also

The Google APIs project on Google Code (*http://code.google.com/android/add-ons/google-apis*); the Google API key sign-up page (*http://code.google.com/android/maps-api-signup.html*)

Source Download URL

You can download the source code for this example from *https://github.com/downloads/jpelgrim/androidcookbook/MapTest.zip*.

16.7 Adding a Device's Current Location to Google Maps

Rachee Singh

Problem

You want to show the current location of the device on Google Maps.

Solution

Using the `MyLocationOverlay` class, the current location of the device can be depicted on the map.

Despite its name, which makes it sound like it's an example we made up for use in this book, `MyLocationOverlay` is a standard Android class, in the package `com.goo gle.android.maps`.

Discussion

Add the following permissions to the Android manifest file:

```
<uses-permission android:name="android.permission.ACCESS_FINE_LOCATION" />
<uses-permission android:name="android.permission.ACCESS_COARSE_LOCATION" />
```

When adding a `MapView` to your application, the following lines of code should be present in the XML layout. The ID of the `MapView` is `map`.

```
<com.google.android.maps.MapView
android:id="@+id/map"
android:layout_width="fill_parent"
android:layout_height="wrap_content"
android:layout_below="@id/map_location_button"
android:layout_above="@+id/use_this_location_button"
android:clickable="true"
android:apiKey="Your API Key Should be placed here"/>
```

In the Java class for the activity that displays the `MapView`, add a field:

```
private MyLocationOverlay myLocationOverlay;
```

Also, get a handle to the `MapView` defined in the XML and add a `MyLocationOverlay`. After that, call the `invalidate()` method.

```
mapView = (MapView)findViewById(R.id.map);
myLocationOverlay = new MyLocationOverlay(this, mapView);
mapView.getOverlays().add(myLocationOverlay);
mapView.invalidate();
```

To prevent depletion of battery power, in the `onPause` method of the class the `disable MyLocation()` method should be called, similar to what was done in Example 16-2. (See Example 16-11.)

Example 16-11. Providing onPause and onResume to conserve battery life

```
@Override
    protected void onPause() {
            super.onPause();
        myLocationOverlay.disableMyLocation();
    }

    @Override
    protected void onResume() {
        super.onResume();
```

```
    myLocationOverlay.enableMyLocation();
}
```

Source Download URL

You can download the source code for this example from *https://docs.google.com/leaf ?id=0B_rESQKgad5LZGU1ZmIzYjUtZTY3OS00MjczLWIxNDAtN zY4NjI5ZWJmMzZj&hl=en_US&authkey=CNb-xe8C.*

16.8 Drawing a Location Marker on a Google MapView

Johan Pelgrim

Problem

You have a geolocation and you want to display it on a Google `MapView`.

Solution

Create an instance of `Overlay`, draw your marker in it, and add it to the `MapView` overlays. Animate to the given geopoint.

Discussion

Create a new project called "Location on Map" and use Recipe 16.6 to set it up correctly (or simply use the `MapTest` code from that recipe). If all's well you should have an `onCreate` that looks like this:

```
@Override
public void onCreate(Bundle savedInstanceState) {
    super.onCreate(savedInstanceState);
    setContentView(R.layout.main);

    MapView mapView = (MapView) findViewById(R.id.mapview);
    mapView.setBuiltInZoomControls(true);

}
```

We are going to make this app a little more interesting. First we are going to set the view type to *satellite* so that we are shown some more recognizable terrain information:

```
mapView.setSatellite(true);
```

Run your application to see the effect.

You can add traffic information by calling `setTraffic`, but that works best with map information, not terrain information.

We can drag and zoom around on this map, but let's automatically animate to a certain geolocation. First, create a private field called `geoPoint` and set it to some geolocation. Note that the `GeoPoint` constructor takes integer arguments for the latitude and longitude values and not floating points! You can convert a floating-point latitude-longitude pair by multiplying it by 1 million, or `1E6` in Java terms:

```
GeoPoint geoPoint = new GeoPoint( (int) (52.334822 * 1E6), (int) (4.668907 * 1E6));
```

We need a handle to the `MapView`'s `MapController` to set the zoom level and animate to a given `GeoPoint`:

```
MapController mc = mapView.getController();
mc.setZoom(18);
mc.animateTo(geoPoint);
```

Pretty easy. Fire up the application to see what we've done here. Play around with the zoom level. What is the minimum value you can set? What is the maximum value?

The technique used to display way markers, your current location and other points of interest, on a map is done with *overlays* (see Figure 16-4). You can think of an overlay as you've probably seen them in the old days, used in combination with an overhead projector. Overlays can be seen as those transparent plastic sheets, which sometimes had graphics or text on them. You can layer several overlays on a single `MapView`.

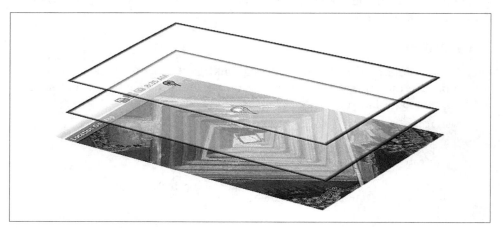

Figure 16-4. Map overlays

Create a private inner class that extends `Overlay` and override the `draw` method. We're calling this class `MyOverlay`, which (unlike in Recipe 16.7) actually is an example class (see Example 16-12).

Example 16-12. The MyOverlay class

```
private class MyOverlay extends com.google.android.maps.Overlay {

    @Override
    public void draw(Canvas canvas, MapView mapView, boolean shadow) { ❶
        super.draw(canvas, mapView, shadow);

        if (!shadow) { ❷

            Point point = new Point();
            mapView.getProjection().toPixels(geoPoint, point); ❸

            Bitmap bmp =
                BitmapFactory.decodeResource(getResources(), R.drawable.marker_default); ❹

            int x = point.x - bmp.getWidth() / 2; ❺

            int y = point.y - bmp.getHeight(); ❻

            canvas.drawBitmap(bmp, x, y, null); ❼
        }

    }

}
```

A couple of things are done here:

❶ The draw method has a couple of arguments. The first argument is a handle to an instance of `Canvas` which we will use to draw our marker on. The second is an instance of `MapView` on which this overlay is displayed. The third argument is a boolean that indicates whether we are drawing the actual image, or the shadow. In fact, this method is called twice: once to draw the shadow and once to draw the actual thing you want to draw.

❷ We don't want to draw a shadow.

❸ We translate the geopoint to actual pixels and store this information in the `point` variable.

❹ We use the resource identifier to decode it to an actual instance of `Bitmap` so that we can draw it on the canvas

❺ We calculate the *x* coordinate of where to draw the marker. We shift it to the left so that the *center* of the image is aligned with the *x* coordinate of the geopoint.

❻ We calculate the *y* coordinate of where to draw the marker. We shift it upward so that the *bottom* of the image is aligned with the *y* coordinate of the geopoint.

❼ We draw the bitmap at the calculated x and y locations.

You can use this image as the *marker_default.png*. Drop it in your *./res/drawable* directory.

You can manipulate the overlays by calling `getOverlays()` on the `MapView` instance:

```
List<Overlay> overlays = mapView.getOverlays();
overlays.clear();
overlays.add(new MyOverlay());

mapView.invalidate();
```

To force a view to draw, call the `invalidate()` method, which is implemented in the `View` class.

That's it. Fire it up and you should see something like Figure 16-5.

Figure 16-5. The marker on a Google map

See Also

Recipe 16.6

Source Download URL

You can download the source code for this example from *https://github.com/downloads/jpelgrim/androidcookbook/LocationOnMap.zip*.

16.9 Drawing Multiple Location Markers on a MapView

Johan Pelgrim

Problem

You have several geopoints that you want to display on a Google `MapView`.

Solution

Implement the `ItemizedOverlay` *abstract* class and add various `OverlayItem`s to it.

Discussion

Introduction

If you want to draw multiple location markers in your `MapView` you can, of course, take the approach of implementing the `Overlay` interface and do all the resource gathering and drawing in an overridden `draw()` method, as was done in Recipe 16.8. This can become cumbersome and hard to maintain. If you want to do *core* drawing of lines and shapes you cannot avoid overriding the `draw()` method, but when it comes down to drawing several simple location markers and handling user clicks on those markers (to name something) the Google Maps API has introduced the `ItemizedOverlay`. This *abstract* class is meant to maintain a list of `Overlay` items and display it as an aggregated `Overlay` on the `MapView`. `ItemizedOverlay` itself implements the `Overlay` interface. Besides that, it implements sorting *north-to-south* for drawing, creating span bounds, drawing a marker for each point, and maintaining a focused item. It also matches screen-taps to items, and dispatches focus-change events to an optional listener. This looks like the right candidate to display a couple of location markers on our `MapView`.

Adding the ItemizedOverlay to your MapView

Let's begin with the skeleton Google Maps project described in Recipe 16.6; alternatively, you can create your own and refer to the checklist at the end of this recipe to make sure you are good to go.

Add an inner class to your `MapActivity` that extends `ItemizedOverlay` and implements the abstract methods and the default constructor. The `ItemizedOverlay` uses your implementations of the `createItem` and `size()` methods to get hold of all the overlay items in your implementation and do the aggregation. (See Example 16-13.)

Example 16-13. The ItemizedOverlay implementation

```
private class MyItemizedOverlay extends ItemizedOverlay<OverlayItem> {

    public MyItemizedOverlay(Drawable defaultMarker) {
        super(defaultMarker);
    }

    @Override
    protected OverlayItem createItem(int i) {
        return null;
    }

    @Override
    public int size() {
        return 0;
    }
}
```

The `defaultMarker` is a drawable that is drawn on every `OverlayItem` we add to our `ItemizedOverlay`. Whenever you add a drawable to an `OverlayItem` you must set its bounding rectangle via the `setBounds` method. Or you can use one of the two convenience methods `boundCenterBottom` or `boundCenter`, which sets the bounding rectangle to the center-bottom or the center, respectively. Note: a call to `boundCenterBottom` basically results in this call to `setBounds` (given `marker` is an instance of `Drawable`: `marker.setBounds(-marker.getIntrinsicWidth()/2, -marker.getIntrinsicHeight(), marker.getIntrinsicWidth() /2, 0);`. Typically the constructor is rewritten like this:

```
public MyItemizedOverlay(Drawable defaultMarker) {
    super(boundCenterBottom(defaultMarker));
}
```

We want to add several `OverlayItem` instances, so we add a `List` to this inner type and modify the `createItem(int i)` and `size()` methods to use our new list (see Example 16-14).

Example 16-14. Multiple OverlayItems

```
private List<OverlayItem> mOverlays = new ArrayList<OverlayItem>();

@Override
protected OverlayItem createItem(int i) {
```

```
        return mOverlays.get(i);
    }

    @Override
    public int size() {
        return mOverlays.size();
    }
```

So far so good. Now we add a convenience method to add OverlayItems to our internal list.

```
    public void addOverlayItem(OverlayItem overlayItem) {
        mOverlays.add(overlayItem);
        populate();
    }
```

The populate() method is a utility method that performs all processing on a new ItemizedOverlay. We provide Items through the createItem(int) method. A good rule of thumb is to call this as soon as we have data in our ItemizedOverlay, before anything else gets called.

We're basically done with our inner class. Let's add some statements to our onCreate method of the surrounding MapActivity to add some OverlayItems to our implementation of ItemizedOverlay.

Using MyItemizedOverlay in onCreate

Let's expand our onCreate method and create an instance of our MyItemizedOverlay inner type.

```
    Drawable markerDefault = this.getResources().getDrawable(R.drawable.marker_default);
    MyItemizedOverlay itemizedOverlay = new MyItemizedOverlay(markerDefault);
```

Now let's add some overlay items. When creating an OverlayItem we must provide three things to the constructor: one GeoPoint and two Strings, one for the title and one for an additional snippet of text. Let's add an OverlayItem for the city of Amsterdam.

```
    GeoPoint point = new GeoPoint(52372991, 4892655);
    OverlayItem overlayItem = new OverlayItem(point, "Amsterdam", null);
    itemizedOverlay.addOverlayItem(overlayItem);
```

Let's add another convenience method to our MyItemizedOverlay inner type that basically takes two int values for *latitude* and *longitude* and a String for a title.

```
    public void addOverlayItem(int lat, int lon, String title) {
        GeoPoint point = new GeoPoint(lat, lon);
        OverlayItem overlayItem = new OverlayItem(point, title, null);
        addOverlayItem(overlayItem);
    }
```

We can now rewrite our addition of the Amsterdam OverlayItem and add two more, one for London and one for Paris.

```
itemizedOverlay.addOverlayItem(52372991, 4892655, "Amsterdam");
itemizedOverlay.addOverlayItem(51501851, -140623, "London");
itemizedOverlay.addOverlayItem(48857522, 2294496, "Paris");
```

The next step is to add our itemized overlay to the MapViews overlays. We get a handle to the list of overlays with a call to getOverlays().

```
mapView.getOverlays().add(itemizedOverlay);
```

Finally, we manipulate the MapView's MapController to show the right area and zoom level on our MapView. We set the center to a GeoPoint of Dunkerque, which appears to be a nice center. There is no getCenter() convenience method in the ItemizedOverlay class, but this is something you can easily implement yourself if you want to. We can set the zoom level to a fixed level, but the ItemizedOverlay class does have some nice methods to calculate the span that covers all its overlay items. We use this to call zoomToSpan on the MapController instance.

```
MapController mc = mapView.getController();
mc.setCenter(new GeoPoint(51035349, 2370987)); // Dunkerque, Belgium
mc.zoomToSpan(itemizedOverlay.getLatSpanE6(), itemizedOverlay.getLonSpanE6());
```

We're done! When you fire up your app you should see something like Figure 16-6.

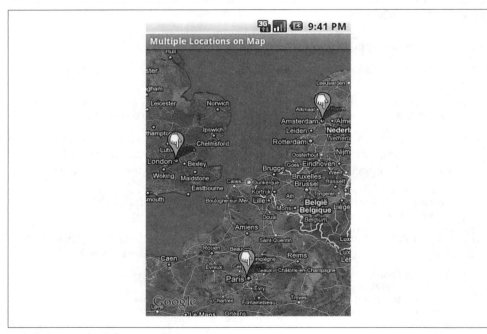

Figure 16-6. Multiple location markers on one map

Extra exercise: Draw an alternate marker. Search Google for some nice 100 × 100 pixel markers and place them in your *./res/drawable* directory. Add these drawables as an extra argument to your `addOverlayItem` convenience method. When you create your `OverlayItem` instance use the `setMarker(Drawable drawable)` method to assign a different marker drawable. Remember to set the bounds by calling the `boundCenterBottom` or `boundCenter` convenience method, or do the math yourself and call `setBounds`. Good luck! (The accompanying source code has the solution if these hints are not sufficient.)

Do something when the user clicks your marker. Finally, the `ItemizedOverlay` class has some nice features to handle taps and focus changes on your overlay items. In this final section we will implement the `onTap(int index)` method to show a `Toast` message which displays our overlay item's title. Of course, you can do whatever you want when a user taps your marker: show a dialog or another activity, draw a view on the map with `addView`, and so on. As you will see, this could not be simpler!

```
@Override protected boolean onTap(int index) {
    Toast.makeText(MainActivity.this, getItem(index).getTitle(),
    Toast.LENGTH_LONG).show();
    return true;
}
```

We return `true` to indicate we have handled the tap event. If we return `false` the `onTap` is executed for all the overlay items in our `ItemizedOverlay`.

Again, when taking your app for a spin, you should see something like Figure 16-7 when you tap near your Paris location marker.

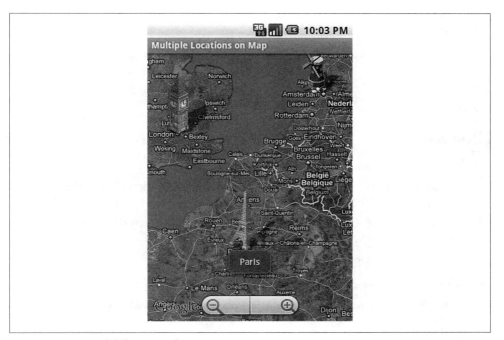

Figure 16-7. Several different markers on one map

See Also

Recipe 16.6

Source Download URL

You can download the source code for this example from *https://github.com/downloads/jpelgrim/androidcookbook/MultipleLocationsOnMap.zip*.

16.10 Creating Overlays for a Google MapView

Rachee Singh

Problem

You need to demarcate a point on a Google map using an image.

Solution

Use the concept of map overlays.

Discussion

Creating your own map overlay is a two-step process:

1. Extend the `Overlay` class and implement the required functionality (the type and characteristics of the overlay) in that class. This is shown in Example 16-15.

2. Another class that controls that Google map on the screen then instantiates the class that extends `Overlay`.

```
public class AddressOverlay extends Overlay
```

Example 16-15. Constructor initialization in the AddressOverlay class

```
public AddressOverlay(Context context, Address address, int drawable) {
        super();
        this.context=context;
        this.drawable=drawable;
```

```
        assert(null != address);
        this.setAddress(address);
        Double convertedLongitude = address.getLongitude() * 1E6;
        Double convertedLatitude = address.getLatitude() * 1E6;

        setGeopoint(new GeoPoint(
                convertedLatitude.intValue(),
                convertedLongitude.intValue()));
    }
```

Override the `draw()` method of the `Overlay` class, as shown in Example 16-16.

Example 16-16. Drawing the overlay

```
@Override
    public boolean draw(Canvas canvas, MapView mapView, boolean shadow, long when) {
        super.draw(canvas, mapView, shadow);
        Point locationPoint = new Point();
        Projection projection = mapView.getProjection();
        projection.toPixels(getGeopoint(), locationPoint);

        // Reading the image
        Bitmap markerImage =
            BitmapFactory.decodeResource(context.getResources(), drawable);

        // Drawing the image, keeping the center of the image at the address's location
        canvas.drawBitmap(markerImage,locationPoint.x - markerImage.getWidth() / 2,
        locationPoint.y - markerImage.getHeight() / 2, null);
        return true;
    }
```

In the class that is implementing the map view's function, add the code in Example 16-17 to add an overlay on the map.

Example 16-17. Instantiating the overlay implementation

```
List<Overlay> mapOverlays = mapView.getOverlays();
// Instantiating the AddressOverlay class we just defined
// 'androidmarker' is the name of the image that you wish to place on the map
AddressOverlay addressOverlay =
    new AddressOverlay(this, address, R.drawable.androidmarker);
// adding the overlay to the map
mapOverlays.add(addressOverlay);
mapView.invalidate();
```

16.11 Changing Modes of a Google MapView

Rachee Singh

Problem

You want to set the appropriate mode of a `MapView`—map, street, or satellite—based on the context in the application.

Solution

The `MapView` class provides methods for changing the mode of a map from the default (map) mode to satellite or street mode.

Discussion

If the application needs to display distance information between two locations on the map, keeping the map in street mode is more suitable. Similarly, some applications might need to use the satellite view of Google maps. You can do this programmatically using the following code:

```
//For street view
mapView.setStreetView(true);

//For satellite view
mapView.setSatellite(true);
```

16.12 Drawing an Overlay Icon Without Using a Drawable

Keith Mendoza

Problem

You want to display a map overlay in a `MapView` without using `Drawable` objects.

Solution

Override the `ItemizedOverlay`'s `draw()` function.

Discussion

This recipe assumes that you have at least done the "Hello, MapView" tutorial in Recipe 16.1, so I will not cover what abstract functions you need to implement from `ItemizedOverlay`. The complete source code for the sample app, Nearby Metars 01.01.0.2, is available for download, so some of the code for the classes mentioned will not be shown in full.

Overview

Nearby Metars displays the cloud condition icon and the direction part of the wind near an airport as an overlay on a `MapView`. This icon is drawn in such a way that the cloud condition covers the scale equivalent of about one mile around the airport. For anyone curious here is the description of METAR taken from the METARs help page (*http://aviationweather.gov/adds/metars/description.php*) provided by NOAA's Aviation Weather Center:

Weather stations all over the world report weather conditions every hour using a data format referred to as METAR (this is a French acronym with a loose English translation to "routine aviation weather observation"). These data are collected centrally by the U.S. National Weather Service (and other country's equivalents) and distributed.

Page 4 (*http://aviationweather.gov/adds/metars/description/page_no/4*) of the help page shows the cloud coverage icons. These are the icons that need to be drawn as an overlay over the airport to depict the cloud coverage. The wind barb points the wind direction (it's actually the direction the wind is coming from).

Overriding the ItemizedOverlay::draw() function

`ItemizedOverlay::draw()` is called whenever the `MapView` needs to be redrawn for whatever reason. Here is the function signature of the `draw()` function:

```
public void draw(android.graphics.Canvas canvas,
                 MapView mapView,
                 boolean shadow)
```

Here are the parameter descriptions taken from the API document:

canvas
> The `Canvas` upon which to draw. Note that this may already have a transformation applied, so be sure to leave it the way you found it.

mapView
> The `MapView` that requested the draw. Use `MapView.getProjection()` to convert between on-screen pixels and latitude/longitude pairs.

shadow
> If `true`, draw the shadow layer. If `false`, draw the overlay contents.

Each time the screen is redrawn the `draw()` function will be called twice: once when `shadow` is `true`, and again when `shadow` is `false`. For Nearby Metars there is no need to draw shadows in overlay items.

For Nearby Metars, `MetarList` is the `MetarItem`-specific implementation of `ItemizedOverlay`. This class overrides the abstract functions, and the `draw()` function. This is the code for `MetarList::draw()`:

```
public void draw(android.graphics.Canvas canvas, MapView mapView, boolean shadow) {
    if(!shadow) {
    Log.v("NearbyMetars", "Drawing items");
    MetarItem item;
    for(int i=0; i<mOverlays.size(); i++) {
        item = mOverlays.get(i);
        item.draw(canvas, mapView);
        }
    }
}
```

`mOverlays` is an instance of `ArrayList<MetarItem>`. Whenever `draw()` is called, we iterate through `mOverlays` and call `MetarItem::draw()`. This implementation makes `Metar List` and `MetarItem` tightly coupled for the sake of performance.

Overview of the MetarItem class

This class is a subclass of `OverlayItem`. The `mTitle` and `mSnippet` fields inherited from `OverlayItem` are used for the ICAO (International Civil Aviation Organization) airport codes, and the raw metar string, respectively. Two fields are added in `MetarItem`:

skyCond
> This is an instance of the `SkyConds` enumerated type defined inside `MetarItem`.

windDir
> This is a `float` value to store the wind direction.

Overview of the MetarItem::draw() function

This is where the real work of drawing the icon onto the canvas happens. In the METAR charts from ADDS, the cloud condition icons are drawn using the colors to depict the flight category in effect for that airport; however, as of version 01.01.0.2 Nearby Metars doesn't depict the flight category, so the icons are all black. For clarity, the code is broken into sections and the explanation follows each code snippet.

```
public void draw(Canvas canvas, MapView mapView) {
```

This function takes two parameters: `canvas` and `mapView`. These two parameters have the same types as the first two parameters of `ItemizedOverlay::draw()`.

```
//Get the bounds of the icon
Point point = new Point();
Projection projection = mapView.getProjection();
projection.toPixels(mPoint, point);
```

First we convert the latitude, longitude coordinates of the airport to (x,y) coordinates. `Projection::toPixels()` takes a `GeoPoint` object that stores the latitude, longitude of the location that will be marked by the overlay as the first parameter, and a `Point` instance to store the (x,y) coordinates of that location in the `MapView` canvas.

```
final float project =
(float)((projection.metersToEquatorPixels((float)1609.344) > 10) ?
    projection.metersToEquatorPixels((float)1609.344) : 10.0);
Log.d("NearbyMetars", "Value of project: " + Float.toString(project));
final RectF drawPos = new RectF(point.x-project, point.y-project,
    point.x+project, point.y+project);
```

We then calculate how many pixels one mile would be, given the map's current zoom level. Next, we calculate the bounding coordinates of the icon to be drawn in as a `RectF` instance (*http://developer.android.com/reference/android/graphics/RectF.html*).

```
//Get the paint to use for drawing the icons
Paint paint = new Paint();
paint.setStyle(Paint.Style.STROKE);
```

```
paint.setARGB(179, 0, 0, 0);
paint.setStrokeWidth(2.0f);
paint.setStrokeCap(Paint.Cap.BUTT);
```

A `Paint` object (*http://developer.android.com/reference/android/graphics/Paint.html*) is instantiated and set to draw a 2-pixel thick black line at about 70% transparency. The reason to not make the cloud condition icons drawn completely opaque is to allow the user to read the labels on the map. Remember, the cloud icons are drawn on top of the map in a layered fashion. See Example 16-18.

Example 16-18. Drawing the icon

```
switch(skyCond) {
    case CLR:
        canvas.drawRect(drawPos, paint);
        break;
    case SKC:
        canvas.drawCircle(point.x, point.y, project, paint);
        break;
    case FEW:
        canvas.drawCircle(point.x, point.y, project, paint);
        canvas.drawLine(point.x, drawPos.top, point.x, drawPos.bottom, paint);
        break;
    case SCT:
        canvas.drawArc(drawPos, 0, 270, false, paint);
        paint.setStyle(Paint.Style.FILL_AND_STROKE);
        canvas.drawArc(drawPos, 270, 90, true, paint);
        break;
    case BKN:
        canvas.drawArc(drawPos, 180, 90, false, paint);
        paint.setStyle(Paint.Style.FILL_AND_STROKE);
        canvas.drawArc(drawPos, 270, 270, true, paint);
        break;
    case OVC:
        paint.setStyle(Paint.Style.FILL_AND_STROKE);
        canvas.drawCircle(point.x, point.y, project, paint);
        break;
    case OVX:
        canvas.drawArc(drawPos, 45, 180, true, paint);
        canvas.drawArc(drawPos, 135, 180, true, paint);
        canvas.drawArc(drawPos, 315, 90, true, paint);
        break;
}
```

The code in Example 16-18 renders the cloud condition icons based on the value of `skyCond`. Please see the `Canvas` reference (*http://developer.android.com/reference/android/graphics/Canvas.html*) for the description of the `draw*()` functions. Drawing the icons for `CLR` and `SKC` is straightforward: call the appropriate `draw*()` function. `FEW` calls a `drawCircle()` to draw the circular outline, and then calls `drawLine()` to draw the vertical line. In the case of this icon, it won't matter if `drawLine()` was called first instead of `drawCircle()`. However, it would be good to remember that successive calls to the `draw*()` function over the same area will draw shapes on top of one another.

Conditions such as SKT, BKN, and OVC first call drawArc() to draw the unfilled portion of the icon, and then switch the pen style to FILL_AND_STROKE and call drawArc() again to complete the circle with the filled portion of the icon. The use of drawArc() on these icons is actually an optimization. Canvas::drawCircle() actually calls Canvas::drawArc() under the hood. Why render a graphic that will simply be covered by another graphic drawn in the same location?

```
//Draw the wind bar if wind is NOT variable
if(windDir > 0)
{
    final float barLen = project * 3;

    //This has been modified to go the opposite direction of
    //standard polar to Cartesian plotting
    canvas.drawLine(point.x, point.y,
        (float)(point.x + barLen * Math.sin(windDir)),
        (float)(point.y - barLen * Math.cos(windDir)), paint);
}
}
```

This last portion of code draws the wind barb without the wind speed lines. As the comment states, this function calculates the Cartesian coordinate with the angle going in a clockwise direction since that's how compass directions go. The standard mathematic polar coordinates have angles going in a counterclockwise direction. Another thing to note is that the value of project is actually the radian equivalent of the wind compass direction.

Final thoughts

Using the Canvas::draw*() functions is not necessarily the best way to draw the overlay icons. Android can render drawable resources (*http://developer.android.com/guide/top ics/resources/drawable-resource.html*) in a more optimized manner than calling the Canvas::draw*() functions; and it's easier to create great-looking images using an image editor. If the overlays for Nearby Metars were done using drawable resources, editing the XML files would be cumbersome; using bitmaps will just be a resource hog. Whether to use drawable or to programmatically draw the overlay icon will depend largely on the project's requirements.

See Also

Hello, MapView tutorial (*http://developer.android.com/guide/tutorials/views/hello-map view.html*); Canvas class reference (*http://developer.android.com/reference/android/ graphics/Canvas.html*); ItemizedOverlay class reference (*http://code.google.com/an droid/add-ons/google-apis/reference/com/google/android/maps/ItemizedOverlay.html*); OverlayItem class reference (*http://code.google.com/android/add-ons/google-apis/refer ence/com/google/android/maps/OverlayItem.html*); Google Add-On API reference (*http: //code.google.com/android/add-ons/google-apis/reference/index.html*)

Source Download URL

You can download the source code for this example from *https://github.com/keithmendozasr/NearbyMetars/zipball/01.01.0.2.*

Binary Download URL

You can download the executable code for this example from *https://github.com/downloads/keithmendozasr/NearbyMetars/NearbyMetars-01.01.0.2.apk.*

16.13 Implementing Location Search on Google Maps

Rachee Singh

Problem

You want to let the user type in the name of a place and find it using Google Maps, giving the user a list of all the results and displaying the most appropriate location result.

Solution

The text the user enters into an EditText is extracted. It is searched and the search results are extracted. The best out of the location search results is displayed (in this sample, the results are just displayed as a toast; in a real app much more could be done with the data).

Discussion

This method obtains text from an EditText named addressText. Then this text is searched for using the getFromLocationName() method of the Geocoder class. From the search results obtained the first result is extracted and displayed as a toast. If the string returned is of size=0, an appropriate message is displayed. Example 16-19 shows the code. Figure 16-8 shows the result.

Example 16-19. Searching for a location with Google Maps

```
protected void mapCurrentAddress() {
    String addressString = addressText.getText().toString();
    Geocoder g = new Geocoder(this);
    List<Address> addresses;
    try {
        addresses = g.getFromLocationName(addressString, 1);
        String add = "";
        if (addresses.size() > 0) {

            address = addresses.get(0);
            for (int i=0; i < address.getMaxAddressLineIndex();i++) {
                add += address.getAddressLine(i) + "\n";
            }
            Toast.makeText(getBaseContext(), add, Toast.LENGTH_SHORT).show();

        } else {
            Toast.makeText(getBaseContext(),
                "Failed to locate this address.", Toast.LENGTH_SHORT).show();
        }
    } catch (IOException e) {
        e.printStackTrace();
    }
}
```

Figure 16-8. Map showing on the first tab

16.14 Placing a MapView Inside a TabView

Vladimir Kroz

Problem

You want to place a `MapView` object within a `TabView`.

Solution

Create a `MapView` and corresponding XML layout, and make sure it runs in standalone mode. Then create a `TabView` and corresponding XML layout. Finally, attach a `Map View` activity to one of the tabs using `TabSpec.setContent()`. That's it!

Discussion

For this recipe to work, you need a Google Maps API key, as we obtained in Recipe 16.6.

The structure of the typical `TabLayout` (Figure 16-9) includes `TabHost` as a container, `TabWidget` to draw tabs, and `FrameLayout` with a predefined ID of `@android:id/tabcon tent` to contain the interchangeable content. Example 16-20 shows the code for the XML layout.

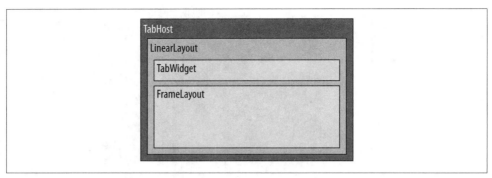

Figure 16-9. Tab layout

Example 16-20. XML layout for tabs

```xml
<?xml version="1.0" encoding="utf-8"?>
<TabHost xmlns:android="http://schemas.android.com/apk/res/android"
android:id="@android:id/tabhost"
android:layout_width="fill_parent" android:layout_height="fill_parent">
<LinearLayout android:orientation="vertical"
android:layout_width="fill_parent" android:layout_height="fill_parent">
<TabWidget android:id="@android:id/tabs"
android:layout_width="fill_parent" android:layout_height="wrap_content"/>
<FrameLayout android:id="@android:id/tabcontent"
android:layout_width="fill_parent" android:layout_height="fill_parent">
<RelativeLayout android:id="@+id/emptylayout1" android:orientation="vertical"
android:layout_width="fill_parent" android:layout_height="fill_parent"/>
<TextView android:id="@+id/textview2"
android:layout_width="fill_parent"
android:layout_height="fill_parent"
android:text="Details Details Details Details"/>
</FrameLayout>
</LinearLayout>
</TabHost>
```

Code for the `MapView` layout follows, in Example 16-21.

Example 16-21. XML layout for MapView

```xml
<?xml version="1.0" encoding="utf-8"?>
<RelativeLayout xmlns:android="http://schemas.android.com/apk/res/android"
android:id="@+id/maptablayout" android:orientation="vertical"
android:layout_width="fill_parent" android:layout_height="fill_parent">
<com.google.android.maps.MapView android:id="@+id/mapview"
android:layout_width="fill_parent" android:layout_height="fill_parent"
android:clickable="true"
android:apiKey="OpFtdSwta8EMTfArj32ycOw2kZgOLSEqa4fUGFA"/>
</RelativeLayout>
```

The code in Example 16-22 is the application entry point.

Example 16-22. AppMain.java

```java
package org.kroztech.cookbook;

import android.app.TabActivity;
import android.content.Context;
import android.content.Intent;
import android.os.Bundle;
import android.widget.FrameLayout;
import android.widget.TabHost;
import android.widget.TabHost.TabSpec;

public class AppMain extends TabActivity  {
 TabHost mTabHost;
 FrameLayout mFrameLayout;

 /** Called when the activity is first created.*/
 @Override
 public void onCreate(Bundle savedInstanceState) {
     super.onCreate(savedInstanceState);
     setContentView(R.layout.main);
     mTabHost = getTabHost();
     TabSpec tabSpec = mTabHost.newTabSpec("tab_test1");
     tabSpec.setIndicator("Map");
     Context ctx = this.getApplicationContext();
     Intent i = new Intent(ctx, MapTabView.class);
     tabSpec.setContent(i);
     mTabHost.addTab(tabSpec);
     mTabHost.addTab(
         mTabHost.newTabSpec("tab_test2").setIndicator("Details").setContent(R.id.textview2));
     mTabHost.setCurrentTab(0);
 }
}
```

The `MapActivity` follows, in Example 16-23.

Example 16-23. The MapActivity

```java
package org.kroztech.cookbook;

import android.os.Bundle;
import com.google.android.maps.MapActivity;

public class MapTabView extends MapActivity {
 @Override
 protected void onCreate(Bundle icicle) {
     super.onCreate(icicle);
     setContentView(R.layout.maptabview);
 }
 @Override
 protected boolean isRouteDisplayed() {
   return false;
 }
}
```

Finally, Example 16-24 shows the manifest file.

Example 16-24. The AndroidManifest.xml file

```xml
<?xml version="1.0" encoding="utf-8"?>
<manifest xmlns:android="http://schemas.android.com/apk/res/android"
   package="com.kroz.tag" android:versionCode="1" android:versionName="1.0">
 <application android:icon="@drawable/icon" android:label="@string/app_name">
    <uses-library android:name="com.google.android.maps"/>
    <activity android:name=".AppMain" android:label="@string/app_name">
       <intent-filter>
           <action android:name="android.intent.action.MAIN"/>
           <category android:name="android.intent.category.LAUNCHER"/>
       </intent-filter>
    </activity>
    <activity android:name="MapTabView" android:label="@string/mapview_name">
       <intent-filter>
           <category android:name="android.intent.category.EMBED"></category>
           <action android:name="android.intent.action.MAIN"></action>
       </intent-filter>
    </activity>
 </application>
 <uses-sdk android:minSdkVersion="3"/>
 <uses-permission android:name="android.permission.INTERNET"/>
 <uses-permission android:name="android.permission.ACCESS_COARSE_LOCATION"/>
 <uses-permission android:name="android.permission.ACCESS_FINE_LOCATION"/>
 <uses-permission android:name="android.permission.ACCESS_LOCATION_EXTRA_COMMANDS"/>
</manifest>
```

Source Download URL

You can download the source code for this example from *http://www.kroztech.com/res/ android_cookbook/src/MapTabViewDemo.zip*i.

16.15 Handling a Long-Press in a MapView

Roger Kind Kristiansen

Problem

For some map applications you might want to let the user trigger an action related to an arbitrary point on the map—for example, through a context menu. Enabling the user to do a long-press on the map is among the more intuitive ways to expose this kind of functionality, but support for this is not built into Android.

Solution

Add this support yourself. Start by creating a subclass of `MapView`, in which you define your own `OnLongpressListener` interface as well as overriding `MapView.onTouchEvent()` to insert your long-press detection logic. `onTouchEvent()` is triggered every time the user touches, moves, or releases her finger on the map, which makes this the perfect place for your purposes.

After modifying your map layout file and using this map as the content of a `MapActivity`, you can finally create an `OnLongPressListener` object, add it to your `MapView` subclass object, and enjoy some long-press action.

Discussion

We will start with the meat of the solution: subclassing `MapView`, defining our `OnLongpressListener` interface, and implementing the logic to catch when a user performs a long-press (see Example 16-25).

Example 16-25. A long-pressable MapView

```
public class MyCustomMapView extends MapView {

    // Define the listener interface we will make use of in our MapActivity later.
    public interface OnLongpressListener {
        public void onLongpress(MapView view, GeoPoint longpressLocation);
    }

    // Time in ms before the OnLongpressListener is triggered.
    static final int LONGPRESS_THRESHOLD = 500;

    /*
     * The Timer will be instrumental in detecting our long-presses. It executes a
     * task after a given amount of time.
     */
    private Timer longpressTimer = new Timer();

    /*
     * Our OnLongPressListener instance. When a long-press is detected, its
     * onLongPress() method is called.
     */
```

```
private MyCustomMapView.OnLongpressListener longpressListener;

/*
 * Keep a record of the center of the map, to know if the map
 * has been panned.
 */
private GeoPoint lastMapCenter;

public MyCustomMapView(Context context, String apiKey) {
    super(context, apiKey);
}

public MyCustomMapView(Context context, AttributeSet attrs) {
    super(context, attrs);
}

public MyCustomMapView(Context context, AttributeSet attrs, int defStyle) {
    super(context, attrs, defStyle);
}

public void setOnLongpressListener(MyCustomMapView.OnLongpressListener listener) {
    longpressListener = listener;
}

/*
 * This method is called by Android every time the user touches the map,
 * drags a finger on the map, or removes a finger from the map.
 */
@Override
public boolean onTouchEvent(MotionEvent event) {
    // Perform our custom logic.
    handleLongpress(event);

    return super.onTouchEvent(event);
}

/*
 * This method takes MotionEvent as an argument and decides whether
 * or not a long-press has been detected.
 *
 * The Timer class executes a TimerTask after a given time,
 * and we start the timer when a finger touches the screen.
 *
 * We then listen for map movements or the finger being
 * removed from the screen. If any of these events occur
 * before the TimerTask is executed, it gets cancelled. Else
 * the OnLongPressListener.onLongpress() method is fired.
 */
private void handleLongpress(final MotionEvent event) {

    if (event.getAction() == MotionEvent.ACTION_DOWN) {
        // Finger has touched screen.
        longpressTimer = new Timer();
        longpressTimer.schedule(new TimerTask() {
            @Override
```

```
            public void run() {
                GeoPoint longpressLocation =
                    getProjection().fromPixels((int)event.getX(),
                    (int)event.getY());

                /*
                 * Fire the listener. We pass the map location
                 * of the long-press as well, in case it is needed
                 * by the caller.
                 */
                longpressListener.onLongpress(
                    MyCustomMapView.this, longpressLocation);
            }

        }, LONGPRESS_THRESHOLD);

        lastMapCenter = getMapCenter();
    }

    if (event.getAction() == MotionEvent.ACTION_MOVE) {

        if (!getMapCenter().equals(lastMapCenter)) {
            // User is panning the map, this is no long-press
            longpressTimer.cancel();
        }

        lastMapCenter = getMapCenter();
    }

    if (event.getAction() == MotionEvent.ACTION_UP) {
        // User has removed finger from map.
        longpressTimer.cancel();
    }

        if (event.getPointerCount() > 1) {
                // This is a multitouch event, probably zooming.
            longpressTimer.cancel();
        }
    }
}
```

We will need to modify our map layout file so that we make use of the MyCustomMap
View we just defined:

```
<?xml version="1.0" encoding="utf-8"?>
<RelativeLayout xmlns:android="http://schemas.android.com/apk/res/android"
    android:layout_width="fill_parent"
    android:layout_height="fill_parent">
    <com.example.MyCustomMapView android:id="@+id/mapview"
    android:layout_width="fill_parent"
    android:layout_height="fill_parent"
    android:apiKey="<YOUR MAP API KEY HERE>"
    android:clickable="true"/>
</RelativeLayout>
```

Make note of the android:clickable attribute. As you might know, this must be set to be able to pan, zoom, or in other ways interact with your map.

The last thing we need to do is add our onLongpressListener instance to the MapView in our MapActivity. For the sake of the example, let's say the previous layout file is named *res/layout/map.xml*. The necessary code for adding an OnLongPressListener will look something like Example 16-26.

Example 16-26. The map activity

```
public class Map extends MapActivity {
    private MyCustomMapView mapView;

    @Override
    public void onCreate(Bundle savedInstanceState) {
        super.onCreate(savedInstanceState);

        // Add our map layout to this MapActivity
        setContentView(R.layout.map);

        // Add the OnLongPressListener to our custom MapView
        mapView = (MyCustomMapView)findViewById(R.id.mapview);
        mapView.setOnLongpressListener(new MyCustomMapView.OnLongpressListener() {
        public void onLongpress(final MapView view, final GeoPoint longpressLocation) {
            runOnUiThread(new Runnable() {
            public void run() {
                /*
                 * Insert your long-press action here!
                 */
            }
        });
        }
    });
}
```

To actually have your long-press open up a context menu, you need to perform some additional setup of the context menu itself. I've avoided including this, to make the example shorter and hopefully clearer. To test that it works, try, for example, adding a log statement.

16.16 Using OpenStreetMap

Rachee Singh

Problem

You want to use OpenStreetMap (OSM) map data in your application in place of Google Maps.

Solution

Use the third-party osmdroid library to interact with OpenStreetMap data.

Discussion

OpenStreetMap is a free, editable map of the world. The `OpenStreetMapView` is an (almost) full/free replacement for Android's `MapView` class. See the osmdroid Google code page (*http://code.google.com/p/osmdroid/*) for more details.

To use OSM map data in your Android app, your project must be Android API level 3 (version 1.5) or higher. You need to include two JARs in the Android project, namely *osmdroid-android-x.xx.jar* and *slf4j-android-1.x.x.jar*. osmdroid is a set of tools for OpenStreetMap data; SLF4J is (yet another) simplified logging facade. You can download them from the following links:

- osmdroid   (*http://code.google.com/p/osmdroid/downloads/detail?name=osmdroid-android-3.0.5.jar*)
- slf4j (*http://www.slf4j.org/android/slf4j-android-1.5.8.jar*)

See Recipe 1.10 to learn how to use external libraries in your Android project.

After adding the JARs to the project you can start coding.

You need to add an OSM `MapView` to your XML layout, like so:

```
<LinearLayout xmlns:android="http://schemas.android.com/apk/res/android"
    android:orientation="vertical"
    android:layout_width="fill_parent"
    android:layout_height="fill_parent">
  <org.osmdroid.views.MapView
      android:layout_width="fill_parent"
      android:layout_height="fill_parent"
      android:id="@+id/mapview">
  </org.osmdroid.views.MapView>
</LinearLayout>
```

Remember that you need to include the `INTERNET` permission in the *AndroidManifest.xml* file for any app that downloads information over the Internet. The osmdroid code also needs `ACCESS_NETWORK_STATE` permission:

```
<uses-permission android:name="android.permission.ACCESS_NETWORK_STATE" />
<uses-permission android:name="android.permission.INTERNET" />
```

Now we have to use this `MapView` in the activity code. The process is similar to the case of using Google Maps (see Example 16-27).

Example 16-27. Using the MapView in the application

```
private MapView mapView;
private MapController mapController;
mapView = (MapView) this.findViewById(R.id.mapview);
mapView.setBuiltInZoomControls(true);
```

```
mapView.setMultiTouchControls(true);
mapController = this.mapView.getController();
mapController.setZoom(2);
```

Figure 16-10 shows how the application should look on initial startup. Figure 16-11 shows how it might look after the user has touched the zoom controls.

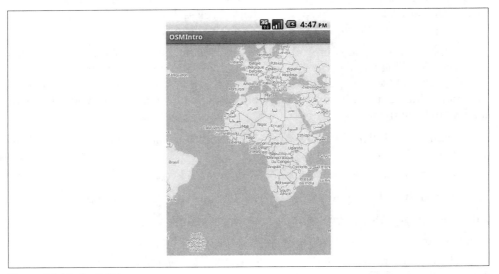

Figure 16-10. An OSM map

Figure 16-11. OSM map zoomed in

Source Download URL

You can download the source code for this example from *https://docs.google.com/leaf ?id=0B_rESQKgad5LYjIwYTM1NTctZTU3OS00NTE5LTg1NmItZTU4MGRkYTM zODJl&hl=en_US*.

Binary Download URL

You can download the executable code for this example from *https://docs.google.com/ leaf?id=0B_rESQKgad5LY2U5MzVlMGYtOWY1Ni00NThhLTg0MmItM zI2MDgyYzRjNzI5&hl=en_US*.

16.17 Creating Overlays in OpenStreetMap Maps

Rachee Singh

Problem

You want to display graphics such as map markers on your OpenStreetMap view. Most map mechanisms provide an overlay feature that lets you draw these graphics in front of the main picture or map. Refer back to Figure 16-4.

Solution

Instantiate an `Overlay` class and add the overlay to the point you wish to demarcate on the map.

Discussion

To get started with OpenStreetMap, see Recipe 16.16.

To add overlays, first we need to get a handle on the `MapView` defined in the XML layout of the activity.

```
mapView = (MapView) this.findViewById(R.id.mapview);
```

Then we enable zoom controls on the `MapView` using the `setBuiltInZoomControls` method and also set the zoom level to a reasonable value.

```
mapView.setBuiltInZoomControls(true);
        mapController = this.mapView.getController();
        mapController.setZoom(12);
```

Now we create two `GeoPoint`s; the first one (`mapCenter`) is to center the OSM map around the point when the application starts, and the second (`overlayPoint`) is where the overlay will be placed.

```
GeoPoint mapCenter = new GeoPoint(53554070, -2959520);
        GeoPoint overlayPoint = new GeoPoint(53554070 + 1000, -2959520 + 1000);
        mapController.setCenter(mapCenter);
```

To add the overlay, we create an `ArrayList` of `OverlayItems`. To this list, we will add the overlays we wish to add to the OSM map.

```
ArrayList<OverlayItem> overlays = new ArrayList<OverlayItem>();
        overlays.add(new OverlayItem("New Overlay", "Overlay Description", overlayPoint));
```

To create the overlay item, we need to instantiate the `ItemizedIconOverlay` class (along with appropriate arguments specifying the point at which the overlay has to be placed, resource proxy, etc.). Then we add the overlay to the OSM map.

```
resourceProxy = new DefaultResourceProxyImpl(getApplicationContext());
        this.myLocationOverlay = new ItemizedIconOverlay<OverlayItem>(
            overlays, null, resourceProxy);
        this.mapView.getOverlays().add(this.myLocationOverlay);
```

Then a call to the `invalidate` method is needed to update the `MapView` so that the user will see the changes we made to it.

```
mapView.invalidate();
```

The end result should look like Figure 16-12 and Figure 16-13.

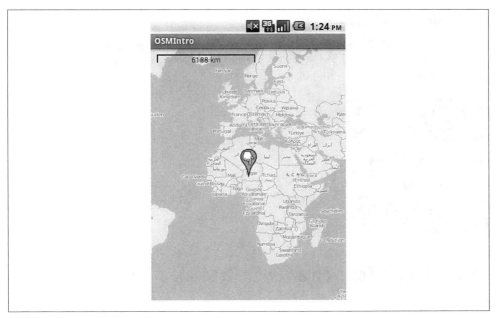

Figure 16-12. OSM map with marker overlay

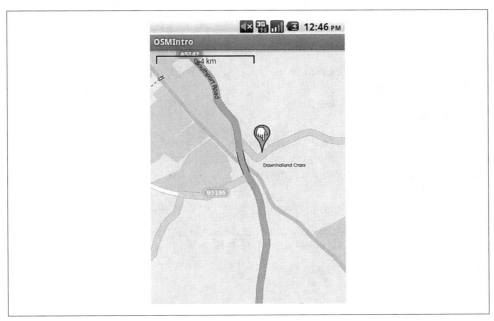

Figure 16-13. OSM map with marker overlay after zooming

Source Download URL

You can download the source code for this example from *https://docs.google.com/leaf ?id=0B_rESQKgad5LMThlYmI3ZjctMGU4ZS00ZDhjLWJjMGMtY WYwMTBmNzcxNzJl&hl=en_US*.

16.18 Using a Scale on an OpenStreetMap Map

Rachee Singh

Problem

You need to show a map scale on your OSM map to indicate the level of zoom on the `MapView`.

Solution

You can add a scale on the OSM map as an overlay using the osmdroid `ScaleBarOver lay` class.

Discussion

Putting a scale on your `MapView` helps the user keep track of the map's zoom level (as well as estimate distances on the map). To overlay a scale on your OSM `MapView`, instantiate the `ScaleBarOverlay` class and add it to the list of overlays in your `MapView` using the `add()` method.

Here is how the code would look:

```
ScaleBarOverlay myScaleBarOverlay = new ScaleBarOverlay(this);
this.mapView.getOverlays().add(this.myScaleBarOverlay);
```

The scale bar overlay is shown in Figure 16-14.

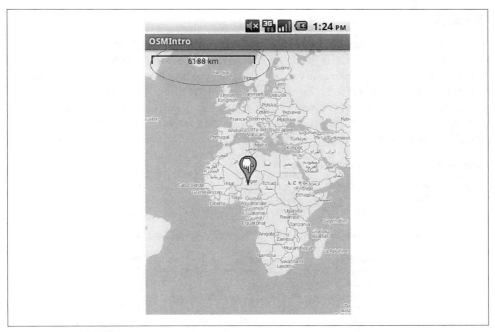

Figure 16-14. OSM map with scale

16.19 Handling Touch Events on an OpenStreetMap Overlay

Rachee Singh

Problem

You need to perform actions when the overlay on an OpenStreetMap map is tapped.

Solution

Override the methods of the OnItemGestureListener method for single-tap events and long-press events.

Discussion

To address touch events on the map overlay, we modify the way we instantiate an overlay item (for more details on using overlays in OSM, refer back to Recipe 16.17). While instantiating the `OverlayItem`, we make use of an anonymous object of the `OnI temGestureListener` class as an argument and provide our own implementation of the `onItemSingleTapUp` and `onItemLongPress` methods. In these methods, we simply display a toast depicting which action took place—single-tap or long-press—and also the title and description of the overlay touched. Example 16-28 shows the code for this.

Example 16-28. Code for touch events in OSM

```
ArrayList<OverlayItem> items = new ArrayList<OverlayItem>();
items.add(
    new OverlayItem("New Overlay", "Overlay Sample Description", overlayPoint));

resourceProxy = new DefaultResourceProxyImpl(getApplicationContext());

this.myLocationOverlay = new ItemizedIconOverlay<OverlayItem>(items,
        new ItemizedIconOverlay.OnItemGestureListener<OverlayItem>() {
            @Override
            public boolean onItemSingleTapUp(
                final int index, final OverlayItem item) {
                Toast.makeText( getApplicationContext(), "Overlay Titled: " +
                item.mTitle + " Single Tapped" + "\n" + "Description: " +
                item.mDescription, Toast.LENGTH_LONG).show();
                return true;
            }
            @Override
            public boolean onItemLongPress(
                final int index, final OverlayItem item) {
                Toast.makeText( getApplicationContext(), "Overlay Titled: " +
                item.mTitle + " Long pressed" + "\n" + "Description: " +
                item.mDescription ,Toast.LENGTH_LONG).show();
                return false;
            }
        }, resourceProxy);
this.mapView.getOverlays().add(this.myLocationOverlay);
mapView.invalidate();
```

After a single-tap of the overlay, the application should look like Figure 16-15.

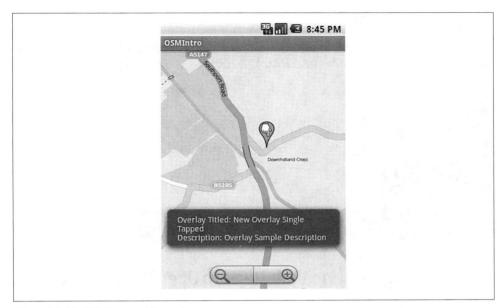

Figure 16-15. OSM map with touch event

Figure 16-16 shows how the application might look after a long-press of the overlay.

Figure 16-16. Long-press overlay reaction

Source Download URL

You can download the source code for this example from *https://docs.google.com/leaf ?id=0B_rESQKgad5LMzZmMjJkZjYtN2M1OC00MGEzLWI2ZTQtNTUxMzFhZ jEzMGIx&hl=en_US*.

16.20 Getting Location Updates with OpenStreetMap Maps

Rachee Singh

Problem

You need to react to the changes in the device's location and move the map to display the changed location.

Solution

Using `LocationListener`, you can make an application request location updates (see Recipe 16.2) and then react to these changes in location by moving the map.

Discussion

- The activity that includes the OSM `MapView` needs to implement `LocationListener` to be able to request changes in the device's location. An activity implementing `LocationListener` will also need to add the unimplemented (abstract) methods from the `LocationListener` interface (Eclipse will do this for you). We set the center of the map to the `GeoPoint` named `mapCenter` so that the application starts with the map focused on that point.

- Now we need to get an instance of `LocationManager` and use it to request location updates using the `requestLocationUpdates` method.

- In one of the overridden methods (which were abstracted in the `LocationListener` interface), named `onLocationChanged`, we can write the code that we want to be executed when the location of the device changes.

- In the `onLocationChanged` method we obtain the latitude and longitude of the new location and set the map's center to the new `GeoPoint`. Example 16-29 shows the relevant code.

Example 16-29. Managing location changes with OSM

```
public class LocationChange extends Activity implements LocationListener {
    private LocationManager myLocationManager;
    private MapView mapView;
    private MapController mapController;

    @Override
    public void onCreate(Bundle savedInstanceState) {
        super.onCreate(savedInstanceState);
        setContentView(R.layout.main);
        mapView = (MapView)findViewById(R.id.mapview);
        mapController = this.mapView.getController();
        mapController.setZoom(15);
        GeoPoint mapCenter = new GeoPoint(53554070, -2959520);
        mapController.setCenter(mapCenter);
        myLocationManager = (LocationManager) getSystemService(LOCATION_SERVICE);
        myLocationManager.requestLocationUpdates(
            LocationManager.GPS_PROVIDER, 1000, 100, this);
    }

    @Override
    public void onLocationChanged(Location location) {
        int latitude = (int) (location.getLatitude() * 1E6);
        int longitude = (int) (location.getLongitude() * 1E6);
        GeoPoint geopoint = new GeoPoint(latitude, longitude);
        mapController.setCenter(geopoint);
        mapView.invalidate();
    }

    @Override
    public void onProviderDisabled(String arg0) {

    }

    @Override
    public void onProviderEnabled(String arg0) {

    }

    @Override
    public void onStatusChanged(String arg0, int arg1, Bundle arg2) {

    }
}
```

When the application starts, the map is centered on the `mapCenter GeoPoint`. Since the application is listening to location changes, the icon in the top bar of the phone is visible (see Figure 16-17).

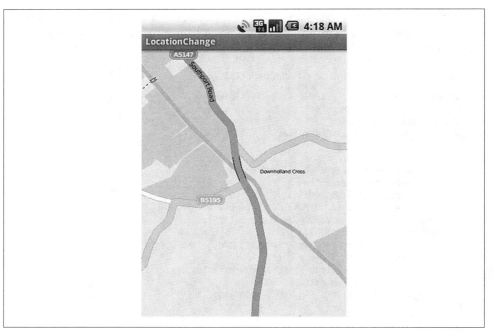

Figure 16-17. Moving the map, start of move

Now, using the emulator controls, new GPS coordinates (–122.094095, 37.422006) are sent to the emulator. The application reacts to this and centers the map on the new coordinates (see Figure 16-18).

Similarly, different GPS coordinates are given from the emulator controls and the application centers the map on the new location (see Figure 16-19).

Also, to allow the application to listen for location changes, include these permissions in the *AndroidManifest.xml* file.

```
<uses-permission android:name="android.permission.ACCESS_COARSE_LOCATION"/>
<uses-permission android:name="android.permission.ACCESS_FINE_LOCATION"/>
<uses-permission android:name="android.permission.ACCESS_NETWORK_STATE" />
<uses-permission android:name="android.permission.INTERNET" />
```

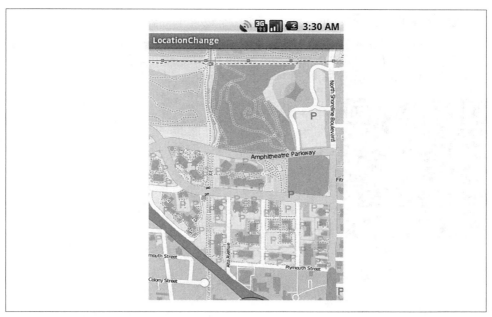

Figure 16-18. Moving the map, end of move

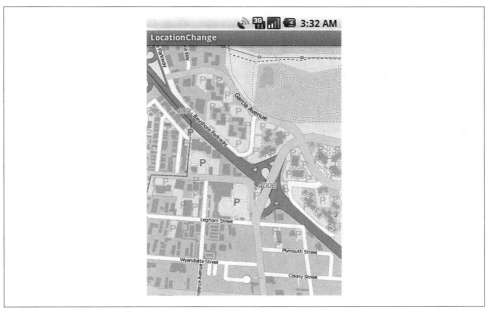

Figure 16-19. Changing the location via the emulator

Source Download URL

You can download the source code for this example from *https://docs.google.com/leaf ?id=0B_rESQKgad5LNGViMzhmM2ItZG FiZC00NGVhLWJmNjctNTRjNTA0M2QzMjdh&hl=en_US.*

Accelerometer

17.1 Introduction: Sensors

Ian Darwin

Discussion

Accelerometers are one of the more interesting bits of hardware in smartphones. Earlier devices such as the OpenMoko "Neo" smartphone and the Apple iPhone included them. Before Android was released I was advocating for OpenMoko at open source conferences. One of my favorite imaginary applications was private key generation. Adhering to the theory that "When privacy is outlawed, only outlaws will have privacy," several people were talking about this as early as 2008 (when I presented the idea, to great applause, at the Ontario Linux Fest). The idea is: if you can't or don't want to exchange private keys over a public channel, you meet on a street corner and shake hands—with each hand having a cell phone concealed in the palm. The devices are touching each other, thus their sensors should record exactly the same somewhat random motions. With a bit of mathematics to filter out the leading and trailing motion of the hands moving together, both devices should have quite a few bits' worth of identical, random data that nobody else has—just what you need for crypto key exchange. I've yet to see anybody implement this, and I must admit I still hope somebody will come through.

Meanwhile, we have many other recipes on accelerometers and other sensors in this chapter...

17.2 Checking for the Presence or Absence of a Sensor

Rachee Singh

Problem

You want to use a given sensor. Before using an Android device for a sensor-based application, you should ensure that the required sensor is supported by the device you are currently running on.

Solution

Check for the availability of the sensor on the Android device.

Discussion

The SensorManager class is used to manage the sensors available on an Android device. So we require an object of this class:

```
SensorManager deviceSensorManager =
    (SensorManager) getSystemService(SOME_SENSOR_SERVICE);
```

Then, using the getSensorList() method, we check for the presence of sensors of any type (accelerometer, gyroscope, pressure, etc.). If the list returned contains any elements, this implies that the sensor is present. A TextView is used to show the result: either "Sensor present!" or "Sensor absent.". Example 17-1 shows the code.

Example 17-1. Checking for the accelerometer

```
List<Sensor> sensorList =
deviceSensorManager.getSensorList(Sensor.TYPE_ACCELEROMETER);

if (sensorList.size() > 0) {
    sensorPresent = true;
    sensor = sensorList.get(0);

}
else
    sensorPresent = false;

/* Set the face TextView to display sensor presence */
face = (TextView) findViewById(R.id.face);

if (sensorPresent)
    face.setText("Sensor present!");
else
    face.setText("Sensor absent.");
```

17.3 Using the Accelerometer to Detect Shaking of the Device

Thomas Manthey

Problem

Sometimes it makes sense to evaluate not only on-screen input, but also gestures like tilting or shaking the phone. You need to use the accelerometer to detect whether the phone has been shaken.

Solution

Register with the accelerometer and compare the current acceleration values on all three axes to the previous ones. If the values have repeatedly changed on at least two axes and those changes exceed a high enough threshold, you can clearly determine shaking.

Discussion

Let us first define shaking as a fairly rapid movement of the device in one direction followed by a further one in another direction, mostly but not necessarily the opposite. If we want to detect such a shake motion in an activity, we need a connection to the hardware sensors; those are exposed by the class **SensorManager**. Furthermore, we need to define a **SensorEventListener** and register it with the **SensorManager**.

So the source of our activity starts like this (see Example 17-2).

Example 17-2. ShakeActivity—getting accelerometer data

```
public class ShakeActivity extends Activity {
    /* The connection to the hardware */
    private SensorManager mySensorManager;

    /* The SensorEventListener lets us wire up to the real hardware events */
    private final SensorEventListener mySensorEventListener = new SensorEventListener() {

        public void onSensorChanged(SensorEvent se) {
         /* we will fill this one later */
        }

    public void onAccuracyChanged(Sensor sensor, int accuracy) {
        /* can be ignored in this example */
        }
    };

    ....
```

In order to implement `SensorEventListener`, we have to implement methods: `onSensorChanged(SensorEvent se)` and `onAccuracyChanged(Sensor sensor, int accuracy)`. The first one gets called whenever new sensor data is available, and the second one whenever the accuracy of the measurement changes—for example, when the location service switches from GPS to network-based. In our example we just need to cover onSensorChanged.

Before we continue, let us define some more variables, which will store the information about values of acceleration and some state (see Example 17-3).

Example 17-3. Variables for acceleration

```
/* Here we store the current values of acceleration, one for each axis */
private float xAccel;
private float yAccel;
private float zAccel;

/* And here the previous ones */
private float xPreviousAccel;
private float yPreviousAccel;
private float zPreviousAccel;

/* Used to suppress the first shaking */
private boolean firstUpdate = true;

/*What acceleration difference would we assume as a rapid movement? */
private final float shakeThreshold = 1.5f;

/* Has a shaking motion been started (one direction) */
private boolean shakeInitiated = false;
```

I hope that the names and comments do explain enough about what is stored in these variables; if not, it will become clearer in the next steps. Now let us connect to the hardware sensors and wire up for their events. onCreate is the perfect place to do so (Example 17-4).

Example 17-4. Initializing for accelerometer data

```
@Override
public void onCreate(Bundle savedInstanceState) {
    super.onCreate(savedInstanceState);
    setContentView(R.layout.main);
    mySensorManager = (SensorManager) getSystemService(Context.SENSOR_SERVICE); ❶
    mySensorManager.registerListener(mySensorEventListener, mySensorManager
            .getDefaultSensor(Sensor.TYPE_ACCELEROMETER),
            SensorManager.SENSOR_DELAY_NORMAL); ❷
}
```

❶ We get a reference to Android's sensor service.

❷ We register the previously defined SensorEventListener with the service. More precisely, we register only for events of the accelerometer and for a normal update rate—this could be changed, if we needed to be more precise.

Now let us define what we want to do when new sensor data arrives. We have defined a stub for theSensorEventListener's method onSensorChanged, so now we will fill it with some life (see Example 17-5).

Example 17-5. Using the sensor data

```java
public void onSensorChanged(SensorEvent se) {
    updateAccelParameters(se.values[0], se.values[1], se.values[2]); ❶
    if ((!shakeInitiated) && isAccelerationChanged()) { ❷
        shakeInitiated = true;
    } else if ((shakeInitiated) && isAccelerationChanged()) { ❸
        executeShakeAction();
    } else if ((shakeInitiated) && (!isAccelerationChanged())) { ❹
        shakeInitiated = false;
    }
}
```

❶ We copy the values of acceleration that we received from the SensorEvent into our state variables. The corresponding method is declared like this:

```java
/* Store acceleration values from sensor */
private void updateAccelParameters(float xNewAccel, float yNewAccel,
        float zNewAccel) {
        /* we have to suppress the first change of acceleration,
     * it results from first values being initialized with 0 */
    if (firstUpdate) {
        xPreviousAccel = xNewAccel;
        yPreviousAccel = yNewAccel;
        zPreviousAccel = zNewAccel;
        firstUpdate = false;
    } else {
        xPreviousAccel = xAccel;
        yPreviousAccel = yAccel;
        zPreviousAccel = zAccel;
    }
    xAccel = xNewAccel;
    yAccel = yNewAccel;
    zAccel = zNewAccel;
}
```

❷ We test for a rapid change of acceleration and whether any has happened before; if not, we store the information that now has happened.

❸ We test again for a rapid change of acceleration, this time with the information from before. If this is true, we can assume a shaking movement according to our definition and commence action.

❹ At last we reset the shake status if we detected shaking before but do not get a rapid change of acceleration anymore.

To complete the code, we add the last two methods. The first is theisAcceleration Changed() method (see Example 17-6).

Example 17-6. The isAccelerationChanged() method

```java
/* If the values of acceleration have changed on at least two axes,
   we are probably in a shake motion */
private boolean isAccelerationChanged() {
    float deltaX = Math.abs(xPreviousAccel - xAccel);
```

```
        float deltaY = Math.abs(yPreviousAccel - yAccel);
        float deltaZ = Math.abs(zPreviousAccel - zAccel);
        return (deltaX > shakeThreshold && deltaY > shakeThreshold)
                || (deltaX > shakeThreshold && deltaZ > shakeThreshold)
                || (deltaY > shakeThreshold && deltaZ > shakeThreshold);
    }
```

Here we compare the current values of acceleration with the previous ones, and if at least two of them have changed above our threshold, we return true.

The last method is executeShakeAction(), which does whatever we wish to do when the phone is being shaken.

```
        private void executeShakeAction() {
        /* Save the cheerleader, save the world
            or do something more sensible... */
    }
```

17.4 Checking Whether a Device Is Facing Up or Facing Down Based on Screen Orientation Using an Accelerometer

Rachee Singh

Problem

You want to check for the orientation (facing up/facing down) of the Android device.

Solution

Use a SensorEventListener to check for appropriate accelerometer values.

Discussion

To implement a SensorEventListener, the onSensorChanged method is called when sensor values change. Within this method, we check to see if the values lie within a particular range for the device to be facing down or facing up.

Here is the code to obtain the sensor object for an accelerometer:

```
List<android.hardware.Sensor> sensorList =
    deviceSensorManager.getSensorList(Sensor.TYPE_ACCELEROMETER);
sensor = sensorList.get(0);
```

Example 17-7 shows the SensorEventListener implementation.

Example 17-7. The SensorEventListener implementation

```
private SensorEventListener accelerometerListener = new SensorEventListener() {
    @Override
    public void onSensorChanged(SensorEvent event) {
        float z = event.values[2];
        if (z >9 && z < 10)
```

```
            face.setText("FACE UP");
        else if (z > -10 && z < -9)
            face.setText("FACE DOWN");
    }

    @Override
    public void onAccuracyChanged(Sensor arg0, int arg1) {

    }

};
```

After implementing the listener along with the methods required, we need to register the listener for a particular sensor (which in our case is the accelerometer). `sensor` is an object of the `Sensor` class; it represents the sensor being used in the application (accelerometer).

```
deviceSensorManager.registerListener(accelerometerListener, sensor, 0, null);
```

17.5 Finding the Orientation of an Android Device Using an Orientation Sensor

Rachee Singh

Problem

You want to detect which side of the Android device is facing upward compared to the rest (top/bottom/right/left side).

Solution

By checking if the pitch and roll values of the orientation sensor of an Android device lie within certain intervals, you can determine which side is facing upward.

Discussion

As we do in the case of every other sensor supported by Android, first we need to instantiate the `SensorManager` class.

```
SensorManager sensorManager = (SensorManager)getSystemService(SENSOR_SERVICE);
```

Using the object of the `SensorManager` class we can get a handle on the sensors available on the device. The `getSensorList()` method returns a list of all sensors of a particular type (in this case orientation). We need to check if the orientation sensor is supported by the device; if it is, we get the first sensor from the list of sensors. If the sensor is not supported, an appropriate message is displayed. See Example 17-8.

Example 17-8. Finding the orientation sensor

```
List<android.hardware.Sensor> sensorList =
    sensorManager.getSensorList(Sensor.TYPE_ORIENTATION);
if (sensorList.size() > 0) {
    sensor = sensorList.get(0);
}
else {
    orient.setText("Orientation sensor not present");
}
```

To register a `SensorEventListener` with this sensor, use this code:

```
sensorManager.registerListener(orientationListener,sensor, 0, null);
```

Now, we define the `SensorEventListener`. We must implement two methods: `onAccur` `acyChanged()` and `onSensorChanged()`. `onSensorChanged()` is called when the sensor values change. In this case it's the orientation sensor values that change on moving the device. The orientation sensor returns three values: azimuth, pitch, and roll angles. Now we check the returned values; if they lie within a particular range, and depending upon the range they lie in, appropriate text is displayed. See Example 17-9.

Example 17-9. The SensorEventListener implementation

```
private SensorEventListener orientationListener = new SensorEventListener() {

    @Override
    public void onAccuracyChanged(Sensor arg0, int arg1) {
    }

    @Override
    public void onSensorChanged(SensorEvent sensorEvent) {
        if (sensorEvent.sensor.getType() == Sensor.TYPE_ORIENTATION) {
            float azimuth = sensorEvent.values[0];
            float pitch = sensorEvent.values[1];
            float roll = sensorEvent.values[2];
            if (pitch < -45 && pitch > -135) {
                orient.setText("Top side of the phone is Up!");

            } else if (pitch > 45 && pitch < 135) {

                    orient.setText("Bottom side of the phone is Up!");

            } else if (roll > 45) {

            orient.setText("Right side of the phone is Up!");

            } else if (roll < -45) {

                    orient.setText("Left side of the phone is Up!");
            }

        }
    }
```

```
};
```

Source Download URL

You can download the source code for this example from *https://docs.google.com/leaf ?id=0B_rESQKgad5LNzZiODY5YmMtNDAxMi00OGQwL WI3NmQtMGY1ZTdlN2E5MmI5&hl=en_US&authkey=COHZxYkE.*

17.6 Reading the Temperature Sensor

Rachee Singh

Problem

You need to get temperature values using the temperature sensor.

Solution

Use the SensorManager and SensorEventListener to track changes in temperature values detected by the temperature sensor.

Discussion

We need to create an object of SensorManager to use sensors in an application. Then we register a listener with the type of sensor we require. To register the listener we provide the name of the listener, a Sensor object, and the type of delay (in this case it is SENSOR_DELAY_FASTEST) to the registerListener method. In this listener, within the overridden onSensorChanged method, we can print the temperature value into a Text View named tempVal.

```
SensorManager sensorManager = (SensorManager)getSystemService(SENSOR_SERVICE);
sensorManager.registerListener(temperatureListener,
    sensorManager.getDefaultSensor(Sensor.TYPE_TEMPERATURE),
    SensorManager.SENSOR_DELAY_FASTEST);
```

Example 17-10 shows the SensorEventListener implementation.

Example 17-10. The SensorEventListener implementation

```
private final SensorEventListener temperatureListener = new SensorEventListener(){
    @Override
    public void onAccuracyChanged(Sensor sensor, int accuracy) {}
    @Override
    public void onSensorChanged(SensorEvent event) {

        tempVal.setText("Temperature is:"+event.values[0]);

    }
};
```

See Also

Recipe 17.2

Bluetooth

18.1 Introduction: Bluetooth

Ian Darwin

Discussion

Bluetooth technology allows users to connect a variety of peripherals to a computer, tablet, or phone. Headsets, speakers, keyboards, and printers; medical devices such as glucometers and ECG machines; these are only some of the numerous types of devices that can be connected via Bluetooth. Some, such as headsets, are supported automatically by Android; the more esoteric ones will need some programming. Some of these other devices use Serial Port Protocol (SPP), which is basically an unstructured protocol that requires you to write code to format data yourself.

This chapter has recipes on how to ensure that Bluetooth is turned on, how to make your device discoverable, how to discover other devices, and how to read from and write to another device over a Bluetooth connection.[1]

A future edition of this work will provide coverage of the Bluetooth Health Device Profile (HDP) standardized by the Continua Health Alliance.

18.2 Enabling Bluetooth and Making the Device Discoverable

Rachee Singh

Problem

The application requires that the Bluetooth adapter be switched on, so you need to check if this capability is enabled. If it is not enabled, you need to prompt the user to

---

1. Bluetooth (the *t* is not capitalized) is a trademark of The Bluetooth Special Interest Group (*https://www .bluetooth.org/*).

enable Bluetooth. To allow remote devices to detect the host device, you must make the host device discoverable.

Solution

Use intents to prompt the user to enable Bluetooth and make the device discoverable.

Discussion

Before performing any action with an instance of the `BluetoothAdapter` class, you should check if the device had enabled the Bluetooth adapter using the `isEnabled()` method. If the method returns `false`, the user should be prompted to enable Bluetooth.

```
BluetoothAdapter BT = BluetoothAdapter.getDefaultAdapter();
if (!BT.isEnabled()) {
//Taking user's permission to switch the bluetooth adapter On.
Intent enableIntent = new Intent(BluetoothAdapter.ACTION_REQUEST_ENABLE);
startActivityForResult(enableIntent, REQUEST_ENABLE_BT);
}
```

The preceding code will show an `AlertDialog` to the user prompting her to enable Bluetooth (see Figure 18-1).

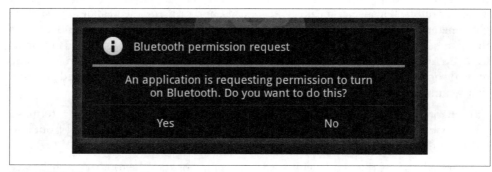

Figure 18-1. Bluetooth enable prompt

On returning to the activity that started the intent, `onActivityResult()` is called, in which the name of the host device and its MAC address can be extracted (see Example 18-1).

Example 18-1. Getting the device and its Bluetooth MAC address

```
protected void onActivityResult(int requestCode, int resultCode, Intent data) {
    if(requestCode==REQUEST_ENABLE_BT && resultCode==Activity.RESULT_OK) {
            BluetoothAdapter BT = BluetoothAdapter.getDefaultAdapter();
        String address = BT.getAddress();
            String name = BT.getName();
            String toastText = name + " : " + address;
            Toast.makeText(this, toastText, Toast.LENGTH_LONG).show();
}
```

To request the user's permission to make the device discoverable to other Bluetooth-enabled devices in the vicinity, you can use the following lines of code:

```
//Requesting user's permission to make the device discoverable for 120 secs.
Intent discoverableIntent = new Intent(BluetoothAdapter.ACTION_REQUEST_DISCOVERABLE);
startActivity(discoverableIntent);
```

The preceding code will show an `AlertDialog` to the user prompting her to make her device discoverable by other devices for 120 seconds (Figure 18-2).

Figure 18-2. Bluetooth configuration

18.3 Connecting to a Bluetooth-Enabled Device

Ashwini Shahapurkar

Problem

You want to connect to another Bluetooth-enabled device and communicate with it.

Solution

Use the Android Bluetooth API to connect to the device using sockets. The communication will be over the socket streams.

Discussion

For any Bluetooth application you need to add these two permissions to *AndroidManifest.xml* file:

```
<uses-permission android:name="android.permission.BLUETOOTH_ADMIN" />
<uses-permission android:name="android.permission.BLUETOOTH" />
```

You will create the socket connection to the other Bluetooth device. Then you should continuously listen for the data from the socket stream in a thread. You can write to the connected stream outside the thread. The connection is a blocking call, and with Bluetooth device discovery being a heavy process, this may slow down the connection. So it is a good practice to cancel the device discovery before trying to connect to the other device.

The Bluetooth socket connection is a blocking call and returns only if a connection is successful or if an exception occurs while connecting to the device.

The BluetoothConnection will, once instantiated, create the socket connection to the other device, and start listening to the data from the connected device.

Example 18-2. Reading from and writing to a Bluetooth Device

```
private class BluetoothConnection extends Thread {
    private final BluetoothSocket mmSocket;
    private final InputStream mmInStream;
    private final OutputStream mmOutStream;
    byte[] buffer;

    // Unique UUID for this application, you should use different
    private static final UUID MY_UUID = UUID
            .fromString("fa87c0d0-afac-11de-8a39-0800200c9a66");

    public BluetoothConnection(BluetoothDevice device) {

        BluetoothSocket tmp = null;

        // Get a BluetoothSocket for a connection with the given BluetoothDevice
        try {
            tmp = device.createRfcommSocketToServiceRecord(MY_UUID);
        } catch (IOException e) {
            e.printStackTrace();
        }
        mmSocket = tmp;

        //now make the socket connection in separate thread to avoid FC
        Thread connectionThread = new Thread(new Runnable() {

                @Override
                public void run() {
                    // Always cancel discovery because it will slow down a connection
                    mAdapter.cancelDiscovery();

                    // Make a connection to the BluetoothSocket
                    try {
                        // This is a blocking call and will only return on a
                        // successful connection or an exception
                        mmSocket.connect();
                    } catch (IOException e) {
                        //connection to device failed so close the socket
                        try {
                            mmSocket.close();
                        } catch (IOException e2) {
                            e2.printStackTrace();
```

```
                    }
                }
            }
        });

    connectionThread.start();

    InputStream tmpIn = null;
    OutputStream tmpOut = null;

    // Get the BluetoothSocket input and output streams
    try {
        tmpIn = socket.getInputStream();
        tmpOut = socket.getOutputStream();
        buffer = new byte[1024];
    } catch (IOException e) {
        e.printStackTrace();
    }

    mmInStream = tmpIn;
    mmOutStream = tmpOut;
}

public void run() {

    // Keep listening to the InputStream while connected
    while (true) {
        try {
            //read the data from socket stream
            mmInStream.read(buffer);
            // Send the obtained bytes to the UI Activity
        } catch (IOException e) {
            //an exception here marks connection loss
            //send message to UI Activity
            break;
        }
    }
}

public void write(byte[] buffer) {
    try {
        //write the data to socket stream
        mmOutStream.write(buffer);
    } catch (IOException e) {
        e.printStackTrace();
    }
}

public void cancel() {
    try {
        mmSocket.close();
    } catch (IOException e) {
        e.printStackTrace();
    }
```

```
    }
}
```

See Also

Recipe 18.5

18.4 Listening for and Accepting Bluetooth Connection Requests

Rachee Singh

Problem

You want to create a listening server for Bluetooth connections.

Solution

Before two Bluetooth devices can interact, one of the communicating devices must act like a server. It obtains a `BluetoothServerSocket` instance and listens for incoming requests. This instance is obtained by calling the `listenUsingRfcommWithServiceRecord()` method on the Bluetooth adapter.

Discussion

With the `BluetoothServerSocket` instance, we can start listening for incoming requests from remote devices through the `start()` method. Listening is a blocking process, so we have to make a new thread and call it within the thread; otherwise, the UI of the application becomes unresponsive. Example 18-3 shows the relevant code.

Example 18-3. Creating a Bluetooth server and accepting connections

```
//Making the host device discoverable
startActivityForResult(new Intent(BluetoothAdapter.ACTION_REQUEST_DISCOVERABLE),
DISCOVERY_REQUEST_BLUETOOTH);
    @Override
    protected void onActivityResult(int requestCode, int resultCode, Intent data) {
        if (requestCode == DISCOVERY_REQUEST_BLUETOOTH) {
            boolean isDiscoverable = resultCode > 0;
            if (isDiscoverable) {
                UUID uuid = UUID.fromString("a60f35f0-b93a-11de-8a39-08002009c666");
                String serverName = "BTserver";
                final BluetoothServerSocket bluetoothServer =
                bluetoothAdapter.listenUsingRfcommWithServiceRecord(serverName, uuid);

                Thread listenThread = new Thread(new Runnable() {

                    public void run() {
                        try {
                            BluetoothSocket serverSocket = bluetoothServer.accept();
```

```
                    myHandleConnectionWith(serverSocket);
            } catch (IOException e) {
                Log.d("BLUETOOTH", e.getMessage());
            }
        }
    });
    listenThread.start();
    }
  }
}
```

18.5 Implementing Bluetooth Device Discovery

Shraddha Shravagi

Problem

You want to display a list of Bluetooth devices that are within communication range of your device.

Solution

Create an XML file to display the list, create a class file to load the list, and then edit the manifest file.

It's that simple.

Note that, for security reasons, devices to be discovered must be in "discoverable" mode (also known as "pairing"); for Android devices there is a Discoverable setting in the Bluetooth Settings, while for "conventional" Bluetooth devices you may need to refer to the device's instruction manual.

Discussion

Use the following code to create the XML file to display the list:

```
<ListView
    android:id="@+id/pairedBtDevices"
    android:layout_width="fill_parent"
    android:layout_height="wrap_content"
/>
```

The code in Example 18-4 creates a class file to load the list.

Example 18-4. Activity with BroadcastReceiver for connections

```
//IntentFilter will match the action specified
IntentFilter filter = new IntentFilter(BluetoothDevice.ACTION_FOUND);
//broadcast receiver for any matching filter
this.registerReceiver(mReceiver, filter);

//attach the adapter
ListView newDevicesListView = (ListView)findViewById(R.id.pairedBtDevices);
```

```
newDevicesListView.setAdapter(mNewDevicesArrayAdapter);

filter = new IntentFilter(BluetoothAdapter.ACTION_DISCOVERY_FINISHED);
this.registerReceiver(mReceiver, filter);

// Create a receiver for the Intent
private final BroadcastReceiver mReceiver = new BroadcastReceiver() {

    @Override
    public void onReceive(Context context, Intent intent) {

        String action = intent.getAction();

        if(BluetoothDevice.ACTION_FOUND.equals(action)){
            BluetoothDevice btDevice =
                intent.getParcelableExtra(BluetoothDevice.EXTRA_DEVICE);

            if(btDevice.getBondState() != BluetoothDevice.BOND_BONDED){
                mNewDevicesArrayAdapter.add(btDevice.getName()+"\n"+
                btDevice.getAddress());
            }
        }
        else
            if(BluetoothAdapter.ACTION_DISCOVERY_FINISHED.equals(action)){
                setProgressBarIndeterminateVisibility(false);
                setTitle(R.string.select_device);
                if(mNewDevicesArrayAdapter.getCount() == 0){
                    String noDevice =
                        getResources().getText(R.string.none_paired).toString();
                    mNewDevicesArrayAdapter.add(noDevice);
                }
            }

    }
};
```

The *AndroidManifest.xml* file must specify that you need the following permissions:

- android.permission.BLUETOOTH
- android.permission.BLUETOOTH_ADMIN

Source Download URL

The source code for this example is in the Android Cookbook repository at *http://github.com/AndroidCook/Android-Cookbook-Examples*, in the subdirectory BlueToothDemo (see "Getting and Using the Code Examples" on page xvii).

System and Device Control

19.1 Introduction: System and Device Control

Ian Darwin

Discussion

Android provides a good compromise between the needs of the carriers for control and the needs of developers for device access. This chapter looks at some of the informational and control APIs that are publicly available to the Android developer to explore and control the extensive hardware facilities provided by the system, and to deal with the wide range of hardware it runs on, from 2-inch cell phones to 10-inch tablets and netbooks.

19.2 Accessing Phone Network/Connectivity Information

Amir Alagic

Problem

You want to find information about the device's current network connectivity.

Solution

You can determine whether your phone is connected to the network, its type of connection, and whether your phone is in roaming territory, using the `ConnectivityMan ager` and a `NetworkInfo` object.

Discussion

Often you need to know whether the device you are running on can connect to the Internet at the moment, and, since roaming can be expensive, it is also very useful if you can tell the user whether he is roaming (the user who is truly worried about this will disable data roaming using the Settings application). To do this and more we can use the `NetworkInfo` class in the `android.net` package, as in Example 19-1.

Example 19-1. Getting network information

```
ConnectivityManager connManager =
(ConnectivityManager)this.getSystemService(Context.CONNECTIVITY_SERVICE);
 NetworkInfo ni = connManager.getActiveNetworkInfo();
 /*Indicates whether network connectivity is possible.
 A network is unavailable when a persistent or semi-persistent
 condition prevents the possibility of connecting to
 that network.*/
 boolean available = ni.isAvailable();
 /*Indicates whether network connectivity is possible.
  A network is unavailable when a persistent
  or semi-persistent condition prevents the possibility
  of connecting to that network. Examples include*/
 boolean connected = ni.isConnected();
 boolean roaming = ni.isRoaming();
 /* Reports the type of network (currently mobile or Wi-Fi) to which the info
    in this object pertains.*/
 int networkType = ni.getType();
```

19.3 Obtaining Information from the Manifest File

Colin Wilcox

Problem

You want to obtain project settings (e.g., app version) data from the *AndroidManifest.xml* file during program execution.

Solution

Use the `PackageManager`. Rather than hardcoding values into the application that need to be changed each time the application is modified, it is easier to read the version number from the manifest file. Other settings can be read in a similar manner.

Discussion

The `PackageManager` is fairly straightforward to use. The two `import`s in the following code need to be added to the `Activity`:

```
import android.content.pm.PackageInfo;
import android.content.pm.PackageManager;
```

The main part of the code is shown in Example 19-2.

Example 19-2. Code to get information from the manifest

```
// In the main Activity...
public String readVersionNameFromManifest() {
```

```
    PackageInfo packageInfo = null;

    // Read package name and version number from manifest
    try {
        // load the package manager for the current context
        PackageManager packageManager = this.getPackageManager();

        // get the package info structure and pick out the fields you want
        packageInfo = packageManager.getPackageInfo(this.getPackageName(), 0);
    } catch (Exception e) {
      Log.e(TAG, "Exception reading manifest version " + e);
    }
    return (packageInfo.versionName);
}
```

19.4 Changing Incoming Call Notification to Silent, Vibrate, or Normal

Rachee Singh

Problem

You need to set the Android device to silent, vibrate, or normal mode.

Solution

Use Android's `AudioManager` system service to set the phone to normal, silent, and vibrate modes.

Discussion

This recipe presents a simple application that has three buttons to change the phone mode to Silent, Vibrate, and Normal, as shown in Figure 19-1.

We instantiate the `AudioManager` class to be able to use the `setRingerMode` method. For each of these buttons (`silentButton`, `normalButton`, and `vibrateButton`) we have `OnClick Listeners` defined in which we used the `AudioManager` object to set the ringer mode. We also display a toast notifying the user of the mode change. See Example 19-3.

Example 19-3. Setting the audio mode

```
am= (AudioManager) getBaseContext().getSystemService(Context.AUDIO_SERVICE);
silentButton = (Button)findViewById(R.id.silent);
normalButton = (Button)findViewById(R.id.normal);
vibrateButton = (Button)findViewById(R.id.vibrate);

//For Silent mode
silentButton.setOnClickListener(new View.OnClickListener() {
    @Override
    public void onClick(View arg0) {
        am.setRingerMode(AudioManager.RINGER_MODE_SILENT);
```

```java
            Toast.makeText(getApplicationContext(), "Silent Mode Activated.",
               Toast.LENGTH_LONG).show();
        }
    });


    //For Normal mode
    normalButton.setOnClickListener(new View.OnClickListener() {
        @Override
        public void onClick(View arg0) {
            am.setRingerMode(AudioManager.RINGER_MODE_NORMAL);
            Toast.makeText(getApplicationContext(),
                "Normal Mode Activated", Toast.LENGTH_LONG).show();
        }
    });


    //For Vibrate mode
    vibrateButton.setOnClickListener(new View.OnClickListener() {
        @Override
        public void onClick(View arg0) {
            am.setRingerMode(AudioManager.RINGER_MODE_VIBRATE);
            Toast.makeText(getApplicationContext(),
                "Vibrate Mode Activated", Toast.LENGTH_LONG).show();
        }
    });
```

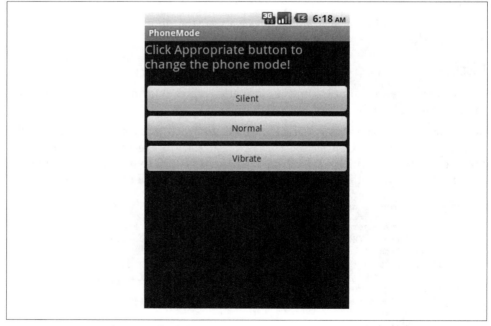

Figure 19-1. Setting phone notification mode

Figure 19-2 shows the application when the Silent button is clicked (notice also the silent icon in the status bar of the phone).

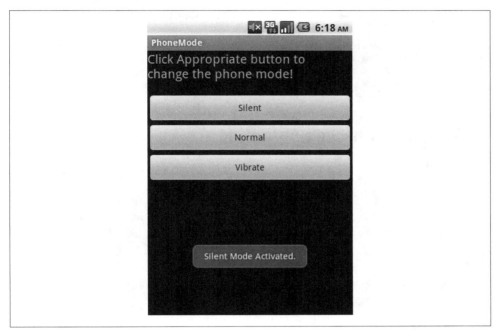

Figure 19-2. Silent mode activated

19.5 Copying Text and Getting Text from the Clipboard

Rachee Singh

Problem

You need to copy text to the clipboard and access the text stored on the clipboard; this allows you to provide full copy and paste functionality for text.

Solution

With the help of the `ClipboardManager` class, you can access the items stored on the clipboard of an Android device.

Discussion

The `ClipboardManager` class allows you to copy text to the clipboard using the `set Text()` method and get the text stored on the clipboard using the `getText()` method. `getText()` returns a `charSequence` that is converted to a string by the `toString()` method.

Example 19-4 is sample code that demonstrates how to obtain an instance of the `ClipboardManager` class and how to use it to copy text to the clipboard. Then the `get Text()` method is used to get the text on the clipboard, and the text is set to a `TextView`.

Example 19-4. Copying text to the clipboard

```
ClipboardManager clipboard = (ClipboardManager)getSystemService(CLIPBOARD_SERVICE);
clipboard.setText("Using the clipboard for the first time!");
String clip =  clipboard.getText().toString();
clipTextView = (TextView) findViewById(R.id.clipText);
clipTextView.setText(clip);
```

19.6 Using LED-Based Notifications

Rachee Singh

Problem

Most Android devices are equipped with an LED for notification purposes. You want to flash different colored lights using the LED.

Solution

Using the `NotificationManager` and `Notification` classes allows you to provide notifications using the LED on the device.

Discussion

As in case of all notifications, we instantiate the `NotificationManager` class. Then we create a `Notification` class's object. Using the method `ledARGB()` we can specify the color of the LED light. The constant `ledOnMS` is used to specify the time in milliseconds for which the LED will be on; `ledOffMS` specifies the time in milliseconds for which the LED is off. The `notify()` method starts the notification process. Example 19-5 shows the code corresponding to the actions just described.

Example 19-5. Making the LED flash in blue

```
NotificationManager notificationManager =
(NotificationManager)getSystemService(NOTIFICATION_SERVICE);
Notification notification = new Notification();
notification.ledARGB = 0xff0000ff;          // Blue color light flash
notification.ledOnMS = 1000;                // LED is on for 1 second
notification.ledOffMS = 1000;               // LED is off for 1 second
notification.flags = Notification.FLAG_SHOW_LIGHTS;
notificationManager.notify(0, notification);
```

19.7 Making the Device Vibrate

Rachee Singh

Problem

You wish to notify the user of some event by means of device vibration.

Solution

Use notifications to set a vibration pattern.

Discussion

To allow device vibration, include this permission in the *AndroidManifest.xml* file:

```
<uses-permission android:name="android.permission.VIBRATE"/>
```

In the Java code, we need to get an instance of the `NotificationManager` class and of the `Notification` class:

```
NotificationManager notificationManager =
    (NotificationManager) getSystemService(NOTIFICATION_SERVICE);
Notification notification = new Notification();
```

To set a pattern for the vibration, assign a sequence of long values (time in milliseconds) to the `Notification`'s `vibrate` property. This sequence represents the time for which the device will vibrate and the time for which it will pause vibration. For instance, the pattern used in this example will cause the device to vibrate for one second and then pause for one second, then vibrate again for one second, and so on:

```
notification.vibrate =
    new long[]{1000, 1000, 1000, 1000, 1000};
notificationManager.notify(0, notification);
```

Source Download URL

You can download the source code for this example from *https://docs.google.com/leaf ?id=0B_rESQKgad5LZjJiMTU5MzEtYzk3NC00NTcxLWE0NDAtMDV jY2I3ZWFmMGI3&hl=en_US&authkey=CJ2SjpAC.*

19.8 Running Shell Commands from Your Application

Rachee Singh

Problem

You need to run a Unix/Linux shell command (command-line program) from your application (e.g., pwd, ls, etc.).

Solution

Use the exec() method of the Runtime class, passing the shell command you wish to run as an argument.

Discussion

As in standard Java, your applications cannot create an instance of the Runtime class, but rather get an instance by invoking the static getRuntime() method. Using this instance we call the exec() method, which executes the specified program in a separate native process. It takes the name of the program to execute as an argument. The exec() method returns the new Process object that represents the native process.

As an example, we run the ps command that lists all the processes running on the system. The full location of the command is specified (*/system/bin/ps*) as an argument to exec().

We get the output of the command and return the string. Then process.waitFor() is used to wait for the command to finish executing. See Example 19-6.

Example 19-6. Running a shell command

```
try {
    Process process = Runtime.getRuntime().exec("/system/bin/ps");
    InputStreamReader reader = new InputStreamReader(process.getInputStream());
    BufferedReader bufferedReader = new BufferedReader(reader);
    int numRead;
    char[] buffer = new char[5000];
    StringBuffer commandOutput = new StringBuffer();
    while ((numRead = bufferedReader.read(buffer)) > 0) {
        commandOutput.append(buffer, 0, numRead);
    }
    bufferedReader.close();
    process.waitFor();

    return commandOutput.toString();
} catch (IOException e) {
    throw new RuntimeException(e);
} catch (InterruptedException e) {
    throw new RuntimeException(e);
}
```

Figure 19-3 shows the output of the ps command.

<figure>

USER	PID	PPID	VSIZE	RSS	WCHAN	PC	
NAME							
root	1	0	312	220	c009b74c	0000ca4c	S
/init							
root	2	0	0	0	c004e72c	00000000	S
kthreadd							
root	3	2	0	0	c003fdc8	00000000	S
ksoftirqd/0							
root	4	2	0	0	c004b2c4	00000000	S
events/0							
root	5	2	0	0	c004b2c4	00000000	S
khelper							
root	6	2	0	0	c004b2c4	00000000	S
suspend							
root	7	2	0	0	c004b2c4	00000000	S
kblockd/0							
root	8	2	0	0	c004b2c4	00000000	S
cqueue							
root	9	2	0	0	c018179c	00000000	S
kseriod							
root	10	2	0	0	c004b2c4	00000000	S
kmmcd							
root	11	2	0	0	c006fc74	00000000	S
pdflush							
root	12	2	0	0	c006fc74	00000000	S
pdflush							
root	13	2	0	0	c00744e4	00000000	S

</figure>

Figure 19-3. Android ps(1) command output

Source Download URL

You can download the source code for this example from *https://docs.google.com/leaf ?id=0B_rESQKgad5LNTkxMDIyYTgtMzlmMS00ZDViLThkOTUtY WY4MjQ5NGY1NzFk&hl=en_US*.

19.9 Determining Whether a Given Application Is Running

Colin Wilcox

Problem

You want to know whether your app or some other app is running.

Solution

The system activity manager maintains a list of all active tasks. This provides the name of all running tasks and can be interrogated for various system-specific information.

Discussion

The code in Example 19-7 takes the name of an application and returns true if the ActivityManager thinks it is currently running.

Example 19-7. Checking for a running app

```
import android.app.ActivityManager;
import android.app.ActivityManager.RunningAppProcessInfo;

public boolean isAppRunning (String aApplicationPackageName)
{
    ActivityManager activityManager =
        (ActivityManager) this.getSystemService(ACTIVITY_SERVICE);
    if (activityManager == null)
    {
        return false; // should report: can't get Activity Manager
    }

    List<RunningAppProcessInfo> procInfos =
            activityManager.getRunningAppProcesses();
    for(int idx = 0; idx < procInfos.size(); idx++)
    {
        if(procInfos.get(i).processName.equals(aApplicationPackageName))
        {
            return true;
        }
    }

    return false;
}
```

Other Programming Languages and Frameworks

20.1 Introduction: Other Programming Languages

Ian Darwin

Discussion

Developing new programming languages is a constant process in this industry. Several new (or not-so-new) languages have become popular recently: Scheme, Erlang, Scala, Clojure, Groovy, C#, F#, and more. While the Apple approach on the iPhone has been to mandate use of Objective-C and to ban (at least initially, it has been relaxed somewhat recently) use of other languages, particularly JVM-style translated languages, Android positively encourages the use of many languages. You can write your app in pure Java using the SDK, of course—that's the subject of most of the rest of the book. You can mix some C/C++ code into Java using native code (see Recipe 20.3), using Android's NDK. People have made most of the major compiled languages work, especially (but not exclusively) the JVM-based ones. You can write using a variety of scripting languages such as Perl, Python, and Ruby (see Recipe 20.4). And there's more...

If you want a very high-level, drag-and-drop development process, look at Android App Inventor, a Google-originated environment for building applications easily using the drag-and-drop metaphor and "Blocks" that snap together. We have a recipe in progress (*http://androidcookbook.com/r/3224*). App Inventor is now maintained at MIT; you can also visit the official MIT site (*http://appinventor.mit.edu*).

If you are a web developer used to working your magic in HTML, JavaScript, and CSS, there is a route for you to become an Android developer using the tools you already know. There are, in fact, five or six technologies that go this route, such as AppCelerator Titanium, PhoneGap (see Recipe 20.9), and more. These generally use CSS to build a style that looks close to the native device toolkit, JavaScript to provide actions, and W3 standards to provide device access such as GPS. Most of these work by packaging up a JavaScript interpreter along with your HTML and CSS into an APK file. Many of these have the further advantage that they can be packaged to run on iPhone, BlackBerry, and other mobile platforms. The risk I see with these is that, since they're not using native toolkit items, they may easily provide strange-looking user interfaces that don't conform either to the Android Guidelines or to users' expectations of how apps should behave on the Android platform. That is certainly something to be aware of if you are using one of these toolkits.

One of the key ideas in Android was to keep it as an open platform. The wide range of languages that you can use to develop Android apps testifies that this openness has been maintained.

20.2 Running an External/Native Unix/Linux Command

Amir Alagic

Problem

Sometimes it can be convenient to start one of the Linux commands available on the phone, such as `rm`, `sync`, `top`, or `uptime`.

Solution

To run Linux commands available on the Android OS you should use classes that are available in standard Java and are used to start external processes. First you have to know which command you want to run, get/obtain the runtime object, and then execute the native command in a separate native process. Often you will need to read results, and to do that, use streams.

Discussion

Java (both desktop and under Android) makes it pretty simple to start external processes.

With the a file manager such as the AndroZip File Manager you can find Linux commands in the *./system/bin* folder. One of the commands is `ls`, which lists the files (and subfolders) in a folder. To run this command we will send its path to the `Runtime.exec()` method.

You cannot create a `Runtime` object directly since it is a singleton; to obtain its instance you call the static `getRuntime()` method and then pass the path to the Linux command you want to run.

```
Process process = Runtime.getRuntime().exec("/system/bin/ls");
```

The `Process` class is used in the preceding code to create the process; it will also help us read from the process, and we obtain an `InputStream` that is connected to the standard output stream (stdout) of the native process represented by this object.

```
DataInputStream osRes = new DataInputStream(process.getInputStream());
```

Then we create a `BufferedReader` object that will help us to read results line by line.

```
BufferedReader reader = new BufferedReader(new InputStreamReader(osRes));
String line;

while ((line = reader.readLine()) != null || reader.read() !=-1) {
    Log.i("Reading command result", line);
}
```

As you can see, we read all the lines and show them on the LogCat console. You can see the output for the example in your Eclipse IDE.

You could, of course, capture the output of any system command back into your program and either parse it for display in, for example, a `ListView`, or display it as text in a `TextView`.

20.3 Running Native C/C++ Code with JNI on the NDK

Ian Darwin

Problem

You need to run parts of your application natively in order to use existing C/C++ code or, possibly, to improve performance of CPU-intensive code.

Solution

Use JNI (Java Native Interface) via the Android Native Development Kit or NDK (*http://developer.android.com/sdk/ndk/1.6_r1/index.html*).

Discussion

Standard Java has always allowed you to load *native* or compiled code into your Java program, and Android's Dalvik runtime supports this in a way that is pretty much identical to the original. Why would you as a developer want to do such a thing? One reason might be to access OS-dependent functionality. Another is speed: native code will likely run faster than Java, at least at present, although there is some contention as to how much of a difference this really makes. Search the Web for conflicting answers.

The native code language bindings are defined for code that has been written in C or C++. If you need to access a language other than C/C++, you could write a bit of C/C++ and have it pass control to other functions or applications, but you should also consider using the Android Scripting Environment (see Recipe 20.4).

For this example I use a simple numeric calculation, computing the square root of a `double` using the Newton-Raphson iterative method. The code provides both a Java and a C version, to compare the speeds.

Ian's basic steps: Java calling native code

To call native code from Java follow these steps:

1. Install the NDK in addition to the Android Development Kit (ADK).
2. Write Java code that declares and calls a native method.
3. Compile this Java code.
4. Create an *.h* header file using *javah.*
5. Write a C function that includes this header file and implements the native method to do the work.
6. Prepare the *Android.mk* (and optionally *Application.mk*) configuration files.
7. Compile the C code into a loadable object using `$NDK/ndk-build`.
8. Package and deploy your application, and test it.

The preliminary step is to download the NDK as a TAR or ZIP file, extract it someplace convenient, and set the environment variable such as `NDK` to where you've installed it, for referring back to the NDK install. You'll want this to read documentation as well as to run the tools.

The first step is to write Java code that declares and calls a native method (see Example 20-1). To declare the method, use the keyword `native` to indicate that the method is native. To use the native method, no special syntax is used, but your application—typically in your main activity—must provide a static code block that loads your native method using `System.loadLibrary()`, as shown in Example 20-2. (The dynamically loadable module will be created in step 6.) Static blocks are executed when the class containing them is loaded; loading the native code here ensures that it is in memory when needed!

Object variables that your native code may modify should carry the `volatile` modifier. In my example, *SqrtDemo.java* contains the native method declaration (as well as a Java implementation of the algorithm).

Example 20-1. The Java code

```
public class SqrtDemo {

    public static final double EPSILON = 0.05d;

    public static native double sqrtC(double d);

    public static double sqrtJava(double d) {
        double x0 = 10.0, x1 = d, diff;
        do {
            x1 = x0 - (((x0 * x0) - d) / (x0 * 2));
            diff = x1 - x0;
            x0 = x1;
        } while (Math.abs(diff) > EPSILON);
        return x1;
```

```
        }
}
```

Example 20-2. The Activity class Main.java uses the native code

```
// In the Activity class, outside any methods:
static {
    System.loadLibrary("sqrt-demo");
}

// In a method of the Activity class where you need to use it:
double d = SqrtDemo.sqrtC(123456789.0);
```

The next step is simple; just build the project normally, using the ADK Eclipse Plugin or Ant.

Next, you need to create a C-language *.h* header file that provides the interface between the JVM and your native code. Use javah to produce this file. javah needs to read the class that declares one or more native methods, and will generate an *.h* file specific to the package and class name.

```
mkdir jni // keep everything JNI-related here
javah -d jni -classpath bin foo.ndkdemo.SqrtDemo // produces foo_ndkdemo_SqrtDemo.h
```

The *.h* file produced is a "glue" file, not really meant for human consumption and particularly not for editing. But by inspecting the resultant *.h* file, you'll see that the C method's name is composed of the name Java, the package name, the class name, and the method name:

```
JNIEXPORT jdouble JNICALL Java_foo_ndkdemo_SqrtDemo_sqrtC
  (JNIEnv *, jclass, jdouble);
```

Now create a C function that does the work. You must import the *.h* file and use the same function signature as is used in the *.h* file.

This function can do whatever it wishes. Note that it is passed two arguments before any declared arguments: a JVM environment variable and a "this" handle for the invocation context object. Table 20-1 shows the correspondence between Java types and the C types (JNI types) used in the C code.

Table 20-1. Java and JNI types

Java type	JNI	Java array type	JNI
byte	jbyte	byte[]	jbyteArray
short	jshort	short[]	jshortArray
int	jint	int[]	jintArray
long	jlong	long[]	jlongArray
float	jfloat	float[]	jfloatArray
double	jdouble	double[]	jdoubleArray
char	jchar	char[]	jcharArray

Java type	JNI	Java array type	JNI
boolean	jboolean	boolean[]	jbooleanArray
void	jvoid		
Object	jobject	Object[]	jobjectArray
Class	jclass		
String	jstring		
array	jarray		
Throwable	jthrowable		

Example 20-3 shows the complete C native implementation. It simply computes the square root of the input number, and returns that. The method is static, so the "this" pointer is not used.

Example 20-3. The C code

```
// jni/sqrt-demo.c

#include <stdlib.h>

#include "foo_ndkdemo_SqrtDemo.h"

JNIEXPORT jdouble JNICALL Java_foo_ndkdemo_SqrtDemo_sqrtC(
    JNIEnv *env, jclass clazz, jdouble d) {

    jdouble x0 = 10.0, x1 = d, diff;
    do {
        x1 = x0 - (((x0 * x0) - d) / (x0 * 2));
        diff = x1 - x0;
        x0 = x1;
    } while (labs(diff) > foo_ndkdemo_SqrtDemo_EPSILON);
    return x1;
}
```

The implementation is basically the same as the Java version. Note that javah even maps the final double EPSILON from the Java class SqrtDemo into a #define for use within the C version.

The next step is to prepare the file *Android.mk*, also in the *jni* folder. For a simple shared library, Example 20-4 will suffice.

Example 20-4. An Android.mk makefile example

```
# Android.mk

LOCAL_PATH := $(call my-dir)

include $(CLEAR_VARS)

LOCAL_MODULE    := sqrt-demo
LOCAL_SRC_FILES := sqrt-demo.c
```

```
include $(BUILD_SHARED_LIBRARY)
```

Finally, you compile the C code into a loadable object. Under desktop Java, the details depend on platform, compiler, and so on. However, the NDK provides a build script to automate this. Assuming you have set the NDK variable to the install root of the NDK download from step 1, you only need to type the following:

```
$ $NDK/ndk-build  # for Linux, Unix, OS-X?
> %NDK%/ndk-build # for MS-Windows

Compile thumb  : sqrt-demo <= sqrt-demo.c
SharedLibrary  : libsqrt-demo.so
Install        : libsqrt-demo.so => libs/armeabi/libsqrt-demo.so
```

And you're done! Just package and run the application normally. The output should be similar to Figure 20-1.The full download example for this chapter includes buttons to run the **sqrt** function a number of times in either Java or C and compare the times. Note that at present it does this work on the event thread, so large numbers of repetitions will result in "Application Not Responding" (ANR) errors, which will mess up the timing.

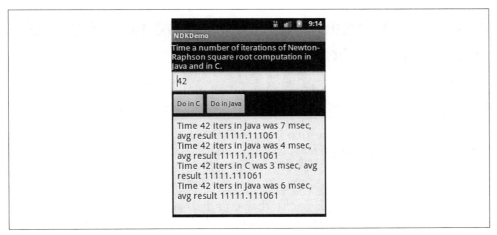

Figure 20-1. NDK demonstration output

Congratulations! You've called a native method. Your code may run slightly faster. However, you will require extra work for portability; as Android begins to run on more hardware platforms, you will have to (at least) add them to the *Application.mk* file. If you have used any assembler code, the problem is much worse.

Beware that problems with your native code can and will crash the runtime process right out from underneath the Java Virtual Machine. The JVM can do nothing to protect itself from poorly written C/C++ code. Memory must be managed by the programmer; there is no automatic garbage collection of memory obtained by the system runtime allocator. You're dealing directly with the operating system and sometimes even the hardware, so, 'Be careful. Be very careful.'

See Also

There is a recipe in Chapter 26 of my *Java Cookbook* (*http://shop.oreilly.com/product/ 9780596007010.do*), published by O'Reilly, that shows variables from the Java class being accessed from within the native code. The official documentation for Android's NDK is on the Android Native SDK information page (*http://developer.android.com/ sdk/ndk/1.6_r1/index.html*). Considerable documentation is included in the *docs* folder of the NDK download. If you need more information on Java native methods, you might be interested in the comprehensive treatment found in *Essential JNI: Java Native Interface* by Rob Gordon (Prentice Hall), originally written for Desktop Java.

Source Download URL

The source code for this example is in the Android Cookbook repository at *http://github .com/AndroidCook/Android-Cookbook-Examples*, in the subdirectory NdkDemo (see "Getting and Using the Code Examples" on page xvii).

20.4 Getting Started with the Scripting Layer for Android (SL4A, Formerly Android Scripting Environment)

Ian Darwin

Problem

You want to write your application in one of several popular scripting languages, or you want to program interactively on your phone.

Solution

One of the best approaches is to use the Scripting Layer for Android (SL4A). This provides support for several popular scripting languages (including Python, Perl, Lua, and BeanShell). An `Android` object is provided that gives access to most of the underlying Android APIs from this language. This recipe shows how to get started; several other recipes explore particular aspects of using SL4A.

Here's how to get started:

1. Download the Scripting Layer for Android (formerly Android Scripting Environment) from *http://code.google.com/p/android-scripting/*.
2. Add the interpreter(s) you want to use.
3. Type in your program.
4. Run it immediately—no compilation or packaging steps are needed!

Discussion

The SL4A application is not at the time of this writing in the Android Market, so you have to visit the website and download it (there is a Quick Response or QR code for downloading, so start in your laptop or desktop browser). And since it's not in the Market, before you can download it you'll have to go into Settings→Applications→Unknown Sources and enable unknown-sourced applications. Also note that since this is not downloaded via the Market, you will not be notified when the Google project releases a new binary.

Once you have the SL4A binary installed, you must start it and download the particular interpreter you want to use. The following are available as of this writing:

- Python
- Perl
- JRuby
- Lua
- BeanShell
- JavaScript
- Tcl
- Unix shell

Some of the interpreters (e.g., JRuby) run in the Dalvik VM, while others (e.g., Python) run the "native" versions of the language under Linux on your phone. Communication happens via a little server that is started automatically when needed or can be started from the Interpreters menu bar.

The technique for downloading new interpreters is a bit subobvious. When you start the SL4A application it shows a list of scripts, if you have any. Click the Menu button, then go to the View menu and select Interpreters (while here, notice that you can also view the LogCat, the system exception logfile). From the Interpreters list, clicking Menu *again* will get you a menu bar with an Add button, and this lets you add another interpreter.

Pick a language (Python)

Suppose you think Python is a great language (which it is).

Once your interpreter is installed, go back to the SL4A main page and click the Menu button, then Add (in this context, Add creates a new file, not another interpreter). Select the installed interpreter and you'll be in Edit mode. We're trying Python, so type in this canonical "hello world" example:

```
import android
droid = android.Android()
droid.makeToast("Hello, Android")
```

Click the Menu button, and Save and Run if enabled, or Save and Exit otherwise. The former will run your new app; the latter will return you to the list of scripts, in which case you want to tap your script's name. In the resultant pop up, the choices are (left to right):

- Run ("DOS box" icon)
- Disabled
- Edit ("pencil" icon)
- Save ("1980 floppy disk icon")
- Delete (trash can icon)

If you long-press a filename, a pop up gives you the choice of Rename or Delete.

When you run this trivial application, you will see the toast near the bottom of your screen.

Source editing

If you want to keep your scripts in a source repository, and/or if you prefer to edit them on a laptop or desktop with a traditional keyboard, just copy the files back and forth (if your phone is rooted, you can probably run your repository directly on the phone). Scripts are stored in *sl4a/scripts* on the SD card. If you have your phone mounted on your laptop's */mnt* folder, for example, you might see the code shown in Example 20-5 (on Windows it might be *E:* or *F:* instead of */mnt*):

Example 20-5. List of scripting files

```
laptop$ ls /mnt/sl4a/
Shell.log demo.sh.log dialer.py.log hello_world.py.log ifconfig.py.log
notify_weather.py.log phonepicker.py.log say_chat.py.log say_time.py.log
say_weather.py.log scripts/ sms.py.log speak.py.log take_picture.py.log
test.py.log
laptop$ ls /mnt/sl4a/scripts
bluetooth_chat.py demo.sh dialer.py foo.sh hello_world.py ifconfig.py
notify_weather.py phonepicker.py say_chat.py say_time.py say_weather.py
sms.py speak.py take_picture.py test.py weather.py weather.pyc
laptop$
```

See Also

The official SL4A website is *http://code.google.com/p/android-scripting/*; a QR code is available there to download the latest binary. In addition, several textbooks are now available on SL4a, also listed there.

20.5 Creating Alerts in SL4A

Rachee Singh

Problem

You need to create an alert box or pop-up dialog using Python in the Scripting Layer for Android (SL4A).

Solution

You can create many kinds of alert dialogs using Python in SL4A. They can have buttons, lists, and other features.

Discussion

Begin by starting the SL4A app on your emulator/device. Then add a new Python script by clicking the Menu button and choosing Add (see Figure 20-2).

Choose the Python 2.x option from the submenu that appears, as shown in Figure 20-3.

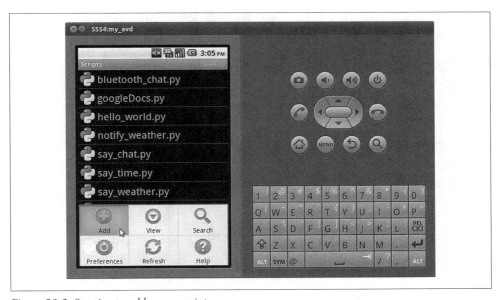

Figure 20-2. Starting to add a new script

This opens an editor, with the first two lines (shown in Figure 20-4) already filled in for you. Enter the name of the script (I have named mine *alertdialog.py*; see Figure 20-4).

Now we are ready to enter the code to create the alert dialogs. Type in the code shown in Example 20-6:

Example 20-6. A simple SL4A Python script

```
title = 'Sample Alert Dialog'
text = 'Alert Dialog Type 1!'
droid.dialogCreateAlert(title, text)
droid.dialogSetPositiveButtonText('Continue')
droid.dialogShow()
```

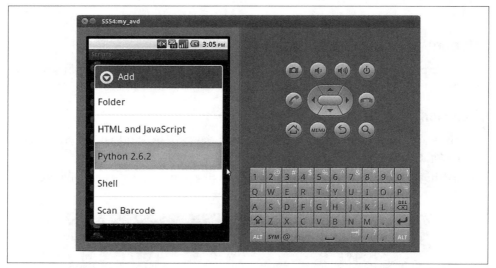

Figure 20-3. Choosing the language

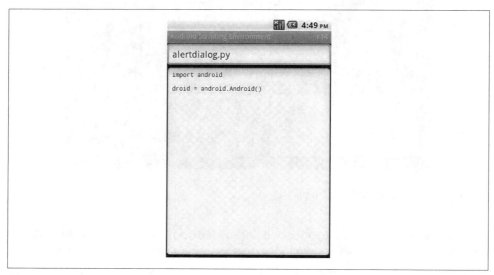

Figure 20-4. Composing the script

Press the Menu button and choose Save and Run from the menu. This runs the script. The alert dialog should look like Figure 20-5.

Figure 20-5. Sample alert dialog

Now let's create an alert dialog with two buttons, using the code in Example 20-7.

Example 20-7. Composing an alert with three choices

```
title = 'Sample Alert Dialog'
text = 'Alert Dialog Type 2 with Buttons!'
droid.dialogCreateAlert(title, text)
droid.dialogSetPositiveButtonText('Yes')
droid.dialogSetNegativeButtonText('No')
droid.dialogSetNeutralButtonText('Cancel')
droid.dialogShow()
```

Figure 20-6 shows how this alert dialog looks.

Figure 20-6. Alert dialog with two choices in action

Now try the code in Example 20-8 to create an alert dialog with a list.

Example 20-8. Another approach to composing an alert with three choices

```
title = 'Sample Alert Dialog'
droid.dialogCreateAlert(title)
droid.dialogSetItems(['mango', 'apple', 'strawberry'])
droid.dialogShow()
```

Figure 20-7 shows how this alert dialog looks.

Figure 20-7. Dialog with three choices

20.6 Fetching Your Google Documents and Displaying Them in a ListView Using SL4A

Rachee Singh

Problem

You need to get the details of your Google documents after logging in with your Google ID and password.

Solution

Google Documents is a widely used document editing and sharing service. Using the library gdata.docs.service, we can log in (getting the username and password from the user) and then get the "Google documents feed" or list of documents.

Discussion

Fire up the Scripting Layer for Android on your device (or emulator). Open a new Python script and add to the script the code shown in Example 20-9. If you have not worked in Python before, be aware that indentation, rather than braces, is used for statement grouping, so you must be very consistent about leading spaces.

Example 20-9. Composing a script to fetch Google documents

```python
import android
import gdata.docs.service

droid = android.Android()

client = gdata.docs.service.DocsService()

username = droid.dialogGetInput('Username').result
password = droid.dialogGetPassword('Password', 'For ' _username).result

def truncate(content, length=15, suffix='...'):
    if len(content) <=length:
        return content
    else:
        return content[:length] + suffix
try:
    client.ClientLogin(username, password)
except:
    droid.makeToast("Login Failed")

docs_feed = client.GetDocumentListFeed()

documentEntries = []

for entry in docs_feed.entry:
    documentEntries.append('%-18s %-12s %s' % (truncate(entry.title.text.encode('UTF-8')),
    entry.GetDocumentType(), entry.resourceId.text))

droid.dialogCreateAlert('Documents:')
droid.dialogSetItems(documentEntries)
droid.dialogShow()
```

Figure 20-8 shows how the editor should look after you have finished entering the code.

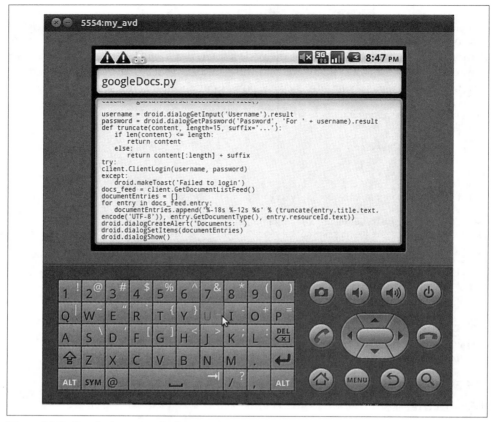

```
username = droid.dialogGetInput('Username').result
password = droid.dialogGetPassword('Password', 'For ' + username).result
def truncate(content, length=15, suffix='...'):
    if len(content) <= length:
        return content
    else:
        return content[:length] + suffix
try:
client.ClientLogin(username, password)
except:
    droid.makeToast('Failed to login')
docs_feed = client.GetDocumentListFeed()
documentEntries = []
for entry in docs_feed.entry:
    documentEntries.append('%-18s %-12s %s' % (truncate(entry.title.text.
encode('UTF-8')), entry.GetDocumentType(), entry.resourceId.text))
droid.dialogCreateAlert('Documents: ')
droid.dialogSetItems(documentEntries)
droid.dialogShow()
```

Figure 20-8. Google document fetcher in action

In this Python code, we use the gdata.docs.service.DocsService() method to connect to the Google account of a user. The username and password are taken from the user. Once the login is done successfully, the GetDocumentListFeed() method is used to get the feed list of the Google documents. We format the details of each entry and append them to a list named documentEntries. This list is then passed as an argument to the alert dialog, which displays all the entries in a list.

Figure 20-9 shows how my own document list looks.

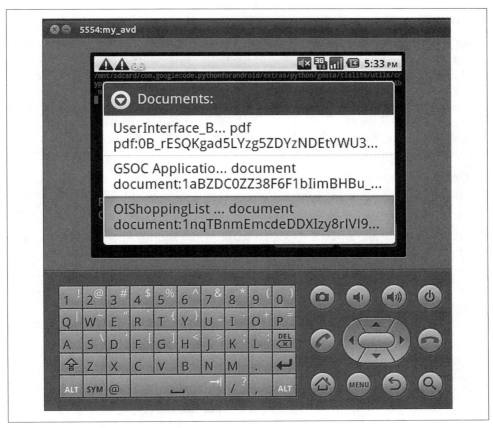

Figure 20-9. List of Google documents

20.7 Sharing SL4A Scripts in QR Codes

Rachee Singh

Problem

You have a neat/useful SL4A script and want to distribute it packed in a Quick Response (QR) code.

Solution

Use *http://zxing.appspot.com/generator/* or one of several other QR code generators to generate a QR code that contains your entire script in the QR code graphic, and share this image.

Discussion

Most people think of QR codes as a convenient way to share URL-type links. Indeed, the printed edition of this book uses QR codes for individual downloads of sample applications. However, the QR code format is much more versatile, and can be used to package all sorts of things, like VCard (name and address) information. Here we use it to wrap the "plain text" of an SL4A script so that another Android user can get the script onto his device without retyping it. QR codes are a great way to share your scripts if they are short (QR codes can only encode 4,296 characters of content). Follow these simple steps to generate a QR code for your script:

1. Visit *http://zxing.appspot.com/generator/* in your mobile device's browser.
2. Select Text from the drop-down menu.
3. In the "Text content" box, put the script's name in the first line.
4. From the next line onward, enter the script. As an alternative to these steps, copy the script from an SL4A editor window and paste it into the "Text content" box in the browser.
5. Choose Large for the barcode size and click Generate.

Figure 20-10 shows how this looks in action.

Figure 20-10. Barcode generated from the SL4A script

Many QR code readers are available for Android. Any such application can decipher the text that the QR code encrypts. For example, with the common ZXing barcode scanner, the script is copied to the clipboard (this is controlled by a "When a Barcode is found..." entry in the Settings for ZXing). Then start the SL4A editor, pick a name for your script, ideally the same as the original if you know it—depending on how it was pasted into the QR code generator it may appear as the first line—then long-press in the body area and select Paste. You are now ready to save the script and run it! It should look like Figure 20-11.

Figure 20-11. The script, downloaded

I was able to run the script from the QR code with no further work other than commenting out the script name in the body and typing it into the filename field, then clicking "Save and Run" (see Figure 20-12).

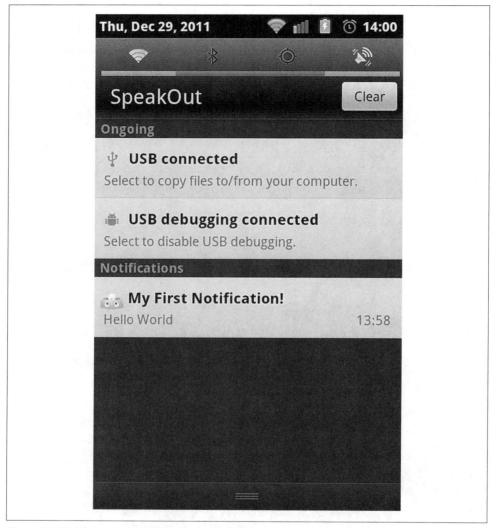

Figure 20-12. The script running, showing a Notification

20.8 Using Native Handset Functionality from WebView via JavaScript

Colin Wilcox

Problem

The availability of HTML5 as a standard feature in many browsers means that developers can exploit the features of the HTML5 standard to create applications much more quickly than they can in native Java. This sounds great for many applications, but, alas, not all of the cool functionality on the device is accessible through HTML5 and JavaScript. Webkits attempt to bridge the gap, but they may not provide all the functionality needed in all cases.

Solution

You can invoke Java code in response to JavaScript events using a bridge between the JavaScript and Java environments.

Discussion

The idea is to tie up events within the JavaScript embedded in an HTML5 web page and handle the event on the Java side by calling native code.

The following code creates a button in HTML5 embedded in a web view which, when clicked, causes the contacts application to be invoked on the device through the Intent mechanism:

```
import android.content.Context;
import android.content.Intent;
import android.util.Log;
```

Now we write some thin bridge code, as shown in Example 20-10.

Example 20-10. The bridge code

```
public class JavaScriptInterface
{
    private static final String TAG = "JavaScriptInterface";
    Context iContext = null;

    /** Instantiate the interface and set the context */
    JavaScriptInterface(Context aContext)
    {
        // save the local content for later use
        iContext = aContext;
    }

    public void launchContacts();
    {
        iContext.startActivity(contactIntent);
```

```
        launchNativeContactsApp ();
    }
}
```

The Java code to actually launch contacts is shown in Example 20-11.

Example 20-11. Java code to launch contacts

```java
private void launchNativeContactsApp()
{
    String packageName = "com.android.contacts";
    String className = ".DialtactsContactsEntryActivity";
    String action = "android.intent.action.MAIN";
    String category1 = "android.intent.category.LAUNCHER";
    String category2 = "android.intent.category.DEFAULT";

    Intent intent = new Intent();
    intent.setComponent(new ComponentName(packageName, packageName + className));
    intent.setAction(action);
    intent.addCategory(category1);
    intent.addCategory(category2);
    startActivity(intent);
}
```

The JavaScript that ties this all together is shown in the following snippet. In this case the call is triggered by a click event.

```html
<input type="button" value="Say hello" onClick="showAndroidContacts())" />
<script type="text/javascript">
    function showAndroidContacts()
    {
        Android.launchContacts();
    }
</script>
```

The only preconditions are that the web browser has JavaScript enabled and the interface is known. This is done by:

```java
WebView iWebView = (WebView) findViewById(R.id.webview);
iWebView.addJavascriptInterface(new JavaScriptInterface(this), "Android");
```

20.9 Creating a Platform-Independent Application Using PhoneGap/Cordova

Shraddha Shravagi

Problem

You want an application to run on different platforms, such as iOS, Android, BlackBerry, Bada, Symbian, and Windows Mobile.

Solution

Cordova (better known as PhoneGap) is an open source mobile development framework. If you plan to develop an application for multiple platforms, PhoneGap is one good solution, so much so that Oracle and BlackBerry, among others, either endorse it or base products on it. PhoneGap does not use traditional platform GUI controls; rather you write a web page with buttons—made to approximate the native look by careful use of CSS—and PhoneGap runs this "mobile app" for you.

PhoneGap was written by Nitobi, a small company that Adobe Systems Inc. acquired in fall 2011. Adobe has donated the framework source code to the Apache Software Foundation, where its development continues, briefly under the name "Callback" and now under the name "Cordova."

Discussion

We will start with an Android application. We don't use the normal Android layouts nor the notion of "one activity per screen"; instead, we create HTML and JavaScript files, which can run on different platforms. In fact, the app is mostly a "mobile web app" that is packaged as an Android app! We keep minimal code in the activity since such code would have to be rewritten for each platform.

Here are the steps for a basic PhoneGap application:[1]

1. Create a new Android application.
2. Download the *phonegap-version.zip* file (the version as of this writing is 1.5.0) from *http://phonegap.com/* (this URL will soon be changed to the Apache download site). Copy the *cordova-version.jar* file from the *lib/android* folder of the ZIP file you downloaded, and add it to the *lib* folder and, of course, to the project's build path.
3. Create a new folder in the *assets* folder; for example, *www*.
4. Copy the *phonegap-1.0.0.js* and *jquery.min.js* files into *assets/www*.
5. Create a new file, *helloworld.html*, in the *assets/www* folder.
6. In the body of this HTML page, add:

   ```
   <h1> Hello World </h1>
   ```

   You can add all your HTML/jQuery mobile code here. For example, to add a button:

   ```
   <a data-role="button" data-icon="grid" data-theme="b" onClick="showAlert()">
   Click Me!!!</a>
   ```

7. Create a new file, *helloresponse.js*, in the *assets/www* folder. In this JavaScript file you can add all your jQuery mobile and JavaScript code:

---

1. Note that, as of the current version as we go to press, some of the filenames contain "phonegap," while others contain "cordova."

```
function showAlert(){
    alert('Hello World from PHONE GAP using Javascript!!! ');
}
```

8. In your main activity file, import `com.phonegap.DroidGap`; then change `extends Activity` to `extends DroidGap`.

9. In the `Activity`'s `onCreate()` method, pass the URI of your HTML file into the `DroidGap` `loadUrl` method so that the HTML file will be invoked.

The Java code should look just like Example 20-12.

Example 20-12. The PhoneGap activity

```
import com.phonegap.DroidGap;

public class HomeScreen extends DroidGap {
    /** Called when the activity is first created. */
    @Override
    public void onCreate(Bundle savedInstanceState) {
        super.onCreate(savedInstanceState);

        //set the URL from assets which is to be loaded.
        super.loadUrl("file:///android_asset/www/helloworld.html");
    }
}
```

That's it. You should be able to run the application.

Take a look at the source download for some more great jQuery mobile examples.

See Also

http://phonegap.com/. Also, *Building Android Apps with HTML, CSS, and JavaScript* (*http://shop.oreilly.com/product/0636920010067.do*) by Jonathan Stark (O'Reilly) gives a PhoneGap-centric coverage of these "background" technologies as well as more information on PhoneGap development.

Source Download URL

The source code for this example is in the Android Cookbook repository at *http://github.com/AndroidCook/Android-Cookbook-Examples*, in the subdirectory PhoneGapDemo (see "Getting and Using the Code Examples" on page xvii).

CHAPTER 21

Strings and Internationalization

21.1 Introduction: Internationalization

Ian Darwin

Discussion

"All the world's a stage," wrote William Shakespeare. But not all the players on that great and turbulent stage speak the great Bard's native tongue. To be usable on a global scale, your software needs to communicate in many different languages. The menu labels, button strings, dialog messages, title bar titles, and even command-line error messages must be settable to the user's choice of language. This is the topic of internationalization and localization. Because these words take a long time to say and write, they are often abbreviated with their first and last letters and the count of omitted letters, that is, I18N and L10N.

If you've got your strings in a separate XML file as we advised in Chapter 1, you have already done part of the work of internationalizing your app. Aren't you glad you followed our advice?

Android provides a `Locale` class to discover/control the internationalization settings. A default `Locale` is inherited from the user's language settings when your app starts up.

Note that if you know internationalization from Desktop Java, it's pretty much the same. We'll explain as we go along, with examples, in this chapter.

Ian's basic steps: Internationalization

Internationalization and localization consist of:

Sensitivity training (internationalization or I18N)
    Making your software sensitive to these issues.

Language lessons (localization or L10N)
    Writing configuration files for each language.

Culture lessons (optional)

Customizing the presentation of numbers, fractions, dates, and message-formatting. Images can mean different things in different cultures.

This chapter's recipes provide examples of doing all three.

See Also

Wikipedia has a good article on localization at *http://en.wikipedia.org/wiki/Internation alisation_and_localisation.*

See also *Java Internationalization* (*http://shop.oreilly.com/product/9780596000196.do*) by Andy Deitsch and David Czarnecki (O'Reilly).

Microsoft's *The GUI Guide: International Terminology for the Windows Interface* (*http://www.amazon.com/dp/1556155387*) was, despite the title, less about UI design than about internationalization; it came with a 3.5-inch floppy disk holding suggested translations of common Microsoft Windows GUI element names into a dozen or so common languages. This book is rather dated today, but it might be a start for translating simple texts into some common languages. It can often be found on the usual used-book websites.

21.2 Internationalizing Application Text

Ian Darwin

Problem

You want the text of your buttons, labels, and so on to appear in the user's chosen language.

Solution

Create a *strings.xml* file in the *res/values-XX/* subdirectory of your application. Translate the string values into the given language.

Discussion

Every Android project created with the SDK has a file called *strings.xml* in the *res/values* directory. This is where you are advised to place your application's strings, from the application title through to the button text and even down to the contents of dialogs.

You can refer to a string by name in the following two ways:

- By a reference in a layout file, to apply the correct version of the string directly to a GUI component; for example, `android:text="@string/hello"`
- If you need the value in Java code, by using a lookup such as `get String(R.string.hello)` to look up the string's value from the file

---

To make all of these strings available in a different language, you need to know the correct ISO-3166 language code; a few common ones are shown in Table 21-1.

Table 21-1. Common languages and codes

Language	Code
Chinese (traditional)	cn-tw
Chinese (simplified)	cn-zh
English	en
French	fr
German	de
Italian	it
Spanish	es

With this information, you can create a new subdirectory, *res/values-<LL>/* (where *LL* is replaced by the ISO language code). In this directory you create a copy of *strings.xml*, and in it you translate the individual string values (but not the names). For example, a simple application might have the following in *strings.xml*:

```
<?xml version="1.0" encoding="utf-8"?>
<resources>
    <string name="app_name">MyAndroid</string>
    <string name="hello">Hello Android</string>
</resources>
```

You might create *res/values-es/strings.xml* containing the following Spanish text (see Figure 21-1):

```
<?xml version="1.0" encoding="utf-8"?>
<resources>
    <string name="app_name">MiAndroid</string>
    <string name="hello">Hola Android</string>
</resources>
```

You might also create the file *res/values-fr/strings.xml* containing the following French text:

```
<?xml version="1.0" encoding="utf-8"?>
<resources>
    <string name="hello">Bonjour Android</string>
    <string name="app_name">MonAndroid</string>
</resources>
```

Note that the order of entries within this file does not matter, so the fact that this example has the *app_name* last is unimportant.

Now when you look up the string "hello" using either of the methods described earlier, you will get the version based on the user's language choice. If the user selects a language that you don't have a L10N file for, the app will still work, but it will get the value from the default file—the one in the *values* directory with no language code. For most of us, that will contain the English values, but it's up to the developer.

This lookup is done per string, so if there is a string that's not defined in a language-specific file, the app will find the version of it from the default *strings.xml* file.

Is it really that simple?

Yes. Just package your application and deploy it (if you're using Eclipse, just Run As Android Application). Go into the Settings app of your emulator or device, choose Language, and select French or Spanish and the program title and window contents should reflect the change (Figure 21-1).

Figure 21-1. Hello app in Spanish

You just have to remember to keep the versions of *strings.xml* in sync with the "master" copy.

Regional variants

OK, so it's not quite that simple. There are also regional variations within a language. In English there are, for example, UK English (a.k.a. "the real thing" by some), U.S. English, Canadian, Australian, and so on. These, fortunately, have tended to use the same vocabulary for technical terms, so using the regional variations is not as important for English. On the other hand, French and Spanish, to name two that I am familiar with, are languages where there is significant variation in vocabulary from one region to another. Parisian French and French Canadian have used different vocabularies for many words coined since the 1500s when the exodus to Canada began. The many Spanish colonies were likewise largely isolated from hearing and reading one another's words for hundreds of years—from their founding until the age of radio—and they have diverged even more than French. So you may want to create "variant" files for these languages, as for any other that has significant regional variation.

Android's practice here diverges slightly from Java's, in that Android uses a letter *r* to denote regional variations; for example, you'd create a *values-fr-rCA* directory for French Canadian. Note that, as in Java, language codes are in lowercase and variations (which are usually the two-letter ISO country code) are written in capital letters (except for the leading *r*). So we might wind up with the set of files listed in Table 21-2.

Table 21-2. L10N directory examples

Directory	Meaning
values	English; default.
values-es	Spanish ("Castilian," generic)
values-es-rCU	Spanish - Cuban
values-es-rCL	Spanish - Chilean

See Also

There is a bit more detail in the official Android Localization documentation (*http://developer.android.com/guide/topics/resources/localization.html*).

21.3 Finding and Translating Strings

Ian Darwin

Problem

You need to find all the strings in your application, internationalize them, and begin the process of translating them.

Solution

There are several good tools for finding string literals, as well as collaborative and commercial services that translate text files.

Discussion

Suppose you have a mix of old and new Java code in your app; the new code was written specifically for Android, while the older code may have been used in some other Java environment. You need to find every `String` literal, isolated it into a *Strings.xml* file, and translate it into any necessary languages.

The Android Localizer from ArtfulBits Inc. (*http://artfulbits.com/products/free/ailocal izer.aspx*) is a free and open source tool that you can use to handle both steps of this process.

MOTODEV Studio (*http://developer.motorola.com/docstools/motodevstudio*) is a freely available (with sign-up) commercial tool that includes this functionality (as well as quite a bit more). Both tools will feed your strings through Google Translate to get a rough working version.

Imagine a slightly different scenario: suppose your organization has a "native" (Objective-C) application from iOS and you are building the "native" Java version for Android. Here, the properties files are in very different formats—on iOS there is a Java Properties-like file but with the default (probably English) strings on the left and the translations on the right. No names are used, just the actual strings, so you might find something like the following:

```
You-not us-are responsible=You-not us-are responsible
```

You cannot translate this directly into XML, since the "name" is used as an identifier in the generated `R` (`Resources`) class, and the hyphen (-) and straight quotes (") characters are not valid in Java identifiers. Doing it manually, you might come up with something like this:

```
<string name="you_not_us_are_responsible">You-not us-are responsible</string>
```

User "johnthuss" has developed a version of a Java program that performs such translations from iOS to Android format (*http://stackoverflow.com/questions/3141118/are -there-any-tools-to-convert-an-iphone-localized-string-file-to-a-string-resou/5838915 #5838915*), handling characters that are not valid identifiers.

Now, at any rate, you are ready to begin translating your master resource file into other languages. While it may be tempting to scrimp on this part of the work, it is generally worthwhile to engage the services of a professional translation service skilled in the particular language(s) you target. Alternatively, you may wish to investigate the commercial collaborative translation service at Crowdin.net (*http://crowdin.net/page/an droid-localization*).

When using any third-party translation service, especially for languages with which you or your staff are not personally "first or second childhood language" familiar, you should normally *get a second opinion*. Embarrassing errors in software shipped with "bad" translations can be very expensive. There is an apocryphal story, widely used as a warning of this point, of Microsoft inadvertently hiring Taiwanese-sympathetic translators to translate the mainland Chinese version of Microsoft Windows. Here is one reference to this incident: "... The discovery, in the summer of 1996, that some Microsoft programs localized in Chinese carried hidden slogans has again strained

Microsoft-PRC relations." The citation given is to the *South China Morning Post*, October (day unknown), 1996.[1]

A quick web search will find many commercial services that perform translations for you, as well as some that help with the internationalization part of the work.

21.4 Handling the Nuances of strings.xml

Daniel Fowler

Problem

Entering text in the *strings.xml* file on most occasions is easy enough, but sometimes peculiar results crop up.

Solution

Understanding how some text strings and characters work in *strings.xml* will prevent strange results.

Discussion

When some text is required on a screen it can be declared in a layout file, as shown in the following `android:text` attribute:

```
<TextView android:id="@+id/textview1"
    android:layout_width="fill_parent"
    android:layout_height="wrap_content"
    android:text="This is text"/>
```

The text can be also be set in code:

```
TextView tview = (TextView) findViewById(R.id.textview1);
tview.setText("This is text");
```

However, hardcoding strings like this is not recommended, because it reduces maintainability. Changing text at a later date may mean hunting down declarations across several Java source files and layout files. Instead, text in a project can be centralized into a *strings.xml* file. The file is located in the directory *values* under *res* in the project folders. Centralizing text means there is only one place to go to change it. It also makes localization much easier; see Recipe 21.2. Here is an example of a *strings.xml* file:

```
<?xml version="1.0" encoding="utf-8"?>
<resources>
    <string name="app_name">Strings XML</string>
    <string name="text1">This is text</string>
```

---

1. This appears in "Software Localization: Notes on Technology and Culture" by Kenneth Keniston, January 17, 1997, Working Paper #26, Program in Science, Technology, and Society, Massachusetts Institute of Technology, Cambridge, Massachusetts 02139. Online (PDF) available at *http://web.mit.edu/sts/pubs/pdfs/MIT_STS_WorkingPaper_26_Keniston_2.pdf*; viewed November 4, 2011.

```
                  <string name="text2">And so is this</string>
              </resources>
```

To access the declared string from another project XML file use @ followed by **string** and then a slash and the string's name. Using the preceding example, the text for two **TextView**s is set with the following layout XML file:

```
<LinearLayout xmlns:android="http://schemas.android.com/apk/res/android"
    android:orientation="vertical"
    android:layout_width="fill_parent"
    android:layout_height="fill_parent">
  <TextView android:id="@+id/textview1"
            android:layout_width="fill_parent"
            android:layout_height="wrap_content"
            android:text="@string/text1"
            android:textSize="16dp"/>
  <TextView android:id="@+id/textview2"
            android:layout_width="fill_parent"
            android:layout_height="wrap_content"
            android:text="@string/text2"
            android:textSize="16dp"/>
</LinearLayout>
```

When the *strings.xml* file is saved, the **R.string** class is generated (see *R.java* in the *gen* directory for the project). This provides a **static int** that can be used to reference the string in code:

```
tview = (TextView) findViewById(R.id.textview1);
    tview.setText(R.string.text1);
```

The **R** class should never be edited, because it is generated by the SDK and any changes you do make will be overwritten.

In the *strings.xml* file an entry can duplicate another string by referencing it the same way as a layout file:

```
<string name="text1">This is text</string>
<string name="text2">@string/text1</string>
```

Since @ is used to indicate another string resource trying to set the text to a single @, using <string name="text1">@</string> will not work. Nor will text that starts with an @, such as <string name="text2">@mytwittername</string>.

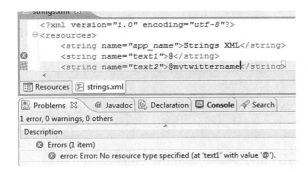

The first @ needs to be *escaped* with a \ (backslash), that is, \@ and \@mytwittername. If the @ does not start a string or is being set in code it does not need to be escaped; for example, `android:text=Twitter:@mytwittername` or `tview.setText("@mytwittername");`. This problem of @ as the first character, or only character, also applies to the ? (question mark). If it appears at the start of a string it also needs escaping, `android:text=\?`.

An alternative to escaping the @ or ? is to use quotes (speech marks); the closing quote mark is optional:

```
<string name="text1">"@"</string>
<string name="text2">"?"</string>
```

If fact, any number of quotes or whitespace before and after text is dropped. The two lines in the preceding code snippet produce an identical result to these two lines:

```
<string name="text1">"""""""""@"""""""</string>
<string name="text2">        "?"        </string>
```

There is a character for which this approach will not work:

```
<string name="text1">War & Peace</string>
<string name="text2">War and Peace</string>
```

The first line will result in an error because of the &. This is because of the XML file format itself. XML requires balanced pairs of tags—for example, `<string>` and `</string>`—and each start tag and end tag is enclosed in opening (<) and closing (>) angle brackets. Once a start tag is encountered the editor is on the lookout for the opening bracket of the end tag. This produces a problem if the content of the XML tags contains the open angle bracket itself:

```
<string name="question">Is 5 &lt; 6?</string>
```

This will not work. The solution is to use an XML internal entity; this is similar to using an escape character but is in a specific format for XML. The format is an ampersand, &, followed by the entity name and then a semicolon. For the open angle bracket, or less-than symbol, the name is lt, and therefore the full entity is < as in:

```
<string name="question">Is 5 &lt; 6?</string>
```

Depending on what is required in an XML file at a particular point, there are five internal entities defined for XML that can be used, as shown in Table 21-3:

Table 21-3. The predefined entities in XML

Entity	Name	Usage
The left angle bracket (<)	lt	&lt;
The right angle bracket (>)	gt	&gt;
The ampersand (&)	amp	&amp;
The single quote or apostrophe (')	apos	&apos;
The double quote (")	quot	&quot;

Now we can see why the ampersand causes us a problem. It is used to define an internal entity, and thus when one is required the amp entity itself must be used. Therefore, `<string name="text1">War & Peace</string>` becomes `<string name="text1">War &amp; Peace</string>`.

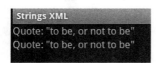

However, the XML internal entity apos, while valid for XML, is reported as an error when the file is saved:

```
<string name="text1">This isn't working</string>
<string name="text2">This isn&apos;t working either</string>
```

It is another character that requires escaping or wrapping in quotes:

```
<string name="text1">This\'ll work</string>
<string name="text2">"This'll work as well"</string>
```

To use quotes (speech marks) themselves, even the XML internal entity version, escape them:

```
<string name="text1">Quote: \"to be, or not to be\"</string>
<string name="text2">Quote: \&quot;to be, or not to be\&quot;</string>
```

When defining a string that requires pre or post space, again use quotes:

```
<string name="text1">  No spaces before and after  </string>
<string name="text2">"  Two spaces before and after  "</string>
```

The strings will support a new line by escaping the letter *n*:

```
<string name="text1">Split over\ntwo lines</string>
<string name="text2">2 TextViews\n4 Lines</string>
```

Escaping a *t* adds a tab to the defined string:

```
<string name="text1">Tab stops\ta\t\tb</string>
<string name="text2">\t\t\t\tc\t\td</string>
```

To see the escape character (backslash), use two of them:

```
<string name="text1">Backlash:\\</string>
<string name="text2">Slash:/</string>
```

The `android:textstyle` attribute of a `TextView` in a layout file can be used to set the text to bold or italic (or both):

```
android:textStyle="bold"
android:textStyle="italic"
android:textStyle="bold|italic"
```

This can be achieved in the *strings.xml* file using a bold (`<b>`) or italic tag (`<i>`), plus it supports an underline tag (`<u>`). However, instead of applying it to the whole text of the `TextView`, it can be used for individual portions of the text:

```
<string name="text1">Hey look:<b>bold</b> and <i>italic</i>.</string>
<string name="text2">And look: <u>underline</u> and <b><i><u>bold italic underline
</u></i></b>.</string>
```

See Also

http://developer.android.com/guide/topics/resources/string-resource.html

Packaging, Deploying, and Distributing/Selling Your App

22.1 Introduction: Packaging, Deploying, and Distributing

Ian Darwin

Discussion

The success of Android has led to a proliferation of application markets. But the official Android Market remains the largest marketplace for distributing your app, so we will cover that, along with information on preparing your app, making it harder to reverse-engineer, and other information you may need along the way.

22.2 Creating a Signing Certificate

Zigurd Mednieks

Problem

You want to publish an application, and you need a "signing key" to complete the process.

Solution

Use the standard JDK tool *keytool* to generate a self-signed certificate.

Discussion

Google has stated that one of its intentions with Android was to minimize the hassle of getting applications signed. You don't have to go to a central signing authority to get a signing certificate; you can create the certificate yourself. Once you generate the certificate, you can sign your application using the jarsigner tool that comes with the

Java JDK. Once again, you don't need to apply for or get anyone's approval. As you'll see, it's about as straightforward as signing can be.

In this recipe, you are going to create an encrypted signing certificate and use it to sign your application. You can sign every Android application you develop with the same signing certificate. You can create as many signing certificates as you want, but you really need only one for all your applications. And using one certificate for all your applications lets you do some things that you couldn't do otherwise:

Simplify upgrades

> Signing certificates are tied to the application package name, so if you change the signing certificate you use with subsequent versions of your application, you'll have to change the package name, too. Changing certificates is manageable, but messy.

Run multiple applications per user ID

> When all your applications share the same signing certificate, they can run in the same Linux process. You can use this to separate your application into smaller modules (each one an Android application) that together make up the larger application. If you were to do that, you could update the modules separately and they could still communicate freely.

Share code/data

> Android lets you enable or restrict access to parts of your application based on the requester's signing certificate. If all your applications share the same certificate, it's easy for you to reuse parts of one application in another.

When you generate a key pair and certificate you'll be asked for the validity period you desire for the certificate. Although usual practice in website development is to use one or two years, Google recommends that you set the validity period to at least 25 years, and in fact, if you're going to use the Android Market to distribute your application, it requires a validity date at least until October 22, 2033 (25 years to the day from when Google opened the Android Market) for your certificate.

Generating a key pair (public and private keys) and a signing certificate

To generate a pair of public/private keys, use a tool called keytool, which came with the Sun JDK when you installed it onto your development computer. keytool asks you for some information and uses that to generate the pair of keys:

- A private key that will be kept in a keystore on your computer, secured with passwords. You will use the private key to sign your application, and if you need a Map API Key for your application, you will use the MD5 fingerprint of the signing certificate to generate the Map API Key.

- A public key that Android can use to decrypt your signing certificate. You will send the public key along with your published application so that it can be made available in the runtime environment. Signing certificates are actually checked only at install time, so once installed, your application is good to run, even if the certificate or keys expire.

keytool is pretty straightforward. From your operating system's command line, enter something like the following:

```
$ keytool -genkey -v -keystore myapp.keystore -alias myapp -keyalg RSA
 -validity 10000
```

This asks keytool to generate a key pair and self-signed certificate (-genkey) in verbose mode (-v), so you get all the information, and put it in a keystore called myapp.key store (-keystore). It also says that in the future you want to refer to that key by the name myapp (-alias), and that keytool should use the RSA algorithm for generating public/private key pairs (-keyalg). Finally, we say that we'd like the key to be valid for 10,000 days (-validity), or about twenty-seven years.

keytool will prompt you for some things it uses to build the key pair and certificate:

- A password to be used in the future when you want to access the keystore
- Your first and last names
- Your organizational unit (the name for your division of your company, or something like "self" if you aren't developing for a company)
- Your organization name (the name of your company, or anything else you want to use)
- The name of your city or locality
- The name of your state or province
- The two-letter country code where you are located

keytool will then echo all this information back to you to make sure it's accurate, and if you confirm the information, will generate the key pair and certificate. It will then ask you for another password to use for the key itself (and give you the option of using the same password you used for the keystore). Using that password, keytool will store the key pair and certificate in the keystore.

See Also

If you're not familiar with the algorithms used here, such as RSA and MD5, well, you don't actually need to know much about them. Assuming you've a modicum of intellectual curiosity, you can find out all you need to know about them with any good web search engine.

You can get more information about security, key pairs, and the keytool utility on Sun's website (*http://java.sun.com/j2se/1.5.0/docs/tooldocs/#security*).

22.3 Signing Your Application

Zigurd Mednieks

Problem

You want to sign your application prior to uploading it to the Android Market.

Solution

An APK file is a standard Java Archive (JAR) format, so you just use the standard JDK tool jarsigner.

Discussion

Having created a key, and a Map API Key if needed, you are almost ready to sign your application, but first you need to create an unsigned version that you can sign with your digital certificate. To do that, in the Package Explorer window of Eclipse, right-click on your project name. You'll get a long pop-up menu; toward the bottom, click on Android Tools. You should see another menu that includes the item you want: "Export Unsigned Application Package...". This item takes you to a File Save dialog box, where you can pick the place to save the unsigned version of your APK file. It doesn't matter where you put it, just pick a place you can remember. Now that you have an unsigned version of your APK file, we can go ahead and sign it using jarsigner.

Open a terminal or command window in the directory where you stored the unsigned APK file. To sign MyApp, using the key you generated in Recipe 22.2:

```
$ jarsigner -verbose -keystore myapp.keystore MyApp.apk mykey
```

You should now have a signed version of your application that can be loaded and run on any Android device. But before you send it in to the Android Market, there's one more intervening step: you have rebuilt the application, so you must test it again, on real devices. If you don't have a real device, get one. If you only have one, get more, or make friends with somebody who owns a device from a different manufacturer.

Note that in the latest version of the Eclipse plug-in, there is also an Export Signed Application Package, which will combine these actions (Recipe 22.2 and Recipe 22.3) into a single wizard. This new action is available in the project's context menu (as discussed in the first paragraph of this recipe's Discussion), and also in the File Menu under Export, where it is known simply as Export Android Project. This new action also allows you to create the keystore and generate the keys within the wizard, which is so much more convenient that it probably makes it more likely that you will forget where you put the keystore. Don't do that!

22.4 Distributing Your Application via Android Play (formerly the Android Market)

Zigurd Mednieks

Problem

You want to give away or sell your application via Android Play, the app store formerly known as Android Market. Note that the Android Market was combined with Google Books and other services under the Google Play rubric, just as this book was going to press.

Solution

Use the Android Play app market.

Discussion

After you're satisfied that your application runs as expected on real Android devices, you're ready to upload it to the Android Play market, Google's service for publishing and downloading Android applications. The procedure is pretty straightforward:

1. Sign up as an Android developer (if you're not already signed up).
2. Upload your signed application.

Signing up as an Android developer

Go to Google's website (*http://market.android.com/publish*), and fill out the forms provided. You will be asked to:

- Use your Google account to log in (if you don't have a Google account, you can get one for free by following the Create Account link on the login page)
- Agree to the Android Market Terms of Service
- Pay a one-time fee of $25 (payable by credit card via Google Checkout; again, if you don't have an account set up, you can do so quickly)
- If the game is being charged for, specify your payment processor (again, you can easily sign up for a Google Payments account)

The forms ask for a minimal amount of information—your name, phone number, and so on—and you are signed up.

Uploading your application

Now you can go to *http://play.google.com/apps/publish/Home* to upload your application. To identify and categorize your application, you will be asked for the following:

Application APK file name and location

This refers to the APK file of your application, signed with your private signature certificate.

Title and description

These are very important, because they are the core of your marketing message to potential users. Try to make the title descriptive and catchy at the same time, and describe the application in a way that will make your target market want to download it.

Application Type

There are currently two choices: Applications or Games.

Category

The allowable list of categories varies depending on application type. The currently available categories for applications are Communications, Demo, Entertainment, Finance, Lifestyle, Multimedia, News & Weather, Productivity, Reference, Shopping, Social, Software Libraries, Tools, and Travel. For games, the currently available categories include Arcade & Action, Brain & Puzzle, Cards & Casino, and Casual.

Price

This may be "Free" or a fixed price. Refer to the agreement you agreed to earlier to see what percentage you actually get to keep.

Geography

You can limit where your application is available, or choose to make it available everywhere.

Finally, you are asked to confirm that your application meets the Android Content Guidelines and that it does not knowingly violate any export laws. After that, you can upload your APK file, and within a few days your application will appear on the Android Market online catalog, accessible from any connected Android device. There is currently no way to access the Android Market directly from your PC or Mac, so you'll have to use your Android phone to find out when your application is available for download. Use the Search box in the Market, or load in the browser a file with a link of the form URL of *market://details?id=com.yourorg.yourprog*, but with your application's actual package name.

Then what?

Then sit back and watch the fame or money—and the support emails—roll in. Be patient with end users, for they do not think as we do.

22.5 Integrating AdMob into Your App

Enrique Diaz

Problem

You want to monetize your free app by showing ads within it.

Solution

Using AdMob Libraries, you can start using ads in your free app, getting money each time a user taps/clicks on the ad.

Discussion

AdMob is one of the world's largest mobile advertising networks, offering solutions for discovery, branding, and monetization on mobile phones.

The AdMob Android SDK contains the code necessary to install AdMob ads in your application.

Step 1

In your project's root directory create a subdirectory named *libs*. This will already be done for you if you used Android's activitycreator tool. Copy the AdMob JAR file (*admob-sdk-android.jar*) into that *libs* directory.

For Eclipse projects:

1. Right-click on your project from the Package Explorer tab and select Properties.
2. Select Java Build Path from the left panel.
3. Select the Libraries tab from the main window.
4. Click on Add JARs.
5. Select the JAR file copied to the *libs* directory.
6. Click OK to add the SDK to your Android project.

Step 2

Add your publisher ID to your *AndroidManifest.xml* file. Just before the closing </application> tag add a line to set your publisher ID. If your publisher ID were 149afxxxx, the line would look like this:

```
<meta-data android:value="a149afxxxx" android:name="ADMOB_PUBLISHER_ID"/>
```

To find your publisher ID, log in to your AdMob account, select the Sites and Apps tab, and click on the Manage Settings link for your site. On this page, you can find your publisher ID as shown in Figure 22-1.

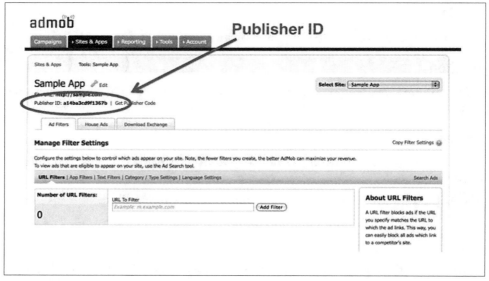

Figure 22-1. AdMob: Where to find your publisher ID

Step 3

Add the `INTERNET` permission to your *AndroidManifest.xml* file just before the closing `</manifest>` tag:

```
<uses-permission android:name="android.permission.INTERNET" /> </manifest>
```

Optionally, you can add the `ACCESS_COARSE_LOCATION` and/or `ACCESS_FINE_LOCATION` permissions to allow AdMob the ability to show geotargeted ads.

Your final *AndroidManifest.xml* file may look something like Figure 22-2.

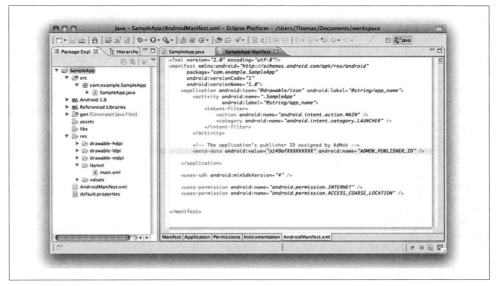

Figure 22-2. After pasting some code

Step 4

Paste the following into your *attrs.xml* file:

```
<declare-styleable name="com.admob.android.ads.AdView">
<attr name="backgroundColor" format="color" />
<attr name="primaryTextColor" format="color" />
<attr name="secondaryTextColor" format="color" />
<attr name="keywords" format="string" />
<attr name="refreshInterval" format="integer" />
</declare-styleable>
```

If your project does not already have an *attrs.xml* file, create one in the */res/values/* directory of your project, and paste the following:

```
<?xml version="1.0" encoding="utf-8"?> <resources>
<declare-styleable name="com.admob.android.ads.AdView">
<attr name="backgroundColor" format="color" />
<attr name="primaryTextColor" format="color" />
<attr name="secondaryTextColor" format="color" />
<attr name="keywords" format="string" />
<attr name="refreshInterval" format="integer" />
</declare-styleable>
</resources>
```

Step 5

Create a reference to the *attrs.xml* file in your layout element by adding an xmlns line that includes your package name specified in *AndroidManifest.xml* file. For example, if your package name were com.example.sampleapp you would include this line:

```
xmlns:myapp="http://schemas.android.com/apk/res/com.example.sampleapp"
```

So, for a simple screen with only one ad, your layout element would look like Example 22-1.

Example 22-1. Layout with one ad

```
<?xml version="1.0" encoding="utf-8"?>
<LinearLayout
xmlns:android="http://schemas.android.com/apk/res/android"
xmlns:myapp="http://schemas.android.com/apk/res/com.example.SampleApp"
android:orientation="vertical"
android:layout_width="fill_parent"
android:layout_height="fill_parent">

<com.admob.android.ads.AdView
android:id="@+id/ad"
android:layout_width="fill_parent"
android:layout_height="wrap_content"
myapp:backgroundColor="#000000"
myapp:primaryTextColor="#FFFFFF"
myapp:secondaryTextColor="#CCCCCC"
</LinearLayout>
/>
```

Step 6

When integrating AdMob ads into your application it is recommended that you use test mode. In a test mode test, ads are always returned. Test mode is enabled on a per-device basis. To enable test mode for a device, first request an ad, then look in LogCat for a line like the following:

```
To get test ads on the emulator use AdManager.setTestDevices...
```

Once you have the device ID you can enable test mode by calling in your main activity, AdManager.setTestDevices:

```
AdManager.setTestDevices( new String[] { AdManager.TEST_EMULATOR,
"E83D20734F72FB3108F104ABC0FFC738", //Phone ID
} );
}
```

Once you have successfully requested test ads, try clicking on each type of test ad to make sure it works properly from your application. The type of test ad returned is changed with AdManager.setTestAction. You can see the result in Figure 22-3.

Figure 22-3. The ad in your app

See Also

http://www.admob.com/; *http://androidtitlan.org/2010/09/como-agregar-publicidad -con-admob-a-tu-android-app/*; *http://groups.google.com/group/admob-publisher-dis cuss*

22.6 Obfuscating and Optimizing with ProGuard

Ian Darwin

Problem

You want to obfuscate your code, or optimize it (for speed or size), or all of the above.

Solution

The optimization and obfuscation tool ProGuard is supported by the Ant script provided with the Android New Project Wizard in Eclipse, needing only to be enabled.

Discussion

Obfuscation of code is the process of trying to hide information (such as compile-time names visible in the binary) that would be useful in reverse-engineering your code. If your application contains commercial or trade secrets, you probably do want to obfuscate it. If your program is open source, there is probably no need to obfuscate the code. You decide.

Optimization of code is analogous to refactoring at the source level; but it usually aims to make the code either *faster*, *smaller*, or both.

The normal development cycle with Android and Eclipse involves compilation to standard Java bytecode (done by the Eclipse Compiler) and then conversion to the Android-specific DEX (Dalvik Executable) format. ProGuard (*http://proguard.sourceforge.net*) is Eric Lafortune's open source, free software program for optimizing and obfuscating Java code. ProGuard is not Android-specific; it works with console-mode applications, applets, Swing applications, Java ME midlets, Android, or just about any type of Java program. ProGuard works on compiled Java, so it must be interposed in the development cycle before conversion to DEX. This is most readily achieved using the standard Java build tool Ant. The Eclipse Android New Project Wizard, as of Gingerbread (2.3), includes support for ProGuard in the generated *build.xml* file. You only need to edit the file *build.properties* to include the following line, which gives the name of the configuration file:

```
proguard.config=proguard.cfg
```

For older versions, please refer to the ProGuard Reference Manual (*http://proguard.sourceforge.net/index.html*).

Configuration file

The ProGuard processing is controlled by the configuration file (normally called *proguard.cfg*), which has its own syntax. Basically, keywords begin with a "-" character in the first character position, followed by a keyword, followed by optional parameters. Where the parameters reference Java classes or members, the syntax somewhat mimics Java syntax to make your life easier. Here is a minimal ProGuard configuration file for an Android application:

```
-injars      bin/classes
-outjars     bin/classes-processed.jar
-libraryjars /usr/local/java/android-sdk/platforms/android-9/android.jar

-dontpreverify
-repackageclasses ''
-allowaccessmodification
-optimizations !code/simplification/arithmetic

-keep public class com.example.MainActivity
```

The first section specifies the paths of your project, including a temporary directory for the optimized classes.

The next section lists various options. Preverification is only for full Java projects, so it's turned off. The optimizations shown are for an Android 1.5 project and could probably be omitted today.

Finally, the class `com.example.MainActivity` has to be present in the output of the optimization and obfuscation process, since it is the main activity and is referred to by name in the *AndroidManifest.xml* file.

A full working *proguard.cfg* file will normally be generated for you by the Eclipse Android New Project Wizard. Example 22-2 is the configuration file generated for an Android 2.3.3 project.

Example 22-2. Example proguard.cfg file

```
-optimizationpasses 5
-dontusemixedcaseclassnames
-dontskipnonpubliclibraryclasses
-dontpreverify
-verbose
-optimizations !code/simplification/arithmetic,!field/*,!class/merging/*

-keep public class * extends android.app.Activity
-keep public class * extends android.app.Application
-keep public class * extends android.app.Service
-keep public class * extends android.content.BroadcastReceiver
-keep public class * extends android.content.ContentProvider
-keep public class * extends android.app.backup.BackupAgentHelper
-keep public class * extends android.preference.Preference
-keep public class com.android.vending.licensing.ILicensingService

-keepclasseswithmembernames class * {
    native <methods>;
}

-keepclasseswithmembernames class * {
    public <init>(android.content.Context, android.util.AttributeSet);
}

-keepclasseswithmembernames class * {
    public <init>(android.content.Context, android.util.AttributeSet, int);
}

-keepclassmembers enum * {
    public static **[] values();
    public static ** valueOf(java.lang.String);
}

-keep class * implements android.os.Parcelable {
  public static final android.os.Parcelable$Creator *;
}
```

The prolog is mostly similar to the earlier example. The `keep`, `keepclasseswithmember` `names`, and `keepclassmembers` specify particular classes that must be retained. These are mostly obvious, but the `enum` entries may not be: the Java 5 enum methods `values()` and `valueOf()` are sometimes used with the Reflection API, so they must remain visible, as must any classes that you access via the Reflection API.

The `ILicensingService` entry is only needed if you are using Android's License Validation Tool (LVT):

```
-keep class com.android.vending.licensing.ILicensingService
```

See Also

The *ProGuard Reference Manual* (*http://proguard.sourceforge.net/index.html*) has many more details. There is also information at Google's Developers site (*http://developer .android.com/guide/developing/tools/proguard.html*). Finally, Matt Quigley has an article at the Android Engineer blog titled "Optimizing, Obfuscating, and Shrinking your Android Applications with ProGuard" (*http://www.androidengineer.com/2010/07/opti mizing-obfuscating-and-shrinking.html*).

22.7 Providing a Link to Other Published Apps in the Google Play Market

Daniel Fowler

Problem

Your developed app is running on a device; you want a link to your other apps on the Android Market to encourage users to try them.

Solution

Use an `Intent` and a URI that contains your publisher name or package name.

Discussion

Android's `Intent` system is a great way for your application to leverage functionality that has already been written by other developers. The Android Market application, which is used to browse and install apps, can be called from an application by using an `Intent`. This allows an existing app to have a link to other apps on the Android Market, thus allowing app developers and publishers to encourage users to try their other apps.

To search via the Android Market app, the standard `Intent` mechanism is used, as described in Recipe 4.2. The Uniform Resource Identifier (URI) used is *market://search? q=search term* where *search term* is replaced with the appropriate text, such as the program name or keyword. The `Intent Action` is `ACTION_VIEW`.

The URI can also point directly to the Android Market details page for a package by using *market://details?id=package name* where *package name* is replaced with the unique package name for the app.

The program shown in this recipe (and whose output is shown in Figure 22-4) will allow a text search of the Android Market or show the details page for a given app. Example 22-3 is the layout.

Example 22-3. The main layout

```xml
<LinearLayout xmlns:android="http://schemas.android.com/apk/res/android"
    android:orientation="vertical"
    android:layout_width="fill_parent"
    android:layout_height="fill_parent">
    <EditText android:id="@+id/etSearch"
        android:layout_width="fill_parent"
        android:layout_height="wrap_content"
        android:textSize="20sp"
        android:singleLine="true"/>
    <RadioGroup android:layout_width="wrap_content"
        android:layout_height="wrap_content">
        <RadioButton android:id="@+id/rdSearch"
            android:layout_height="wrap_content"
            android:layout_width="wrap_content"
            android:checked="true"
            android:text="search"
            android:textSize="20sp"/>
        <RadioButton android:id="@+id/rdDetails"
            android:layout_height="wrap_content"
            android:layout_width="wrap_content"
            android:text="details"
            android:textSize="20sp"/>
    </RadioGroup>
    <Button android:id="@+id/butSearch"
        android:layout_width="wrap_content"
        android:layout_height="wrap_content"
        android:textSize="20sp"
        android:text="Search Android Market"/>
</LinearLayout>
```

An EditText allows entry of the search term, a RadioButton can be used to do a straight search or show an app's details page (provided the full package name is known). The Button starts the search.

Figure 22-4. Market search

The important point to notice in the code shown in Example 22-4 is that the search term is encoded.

Example 22-4. The main activity

```
public class Main extends Activity {
    RadioButton publisherOption;    //Option for straight search or details
    @Override
    public void onCreate(Bundle savedInstanceState) {
        super.onCreate(savedInstanceState);
        setContentView(R.layout.main);
        //Search button press processed by inner class HandleClick
        findViewById(R.id.butSearch).setOnClickListener(new OnClickListener(){
        public void onClick(View arg0) {
        String searchText;
        //Reference search input
        EditText searchFor=(EditText)findViewById(R.id.etSearch);
        try {
            //URL encoding handles spaces and punctuation in search term
            searchText = URLEncoder.encode(searchFor.getText().toString(),"UTF-8");
        } catch (UnsupportedEncodingException e) {
            searchText = searchFor.getText().toString();
        }
        Uri uri; //Stores intent URI
        //Get search option
        RadioButton searchOption=(RadioButton)findViewById(R.id.rdSearch);
        if(searchOption.isChecked()) {
                uri=Uri.parse("market://search?q=" + searchText);
            } else {
                uri=Uri.parse("market://details?id=" + searchText);
            }
            Intent intent = new Intent(Intent.ACTION_VIEW, uri);
            try {
                main.this.startActivity(intent);
            } catch (ActivityNotFoundException anfe) {
                Toast.makeText(main.this, "Please install the Android Market App",
                Toast.LENGTH_SHORT);
    }
    }
```

```
    });
  }
}
```

A straight text search is simply the text appended to the URI *market://search?q=*. To search by publisher name use the *pub:* qualifier, that is, append the publisher's name to *market://search?q=pub:*. However, at the time of this writing, a bug exists in some versions of the Android Market that causes publisher names of more than one word to return no results. So, while *market://search?q=pub:IMDb* works, *market://search? q=pub:O'Reilly+Media* does not. The workaround is to use the straight text search for publisher names of two words or more—for example, *market://search?q=oreilly+media*.

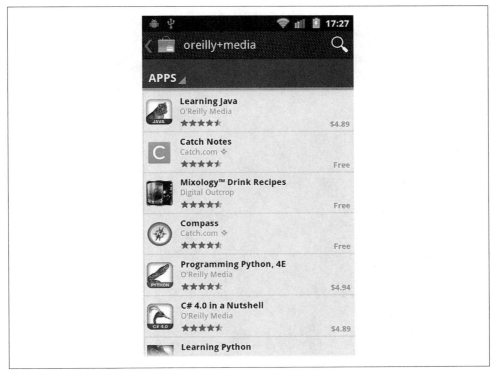

Figure 22-5. Market search results

The *pub:* search qualifier is also case-sensitive, thus *market://search?q=pub:IMDb* returns a result but *market://search?q=pub:imdb* does not.

It is also possible to search for a specific application if the package name is known by using the *id* qualifier. So, if an app has a package name of `com.example.myapp` the search term will be *market://search?q=id:com.example.myapp*. Even better is to go straight to the Apps details page with *market://details?q=id:com.example.myapp*. For example,

O'Reilly has a free app, the details of which can be shown using *market://details? id=com.aldiko.android.oreilly.isbn9781449388294*.

Figure 22-5 shows the output of the search entered in Figure 22-4.

Using these techniques it is very easy to put a button or menu option on a screen to allow users to go directly to other apps that you have published.

See Also

http://developer.android.com/guide/publishing/publishing.html#marketintent

Index

We'd like to hear your suggestions for improving our indexes. Send email to *index@oreilly.com*.

---

obfuscating and optimizing code, 633–636
providing links to published apps, 636–640
signing applications, 626
padding attribute, 308
Paint.NET software
creating launcher icons, 217–223
scaling view backgrounds, 225
parsing
Atom feeds, 476–480
JSON using JSONObject, 432–433
RSS feeds, 476–480
XML documents using DOM API, 433–435
XML documents using XmlPullParser, 435–438
password attribute, 267
PendingIntent class, 354
permissions, 81
(see also specific permissions)
controlling device vibrator, 278, 280, 316
dialing phones, 454
receiving SMS messages, 457
sending SMS messages, 455
Persson, Tomas, 292
phone numbers, opening with intents, 142–143
PhoneGap development framework, 608–610
Photo Gallery (Android), 321–324
PictureCallback interface, 204
pictures
taking using Camera class, 201–204
taking using intents, 199–200
pinch movements, adding to zoom, 234
PNG (Portable Network Graphics) format, 211, 220
pop-up/alert dialogs, creating, 336
Portable Network Graphics (PNG) format, 211, 220
POST message (HTTP), 472
Preference class, 416
PreferenceActivity class
onSharedPreferenceChanged() method, 419
providing user preference information, 415–418
PreferenceCategory class, 416
PreferenceManager.getDefaultSharedPrefences() method, 418
preferences

checking consistency of default shared, 419–421
providing information about, 415–418
setting for first-run, 88–89
PreferenceScreen class, 415–418
printf() function, 286
priority attribute, 451
private keys, 624
Process class
about, 588
waitFor() method, 584
PROCESS_OUTGOING_CALLS permission, 450
programming languages, 587
(see also specific programming languages)
about, 587
creating alerts in SL4A, 597–600
creating platform-independent applications, 608–610
fetching and displaying Google Documents, 600–602
getting started with SL4A, 594–596
native handset functionality from WebView, 607–608
running apps natively, 589–594
running Linux command, 588
sharing SL4A scripts in QR codes, 603–606
ProgressBar class, 272
ProgressDialog class
about, 161, 346
STYLE_HORIZONTAL constant, 161
ProGuard tool, 633–636
Projection::toPixels() method, 532
projects
creating, 3, 7
naming, 7
referenced, 23
setting up for Google Maps, 516
setting up test-driven development, 104
test, 114–118
Proximity support property (AVD), 109
ps command, 584, 585
public keys, 624
publisher ID, 629
Python language
about, 595
creating alerts in SL4A, 597–600
fetching and displaying Google Documents, 600–602

About the Author

Ian F. Darwin has worked in the computer industry for three decades. He wrote the freeware *file(1)* command used on Linux and BSD and is the author of *Checking C Programs with Lint*, *Java Cookbook*, and more than a hundred articles and courses on C, Unix, and Java and Android. In addition to programming and consulting, Ian teaches Unix, Java, and Android for Learning Tree International, one of the world's largest technical training companies.

Colophon

The animal on the cover of the *Android Cookbook* is a marine iguana (*Amblyrhynchus cristatus*). These lizards are found exclusively in the Galapagos (with a subspecies particular to each island). They are believed to be descended from land iguanas carried to the islands on log rafts from mainland South America.

The marine iguana is the only type of lizard that feeds in the water. Darwin found the reptiles unattractive and awkward, labeling them "disgusting clumsy lizards" and "imps of darkness," but these streamlined large animals (up to 5 or 6 feet long) are graceful in the water, with flattened tails designed for swimming.

These lizards feed on seaweed and marine algae. They can dive deeply (as far as 50 feet), though their dives are usually shallow, and they can stay underwater for up to an hour (though 5 to 10 minutes is more typical). Like all reptiles, marine iguanas are cold-blooded and must regulate their body temperature by basking in the sun; their black or gray coloration maximizes their heat absorption when they come out of the cold ocean. Though these harmless herbivores often allow humans to approach them closely, they can be aggressive when cold.

Marine iguanas have specialized nasal glands that filter ocean salt from their blood. They sneeze up the excess salt, which often accumulates on their heads or faces, creating a distinctive white patch or "wig." These iguanas are vulnerable to predation by introduced species (including dogs and cats), as well as to ocean pollution and fluctuations in their food supply caused by weather events such as El Niño.

The cover image is from *Wood's Animate Creation*. The cover font is Adobe ITC Garamond. The text font is Linotype Birka; the heading font is Adobe Myriad Condensed; and the code font is LucasFont's TheSansMonoCondensed.

Get even more for your money.

Join the O'Reilly Community, and register the O'Reilly books you own. It's free, and you'll get:

- $4.99 ebook upgrade offer
- 40% upgrade offer on O'Reilly print books
- Membership discounts on books and events
- Free lifetime updates to ebooks and videos
- Multiple ebook formats, DRM FREE
- Participation in the O'Reilly community
- Newsletters
- Account management
- 100% Satisfaction Guarantee

Signing up is easy:

1. Go to: oreilly.com/go/register
2. Create an O'Reilly login.
3. Provide your address.
4. Register your books.

Note: English-language books only

To order books online:

oreilly.com/store

For questions about products or an order:

orders@oreilly.com

To sign up to get topic-specific email announcements and/or news about upcoming books, conferences, special offers, and new technologies:

elists@oreilly.com

For technical questions about book content:

booktech@oreilly.com

To submit new book proposals to our editors:

proposals@oreilly.com

O'Reilly books are available in multiple DRM-free ebook formats. For more information:

oreilly.com/ebooks

Spreading the knowledge of innovators   oreilly.com

©2010 O'Reilly Media, Inc. O'Reilly logo is a registered trademark of O'Reilly Media, Inc. 00000

Have it your way.

O'Reilly eBooks

- Lifetime access to the book when you buy through oreilly.com
- Provided in up to four DRM-free file formats, for use on the devices of your choice: PDF, .epub, Kindle-compatible .mobi, and Android .apk
- Fully searchable, with copy-and-paste and print functionality
- Alerts when files are updated with corrections and additions

oreilly.com/ebooks/

Safari Books Online

- Access the contents and quickly search over 7000 books on technology, business, and certification guides
- Learn from expert video tutorials, and explore thousands of hours of video on technology and design topics
- Download whole books or chapters in PDF format, at no extra cost, to print or read on the go
- Get early access to books as they're being written
- Interact directly with authors of upcoming books
- Save up to 35% on O'Reilly print books

See the complete Safari Library at safari.oreilly.com

O'REILLY®

Spreading the knowledge of innovators.   oreilly.com

©2011 O'Reilly Media, Inc. O'Reilly logo is a registered trademark of O'Reilly Media, Inc. 00000